Early China

Early China

The Making of the Chinese Cultural Sphere

HAN JIANYE

Translated by MARK LAW

Books Beyond Boundaries
ROYAL COLLINS

Early China: The Making of the Chinese Cultural Sphere

Han Jianye
Translated by Mark Law

First published in 2024 by Royal Collins Publishing Group Inc.
Groupe Publication Royal Collins Inc.
550-555 boul. René-Lévesque O Montréal (Québec) H2Z1B1 Canada

10 9 8 7 6 5 4 3 2 1

Copyright © Shanghai Ancient Books Publishing House, 2024
Original Edition © Shanghai Ancient Books Publishing House
Arranged by China Renmin University Press.

All rights reserved. Without limiting the rights under copyright reserved above, no part of this publication may be reproduced, stored in or introduced into a retrieval system, or transmitted in any form or by any means (electronic, mechanical, photocopying, recording, or otherwise), without the prior written permission of both the copyright owner and the above publisher of this book.

ISBN: 978-1-4878-1213-3

To find out more about our publications, please visit www.royalcollins.com.

Contents

Foreword — xiii
Preface — xvii
Introduction — 1

Chapter 1 Introduction — 7
  I. The Cultural and Political Significance of China — 7
  II. The Concept of Early China in a Cultural Sense — 9
  III. The Purpose of This Book — 13
  IV. Research and Writing Approach — 14

Chapter 2 China before Early China — 17
  I. The Ancient Basis of Early Chinese Race and Culture — 17
  II. Five Major Cultural Systems — 26
  III. The Sprouts of Early China — 38
  IV. Three Major Cultural Systems — 65

Chapter 3 The Miaodigou Era and the Formation of Early China — 93
  I. The Flourishing Development of Core Culture — 94
  II. Yangshao Culture's "Miaodigou Transformation" — 97
  III. The New Stage of Hongshan Culture — 107
  IV. Convergence of Cultures in the Lower Reaches of the Yellow River and the Middle and Lower Reaches of the Yangtze River — 109

V.	Cultures in South China, Northeast, Northwest, and Southwest Regions	118
VI.	Three-Tiered Cultural Community in the Miaodigou Era	119
VII.	Conclusion	122

Chapter 4   *The Archaic State Stage of Early China*   129

I.	Late Yangshao Culture: Diversification and Integration	129
II.	Longshan Era: From a Multitude of States to the Central Plain's Core	194

Chapter 5   *The Dynastic State Stage of Early China*   239

I.	The Majority of the Yellow River, Yangtze River, and Liao River Basins	240
II.	From the Upper Reaches of the Yellow River to Eastern Xinjiang	260
III.	Sanxingdui Culture in the Upper Reaches of the Yangtze River Region	264
IV.	Culture in South China	265
V.	Culture of Early China Outer Margin Zone	266
VI.	Cultural Exchange in the Erlitou–Erligang Era	267
VII.	Conclusion	270

Chapter 6   *Early China and Ancient Legends*   285

I.	The Yan Emperor and the Yellow Emperor Period	286
II.	Zhuanxu and Emperor Ku Period	295
III.	Emperors Yao and Shun Period	303
IV.	Xia Dynasty	307
V.	Early Shang Dynasty	314
VI.	Conclusion	316

Chapter 7   *The Geographical Environmental Basis of Early China*   319

I.	The Geographical Environmental Basis of Early China	319
II.	Environmental Evolution and Cultural Changes	323
III.	Conclusion	331

Chapter 8   Conclusion   333

Postscript   341
Notes   345
Index   417

List of Figures

Figure 2.1	Diagram of the lineage of flexed burial in ancient China (13000 BCE–900 CE)	27
Figure 2.2	Cultural regions of early Neolithic China (18000–7000 BCE)	29
Figure 2.3	Three stages of spatial expansion of rice agriculture in China's Neolithic (13000–2000 BCE)	37
Figure 2.4	Seven-holed bone flute from the Jiahu site	43
Figure 2.5	Turtle shell and engraved symbols from the Jiahu site (M244: 18)	43
Figure 2.6	Pottery of Peiligang culture and Peiligang cultural elements in surrounding cultures (6200–5000 BCE)	44
Figure 2.7	The spatial arrangement of pottery high-foot plates and round-foot plates in China's Neolithic	46
Figure 2.8	Cultural regions of the middle stage of the middle China's Neolithic (6200–5500 BCE)	47
Figure 2.9	Cultural interactions between the middle and lower reaches of the Yangtze River during the middle Neolithic	48
Figure 2.10	Canoe at the Kuahuqiao site	49
Figure 2.11	The spatial expansion of Chinese Neolithic pottery *ding*	58
Figure 2.12	The spatial expansion of two major painted pottery traditions before the late Shang Dynasty	60
Figure 2.13	Development and evolution of symbols (primitive characters) before the late Shang Dynasty	61
Figure 2.14	Development and dissemination of octagonal patterns in Chinese Neolithic	62
Figure 2.15	Development and evolution of symbols (primitive characters) before the late Shang Dynasty	63
Figure 2.16	Human figurines in the Neolithic of Northeast China	64

LIST OF FIGURES

Figure 2.17	The distribution of the remains of the moat-enclosed settlement at Jiangzhai phase I	73
Figure 2.18	The reconstruction of the moat-enclosed settlement in Jiangzhai phase I (by Zhang Xiaoguang)	73
Figure 2.19	The distribution of imprinted-pattern white pottery in the middle to late China's Neolithic (6000–4200 BCE)	74
Figure 2.20	The spatial expansion of *gui* (*he, jue*) before the Late Shang Dynasty	77
Figure 2.21	Cultural regions of late China's Neolithic (5000–4200 BCE)	83
Figure 2.22	The spatial expansion of jade artifacts in China's Neolithic	87
Figure 2.23	The ivory carving with twin birds (phoenix) facing the sun pattern from the Hemudu site (T226 [3B]: 79)	89
Figure 2.24	Dragon and tiger tomb with clam sculpture from the Xishuipo site (M45)	91
Figure 2.25	The human face image of Banpo type of Yangshao culture	91
Figure 3.1	The plan of the large house F105 at the Xipo site	97
Figure 3.2	Comparison of double-lipped small-mouth pointed-bottom bottles from various regions during the Miaodigou era	98
Figure 3.3	Comparison of black colored-band-pattern pottery earthen bowls from various regions during the Miaodigou era	99
Figure 3.4	Comparison of petal-pattern painted pottery basins from various regions during the Miaodigou era	100
Figure 3.5	Plan of the Shijia cemetery M25	102
Figure 3.6	*Stork Fish and* Yue of the Yan Village type of Yangshao culture (Yan Village, Ruzhou City)	106
Figure 3.7	Plan and section of the M2005 excavation at the Dawenkou cemetery	111
Figure 3.8	Spatial expansion of pottery *yan* before the late Shang Dynasty	114
Figure 3.9	Early China in the cultural sense during the Miaodigou era (4200–3500 BCE)	121
Figure 4.1	Plan and section of the M27 Xipo cemetery	133
Figure 4.2	Spatial expansion of pottery *jia* and *li* before the late Shang Dynasty	135
Figure 4.3	Distribution of divination bones before the late Shang Dynasty	146
Figure 4.4	Plan of F901 at the Dadiwan site	147
Figure 4.5	Two types of pottery from the Zongri type of Majiayao culture	151
Figure 4.6	Plan of Yuchisi moated settlement	155
Figure 4.7	Plan and reconstruction of building No. 2 at Yuchisi (F8–F13)	156
Figure 4.8	Plan of Dawenkou cemetery M10	157
Figure 4.9	Plan of Liangzhu ancient city	162
Figure 4.10	Large jade *cong* from tomb M12 in Liangzhu Fanshan cemetery (M12: 98)	162

LIST OF FIGURES ix

Figure 4.11	Large jade *yue* from tomb M12 in Liangzhu Fanshan cemetery (M12: 100)	162
Figure 4.12	The mud-brick wall connected-room house at the Menbanwan site	171
Figure 4.13	Jade dragon from Hongshan culture at the Niuheliang site (N2Z1M4: 2)	172
Figure 4.14	Jade phoenix from Hongshan culture at the Niuheliang site (N16M4: 1)	172
Figure 4.15	Panorama of the second location at Niuheliang site (west–east)	174
Figure 4.16	Three levels of the southern influence of late Hongshan culture	181
Figure 4.17	Schematic diagram of the "painted pottery road"	185
Figure 4.18	Majiayao culture painted pottery dancing-pattern basin	185
Figure 4.19	Early China in the cultural sense of the late Yangshao (3500–2500 BCE)	193
Figure 4.20	Longshan culture eggshell black pottery cups from the Sanlihe site	196
Figure 4.21	Plan and section of Xizhufeng cemetery M202	199
Figure 4.22	Jade hairpin from Xizhufeng burial (M202: 1, 2)	199
Figure 4.23	Painted coiling dragon-pattern pottery plate from the Taosi site (M3072: 6)	201
Figure 4.24	Black *gu*-shaped pottery cup from the Wadian site (IT3H12: 11)	205
Figure 4.25	Plans of cave-style houses of part Laohushan culture in Yuanzigou site section II	210
Figure 4.26	Cylindrical tiles from Qijia culture at the Qiaozhen site	212
Figure 4.27	Pottery figures of Shijiahe culture at Dengjiawan site	215
Figure 4.28	The southward trend of late Longshan culture	228
Figure 4.29	Early China in a cultural sense during the Longshan era (2500–1800 BCE)	238
Figure 5.1	Bronze vessels from Erlitou culture	241
Figure 5.2	Turquoise-inlaid bronze plaque ornaments from Erlitou culture	242
Figure 5.3	Plan of palace No. 1 base at the Erlitou site	243
Figure 5.4	The bronze square *ding* of Erligang culture	247
Figure 5.5	Plan of Yanshi Shangcheng	248
Figure 5.6	Courtyard group at the Erdaojingzi site (west–east)	257
Figure 5.7	Map of the distribution of early Bronze Age cultures in Northwest China (2000–1500 BCE)	269
Figure 5.8	Two major traditions of bronzeware before the late Shang Dynasty	275
Figure 5.9	Early China in a cultural sense during the Erlitou–Erligang era (1800–1300 BCE)	283

List of Tables

Table 2.1	Cultural regions of early Neolithic of China (18000–7000 BCE)	28
Table 2.2	Cultural regions of middle China's Neolithic (7000–5000 BCE)	39
Table 2.3	Cultural regions of the early stage of late China's Neolithic (5000–4200 BCE)	66
Table 3.1	Cultural regions of the late stage of the late China's Neolithic (4200–3500 BCE)	94
Table 4.1	Cultural regions in early Chalcolithic China (3500–2500 BCE)	130
Table 4.2	Cultural regions of the late Chalcolithic in China (2500–1800 BCE)	195
Table 5.1	Cultural regions of the early Bronze Age in China (1800–1300 BCE)	240

Foreword

Although China did not emerge very early as a political entity, from the first dynasty onwards, the lineage has been very clear, one generation after another. Even in times of division and unity, unity was not forgotten in times of division, and efforts were made to maintain unity in times of unity, making China the only ancient civilization in the world that has developed continuously without interruption. Why is this the case? There are many reasons, the most important of which is the existence of a cultural foundation in China.

Han Jianye noticed early on that there was an early China or early Chinese cultural sphere in the pre-Qin and even prehistoric periods. Through in-depth research, he believes that this cultural early China sprouted in the mid-Neolithic period around 6000 BCE and formally formed around 4000 BCE in the late Neolithic period, lasting until before the late Shang Dynasty.

This book thoroughly organizes the archaeological data before the late Shang Dynasty, from which the formation and development process of the early Chinese cultural sphere can be clearly seen. In the Paleolithic Age, which lasted two million years, many fossil specimens from Homo erectus, early Homo sapiens, to late Homo sapiens all show shovel-shaped incisors. The famous paleoanthropologist Wei Dunrui, who first studied the fossils of Peking Man, discovered shovel-shaped incisors and pointed out that this is a characteristic of modern Proto-East Asians. The stone tools of the Paleolithic Age in China belong mostly to the gravel-lithic flake tradition, which is quite different from the Western Paleolithic Age and forms its own system. However, given the vast geographical range of China, the cultures of different regions naturally have significant differences. The Paleolithic Age can be divided into two regions, the North and the South, and five or six smaller areas. In the early Neolithic, five cultural systems appeared. This shows that China's prehistoric culture presented a diverse state very early, closely related to each region's different natural environments and geographical locations. By the middle of the Neolithic period, the situation began subtly changing. Due to the development of agriculture, the economic and cultural tiers of the Yellow River Basin and the Yangtze River Basin significantly exceeded the surrounding areas, and their dominant status began to emerge. The Peiligang culture, located in the Central Plain, came into prominence, expanding to the surrounding areas on the one hand and absorbing the advantageous factors of the surrounding cultures on the other, strengthening the connections between them. A layered structure with the Central Plain as the core, the Yellow River Basin, and the Yangtze River Basin as the main body began to emerge. This is the sprout of the early Chinese cultural sphere. Why did the early Chinese cultural sphere sprout so early? Han Jianye summarizes five major characteristics in this book, all unique to China and greatly different from the prehistoric states of ancient civilizations in other parts of the world. At the same time, they are closely related to the subsequent development of Chinese culture and are very persuasive.

By the late Neolithic, around 4000 BCE, Yangshao culture in the Central Plain developed rapidly, with a significantly expanded distribution range, and its influence on surrounding cultures was also significantly strengthened. Especially during its Miaodigou phase, the culture developed very strongly, to the point where it could be referred to as the Miaodigou period. Due to cultural expansion, a three-tiered structure naturally formed: the core area was in southern Shanxi Province, western Henan Province, and eastern Guanzhong; the main area was in the middle reaches of the Yellow River and slightly to the south, that is, the entire distribution area of Yangshao culture; and the outer tiered was the area influenced by Yangshao culture. The formation of this three-tiered cultural community, both geographically and culturally, laid the foundation for China's later development. The early Chinese cultural sphere was officially formed at this time.

The subsequent Chalcolithic roughly corresponds to the legendary archaic state era. Many cultural centers appeared nationwide, a large number of ancient cities emerged on the land, and exquisite jade, lacquerware, ivory, silk, and high-end pottery, as well as the emergence or widespread popularity of a small amount of copperware, all shone with the light of primitive civilization. The three development patterns of the Central Plain, the East, and the North formed earlier still manifested in this era. Still, the influence, penetration, and exchange between them became more extensive and closer, and the early Chinese cultural sphere expanded further. A large number of artifacts with Chinese characteristics, such as jade *cong, bi, gui*, jade *zhang*, and *yue*; the *li, jia, yan, gui*, and *he* in pottery; the *gu* in lacquerware; and silk, all emerged during this era. The pottery *ding* was a traditional artifact that had existed for a long time, and these were all inherited and developed in the subsequent dynastic state stage.

Around 2000 BCE or slightly later, we entered the Bronze Age, which also marked the beginning of the dynastic state stage. The Xia was China's first hereditary dynasty. After several early upheavals, it stabilized under the revival of Shaokang. According to research, the Erlitou site in Yanshi, Henan, may have been the capital of Shaokang until the end of the Xia Dynasty. There, a palace city covering more than 100,000 square meters was found, with over ten palaces built successively. The "establishing the center and setting up the pole" pattern was quite evident. Around the palace city was the noble residential area, with workshops for casting copper, pottery making, and bone crafting. For the first time, bronze ritual vessels such as *ding, jia, jue*, and *he* were unearthed. Erlitou culture, represented by the Erlitou site, was dominant, its influence reaching almost half of present-day China. Erlitou culture followed Erligang culture, with the unprecedentedly grand Zhengzhou Shangcheng. Within the city were large palace areas and various handicraft workshop areas, from which many bronze ritual vessels were unearthed. Among them, the big square *ding* with animal-face patterns stood as high as one meter, a true national treasure. Roughly concurrent with Zhengzhou Shangcheng was Yanshi Shangcheng, along with smaller Shangcheng distributed in various places. Erligang culture even extended to most parts of the country, clearly forming a four-tiered structure with the Zhengzhou and Luoyang region as the core, Erlitou culture and Erligang culture as the main body, many bronze cultures deeply influenced by these two cultures on the periphery, and further local cultures. This marked the peak of the early Chinese cultural sphere. The concept of ancient China—the Five *Fu* system—objectively reflects this layered structure.

The above is the basic framework of this book's discourse on early China culturally. My summary may be inaccurate, but the general outline is clear. I think the author writes up to the late Shang Dynasty because the late Shang had not only a small amount of literature and bronze inscriptions but also a large amount of oracle bone inscriptions, falling within the scope of documented history. As for whether the period before the late Shang can be called early China and when early China should begin, there are still different understandings. This book discusses archaeology, collecting all available archaeological data as much as possible and conducting a detailed analysis of the lineage and cultural characteristics marked by pottery combinations. The reason for doing this, I believe, is because prehistoric pottery in China is the richest and most diverse in the world, and the characteristics and evolution of pottery are obvious and easy to grasp. Based on such meticulous analysis, referring to ancient historical legends as much as possible is necessary. This is because legends mainly reflect the historical memory of the Huaxia ethnic group. The Huaxia ethnic group attaches great importance to clan traditions and ancestor worship, and the related ancient legends should have a high degree of credibility. If they can be cross-referenced with relevant archaeological cultures, it will further enhance their academic value. Jianye has followed this approach in his years of research into ancient historical legends. He also places special emphasis on studying natural environments and human-land relationships, because the natural environment has played an important role in forming and evolving Chinese cultural characteristics. The book also devotes a chapter to this discussion.

The combination of archaeological-based research, the study of ancient historical legends, and the analysis of historical environments form an important feature of this book, making it unique among many discussions on early China. Its advantages are evident. It is a must-read for readers interested in early China.

Yan Wenming
At residence in Lanqiying, Peking University
August 15, 2014

Preface

At the International Academic Conference on "Ancient Chinese History and General Laws of Social Science" held at the Airlie Hotel in Warrenton, Virginia, in 1986, Yan Wenming submitted a paper titled "The Unity and Diversity of Chinese Prehistoric Culture." In it, he proposed that the unified multi-ethnic modern Chinese structure was already embryonic in the distant prehistoric period—prehistoric Chinese culture itself encompasses both unity and diversity or what he referred to as a "multi-petaled flower" or "pluralistic unity" structure, with the Central Plain as its core:

> Modern China is a unified multi-ethnic country with the Han ethnicity as the majority and over fifty other minority ethnicities. This social structure, which has a main body and many siblings, is unified and retains each ethnicity's characteristics. It results from long-term historical development, with its roots deeply planted in the distant prehistoric period … In the Neolithic Age … in addition to having certain common factors within a certain range, a multi-petaled flower structure was also formed, centered in the Central Plain, and included different economic cultural types and different cultural traditions at different tiers. This development profoundly impacted the emergence and characteristics of early Chinese civilization.[1]

At the same time, Zhang Guangzhi, in his book *Archaeology of Ancient China* (Fourth Edition), proposed that from around 4000 BCE, due to profound cultural exchanges, a "Chinese interaction sphere" was formed.

How should we refer to this "Interaction Sphere" that began to form around 4000 BCE, stretching north to the Liao River Basin, south to Taiwan [China] and the Pearl River Delta, east to the coast, and west to Gansu, Qinghai, and Sichuan? We could also choose a completely neutral term and call it X. Still, we might as well call it the Chinese Interaction Sphere or Former Chinese Interaction Sphere because this prehistoric circle formed the geographical core of China during the historical period. All regional cultures within this circle played a specific role in forming the Chinese historical civilization unified under the Qin and Han empires.[2]

The views of the two scholars have certain differences. In Zhang Guangzhi's "Chinese Interaction Sphere," all cultures are "equal," and the Central Plain does not hold a special position, which is similar to the "regional type" theory of Su Bingqi, which emphasizes the parallel development of various cultural areas.[3] Yan Wenming's "multi-petaled flower" structure, on the other hand, has a primary and secondary structure. The "heart of the flower" is the core of the Central Plain, and the "double-petals" represent the surrounding cultures that have layered connections with the Central Plain, varying in closeness and distance. It retains the rational components of the previously popular "Central Plain Centrism" theory while absorbing the essence of the "regional type" theory. However, overall, the two scholars' understandings are quite similar: that is, they both believe that Chinese civilization has the characteristics of continuity and wholeness. In the Neolithic Age, there was already an embryonic form of the basic structure of "China" or modern China after the Qin and Han dynasties.[4] Xia Nai also once said: "Based on archaeological evidence, although China is not completely isolated from the outside world, Chinese civilization is indeed indigenous. Chinese civilization has its own personality, unique style, and characteristics. The primary cultures of the Chinese Neolithic Age already possessed some cultural elements with Chinese characteristics. The formation process of Chinese civilization developed based on these elements."[5]

However, there are views that differ significantly from theirs.

In a book review criticizing Wu Hung's *Monumentality in Early Chinese Art and Architecture*,[6] Robert Bagley was highly dissatisfied with Wu's "ignorance" of cultural diversity and his assumption that all prehistoric cultures were "Chinese" culture and for labeling many prehistoric inhabitants as "Chinese."

Throughout the periods covered in this book, Wu Hung overlooks cultural diversity. From beginning to end, he assumes that all he is dealing with is Chinese culture. Regarding the Neolithic period, he wants to say that the inhabitants of the lower Yangtze and Shandong Peninsula are all Chinese. But what does this mean? We surely cannot say they spoke Chinese, as we don't know their language. If all he wants to say is that the material culture of these people certainly had something to do with the material culture of those who spoke Chinese in historical times, then that is acceptable, but beyond that, it explains nothing. Because at least a dozen or so very different prehistoric ethnic groups could also be called Chinese for the same (and similarly insignificant) reasons. We cannot comfortably apply the same label of "Chinese" to the people represented by the distinct archaeological cultures of Liangzhu, Dawenkou, Hongshan, Longshan, Shilingxia, Majiayao, and Miaodigou.[7]

In Bagley's view, due to the lack of linguistic evidence, even the surrounding bronze cultures during the late Shang period in Yin Ruins should not be considered part of early Chinese civilization: "Although it is acceptable to call the people of Anyang in the second half of the second millennium BCE 'Chinese' because of strong linguistic evidence, we do not know how many or which of their neighbors spoke the same language."[8] This understanding is further elaborated in his writing of the third chapter of the *Cambridge History of Ancient China*.[9] It's no wonder that Wu Hung, who even labels Neolithic cultures as "Chinese," faced such severe criticism from him.

Later, Wu Hung retorted,[10] and due to the strong confrontational nature of both sides, it was referred to as an "academic Kosovo" by Li Ling. Li Ling said, "The target of Western scholars' criticism of Wu Hung is primarily focused on 'deconstructing eternal China,' that is, breaking the 'continuity' and 'unity' of Chinese culture that we are accustomed to talking about … The criticism of Western scholars is not only aimed at Wu Hung but also includes the academic background and habits that Wu Hung was educated in and is still in contact with, as well as the research of his Chinese colleagues that he still cites."[11] Li Feng also pointed out that "traditional Chinese historians depict early China as a unified regime … But many Western scholars tend to see a smaller and more fragmented early 'China.'"[12] Indeed, the academic debate between Wu Hung and Bagley is just the tip of the iceberg of the huge disagreements in the international academic community on the issue of "early China."

The issue of "early China" is ultimately an academic issue, which must be treated with an academic attitude and solved through academic research. The only way to narrow the disagreements about "early China" should be to conduct systematic research on its origins, formation, and development process.

Introduction

"Early China" as a cultural unity was a result of the long-term interaction and assimilation between different regional cultures before the late Shang in a large part of modern-day China, revolving around the Central Plain area. It laid the geographic, cultural, and political foundation for the future Zhou Dynasty as well as Qin and Han empires. It may be alternately named "early Chinese cultural sphere."

That the history of early China centers around the Central Plain, undergoing by and large continuous development at least since the Five-Emperor Period, was once a standard account in traditional Chinese historiography. But since the late Qing Dynasty and due to the Sino-Western cultural collision and the decline of China, the "Doubt in the Past" sentiment took a grip on the international and domestic Sinological communities, posting an unprecedented challenge to this established account. This is particularly well manifested in the *Doubting Antiquity* (古史辨) series edited by Gu Jiegang. After discovering the oracle bone inscriptions, the subsequent research works of Wang Guowei and Xu Xusheng, and the archaeological investigation of Yin Ruins and other sites since the 1920s. However, the radical "Doubt in the Past" sentiment gradually waned in Chinese historiography. The Chinese history composed since the late Shang is credible, and the origin of Chinese civilization predates the late Shang and has been widely accepted by Chinese scholars. But some fundamental issues, such as whether a culturally continuously developing early China ever existed and how the pattern, characteristics, and developmental process of the culture of early China should be defined, have remained unsolved or unclear. Since the 1980s, Chinese scholars have debated the origin of Chinese civilizations; often, they have defined and employed the term "China" simply. This has duly invited criticism from Western scholars.

The book presents the following research results:

1. Having its beginning in the Paleolithic Age, the cultural genealogy of early China took shape in the middle Neolithic (6000 BCE). It culminated in the Miaodigou period (4000 BCE), undergoing developmental stages like the archaic state stage and dynastic state.

In terms of cultural genealogy, early China bears its root in the Paleolithic and the early and middle Neolithic. Throughout the two million years during the Paleolithic Age, residents in China were physically characterized by spade-shaped incisors, a feature that is typical of the later Proto-East Asians. The persistence of gravel-lithic flake technological traditions and the protracted existence of pebble tools in the south and microlithic tools in the north indicate the remarkable continuity, homogeneity, and diversity of human evolution and cultural development in China at the time. Around 18000 BCE, the intermediate zone between South China and the Yangtze River Basin witnessed the advent of the Neolithic. Around 10000 BCE, the Neolithic cultures expanded into Middle-East China, giving rise to five great cultural systems. Variations in economic features notwithstanding, these cultures shared some salient common features, as seen most importantly in their well-established cultural triad—agriculture, pottery, and ground stone tools.

Early China took a rudimentary configuration in the middle Neolithic around 6000 BCE. After 7000 BCE, when the middle Neolithic began, agriculture developed quickly. When it came to 6200 BCE, cross-regional cultural interaction intensified; under the forceful expansion and influence of the Peiligang culture of the Central Plain, the five cultural systems were merged into four, forming thus an embryo early Chinese cultural sphere. Around 5000 BCE in the late Neolithic, they were further fused into three cultural systems, and the early Chinese cultural sphere continued to develop. The societies of the time were simple and egalitarian.

Early China reached its maturity around 4000 BCE in the Miaodigou period. In this period, the robust Dongzhuang–Miaodigou phase of Yangshao culture in Southern Shanxi and Western Henan expanded its influence substantially. As a result, the three cultural systems were transformed into a cultural unity consisting of three tiers: now early China took shape in the cultural sense. The same period also saw the beginning of social divisions and hence the emergence of Chinese civilization.

From 3500 BCE to 1800 BCE, early China entered the archaic state stage. The beginning of the Chalcolithic Age around 3500 BCE concurs with the decline of the cultural power of the Central Plain and the rise of the surrounding cultures, but aforementioned early China remained structurally intact. Cross-cultural collision intensified to an unprecedented extent, and social differentiation grew significantly; early China entered the initial stage of civilization. Around 2500 BCE or in the late Chalcolithic (Longshan period), the Central Plain core resumed its dominance over the surrounding regions. Still, it was generally an era of multiple competing cultural centers and polities: the newly civilized societies continued to develop. Around 2100 BCE or at the end of the Longshan period, Wangwan culture phase III advanced into the middle Yangtze River Basin, indicating that the Central Plain regained its dominant status. This period corresponds to the early and middle Xia Dynasty, and the Longshan period is a stepping stone from the archaic state stage to the dynastic state.

The period of 1800 BCE to 1300 BCE was the dynastic state stage of early China. After 1800 BCE, Erlitou and Erligang cultures of the Central Plain core consecutively commanded a powerful influence over the surrounding regions, and the cultures of the greater part of China were united into a larger unity that consisted of four tiers. This period witnessed the rise of large urban centers and palace compounds and the maturation of bronze ritual vessels and ritual institutions; the Erlitou site was transformed into a royal capital that ruled a large territory. By now, a true civilization and the dynastic state stage have arrived, and two developmental patterns, one eastern and the other western are in operation. This period roughly corresponds to the late Xia Dynasty and early Shang Dynasty in the legendary history of China.

2. Early China differs from other civilizations in its agriculture, stability, holistic way of thinking, and ancestral worship.

a. Agriculture, stable inward-oriented structure, and ritual institution

Among the multiple food-acquiring strategies that comprise hunting, gathering, and stock-raising, agriculture has the greatest potential for development. Located in the middle-latitudinal zone, in the Yellow and Yangtze River basins, early China owned a vast territory suitable for agriculture; after the invention of rice- and millet-based agriculture, two complimentary agricultural systems and agriculture-centered mentalities took shape. Early China focused on maintaining internal stability, cultivating sophisticated ritual institutions, and formulating self-restrained and introspective characters. In its thousands of years of development, early China was largely confined to the east of the Hexi Corridor, with no indication of having waged large-scale territorial expansions.

The ritual vessels as "conveyors of *li*" have a long history. The pottery wares invented 20,000 years ago, evolved into ritual paraphernalia centered on *ding* around 4000 BCE. Through the Spring and Autumn and Warring States periods, the *ding* remained the primary ritual vessel. Jade artifacts, which appeared in 6000 BCE, likewise became a part of the ritual paraphernalia around 4000 BCE. Since the Bronze Age began around 2000 BCE, bronze wares were catapulted to dominate ritual paraphernalia. Albeit the form and combination of the ritual paraphernalia changed over time, the ritual institution was solidified as an integral component of the Chinese culture. It lasted through the Qin and Han dynasties and beyond.

b. Holistic thinking, secularism, and ancestral worship

The cultures of early China favored holistic thinking, emphasizing comprehensive, holistic, systematic, and organic approaches toward the world. The holistic worldview may have been rooted in Paleolithic experimentation with circles and was manifest in the possibly shamanistic activities of Peiligang culture around divination, music, medicine, and astronomy. When early China took shape, it was embodied in the octagons, *Taiji* designs, the jade *cong*-tubes, and bronze vessels with animal mask designs. In addition, the painted pottery of early China was mostly decorated with geometric designs, which evinced abstract holistic thinking.

Early China is, in general, characterized by secularism. Primitive religious beliefs were primarily latent in daily production and life; altars and iconic images were rarely seen in houses, while ancestral worship constituted the core of the belief system. The inhumation custom (burying a corpse) provided eternal abodes for the deceased ancestors; the cemeteries were spatially divided into zones and groups, indicating the existence of lineage organization, respect for ancestors, and an emphasis on social order.

c. Early China is a multi-component unity

The persistence of the pebble-flake stone industry throughout the Paleolithic Age and the co-existence of pebble stone tools in the south and microlithic tools in the north exhibit the homogeneity and diversity of cultural development in China. In the Neolithic, the five cultural systems were fused into three cultural systems, and the Yellow River and the Yangtze River basins, especially the Central Plain, became prominent from the middle Neolithic. During the Miaodigou period, a three-tiered structure centered upon the Central Plain emerged in early China, which evolved into a four-tiered structure during the Erlitou–Erligang periods, when the Central Plain slightly diminished in power, yet the structure remained intact. Such a "multi-petaled flower" structure lasted through the late Shang, Western Zhou, Qin, and Han dynasties and beyond. Chinese civilization's origin, formation, and development embodied the same multi-component unity structure. Since the Miaodigou period, three models of the origin of civilization and social development arose: Eastern, Northern, and Central Plain. The Central Plain Mode is characterized by the hierarchical treatment of the deceased, the emphasis on the elite status rather than wealth, the rigid ritual institution, and the self-restrained decorum, which are to become the essential features of the Chinese civilization of later times.

The multi-component unity of early China is the fundamental force that set into motion the uninterrupted development of Chinese civilization. This is conditioned by the relatively enclosed yet internally diverse geographical setting and the favorable environment for agriculture in the two river basins.

d. Early China experiences continuous yet vicissitudinous development

Given that the Central Plain is the heart of early China, the rise and fall of its cultures largely determined the checkered development of early China. In its prime times, the Central Plain led the entire of early China, whereas in its low times, it absorbed the advantages of the surrounding cultures. Thus, in the Miaodigou, Erlitou, and Erligang periods, which are the prime times of the Central Plain cultures, the unity of the Central Plain consolidated and commanded a tremendous power over the surrounding regions, which denotes the "unity"; in its low or incubation times, the unity of the Central Plain fell apart and gave its way to external influence, which denotes the "breakdown." While one would not downplay the significance of the Central Plain during its prime time, neither would one ignore the significance of the opportunities that the transitional or low period afforded the Central Plain to learn from the surrounding regions. These two phases are complimentary and interchangeable. It is in this very dialectical process consisting of the binary inhaling and exhaling, waxing and waning, and unity and breakdown that enabled the Central Plain cultures to develop spirally. The "early Chinese cultural sphere" gradually grows in size, internal bonding, and self-identifying; in the meantime, the historically significant "early China" evolves from its embryo state to maturity and lives on. Such a "unity-division" cycle lingered in Shang, Zhou, Qin, and Han times.

The vicissitudinous continuous development of early China makes the devotion to tradition part of the Chinese collective character, the underlying force of which lies with the cyclic climatic change.

In retrospect, we can see that early China as a cultural entity has a profound impact on the later development of China and the continuous development of China as a political entity. The multi-component unity lays the foundation for the hierarchical domains of the Shang and Zhou periods, the multi-ethnic state of the Qin and Han dynasties, and beyond. It directly affects the formation of the Chinese model of civilization formation, the "Chinese path" after the founding of the New China, the formation of the "imperial tributary system," and the independent foreign-relation policies of the New China. The vicissitudinous cultural development constitutes the basis for the continuous development of China and China's desire to maintain unity. The various traits of early China—agriculture-based, stable and introspective, ritualism, holistic thinking, secularism, and ancestral worship—nurtured the philosophies of Pre-Qin Confucians and Taoists, which practically became the cultural DNA of China. One may gain more insights for pondering over what path for China to take for further development: for instance, enforcing the principles of cultural diversity and unity, reformation and staying open to the world; carrying on the strategy of national cultural development, in which tradition-based yet open-minded advanced culture ensures that China walks a healthy developmental path; respecting the diverse cultures over the world, and employing the policies of peaceful co-existence, hand-in-hand development, fighting against expansion and invasion, colonialism, and cultural prejudice. In the meantime, we must keep ourselves aware that early China placed too much emphasis on maintaining the internal social order and was conservative regarding cultural exchange with other cultures. The agriculture-based culture and the lineage-centered social structure constrain the developmental space of urban centers, commerce, and public affairs. We must inherit the viable elements, discard the decadent ones, and learn what is wanted. Only when we vigorously keep our traditional culture alive and learn about the advanced cultures of the West and the world can we rejuvenate our country and nation.

HAN JIANYE

CHAPTER 1

Introduction

I. The Cultural and Political Significance of China

The term "China" first appeared in Western Zhou Dynasty (1046–771 BCE) literature. During the reign of King Cheng of Zhou, the following words were inscribed on the bronze vessel He *zun*: "King Cheng moved the capital to Chengzhou … When King Wu conquered the great city of Shang, he proclaimed to the heavens, 'I shall dwell in this Central Land, and from here govern the people.'"[1] The *Book of Documents · Timber of Rottlera* says, "God has committed the Central Land and its people, with their territories, to our former kings." The word "China" appears in several places in the *Book of Songs*, and in the *Book of Songs · Major Court Hymns · Decade of Sheng Min · Min Lao*, it is stated, "Love the people in the capital, and thus pacify the Four Directions." At that time, "China" was similar in meaning to "Central Land" or "Central Plain" and was contrasted with the "Four Directions." Together, they formed what is referred to as "Under the heavens, all land belongs to the king; on the edges of the land, all people are his subjects" in the *Book of Songs · Lesser Court Hymns · Decade of Gu Feng · Bei Shan*. "China" not only denoted the "country of the Central Land," namely the capital Chengzhou and Luoyi[2] but also represented the core of the "All under Heaven" that possessed the mandate of Heaven and royal power. Although it was not a modern term for a nation, it carried profound political significance.[3] From the Spring and Autumn and Warring States periods (770–221 BCE) to the Qin (221–207 BCE) and Han dynasties (202 BCE–220 CE), "China" was often contrasted with the "four barbarians." Its scope expanded to the Central Plain and even further to the "orthodox calendar" dynasties established mainly by the

Han people.[4] However, it was still not a term for a nation, and its connotation was more minor than "all under Heaven." It was not until the Qing Dynasty (1616–1911 CE) Kangxi, Yongzheng, and Qianlong emperors unified the country and established the basic spatial structure of modern China that "China" became an actual national name. After the Xinhai Revolution (1911 Revolution), "China" became the abbreviation for the "Republic of China."

"China," commonly used today, refers to the abbreviation for the People's Republic of China, also called modern China. Modern China can be observed from both cultural and political perspectives. Culturally, modern China is characterized by a "pluralistic unity" of multiple ethnic groups and regional cultures. Politically, it is a fundamentally unified country capable of exercising sovereignty over approximately 9.6 million square kilometers of territory and a specific range of territorial waters and airspace. It is further divided into over 30 provincial administrative units. Although the divisions of internal units in modern China are not consistent in terms of cultural and political significance, they generally share unifying characteristics, and their geographical spaces are largely consistent.[5]

Before modern China, there was historical China, and opinions on its spatial or territorial scope were diverse, with at least five viewpoints summarized by some.[6] Among them, the most representative view is advocated by Tan Qixiang, the editor-in-chief of the *Historical Atlas of China*, who argues for the territory of the Qing Dynasty before the Opium War (1840 CE) as the scope of historical China. He asserts:

> We can neither use the ancient concept of "China" for historical China nor limit the scope of our historical China to today's China. We should adopt the whole historical period and the China that has naturally formed over thousands of years of historical development as historical China. We believe that the scope of China between the mid-18th century and 1840 is the China that has naturally formed through thousands of years of historical development, and this is our historical China. As for the current territory of China, it is no longer the naturally formed range in history but rather the result of the partition of our territory by capitalist and imperialist powers in the past century or so. Therefore, it cannot represent the territory of historical China.[7]

Under Tan Qixiang's guidance, we can make at least three observations from a macro perspective on the development of historical China since the Qin and Han empires.

First, the so-called unification and division primarily pertain to the political realm, while culturally, China has maintained considerable stability. The cultural significance of China serves as an essential foundation for the aspiration of unity during political division and the maintenance of unity during political unification. Although the Central Plain and border regions experience unification and division, war and peace at different times, their economic interdependence and constant cultural exchange lead to an overall trend of increasing unity in the cultural sense of China. The geographical scope also generally expanded, ultimately giving rise to a politically unified multiethnic nation after the mid-18th century.

Second, in the interaction between the Central Plain and border regions, the Central Plain and its "Han culture" generally play a core and leading role. Although the strength of the Central Plain varies, it overall holds a dominant position. Despite the coexistence of multiple ethnic cultures and their complex exchange and integration processes, "Han culture" occupies the main body, with the assimilation of other ethnic cultures by "Han culture" being mainstream. Even during the Yuan (1206–1368 CE) and Qing dynasties, when minority ethnic groups ruled the Central Plain, China did not perish but saw its territory expand significantly due to a broader integration and "Sinicization."

Third, regarding foreign relations, China relies on the radiating influence of its distinctive culture rather than political and economic intervention. It advocates "royal power" instead of "hegemony," respects the different cultures of various countries and ethnic groups and wins people over with virtue. It has established a tribute system with China as the suzerain state, which contributes more than it takes, thereby maintaining long-term stability and harmony in the international order of East Asia and beyond.

II. The Concept of Early China in a Cultural Sense

The concept of "early China" was proposed by American scholar David N. Keightley in 1975 when he founded the publication *Early China*. The time range spans from prehistory to the Han Dynasty,[8] but "China" is more of a geographical concept. Here, when I refer to "early China" or the cultural sense of early China, I mean the relatively cultural community formed by the interaction and integration of cultures in most parts of China before the Qin and Han dynasties, which can also be called the "early Chinese cultural sphere."[9] This is obviously a concept with specific historical connotations. Compared to historical China after the Qin and Han empires, "early China" has distinct characteristics: it was a "pre-imperial" period without the emergence of true centralized power, although the Huns and other nomadic peoples of the North had appeared in the historical stage, their strength was limited, and the pressure on the predominantly agricultural population of the Central Plain was far less than in later times.

Early China centered around the Central Plain, and at least since the Five Emperors, it has been understood to have developed continuously in traditional Chinese historiography. However, since the late Qing Dynasty, with the collision of Chinese and Western cultures and the exposure of China's vulnerable position, the thought of doubting the ancient has gradually become popular at home and abroad. This understanding has faced unprecedented challenges, as seen in the work of *Doubting Antiquity*, edited by Gu Jiegang and others.[10] Of course, with the discovery and research of oracle bone inscriptions, the study and collation of ancient history by scholars such as Wang Guowei,[11] Xu Xusheng,[12] and Meng Wentong,[13] as well as the archaeological discoveries and research of essential sites such as Yin Ruins since the 1920s,[14] extreme thought of doubting the ancient has faded from the field of historiography. It has become an academic consensus that the history of China since the late Shang Dynasty (1600–1046 BCE) is credible and that the origins of Chinese civilization predate the late Shang Dynasty.

According to the *Book of Documents · Announcement about Drunkenness*, the officials and nobles of the Shang Dynasty can be divided into two categories: "inner *Fu*" and "outer *Fu*";[15] according to oracle bone inscriptions, the area directly governed by the Shang king was "Da Yi Shang," "Tian Yi Shang," or "Shang," while the surrounding governed or related regions were "Four Directions" and "Four Lands."[16] According to *Discourses of the States · Discourses of Zhou*, there was a system of Five *Fu*, including *Dian, Hou, Bin, Yao,* and *Huang*, during the Western Zhou period.[17] Perhaps these records, especially the Five *Fu* system of the Western Zhou, have some idealized elements. Still, implementing a hierarchical administrative system during the Shang and Zhou periods is beyond doubt. This system was based on basic blood and clan relationships, with kinship relationships extending from the inside out and spatially from near to far. At least from the Western Zhou period, the feudal system was implemented,[18] adopting different governance methods according to different levels, advocating "kingly power" rather than "hegemony," ruling with virtue, relying on the radiating influence of excellent culture rather than merely political and economic intervention, respecting the different cultures of each region, and forming a fairly stable cultural or political community. It can be said that there was a clear existence of early China in the cultural sense during the late Shang Dynasty, which continued during the Western Zhou period amid changes.

However, whether there was a continuous development of early China in the cultural sense before the late Shang Dynasty or what kind of cultural patterns, characteristics, and development processes this early China had still needed to be more conclusive and clearer. Even during the late Shang Dynasty and the Western Zhou, the scope and pattern of "early China" were diverse and disputed.

In the heated discussion on the origin of Chinese civilization since the 1980s, most of the research, mainly conducted by Chinese scholars, directly discussed the timing, symbols, and processes of the origin of ancient Chinese civilization or the state and used the term "China" without further investigating the concept of "China" or defining the scope of "China." This naturally led to some criticism from sensitive Western counterparts, even associating it with nationalism and chauvinism.

There are at least three different understandings in the academic community on the issue of early China.

The first acknowledges that the cultural origins of China after the Qin and Han dynasties can be found in the local prehistoric culture. However, as late as the late Shang Dynasty, there was no prototype for the future basic structure of China, let alone the Neolithic.* This view criticizes the concept of the so-called "eternal China," with Bagley as its representative.

The second holds that "early China" or "the earliest China" formed during the Xia (2070–1600 BCE) and Shang periods. For example, Xu Hong proposed that "the earliest China" began with the Erlitou[19] or late Xia culture. Ai Lan also pointed out, "The upper culture formed in Erlitou, the range of which is imitated far exceeded its political territory, and its specific form set a trajectory for a superstructure. Through this superstructure, future Chinese people determined their civilization. Although the discovery of bronze vessels does not necessarily reflect political authority and local cultural diversity still exists, this upper culture lays the foundation for a common culture. In the time of Confucius, this common culture was defined according to shared rituals. Therefore, we may have reason to call it 'Chinese Civilization.'"[20]

---

* The Neolithic Age in China is approximately 10,000 to 2,000 years before the present.—Trans.

The third believes that the basic structure of China after the Qin and Han dynasties already had a prototype in the Neolithic. The opinions of Yan Wenming and Zhang Guangzhi represent this. Su Bingqi also pointed out a "consensus China"[21] existed in the pre-Qin period. As a summary of the phased achievements of the "Chinese Civilization Source Exploration Project," a large exhibition entitled *Early China: The Origin of Chinese Civilization* was held in 2009. According to Yan Wenming, "early China" was clearly in the time range from the Chalcolithic (the transitional period between the Neolithic and the Bronze Age) to before the late Shang Dynasty (3500–1400 BCE).[22] Similar to Yan Wenming's view, Zhao Hui particularly emphasized the special position of the Central Plain: "The Central Plain stands out as a cultural entity, not only preparing the regional stage for the three future generations of civilization but also forming the multiple spatial structures of Chinese culture." He believed that the formation of the historical trend centered on the Central Plain "started between 3000 BCE and 2500 BCE."[23] Subsequently, he further demonstrated the prehistoric foundation of China centered on the Central Plain.[24]

Among these three understandings, only the third is a conclusion drawn after carefully reviewing the archaeological and cultural spectrum structure since the Neolithic. It has even initially established the basic framework of the early Chinese cultural sphere. The first and second understandings are mainly inferred, based on the situation during the Xia (2070–1600 BCE) and Shang periods. Even for the third understanding, the spatial structure of the "Chinese interaction circle" or the "consensus-based China" still deserves further study. Its characteristics must be summarized, the formation and development process must be systematically sorted out, and the mechanism needs to be explored in depth. In particular, the issue of the continuous development of early Chinese civilization and whether it is centered on the Central Plain deserves further discussion.

I have been committed to the research of early China issues since 2000. In 2004, I discussed the special status of the Central Plain culture in the Chinese Neolithic.[25] In 2005, I explicitly proposed the concept of the "early Chinese cultural sphere" and the culturally defined "early China."[26] In 2009, I suggested that early China, in the cultural sense, emerged in the mid-Neolithic around 6000 BCE and officially formed in the late Neolithic around 4000 BCE.[27] However, most of these studies focus on a specific period or issue and need a more systematic and comprehensive discussion.

III. The Purpose of This Book

The relationships between the Shang *Wangji* (inner *Fu*) and neighboring states, revealed by oracle bone inscriptions, and the multilevel structured community centered around the Yin Ruins revealed by archaeological remains,[28] all indicate that there was an early China in a cultural sense during the late Shang Dynasty. However, this is still a contentious issue. Therefore, this book mainly studies early China in a cultural sense before the late Shang Dynasty.

What are the characteristics of early China in a cultural sense that distinguish it from other early civilizations? What is its spatial scope and pattern? When was it formed, and what is its process of development and evolution? What is the environmental background and the driving mechanism for the formation and development of early China? These are all key topics for discussion in this book. Clarifying these issues can lay a foundation for in-depth research into the origins and development of early Chinese civilization and objectively evaluate the position of early Chinese civilization in the history of global civilization, which is one of the purposes of writing this book.

What impact has early China in a cultural sense had on the continuous development of cultural China afterward, and how has it influenced the "long united, must divide; long divided, must unite" in the political sense of China and the formation of the Chinese civilization model in the world civilization system? Understanding the experience of thousands of years of continuous development of early China in a cultural sense should provide important insights for clarifying the future direction of China's development, choosing a development path suitable for China, and for the harmonious coexistence and sustainable development of all human beings. This is the second purpose of writing this book.

Ge Zhaoguang's book *Dwelling in China* begins by introducing "China as a problem and the problem of China."[29] Historical China has already been fraught with ambiguity, and modern China is even more likely to cause controversy in the context of revitalization. Leaving aside the prejudices brought about by different standpoints and perspectives of the theorist, the lack of systematic and in-depth research on early China should be an essential reason for the controversy. The hope is that the research in this book can clarify some facts and resolve some disputes, which is the third purpose of writing this book.

IV. Research and Writing Approach

The exploration of early China or early Chinese cultural sphere in a cultural sense before the late Shang Dynasty should be based on early China during the late Shang and Western Zhou periods. This exploration should first examine the spatiotemporal scope and characteristics, or traits, of its cultural community, with the spatiotemporal scope being based on these characteristics and traits. Simply put, the characteristics here mainly refer to the observable external features of archaeological remains, while the traits mainly refer to the inherent nature reflected by the archaeological remains.

Early China, from the late Shang Dynasty to the Qin and Han periods, and even China throughout history, has always centered on the Yellow and Yangtze River basins. Once a cultural community is formed that can roughly encompass the Yellow River and Yangtze River basins with similar characteristics and traits, it marks the formation of early China in a cultural sense. The formation of early China took time. It should have had a long origin process, and after its formation, it underwent several stages of development. Therefore, this book's main chapters are arranged chronologically to discuss early China's origin, formation, and development process, from the Paleolithic Age (300000–10000 BCE) to the early Shang Dynasty. The research is based on comprehensive archaeological data, mainly using the methods of archaeological typology, archaeological stratigraphy, and archaeological culture, focusing on sorting out cultural lineages.

Early China was formed due to cultural blending and connections. However, it's quite common for neighboring cultures to have exchanges, and it is not easy to determine what level of connection is considered close, what common characteristics and traits should be included in early China, or how to define the boundary of early China. Even in the Western Zhou period, the definition of the outer edge of "the world" was rather vague. This book defines early China's basic cultural characteristics and traits based on the Central Plain as the core and the Yellow River and Yangtze River basins as the main body. The further away from this, the fewer similar cultural characteristics and traits must be distinguishable and cannot be completely another cultural system, especially toward the west. It cannot be a Western cultural system. The discussion of the spatial scope of early China and its developmental changes thus becomes the basic content running through the main chapters of this book.

The formation of civilization and the formation of early China can be two different things: the formation of civilization in a general sense emphasizes the degree of social complexity, which does not necessarily occur when early China forms, and the formation of early China does not necessarily have to be after the formation of civilization. However, the formation of "Chinese civilization" must be after the formation of early China. Connecting most of China's regions into a relative cultural community would be unimaginable without the strong energy from the core area and a certain degree of social uncivilization. Therefore, the formation and development of early China is generally also the process of forming and developing early Chinese civilization, so this book discusses the two together. As Yan Wenming did, research on the origin of civilization needs to combine settlement archaeology and archaeological cultural lineage research, rather than relying solely on settlement archaeology to discuss issues of social complexity.

After the late Shang Dynasty, the economy of the Yellow River and Yangtze River basins in China has always been dominated by the dual agricultural system of dry and rice farming, which is also the largest agricultural economic community in the world. What was the economic form of early China before this? This is also content that this book will cover. This section will, of course, absorb many results of agricultural archaeological research.

These constitute the main content of chapters two to five of this book.

Chapter six of this book mainly discusses the relationship between early China and ancient legends. This involves discussions of ancient legends about the early Shang, Xia, and even the Five Emperors' Period, focusing on corroborative research with archaeology. According to my understanding, China's ancient legends mainly consist of a historical system centered on Huaxia,* and one should not expect this ancient historical system to encompass the entire range of early China, not to mention that there are many errors and exaggerations in it. But we should not throw the baby out with the bathwater and give up using the materials from ancient legends. These pieces of ancient history have been passed down orally to the Shang, Zhou (1046–256 BCE), Qin, and Han periods and recorded and organized at different times. As long as they are carefully analyzed, the falsely

---

* "Huaxia" is equivalent in meaning to "Zhonghua" (or "China"). Initially, it referred to several tribes or political communities distributed in the middle and lower reaches of the Yellow River in prehistoric times. These Huaxia people are considered by later generations as one of the origins of Han culture and Chinese civilization.—Trans.

discarded, and the truly preserved, their value is immeasurable because they directly point to early China, far beyond ethnographies, anthropology, and other marginal materials for comparison. Fortunately, we have the base of Gu Jiegang and others' skeptical collation of ancient books and history and the constructive achievements of Wang Guowei, Xu Xusheng, and others to utilize. I have also done some research in this area.

Chapter seven of this book discusses the environmental foundation of early China, attempting to discuss why such a huge early Chinese cultural sphere would emerge in this region centered on the Yellow River and Yangtze River basins in East Asia from the perspective of the characteristics and development and evolution of the natural environment, why such characteristics and traits would form, and the possible relationship between the changes in each stage of early China and environmental evolution. I am certainly not an environmental determinist, but I still believe that the natural environment has a crucial impact on cultural development. Although the environment cannot determine the direction of cultural development, the same environmental changes may have different consequences for different cultures. Still, it is undeniable that the specific environment profoundly affects the characteristics and traits of culture, and environmental changes will certainly have this or that impact on cultural changes. Many geological and environmental archaeological research results can be used in this regard, especially Yan Wenming's excellent macroscopic discussion on the environmental basis of early China.

CHAPTER 2

China before Early China

(Before 4200 BCE)

I. The Ancient Basis of Early Chinese Race and Culture

Everything has a source. Early China's racial and cultural foundation should naturally be sought in the earliest chapters of human history on the Chinese land—the Paleolithic Age. Based on existing data, it is generally believed that the cultural development of the Paleolithic Age in China is roughly divided into early, middle, and late phases. Ancient humans of different evolutionary levels, such as Homo erectus, early Homo sapiens, and late Homo sapiens, have successively lived on the Chinese land.[1] So, what is the basic situation of these cultures and ancient humans in the Paleolithic Age in China, and what is their connection with the culture and humans after the Neolithic? This is the first question we need to clarify.

1. The Theory of "Continuous Evolution Accompanied by Hybridization" in Human Evolution

Is China one of the cradles of early human origins? This is still a matter of debate. The African origin theory of early humans believes that since the earliest members of the human family—the Australopithecines from two to four million years ago—were primarily found in Africa, early humans must have originated in Africa and then spread to the Eurasian continent after the appearance of Homo erectus about 1.5 million years ago. However, some scholars believe East Asia, especially

China, is also one of the origins of early humans, but more evidence is needed to prove this. After the late period of the early Pleistocene,* Homo erectus, early Homo sapiens, and late Homo sapiens lived successively on the Chinese land. Did they develop continuously, and were there foreign genes involved in the process? Are the late Homo sapiens in China resulting from the second "Out of Africa"?

Early Homo Erectus

In the late period of the early Pleistocene in geology, the earliest humans to appear on Chinese land were the early Homo erectus, the most definite of which is the Lantian man from Gongwangling, Lantian County, Shaanxi,[2] generally believed to be about 1.1 million years old. Other Homo erectus discoveries, such as in Shangnabang, Yuanmou, Yunnan Province, and Quyuanhekou, Yun County, Hubei Province, have different theories on their ages, ranging from 500,000 to 600,000 years to the earliest 1.7 million years. These earliest human materials are scarce, their ages are highly controversial, and their overall physical features still need clarification. The most representative Lantian man and Yun County man have significant differences in skulls, such as the larger brain capacity of Yun County man and the skull less robust than Lantian man. However, some standard features can already be observed. In addition to the primitive features determined by the era, there are characteristics associated with the later Proto-East Asian race,[3] such as shovel-shaped incisors, and the orientation of the frontonasal and front maxillary sutures approximately at the same horizontal position. These features are significantly different from the skull of the early African Homo erectus.

It should be said that the early Homo erectus in China already had traces of the later Proto-East Asian race. Considering that the humans within the cultural scope of early China were basically of the Proto-East Asian race, the early Homo erectus in China is likely to be one of the earliest gene sources of the race in "early China."

Late Homo Erectus and Early Homo Sapiens

The human fossils discovered in the middle Pleistocene are numerous and complete, with the Beijing Homo erectus from Zhoukoudian site No. 1 being the most representative. Others include the Hexian man in Anhui Province and the Tangshan man in Nanjing City, roughly dated between 780,000 and 128,000 years ago. The cranial capacity increased to over 1,000 milliliters (compared to

---

* The Pleistocene is estimated to have begun approximately 2.5882 million years ago and ended 117,000 years ago.—Trans.

the previous 780 milliliters of the Lantian man), the skull became taller, the bone wall thinned, and the brow ridge and teeth were not as robust as before, showing clear progressive characteristics, entering the late Homo erectus stage. What is particularly noteworthy is that human evolution showed a significant imbalance at this time. For instance, the cranial capacity of the Jinniushan man, who lived roughly at the same time as the late Beijing Homo erectus, had reached 1,300 milliliters, showed obvious progress, and belonged to the early type of early Homo sapiens. Regardless, the middle Pleistocene humans in China generally had characteristics such as shovel-shaped incisors, sagittal crests, Inca bones, broad noses, round infraorbital margins, and round occipital bones of the mandible. Some of these characteristics were already present in the early Pleistocene humans in China, showing obvious regional inheritance traits.

The human fossils from the early period of the late Pleistocene are mostly early Homo sapiens, which can be further subdivided into early types like the Dali man and later types like the Maba man, Dingcun man, and Xujiayao man, dating approximately between 128,000 and 35,000 years ago. These human fossils have progressive characteristics similar to those in other parts of the world, such as a significant increase in cranial capacity, taller skulls, thinner bone walls, "inverted 八" (*ba*)-shaped brow ridges, higher temporal scales, etc. At the same time, they still have shovel-shaped incisors, Inca bones, sagittal crests, lower nasal bones, high cheekbones, and broader cheeks, like the later Proto-East Asian features, indicating their evolutionary continuity with Homo erectus in China.[4] Moreover, although there are minor physical differences among these early Homo sapiens in China, they are significantly different from the Neanderthals in Europe and Western Asia.

Late Homo Sapiens

The late period of late Pleistocene spanned approximately between 35,000 and 12,000 years ago. Most of China was occupied by late Homo sapiens—modern humans. Their extent and speed of expansion into surrounding areas were unprecedented, in line with their advanced intellectual capacity. The human fossils found in China still had some differences. Still, all showed decreased tooth and facial size compared to early Homo sapiens, a weakened brow ridge, and an increased cranial size within the range of contemporary human variation. Of course, some primitive traces were retained in early modern humans (such as the Liujiang man, Shandingdong man, etc.), such as a more robust skull, more developed brow ridges and sagittal crests, and thicker bone walls.

Some people believe modern humans, represented by the Liujiang man, had already appeared in the early Pleistocene. Not only that, but a segment of human mandible fossil unearthed in a cave in Chongzuo City in Guangxi Province, dating back to about 100,000 years ago, has already shown a series of derivative features of modern humans, such as a prominent genial tubercle, an obvious mental fossa, moderately developed lateral projections, an almost vertical mandibular symphysis, and a clear curvature of the mandibular symphysis cross section. Some believe that the ancient humans of Chongzuo belong to the emerging early modern humans,[5] and their time predates when modern humans arrived in East Asia, according to the "Out of Africa" theory.[6]

The Origin of Proto-East Asian Race

The earliest modern humans in China and East Asia—late Homo sapiens—have a history of about 100,000 years. These late Homo sapiens already have the basic features of modern Proto-East Asians, such as shovel-shaped incisors, round occipital bones of the mandible, large and prominent cheekbones, broad and flat nasal bones, and wide piriform apertures. They already belong to the category of primitive Proto-East Asian and have an apparent inheritance from the early Homo sapiens and Homo erectus previously found in China. Therefore, the main theme of human evolution in China and East Asia is the continuous evolution of indigenous humans. However, it is undeniable that there is a more popular theory that the global origin of modern humans is in Africa, the "Eve" theory. Furthermore, since the late period of late Pleistocene, the culture in East Asia, like the western part of the Old World, has developed rapidly and instep, which may indeed be the result of genetic and cultural exchanges with modern Western human groups. Given this, scholars like Wu Xinzhi have proposed the "continuous evolution with additional hybridization" model for the evolution of human beings in the Paleolithic Age in China, which may essentially align with reality.[7]

2. The Unity and Diversity of Culture

China is vast and rich in Paleolithic culture. Do these cultures have a process of continuous evolution? What is the status of foreign factors in them? Does the culture of the Paleolithic Age in China have the characteristics of unity and diversity, and in what aspects of culture have laid the foundation for the culture after the Neolithic?

Early Paleolithic Culture in the Early Paleolithic Age
China's earliest human culture naturally comes from the late period of the early Pleistocene's early Paleolithic culture in the early Paleolithic Age, which is the culture created by early Homo erectus. In addition to the culture of the Lantian man mentioned above, there are also Paleolithic cultures in the early Pleistocene, such as Xihoudu in Ruicheng County, Shanxi Province, Maquangou and Xiaochangliang in Yangyuan County, Hebei Province, dating between 1.7 and 1 million years ago. These earliest cultures are mainly distributed in China's Second Ladder (in the central and northern part of China), where the relatively developed culture of the north and south of the Qin Mountains just happened to be the core of the "early China," which is thought-provoking.

These cultures can be divided into at least two systems. One system is represented by the stone tools of Yun County man and Lantian man, which are mainly extensive stone tools made directly from gravel, such as chopping tools, primitive handaxes, etc., being the originator of the South China gravel industry, whose economic mode may mainly be the digging and gathering of tuberous plants in the forest environment. The other system is represented by the early Pleistocene stone tools in the Nihewan Basin, which are mainly small stone tools such as scrapers made by striking and peeling off lithic flakes from bedrock fragments, being the prototype of the North China lithic flakes and stone tool industry, whose economic mode may mainly be hunting medium and small animals in the grassland environment. Regardless, the processing technology of both systems is just a simple lithic core-chopper technique, belonging to the Mode I stone tool technology in Clark's classification.[8] As pointed out by Wang Youping, it is very close to the earliest Olduvai stone tool industry in East Africa, showing its primitive nature.[9]

Late Paleolithic Culture in the Early Paleolithic Age
The culture was created mainly by the late Homo erectus in the middle Pleistocene, namely the late Paleolithic culture in the early Paleolithic Age. Wang Youping roughly divided it into two major areas, the South and the North, along the Qin Mountains–Huai River line, and divided it into two types from the perspective of the stone tool industry, namely, the large gravel industry in the eastern South and the southern North, and the small lithic flake industry in the western South and northern North.[10] The eastern South and the southern North,

dominated by the large gravel industry, are connected, which can be regarded as a large area—the southeastern cultural region; the western South and the northern North, dominated by the small lithic flake industry are far apart and should be divided into different areas.

The southeastern cultural region is mainly located on China's Third Ladder and its western edge, extending west to the Loess Plateau in eastern Gansu Province and Hanzhong Basin, north to both sides of the southern Taihang Mountains, east to the lower reaches of the Yangtze River, and south to the south of Nanling Mountains. The Paleolithic sites or groups of sites are most concentrated in the border areas of Shanxi, Shaanxi, and Henan provinces, Luonan Basin, Hanzhong Basin in southern Shaanxi Province, the northwest region of Hubei Province, the middle and lower reaches of Li River in Hunan Province, and Baise Basin in the Guangxi Zhuang Autonomous Region, most of which are near rivers, represented by the Paleolithic sites such as Kehe in Ruicheng County in Shanxi Province, Longgangsi in Nanzheng District in Shaanxi Province, and Jigongdang in Li County in Hunan Province. The stone tools are mostly large chopping tools, pointed tools, primitive handaxes, and stone balls made mainly by percussion method, among which, there are also some chopping tools made from large lithic flakes in the north of the Qin Mountains–Huai River, mainly single-sided processing, belonging to the large gravel tool industry.

The cultural region of the northern North and western South is mainly on China's Second Ladder, with the Nihewan Basin being the most concentrated site, many of which are cave sites, represented by the first site of Zhoukoudian in Fangshan District of Beijing, Jinniushan in the Yingkou City of Liaoning Province, and Guanyin Cave in Qianxi County in Guizhou Province. The stone tools are mainly small scrapers and other lithic flake tools, with the percussion and battering methods being important, with few chopping tools belonging to the small lithic flake industry.

The most significant change is the large-scale human expansion from the Second Ladder to the Third Ladder. Regional features are also more clearly seen, but the southeastern cultural region and the northern cultural region in the North, to a considerable extent, are the continuations of the previous two large regions of the South and North. Overall, the stone tool processing technology still mainly inherits the previous simple lithic core-chopper technique, showing obvious consistency and inheritance of local traditions, which is quite different from the delicate handaxe industry popular on the western side of the Old World.

Mid-Paleolithic Age Culture

The culture created mainly by early Homo sapiens in the early late Pleistocene, namely the mid-Paleolithic culture, is the same as the previous structure. The southeastern cultural region is represented by locations or sites such as Dingcun in Xiangfen County, Shanxi Province, Beiyao in Luoyang City, Henan Province, Jigong Mountain in Jiangling County, Hubei Province, and Maba in Qujiang District, Guangdong Province. Meanwhile, the northern North and the western South cultural regions are represented by locations or sites such as the site No. 15 of Zhoukoudian in Beijing, Gezidong in Kazuo County, Liaoning Province, Xujiayao in Yanggao County, Shanxi Province, Salawusu in Wushen Banner, Inner Mongolia Autonomous Region, Ziyang City in Sichuan Province, and Gaojiazhen in Fengdu County. The former still generally belongs to the large gravel industry, except that the stone tool repair is more exquisite, and the proportion of stone tools processed from lithic flakes has increased. However, it is worth noting that in the northwest edge, such as in the Jing and Wei River basins, there appears the phenomenon of the large gravel industry being replaced by the small lithic flake industry with scrapers as the main body. The latter still belongs to the small lithic flake industry, with no significant difference from before. Neither of the two major regions in China shows the influence of Levallois and Mousterian techniques, forming a stark contrast with the western side of the Old World.

Late Paleolithic Age Culture

The culture of modern humans in the late period of the late Pleistocene was the late Paleolithic culture. The most notable is the significant expansion of the cultural range currently. It has reached the Xizang Plateau to the west,[11] as seen in the stone tool sites by Siling Lake[12] and Pangong Lake.[13] It has also extended to the Xinjiang Autonomous Region.[14] To the north, it has expanded to the Songhua River, Nen River, and Heilong River basins in the middle and north of Northeast China, seen at the Dabusu in Qian'an, Jilin Province, Zhoujiayoufang in Yushu, Harbin, Heilongjiang Province, and Guxiangtun, Yanjiagang, and Ang'angxi in the city of Qiqihaer.[15] To the east, it crossed the continental shelf that was widely exposed, creating the Changbin culture. Second, there were significant changes in cultural patterns and features, which can roughly be divided into the northwest and southeast regions. The northwestern grassland area itself can be divided into three cultural traditions: one is the small stone tool industry tradition inherited from the local earlier traditions, such as the Shiyu site; the second is the microlithic industry tradition that developed slightly later based on this, with a large number of microlith leaves used to make compound tools appearing, and end scrapers occupying an important position, such as the Xiachuan culture; the third is the stone leaf culture tradition, characterized by a large number of regularly shaped stone leaves produced by the direct percussion method, seen at the Shuidonggou site in Lingwu, Ningxia Province.[16] Among them, the stone leaf culture might have been introduced from places like Altay, and the microlithic technique may have been generated based on the small stone tool industry in the North China region under the influence of the West, indicating that there was a relatively close cultural exchange with the West in this region. The southeastern region has gradually developed into a region dominated by small lithic flake tools such as scrapers and pointed tools. In addition to the sites originally belonging to the small stone tools tradition, such as Shandingdong in Zhoukoudian, Beijing, and Xiaogushan Xianren Cave in Haicheng City in Liaoning Province, even the southeastern region that used to belong to the large gravel tool industry is no exception. However, its production technology remains simple and primitive, only "northernized" rather than "westernized." The round plate-shaped decorative bone tools found in Xiaogushan are common in the western part of the Old World, indicating that there was also cultural exchange with the West in this region.

Scrapers, pointed tools, engravers, conical tools, and stone leaves are mainly tools for dismembering animals. Some stone leaves can also be embedded in grooved bone stems to make bone-handle stone-blade knives, a compound tool that can potentially dismember animals and harvest plants. The occasional appearance of stone arrowheads indicates that long-range projectile tools had already appeared, which was of significant importance for the hunting economy. Although these small stone tools vary in shape, they are all practical tools for hunting and gathering economies adapted to the grassland environment. The miniaturization of some stone tools in the Southern regions indicates the expansion of the economic mode of hunting mammals from the north to the south. The appearance of fish harpoons reflects the significant development of fishing and hunting economies.

During this period, decorations made of various materials such as stones, bones, antlers, and teeth, often with holes for stringing, were discovered. As the Shandingdong site shows, these decorations were often found near human fossil bones, likely personal ornaments or pendants. This suggests that people at the time already had a clear concept of beauty and paid attention to their adornments. More importantly, the discovery of bone needles proves that people could already sew clothes. Dyeing ornaments red with ocher powder or scattering the powder next to a corpse indicates that early humans paid particular attention to red, which may have been related to blood or people's views on life and death. Therefore, Shandingdong is believed to contain the earliest graves in China. Engraved bone fragments and engraved deer antlers were also found at sites like Shiyu and Xinglongdong.[17] All of these significantly improved people's abstract thinking abilities.

3. Conclusion

Looking back at the Paleolithic Age in China, which lasted about two million years, one would find that despite the differences in time and space and occasional genetic and cultural exchanges with the West, the overall characteristics such as the shovel-shaped incisors of later Proto-East Asian races are prevalent. The tradition of the gravel-lithic flake industry runs through, demonstrating significant continuity and unity in human evolution and cultural development. The formation of this unity is mainly due to the continuous exchanges within China over a long period.[18] It is in this sense that Su Bingqi said, "The majority of Chinese people are indigenous inhabitants of the East Asian continent, descendants of Peking Man; Chinese culture is an indigenous culture with a tradition of nearly two million years."[19]

Compared to the western Old World, most of the stone tools made during the Paleolithic Age in China belong to the gravel-lithic flake industry tradition, with few finely double-sided processed tools and less symmetry in tool shape, often classified into the Mode I of Clark's classification of stone tool technology.[20] These characteristics may be related to the relative lack of flint resources in most of China. While it may seem primitive on the surface, it should be seen as a long continuation of an ancient cultural tradition. Especially noteworthy is the discovery of round ornaments and beads with circular holes made of stone, bone, or ostrich eggshells at sites like Shandingdong, Shuidonggou, Xiaogushan, and Shiyu. However, these sites lack the "Venus" style sculptures[21] and cave paintings popular in the western Eurasian continent. These findings reflect the characteristics of the Proto-East Asian ancestors: they made use of local materials, preferred practicality, and tended to integrate "art" or primitive beliefs into everyday objects, resulting in a subdued religious tone. According to Zhang Guangzhi, these characteristics, which coincided with witchcraft or shamanistic culture, form a "Maya-Chinese cultural continuum"[22] and have persisted for tens of thousands of years. They have become the most "fundamental" cultural basis for early China, the East Asian region, and even the entire Proto-East Asian region.

II. Five Major Cultural Systems

Childe once proposed the concept of the "Neolithic Revolution," referring to the massive changes in human society following the advent of the Neolithic or the onset of agriculture.[23] However, the earliest appearance of agriculture was neither instantaneous nor widespread. The origin and spread of agriculture, or the transition from the Paleolithic Age to the Neolithic, was a complex process involving different paths and methods. This was true on a global scale, and it was also true in China.

1. The Earliest Appearance of Pottery and Agriculture

When did China enter the Neolithic? Or how do we define the early culture of the early Neolithic in China? Let us start by analyzing the earliest pottery in South China and nearby areas.

The earliest pottery remnants in South China and adjacent areas are represented by early finds from the Xianren Cave and Diaotonghuan sites in Jiangxi Province,[24] phase I of the Zengpiyan site in Guilin,[25] also in Guangxi Province, and early remains from the Yuchanyan site in Dao County in Hunan Province.[26] Evidence of fire-burning ash heaps, stone tool manufacturing sites, and squatting flexed burials have been discovered. In the late Paleolithic Age of China, only one site, Shandingdong in Beijing, could barely be considered a burial site, and the burial method is unclear. However, flexed burials are the main burial type found in the western Old World during the late Paleolithic Age.[27] If the hypothesis that modern humans migrated out of Africa in the late Paleolithic is somewhat valid, then flexed burials might be the earliest popular burial method among modern humans (fig. 2.1).[28]

The observed pottery includes only two types: round-bottom cauldrons and round-bottom earthen bowls, most of which are coarse in texture, low-fired, and unevenly finished, represented by coarse-grained brown pottery; common designs include imprinted cord-mark patterns, imprinted woven patterns, scraped stripes, and plain pottery. According to Zhang Chi's analysis, pottery blanks might have been created using the clay strip coiling and slab-building methods, with the earliest evidence of pottery with stripe patterns found in Xianren Cave, followed by double-sided cord-mark pottery, and finally, single-sided cord-mark pottery.[29] The absolute dating is estimated to be around 18000 BCE to 9000 BCE,[30] still at the end of the Pleistocene. Apart from a small amount of pottery, there were

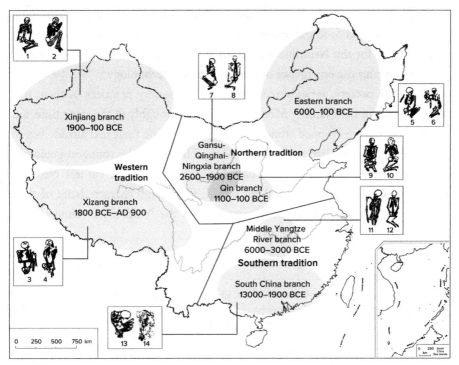

Figure 2.1 Diagram of the lineage of flexed burial in ancient China (13000 BCE–900 CE)

1. M244: Chawuhugou cemetery No. 4
2. M024: Yanghai II cemetery
3. M109: Qugong
4. M207: Qugong
5. M6: Baiyinchanghan
6. M73: Danangou
7. M3: Tugutai
8. M26: Qiedaoba
9. M26: Maojiaping
10. M25086: Taerpo
11. M187: Daxi
12. M79: Daxi
13. M5: Zengpiyan
14. M83: Dingsishan

also several bone, horn, and shell tools, and more importantly, various gravel stone tools inherited from the late Paleolithic Age. However, the discovery of stone hammers, stone drills, whetstones, and especially perforated weights, indicates a transition from chipped stone tools to ground stone tools.

In addition, the rice remains found at the Yuchanyan site and the phytoliths of rice at the Xianren Cave site suggest the possible emergence of primitive rice farming during this period,[31] and the Zengpiyan site might have seen the beginnings of domestic pig farming.[32] Of course, the proportions of agriculture and livestock farming in the socioeconomic structure were still limited, with the primary modes of production likely being gathering, fishing, and hunting. The large number of gravel stone tools found at various sites might have been used for digging up various root crops[33] and catching fish, snails, and shellfish. Some call this diversified food gathering a "broad spectrum revolution," considering it a prerequisite for the Neolithic revolution.[34] The appearance of marked cords on pottery indicates the emergence of primitive textile technology.

The early pottery, agriculture, and animal husbandry practices in these sites on both sides of the Nanling Mountains appeared roughly at the same time, and the transition from chipped stone tools to ground stone tools had already begun. Although this period had not yet entered the Holocene (the youngest geological age, from 11,700 years ago), it should already be one of the earliest Neolithic remains in China, East Asia, and the world. The overall characteristics of these remains are similar and can be summarized as the "cord-mark round-bottom cauldron cultural system" (table 2.1).

Table 2.1 Cultural regions of early Neolithic of China (18000–7000 BCE)

	Early stage (18000–9000 BCE)	Late stage (9000–7000 BCE)
South China	Cord-mark round-bottom cauldron cultural system (Early Xianren Cave, Zengpiyan phase I, and early Yuchanyan)*	Cord-mark round-bottom cauldron cultural system (Zengpiyan phase II, Dingsishan phase I, and Qihe Cave phase II)
Lower reaches of the Yangtze River	The end Paleolithic culture (Longwangchan, Shizitan, and Xiachuan remains)	Flat-bottom basin–round-foot plate–double-handle jar cultural system (Shanshan culture)
Central Plain		Deep-belly jar cultural system (Lijiagou culture)
Lower reaches of the Yellow River		Plain round-bottom cauldron cultural system (Early Bianbian Cave remains)
North China and the Northeast of China		Cylindrical jar cultural system (Nanzhuangtou, Donghulin, Zhuannian, Yujiagou remains, and Shuangta culture phase I)
Other regions		Mesolithic culture

* Typical remains or archaeological cultures belonging to the respective cultural systems are listed in parentheses. The same applies to subsequent entries.

2. The Formation of the Five Major Cultural Systems

From about 9000 BCE to 7000 BCE, in the Holocene, the landscape of China was characterized by the coexistence of five major cultural systems (table 2.1, fig. 2.2).[35] In addition to the areas around South China, the lower reaches of the Yangtze River, the Central Plain, the lower reaches of the Yellow River, the Northeastern regions, and North China also began to show evidence of Neolithic culture in the late early phases, including pottery artifacts.

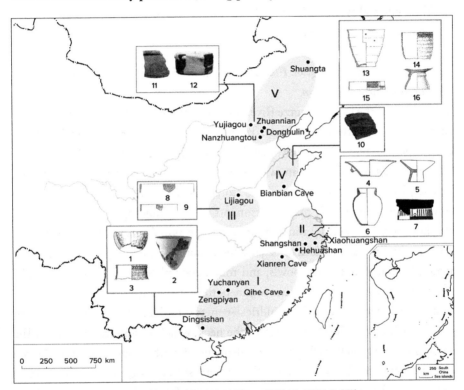

Figure 2.2 Cultural regions of early Neolithic China (18000–7000 BCE)

I. Cord-mark round-bottom cauldron cultural system
II. Flat-bottom–round-foot plate–double-handle jar cultural system
III. Deep-belly jar cultural system
IV. Plain round-bottom cauldron cultural system
V. Cylindrical jar cultural system

1–3. Cauldron (Zengpiyan DT628: 072, Yuchanyan 95DMT9: 26, Dingsishan T2206④: 1)
4. Basin (Shangshan H301: 1)
5, 16. High-foot plate (Shangshan H193: 1, Shuangta II T130②: 2)
6. Double-handle jar (Shangshan H226: 5)

7. Round-foot plate (Xiaohuangshan M2: 2)
8, 9. Deep-belly jar (Lijiagou 09XLL: 612, 738)
10. Plain cauldron (Bianbian Cave)
11–15. Cylindrical jar (Donghulin T9⑤: 20, Zhuannian, Shuangta II T406②: 4, II C2: 1, II T117②: 11)
(All pottery.)

South China: Cord-Mark Round-Bottom Cauldron Cultural System

The culture of South China and nearby regions is represented by the Zengpiyan phase II, Yongning Dingsishan phase I,[36] and Zhangping Qihe Cave phase II remains[37] in Fujian Province. These also generally include contemporary remains from Hainan Island and northern Vietnam. The pottery mainly consists of small-mouth high-neck cord-mark cauldrons, often with floral rims by impressed added relief decorations. This is a continuation of the previous cord-mark round-bottom cauldron cultural system. However, Qihe Cave phase II shows more stamped-dot patterns and jar-type vessels.

Lower Yangtze River Region: Flat-Bottom Basin–Round-Foot Plate–Double-Handle Jar Cultural System

The culture of the lower Yangtze River region is represented by the Pujang Shangshan phase I,[38] early Shengzhou Xiaohuangshan,[39] and Longyou Hehuashan[40] contemporary remains, mainly distributed in the region south of Hangzhou Bay. Findings include ash pits with stone grinding plates, stone grinding rods, or complete pottery, which may have storage or food processing functions, and rows of postholes which may be remnants of stilt buildings. Most pottery has flat bottoms, followed by round-foot ware. The popular types are open-mouth flat-bottom basins, double-handle jars, open-mouth high-foot plates, flat-bottom plates, flat-bottom earthen bowls, and round-foot plates, round-foot jars, high-neck pots, straight-belly cups, and round-bottom cauldrons. Common features are double ring-handles, double cylindrical-penetrating handles, or double handles, some of which are closely attached to the neck, which is quite characteristic. The main pottery is thick-wall and charcoal-included, with a loose texture and more sandy pottery in the later stages. The pottery surface is generally plain with a red coat, and a few are decorated with engraved folding lines and stamped-dot patterns on the outer edge. Some round feet are decorated with round or vertical hollowed-out holes. They were made by the clay strip coiling and the slab-building method. The stone tools are mainly lithic flakes and gravels, with a small number of stone grinding plates, rods, perforated weights, stone balls, and a very small amount of fully polished adzes and chisels. These remains have a wide variety of artifacts, complex accessories, decorations, and a higher level of development. They can be called the "flat-bottom basin–round-foot plate–double-handle jar cultural system." Due to its clear connotations, it has been named Shangshan culture. According to the analysis of rice husks found in the pottery, it can be known that this culture may have involved the cultivation of primitive japonica rice.[41]

Central Plain: Deep-Belly Jar Cultural System

The culture of the Central Plain is represented by the "microlithic cultural remains" and "early Neolithic remains" of Lijiagou in Xinmi City in Henan Province, also known as Lijiagou culture.[42] Findings include piles of stones containing grinding stones, anvils, burned stones, and fragments of animal bones, possibly left from processing edible plants and animals. The pottery is mainly straight-mouth deep-belly jar types, all of which are coarse sandy brown pottery with mottled colors. The exterior is often decorated with impressed round pit patterns and marked cords; a few are decorated with fine-tooth comb patterns with clustered dots and engraved patterns. Some pottery shards are rather hard, indicating they were fired at a high temperature. Numerous microliths, large sandstone products, flat stones, locally polished stone adzes, grinding stones, and anvils exist. It can be tentatively called the "deep-belly jar cultural system."

Lower Yellow River Region: Plain Round-Bottom Cauldron Cultural System

The early remains of Bianbian Cave in Yiyuan County in Shandong Province represent the culture of the lower Yellow River region.[43] Finds include burned earth surfaces, ash pits, and other traces. The pottery includes only fragments of the round-bottom cauldron and earthen bowls, thick-wall sandy brown pottery with uneven mottled surfaces, and uneven firing. They are mainly made by the clay strip coiling, with some surfaces slightly polished and some rims added with a clay ring. These include grinding stones, rods, and bone and antler tools such as awls, needles, and darts. This can be temporarily called the "plain round-bottom cauldron cultural system." Considering the middle and late Neolithic situation, this cultural system may extend to the Jianghuai region (between the Yangtze River and the Huai River).

North China and Northeast Region: Cylindrical Jar Cultural System

The culture of North China is represented by the early remains of Xushui Nanzhuangtou in Hebei Province,[44] Yangyuan Hutouliang Yujiagou,[45] Mentougou Donghulin,[46] and Huairou Zhuannian in Beijing,[47] mainly distributed at the foot of the Taihang and Yan Mountains; the Northeast region is represented by Jilin Province Baicheng Shuangta phase I.[48] At the Donghulin site, firepits and graves were found. The graves are all vertical pit burials, with the burial position mostly supine extended, occasionally supine flexed, and the deceased wearing bone bracelets, bone hairpins, and neck ornaments made of shells and animal bones. The supine extended burial position seems to be the natural state of the body after death, widely used in later China and being the earliest example, but its origin is still a mystery. Postholes were found at the Shuangta site, indicating the existence of buildings supported by wooden posts. Particularly noteworthy is the discovery of a flexed burial similar to those in South China at both the Donghulin and Shuangta sites.

Judging from the Donghulin site, pottery can be divided into two phases. Phase I pottery contains a large amount of talcum powder in fine sand, the thin walls are relatively dense, and the surface is uniform reddish-brown. The vessels are likely deep-arched jars and cauldrons, with added relief decorations with impressed patterns around the mouth, and the overall surface is plain. Phase II pottery contains a lot of coarse sand, the texture is loose, and the surface is unevenly brown. The pottery is shallow-belly cylindrical jars with large and round lips decorated with imprinted patterns. Comparatively speaking, the pottery from Nanzhuangtou and Yujiagou is similar to phase I of Donghulin, while Zhuannian pottery is similar to phase II of Donghulin. These two phases of pottery are quite different. They may belong to two cultural systems: if phase I pottery is round-bottom cauldrons, it is similar to the pottery of Bianbian Cave and belongs to the "plain round-bottom cauldron cultural system," but the overall situation is still unclear; phase II pottery can be classified as the "cylindrical jar cultural system." The Shuangta phase I is mostly coarse sandy brown pottery. Most are cylindrical jars, plain, or decorated with added relief decorations out rims, *Hui* patterns* with raised clay strips, etc. In addition, there are also parts of bulbous-belly jars, basins, high-foot plates, bowls, cups, and other pottery, especially the appearance of round-foot high-foot plate types attracts attention, referred to as Shuangta culture phase I. Overall, it also belongs to the "cylindrical jar cultural system."

The habit of bundling hair with hairpins and wearing bracelets on the arms became a widespread decorative custom in China later.[49] After the Zhou Dynasty, the hairpin even became a symbol of women's coming of age, and these two decorations first appeared in North China and the Northeast region. Shuangta culture phase I also discovered the earliest jade—jade beads, marking the beginning of the brilliant jade culture in eastern China later. Its origin can be traced back to the circular decorations with round holes in the late Paleolithic Age. The pottery shards with human or monkey faces found in Shuangta phase I may be ancestors worshipped by people at that time, reflecting a certain tradition of idol worship in the Northeast region ten thousand years ago.

---

* *Hui* (回) pattern is derived from the thunder patterns on ancient pottery and bronze ware. Since it is composed of square or circular looping patterns made of horizontal and vertical short lines and resembles the Chinese character "回," it is referred to as the *Hui* pattern.—Trans.

Stone tools mainly include chipped stone tools and microliths, as well as ground and abraded stone tools such as grinding stones, grinding rods, stone mortars, and stone grinding tools, and a small number of ground stone tools such as axes and adzes, as well as bone and antler tools and composite tools such as awls, fish darts, bone-handle stone-blade knives. Foxtail millet seeds were floated out of the Donghulin site,[50] and the starch grains remaining on the grinding stones, grinding rods, and pottery belonged to foxtail millets or nuts (acorns). The starch grains on the grinding stones and rods of Nanzhuangtou mainly belong to graminoids,[51] indicating that dry farming may have already appeared. Thus, North China became the earliest origin of sorghum and millet grain agriculture in China and even the world. The production tools of Shuangta culture phase I show that the economy was mainly based on fishing, hunting, and gathering, and the possibility of primitive dry farming cannot be ruled out.

It is worth noting that the earliest pottery spinning wheel was found at the Shuangta site, reflecting the further development of spinning technology. In fact, simple twisting rope technology should have already existed in the early stage of the early Neolithic, which can be seen in the popular cord-mark pottery in South China.

The Interrelationships of the Five Cultural Systems

Due to limitations in available data, it is still difficult to delve deeply into the relationships between these five cultural systems. Generally speaking, they seem to lack direct links due to their large spatial distances and significant differences, but there are commonalities, especially between neighboring cultural systems. These commonalities fall into two categories.

First, these could be due to similar economic models or shared stages of development. For example, crude pottery, coarse sand inclusions, and brown-painted decorations reflect pottery-making technology in its initial stages. The widespread appearance of grinding stones and rods in systems outside of South China may be related to the processing and utilization of cereal plant seeds brought about by changes in the natural environment.

Second, these could reflect certain connections between them. For example, the possible round-bottom cauldrons pottery of the Donghulin phase I may have originated from the lower reaches of the Yellow River, and the occasional flexed burials might have been influenced by the South China factors. The minor double-handle jars with collars and cord-mark round-bottom cauldrons at the Xiaohuangshan site in the lower reaches of the Yangtze River may have been influenced by the cord-mark round-bottom cauldron cultural system in South China. The impressed round pit patterns and marked cords deep-belly jar at the Lijiagou site in the middle reaches of the Yellow River may also have some connection with South China, and cord-mark pottery is also found at the Nanzhuangtou site in North China. Although no marked cords have been found at the Bianbian Cave site in the lower reaches of the Yellow River, pottery cauldrons are popular there, which may also suggest some relationship with South China. As for the presence of high-foot plate type round-foot vessels in both Shangshan culture and Shuangta culture phase I, whether this is a coincidence or a connection is currently difficult to judge. For instance, in well-documented areas like North China, Northeast China, and the lower reaches of the Yangtze River, the discovery of polished stone tools related to chopping or woodworking, such as stone axes, adzes, and chisels, indicates a similar tradition of woodworking, with the appearance of chisels suggesting the possible existence of mortise and tenon wood construction, thousands of years earlier than the appearance of copper chisels and mortise and tenon in Western Asia. This should reflect a tendency toward sedentism and the widespread use of timber for building houses.[52] In addition, South China and the lower Yangtze River region are known for chipped gravel tools and perforated weights, likely related to gathering and processing root and tuber plants. In the middle and lower reaches of the Yellow River and North China, microliths are common and likely related to hunting small animals. The formation of connections between the different systems could be due to contemporary exchange or possibly common origins. Pottery first appeared in South China, and "evidence suggests a single origin for pottery-making technology."[53] Considering that the continental shelf between Eastern China and Japan was exposed during the Last Glacial Period that began around 110,000 years ago and ended around 12,000 years ago, the appearance of pottery in Japan and the Heilongjiang Basin ten thousand years ago does not exclude the possibility of links to South China.

3. Cultures outside the Neolithic Cultural Zones

The End Paleolithic Culture
At the end Pleistocene, when South China and its nearby regions entered the early Neolithic, large north parts of China still had end Paleolithic remains, including sites like Longwangshan in Yichuan County in Shaanxi Province,[54] Shizitan in Ji County in Shanxi Province,[55] Xiachuan in Qinshui County, Shanxi Province,[56] and Jiangxigou site I near Qinghai Lake in Qinghai Province,[57] with absolute

dates ranging from around 18000 BCE to 10000 BCE. The pottery had not yet appeared, and the abundance of microliths, such as scrapers and end scrapers, indicated that hunting was still an important part of the economy. Notably, there were individual locally polished and used stone shovels and grinding stones, and pestles. The grinding stones and pestles were used mainly for shelling and grinding graminoids and acorns.[58] Their appearance likely related to the concentrated gathering of these plants, which prepared the ground for the origin of dry farming. The individually polished stone shovels may have been related to digging and house building, suggesting a marked increase in sedentism, which is also closely linked to the concentrated gathering of grass-family plants. Thus, while there is no direct evidence of agriculture, there were significant changes in the economy and lifestyle.

Mesolithic Culture

At the beginning of the Holocene, while the five major cultural systems of the late stage of the early Neolithic formed in South China and Central Eastern China, the overall situation of the contemporaneous period in Southwest China, Northeast China, and especially Northwest China is unclear. Considering the widespread human activity in these areas during the late Paleolithic, it is unlikely that these populations disappeared suddenly after the Holocene, and they likely continued their hunting and gathering lifestyles, using production tools represented by microliths.

The Shayuan site in Dali County, Shaanxi Province, which contains many microlithic remains, might belong to this period.[59] Among them, arrowheads and spear-shaped weapons were also seen at the late Paleolithic site Xiachuan in Shanxi Province. The only difference is that the former has concave-bottom points while the latter only has convex-bottom points. Similar concave-bottom arrowheads were prevalent in central and southern Inner Mongolia after the late Neolithic. Considering that microliths are virtually absent in the middle Neolithic Baijia culture in the Guanzhong area, the date of the Shayuan microlithic remains might correspond to the early Neolithic in South China and other places.

Regardless, this situation is similar to the persistence of hunting and gathering economies, represented by microliths, in large parts of Europe around 10,000 years ago, after the emergence of agriculture and animal husbandry in West Asia. This phase in Europe is generally referred to as the "Mesolithic."[60] Therefore, these beginning Holocene remains in China should also be considered part of the "Mesolithic."[61]

Currently, it is difficult for us to explore the interactions between the populations of the early Neolithic cultures and those of the end Paleolithic and Mesolithic.

4. Conclusion

The coexistence of the early Paleolithic culture in the early Neolithic in South China and the late Paleolithic culture in other regions at the end Pleistocene manifests the diversity of Chinese culture. It is conceivable that while some people on both sides of the Nanling Mountains had begun to live an early pastoral life of eating rice soup, fish, and pork, most people in the vast Northern Central Plain were still hunting and gathering on the grasslands. Their lifestyle, customs, and consciousness would thus differ significantly. After the beginning of the Holocene, the Neolithic culture spread from South China to Central and Eastern China, and the Mesolithic culture, represented by microlithic remains, largely retreated toward the northwest. The confrontation of these two different types of cultures is somewhat reminiscent of the situation during the early and middle Paleolithic periods. Moreover, even within the Neolithic cultural areas, there were five major cultural systems with local cultural differences, especially the complex pottery shapes and diverse types of tools in Shangshan culture in the lower Yangtze River area, which stood out. Different economic forms also existed. The North mainly relied on hunting and gathering economy, and dry farming of sorghum had already appeared; South China mainly relied on gathering, fishing, and hunting, or had already seen "garden farming"; rice farming was still primarily confined to the Yangtze River Basin; a dual agricultural system of "rice in the south and millet grain in the north" had started to take shape (fig. 2.3).

However, we should not overlook the unifying aspects of these cultures. As mentioned above, not only were these cultures based on a unified late Paleolithic culture, but the pottery of the various cultural systems of the early Neolithic may have had a common origin. There was no stark difference between the Neolithic culture, the end Paleolithic culture, and the Mesolithic culture. Although some early Neolithic populations in the Yangtze River Basin and North China were already cultivating rice and sorghum, it was still in the initial stage, occupying a limited portion of the food structure. It may have been only a supplement to the gathering and hunting economy, belonging to the so-called "low-level food production economy."[62] However, most Northern areas still belonged to the late Paleolithic or Mesolithic culture then; the concentrated gathering had prepared conditions for relative sedentism. There was no significant difference between the lifestyles of the North and the South.

Overall, China is one of the earliest regions in the world to see the emergence of agriculture, pottery (clay containers), and polished stone tools, and all three essentially appeared in combination. Although the initial occurrence of the three may not necessarily be related, they were interconnected in the development process. Agriculture provided the basis for sedentism, preparing conditions for the prosperity of fragile pottery and the meticulous crafting of polished stone tools; pottery served as cooking utensils, tableware, and storage containers, providing the greatest convenience for food preparation, sharing, and storage of agricultural products; polished stone tools gradually became the mainstream of agricultural production tools and provided conditions for early woodworking, especially the production of mortise and tenon structures. This laid a solid foundation for China to become the world's largest and most stable agricultural area and the country with the most characteristic ceramic culture. Developing agriculture requires long-term settlement and continuous adjustment of the internal social structure to maintain stability and does not require unrestricted expansion, especially

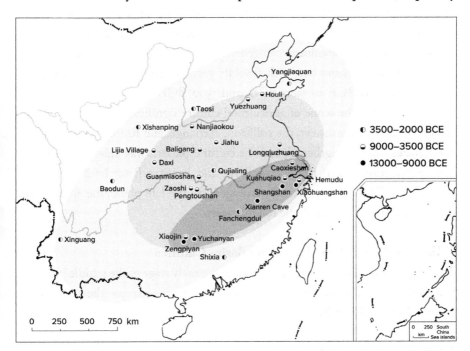

Figure 2.3 Three stages of spatial expansion of rice agriculture in China's Neolithic (13000–2000 BCE)

expansion into areas unsuitable for agriculture. This has made the Chinese culture gradually develop a simple, robust, holistic thinking, respect for tradition, and stable and introverted character or temperament. In addition, China developed textile technology and jade artifacts ten thousand years ago, foreshadowing the brilliant development of the Chinese silk weaving industry and jade culture in later generations. In comparison, wheat agriculture and polished stone tools in West Asia appeared only about 10,000 years ago, which is 5,000 to 6,000 years later than China; pottery appeared no earlier than 8,000 to 9,000 years ago, more than 10,000 years later than China, resulting in a "Pre-Pottery Neolithic"; house construction was mainly mud-brick and stone masonry. Such a society, whose agricultural foundation was not stable enough, had its development direction influenced by the northern pastoral nomadic tribes, creating a turbulent, conflicting, and outward-looking character.

III. The Sprouts of Early China

Around 7000 BCE, the culture in most parts of present-day China began to flourish, entering the middle Neolithic, with nearly 20 archaeological cultures emerging in succession. These cultures can generally be divided into three developmental stages: early, middle, and late, with absolute years roughly between 7000 BCE to 6200 BCE, 6200 BCE to 5500 BCE, and 5500 BCE to 5000 BCE (table 2.2). During this time, the scope of agricultural culture significantly expanded toward the northeast and northwest, the collision, exchange, and fusion trends of different cultures were strengthened, and the cultural pattern was drastically adjusted. The special positions of the Yellow River and Yangtze River basins, especially the Central Plain region, gradually emerged. By the late phase, the approximate outline of future China could be roughly seen.

1. The First Rise of Two Major River Basins Cultures
The biggest change in the cultural pattern of the early stage of the middle Neolithic is the first rise of the cultures of China's two major river basins—the Yellow River and the Yangtze River basins.

Yellow River Basin and Upper and Middle Reaches of the Huai River
The culture of the early stage of the middle Neolithic in the Yellow River Basin and the upper and middle reaches of the Huai River includes the early Peiligang

culture and the early Houli culture. The former is represented by Jiahu phases I to IV in Wuyang County, Henan Province,[63] and the latter by the 12th layer of Houli in Linzi City, Shandong Province,[64] and Xiaojingshan stage I in Zhangqiu.[65] The absolute age is roughly between 7000 BCE to 6200 BCE.

Table 2.2 Cultural regions of middle China's Neolithic (7000–5000 BCE)

	Early stage (7000–6200 BCE)	Middle stage (6200–5500 BCE)	Late stage (5500–5000 BCE)
Yellow River Basin and upper and middle reaches of the Huai River	1. Deep-belly jar–double-handle pot–earthen bowl cultural system (Early Peiligang culture) 2. Plain round-bottom cauldron cultural system (Early Houli culture)	1. Deep-belly jar–double-handle pot–earthen bowl cultural system (Middle Peiligang culture and early Baijia culture) 2. Plain round-bottom cauldron cultural system (Middle Houli culture)	1. Deep-belly jar–double-handle pot–earthen bowl cultural system (Late Peiligang culture, late Baijia culture, and Shuangdun culture) 2. Plain round-bottom cauldron cultural system (Late Houli culture)
Middle and lower reaches of the Yangtze River and South China	1. Cord-mark round-bottom cauldron cultural system (Early Dingsishan culture and early Pengtoushan culture) 2. Flat-bottom basin–round-foot plate–double-handle jar cultural system (Shangshan culture)	1. Cord-mark round-bottom cauldron cultural system (Late Dingsishan culture and late Pengtoushan culture) 2. Cauldron–round-foot plate–high-foot plate cultural system (Early Kuahuqiao culture)	Cauldron–round-foot plate–high-foot plate cultural system (Late Kuahuqiao culture, lower Zaoshi culture, Gaomiao culture, Chengbeixi culture, and Nanmuyuan culture)
North and Northeast China		Cylindrical jar cultural system (Early Cishan culture, Xinglongwa culture, and Hakou phase I type remains)	Cylindrical jar cultural system (Late Cishan culture, early Zhaobaogou culture, lower Xinle culture, early lower Zuojiashan culture, Xinkailiu culture, and Hakou phase I type remains)
Other regions		Mesolithic culture (Layihai site)	Mesolithic culture

During the early Peiligang culture, there were semi-subterranean round buildings with elevated platforms and oxidized flame pottery kilns. Rectangular vertical pit graves and extended supine were prevalent. Commonly found burial goods included everyday pottery vessels, tools, and the earliest instances of infant urn burials.[66] Ground and polished stone tools such as axes, adzes, chisels, shovels, serrated or non-serrated sickles, as well as stone grinding plates, stone grinding rods and net pendants, were also present. Cultivated rice was discovered at sites like Jiahu in Wuyang and Baligang in Dengzhou.[67] The Jiahu site also exhibited evidence of pig domestication. The predominant pottery vessels were deep-belly jars with angular handles made of sand-tempered brown pottery with variegated colors. They had a cylindrical small flat bottom, often decorated with marked cords and round pit patterns. They were primarily constructed using slab-building method and likely had an ancestral relationship with the Lijiagou pottery of the early Neolithic.[68] The ovate double-handle jar resembles the early period double-handle jar of Pengtoushan in Li Couny, Hunan Province. However, the former has a slightly larger mouth, less obvious neck, and a small flat bottom, while the latter has a small mouth, tall neck, and rounded bottom. These differences suggest that the ovate double-handle jars are likely a product of the integration between the Central Plain tradition and the tradition of the middle reaches of the Yangtze River. Similarly, double-handle pots, square-mouth basins, deep-belly basins with handles, flat-bottom earthen bowls, and other pottery vessels likely exhibit similar characteristics.

In the early Houli culture, there were relatively large rectangular semi-subterranean houses. The burial practices were similar to those of Peiligang culture, but grave goods were less common. The polished stone tools included axes, shovels, and others. Analyzing sites such as Yuezhuang in Changqing District and Xihe in Zhangqiu City, Shandong Province, indicates that rice and dry farming might have coexisted during this period.[69] They also engaged in animal husbandry, raising pigs, dogs, and other animals. The predominant pottery during this period was coarse and made of sand mixed with brown clay. The cauldron had a straight belly and a rounded bottom, with multiple outward-folded mouths. Some had handles and were constructed by slab-building method. There is a direct connection between this pottery and the earlier pottery from the Bianbian Cave. A few short-neck earless ovate jars were also present, distinguishing them from the ceramics of Peiligang culture.

Overall, at this time, the culture in the middle and lower reaches of the Yellow River still belonged to two less interconnected cultural systems, Peiligang culture could be called the "deep-belly jar–double-handle pot–earthen bowl cultural system," and Houli culture still belonged to the "plain round-bottom cauldron cultural system."

Middle and Lower Yangtze River and South China Regions
This includes Shangshan culture that continued from the early Neolithic, the early Dingsishan culture represented by phases III and IV of the Zengpiyan and phase II of the Dingsishan remains, phase III of the Qihe Cave remains, and the newly emerged early Pengtoushan culture represented by phases I and II of the Pengtoushan and Bashidang remains in Li Couny, Hunan Province.[70] The absolute age is roughly between 7000 BCE to 6200 BCE.

The early Dingsishan culture featured wide and short rectangular vertical pit graves, with most bodies in a severely squatting flexed burial. There were crude polished axes and other stone tools and perforated sinkers. Most pottery were brown round-bottom jars and cauldrons with imprinted cord-mark patterns, including small-mouth, thin tall-neck varieties and large-mouth short-neck or neckless types. Qihe Cave phase III remains featured timber-framed earthen wall construction ground houses, polished stone tools such as axes, adzes, net pendants, as well as fish-shaped stone ornaments, and cauldrons, jars, and earthen bowls decorated with cord-mark and shell-tooth imprinted patterns. They still belonged to South China's cord-mark round-bottom cauldron cultural system. No signs of rice farming have been discovered in this culture, and it should be predominantly based on a gathering economy.

Pengtoushan culture had moated settlements, ground-level or stilt houses, graves were wide and short rectangular or round vertical pit graves, and like the early Neolithic in South China, it probably predominantly practiced flexed burials,[71] with a small amount of daily-use pottery or stone tools buried with the dead. In addition to many chipped stone tools, there were also polished stone tools such as axes, adzes, chisels, and agricultural tools like bone *sis*.* The discovery of a large amount of carbonized cultivated rice remains at the Bashidang and Pengtoushan sites suggests that rice farming had developed to some extent. However, the gathering of wild plants still held a prominent place. The main pottery types were brown round-bottom jars and cauldrons and basins and earthen bowls with imprinted cord-mark patterns, similar to the pottery from phases III and IV of the Zengpiyan site. They also shared identical parallel line decorations on the neck. It is speculated that the main source was the cord-mark round-bottom cauldron

---

* An ancient Chinese agricultural tool with a curved handle for turning soil.—Trans.

cultural system on both sides of the Nanling Mountains.[72] Of course, Pengtoushan culture also had many of its characteristics, such as the popular charcoal-containing pottery, a certain number of double-shoulder tall-neck jars, short-foot vessels, and animal-shaped supports, with pottery mouth parts imprinted with serrated floral rims rather than marked cords, and more complex patterns composed of stamped dots, circles, fine-tooth comb patterns with clustered dots, etc.

2. Collisions and Blends

Yellow River Basin and Upper and Middle Reaches of the Huai River Regions

The middle stage of the middle Neolithic includes the middle Peiligang culture represented by the Jiahu site 5 to 6 phases in Wuyang and the Peiligang site in Xinzheng, Henan,[73] the middle Houli culture represented by the 11th and 10th layers of the Houli site and the Xiaojingshan II to III phases, and the early Baijia culture represented by the Baijiacun site in Lintong District, Shaanxi Province, and phase I of Dadiwan site in Qin'an County, Gansu Province.[74] The absolute dates are roughly between 6200 BCE to 5500 BCE.

During this period, millet grain was discovered at the Shawaoli and other Peiligang culture sites in Xinzheng City in Henan Province. Analysis of the starch grains on some stone grinding plates and stone grinding rods showed that they were used for processing a variety of foods, including millet grains and nuts.[75] More complex pottery forms, such as *dings*,* tri-legged earthen bowls, round-foot earthen bowls (bowls), etc., emerged, and there was a greater diversity of cauldron types, even individual tubular spouted pots. The use of clay pottery greatly increased, and clay strip coiling became prevalent, with standardized shapes and uniform firing temperatures, reflecting significant advancements in pottery-making technology and more specialized pottery functions. Settlements had started to differentiate, varying in size from several thousand square meters to tens of thousands of square meters. Graves were buried in separate areas. Smaller tombs had only a few grave goods. In contrast, larger ones had dozens of items, including exquisite new items such as bone flutes (fig. 2.4), bone tablets, ivory carvings, turquoise ornaments, and turtle shells (some of which were inscribed) (fig. 2.5) found in the Jiahu large tomb, suggesting that the tomb's occupant likely held a high position in religious matters. The relatively developed material culture prepared Peiligang culture for

---

* A type of prehistoric and ancient Chinese cauldrons, standing upon legs with a lid and two facing handles.—Trans.

exerting a considerable influence externally, most notably its expansion toward the Wei River Basin and the upper reaches of the Han River.

Figure 2.4 Seven-holed bone flute from the Jiahu site
1, 2. M282: 21, 20

In the early Baijia culture in the Wei River Basin and the upper reaches of the Han River, the main types of pottery, such as round-bottom earthen bowls, tri-legged earthen bowls, round-foot earthen bowls, and deep-belly jars could all find their prototypes in Peiligang culture. There is also an evident connection between the former's sawtooth-shaped clams or bone sickles and the latter's stone sickles, and both cultures had polished stone spades. Both lived in crude semi-subterranean houses with tabletops, had oxidation-fired pottery kilns, practiced extended supine with joint burials, had the custom of being buried with deer teeth and pig lower jawbones, and had infant urn burials.[76] Carbonized sorghum was found in phase I of Dadiwan, indicating the existence of dry farming.[77] Since no earlier agricultural culture remains in the Wei River Basin and the upper reaches of the Han River, and the initial dates of Baijia culture are about 1,000 years later than Peiligang culture, it is reasonable to speculate that Baijia culture might be the result of the westward expansion of Peiligang culture and its fusion with the local culture (fig. 2.6).[78] Of course, there are certain

Figure 2.5 Turtle shell and engraved symbols from the Jiahu site (M244: 18)

differences between the two, such as the prevalence of herringbone marked cords in Baijia culture, simple brownish-red painted pottery, small-mouth tall-neck bulbous-belly jars, etc., all of which are different from Peiligang culture. Perhaps influenced by the Pengtoushan type Zhichengbei culture in the Xiajiang region,

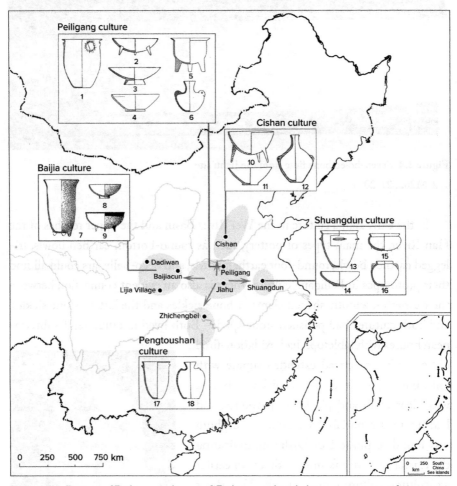

Figure 2.6 Pottery of Peiligang culture and Peiligang cultural elements in surrounding cultures (6200–5000 BCE)

1, 7, 13, 17. Deep-belly jar (Jiahu H190: 2, Baijia T309③: 4, Shuangdun 91T071913: 61, Zhichengbei H1: 5)

2–4, 8–11, 14. Earthen bowl (Shuiquan M20: 2, M2: 2, Jiahu H209: 1, Baijia T117③: 4, T116H4: 2, Cishan T87②: 32, H77: 3, Shuangdun 92T072117: 16)

5, 15. *Ding* (Jiahu H102: 3, Shuangdun 92T062320: 85)

6, 12, 16, 18. Pot (Jiahu M231: 2, Cishan T87②: 25, Shuangdun 92T072129: 29, Zhichengbei H1: 35)

a few flexed burials may also be related.[79] In addition, Baijia culture had already produced roughly rectangular stone knives, some with cord-binding grooves on the sides, which essentially embodied the prototype of the typical stone small sickle—*zhi* of the late Neolithic and after that.

The situation of Houli culture at this stage was the same as before. Notably, in the middle reaches of the Huai River, a type of culture represented by the early Xiaoshankou site in Suzhou City in Anhui Province,[80] and phases I and II of the Shunshanji remains in Sihong County, Jiangsu Province,[81] emerged. The main plain round-bottom cauldron, rod-shaped legs, and small-mouth double-handle pots of this culture were similar to those of Houli culture. However, their cauldrons were short and chubby, and some had polygonal rims, which differed from Houli culture. Others, such as the double-handle flat-bottom jars, double-handle multiple-mouth vessels, folded-belly earthen bowls, and high-foot plates, were likely indigenous elements of the Jianghuai region, remotely inherited from Shangshan culture (fig. 2.7). The round-shaped pottery range found at Shunshanji is one of the earliest pottery ranges in China. Its clay human and animal faces are also distinctive, along with jade tubes, etc. These remains were once classified into Houli culture,[82] but they ultimately have their characteristics and can be independently called the Shunshanji culture. This culture also discovered the earliest circular ditched settlements in the Yellow and Huai River basins, like the semi-subterranean oval-shaped houses of Peiligang culture, and ground houses and pits containing buried whole dogs were found. Graves commonly practiced extended supine burials, with no grave goods or 1 to 3 grave goods.

Thus, through the strong expansion of Peiligang culture, the upper reaches of the Yellow River had been incorporated into the "deep-belly jar–double-handle pot–earthen bowl cultural system." Still, the overall cultural pattern of the Yellow River Basin remained largely unchanged (fig. 2.8).

Middle and Lower Reaches of the Yangtze River and South China Region
In the middle and lower reaches of the Yangtze River and South China region, the middle stage of the middle Neolithic includes the late Dingsishan culture represented by phase III of the Dingsishan site and the late Baozitou site in Nanning, Guangxi Zhuang Autonomous Region,[83] the late Pengtoushan culture represented by the Pengtoushan and Bashidang phase III remains, and the early Kuahuqiao culture represented by phase I of the Kuahuqiao site in Xiaoshan, Zhejiang Province.[84] The absolute dates are roughly between 6200 BCE to 5800 BCE.

The late Dingsishan and Pengtoushan cultures are continuations of their early stages. The early Kuahuqiao culture mainly used polished stone tools such as adzes, axes, and chisels, as well as bone *sis*, stones, or bone arrowheads. Its economic form should be close to Pengtoushan culture. Spindle whorls indicate the early maturity of textile handicrafts. There were bone hairpins used as ornaments. Pottery can be roughly divided into two groups: the first group includes double-

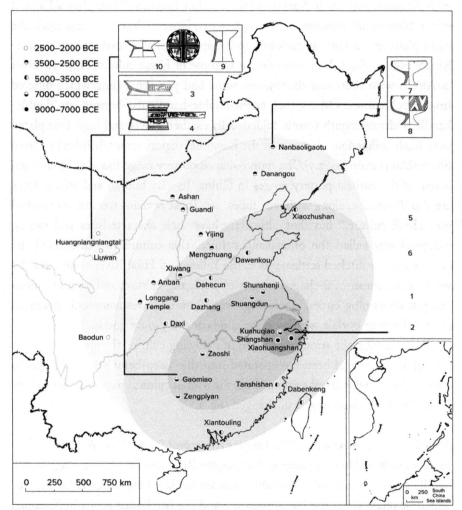

Figure 2.7 The spatial arrangement of pottery high-foot plates and round-foot plates in China's Neolithic

| 1, 5–10. High-foot plate (Shangshan H193: 1, Dawenkou M2004: 8, M2012: 3, Danangou | M24: 3, M31: 6, Liuwan M308: 3, Huangniangniangtai M47: 10) | 2–4. Round-foot plate (Xiaohuangshan M2: 2, Zaoshi T4⑤: 22, Gaomiao 200321: 12) |

handle folded-shoulder jars, round-foot plates, and high-foot plates, etc., which were already seen in Shangshan culture, and their detailed forms are similar. Both also mainly used pottery with embedded charcoal, and there were phenomena of applying red coats to the surfaces of vessels, indicating that the main body of Kuahuqiao culture should be derived from Shangshan culture. The second group

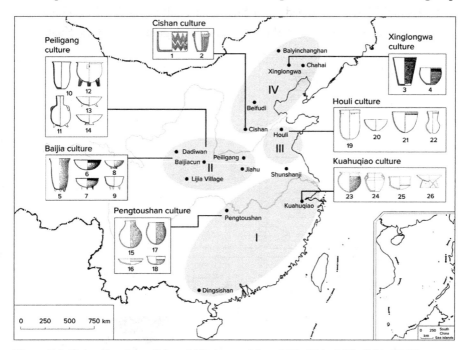

Figure 2.8 Cultural regions of the middle stage of the middle China's Neolithic (6200–5500 BCE)

I. Cauldron–round-foot plate–high-foot plate cultural system
II. Deep-belly jar–double-handle pot–earthen bowl cultural system
III. Plain round-bottom cauldron cultural system
IV. Cylindrical jar cultural system
1–4. Cylindrical jar (*yu*)[a] (Cishan T96②: 38, 25, Xinglongwa F171④: 10, F180④: 8)
5, 10. Deep-belly jar (Baijia T309③: 4, Peiligang M37: 3)
6–9, 13, 14, 16, 18, 20, 25. Earthen bowl (Baijia T204H25: 1, T116H4: 2, T117③: 4, T121③: 8, Peiligang M38: 11, M56: 4, Pengtoushan T5⑤: 4, F2: 1, Houli H1546: 1, Kuahuqiao T0410 Lake III: 17)
11, 22. Pot (Peiligang M100: 10, Houli H1677: 1)
12. *Ding* (Jiahu H104: 6)
15, 17, 19, 21, 23. Cauldron (jar) (Pengtoushan H2: 47, H1: 6, Houli H3827: 1, H3832: 1, Kuahuqiao T0411⑧A: 132)
24. Double-handle jar (Kuahuqiao T0411⑧A: 24)
26. Round-foot plate (Kuahuqiao T0513⑨C: 2)
(All pottery.)

[a] An ancient Chinese vessel for holding water. As time progressed, its functions expanded, such as serving rice, bathing, etc.—Trans.

includes cord-mark round-bottom cauldrons and folded-belly round-bottom earthen bowls with various forms of marked cords, which are not or rarely seen in Shangshan culture but are close to Pengtoushan culture in the middle reaches of the Yangtze River. This shows that the formation of Kuahuqiao culture should include contributions from the Pengtoushan culture. In other words, Kuahuqiao culture should have developed from Shangshan culture under the influence of Pengtoushan culture (fig. 2.9).[85] The discovery of a dugout canoe at the Kuahuqiao

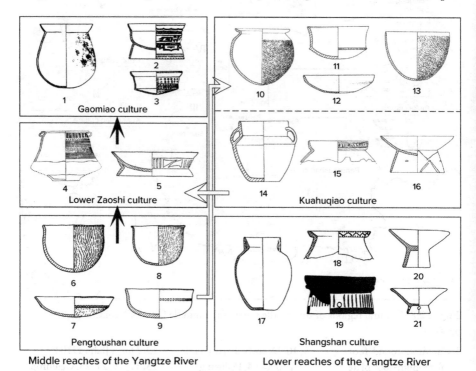

Figure 2.9 Cultural interactions between the middle and lower reaches of the Yangtze River during the middle Neolithic

1, 6, 8, 10, 13. Cauldron (Gaomiao T2003㉔: 18, Pengtoushan T1⑥: 5, F2: 3, Kuahuqiao T0411⑧A: 132, T0510⑤B: 5)

2, 5, 16, 19. Round-foot plate (Gaomiao T2003㉑: 12, Zaoshi T4⑤: 22, Kuahuqiao T0513⑨C: 2, Xiaohuangshan M2: 2)

3, 7, 9, 11, 12. Earthen bowl (Gaomiao T2104㉔: 20, Pengtoushan T2②: 49, T14④: 53, Kuahuqiao T0410 Lake III: 17, T0512 Lake II: 10)

4, 14, 15, 17, 18. Jar (Zaoshi T3③: 143, Kuahuqiao T0411⑧A: 24, T0411 Lake IV: 45, Shangshan H226: 5, H221: 4)

20, 21. High-foot plate (Shangshan H193: 1, H196: 1)

(All pottery.)

(Solid line arrows in the image represent the developmental relationship of cultures within the same region, while hollow arrows represent the influence relationship between cultures from different regions.)

site (fig. 2.10) provides conditions for connections between the middle and lower reaches of the Yangtze River through waterways. In addition, some local factors in the Pengtoushan type culture remain in Zhichengbei in the Xiajiang region (or can be called the Zhichengbei type of Pengtoushan culture) were likely influenced by Peiligang culture, such as the double-handle flat-bottom or round-foot deep-belly jars, small-mouth shrugged-shoulder flat pots, etc.

Figure 2.10 Canoe at the Kuahuqiao site

North and Northeast China Region

In North China and the Northeast region, the middle of the middle Neolithic includes the early Cishan culture represented by the early Cishan site in Wu'an City in Hebei Province,[86] and phase I of the Beifudi site in Yi County,[87] located east of the Taihang Mountains; Xinglongwa culture, represented by the Xiliao River–Ling River basins and the Yan Mountains in both the south and north, including the Aohan Banner in Inner Mongolia, the F171 site in Xinglongwa,[88] the Linxi Baiyinchanghan phase II class A site,[89] and the Chahai D1 site in Fuxin City, Liaoning Province,[90] as well as the Hag phase I remains in the Hulunbuir City in Inner Mongolia.[91] The absolute dates are roughly between 6200 BCE to 5500 BCE.

Cishan culture has square or rectangular semi-subterranean houses, rectangular cellars, and "sacrificial sites" that contain grouped pottery and jade artifacts of grave goods. There are quite a few polished stone tools like axes, adzes, chisels, and shovels, as well as small stone tools, whetstones, stone grinding plates, stone grinding rods, and net pendants. In the more than 80 cellars of the Cishan site, large amounts of layered sorghums ash were found, along with a very small amount of millet grain,[92] indicating that dry farming had become significant in Cishan culture.

The round-foot stone bowls and ceramic masks are distinctive, with bird head-shaped supports and spinning wheels. The basic pottery containers are mostly sand-tempered brown pottery constructed using the clay strip coiling. Short cylindrical jars (*yus*) are dominant, but there are also deep-belly jars, flat-bottom plates, etc. These show clear origins from the early Neolithic cultures in North China and still belong to the "cylindrical jar cultural system." However, there are differences between the north and the south. The pottery of the Beifudi type in the north has a row of diagonal lines, scales, or fine-tooth comb patterns with clustered dot patterns impressed or engraved on the upper surface of the ware, similar in style to the pottery of the early Neolithic Donghulin phase II. The Z-pattern flat-bottom earthen bowl and jade *jue** could have been influenced by Xinglongwa culture. The Cishan type pottery in the south often has double handles, with the surface mainly featuring imprinted cord-mark patterns, and there are also fine clay coils with added relief decorations, fine-tooth comb patterns with clustered dot patterns, engraved patterns, etc., which may be linked to the early Neolithic Nanzhuangtou site. The appearance of a small number of clay tri-legged earthen bowls results from Peiligang culture seeping northward.

Xinglongwa culture features settlements with rows of large square semi-subterranean houses surrounded by moats. The burials are rectangular vertical pit graves or stone casket graves, mainly featuring extended supine burials, with some flexed burials and unique house burials. Grave goods include all kinds of personal ornaments such as jade *jues*, shell decorations, stones, and jade beads, some even with a whole pig. Its jade *jues*, jade dagger-shaped implements, jade cicadas, inlaid shell masks, bone and shell masks, and stone human figures are distinctive. Its jade ware and ceramic masks continue from Shuangta culture phase I pottery human facial decorations. It is dominated by chipped or slightly ground tools with or

---

* An ancient Chinese form of the round jade pendant with a notch around the jade ring.—Trans.

without shoulders, such as shovels, axes, adzes, etc. There are also stone grinding plates, stone grinding rods, bone-handle stone-blade knives, etc. The large amounts of carbonized sorghum and a small amount of millet grain excavated from the Xinglongwa site,[93] as well as the discovery of millet grain and sorghum starch grains on the stone grinding plates and rods from the Baiyinchanghan site,[94] indicate that Xinglongwa culture practiced dry farming of millet grain and sorghum with sorghum as the main crop. There are a small number of stone containers, such as jars, cups, and mortars. The pottery mainly consists of sand-tempered brown cylindrical jars made by clay strip coiling, followed by flat-bottom earthen bowls, basins, and round-foot bowls. Initially, the surface of the pottery was mainly plain,[95] but later widely decorated with impressed spiral patterns, grid patterns, added relief decorations, multiple-scale patterns, etc., and finally popular with Z-shaped and twisted cord patterns. Like Cishan culture, it belongs to the "cylindrical jar cultural system," and origins from the early Neolithic Shuangta culture phase I. There are also specific regional differences within Xinglongwa culture.

The Hag phase I type of remains includes flat-round houses and simple burials, with flexed or secondary burials. Like Xinglongwa culture, it includes jade dagger-shaped implements as grave goods. There are numerous microliths, like stone leaves, scrapers, end scrapers, arrowheads, drills, etc., perforators, grinding plates, grinding rods, and other ground and polished stone tools, bone awls, spears, arrowheads, and other bone tools, as well as bone-handle stone-blade knives, indicating a predominantly fishing and hunting economy. The pottery consists of plain or cord-mark cylindrical jars, and similar pottery is also found in the region near Lake Baikal. The Hag phase I type of remains, like Xinglongwa culture, belongs to the "cylindrical jar cultural system."

3. The Initial Formation of Three Major Cultural Systems

Yellow River Basin and the Upper and Middle Reaches of the Huai River

The late stage of the middle Neolithic includes the late Peiligang culture represented by the Wayaozui site in Gongyi City, Henan Province[96] and Zhaigen in Mengjin, Henan Province;[97] the late Baijia culture represented by the Shizhaocun phase I in Tianshui, Gansu Province;[98] Shuangdun culture represented by Shuangdun in Bengbu, Anhui Province[99] and Zhangshan Ji in Jining, Shandong Province;[100] and the late Houli culture represented by Xiaojingshan IV in Zhangqiu, Shandong Province. The absolute dates are approximately 5500 BCE to 5000 BCE.

Peiligang culture entered its decline phase at this time, with a significant reduction in the number of pots and the emergence of black pottery, vertical stripes, etc. In some cases, the mouths of earthen bowls were slightly folded. Coincidentally, at this time or slightly later, the elements of Peiligang culture, such as conical-foot *dings*, double-handle flat-bottom pots, tri-legged pots, tri-legged earthen bowls, and round-foot or false round-foot bowls with slightly folded mouths were more commonly seen in the middle reaches of the Huai River. This contributed to the transformation of the Shunshanji culture and Houli culture in the middle reaches of the Huai River and even in the southwest of the Taiyi Mountains into Shuangdun culture, forming a confrontation with Houli culture north of the Taiyi Mountains.[101] The high-foot plates, human-face or animal-face pottery in Shuangdun culture, were already present in the earlier Shunshanji culture. This change in the cultural pattern may have been accompanied by eastward migration of the population. In addition, the late Baijia culture also showed vertical stripes similar to the late Peiligang culture, and the jars, earthen bowls, basins, and the newly emerged flat-mouth pots with double handles all showed a trend of transitioning to Yangshao culture.

In this way, the culture of the majority of the Yellow River Basin and the upper and middle reaches of the Huai River essentially integrated into a "deep-belly jar–double-handle pot–earthen bowl cultural system," and the "Yellow–Huai Rivers basins cultural region" was initially formed. However, the plain round-bottom cauldron cultural system represented by Houli culture in the north of the Taiyi Mountains still existed.

Middle and Lower Reaches of the Yangtze River and South China Regions
This includes the late Kuahuqiao culture, represented by phases II and III of Kuahuqiao; the lower Zaoshi culture, represented by the lower Zaoshi in Shimen County, Hunan Province[102] and the Hujiawuchang site in Linli;[103] Gaomiao culture, represented by the lower Gaomiao in Hongjiang City, Hunan Province;[104] the Chengbeixi culture, represented by the early Chengbeixi site in Yidu City within Yichang City, Hubei Province;[105] and the Nanmuyuan culture, represented by the Nanmuyuan site in Badong County, Hubei Province.[106] The absolute dates are roughly 5800 BCE to 5000 BCE.

Looking at the pottery, the elements prevalent in the lower Zaoshi culture, such as the high-neck or neck-banded round-bottom cauldrons and marked cords, carry on from Pengtoushan culture. Other elements like the slanted arc-belly basins, earthen bowl types, and straight feet are closely related to Pengtoushan culture.

It can be said that the lower Zaoshi culture developed based on Pengtoushan culture.[107] However, compared with Pengtoushan culture, many new elements suddenly appeared in the lower Zaoshi culture, such as many round-foot plates with perforated decorations, folded-belly jars, folded-belly earthen bowls, "line wheels" with a round groove on the edge, and typical features of cauldrons and jars such as double handles, inward-folded rims, folded-shoulders or -bellies, and flat bottoms. These are typical elements of Kuahuqiao culture, with an earlier starting point. The lower Zaoshi culture developed based on Pengtoushan culture by accepting more aspects of Kuahuqiao culture.

Further out, Gaomiao culture in the upper and middle reaches of the Yuan River and the Chengbeixi culture below the Xia River estuary are mainly derived from Pengtoushan culture, with fewer Kuahuqiao culture elements such as round-foot plates than the lower Zaoshi culture, perhaps only transmitted through the lower Zaoshi culture. The local characteristics are more pronounced, such as the exquisite white pottery of Gaomiao culture and the design with animal faces with tusks, octagonal star patterns, sun patterns, etc. As for the Nanmuyuan culture in the Three Gorges area, round-foot plates are no longer seen, and only individual double-handle jars show some indirect connections with Kuahuqiao culture. In contrast, more round-foot bowls are elements of Baijia culture. Particularly worth mentioning is that the remains of phase V of Zengpiyan at this time are pretty close to Gaomiao culture, with the appearance of round-foot plates and white pottery, inward-curved vessel mouths, complex geometric patterns made by stamping or imprinting, etc. Similar remains are also found in eastern Guizhou and northeastern Guangxi, showing that Gaomiao culture had a significant southward influence.

In summary, first, around 7000 BCE, the cord-mark round-bottom cauldron cultural system of South China moved northward, possibly combined with local cultures to give birth to Pengtoushan culture in the Dongting Lake area in the middle reaches of the Yangtze River. At the end of 7000 BCE, Pengtoushan culture advanced eastward to the area south of Hangzhou Bay in the lower reaches of the Yangtze River, causing the local Shangshan culture to develop into Kuahuqiao culture. From then on, cord-mark round-bottom cauldron became an essential cultural element in the southern part of the lower reaches of the Yangtze River for a long time. A few hundred years later, at the beginning of 6000 BCE, the flourishing Kuahuqiao culture, in turn, influenced the Dongting Lake area to the west, facilitating the transformation of Pengtoushan culture into the lower Zaoshi culture, making round-foot plates and other elements important features of the culture in the middle reaches of the Yangtze River. Not only that, through the external influence of the lower Zaoshi culture, Kuahuqiao culture also penetrated the basins of the Yuan River, the Xiang River, the Xia River, and even the Li River. Through such two-way exchange and integration, the culture of the middle and lower reaches of the Yangtze River and the northern part of South China has basically become very similar, forming the "middle and lower reaches of the Yangtze River—South China cultural region" and constituting a new "cauldron–round-foot plate–high-foot plate cultural system."

North and Northeast China Region

The late stage includes the late Cishan culture represented by the late Cishan remains, the early Zhaobaogou culture represented by the Zhaobaogou remains in Aohan Banner, Inner Mongolia within the Xiliao River and north and south parts of Yan Mountains,[108] the lower Xinle culture represented by the lower remains of Xinle in Shenyang City, Liaoning Province in the Xialiao River Basin,[109] the early lower Zuojiashan culture represented by the fourth layer of remains at Zuojiashan in Nongan, Jilin in the second Songhua River Basin,[110] Xinkailiu culture in the Mudan River Basin and the Sanjiang Plain in the northern part of the Northeast,[111] and phase I of the Hag type remains in the Hulunbuir region, etc., with absolute dates roughly from 5500 BCE to 5000 BCE.

At this time, the late Cishan culture in Southern Hebei shows that plain clay ware such as tri-legged earthen bowls, round-bottom earthen bowls, pots, and deep-belly jars have accounted for nearly one-third. Also, semi-subterranean houses with round platforms and four-legged stone grinding plates appear, showing that the influence of Peiligang culture has significantly strengthened.[112]

The early Zhaobaogou culture is characterized by semi-subterranean houses arranged in rows and finely ground stone tools such as *sis* (shoulder shovels), axes, adzes, and chisels. Analysis of starch grains on the stone millstones and grinding rods from the fifth layer of Shangzhai in Pinggu in Beijing shows the processing and utilization of plants such as oak fruits, millet grain, and sorghum.[113] In addition to cylindrical jars and flat-bottom earthen bowls, new pottery types such as *zun*-shaped* vessels, round-foot earthen bowls, and round-foot jars have emerged, characterized by geometric patterns imprinted or engraved all over the vessel, with various subjects linked and combined, complicated and intricate,

---

* *Zun* is a Chinese ritual bronze or ceramic wine vessel with a round or square vase-like form.—Trans.

Z-shaped patterns regular and mature, a similar style of decoration was seen early in Xinglongwa culture in the Chahai.

Square semi-subterranean houses characterize the lower Xinle culture. Pottery mainly comprises regular, mature Z-shaped-pattern cylindrical jars, slanted-mouth vats, and round-foot earthen bowls, quite like Zhaobaogou culture. In addition to grinding plates, grinding rods, net pendants, ground stone axes, adzes, chisels, and arrowheads, there are microliths, such as stone arrowheads with *tings* (unrefined copper or iron), stone leaves, etc. Coal jade artifacts are also distinctive. The early lower Zuojiashan culture is similar to the lower Xinle culture, with its engraved step-like band pattern characteristic. Xinkailiu culture cylindrical jars are popular with imprinted or engraved scale patterns, net patterns, diamond patterns, round pit patterns, etc. Still, Z-shaped patterns are not seen, reflecting a different local tradition. Furthermore, if the Xiaonanshan burial in Raohe County indeed belongs to Xinkailiu culture,[114] then the jade artifacts, such as jade *jues*, rings, dagger-shaped implements, etc., buried with it also convey a close relationship with Xinglongwa culture.

Overall, Zhaobaogou culture, lower Xinle culture, lower Zuojiashan culture, and Xinglongwa culture have a certain heritage relationship; Xinkailiu culture and phase I of the Hag type remains have exchange relationships with Xinglongwa culture.

4. Cultures outside the Neolithic Cultural Region

Middle Neolithic cultures had already occupied the core regions, including the Yellow River and Yangtze River basins in China, but certainly not all. In the Northwest and other places, there are still remnants of the Mesolithic culture, such as those found in Guinan Layihai[115] and Dayutai in Qinghai Province,[116] Qinghai Lake Jiangxigou II site, and Ningxia Province's "Helan Group" microlith sites, etc.[117] The tools are all microlith-like scrapers, with no pottery or polished stone tools, and most importantly, there is no evidence of agriculture.

5. Conclusion

After about 6200 BCE, entering the middle Neolithic, the exchanges between different cultural regions became noticeably frequent. The central Peiligang culture in the Central Plain expanded strongly. Pengtoushan culture and Kuahuqiao culture in the Yangtze River Basin moved east and gradually moved west, thereby integrating into four cultural regions or cultural systems. These are the deep-belly jar–double-handle pot–earthen bowl cultural system in the upper and middle reaches of the Yellow River and the Huai River; the cauldron–round-foot plate–high-foot plate cultural system in the middle and lower reaches of the Yangtze River and South China; the cylindrical jar cultural system in North China and the Northeast; and a small cultural system, the plain round-bottom cauldron cultural system north of the Tai–Yi Mountains. Among these, the three major cultural systems roughly match the three systems identified by Yan Wenming for the Neolithic in China.[118]

Moreover, through the strong expansion and influence of Peiligang culture in the Central Plain, the peripheries of each cultural region began to interact and merge, and certain connections occurred between several cultural systems. Whether it is Pengtoushan culture in the middle reaches of the Yangtze River or Cishan culture in North China, the peripheral areas near Peiligang culture began to exhibit more clay plain ware such as pots, earthen bowls, and deep-belly jars—elements of Peiligang culture. In this way, the various cultural systems developed certain commonalities, forming a prototype of an early Chinese cultural sphere with a layered structure or a "multi-petaled flower" structure, or one could say that the cultural meaning of an "early China" had sprouted. Of course, outside this cultural sphere, there were still populations mainly engaged in hunting and gathering, belonging to the Mesolithic, and the cultural differences inside and outside the cultural sphere significantly increased. The prototype of the early Chinese cultural sphere formed in the middle Neolithic was the largest agricultural, cultural sphere in the world at that time, with characteristics and traits significantly different from other cultures in the world. Moreover, the core Peiligang culture held a unique position compared to surrounding cultures.

(1) Complementary dual grain agricultural system of South rice and North dryland
This prototype of an early Chinese cultural sphere features a dual grain agricultural system of South rice and North dryland. Both systems have significantly expanded in their spatial range. Rice agriculture has extended northward to the middle and lower reaches of the Yellow River (fig. 2.3), and millet grain agriculture has expanded to the Xiliao River Basin and most parts of the Yellow River Basin. The Yellow River and Yangtze River basins became the main regions of grain agriculture. Peiligang culture in the Central Plain, an interlaced zone of the two systems, enjoys the advantage of both rice and millet grain agriculture. Its stone tools are often polished, with exquisite bone tools, and the level of agricultural development is high, making it the core of the cultural sphere. Peripheral cultures generally only have one type of agriculture—either rice cultivation or dry farming.

Some had not even adopted grain farming and are still relying on northern hunting and gathering and southern gathering and gardening, with most tools made by chipping. Their level of productivity is lower than Peiligang culture, except in the middle and lower reaches of the Yangtze River. It is worth noting that the highly developed Gaomiao culture shows no signs of rice agriculture.

Although agriculture (including livestock farming) should not be overestimated in terms of its proportion in people's food structure, hunting and gathering still played a vital role. Yet, it was already the largest agricultural and cultural region in the world and the only cultural region where two major agricultural systems coexisted. Yan Wenming pointed out that these two agricultural systems "are like a binary star system, forming an inseparable relationship."[119] They complement each other well, ensuring the long-term stability of the food supply.

(2) Abundant pottery and sophisticated utensil life
Stable food and a considerable degree of settlement accompany abundant pottery. The daily utensils in this cultural sphere are mainly pottery, specially developed in cooking utensils. Various cooking methods have emerged, starkly contrasting the situation in West Asia, where newly emerged pottery are mainly non-cooking vessels, and the primary cooking method is roasting. Yan Wenming said that by focusing on the origin and development of pottery and agriculture, "we can draw a dividing line between the Ganges and Indus Rivers basins."[120]

The pottery of the core area, Peiligang culture, is delicate and elegant, with complex shapes, refined functions, and exquisite regularity. Especially they invented the *ding*, a stable and practical particular cooking utensil that lasted for thousands of years and served as the foremost ritual vessel for three generations, arguably the first typical artifact of early China (fig. 2.11). They also developed China-specific steaming utensils, *zengs*, and pottery pots, which might have been used for drinking alcohol,[121] reflecting the richness and sophistication of settled social life. The discovery of pottery kilns in the Peiligang and Baijia cultures is a significant event worldwide. With kilns, they could better control firing and increase temperature, which to some extent, prepared China to become the most advanced pottery-making region in the world. Next to it, the pottery in the middle and lower Yangtze River cultures often has decorations with complex shapes, refined functions, and exquisite regularity. They invented China-specific cooking ranges and eating utensils high-foot plates, especially the white pottery plates of Gaomiao culture, are elaborately decorated and finely made. The pottery in more peripheral cultures is cruder, with simpler shapes and multipurpose, indi-

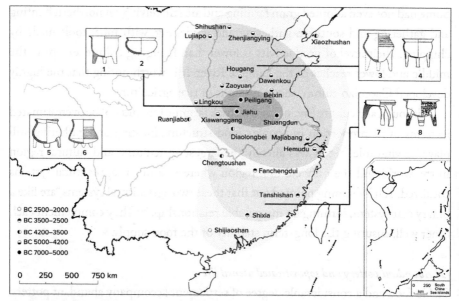

Figure 2.11 The spatial expansion of Chinese Neolithic pottery *ding*
1. Jiahu H102: 3
2. Shuangdun 92T0623⑳: 85
3. Dawenkou H24: 7
4. Hougang H9③: 14
5, 6. Chengtoushan M649: 6, M665: 2
7. Shixia M11: 6
8. Tanshishan M130: 4

cating simpler social life. Furthermore, beautiful jade artifacts appeared in the Xinglongwa and Shunshanji cultures.

(3) Precocious woodworking industry and beam-framed architecture

The woodworking industry has significantly developed due to the widespread findings of stone axes, stone adzes, stone chisels, and other stone tools related to felling and woodworking on both sides of the Yangtze River. Wooden components with mortise and tenon structures have also been discovered at sites such as Kuahuqiao. Semi-subterranean houses in the northern region can be divided into two types. One type is represented by Peiligang culture, with small pit areas but useful outer platforms. The other type, represented by the Xinglongwa and Houli cultures, has larger pit areas but no outer platforms. There is no significant difference in the usable area between the two types of houses. Whether the semi-subterranean houses in the North or the ground-level or stilt houses in the South, all use wooden columns to support the roof. They should have initially formed the beam-framed architectural tradition that later prevailed in China, significantly different from the masonry houses popular in Western Asia. Especially the Xinglongwa and Houli cultures even had large houses of over 100 square meters, highlighting astonishing architectural skills!

(4) Origins of painted pottery, symbols, images, and characters
Kuahuqiao culture has red- or white-geometric-pattern painted pottery, including sun patterns, arranged in separate units, reflecting rhythm in complexity. In contrast, the red-painted pottery of Baijia culture is mostly simply brushed, with a casual layout, indicating that a dual visual art tradition (east and west) was formed 8,000 years ago (fig. 2.12). Painted pottery is bright and eye-catching, and the patterns carry deep meanings, likely serving as an important medium for people to express and transmit information at that time.

However, in terms of the degree of abstraction, the inscriptions from the Jiahu site are the most advanced. The Jiahu inscriptions are quite regular, similar to the characters "田" (*tian*) and "目" (*mu*) in Shang Dynasty oracle bone script, and they are inscribed on mysterious turtle shells, which can be called "character engraved symbols"[122] or character-like symbols, demonstrating the extreme early maturity of the Peiligang people's abstract thinking. Influenced deeply by Peiligang culture, Shuangdun culture also discovered many complex engraved symbols and images (fig. 2.13). Furthermore, Gaomiao culture introduced octagonal star patterns, animal-face patterns, etc., which persisted for thousands of years, influencing more than half of eastern China.[123] They are more figurative than engraved symbols and resemble "clan emblems" (figs. 2.14 and 2.15). The precursors to Chinese characters—symbols and images—have already sprouted during this period, mainly in the Yellow and Yangtze Rivers.

(5) A secular belief system centered on ancestor worship and multi-level holistic thinking
In this cultural sphere, there are few religious remnants similar to the sacrificial niche of shrine statues in West Asia, with primitive religious beliefs primarily embedded in daily production and life, with ancestor worship likely being the core of this belief system. For example, the orderly partitioning and grouping of cemeteries in Peiligang culture might be based mainly on blood relationships, demonstrating respect for ancestors and emphasis on social order, possibly reflecting clan organizations in real society; the extended supine has become the main burial form for later Central Plain and the whole of China. Peiligang and Baijia cultures had China's earliest infant urn burials, showing special care for children. The middle reaches of the Yangtze River and South China had prevalently flexed

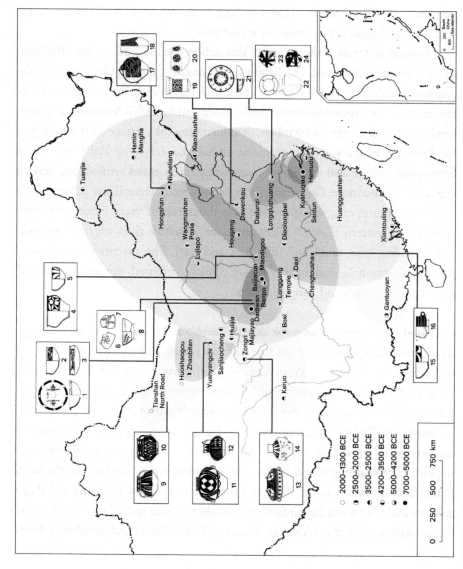

Figure 2.12 The spatial expansion of two major painted pottery traditions before the late Shang Dynasty

1–4. Basin (Jiangzhai T254W156: 1, Banpo P. 1162, Beishouling M169: 1, Miaodigou H11: 75)

5, 8, 15, 20, 21. Earthen bowl (Miaodigou H387: 44, Dadiwan H10: 37, Chengtoushan H210: 3, Dawenkou M2007: 32, Longqiuzhuang M162: 9)

6, 7, 23, 24. Painted pottery shard (Dadiwan H3115: 11, 10, Kuahuqiao T203⑤: 30, T202⑤: 5)

9–14, 17, 18, 22. Jar (pot) (Donghuishan M158: 3, Hami Tianshan North Road, Yuanyangchi M44: 1, M72: 2, Zongri M222: 1, 94TZM68: 5, Niuheliang N2Z4M6: 1, Zhizhu Mountain T1③: 47, Kuahuqiao T0511⑤A: 11)

16. Cup (Chengtoushan M680: 5)
19. Drum (Dawenkou M1018: 24)

Figure 2.13 Development and evolution of symbols (primitive characters) before the late Shang Dynasty

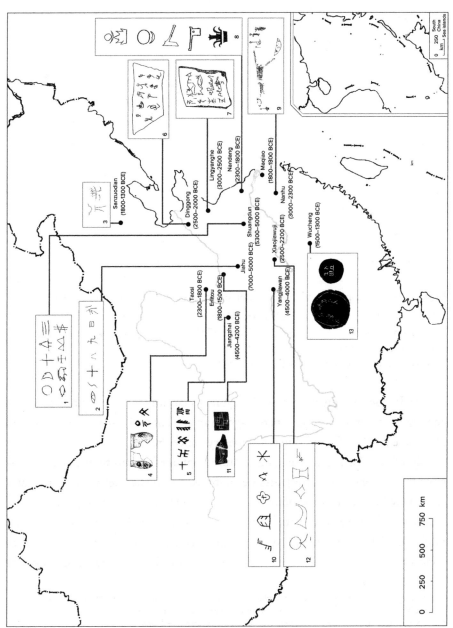

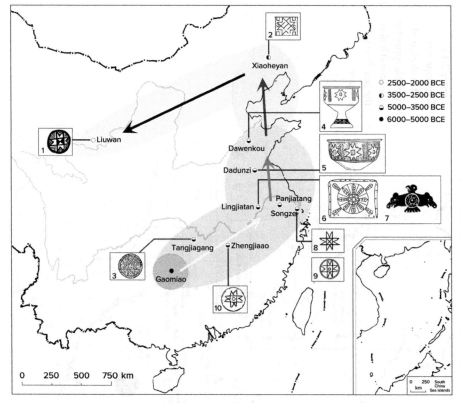

Figure 2.14 Development and dissemination of octagonal patterns in Chinese Neolithic

1. Liuwan (M1275)
2. Xiaoheyan (F4: 3)
3. Tangjiagang (M1: 1)
4. Dawenkou (M2005: 49)
5. Dadunzi (M44: 4)
6, 7. Lingjiatan (87M4: 30, 98M29: 6)
8. Songze (T2: 7)
9. Panjiatang
10. Zhengjiaao (T2M8: 2)

burials. In contrast, phenomena in Xinglongwa culture, such as combined human and pig joint burials and "jade pig-dragon" (an ancient Chinese jade vessel shaped like a jade *jue*),[124] reflected different funerary concepts.

Significant burials of Peiligang culture contained exquisite artifacts such as bone flutes, bone plates, turquoise decorations, and turtle shells. The bone flutes could play heptatonic or pentatonic scales, possibly used for tuning—pioneering traditional Chinese music; the turtle shells containing black and white gravels might be related to divination, or the origin of concepts, such as *Taiji*[*] and *Bagua*;[†] bone needles within the turtle shells could possibly imply medical usage for

---

* The categories used by ancient Chinese philosophy to illustrate the head of the world.—Trans.
† A set of eight symbols that originated in China, used in Taoist cosmology to represent the fundamental principles of reality, seen as a range of eight interrelated concepts.—Trans.

CHINA BEFORE EARLY CHINA

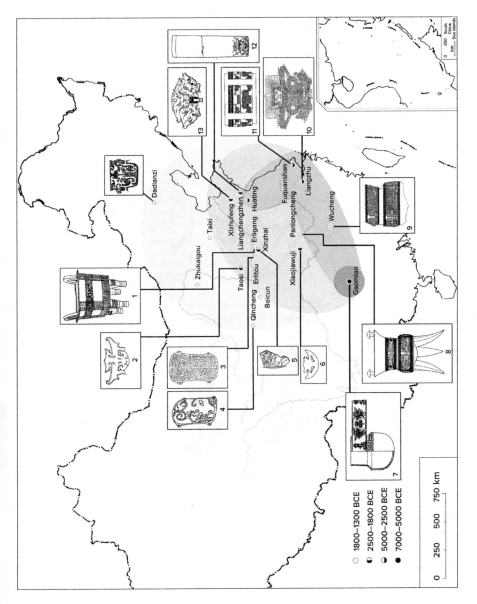

Figure 2.15 Development and evolution of symbols (primitive characters) before the late Shang Dynasty

1. Zhangzhai in Zhengzhou City (Duling No. 1)
2. Taosi (M22: 135)
3. Erlitou (M11: 7)
4. Qincheng in Tianshui City
5. Xinzhai (H24: 1)
6. Xiaojiawuji (W6: 60)
7. Gaomiao (T1015⑧: 16)
8. Panlongcheng (PYWM4: 4)
9. Wucheng (1974QSW [publicly-sourced]: 32)
10. Fanshan (M12: 98)
11. Fuquanshan (M9: 21)
12. Liangchengzhen
13. Xizhufeng (M201: 1)

acupuncture—the tomb owner might be a shaman skilled in divination, music, medicine, and astronomy. Masks, pottery figurines, jade *jues*, etc., characterized the Cishan–Xinglongwa culture in North and Northeast China. These were also thought to be related to the shaman or primitive shamanism. Still, they differed from the former, with slightly more idolatry, reflecting connections with the grassland western regions of the North. For instance, circles of mud and grooved stones behind the ranges of houses AF50, 52, and 17 in the Xinglongwa culture of Baiyinchanghan, were possibly used for erecting statues; a stone-carved human figure was found behind the range of F19. A double-face stone statue was found at the Dongzhai site in Qian'an City, Hebei Province (fig. 2.16).[125] Zhaobaogou culture had *zun*-shaped vessels with animal images such as deer heads, boar heads, and bird heads engraved in their bellies. A large "dragon-shaped pile of stones"

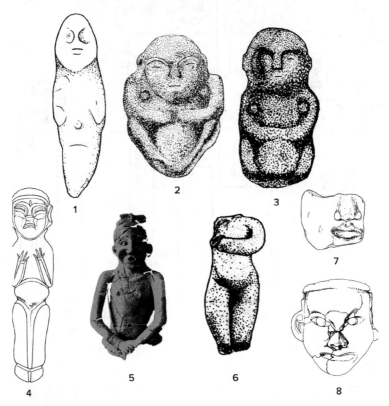

Figure 2.16 Human figurines in the Neolithic of Northeast China

1. Baiyinchanghan (AF19②: 4)
2, 3. Houtaizi (Publicly-sourced: 14, 15)
4, 7, 8. Niuheliang (N16M4: 4, N3G2: 1, N1J1B: 1)
5. Xinglonggou
6. Dongshanzui (TD8②: 5)
(1–3. Stone   4. Jade
5–8. Pottery. The eyeballs of 8 are jade among them.)

from Xinglongwa culture was found in Chahai, Fuxin City, Liaoning Province. Especially the round and notched jade *jue* from Xinglongwa culture, extremely "Chinese" in character, likely originating from phase I of Shuangta culture, profoundly influenced the future jade culture in China and East Asia.[126]

Interestingly, some have noticed that the ornamentation of the pottery cylindrical jars in Xinglongwa culture is divided into upper, middle, and lower sections, with the middle section being the most complex. The houses are divided into ranges, central activity areas, and peripheral areas, with the range as the core. The settlement is divided into houses (actually large central houses), moat interior space, and moat exterior space. Agriculture, gathering, and hunting are roughly divided into three parts based on proximity in the surrounding area.[127] This suggests that people of Xinglongwa culture and even the entire Northeast and North China may have had a holistic underlying thinking of a "centered three-tier structure." The burials in the Central Plain's Peiligang culture are also quite orderly. Still, the arrangement of houses in the settlements is more chaotic, so it is unclear whether this structure exists. According to Zhang Guangzhi, witchcraft and shamanic culture are essential characteristics of the "Maya-Chinese cultural continuum," and "in their worldview, the world is divided into different levels, and shamans can travel between these levels."[128]

In summary, although this early Chinese cultural prototype formed 8,000 years ago still exists in a relatively equal society, it is probably different from the Paleolithic Age where everyone could worship and communicate with spirits. The status of more specialized religious personnel like shamans gradually stood out, laying the foundation for the stable and continuous development of Chinese culture, further refining the characteristics of Chinese culture's stability, moderation, pragmatism, respect for tradition and the internal order, and emphasis on holistic thinking.

IV. Three Major Cultural Systems

Around 5000 BCE marks an important turning point. From this point onwards, Chinese culture reached another peak of development. The exchange and integration of different cultures were further enhanced, establishing the pattern of three major cultural systems. Settlements clustered, social order was well-established, and we entered the late Neolithic, with the embryonic "early China" making considerable progress (table 2.3).

Table 2.3 Cultural regions of the early stage of late China's Neolithic (5000–4200 BCE)

Yellow River Basin	Bottle (pot)–earthen bowl (basin)–jar–*ding* cultural system (The beginning of Yangshao culture, early stage of Yangshao culture phase I, and Beixin culture)
Middle and lower reaches of the Yangtze River and South China	Cauldron–round-foot plate–high-foot plate cultural system (Tangjiagang culture, Daxi culture phase I, Majiabang culture, Hemudu culture, Longqiuzhuang culture, and Xiantouling culture)
Northeast China	Cylindrical jar cultural system (Late Zhaobaogou culture, early Hongshan culture, late lower Zuojiashan culture, middle Zuojiashan culture, lower Xiaozhushan culture, Zhenxing culture, and Yabuli culture)
Other regions	Mesolithic culture

1. The Yellow River Basin Cultural Region

The Yellow River Basin cultural region includes most of the Yellow River Basin, North China, and the upper and middle reaches of the Huai River.

The Formation of Beixin Culture and Its Western Influence

Around 5000 BCE, the standoff between Shuangdun and Houli cultures to the south and north ended, merging into the newly formed Beixin culture.[129] Suppose we divide Beixin culture into an earlier and a later phase. In that case, the earlier phase is represented by the remains of the middle phase delineated by the excavators of the Beixin site.[130] Its features such as conical-foot *dings*, shallow-belly open-mouth flat-bottom earthen bowls, small-mouth double-shoulder pots, round-foot catch-handles or circular catch-handle lids, footed supports, net pendants and other types of items, decorations made by attaching fine clay strips or imprinted, engraved, and stabbing to create net patterns, grouped oblique line patterns, broken line patterns, fine-tooth comb patterns with clustered dots, and the prevalence of clay pottery, all closely align with Shuangdun culture but are distinct from Houli culture. Shuangdun culture was one of the significant sources of Beixin culture. The Peiligang cultural elements in Beixin culture were mainly indirectly inherited from Shuangdun culture. Of course, as previously discussed, the round-bottom and tri-legged cauldrons that hold a significant position in Beixin culture undoubtedly were inherited from Houli culture, and the deep-belly feature of the conical-foot *dings* is also related to Houli culture. In addition, slender-neck jugs, red-topped earthen bowls, and large-mouth jars with bird-beak hook handles (perhaps drum-shaped) have already appeared. Around 4500 BCE, it entered the late Beixin culture, represented by the H24, H2 from the Dawenkou site in Taian City in Shandong Province, excavated in 1974,[131] and Wangyin H11, H1 in Yanzhou,[132] showing changes in the decrease in the number of cauldrons, a significant increase in *dings* with shallower bellies, fine clay strip decorations gradually replaced by stamped patterns, awl-stabbed patterns. Still, overall, it is in line with the earlier phase.

The houses in Beixin culture were simple, near-circular semi-subterranean buildings with platforms. The pit area was usually between 3 to 10 square meters, and items could be placed around the pit is platforms. This is similar to the houses in Peiligang culture but vastly different from Houli culture. The graves were mainly rectangular vertical pit graves, some of which had stone slabs on the grave walls, mainly single burials in extended supine, but there were also joint burials and secondary burials; many had no burial objects, and some had one to three burial objects. Men were buried with arrowheads, and women with awls and needles. The overall situation was similar to Peiligang culture, but no larger graves like those in Jiahu were seen. The phenomenon of adult lateral incisor extraction in the graves of Dongjiabai laid the groundwork for the future tooth extraction tradition of Eastern peoples.[133] Beixin culture had stone axes, stone shovels, stone grinding plates, stone grinding rods, and other tools, and primitive agriculture should have existed, but there is a lack of evidence from plant remains; only judging from the relatively low degree of stone tool grinding and the small number of sickles (claw sickles) for harvesting, there is a big difference from Yangshao culture, where dry farming was developed. It is estimated that the fishing, hunting, and gathering economy occupied a larger proportion, and there was also the livestock industry with pigs and dogs.

The Formation of Yangshao Culture: The Beginning of Yangshao Culture

Beixin culture, formed on the foundation of two major cultural systems, was highly vibrant. From its inception, it began to influence the west, playing a significant role in the frequent cultural exchange and integration in the upper and middle reaches of the Yellow River. This gave birth to the vibrant early Yangshao culture, which spread from east to west, resulting in various subcultures. The Xiapanwang type, represented by the "second type," remains in Ci County in Hebei Province;[134] the Dazhang type, represented by the Dazhang site in Fangcheng County in Henan Province;[135] the Zaoyuan type, represented by phases I and II in Yicheng County in Shanxi Province;[136] and the Lingkou type,[137] represented by the "Lingkou Village cultural remains" in Lintong District of Xi'an City in Shaanxi Province.[138]

The predecessor of Yangshao culture is the middle Neolithic culture in the middle reaches of the Yellow River.[139] Broadly speaking, the main pottery types of the early Yangshao culture, such as earthen bowls, jars, basins, and pots, can be traced back to Peiligang culture, Baijia culture, and Cishan culture, and similarities also exist in production tools, architectural styles, and burial customs. Specifically, the predecessor of the Lingkou type in the Guanzhong and Hanzhong regions should be Baijia culture. The main pottery types of the Lingkou type, such as earthen bowls, false round-foot bowls, small-mouth pots, cord-mark jars with stamped patterns on necks, etc., are also typical artifacts of the late Baijia culture. The characteristics of the former, such as the red top on the earthen bowl, the red-brown colored band, and the stamped pattern on the neck of the marked-cord jar, are all first seen in the latter. In central and southern Henan, the Dazhang type has many links with the late Peiligang culture. Its earthen bowls, basins, jars, round-foot bowls, high-foot plates, small-mouth shoulder-handle pots, conical-foot round-belly *dings*, and other pottery types can all be traced back to Peiligang culture. The Xiapanwang type in Beijing and Hebei Province inherits some elements of the Cishan type of Cishan culture, such as earthen bowls, small-mouth shoulder-handle pots, foot supports, and grooved whetstones.

However, careful analysis reveals many differences, and the transitions are not entirely smooth. For example, the rotary-pattern jars, conical-foot round-belly *dings*, and large-mouth pointed-bottom jars popular in the Lingkou type are not seen in the late Baijia culture. On the other hand, certain features of the late Baijia culture, such as jars with three legs and cord-mark decorations on earthen bowls, do not continue into the Lingkou type. Decorations, such as rotary patterns, fingernail patterns, red-brown painted, large-mouth pointed-bottom jars, and folded-belly *dings* in Dazhang type, are not seen in the earlier Peiligang culture. The Xiapanwang type's rotary-pattern jars, rotary-pattern basins, large-mouth pointed-bottom jars, red-brown painted decorations, and numerous cauldrons also do not have a local origin. Popular trends from Cishan culture, such as the *yus* (short cylindrical jar), cord-mark patterns, and engraved geometric patterns, did not continue, especially in the Yi River Basin, where the difference between the Beifudi type of Cishan culture and the Xiapanwang type is greater. Nevertheless, small-mouth pots (bottles) and conical-foot round-belly *dings* from the Lingkou type can be traced back to central and southern Henan. The red-brown painted decorations of the Dazhang type and Xiapanwang type were earlier seen in

Guanzhong and Hanzhong, and the popularity of rotary patterns or rotating traces on jars and other vessels can be seen because of the popularization of slow wheel pottery technology. This shows that during the formation of the early Yangshao culture, there was a wide range of fast and effective exchanges. It was a very important cultural integration process in the middle reaches of the Yellow River. However, no matter what, large-mouth pointed-bottom jars, folded-lipped features of pot types, cauldrons prevalent in the Xiapanwang type, and ranges and other pottery types that are generally present in the early Yangshao culture, indeed, cannot be traced back to the middle Neolithic cultures in the middle reaches of the Yellow River.

Zooming out, Beixin culture in the Yellow River's lower reaches also has many round-belly ceramic cauldrons similar to the Xiapanwang type. Undoubtedly, the pottery cauldrons of the Xiapanwang type originated from Beixin culture. The small-mouth folded-lipped ball-belly pots and large-mouth pointed-bottom jars share similar features to cauldrons. The small-mouth shoulder-handle pots were very popular during the middle Beixin culture. Thus, these three types of utensils may have been transmitted from Shandong to Hebei rather than vice versa. Ceramic ranges have existed since Shuangdun culture. As such, the westward and northwestward expansion of Beixin culture played a crucial role in the formation of the Xiapanwang type.[140] Not only this, the influence of Beixin culture continues to spread through the Xiapanwang type, promoting frequent exchanges and turbulent recombination of cultures in the entire middle Yellow River region to some extent. It not only integrates and transforms the Neolithic cultures of Beijing, Hebei, Guanzhong, Hanzhong, and central and southern Henan into the completely new early Yangshao culture but also extends its scope to southwest Shanxi Province, connecting various regions into a relatively whole. Large-mouth pointed-bottom jars (perhaps ceramic drums) with bird-beak hook handles seem to have become a special symbol linking Beixin culture and various types of the early Yangshao culture. At the same time, Beixin culture's strong westward influence is also a process of interaction with the early Yangshao culture,[141] and artifacts like red-topped earthen bowls are common factors formed during this exchange process.

The house architecture of the early Yangshao culture is semi-subterranean. Houses in the Yuanqu Ancient City Dongguan Zaoyuan type are still round semi-subterranean, inheriting the tradition of Peiligang culture; the Xiapanwang type houses in Beifudi and other places are square with rounded corners, inheriting the tradition of Cishan culture. Most tombs are rectangular vertical pit tombs, and the tomb owners are single persons in extended supine, which is in line with the tradition of Peiligang culture. But Lingkou type tombs like Fulinbao have several pottery items buried with them,[142] while Yuanqu Ancient City Dongguan Zaoyuan type tombs have none, reflecting differences in funeral thoughts. Infant urn burials have been found at sites such as the Nanyangzhuang site in Zhengding County in Hebei Province,[143] a burial custom seen earlier in Peiligang culture. The overall settlement pattern reflects a society of equals. Additionally, there are more bone or pottery hairpins, stone rings (bracelets), and other decorations.

The production tools of the early Yangshao culture are more ground than chipped. Besides axes, adzes, and chisels, which were woodworking tools used previously, there are most stone shovels. The number of stone or pottery knives (dagger-axes or sickles) used for plucking grain spikes has increased, and more chipped stone or pottery plate-shaped tools might have been used for harvesting. Stone grinding slabs and stone grinding rods can process grain seeds, indicating that dry farming might have developed considerably. It might have been a critical period for transitioning from sorghum to millet grain. Additionally, pottery files can be used for fine processing of wood, leather, etc.

The Initial Development of Yangshao Culture: Yangshao Culture Phase I

Around 4500 BCE, Yangshao culture finally developed into its phase I,[144] which includes the Banpo type, the Hougang type, the Zaoyuan type, and the Lujiaopo type, among others. Although there was no significant change in the cultural pattern, the distribution area expanded significantly. Although there was cultural exchange among different styles, regional differences increased, making this a period where individual characteristics were emphasized.

During phase I of Yangshao culture, the most powerful types were the Banpo type and the Hougang type. The Banpo type, represented by the early remains of Banpo in Xi'an,[145] is the successor of the Lingkou type. The small-mouth pointed-bottom bottle evolved from the small-mouth flat-bottom bottle, and it had spread to northern Shaanxi and the southwestern edge of Ordos.[146] The Hougang type, represented by phase I of remains in Anyang, Henan,[147] is the successor of the Xiapanwang type, and its cauldron-shaped *ding* evolved from a cauldron. Compared to the previous Lingkou and Xiapanwang types, the differences between the Banpo and Hougang types have increased significantly.[148] For instance, the Banpo type features small-mouth pointed-bottom bottles, barely any *dings*, developed painted pottery popularly in black, and common animal patterns like fish. On the other hand, the Hougang type still uses small-mouth flat-bottom bottles, with the *ding* as the main pottery, less developed painted pottery mainly in red and common grouped slant line patterns. The significant differences between the two types may result from the groups they represent intentionally emphasizing their features, which has led to an east and west standoff in Yangshao culture. Not only that, but these two types also advanced into the sparsely populated, narrow Northern region at the same time. This collision and fusion result in the Lujiaopo type and the Shihushan type in the Northern region.[149] The Shihushan type is biased toward a corner of the Daihai region[150] and is quite similar to the Hougang type, only with a small amount of marked cords and other Banpo type elements. In contrast, the Lujiaopo type is widely distributed[151] and is a fusion of the Banpo type and the Hougang type: cord-mark urns, cord-mark jars, or cord-mark and spiral decorations jars, and a few black-painted pottery items are similar to the Banpo type; folded-lipped ball-belly pots, short-neck pots, grouped red stripe painted pottery, and a few *dings*, cauldrons, *zengs*, etc., are similar to the Hougang type. In addition, between the Banpo and Lujiaopo types, the Zaoyuan type continues from the previous period. In Henan Province, there are also the Dahecun and Xiawanggang types, which evolved from the Dazhang type, represented by the first two phases of Dahecun[152] and phase I of Xiawanggang, respectively.

In the phase I of Yangshao culture, circular moat settlements such as Banpo and Jiangzhai were discovered, with Jiangzhai being the most representative.[153] The settlement is generally divided into three major parts: a living area, a pottery kiln, and a cemetery. The living area is mainly within the circular moat, where over 100 houses from the same period are arranged in a circle, all doors facing the center. The houses can be divided into large, medium, and small sizes, in circular or square semi-underground style, arranged around five large square houses forming five groups, possibly representing five clans or large families. The entire settlement constitutes a tribe or clan with over 100 people. There are three cemeteries mainly for adult burials on the moat's east, south, and north sides, roughly corresponding to each group of houses. There are also some infant urn burials arranged near each group of houses. Adult graves are rectangular vertical earth pit graves, most in extended supine, accompanied by several daily-use pottery, production tools, and decorations. There is no apparent wealth disparity or social status difference between men and women, but the types of accompanying items vary by gender. The differences in the production tools buried with men and women reflect a natural division of labor by gender; meanwhile, women are buried with bone hairpins and bone beads, which are not seen with men, reflecting different decorations between men and women. In addition, there is a pottery kiln to the west of the village, possibly an industry for the whole village. At that time, there should have been at least three levels of property ownership (figs. 2.17 and 2.18).[154] The layout of other Banpo type settlements is generally similar to that of Jiangzhai, with a centripetal structure of house arrangement reflecting a society of shared interests, bloodline cohesion, and a sense of order and equality.[155] The emergence of this centripetal structure may be related to the traditional presence in the Northeast and North China regions. Some people believe that such a society conforms to the characteristics of a so-called segmental society.[156] It is worth noting that, in the later part of this period, there are multi-person joint burial tombs represented by Yuanjun Temple and Hengzhen Cemetery, where primary and secondary burials coexist. The secondary burials are mostly arranged in extended supine, emphasizing organization, order, collectiveness, and equality.[157] It is worth noting that graves of the Hougang type, such as those at the Xishuipo site in Puyang City in Henan Province, barely have any accompanying items,[158] which differs from the Banpo type.

In phase I of Yangshao culture, the production tools and economic forms were similar to the early period, with agriculture continuing to develop and lead. Grains and decaying ashes are often found in cellars, and carbonized decaying millet grain and sorghum are found in pottery jars and earthen bowls, with millet grain being the main crop, along with acorns, mustard seeds, and cabbage seeds, suggesting the existence of vegetable farming. Circular and elliptical "scrapers" made from pottery fragments of the Banpo and Hougang types remain dominant, with nearly 2,000 pieces unearthed from Jiangzhai phase I alone, possibly representing harvesting tools.[159] Stone knives (sickle claws) have become the main tools in other areas. Pigs are the main livestock, serving as the primary source of meat. Pottery decorations from Dadiwan seem to imitate bull and sheep horns. Furthermore, the discovery of bone-handle stone-blade knives, arrowheads, fishhooks, and net pendants indicates that fishing, hunting, and gathering still played an important role.

2. The Middle and Lower Yangtze River—South China Cultural Region

Tangjiagang Culture, Daxi Culture Phase I, and Xiantouling Culture
During the early and phase I of Yangshao culture, the middle reaches of the Yangtze River were successively occupied by Tangjiagang culture and phase I of Daxi culture. In contrast, the most clear-cut culture in South China was Xiantouling culture.

Tangjiagang culture is mainly found in sites such as Tangjiagang[160] and Huachenggang in Anxiang County,[161] Hunan Province, and Chengtoushan in Li Couny, Hunan Province.[162] The culture developed from the lower Zaoshi culture, with

CHINA BEFORE EARLY CHINA

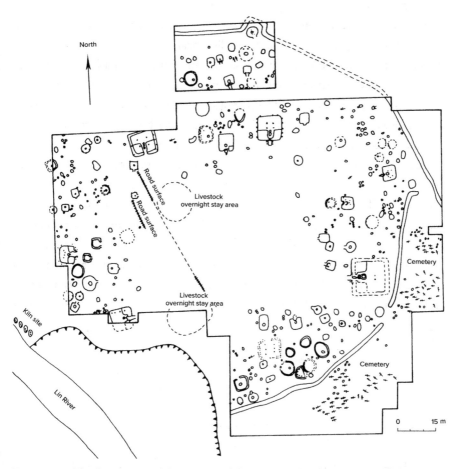

Figure 2.17 The distribution of the remains of the moat-enclosed settlement at Jiangzhai phase I

Figure 2.18 The reconstruction of the moat-enclosed settlement in Jiangzhai phase I (by Zhang Xiaoguang)

its pottery combinations of round-foot plates and cauldrons bearing similarities and its cord-mark and geometric patterns showing a clear succession. But visible changes also emerged, such as the basic disappearance of narrow-waist double-handle jars, and the emergence of fine sand white pottery and a large number of imprinted geometric patterns and fine-tooth comb patterns with clustered dot patterns, especially the imprinted white pottery plates (fig. 2.19). Some believe this was influenced by Gaomiao culture in the Yuan River Basin.[163] In the vicinity of Dongting Lake, there are also some archaeological remains that bear similarities to Tangjiagang culture, such as Songxikou culture in the middle and upper reaches of the Yuan River and Liulinxi culture in the Xiajiang region.[164]

Following Tangjiagang culture is Daxi culture, named after the Daxi site in Wushan County, Sichuan Province.[165] The clearest development stages can be seen in Guanmiaoshan in Zhijiang City, Hubei Province,[166] and Chengtoushan in Li Couny, Hunan Province. Based on these sites, Daxi culture can be divided into three phases,[167] with phase I belonging to this stage. Phase I of Daxi culture developed on the basis of Tangjiagang culture. Main pottery vessels such as

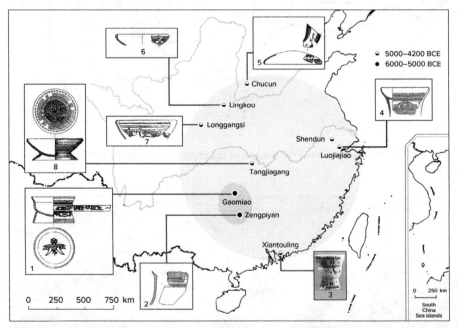

Figure 2.19 The distribution of imprinted-pattern white pottery in the middle to late China's Neolithic (6000–4200 BCE)

1. Gaomiao (T2003㉑: 12)
2. Zengpiyan (KBT3: 013)
3. Xiantouling (T2⑥: 1)
4. Luojiajiao (T118②: 4)
5. Chucun (TG③: 2)
6. Lingkou (T6⑥a: 117)
7. Longgangsi (T5③: 30)
8. Tangjiagang (M1: 1)

cauldrons, round-foot plates, folded-belly earthen bowls, and curved-neck jars continue the lineage of Tangjiagang culture. The major changes are evident in replacing marked-cord cauldrons with plain cauldrons. Additionally, new features include tri-legged plates with perforated foot decorations and plain round-foot bowls, which may have been influenced by Majiabang culture and Longqiuzhuang culture from the lower reaches of the Yangtze River. Daxi culture originated in the Liyang Plain and Xiajiang region, gradually expanding to surrounding areas.

Xiantouling culture, represented by the Xiantouling site in Shenzhen City, Guangdong Province, covers phases I to III in this stage.[168] Its main distribution range is the Pearl River Delta and nearby islands, extending north to Shaoguan City in Guangdong Province.[169] This culture exhibits many cord-mark cauldrons likely inherited from the Dingsishan culture. Still, its frequent stamped-pattern white pottery plates are not a local factor and probably spread from Gaomiao culture and Tangjiagang culture in the middle reaches of the Yangtze River.[170] The white pottery round-foot cups likely emerged under the influence of the white pottery plates. Similar archaeological remains are also found in phase V of Zengpiyan and phase I of Ziyuan Xiaojin in the northeastern Guangxi Zhuang Autonomous Region.[171] Perhaps this region connected the middle reaches of the Yangtze River and the Pearl River estuary.

Tangjiagang culture already featured moated settlements, such as Chengtoushan, Tangjiagang, etc., and ground-level houses. Cemeteries were divided into zones, with white and red pottery plates with white outfits commonly accompanying burials in the northern cemetery. In contrast, the southern cemetery had none, reflecting a certain disparity in the social status represented by different cemetery zones.[172] Daxi culture features the circular city of Chengtoushan, China's earliest known city wall. The city has houses, tombs, altars, and other structures. The ground-level long-row houses, which later became prevalent in the Jianghuai region, were introduced during this period. The burial practices followed traditional rectangular vertical pit graves and flexed burials, with a few instances of urn coffins. Additionally, there are accompanying phenomena of burial objects such as fish and turtles. The emergence of the city wall might prevent flooding, but it might also have a defensive function and a role in emphasizing order. Along with the changes in family structure reflected by the emergence of rectangular houses in a row, these all indicate a significant transition in Daxi culture society, with social order notably strengthening. The Tangjiagang culture and phase I of Daxi culture still had many knapped stone tools and polished stone tools such as axes, adzes, and chisels, as well as wooden tools, such as oars. The remains of rice and rice paddies were found at the Chengtoushan site, indicating that rice agriculture had reached a certain scale, and the gathering of other wild plants also played an important role. The Xiantouling culture mainly consisted of shell mound sites, with livelihoods mainly relying on fishing and gathering, without rice agriculture yet.

Hemudu Culture and Majiabang Culture

The upper limits of the Hemudu and Majiabang cultures in the Lower Yangtze River are generally considered to be around 5000 BCE. However, this raises a question: neither of these cultures is a clear descendant of the middle Neolithic Kuahuqiao culture, and there must be at least a millennium of time difference between them and the early Neolithic Shangshan culture. Where exactly do their cultural origins lie?

Hemudu culture, represented by phases I and II of the Hemudu site in Yuyao City, Zhejiang Province,[173] including the Tianluoshan site,[174] is distributed in the Ningbo–Shaoxing region south of Hangzhou Bay, from Yuhang in the west to the Zhoushan Islands in the east. The pottery is mainly carbonaceous black, with popular cord-mark and engraved geometric patterns and various animal and plant patterns. Its double-handle jars, open-mouth basins, converging-mouth earthen bowls, round-foot plates, and high-foot plates, as well as the style of double-handle outside the rims and polygonal vessel rims, are all inherited from Shangshan culture. Moreover, various cauldrons with cord-mark decorations in their lower bellies may have evolved under the influence of Kuahuqiao culture—the earliest source is still Pengtoushan culture. Still, its features, such as the waist edge and converging mouth, are indeed very local. The real new major pottery is only *he* (a bartending vessel in ancient China) with a tubular spout (fig. 2.20); even ranges have already appeared in the Shunshanji culture. In this view, Hemudu culture is likely to directly inherit Shangshan culture. Its upper limit may be concurrent with Kuahuqiao culture, the dating data of the Tianluoshan site's early remains are close to 6000 BCE, but the lower limit of Hemudu culture extends later. In its later period, it was influenced by Majiabang culture, leading to the appearance of conical-foot *ding*, high-handle high-foot plate, etc.

Majiabang culture is mainly distributed around Tai Lake, and the situation is more complex.[175] The earliest discovered Majiabang culture remains at sites such as the Luojiajiao site in Tongxiang City, Zhejiang Province,[176] the Dongshan Village site in Zhangjiagang City, Jiangsu Province,[177] and the Luotuodun site in Yixing

City, Jiangsu Province.[178] The pottery is mainly red-brown with a clamshell, which is prevalent in plain instead of cord-mark, which is one of its significant differences from Hemudu culture. As for the utensils, there are quite a lot of similarities. Its double-handle jars, open-mouth basins, converging-mouth earthen bowls, round-foot plates, high-foot plates, cups, and other pottery may originate from remains similar to Shangshan culture. Unfortunately, such remains have not been found in the area north of Hangzhou Bay. Still, many wide-rim cauldrons with handles are difficult to find the source in the lower reaches of the Yangtze River. Looking around, Shuangdun culture popularized flat-bottom cauldrons with double

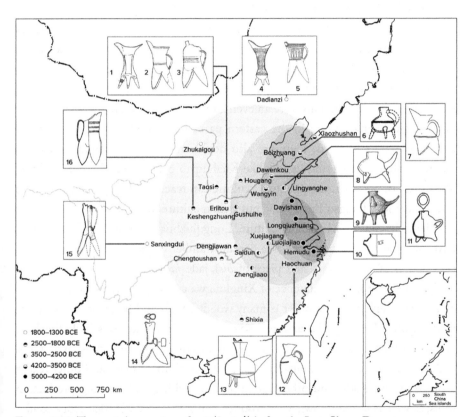

Figure 2.20 The spatial expansion of gui^a (he, jue^b) before the Late Shang Dynasty

1–3. Erlitou (IV M11: 1, V M22: 8, IVM8: 1)
4, 5. Dadianzi (M666: 8, 7)
6. Beizhuang (H101①: 1)
7. Lingyanghe (79M24: 32)
8. Dawenkou (M1001: 4)
9. Longqiuzhuang (T1827⑦: 25)
10. Hemudu (T243 [4A]: 253)
11. Luojiajiao (T135③: 16)
12. Haochuan (M32: 12)
13. Xuejiagang (M5: 1)
14. Dengjiawan (H30: 3)
15. Sanxingdui (DcT1②: 43)
16. Keshengzhuang (H74) (All pottery.)

[a] An ancient China type of pottery cooking utensil, like a *ding*, with a handle and three hollow feet.—Trans.
[b] An ancient China drinking vessel with three legs.—Trans.

handles. Its cultural range once reached Jurong City in Jiangsu Province,[179] so the flat-bottom cauldrons of the Luotuodun type Majiabang culture in the western part of Tai Lake may be related to it. The most common type of Houli culture is the round-bottom cauldron with added relief decorations on the rim. The round-bottom cauldrons of the Luojiajiao type Majiabang culture in the eastern part of Tai Lake may be related to it. But in any case, more *yis* (ancient Chinese vessels for holding water or wine) and *he*-shaped vessels may only be seen as creations of Majiabang or Hemudu culture. In the later development process of Majiabang culture, high-handle high-foot plates and a large number of tri-legged potteries such as the *dings*, *hes*, and tri-legged earthen bowls appeared. The conical-foot *ding* may be related to the influence of Beixin culture. Other tri-legged potteries were also inspired by it, and new characteristic potteries such as pig-shaped jars, double-mouth or three-mouth pots, multi-spout pots, etc., were created, and influenced the emergence of Loujiaqiao type remains in the Puyang River Basin to the south.[180] Similar remains have an even larger distribution area, such as phase I of Longqiuzhuang culture in the eastern part of the Jianghuai region.[181] Apart from wide-rim cauldrons, there are also double ring-handle cauldrons, etc. Its painted pottery is rich and varied, like Kuahuqiao culture, but the details differ. The northern part of Longqiuzhuang culture can reach the Lianyungang–Pizhou line in northern Jiangsu Province,[182] but Beixin culture influences it.

Hemudu culture, Majiabang culture, Longqiuzhuang culture, and others also have two notable features: one is a certain number of jade decorations such as jade *huangs* (shaped like a half piece of *bis*), jade *jues*, beads, etc. The jade *jue* is likely to result from the influence of Xinglongwa culture, and the jade *huang* may be a local innovation. The other is many wooden tools and bone-horn-and-ivory instruments, which are, of course, related to preservation conditions, including boat and oar components, square column tenons and mortises, butterfly-shaped tools, and other building components, spinning wheels, shuttle knives and other textile tools, *sis*, arrowheads, and other agricultural or fishing and hunting production tools, as well as lacquer bowls with wooden cores, hairpins, whistles, ivory combs, etc. Stone tools are still mainly axes, adzes, chisels, etc. A large number of rice remains have been found in several cultures, with the coexistence of japonica rice and indica rice, also raising pigs and dogs, especially the Hemudu site has half a meter thick rice and rice straw remains, pottery has rice ear, pig and other engraved patterns, in the Wuxian Caoxieshan, Kunshan Chuodun[183] and Jiangli sites[184] have also found ancient rice paddies, it can be seen that the utilization of rice is an important part of their livelihood. Analysis of the Tianluoshan site shows that the proportion of cultivated rice continues to increase, indicating the continuous development of agriculture, but the quantity of acorns is also high.[185] There is still a lot of controversy about the level of development of the rice agriculture it represents.[186] The overall livelihood pattern should be close to the Chengtoushan Daxi culture.

Hemudu culture's stilt houses span more than 20 meters in length and are quite noticeable, ingeniously emphasizing collectivity and order, much like the Jiangzhai settlement of Yangshao culture. Majiabang culture and Longqiuzhuang culture feature houses with wooden skeletal structures and mud walls, some of which are also built-in connected series. The burial customs typically involved rectangular vertical pit graves and urn burials. Single burials dominate pit graves, but there are also joint burials of two or three people. These often come with a few everyday ceramic or tool burial objects, and in a few cases, there are pig mandibles or dog heads as burial objects. Hemudu culture graves feature both flexed and extended supine burials. Majiabang culture's prone burials are distinctive, with some grave owners having jade wares in their mouths. Most of Longqiuzhuang culture graves are extended supine burials, with a few prone burials, and the custom of covering the deceased's head and face with red pottery earthen bowls and high-foot plates.

3. Northeast China Cultural Region

After 5000 BCE, the cultural landscape in the Northeast region did not change significantly. The southern part still includes Zhaobaogou culture, the lower Xinle culture, etc., which have slightly altered cultural characteristics, entering their late stages. Specifically, the late Zhaobaogou culture in Inner Mongolia's Linxi Baiyinchanghan phase III class B[187] and the Xiaoshan remains in Aohan Banner[188] are newly revealed with clay red pottery bowls, basins, and other elements from the type of Yangshao culture's Xiapanwang. Around 4500 BCE, as the northeastward push of Yangshao culture's Hougang type became stronger, it eventually generated Hongshan culture on a local cultural basis, represented by the early remains of the Weijiawopu in Chifeng City[189] and Xishuiquan F17.[190] It shares commonalities with the Hougang type including slanted-mouth vats, more earthen bowls, basins, small-mouth double-handle pots, round-bottom cauldrons with fingertip patterns on the rim, and similar red slanting stripe patterns besides cylindrical jars. The southern fringe of the Northeast culture region during the late Zhaobaogou culture's Shangzhai type had more clay red pottery bowls (including red-topped earthen bowls), basins, small-mouth pots, spoons, etc., found in the late middle period of Beijing Pinggu's Shangzhai,[191] Hebei's Qianxi Xizhai phase II,[192] etc. At the time, the Fangshan area in Beijing was part of Yangshao culture, the Yan Mountains area was part of Zhaobaogou culture, and Beijing was precisely where these two cultural systems intersected.[193] Additionally, the lower Zuojiashan culture evolved into the middle Zuojiashan culture, where Z-shaped patterns began to become popular on cylindrical jars, likely due to the influence of Hongshan culture.

The lower Xiaozhushan culture on the Liaodong Peninsula,[194] similar to or influenced by Zhaobaogou culture, also had popular Z-shaped patterns on cylindrical jars. However, the lower Xiaozhushan culture also commonly featured double-handle cylindrical jars, double-handle bulbous-belly jars (pots), mat patterns, horizontal line patterns, etc. Additionally, the north area of the Northeast of the Mudan River Basin and the Sanjiang Plain still had Xinkailiu culture (late stage),[195] Zhenxing culture,[196] Yabuli culture,[197] etc. Cylindrical jars often featured imprinted or engraved scale patterns, net patterns, triangular patterns, rhombic patterns, round pit patterns, fine-tooth comb patterns with clustered dot patterns, and added relief decorations. However, Z-shaped patterns were not found. Thus, the Northeast cylindrical jar culture area can be roughly divided into two sub-areas: those with Z-shaped patterns and those without.

Worth noting is that at that time, in places like the Yaojingzi site in Changling County, Jilin Province,[198] which had the lower Zuojiashan culture, and Yabuli site in Shangzhi City, Heilongjiang Province, which had Yabuli culture, jade artifacts like axes, adzes, chisels, arrowheads, jade *bis*,* linked jade *bis*, and jade tubes were frequently found; the middle Zuojiashan even found primitive-looking stone dragons similar to Hongshan culture. These jade and stone artifacts all predate the widespread popularity of such jade artifacts in the late period of Hongshan culture.

The Northeast cylindrical jar cultural system generally featured rectangular semi-subterranean houses without a platform. Most graves were rectangular vertical pit graves, mostly with extended supine burials. Still, Xinkailiu culture had wide and short-chambered burials with flexed burials, and there were also attached burials such as secondary burials. Apart from the common ground stone tools like axes, adzes, chisels, shovels (*sis*) seen in the Yellow River area, as well as stone grinding plates and grinding rods, there were also many microliths like arrowheads, stone leaves, scrapers, spears (spearheads), bone-handle stone-

---

* A jade ring-shaped object used for sacrificial rituals in ancient China. Any such jade object where the radius is three times that of the inner radius is called a "*bi*."—Trans.

blade knives, net pendants, as well as a large number of bone-horn-and-ivory instruments like arrowheads, spears, fish darts, fishhooks, knives, etc. The Xinkailiu site had a specialized fish pit, and fish bones were buried with the dead in the graves. This reflects the significant position of fishing and hunting in the economy, especially in the northern sub-area. Still, dry farming also occupied a proportion in the southern sub-area like the Liao River Basin. Zhaobaogou culture's stone *si* (shovel) was well-organized, light, and sharp-edge, likely representing a more advanced agricultural tool for tilling the land than the Xinglongwa culture's shoulder-stone shovel (hoe).

4. The Formation of Three Major Cultural Systems and Cultural Exchange between Them

The Formation of Three Major Cultural Systems

Around 5000 BCE, the lower Yellow River and the middle Huai River regions were consolidated into Beixin culture at the beginning of the late Neolithic. This culture then influenced and promoted the development of the early Yangshao culture in the upper and middle Yellow River regions, giving the culture of the Yellow River Basin and the upper and middle Huai River regions a more unified appearance. This led to the formation of the Yellow River Basin cultural area (most of the Yellow River Basin, North China, and the upper and middle Huai River) and its bottle (pot)–earthen bowl (basin)–jar–*ding* cultural system.

The development of the cauldron–round-foot plate–high-foot plate cultural system in the middle and lower reaches of the Yangtze River–South China cultural region continued to blend and develop from an ancient tradition. During the early stage, the imprinted white pottery of Tangjiagang culture from the middle Yangtze River spread to sites such as the Luojiajiao site in Zhejiang Province during the early Majiabang culture in the lower Yangtze River. Conversely, elements of Majiabang culture, such as stone *yues*,[*] were found within Liulinxi culture at the Chaotianzui site in Yichang City, Hubei Province, in the middle Yangtze River. In the later stage, the imprinted white pottery of phase I of Daxi culture spread to sites such as the Shendun site in Liyang City, Jiangsu Province, during the late Majiabang culture.[199] In return, Daxi culture's tri-legged plates with perforated foot decorations possibly came from Majiabang culture. Remarkably, a large amount of imprinted white pottery from the middle Yangtze River was found

---

[*] An ancient Chinese weapon, whose shape resembles an axe and is mainly used for chopping and slashing.—Trans.

along the Pearl River estuary, and northeastern Guangxi might be an important transit point for this spread.

Previously, both Northeast and North China belonged to the cylindrical jar cultural system. However, with the formation and northward expansion of Yangshao culture, North China became part of the bottle (pot)–earthen bowl (basin)–jar–*ding* cultural system. The cylindrical jar cultural system receded northward to form the northeast cultural region. This region roughly split into southern and northern sub-regions based on the presence or absence of Z-shaped patterns.

In this way, the three major early Chinese cultural systems officially formed (fig. 2.21).

Cultural Exchange between Three Major Cultural Systems
At this time, the cultures of various regions were in a period of self-accumulation and parallel development. There was no obvious core culture, but the exchange between the cultural systems was more frequent than before, and the scope of exchange was unprecedentedly wide. Long-distance water transportation appeared. Especially, exchanges were more common at the intersection of the three major cultural systems, presenting a state of mutual interpenetration and intertwining.

For the western part of the border region between the Yellow River and the Yangtze River basins, remains similar to the Xiawanggang type of Yangshao culture have already spread to the northern edge of the Jianghan Plain northeast of the Han River, found at sites such as the Bianfan in Zhongxiang.[200] Conversely, elements of Tangjiagang culture's imprinted white pottery, such as earthen bowls, basins, and lids with multiple wave patterns with patterned imprints like Hui patterns and diamond-shaped patterns filled with beads, are seen in Yangshao culture Lingkou type sites such as Lingkou in Lintong, Shaanxi and Chucun in Houma, Shanxi Province,[201] as well as Yangshao culture Banpo type sites like Longgangsi in Nanzheng, Shaanxi Province.[202] In the east, elements of Beixin culture, such as deep-belly earthen bowls and double-handle pots, have influenced Longqiuzhuang culture in the early Dayishan. In contrast, aspects of the early Longqiuzhuang culture, like net pattern and wave pattern painted pottery, are also found in Beixin culture sites like Yuhuangding site in Jining City of Shandong Province[203] and Dadunzi site in Pizhou County in Jiangsu Province.[204]

As for the border region between the Yellow River Basin and the northeast cultural region, shallow-belly flat-bottom earthen bowls, basins, pots, spoons, small cups, etc., of the Xiapanwang type and the Hougang type in Yangshao

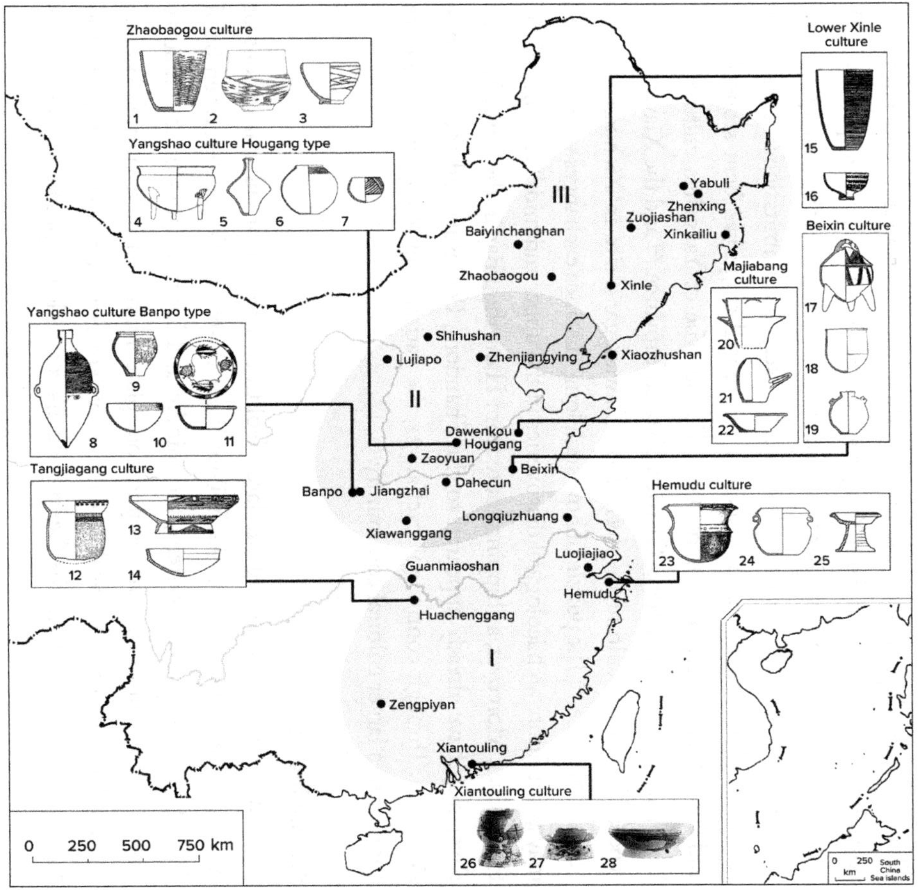

Figure 2.21 Cultural regions of late China's Neolithic (5000–4200 BCE)

I. Cauldron–round-foot plate–high-foot plate cultural system
II. Bottle (pot)–earthen bowl (basin)–jar–*ding* cultural system
III. Cylinder jar culture system

1, 15. Cylinder jar (Zhaobaogou F105②: 28, Xinle)
2. *Zun* (Zhaobaogou F7②: 15)
3, 16. Round-foot earthen bowl (Zhaobaogou F105②: 11, Xinle)
4, 17. *Ding* (Hougang H5: 6, Beixin H706: 7)
5, 8, 19. Bottle (pot) (Hougang, Jiangzhai T181F46: 11, Beixin H1002: 12)
6, 9, 24. Jar (Hougang H2: 2, Jiangzhai T276M159: 4, Hemudu T33 [4]: 109)
7, 10, 14. Earthen bowl (Hougang H2: 1, Jiangzhai T276W222: 1, Huachenggang T28⑥: 1)
11, 22. Basin (Jiangzhai T16W63: 1, Luojiajiao T129④: 3)
12, 18, 20, 23. Cauldron (Huachenggang T13⑦B: 5, Beixin M702: 1, Luojiajiao T128③: 20, Hemudu T26 [4]: 34)
13, 27, 28. Round-foot plate (Huachenggang M156: 1, Xiantouling T9⑤:1, T18⑧: 2)
21. *He* (Luojiajiao T107①: 2)
25. High-foot plate (Hemudu T211 [4B]: 447)
26. Cup (Xiantouling T1⑤: 2)
(All pottery.)

culture are frequently seen in Zhaobaogou culture in Beijing and northeastern Hebei Province. Clay earthen bowls, basins, and cauldrons have even penetrated Zhaobaogou culture in the western Liao River Basin and even reached the lower Zuojiashan culture in the second Songhua River Basin,[205] which later even contributed to the transformation of Zhaobaogou culture into Hongshan culture. The Beizhuang type of Dawenkou culture[206] and the lower Xiaozhushan culture have mutually influenced each other. The former's cylindrical jars were introduced from the latter, and the latter's double-handle jars (pots) were influenced by the former's double-handle pots, indicating that there was sea transport between Shandong Province and the Liaodong Peninsula.

There was still long-distance communication between the Banpo Yangshao culture in the middle Yellow River and Majiabang culture in the lower Yangtze River. Yangshao culture Banpo type's large-mouth pointed-bottom jars with hook handles on the outer lip are found in the burial sites in Dongshan Village, Zhangjiagang City, Jiangsu Province.[207] Their form is standard and authentic, possibly directly imported from Yangshao culture. Similarly, painted pottery with human-face fish patterns similar to the Banpo type is found at the Longqiuzhuang site in Gaoyou City, Jiangsu Province,[208] likely local imitations. Conversely, elements of Majiabang culture, such as perforated stone *yue*, bent stone *huang*, and high-foot plates, are found in the Banpo type of Yangshao culture in the Longgangsi site in Nanzheng District, Shaanxi Province,[209] and the Xiawanggang type of Yangshao culture in phase I of Xiawanggang site in Xichuan County, Henan Province.[210] The puzzle of how such long-distance exchanges were achieved may await future archaeological discoveries in the upper and middle reaches of the Huai River. Moreover, a shipping route from Hangzhou Bay in the lower Yangtze River may have already appeared to the Shandong Peninsula and the Liaodong Peninsula. Through continuous exchanges, the various cultural systems began to connect to a larger cultural community.

5. Conclusion

Around 5000 BCE, entering the late Neolithic, three major cultural regions or systems were finally formed: the Yellow River Basin's bottle (pot)–earthen bowl (basin)–jar–*ding* cultural system, the middle and lower reaches of the Yangtze River–South China's cauldron–round-foot plate–high-foot plate cultural system, and the Northeast's cylindrical jar cultural system. Although each cultural region developed in parallel, with the Central Plain's core role less prominent, exchanges within and between cultural regions became more frequent. The nascent "early Chinese cultural sphere" continued to develop, laying a solid foundation for forming an "early China" in a cultural sense.

(1) The further development of two agricultural systems
The two major agricultural systems further developed, and agriculture's importance grew increasingly in most parts of the Yellow River and Yangtze River basins. Yangshao culture in the middle and upper reaches of the Yellow River region increased in stone spades, advanced stone, or pottery knives (*zhi*) used for reaping grain spikes, and frequent findings of millet grain remain. This evidence suggests agriculture had taken a dominant position, laying the foundation for the subsequent formation of the Central Plain's core role. The proportion of agriculture also significantly increased in the lower Yellow River, the middle and lower reaches of the Yangtze River, and the Xiliao River Basin. However, fishing, hunting, and gathering economies may still have shared equal importance. In most parts of South China, the northern part of the Northeast, and most parts of the Northwestern Mesolithic culture, the economy still mainly relied on fishing, hunting, gathering, or primitive crop agriculture.[211] Especially the vivid scenes of fishing and hunting displayed by the fishing kilns, various fishing and hunting tools, fish-scale patterns on cauldron jars, net patterns, etc., of Xinkailiu culture indicate the joy of a fisherman's life.

(2) "Chinese" characteristic artifacts: Pottery, jade, and lacquerware
Looking globally, pottery, jade, and lacquerware are undoubtedly among the most "Chinese" characteristic artifacts. Pottery, of course, is not unique to China, but it first thrived in China. By the late Neolithic, pottery was prevalent in most parts of China. Not only were large quantities of pottery often found in houses, but burial goods were also predominantly pottery, encompassing cooking utensils, drinking and eating utensils, and storage utensils. This reflected a further increase in the degree of settlement, and more stable social life, with the pottery in the Yellow River and Yangtze River basins being the most developed. The artifacts were simple but relatively standard of the bottle (pot)–earthen bowl (basin)–jar–*ding* cultural system. In contrast, the artifacts of the cauldron–round-foot plate–high-foot plate cultural system in the middle and lower reaches of the Yangtze River–South China cultural area were complex and varied. They also shared specialized cooking utensils like stoves. Influenced by the Yellow and Yangtze River basins, peripheral cultures'

pottery gradually became complex. For instance, the Northeast added earthen bowls and basins made of red clay pottery to its cylindrical jars, while South China added imprinted white pottery plates and high-foot plates to its cauldrons. This undoubtedly would make local social life more nuanced and enriched.

Jade, first seen in the middle Neolithic Xinglongwa and Shunshanji cultures, started to thrive at this time, widely seen in the lower Zuojiashan culture, Yabuli culture in the Northeast, and the Majiabang, Hemudu, and Longqiuzhuang cultures along the southeastern coast. It can be said that the uniquely Chinese jade culture tradition was officially formed. The jade *yue*, a specialized weapon that evolved from stone axes on the Southeast coast, might have symbolized military power. As for decorative pieces like jade *jues*, jade *huangs*, and rings, their use might have been related to certain statuses and occasions (fig. 2.22). The wooden lacquer bowl found in Hemudu culture is one of the earliest lacquerware in China. The large number of spinning wheels found in various places indicates the widespread development of the primitive textile industry. The loom parts, such as the shuttle and the cloth roller from Hemudu culture, might have been used for silk textile production.

The prevalence of the various categories of artifacts mentioned above is closely related to the considerable degree of settled society. Particularly, jade manufacturing is time-consuming, technically demanding, and sophisticated in its use, making it one of the symbols of "Chinese" culture. In addition, each region has its unique and high-quality items, such as the microlith in the Northeast, wooden objects, and bone-horn-and-ivory instruments in the Yangtze River Delta, among others. Decorations such as hairpins and bracelets (rings) were popular nationwide then.

(3) Orderly settlements and three types of beam-framed houses

Whether the grouped houses and centripetal settlement structure of Yangshao culture or the row houses of the Daxi and Hemudu cultures, all major constructions like houses and cellars were arranged in a specific space; some even had moats or city walls around the perimeter, ingeniously emphasizing collective benefits and public order. Among these, Yangshao culture settlements like the Jiangzhai settlement even had infant urn burials near the houses in the settlement, a central public activity space, communal pottery kilns, and graves corresponding to each group of houses outside the settlement. There was still no significant wealth or status differentiation between the settlements. To a large extent, this was an era of equality and friendliness, care for the weak, a focus on collectivity, and orderliness.

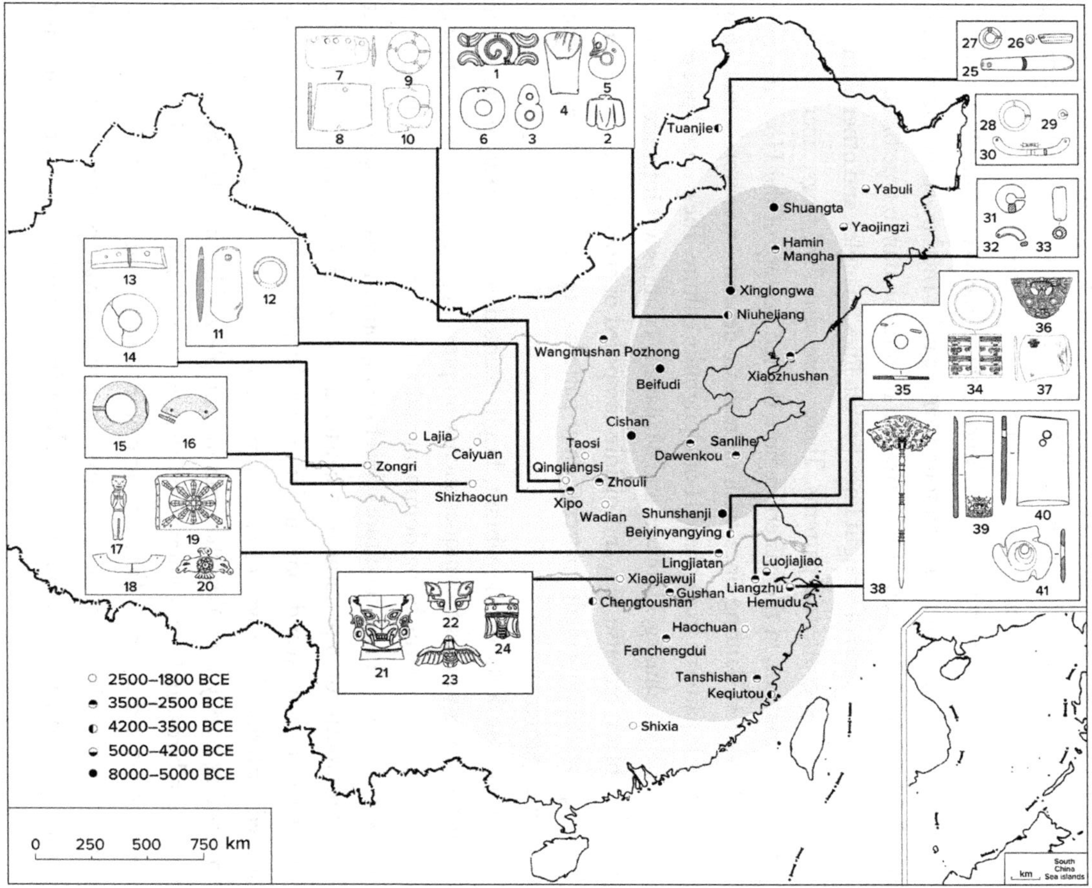

Figure 2.22 The spatial expansion of jade artifacts in China's Neolithic

1–6. Niuheliang (N2Z1M14: 1, N2Z1M15: 4, N2Z1M21: 7, N2Z1M4: 1, 2, N2Z1M21: 14)
7–10. Qingliangsi (M112: 1, M146: 1, M54: 1, M100: 7)
11, 12. Xipo (M22: 1, 2)
13, 14. Zongri (M200: 2, 5)
15, 16. Shizhaocun (T403②: 7, 11)
17–20. Lingjiatan (M1: 1, M4: 34, 30, M29: 6)
21–24. Xiaojiawuji (W6: 32, 16, 7, 12)
25, 27. Chahai (T0307②: 1, T0607②: 1)
26. Xinglongwa (I M117: 2)
28–30. Beiyinyangying (M144: 1, M81: 5, M39: 4)
31–33. Hemudu (T244 [3A]: 6, T213 [3B]: 46, T231 [3B]: 27)
34, 35, 37. Fanshan (M12: 93, M23: 23, M12: 100)
36. Yaoshan (M10: 20)
38, 40. Xizhufeng (M202: 2, 1, M203: 17)
39. Liangchengzhen
41. Sanlihe (M203: 9)

Architectural technology tended to be mature and standardized, and three types of beam-frame structures had been formed on both sides of the Yangtze River: semi-subterranean, with or without platforms in the Yellow River Basin and its northern region; stilt-style and ground-style in the middle and lower reaches of the Yangtze River. Particularly, the stilt-style wooden structures of Hemudu culture were up to 20 to 30 meters long, proficiently employing mortise and tenon joints, indicating that construction technology was quite mature.[212]

(4) Art and symbol system centered on the West and East dual pottery
The most eye-catching art form in China at the time was painted pottery, which formed a pottery system represented by the Yangshao and Longqiuzhuang cultures in the Yellow and Yangtze River basins, a continuation of the previous West and East dual pottery system. Among these, the West Yangshao culture's painted pottery was simple and profound, with a brisk rhythm, strict and plain. It was divided into two regions: in the western region, the Banpo type black pottery was popular, composed of straight lines, broken lines, triangles, and other elements forming various geometric patterns. There were also fish, frogs, deer, and net patterns. In contrast, in the eastern region, the red pottery of the Hougang type only had grouped slanting lines, with no realistic decoration, remotely inheriting the geometric patterns from phase II of Donghulin culture. The painted pottery of the east Longqiuzhuang, Hemudu, and Majiabang cultures was intricate, complex, primarily black, but also red, and mainly composed of straight and curved lines forming overlapping-scale patterns, net patterns, fence patterns, and other geometric patterns.

On the outskirts of the vibrant, bright-painted pottery areas, pottery was decorated using various techniques such as impressing, engraving, and stamping, with geometric patterns being dominant and various animal patterns. Especially noteworthy is Zhaobaogou culture's developed geometric patterns, using straight lines, fine-tooth comb patterns with clustered dots, arc lines, and other elements, which were organized and combined into complex patterns such as *Hui* and hook-shaped patterns. There was often a combination of main and ground patterns, contrasting starkly with Yangshao culture's simple and brisk style. The images of pigs, deer, birds, and other animals on their *zun*-shaped vessels are abstract to a considerable degree. Also, Tangjiagang culture's white pottery featured complex, intricate patterns like octagram patterns, sun patterns, wave patterns, and hanging banner patterns, which were unique. Hemudu culture's images of twin birds (phoenixes) facing the sun are artistic treasures that leave an enduring impression (fig. 2.23).

Patterns and decorations were not merely for ornamental purposes; they were a crucial method for prehistoric humans to express, record, and disseminate thoughts and information. But more abstract and bearing more accurate meanings were symbols. The Banpo type of Yangshao culture unearthed many engraved symbols, typically etched on ceramic earthen bowls, with one symbol per object. If they were markers made by potters, why don't we see them on other pottery? As Guo Moruo and others have suggested, they may be precursors to writing,[213] possibly inherited from the earlier Peiligang culture's pottery symbols. In addition, several symbols have also been discovered in Hemudu and Daxi cultures. Symbols, such as interconnected birds and sprouts engraved at the Hemudu site, may express some specific meaning. The symbols of Daxi culture at Yangjiawan in Yichang City, in Hubei Province, are numerous and varied[214] (fig. 2.23).

Sculptures were mostly small human heads and animal pottery, bone carvings, etc., with few numbers. Among them were exquisite works such as the ivory carving of twin birds (phoenixes) facing the sun at the Hemudu site and the bone carving of a bird's head (swan) at the Xinkailiu site. Of particular note were the stone or pottery sculptures found in the southern part of the Northeast region, including stone eagle-owl, turtles, humans (monkey-shaped stone ornaments), pottery pig heads, silkworm-shaped pottery decorations, seahorse-shaped pottery decorations belonging to Zhaobaogou culture at the Shangzhuang site in Pinggu, Beijing. Other examples include stone human figures from Zhaobaogou culture at the Houtaizi site in Luanping County, Hebei Province,[215] and the lower Xiaozhushan culture at the Houwa site in Dandong City, Liaoning Province.

Figure 2.23 The ivory carving with twin birds (phoenix) facing the sun pattern from the Hemudu site (T226 [3B]: 79)

Also found were percussion or wind instruments such as pottery bell and pottery *xun* (a Chinese wind instrument). Pottery bells first appeared in the Banpo type of Yangshao culture[216] and Beixin culture, later continuing for thousands of years, becoming the origin of the bronze bells in the Longshan period and the *bo** in the Shang and Zhou periods. Bone flutes from the Peiligang culture were no longer seen, but bone whistles were found in the Hemudu culture.

(5) Secularized religious belief system centered on ancestor worship
At that time, there was still a continuation of the secularized religious belief system centered on ancestor worship. Large clan cemeteries were prevalent, and graves in the same cemetery often had roughly the same head direction and burial customs, suggesting close kinship relationships. In particular, cemeteries of Yangshao culture in the Guanzhong region sometimes buried dozens or hundreds of people in one pit, strongly emphasizing a sense of collective belonging. Infant urn burials were found in Yangshao culture, Daxi culture, Hemudu culture, etc. The pottery that covered the top often had holes in the bottom. Some people think it was to facilitate the child's soul to come and go,[217] vividly embodying the care for children in clan society.

There was also evidence of worship or interest in various types of animals. The "dragon and tiger tomb" (fig. 2.24), made of clam molds found at the Xishuipo site in Puyang City, Henan Province, of the Hougang type of Yangshao culture, is probably the prototype of the Azure Dragon and White Tiger in later generations. The tomb could be that of a headed shaman knowledgeable in astronomy and capable of communicating between heaven and earth.[218] Fish patterns and human-face fish patterns are common in the Banpo type of Yangshao culture, suggesting that the population might have a fish-worshipping custom. The 12 human faces on a pointed-bottom cauldron from Longgangsi, some with eyes open and some with eyes closed, are imbued with deep meaning (fig. 2.25). Hemudu culture often features birds, pigs, and fish, especially the ivory carving of twin birds (phoenixes) facing the sun, reflecting the bird-worshipping custom in the eastern regions. There are many small sculptures in the Northeast region. Scholars speculate that these animal or human sculptures might be used in shamanistic activities,[219] with human sculptures possibly related to ancestor worship or fertility rituals.[220] However, compared to the prevalence of pottery figurines in Japan's Jomon period,† this was

---

* A musical instrument with a shape similar to that of a bell; unlike a bell with a curved mouth, it has a flat mouth.—Trans.
† The Jomon period followed the late Paleolithic Age in Japan, beginning around 12000 BCE and ending around 300 BCE.—Trans.

CHINA BEFORE EARLY CHINA 91

quite rudimentary, let alone in comparison to the abundance of sculptures in West Asia during the same period.

Furthermore, the "three-tier structure with a center," previously rooted in Northeast and North China, began to appear in the Central Plain. Yangshao culture's houses were centered around the range, settlements around the central square, the economy around agriculture, and beliefs around ancestors. From the core, at least three tiers extended outward. This likely had certain influences on the formation and development of the multi-tiered basic structure of early China.

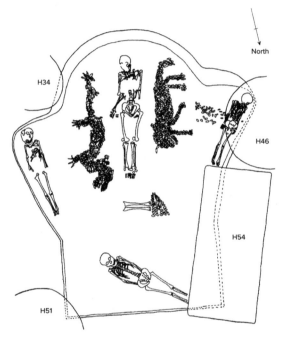

Figure 2.24 Dragon and tiger tomb with clam sculpture from the Xishuipo site (M45)

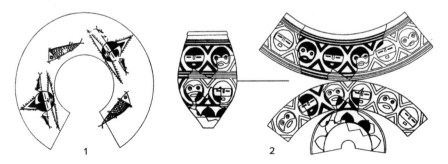

Figure 2.25 The human face image of Banpo type of Yangshao culture
1. Banpo (P. 4691)   2. Longgangsi (H23: 1)

CHAPTER 3

The Miaodigou Era and the Formation of Early China

(4200–3500 BCE)

DURING THE LATE STAGE OF THE late Neolithic, the Dongzhuang–Miaodigou type of Yangshao culture in the core area of Central Plain rose rapidly. It expanded its influence powerfully into surrounding areas, making significant cultural patterns and characteristics adjustments. The depth and breadth of its impact was unprecedented. Through this process, the cultures of most regions of China first integrated and interacted to form a cultural community with the Central Plain as the core. The "early Chinese cultural sphere" or, in a cultural sense, "early China" was officially established (table 3.1). This book refers to the splendid era during which early China formed in a cultural sense as the "Miaodigou era."[1]

The scholarly consensus is that the Miaodigou type of Yangshao culture was a powerful force and significantly impacted other regions. As early as 1965, Su Bingqi noticed that the Miaodigou type had a "great impact on the distant neighboring regions."[2] Afterward, Yan Wenming pointed out that the "Miaodigou era was a relatively prosperous period, which on the one hand was reflected in the strengthening trend of integration and unity among its internal regional types, and on the other hand in the strengthening of its influence on external cultures."[3] Zhang Zhongpei considered this period to be a "relatively unified era,"[4] in which the Xiyin culture (i.e., the Miaodigou type) had a positive influence on the contemporary archaeological cultures in the surrounding areas.[5] Wang Renxiang called the expansion of painted pottery in the Miaodigou era the "artistic wave

Table 3.1 Cultural regions of the late stage of the late China's Neolithic (4200–3500 BCE)

Early Chinese cultural sphere	Upper and middle reaches of the Yellow River	Bottle (pot)–earthen bowl (basin)–jar–*ding* cultural system (Yangshao culture late phase I and phase II)
	Middle and lower reaches of Yangtze River and lower reaches of Yellow River	*Ding*–high-foot plate–pot–cup cultural system (Early Dawenkou culture, early Songze culture, Beiyinyangying culture, Longqiuzhuang culture, and Daxi culture phases II and III)
	Southern and western Northeast	Cylindrical jar–painted pottery jar–earthen bowl cultural system (Middle Hongshan culture and middle Xiaozhushan culture)
Early China outer margin zone	South China	Cauldron–round-foot plate–high-foot plate cultural system (Tanshishan phase I and Xiantouling sections VI–V)
	Eastern Northeast	Cylindrical jar cultural system (Yabuli culture)
	Other regions	Mesolithic culture

of prehistoric China."[6] Based on the previous research, this chapter provides a more detailed review of the specific process of the expansion and influence of the Dongzhuang–Miaodigou type of Yangshao culture and the formation of early China.

I. The Flourishing Development of Core Culture

The Dongzhuang and Miaodigou types of Yangshao culture are mainly distributed in the Southwestern Shanxi Province and the Western Henan Province, with an absolute date of approximately 4200 BCE to 3500 BCE.[7]

1. Dongzhuang Type of Yangshao Culture

The Dongzhuang type, represented by the Yangshao ruins in Dongzhuang Village,[8] Ruicheng, Shanxi Province, and phases I and II of Beigan in Yicheng,[9] is situated temporally between the Banpo and Miaodigou types,[10] with an absolute date approximately between 4200 BCE and 4000 BCE. It was formed based on the local Zaoyuan type of Yangshao culture, heavily influenced by the advancing east forward Banpo type.[11] Specifically, its primary pottery forms, such as earthen bowls, basins, jars, and urns, possess characteristics of both the Zaoyuan and Banpo types. The pointed-bottom bottle with a fledgling double-lipped mouth combines the inward-folded mouth of the Zaoyuan type and the cup-shaped mouth of the Banpo type. The pointed-bottom characteristic of the cup-shaped mouth pointed-bottom bottle and fledgling double-lipped mouth pointed-bottom bottle, as well as the black patterns like marked cords, broadband, triangle, diamond, and fish patterns come from the Banpo type. The plain cauldron and *ding*, the slender characteristic of the pointed-bottom bottle, and other features are based on the Zaoyuan type. New creations include the gourd-shaped bottle, fire seed stove, and painted pottery decorations such as pod and petal patterns. Overall, the influence of the Banpo type is great, and from certain perspectives, it can even be regarded as an eastern variant of the Banpo type.[12]

The Dongzhuang type can be roughly divided into two stages. The early stage, represented by the Beigan phase I, features pointed-bottom bottles without necks and with lower lips of the fledgling double-lipped mouth not protruding. The late stage, represented by the Beigan phase II, features pointed-bottom bottles with necks and more protruding lower lips of the fledgling double-lipped mouth. Yangshao remains of the Dongzhuang type, like those at Sanliqiao in Shan County in western Henan Province[13] and phase I of Yangshao culture at Nanjiaokou in Sanmenxia,[14] only have pointed-bottom bottles with cup-shaped mouths but not pointed-bottom bottles with fledgling double-lipped mouths, nor fire seed stoves. It is speculated that the core of the Dongzhuang type is not in western Henan Province but in the Southwestern Shanxi Province.

The Dongzhuang type has square or circular semi-subterranean houses with round corners, and the surroundings of the pit houses have usable platforms, similar to the Banpo type of Yangshao culture. The unique change is found in burials. Although there are still extended supine burials, new secondary burials, which are unprecedented and involve placing skulls and limb bones together, appear in sites such as Beigan. These burials can be for one person or multiple people. The origin of this should still be in the Banpo type—in Yuanjun Temple in Hua County, Shaanxi Province, and Hengzhen Cemetery in Huayin, which belong to this type, there are already secondary burials roughly arranged in the extended supine burial. However, the burials of the Dongzhuang type have no accompanying goods, which continues the simple characteristic of the Zaoyuan type and differs from the Banpo type, which usually accompanies several pieces of pottery.

The production tools of the Dongzhuang type are basically the same as those of the previous Zaoyuan and Banpo types. From the findings at Nanjiaokou, it can be seen that at least south of the Yellow River, there is a mixed situation of rice farming and dry farming of millet grain and sorghum.

2. Miaodigou Type of Yangshao Culture

The Miaodigou type is represented by phase I of the Miaodigou site in Shan County, Henan Province,[15] with an absolute date approximately between 4000 BCE and 3500 BCE. It generally continues the development based on the Dongzhuang type, and new developments like straight-neck cauldrons and ranges reflect influences from the Zhengzhou–Luoyang area. This type popularizes pottery with bird patterns, as seen on bird-shaped *dings*, ranges, and vessel lids. The Miaodigou type can be roughly divided into three stages: the early stage represented by phases III and IV of Beigan and the early phase II of Yangshao culture at Nanjiaokou, the middle stage represented by phase I of the Miaodigou site and the main Miaodigou type remains at Xiyin Village,[16] and the late stage represented by the Xipo H110.[17] The small-mouth pointed-bottom bottle first became a true double-lipped mouth with an rounded upper lip and a protruding lower lip. Then the double lips gradually became pointed and flat. Finally, the upper lip almost disappeared and changed into a mouth resembling a horn shape, while the bottom of the cauldron changed from pointed to blunt. The upper part of the gourd-shaped bottle changed from a slanting arc to a slanting straight, finally becoming a neck with an edge similar to a horn mouth. The earthen bowl and wide-rim basin developed from shallow arc belly to deep curved-belly, the belly of the jar and urn evolved from short arc to deep and straight, and more and more handles and added relief decorations appeared. In the painted pottery, the petal pattern gradually became complex and mature, then tended to simplify, and the rim of the earthen bowl first changed from a broadband pattern to a narrow band pattern. Finally, the painted band disappeared.

The burial situation of the Miaodigou type is the same as the Dongzhuang type. The most significant change in settlement form is the appearance of several oversized houses in sites such as Xipo in Lingbao City in Henan Province.[18] The largest of these, house F105, has a foundation area of 372 square meters, including the porch and corridor. It covers 516 square meters. The four main load-bearing pillars in the center have diameters of 0.5 to 0.7 meters; the floor is layered with ginger stone and grass mixed with mud, and a red coating can be seen on the surface. This house is grand and elaborately decorated and has the nature of a "primitive palace" (fig. 3.1). Although the relationship between these large houses is not entirely sure yet, and whether there are other medium and small-sized houses nearby is still unclear, just from the scale of their construction and the degree of meticulousness, they should not only be places for public gatherings but may also be related to a certain degree of social differentiation. In addition, chaotic burial pits of humans began to appear at sites like Miaodigou.

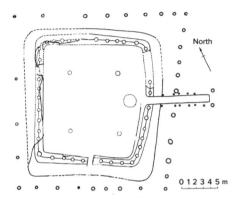

Figure 3.1 The plan of the large house F105 at the Xipo site

Regarding agricultural production tools, there is a significant increase in stone knives (sickle claws) and stone spades. The stone spades are broad and regular, and their polishing is more refined, indicating a substantial agricultural development. The crops remain millet grain, sorghum, and rice, and there are domestic animals such as pigs. Bag-shaped pits with one pit below another have also been discovered, indicating more advanced crop preservation technology. Moreover, the discovery of perforated stone *yue* at the Miaodigou and Nanjiaokou sites reflects the influence of the lower Yangtze River.

II. Yangshao Culture's "Miaodigou Transformation"

Following the formation of the Dongzhuang type, its dynamic features rapidly expanded. The Miaodigou type excelled and further spread its influence, leading to a phenomenon of "Miaodigou Transformation" in Yangshao culture and unprecedented cultural convergence in the upper and middle reaches of the Yellow River (figs. 3.2, 3.3, and 3.4).

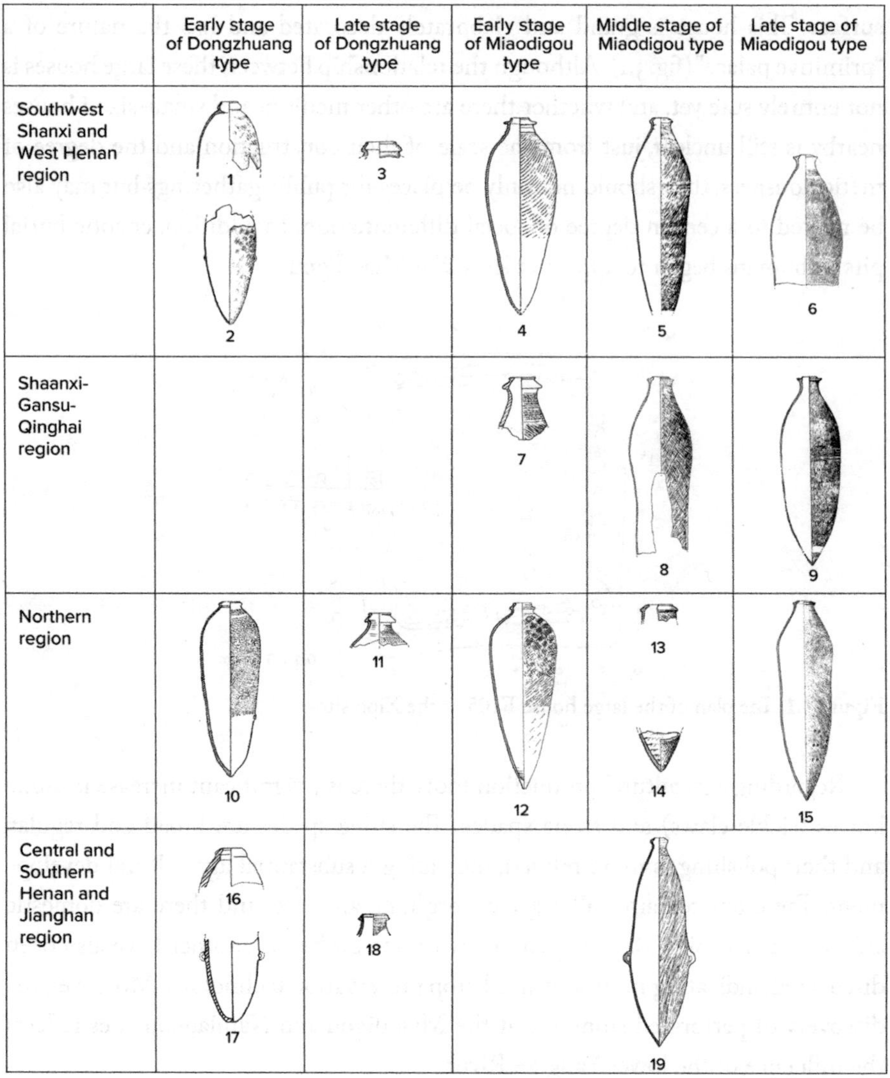

	Early stage of Dongzhuang type	Late stage of Dongzhuang type	Early stage of Miaodigou type	Middle stage of Miaodigou type	Late stage of Miaodigou type
Southwest Shanxi and West Henan region	1, 2	3	4	5	6
Shaanxi-Gansu-Qinghai region			7	8	9
Northern region	10	11	12	13, 14	15
Central and Southern Henan and Jianghan region	16, 17	18	19		

Figure 3.2 Comparison of double-lipped small-mouth pointed-bottom bottles from various regions during the Miaodigou era

1–3. Yangshao culture Dongzhuang type (Beigan H34:27, 5, II T1302④:6)
4–6. Yangshao culture Miaodigou type (Nanjiaokou H90:1, Xiyin G1:28, Xipo H110:5)
7–9. Quanhu type of Yangshao culture (Dadiwan T704③: P50, Anban GNDH24: 7, Fulinbao H37: 8)
10–15. Bainiyaozi type of Yangshao culture (Bainiyaozi F1: 1, Wangmushan Poxia IF1: 21, IF11: 13, Duanjiazhuang H3: 15, 27, Yangjiaping F1: 3)
16, 17. Dahecun type of Yangshao culture (Dahecun T56⑯: 27, 28)
18. Daxi culture (Guanmiaoshan T63⑤A: 27)
19. Yan Village type of Yangshao culture (Shuidihe W1: 2)

THE MIAODIGOU ERA AND THE FORMATION OF EARLY CHINA   99

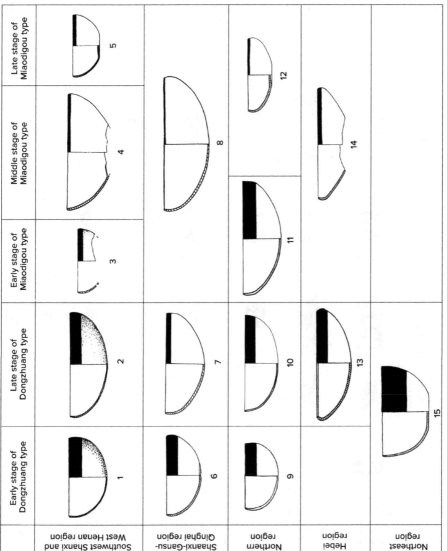

Figure 3.3 Comparison of black colored-band-pattern pottery earthen bowls from various regions during the Miaodigou era

1, 2. Yangshao culture Dongzhuang type (Beigan H34: 20, H32: 2)
3–5. Yangshao culture Miaodigou type (Beigan II T402③: 2, Xiyin H33: 54, H30: 9)
6, 7. Yangshao culture Shijia type (Yuanzitou H126: 1, Dadiwan T302③: 21)
8. Yangshao culture Quanhu type (Dadiwan F709: 1)
9–12. Yangshao culture Bainiyaozi type (Bainiyaozi F1: 11, Wangmushan Poxia IH1: 4, IF6: 13, Duanjiazhuang H3: 5)
13. Yangshao culture Hougang type (Nanyangzhuang T40②: 1)
14. Yangshao culture Diaoyutai type (Diaoyutai H1)
15. Hongshan culture (Xishuiquan T7②: 20)

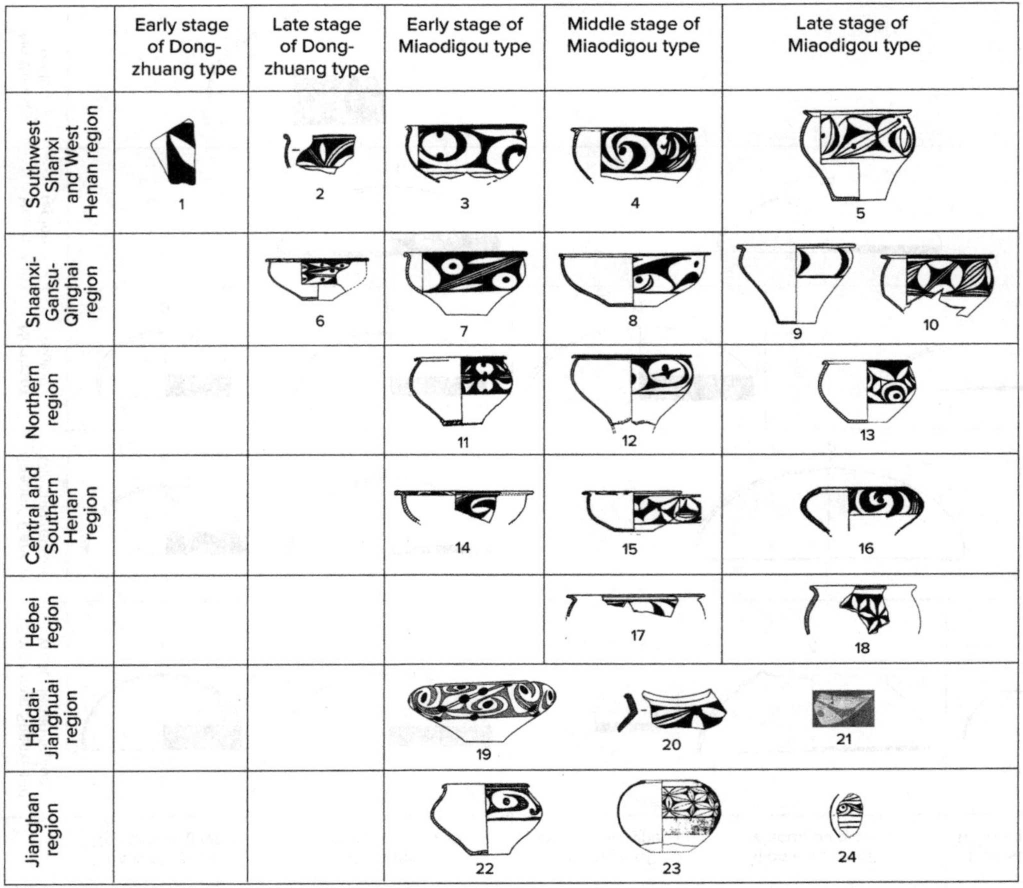

Figure 3.4 Comparison of petal-pattern painted pottery basins from various regions during the Miaodigou era

1, 2 Yangshao culture Dongzhuang type (Beigan H38: 11, Dongzhuang H104: 1: 01)
3–5. Yangshao culture Miaodigou type (Beigan T8⑨: 1, Xiyin H33: 7, H30: 63)
6. Yangshao culture Shijia type (Yuanzitou H42: 1)
7–10. Yangshao culture Quanhu type (Dadiwan T700③: 19, Quanhu H5: 192, H1127: 871, Hulijia H14: 2)
11–13. Yangshao culture Bainiyaozi type (Zhangmaowusu F1: 4, Duanjiazhuang H3: 07, Bainiyaozi site A F2: 2)
14–16. Yangshao culture Yan Village type (Dahecun T1⑥D: 113, Dianjuntai F3: 7, Dahecun T11⑤A: 83)
17, 18. Yangshao culture Diaoyutai type (Nanyangzhuang H108: 1, Diaoyutai T4②)
19. Dawenkou culture (Liulin M72: 1)
20, 21. Songze culture (lower Qingdun culture, Caoxieshan T304: 6)
22–24. Daxi culture (Luosishan tomb No. 1, Guanmiaoshan T37④: 9, T4③: 9)

1. The Influence on Western Regions

Once the Dongzhuang type was formed, it quickly reciprocally influenced the Guanzhong region, driving the Banpo type into its late stage, known as the Shijia type period.[19] The Shijia type remains are represented by Shijia graves in Weinan, Shaanxi Province,[20] and phase II of Jiangzhai in Lintong District, Shaanxi Province.[21] They generally inherit and develop from the early Banpo type, such as transforming earthen bowls and basin-type vessels toward pointed and round bottoms and folded bellies and miniaturizing small-mouth pointed-bottom bottles and narrow-neck pots. However, many elements are influenced by the Dongzhuang type, such as gourd-shaped bottles and petal patterns, and pea pod patterns on painted pottery. Considering that the Banpo type favors fish, and the Dongzhuang type admires birds, the emergence of new fish-and-bird combined patterns can be seen as a symbol of the fusion of the Banpo and Dongzhuang types.[22] This cultural wave even extended to the western part of the Guanzhong region and even to the middle and eastern parts of Gansu Province, forming phases I and II remains of Yangshao culture at Yuanzitou in Long County, Shaanxi Province,[23] and phase II of Dadiwan in Qin'an County, Gansu Province.[24] It may have extended to the eastern edge of the Hexi Corridor in the northwest.[25] However, these western remains predominantly feature extended supine burials and do not show multiple secondary joint burials in the east. Many of these vertical shaft graves with earth pits also have side niches for placing burial objects. Items like double bellied-handle jars, double bellied-handle earthen bowls, gourd-mouth small-mouth pointed-bottom bottles, and human head-shaped flat-bottom bottles also have specific local characteristics.

The influence of the Miaodigou type to the west is even stronger, leading to the development of the Quanhu type from the Shijia type in the region Guanzhong and eastern Gansu Province, as seen in phase I of the Quanhu site in Hua County, Shaanxi Province,[26] Xiahe site in Baishui County, Shaanxi Province,[27] Anban site in Fufeng County,[28] phases I and II of Fulinbao site in Baoji City,[29] and phase III of Dadiwan in Qin'an County, Gansu Province. Typical elements like petal patterns, bird patterns on painted pottery, and double-lipped small-mouth pointed-bottom bottles are very similar to the Miaodigou type, with differences only in details like fewer *dings*. Similar remains even extended northwest to the eastern part of Qinghai Province[30] and the southern part of Ningxia Province,[31] southwest to southern Gansu Province and northwestern Sichuan Province,[32] with painted pottery becoming noticeably more intricate in later stages, in stark contrast to the trend of simplification in eastern Guanzhong, reflecting the divergence between the core area and the "remote areas." As for the remains in Hanzhong, such as Ruanjiaba in Hanyin County, Shaanxi Province, and Majiaying in Ziyang County Shanxi Province,[33] where cauldron-shaped *dings* are slightly different from the Quanhu type, might have been directly influenced by the culture in the core area of southern Shanxi and western Henan.

The settlement form of the Shijia type basically follows the Banpo type, with circular moat settlements and similar house architecture. However, there is a significant difference in the burial customs, especially in the eastern Guanzhong area where multi-person secondary joint burial is prevalent. This form, where skulls and limbs are placed together, is likely influenced by the Dongzhuang type. Tombs are numerous and highly concentrated, with over 2,000 individuals in phase II of Jiangzhai and probably over 1,000 in Shijia graveyards (fig. 3.5). These large graveyards might have served not only the deceased in their villages.

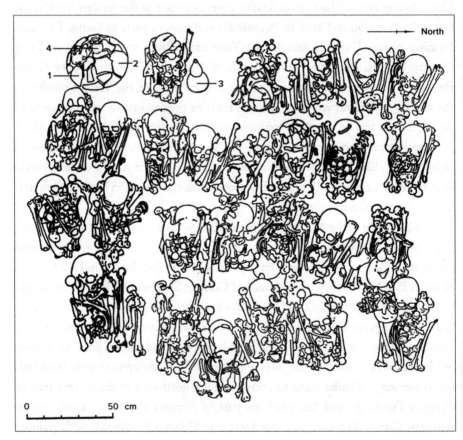

Figure 3.5 Plan of the Shijia cemetery M25

1, 2. Pottery earthen bowl   3. Pottery gourd bottle   4. Pottery jar with a lid

Observations of the skull feature in Shijia graveyards show that individuals in the same grave show more similarities, suggesting a possible kinship among the deceased in the same grave.[34] Another characteristic in the eastern area is that many adults also used urn burials, and there are even a few instances of multiple urn joint burials for adults. Yan Wenming believes that this was the result of the invasion by people from the further east.[35] This aligns with the significant influence of the Dongzhuang type in the east demonstrated in pottery and other aspects. Furthermore, the burial pottery in the Shijia type is often smaller and crude than the pottery found in the settlements, showing a clear trend toward grave goods, and indicating a critical turning point in society at the time. The density of Quanhu type settlements significantly increased, and large-scale settlements with an area of up to 1.3 million square meters, like Yinjia Village in Xianyang City, Shaanxi Province, emerged. More important is the appearance of large houses of 200 to 300 square meters at Xiahe and Quanhu, like the situation at Xipo, indicating that differentiation began to become apparent both within and between settlements.

In Shijia and Quanhu, carbonized or rotten millet grains are often found in house grounds and cellars. Carbonized foxtail millet was found in the Hulijia site far away in Qinghai Province. The biggest change is the increase in rectangular pottery knives and the sharp decrease in round pottery and stone "claw sickles." Although the method of harvesting remains the same, the rise in productivity suggests that agricultural production is continuously improving. Domestic pigs continue to be the most common livestock. Hunting and gathering tools like bone-handle stone-blade knives are still in the west.

2. The Expansion to Northern Regions

The Dongzhuang type also expanded vigorously northward to the north Jinzhong, the central and southern parts of Inner Mongolia, the northern part of northern Shaanxi, and the northwest of Hebei—a narrower definition of the Northern regions, forming the Bainiyaozi and Majiaxiao Village types of Yangshao culture.[36]

In the central and southern parts of Inner Mongolia and the northern part of northern Shaanxi, the Lujiapo and Shihushan types of Yangshao culture were previously distributed, which could be seen as a fusion of the Hougang and Banpo types. However, it turned into the Bainiyaozi type during this period, represented by the early and late stages of the Bainiyaozi C site F1 in Qingshuihe,[37] Inner Mongolia, and phase I of Wangmushan Poxia in Liangcheng County.[38] New double-lipped small-mouth pointed-bottom bottles and fire seed stoves emerged, and wide-band patterns and petal patterns decorated in black were popular on earthen bowls and basins, clearly related to the large influx of Dongzhuang elements. Even the features of the pointed-bottom bottle mouths in the early and late stages correspond perfectly with those in phases I and II of Beigan, showing a synchronous relationship with the southwest of Shanxi Province. However, the Bainiyaozi type lacks *ding*, cauldron, range, etc., and the painted pottery with petal patterns is simpler, reflecting certain local characteristics. The northern Shanxi and northwest Hebei, previously belonging to the Hougang type, evolved into the locally distinct Majiaxiao Village type, represented by the Majiaxiao Village site in Datong City, Shanxi Province.[39] Painted pottery with wide-band patterns and petal patterns is rare and simple, and some pointed-bottom bottles with small mouths have an additional clay ring on the outside of the rim, appearing as double lips, but most are single round-lipped straight mouths. By the early and middle stages of the Miaodigou type, the cultural features of the central and northern Shanxi Province and northwest Hebei Province were the same as those of the Miaodigou type.[40] In contrast, central and southern Inner Mongolia followed the previous style. In the late stage of the Miaodigou type, due to the influence of Hongshan culture moving south, northwest Hebei Province nurtured the earliest Xueshan culture phase I. In the Daihai region, beneath the Wangmushan Poxia, there are remnants of phase III characterized by abundant, red-painted decorations. These remnants belong to the early Haishengbulang type. The cultural relationship with the southwest of Shanxi Province gradually faded.

The settlements of the Bainiyaozi and Majiaxiao Village types in the Northern regions are the same as those of the Dongzhuang–Miaodigou type. Still, they are quite different from the local Shihushan and Lujiapo types, such as house floors are often made of grass-mixed clay rather than white clay. In the Wangmushan Poxia under the settlement, the central position is occupied by a large house F7 with an area of up to 90 square meters, surrounded by a blank area. The periphery is made up of medium and small houses, reflecting its special status, which is different from the situation where large houses and medium and small houses form a group in settlements like Jiangzhai. However, the largest house here is dwarfed compared to those in western Henan Province and Guanzhong region, indicating obvious hierarchical differences between the core and peripheral areas. Moreover, the production tools and economic forms of the Northern region at that time were similar to those of the core area of southern Shanxi–Guanzhong but hunting and gathering were more significant. The frequently found fine stone arrowheads and bone-handle stone-blade knives here are mainly tools adapted to the hunting style of the grassland.

3. The Influence on Central and Southern Henan and Northern Hubei

The Dongzhuang type also had a significant southeast–southward impact on central and southern Henan and northern Hubei. In the Zhengzhou–Luoyang and regions to its south, there was a transformation to the later stage of Dahecun type, with new fledgling double-lipped small-mouth pointed-bottom bottles[41] and bean pot-pattern black-painted petal, elements of the Dongzhuang type. However, the popularity of cauldron-shaped *ding*, the preference for plain and red-painted bands, etc., continued to be a local tradition. The appearance of the small-mouth folded-belly cauldron-shaped *ding* is likely a result of the influence of Beixin culture, and the high-foot plates and cups reflect the cultural connection with the Jianghuai region. In Southwestern Henan and Northwestern Hubei, which previously belonged to the Dazhangzhuang type of Yangshao culture,[42] they developed into the Xiawanggang type, represented by the lower phase II of the Xiawanggang site in Xichuan County, Henan Province,[43] and M53 of Baligang in Dengzhou,[44] with new wide-band patterns, pod patterns, and black-painted petal patterns, elements of the Dongzhuang type. The small-mouth pointed-bottom bottles were often cup-shaped mouths.

The influence of the Miaodigou type was even more profound, and petal-pattern painted pottery became a typical element of these regions. Double-lipped small-mouth pointed-bottom and gourd-shaped bottles were also found in various places, although they became less common the further they were from western Henan. However, local characteristics were still strong. In the Yan Village site in Ruzhou City, Henan Province, the Dahecun phases I and II in Zhengzhou City, the Dianjuntai phase I in Xingyang City,[45] and Shuidihe phases III and IV in Gongyi City,[46] small-mouth pointed-bottom bottles were often cup-shaped mouths, shallow-belly cauldron-shaped *dings* were developed. There were newly emerging plain round-shoulder large-belly high-neck jars that often had black and red decorations on a white surface. In addition, it was popular to have adult urn burials there. This is referred to as the Yan Village type of Yangshao culture.[47] Southwestern Henan and Northwestern Hubei Provinces continued to belong to the Xiawanggang type, represented by the middle and upper Xiawanggang phase II, expanding to Yun County, Zaoyang, and Suizhou in northwestern Hubei Province.[48] Round-belly cauldron-shaped *dings* were popular, small-mouth pointed-bottom bottles often had cup-shaped mouths, and painted pottery was an interesting combination of black, red, and white. In the late stage, it was influenced by Dawenkou, Daxi, and Songze cultures, leading to the appearance of sun patterns, *Hu* patterns,* and other painted pottery patterns. The number of high-foot plates, cups, round-foot bowls, and cup-attached round-foot plates increased. Thus, the difference between the core areas of the southwestern region of Shanxi and western Henan gradually increased.

During the Dongzhuang type period, the Dahecun- and Xiawanggang type settlement situations were similar to those of the local areas in the previous period, but the burials underwent significant changes. They shifted from single-person extended supine burials to mainly multiple-person secondary burials, which resulted from the influence of the Dongzhuang type. But generally, a few ceramic grave goods were accompanied, reflecting the preservation of local traditions. During the Miaodigou type period, the settlement pattern underwent significant changes, with the widespread appearance of ground houses with timber-framed earthen walls, such as at the Baligang, Xiawanggang, and Dianjuntai sites. This may have been influenced by the traditions of the Yangtze River Basin, but it was also a reflection of changes in family and social structure. The burial practices varied from place to place. Yangshao culture graves at Laofengang in Xixia, southwestern Henan, were rectangular vertical shaft stone coffin graves[49] with accompanying perforated stone *yue* and paired round-bottom large-mouth vats. In contrast, adult urn burials were popular in the Luo River Basin, with some graves having hundreds of urn coffins.[50] If you remove the urn coffins, it approaches a multiple-person secondary joint burial. Additionally, the *Stork Fish and* Yue depiction seen on the "Yichuan vat" in Yan Village site in Ruzhou City, Henan Province, where the "axe" has a hole or symbolizes military power,[51] is the *yue*. It is unclear whether it is stone or jade, so it can also be called the *Stork Fish and* Yue. This shows that the Yan Village type already had the *yue* (fig. 3.6).

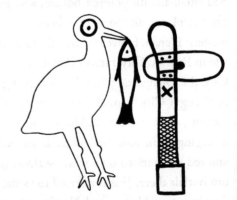

Figure 3.6 *Stork Fish and* Yue of the Yan Village type of Yangshao culture (Yan Village, Ruzhou City)

---

* An interlocking pattern shaped like the Chinese character "耳" (*hu*).—Trans.

4. The Influence on the East of the Taihang Mountains

The influence of the Dongzhuang type to the east of the Taihang Mountains was minimal. Only a small number of Dongzhuang type elements, such as black-painted wide-band earthen bowls, concaved folded-edge marked-cord jars, and spiral-pattern jars, were seen in the remains of phase III of Nanyangzhuang in Zhengding County, Hebei Province, the section VI of middle and late H52 of Shibei in Yongnian County, etc.[52] This is probably related to the staunch resistance of the Hougang type. Around 4000 BCE, after the formal formation of the Miaodigou type, its confrontation with the Hougang type finally ended. At this time, except for a small number of Diaoyutai type sites similar to the Miaodigou type, represented by Diaoyutai in Ci County and phase VI of Nanyangzhuang in Zhengding County,[53] most of the Hebei Plain presented a cultural depression, which may be related to the intense wars caused by the entry of the Miaodigou type into the area east of the Taihang Mountains. This also, from another side, demonstrates the severe degree of the robust expansion of the Miaodigou type.

III. The New Stage of Hongshan Culture

The Dongzhuang and Miaodigou types also impacted the Northeast region outside the Yangshao culture area.

After the formation of the Dongzhuang type, it had a strong influence on the north, forming the Bainiyaozi type and Majiaxiao Village type of Yangshao culture, the former of which had expanded to the territory of Xilingol League in Inner Mongolia, and the latter had reached northwestern Hebei Province.[54] These two types continued to strongly influence the northeast, leading Hongshan culture in the Xiliao River basin to enter the early stage of the middle Hongshan culture, represented by the H2 site of Shuiquan in Chifeng City, Inner Mongolia, and the early remains at the Niuheliang site 5 at the junction of Jianping, Lingyuan[55] and Kazuo counties in Liaoning Province. At this time, many clay-red pottery earthen bowl-, basin-, and pot-type vessels decorated with black paint appeared especially the wide-band patterned black-painted earthen bowls, which are elements of the Dongzhuang type. The sizable overlapping-scale patterns (or parallel arc lines patterns), rhombus patterns, etc., on the painted pottery, belong to the combination of Yangshao culture and local tradition: the form of painted pottery comes from the Central Plain, while the scale patterns and other patterns are local.

The Miaodigou type continued to exert influence toward the northeast, not only leaving behind remains similar to itself in the northwestern part of Hebei Province, such as the Sanguan F3 in Yu County but also leading the late stage of middle Hongshan culture, represented by the middle Niuheliang site 5 and Sandaowanzi H1 in the Aohan Banner,[56] to popularize swirling-pattern painted pottery, which is a variant of petal-pattern paint. New pottery, such as painted pottery jars, cylindrical vessels, and jade bracelets, have also appeared.[57]

Su Bingqi once used the phrase "Hua Mountain's rose and Yan Mountains' dragon"* to highly summarize this cultural connection between the Central Plain and the Northeast. He pointed out that elements of Yangshao culture, such as the petal pattern, started at the foot of Hua Mountain, passed through southern Shanxi Province, Northern regions, and reached the Northeast. He stated that Hongshan culture "is the product of the collision and fusion of the two major cultural regions of the North and the Central Plain in the upper reaches of the Daling River."

As typical representatives of the early stage of the middle period of Hongshan culture, Weijiawopu and Xitai settlements[58] are moated settlements. Inside the moat are square semi-subterranean houses and round ash pits (some are cellars). The houses are large, medium, and small, which are very similar to the situation of the various types of Yangshao culture north of the Yellow River. Their social conditions should be similar. However, the square horizontal-chamber pottery kiln discovered at the Sileng Mountain site in the Aohan Banner has very local characteristics.[59] Most notably, at this time, stone tomb construction had already begun at the Niuheliang site. Among them, a few cylindrical vessels were found between the stones of the two stone tombs at site 5. The tombs were vertical chamber tombs built with stones. The tomb owners were extended supine burials. Among them, one jade bracelet was buried with M7. A sacrificial pit that had been barbecued at the bottom was also discovered near the stone tomb.

The production tools of Hongshan culture also have similarities with Yangshao culture, such as polished axes, adzes, chisels, knives (sickle claws), and shovels, reflecting significant development in dry farming, only the shapes are different. Hongshan culture stone knives are mostly double-holed, and one type is in the form of a laurel leaf; the shovel is shoe-shaped, with a sharp blade, also known as

---

* Specifically, between seven thousand and five thousand years ago, Yangshao culture of the Miaodigou type, originating from the foot of Hua Mountain, achieved the combination of roses and dragons through a southwest–northeast passage in an S shape. This passage intersected with Hongshan culture originating from the northern side of Yan Mountains, resulting in a fusion of these two cultures.—Trans.

"*si*." In addition, the existence of stone grinding plates, stone grinding rods, and a large number of concaved-bottom stone arrowheads, stone blades (knife blades of bone-handle stone-blade knives), scrapers, and other microliths reflect a larger proportion of the grassland hunting and gathering economy.

The northward influence of Hongshan culture led to the appearance of geometric, black-painted patterns in the contemporary remains of the Hulunbuir grassland.[60] As for the pit dot patterns, diamond check-pattern pottery jars, and jade tools, such as axes, square jade *bis* with rounded corners, rings, etc., of the remains, may belong to local traditions. The many finely made concaved-bottom microlithic arrowheads, bone-handle stone-blade knives, bone spears, etc., indicated that it belonged to a hunting and gathering economy. The jade axes were likely woodworking tools, suggesting the possible existence of relatively settled villages.

In addition, during the early phase of the middle Xiaozhushan culture in the Liaodong Peninsula, represented by the middle of Xiaozhushan site in Changhai County, Liaoning Province,[61] and the lower remains of the Guojiacun settlement in Dalian,[62] the development was based on the system of the earlier lower Xiaozhushan culture, the cylindrical jar cultural system. Cylindrical jars changed from straight mouths to flipped rims, Z-shaped patterns disappeared, and engraved and imprinted parallel line patterns, slanted line patterns, stamped point patterns, etc., became popular. More importantly, many elements from Dawenkou culture, such as the cauldron-shaped *ding*, high-foot plate, cup, and swirling-pattern painted pottery, were added.

IV. Convergence of Cultures in the Lower Reaches of the Yellow River and the Middle and Lower Reaches of the Yangtze River

The eastward expansion and influence of the Dongzhuang and Miaodigou types caused a certain degree of change in the newly emerged Dawenkou culture in the Haidai region. It stimulated the "Songze transformation" process in the Jianghuai and Jiangsu–Zhejiang regions, bringing elements such as the *ding*, high-foot plate, and pot to the middle reaches of the Yangtze River. This eventually promoted forming of the "*ding*–high-foot plate–pot–cup cultural system" in Eastern China.

1. The Formation of Dawenkou Culture

Around 4100 BCE, under the backdrop of the northward penetration of Longqiuzhuang culture in the Jianghuai region, the Haidai region added new elements such as the cup, high-foot plate, and *he*, evolving from Beixin culture to the earliest Dawenkou culture, represented by Dawenkou H2003 in Tai'an City, Shandong Province, and Wangyin M2594 in Yanzhou District, Shandong. The *dings*, earthen bowls, and small-mouth double-handle pots belong to Beixin culture elements.[63] Around 4000 BCE, the influence of the Miaodigou type significantly increased, and many Miaodigou type elements, such as petal-pattern painted pottery, converging-mouth protruding-shoulder deep-belly painted pottery earthen bowls, and wide folded-rim painted pottery basins, suddenly appeared in the early Dawenkou culture remains such as Dawenkou and Wangyin. This caused a certain degree of change in the appearance of Dawenkou culture. However, from the perspective of the black, red, and white combination of its painted pottery and the significant converging mouth of the earthen bowl, it is closer to the Yan Village type, indicating that the Miaodigou type indirectly influenced Dawenkou culture through the Yan Village type.

Early Dawenkou culture settlements and tombs are seen at sites like Dawenkou in Tai'an City, Wangyin in Yanzhou District, Qianbuxia in Weifang City,[64] and Beizhuang in Changdao County, Shandong Province.[65] The overall situation of the settlements is far less clear than in Yangshao culture. The houses are generally semi-subterranean or ground level with wooden frames and mud walls, square or rectangular, often with multiple ranges set against the wall, differing from Yangshao culture's single range located in the center of the house. The tombs are divided into zones for burial, arranged neatly. They are rectangular vertical pit tombs, which can be divided into two types. The first is the primary extended supine burial, mostly single, as well as joint burials, which belong to Beixin culture tradition. The second is a multiple secondary joint burial, which belongs to the Yangshao culture Dongzhuang–Miaodigou type tradition. In the later early Dawenkou culture, a significant disparity existed between the rich and the poor. Large tombs like M2005 have a second layer platform, and as many as 104 pieces of pottery and stone artifacts were buried with the body. Some pottery vessels even contained pig mandibles, ox skulls, etc., for sacrificial purposes (fig. 3.7), while most of the smaller tombs had only a few burial objects or none. The custom of burying with turtle shells originally came from the Peiligang culture.

Tongue-shaped stone shovels, angle hoes, and tools made from teeth, clams, and keratin, such as knives and sickles, are agricultural tools, and disk-shaped stone or pottery tools may also be related to agriculture. Axes, adzes, and chisels are primarily woodworking tools, and the "oyster picks" made from pottery shards with one pointed end are likely tools for processing edible clams. There are also bone and antler tools, such as needles, awls, arrowheads, implements with blade-like ends, as well as characteristic net sinkers, and spinning wheels. Perforated whetstones are rather distinctive. Sorghum husks have been found at the Beizhuang site,[66] phytoliths of rice at the Dazhongjia site in Penglai, and rice

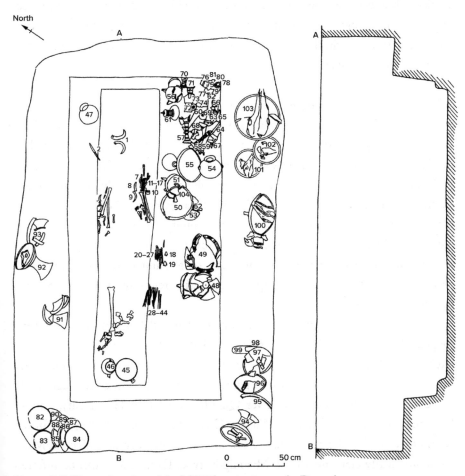

Figure 3.7 Plan and section of the M2005 excavation at the Dawenkou cemetery

1. Tooth-made hair binding device
2, 3. Bone hairpin
4–9. Water deer's tooth
10. Ivory handle
11–17, 20. Rod-shaped horn pendant
18, 19. Tooth-made arrowhead
21–44. Bone implements with blade-like ends
45, 46, 50, 52, 100, 101, 103. Pottery earthen bowl
47, 54. Pottery jar
48, 51, 56. Pottery *ding*
49, 55, 82–97, 102. Pottery high-foot plate
53, 104. Pottery lid
57–70. Pottery *gu*-shaped[a]
71–81. Pottery high-foot cup
98. Stone adze
99. Stone axe

[a] An ancient Chinese ritual vessel used to serve wine, with a round foot, flared mouth, and long body. The mouth and bottom are flared.—Trans.

pollen at the Wangyin site, suggesting an economy primarily based on dry farming of millet grain and sorghum, supplemented by rice cultivation. Raising pigs and dogs, as well as fishing and hunting, still played a significant role.

Unique customs, such as tooth extraction, cranial deformation, holding water deer's tooth, and stone spheres in the mouth were widespread in Dawenkou culture. In particular, the practice of tooth extraction later spread throughout East Asia, Southeast Asia, and the Pacific Islands,[67] demonstrating its significant influence on the eastern coastal areas.

2. The "Songze Transformation" Process

Around 4100 BCE, significant changes occurred in the cultures of the Jianghuai and Jiangzhe regions. The early Songze culture, represented by phases I and II of the Songze site in the Qingpu District of Shanghai,[68] and the early Nanhebang site in Jiaxing City, Zhejiang Province,[69] emerged, along with the early Beiyinyangying culture,[70] represented by phase II of the Beiyinyangying site in Nanjing, Jiangsu Province,[71] the Huangshanzui site in Susong County, Anhui Province[72] and early Saidun site in Huangmei County, Hubei Province,[73] and phase II of Longqiuzhuang culture. Because these cultures look quite similar and their formation processes are interrelated, this paper temporarily refers to it as the "Songze transformation" process.

These remains generally introduced new small-mouth bulbous-belly cauldron-shaped *dings*, some of which have slow wheel-rotated spirals on their shoulders, likely influenced by the Miaodigou–Yan Village type small-mouth folded-belly cauldron-shaped *dings*. Petal-pattern painted pottery found in early Gugeng H2 in Feixi, Anhui Province,[74] the lower Qingdun culture in Haian City, Jiangsu Province,[75] Caoxieshan T304 in Wuxian City,[76] and Sanxing Village in Jintan District,[77] as well as the gourd-shaped bottle from Longqiuzhuang phase II M141, are more clearly elements of the Miaodigou type. From this, it can be inferred that the influence of the Dongzhuang–Miaodigou type, especially the latter, significantly stimulated this "Songze transformation" process.

However, more importantly, there was a convergent change in the culture of the Jianghuai region itself under this stimulation. Based on its predecessors, Majiabang culture, phase I of Longqiuzhuang culture, etc., pottery generally became more complex in design, diverse in shape, and multi-segmented, with mostly tri-legged or round-foot vessels. The most characteristic is the decorations with octagonal star patterns and edge-wrapped triangular sun (or star) patterns. Painted pottery or colored painted pottery includes red, yellow, and black colors.

The main types of vessels are *ding*, high-foot plate, pot, *he*, and cup types. There are also cauldrons, jars, vats, basins, earthen bowls, round-foot bowls, round-foot plates, *yis*, earthen bowl-shaped *zengs*, three-mouth vessels, etc., often with lids. Specifically, the number of *dings* increased significantly, primarily high-foot cauldron-shaped *dings* and some low-foot *dings*. The feet are often chisel-shaped, flat-columnar, and duckbill-shaped. High-foot plates are diverse in shape, many with folded rims and curved handles. Cups are either straight-belly or curved-belly, flat-bottom, round-foot, or tri-legged. Among jade and stone tools, the striking ones are the exquisite *yues*, jade *huangs*, jade *jues*, and jade bracelets. The *yue* comes in many forms, including tongue-shaped, the shape of the Chinese character "风" (*feng*), and some with round holes resembling jade *bi*. Jade *huang* are often long strips that curl up at both ends, some symmetrically connected into halves.

Of course, each culture has its characteristics. For example, in the Songze culture, pottery is mainly made of clay and charcoal-tempered pottery, with distinct edges and corners on the body, a tiled appearance on the surface, often with floral edges on the round foot and many with fish fin-shaped-foot *dings* and round-foot jars. There are also *ding*-shaped *yans** (fig. 3.8), pig snout-shaped feet, basin-shaped mortars and pestles, etc. The cauldrons have a handle on the lower belly, and the woven pattern is characteristic, with many in colored painted pottery painted after firing. The sandy potteries of Beiyinyangying culture and phase II of Longqiuzhuang culture sites are more than clay ones, and the body is more curved. The cauldrons often have double-shoulder handles; round-bottom earthen bowls, etc., are many; and many are colored painted pottery painted before firing. The former has a characteristic wide-mouth double-belly basin, the inner wall decorated with polygonal or multi-angular patterns. There are even more detailed regional differences. For example, in Beiyinyangying culture, the *ding* feet in the eastern Ningzhen region are distinct and often have protuberances; in the western Hubei–Anhui border area, the *ding* feet are flat and round, and the base often has a depression. Single-handle painted pottery cups and impressed geometric patterned white pottery are much more common than in the east, with spiral-pattern spinning wheels full of rotational dynamism. We can tentatively call the eastern remains the Beiyinyangying type and the western ones the Huangshanzui type.

The early Songze culture, Beiyinyangying culture, and phase II of Longqiuzhuang culture's settlement situations are not very clear overall. Houses are generally made of wooden structures with mud walls and ground-level architecture.

---

* An ancient Chinese cooking and ritual vessel. Each consists of two parts; the upper part is the *zeng* mentioned before.—Trans.

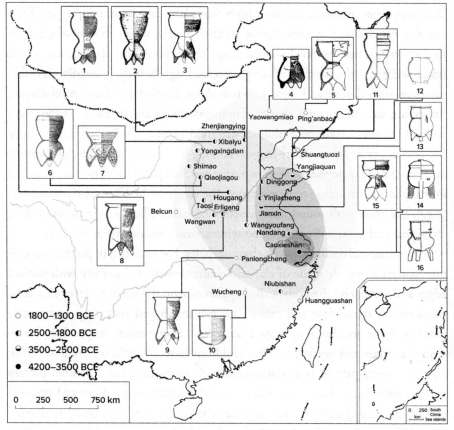

Figure 3.8 Spatial expansion of pottery *yan* before the late Shang Dynasty

1. Hougang H31: 6
2. Zhenjiangying H1101: 12
3. Wangyoufang H5: 5
4. Yaowangmiao T1③: 13
5. Gaotaishan 76XGT1H1: 5
6. Qiaojiagou H1: 11
7. Xibaiyu T2③: 1
8. Erligang C1H1: 39
9. Panlongcheng PWZT80⑥: 2
10. Wucheng 1993ZW (X) T1H7: 1
11. Yinjiacheng H67: 2
12. Yangjiaquan T41④: 44
13. Jianxin F20: 02
14. Fuquanshan M136: 14
15. Nandang T7②: 6
16. Caoxieshan M203: 23

In the western region, there are also semi-subterranean buildings, and different layers of altars piled with soil have been found at the Nanhebang site. There is a phenomenon of burial zones, with rectangular vertical pit graves,[78] some of which have second layer platforms and coffins. Most of the tomb occupants are single persons with extended supine burials. They are generally accompanied by several pieces of pottery, jade, and bone tools. Some potteries are crude, small, and simple and should be considered grave goods. Beiyinyangying culture and Songze culture have accompanying burials of pig mandibles and paired pig tusks, and some of the deceased have jade wares or rain-flower pebbles in their mouths. The differentiation between rich and poor has become relatively noticeable. For example, the cemetery in Dongshan Village, Zhangjiagang, Jiangsu Province, which belongs to the early Songze culture, is generally wealthy. In particular, tomb M90 includes 67 burial objects,[79] including painted stone *yues*, jade *huangs*, and large pottery vats, displaying a style of wealth and importance, which is significantly different from the usual burials where each grave is accompanied by only a few pieces of pottery and stone tools. Beiyinyangying M145 was accompanied by seven jade and stone tool semi-finished products and jade *xins*.* Perhaps it is the tomb of a jade tool professional craftsman, indicating that there has been a more definite division of labor in society.

Ground stone tools often seen are adzes, drills, axes, and knives, especially adzes and drills, showing the development of woodworking. The characteristics are segmented stone adzes and three-holed or seven-holed stone knives. There are also bone shovels, horn hoes, spinning wheels, bone arrowheads, bone darts, net pendants, etc. The craftsmanship of jade and stone tools is advanced, with many thoroughly polished, regular, exquisite, and skilled cutting and tube drilling techniques. Rice agriculture has made great strides, along with rearing domestic animals such as pigs and dogs and fishing and hunting. Rice remains have been found at several sites, such as Songze and Longqiuzhuang, including both indica and japonica rice; at the Chenghu site in Wuxian City, rice field remains have been found, along with carbonized rice grains.[80] A large amount of mulberry tree pollen was found at the Songze site. Perhaps sericulture was already practiced at the time.

3. The Transformation of Daxi Culture

Around 4100 BCE, elements of Yangshao culture's Dongzhuang type, such as petal-pattern painted pottery, wide-band black-painted earthen bowls, fledgling double-lipped small-mouth pointed-bottom bottles, and small-mouth bulbous-belly spiral-pattern *dings* permeated the banks of the Han River, seen in phase II remains of Daxi culture such as the Guanmiaoshan phase II, Chengtoushan phase II, etc. At the same time, Daxi culture also saw the emergence of relatively novel short round-foot potteries such as high round-foot high-foot plates, small-mouth bulbous-belly high-foot plates, single-handle curved-belly round-foot painted pottery cups, round-foot thin-bodied painted pottery bowls, converging-

---

* An ancient Chinese jade vessel with a variety of shapes, including round, semicircular, and irregular.— Trans.

mouth *guis* (ancient Chinese containers or ritual vessels here), high-neck or short-neck round-foot pots and jars, as well as deep-bodied pointed-bottom vats, *yis*, etc. The pottery often came with lids. The main body of these is the short round-foot vessels, which were developed based on similar vessels in phase I of Daxi culture. Though their earlier source was downstream of the Yangtze River, the appearance of high round-foot high-foot plates, small-mouth bulbous-belly high-foot plates, *yis*, and jade *huangs* should be the result of cultural influences from downstream of the Yangtze River at this time. The frequent appearance of painted pottery may have been inspired by Yangshao culture, and the deep-bodied pointed-bottom vats came from the Central Plain or Haidai. In addition, many objects, such as plain cauldrons and round-foot plates, still continue the lineage of phase I of Daxi culture. The pottery of Daxi culture is clearly divided into two series: red pottery and black-gray pottery, with red pottery generally given a red coating and painted pottery generally black.

It is particularly worth noting that at this time, there was a significant adjustment in the cultural pattern of the middle reaches of the Yangtze River. The eastward advance of Daxi culture to areas east of the Han River transformed the local Yangshao culture into phase II of Daxi culture with certain local features, including the early phase I of the Youziling site in Jingshan City, Hubei Province,[81] and phase I of the Tanjialing in Tianmen City, etc.[82] Some call it the Youziling type of Daxi culture.[83]

The influence of the Miaodigou type on phase III of Daxi culture in the middle reaches of the Yangtze River is even more profound. Its typical elements, such as petal-pattern, bird-pattern painted pottery decorations and large-mouth jars with a row of hook handles on rims, were found at the Neolithic phase I of the Zhongbaodao site in Yichang City, Hubei Province,[84] the Qingshuitan site,[85] phase III of Daxi culture at Guanmiaoshan, the Daxi site in Wushan County, Chongqing, etc.[86] In M1 of the Luoshishan in Huanggang City, Hubei Province, even the painted pottery bulbous-belly basin in the style of the Miaodigou type was buried.[87] Daxi culture exhibited more apparent differentiation, with the area east of the Han River being the most active. In the late phase I of the Youziling, phase II of the Tanjialing, etc., new types of vessels such as folded-belly *guis*, curved-belly cups, and round-foot plates with cups attached emerged, and the number of short chisel-foot *dings* and converging-mouth *guis* (ancient Chinese containers or ritual vessels here) significantly increased. The Xiajiang area was second, with new curved-belly cups, cylindrical cups, ball-belly jars with corrugated patterns, etc. Cauldrons and foot supports are common. Liyang Plain area was the most conservative, but new cylindrical cups, basin-shaped mortars and pestles, and jars decorated with woven patterns, etc., emerged. Due to this differentiation, some people propose that the remnants in the area east of the Han River at this time can already be an independent archaeological culture—Youziling culture.[88] But in fact, most types of objects in each area were developed and innovated based on phase II of Daxi culture, with no exception for the area east of the Han River. Therefore, it is still appropriate to call the culture there Daxi culture. These different regional Daxi cultures each have their characteristics and can be divided into some local types.

The settlement pattern of phase II of Daxi culture is roughly the same as before, but some notable changes have also occurred. In the ancient city of Chengtoushan, class A large tombs sometimes come with more than 20 pieces of potteries and jade *huangs*, showing that the tomb owners had higher ranks, and their burial style is extended supine burial. The burial style of other small tombs that do not have accompanying burial items is flexed burial. This shows that there is a difference in the burial customs of tombs of different ranks, and perhaps the clan origins of their tomb owners are also different. Looking at the bigger picture, the burial style of the entire Daxi culture differs somewhat east and west of the Han River. Flexed burial is more common west of the Han River, adhering to the ancient tradition of South China; extended supine burial is more common east of the Han River, in line with the tradition of Yangshao culture. So, was the extended supine burial in Chengtoushan from the north, and was the flexed burial local natives? This might require tools such as DNA analysis to answer further.

The economic mode should be largely the same as phase I of Daxi culture, with rice farming and a considerable proportion of fishing and gathering. Common ground stone tools include somewhat rough axes, adzes, chisels, etc., with the number of axes significantly exceeding that of adzes, which is a notable difference from downstream of the Yangtze River. Tube drilling technology was also used in stone tool making. There are many stone tool workshops in the Xiajiang area, containing a large amount of semi-finished stone tools, stone materials, drilling cores, etc., such as at the Honghuatao site in Yidu City, the Zhongbaodao site in Yichang City in Hubei Province, etc.[89] There are also clam sickles, bone shovels, bone *sis*, bone awls, spinning wheels, net pendants, etc. The Liyang Plain is characteristic of the southern riverine area with oars, paddles, and other wooden tools related to boats and ships, wooden knives, spears, and construction components of mortise and tenon structures.

V. Cultures in South China, Northeast, Northwest, and Southwest Regions

Despite the profound influence of the Dongzhuang–Miaodigou type of Yangshao culture on surrounding cultures, it has not yet spread to the entire historical range of China.

Representative remains in the South China region include phase I of Tanshishan in Minhou County, Fujian Province,[90] the Keqiutou remains in Pingtan County, Fujian Province,[91] as well as the sections IV and V of Xiandouling in Shenzhen City, Guangdong Province, and the middle stage remains of Dabenkeng in Hsinchu City, Taiwan, etc.[92] These are primarily shell mound and sand mound sites, with chipped stone tools and bone tools discovered, and the primary economic activity is hunting and gathering. The discovery of a relatively large number of stone adzes shows that this type of remains has a relatively developed woodworking industry, which should be related to settling down. Pottery includes nothing but cord-mark round-bottom cauldrons, round-foot plates, high-foot plates, foot supports, etc. Popular are marked cords, shell tooth decorations, stamped-dot patterns, circle patterns, etc., with a small number of painted potteries and jade *jues*. This area is generally part of the same cultural region as the middle and lower reaches of the Yangtze River, still being a cauldron–round-foot plate–high-foot plate cultural system. However, these remains do not show obvious influence from the Dongzhuang–Miaodigou type as the middle and lower reaches of the Yangtze River do.

The Northeast region from the Xiliao River Basin and the Liaodong Peninsula to the Hulunbuir grasslands is influenced by the Yellow River Basin. However, further east and north still belong to a relatively pure cylindrical jar cultural system, such as the late Yabuli culture of the Mudan River Basin.

As mentioned earlier, Yangshao culture has reached the eastern part of Qinghai Province to the northwest and the northwestern part of Sichuan Province to the southwest. Still, further west and south, no remains containing pottery and agriculture have been found yet, and these areas should still belong to the cultural category of the Mesolithic.

VI. Three-Tiered Cultural Community in the Miaodigou Era

1. Three-Tiered Cultural Community

Overall, due to the forceful expansion and influence of the Dongzhuang–Miaodigou type of Yangshao culture from the core area of southern Shanxi Province and western Henan Province around 4000 BCE, the previous pattern of the three major cultural areas or cultural systems drastically changed. The cultures in most parts of China have merged and connected into a relative cultural community. Its spatial structure can be divided into at least three tiers from inside to outside:

1. The core area is in southwestern Shanxi, western Henan, and eastern Guanzhong Provinces, the distribution area of the Dongzhuang–Miaodigou type of Yangshao culture and the eastern part of the Quanhu type. The representative petal-pattern painted pottery has smooth lines and is elegantly painted; the specific objects, such as double-lipped pointed-bottom small-mouth bottles and folded-belly cauldron-shaped *dings*, have neat and magnificent shapes. There are also a certain number of palace-style houses.

2. Outside of this is the main area, that is, the middle reaches of the Yellow River (also includes the upper and middle reaches of the Han River, the upper reaches of the Huai River, etc., on the south side), which is the entire distribution area of Yangshao culture outside the core area. The shape of petal-pattern painted pottery varies slightly by location, with the lines being undeveloped or immature. The painted pottery in the eastern part often uses a lively combination of multiple colors, which is lively but not calm enough. The northwest part has more double-lipped pointed-bottom small-mouth bottles and fewer *dings*. In comparison, the southeast part has fewer double-lipped small-mouth pointed-bottom bottles and more *dings*, reflecting regional differences.

3. Further out is the peripheral area, that is, the lower reaches of the Yellow River, the middle and lower reaches of the Yangtze River, and the Northeast, etc., the neighboring areas of Yangshao culture. From time to time, authentic or variant petal-pattern painted pottery, as well as earthen bowls with black-painted bands, folded-belly cauldron-shaped *dings*, double-lipped small-mouth pointed-bottom bottles, and gourd-shaped bottles

can be seen. But the main types of objects are still local traditions, often decorated with Miaodigou type patterns on local objects, integrating both Chinese and Western elements.

This three-tiered structure community was initially established during the Dongzhuang type and matured during the Miaodigou type. It is a relatively stable community lasting 600 to 700 years. The era they lived in constitutes the Miaodigou era (fig. 3.9).

It can be seen that the core and main areas of this three-tiered cultural community essentially correspond to the previous regions of the Yellow River Basin, North China, and the upper and middle reaches of the Huai River. In other words, it mainly developed based on the bottle (pot)–earthen bowl (basin)–jar–*ding* cultural system. Its peripheral area includes the newly integrated *ding*–high-foot plate–pot–cup cultural system of the middle and lower reaches of the Yangtze River and the lower reaches of the Yellow River and the cylindrical jar–painted pottery jar–earthen bowl cultural system of the southern and western Northeast. Outside of this three-tiered cultural community, there are the cauldron–round-foot plate–high-foot plate cultural system of South China, the cylindrical jar cultural system of the majority of the Northeast, and the Mesolithic cultural region, all of which have connections with those above the three-tiered cultural community. From the perspective of modern China, this would be considered the fourth tier.

2. Cultural Exchange in the Miaodigou Era

The cultural exchange during the Miaodigou era is prominently manifested in the unilateral expansion and influence of the Dongzhuang–Miaodigou types outward. The influence in the reverse direction is limited, with only a few elements, such as jade *yues* and jade *huangs*, reflecting the influence of the culture of the lower reaches of the Yangtze River.

The lower reaches of the Yangtze River have extensive and profound influence on the surrounding regions. Northward, it influenced the lower reaches of the Yellow River, causing Beixin culture to transition into Dawenkou culture; westward, it influenced the middle reaches of the Yangtze River, resulting in a large number of high-handle high-foot plates, cups, and other pottery, as well as *yues*, jade *huangs*, jade *jues*, and other jade artifacts in this region, causing a significant change in the development direction of Daxi culture; southward, it first had a significant impact on the Ningshao Plain, transforming Hemudu culture into the locally distinctive Songze culture, then further south, it influenced the South

Figure 3.9 Early China in the cultural sense during the Miaodigou era (4200–3500 BCE)

I. Cauldron–round-foot plate–high-foot plate cultural system
II. Early Chinese cultural sphere
III. Cylindrical jar cultural system
A. Core area B. Main area C. Peripheral area

1, 7, 12, 13. Basin (Zhangmaowusu F1: 4, Miaodigou H11: 75, Hulijia T1②: 1, H14: 2)
2, 8, 20. Jar (Zhangmaowusu F1: 2, Miaodigou H322: 66, Zhizhushan T1③: 47)
3, 10, 14, 16, 22. Earthen bowl (Zhangmaowusu F1: 6, Dadiwan T1③: 1, Hulijia T1004②B: 3, Chengtoushan H210: 3, Xishuiquan H4: 2)
4, 9, 11. Bottle (Miaodigou T203: 43, Dadiwan F2: 14, QD0: 19)
5. Cauldron (Miaodigou H12: 112)
6. Range (Miaodigou H47: 34)
15, 23, 27. *Ding* (Chengtoushan M665: 2, Dawenkou M1013: 5, Songze M10: 3)
17, 24, 28. High-foot plate (Chengtoushan M678: 4, Dawenkou M2005: 49, Songze M30: 4)
18, 25. Cup (Chengtoushan M679: 3, Dawenkou M2002: 8)
19. Cylindrical jar (Xishuiquan F13: 31)
21, 26, 29. Pot (Xishuiquan H2: 21, Dawenkou M1013: 2, Songze M30: 3)
(All pottery.)

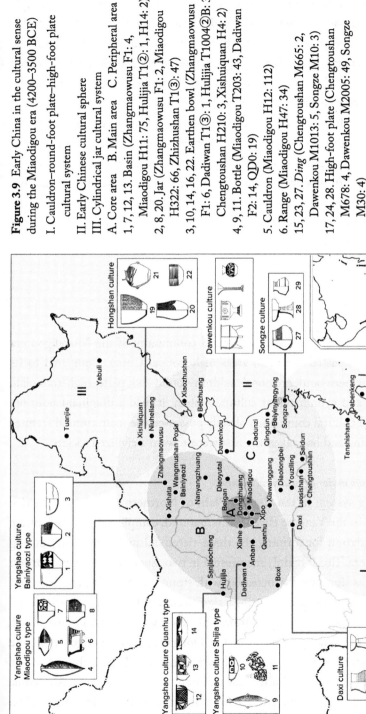

China region, introducing new high-foot plates and other potteries, jade *yues*, jade *jues*, and other jade artifacts based on the cauldron and round-foot plate. Of course, the lower reaches of the Yangtze River were also influenced by the middle reaches of the Yangtze River. For example, white pottery, single-handle painted pottery cups decorated with grid patterns, and round-foot plates of the Saidun type, Beiyinyangying culture, belonging to Daxi culture.

More intense cultural exchanges also existed between other regions. For example, elements from the Northeast, such as cylindrical jars, were found in Dawenkou culture remains at Beizhuang in Changdao County, Shandong Province, and the Z-shaped pattern was even found in the Weifang area. Meanwhile, cultural elements from Dawenkou culture, such as cauldron-shaped *ding*, *gui*, *he*, high-foot plate, and cup, were abundant on the Liaodong Peninsula, leading to the emergence of the middle Xiaozhushan culture.

VII. Conclusion

Around 4000 BCE, the three-tiered cultural community of the Miaodigou era had already encompassed the main areas of historical China. Compared to its southern and northern border regions' cauldron–round-foot plate–high-foot plate cultural system and cylindrical jar cultural system, it held a dominant position. This three-tiered cultural community already possessed the main cultural features of historical China and had taken the first steps toward a civilized society.

(1) Maturity of two major agricultural systems

The dry farming system in the Central Plain of Northern regions and the rice farming system in the Yangtze River Basin matured, complementing each other, laying the foundation for forming the three-tiered cultural community during the Miaodigou era. This is mainly manifested in two aspects: first, the proportion of stone tools has significantly increased, with stone shovels being common and the refinement becoming finer, showing a significant improvement in agricultural production tools; second, the agricultural cultural region has greatly expanded, especially with the rapid expansion of the Dongzhuang–Miaodigou type, the dry farming system of millet grain and sorghum expanded northward to the semi-arid grassland area including the Xilingol League in Inner Mongolia, and westward to eastern Qinghai Province and the eastern edge of the Hexi

Corridor, forming the largest agricultural cultural area in the world. Of course, a large area of hunting and gathering economic culture still exists outside the two major agricultural systems.

(2) Prosperous development of "Chinese" characteristic artifacts
"Chinese" characteristic artifacts such as pottery, jade, lacquerware, and silk textiles are abundant and exquisitely made, entering their first period of prosperity. Pottery *ding*, the symbol of Chinese culture, became popular throughout both sides of the Yangtze River. The jade of the Beiyinyangying–Songze culture in the lower reaches of the Yangtze River was beautifully made and had a wide influence. The jade in the Northeast also further developed. Li Ji once found a halved silkworm cocoon cut in Xiyin Village, Xia County, Shanxi Province. Later, traces of silk textiles were found in the remains of Yangshao culture in the Qingtai site in Xingyang County, Henan Province,[93] indicating that silk textiles had appeared then. Spinning wheels were found throughout both sides of the Yangtze River. Pottery bells, drums with hook handles on the rim, and hollow pottery balls with patterned stones (sound-making devices) were common in the Yangtze and Yellow River basins. Moreover, people in the Yangtze River Basin and northward generally wore bracelets, while people in the Yellow River Basin generally wore hairpins. Of course, the artifacts of each place still have their characteristics. For example, the pottery of Yangshao culture is simple, thick, and generous; the pottery of the Yangtze River and the lower Yellow River is complex, delicate, and small; and the pottery of the Northeast and South China is quite rustic.

(3) Maturity of civil engineering
The three types of beam-frame structure houses, including half underground, raised-floor, and ground-level, became more mature on both sides of the Yangtze River. Especially notable are the palace-like houses of Yangshao culture's Miaodigou type, which are large in scale and beautifully decorated, astonishing to behold. Daxi culture had already seen the earliest city walls in China, built with earth and fortified with moats, reinforced with wooden stakes and reed mats. They no longer looked like the initial appearance of city walls.

(4) Diversity and unity of pottery painting and symbols
This was a period when pottery painting was most prosperous. With the development of pottery painting in various regions, the previous dual-painted pottery

system of east and west pottery painting underwent considerable changes. Yangshao, Hongshan, Dawenkou, Beiyinyangying–Songze, and Daxi cultures stand out in their painted pottery, presenting various brilliant styles. Yangshao culture's Dongzhuang–Miaodigou type of painted pottery showcases a striking and elegant contrast between black and red, exuding a sense of solemnity and grandeur. These pottery pieces demonstrate cohesive unity and vibrant vitality with prevalent curved lines, interconnected patterns, and lively and dynamic designs. Undoubtedly, they hold a central position within the cultural landscape. They had a wide influence, making the overall appearance of Chinese pottery painting present a diversified and unified aspect, laying the tone for the most traditional colors of future China. Generally speaking, the patterns on Chinese painted pottery are mainly abstract geometric decorations, with few animals, humans, and other symbolic patterns. Even the *Stork Fish and* Yue description at Yan Village is only a symbolic representation of tribal conflict and power, unlike the pottery paintings of West Asia and Egypt at the same time that directly depict the image of the victor and complex funeral rituals.

Symbols can also be observed in this regard. Although symbols vary across regions, they share similarities with the later oracle bone script. Mature and regulated patterns such as octagonal star patterns and sun patterns carry profound meanings and have wide-ranging influences, particularly in the coastal regions of China. Some spiral patterns or designs resembling the *Taiji* diagram[*] reflect the budding concepts of *yin* and *yang*.[†] People of that time could distinguish between odd and even numbers and may have attributed special significance to them. For instance, in Beiyinyangying culture, polygonal and double-belly basins are typically adorned with patterns of polygons with an even number of sides. In contrast, stone knives are decorated with three or seven perforations, which are odd numbers.

(5) Ancestor worship system

This era maintained a secular religious belief system centered around ancestor worship. Graves were typically vertical earth pit graves, providing permanent

---

[*] *Taiji* diagram refers to a Chinese symbol representing the concept of *yin* (the receptive principle) and *yang* (the active principle). Sometimes, it also generically refers to geometric patterns similar to the Chinese *Taiji* diagram used in other cultures throughout history. These symbols typically consist of two semicircular tear-shaped curves of different colors (mostly black and white), symbolizing *yin* and *yang*.—Trans.

[†] *Yin* and *yang*, originated from the traditional philosophy of China as a concept of dualism. Ancient China used the concept of *yin* and *yang* to describe the characteristics of mutually opposed and interconnected things. Examples include sun and moon, day and night, hot and cold, female and male, etc. The concept of *yin* and *yang* embodies the abstract implication of "mutual opposition yet interdependence."—Trans.

underground residences for ancestors. The multi-person secondary joint burial of the core area's Dongzhuang–Miaodigou type is discerning, simple, and adheres to neutrality, emphasizing family or clan. Although there were also bird, pig, and dog-shaped decorations or artifacts, there were few pottery figurines, human images were rare, and almost no content of idol worship or ghost worship could be seen, echoing the temperament of the later Western Zhou culture. Moreover, specially made grave goods, small and crude, with outdated forms, began to appear, showing the emergence of ideas about following ancestors and "retro" funeral customs.[94] Peripheral regions were not necessarily the same. For example, Hongshan culture began to have piled stone tombs, sacrificial pits, and female sculptures, inheriting the previously common tradition of pottery figurines in the northeastern region, perhaps still the primitive shamanistic religious system communicating heaven and earth. Moreover, the Miaodigou type has many bird-pattern painted pottery, including tri-legged crow and bird-bearing-the sun patterns, as well as bird-shaped *dings*, bird-shaped lids, etc. Eastern cultures also often feature octagonal patterns and bird and sun patterns, indicating that the Miaodigou type and the vast majority of the eastern region have a tradition of bird and sun worship. The religious worship of the Miaodigou era was already relatively complex, especially with the expansion of sacrificial facilities in the eastern and Yangtze River regions, indicating the emergence of a certain religious authority differentiation.

(6) Origin of civilization and three models
The Miaodigou era was a period when society began to differentiate, with the societal changes and complexification trends of the slightly later age of combined use of bronze and stone starting here.[95] Large "palace-style" houses of 200 to 500 square meters near the core area appeared at sites such as Xipo in Lingbao City, Henan Province, Xiahe in Baishui County, Shaanxi Province, and Quanhu in Hua County, Shaanxi Province. The emergence of perforated stone *yue*, perhaps symbolic of military authority and mass graves, hints at the increasing importance of warfare in society.[96] This shows that society had already become quite complex, standing at the threshold of civilized society. However, graves often lack burial goods, reflecting a custom of distinguishing between life and death and adhering to simplicity, and their differentiation in wealth, social status, and handicrafts is still somewhat limited. Eastern cultures—Dawenkou culture, Songze culture, Beiyinyangying culture, etc., have already seen rich graves with hundreds of burial artifacts and a lot of jades, with clear distinctions between rich burial areas and poor burial areas, and family status quite prominent, showing that their social complexity

is no less than that of the central core area. These cultures' larger graves are buried with many personal belongings and group pottery, some even containing pig and cow bones, reflecting an extravagant lifestyle. Jade and stone artifact productions clearly show a trend toward specialization. However, fundamentally, the rapid development of these cultures still cannot be separated from the inspiration of Yangshao culture's Dongzhuang–Miaodigou type. However, the Bainiyao type of Yangshao culture in the Northern regions shows no differentiation of wealth, and the differentiation of social status is unclear.

Looking at it this way, as early as the Miaodigou era, general trends such as social differentiation, prominence of family, and emphasis on male military power were already beginning to form, and three different models of social development were taking shape, pioneering the origins of early Chinese civilization. We can refer to these three different modes as the "Central Plain Mode," "Eastern Mode," and "Northern Mode."[97] Of course, the formation of these different models is related to the degree of natural resources and wealth accumulation in each area. It is the result of adapting to different natural environments. This general trend of social development and the different models are other manifestations of the multi-centered unity of early Chinese culture and the source of the endless vitality and uninterrupted development of Chinese civilization.[98] Among them, the "Central Plain Mode," with its characteristics of measured life and death, the importance of nobility over wealth, orderliness, and adherence to simplicity, has become the core traits of Chinese civilization in later generations.

(7) The formal formation of early China in cultural significance
The three-tiered cultural community of the Miaodigou era shares striking similarities with the three-tiered structure of the Shang Dynasty in terms of political geography.[99] This community laid the foundation for the Xia, Shang, and even the later Qin and Han periods in both geographic and cultural terms, thus it can be termed the "early Chinese cultural sphere" or "early China" in cultural significance, simply referred to as "early China."

As mentioned earlier, Yan Wenming, Zhang Guangzhi, and Su Bingqi have separately proposed concepts such as the "multi-petaled flower" pattern of prehistoric China, "China interaction sphere," and the consensus "China," which are closely related to the "early China" in cultural significance discussed in this book. Specifically, Zhang Guangzhi pointed out that the "China interaction sphere" formed roughly around 4000 BCE. Still, he did not recognize Central

Plain culture's central position and hierarchical structure at the time. His "China Interaction Sphere" is a circle of interconnected cultures on the historic Chinese territory. Su Bingqi's proposed "Five-Emperor Period" forms a consensus "China" due to the exchange and mutual recognition among major cultural regions. Its meaning is the same as the "China interaction sphere." Yan Wenming's "multi-petaled flower" pattern has a primary and secondary structure, with the "flower heart" being the core of the Central Plain, equivalent to the first tier of early China in this book. The "multi-petaled flower" represent the surrounding cultures connected to the Central Plain in layers based on their closeness or distance: the first layer of petals close to the "flower heart" is equivalent to the second tier of early China in this book, and the second layer of petals is equal to the third tier of early China. However, he did not explicitly mention when this "multi-petaled flower" pattern was formed.

People cannot help but ask: how did such a wide-ranging early China form around 4000 BCE in the Miaodigou era? How did the strong core area permeate its cultural factors into the surrounding regions, making it the primary cognition of the vast surrounding areas? Perhaps war and population migration played a significant role. However, continuing this recognition trend for 600 to 700 years is related to the Central Plain core area's admirable cultural characteristics and convincing cultural strategies. The characteristics of the "Central Plain Mode," being stable and restrained, valuing nobility over wealth, and being orderly and adhering to simplicity, determined that its essential characteristics of social politics lie in coordinating and stabilizing internal order, and the ritual system should have truly emerged. It also determined that its social management was based on basic kinship relations, spatially from near to far, implementing different management methods at different levels, respecting different cultures in other regions, forming a cultural or political community with a super stable structure, and the earliest "tributary system" may have begun to sprout. Furthermore, it determined that it advocated "royal power" rather than "hegemony," relying mainly on the radiating influence of excellent culture rather than military or economic intervention.

CHAPTER 4

The Archaic State Stage of Early China

(3500–1800 BCE)

I. Late Yangshao Culture: Diversification and Integration

Around 3500 BCE, we entered the early Chalcolithic, also known as the late Banpo—Miaodigou phase II type period of Yangshao culture.[1] The situation reversed at this time. The local cultural features of the early China cultural circle greatly intensified, the trend of cultural differentiation was prominent, and the intensity of cultural exchanges and collisions was unprecedented. The influence of Central Plain culture represented by Yangshao culture weakened, and the acceptance of surrounding areas, especially the eastern regions, significantly increased (table 4.1). The reason is directly related to the gradual decline of the Central Plain culture and the gradual loss of the core cultural position of the Central Plain. The influx of foreign cultural factors naturally meant passivity and pain for the people in the Central Plain at that time. Still, after hardships and struggles, the increasingly strong foreign influences gradually transformed into a new energy source, and the new cultural integration process had already begun. Although it was a period of general diversification, the foundation of "early China" was still maintained. The western regions significantly expanded and still intersected with the cylindrical jar cultural system of Northeast Asia and the cauldron–round-foot plate cultural system of South China in the border areas. On the other hand, this was also a time when social differentiation was significantly strengthened, social conflicts were

Table 4.1 Cultural regions in early Chalcolithic China (3500–2500 BCE)

		Early stage (3500–3000 BCE)	Later stage (3000–2500 BCE)
Early Chinese cultural sphere	Upper and middle reaches of the Yellow River, upper reaches of the Yangtze River, eastern Xizang Plateau	Jar–earthen bowl–basin–bottle (Yangshao culture phase III, Majiayao culture Shilingxia type stage, Shaozui culture phase II, Guiyuanqiao type remains, and Karuo culture)	Jar–earthen bowl–basin–bottle (Yangshao culture phase IV, Majiayao culture Majiayao type stage, Shaopengzui culture phase II, Guiyuanqiao type remains, and Karuo culture)
	Middle and lower reaches of the Yangtze River, lower reaches of the Yellow River	*Ding*–high-foot plate–pot–cup cultural system (Middle Dawenkou culture, Daxi culture phase IV, Xuejiagang culture, and late Songze culture–early Liangzhu culture)	*Ding*–high-foot plate–pot–cup cultural system (Late Dawenkou culture, Qujialing culture, middle Liangzhu culture, Fanchengdui culture, Shixia culture, Niubizhan culture, and Tanshishan culture)
	South and west parts of Northeast China	Cylindrical jar–painted pottery jar–earthen bowl cultural system (Late Hongshan culture, Hamin Mangha culture, Xueshan culture phase I, and middle Xiaozhushan culture)	Cylindrical jar–painted pottery jar–earthen bowl cultural system (Xueshan culture phase I, Nanbaoligaotu culture, and Pianbuzi culture)
Early China outer margin zone	South China, part of Southwest China	Cauldron–round-foot plate–high-foot plate cultural system (Damaoshan culture and Dabenkeng culture)	Cauldron–round-foot plate–high-foot plate cultural system (Damaoshan culture and Dabenkeng culture)
	Eastern part of Northeast China	Cylindrical jar cultural system (Upper Zuojiashan culture and lower Yinggeling culture)	Cylindrical jar cultural system (Xiaolaha culture phase I, upper Zuojiashan culture, and lower Yinggeling culture)
	Other regions	Mesolithic culture	Mesolithic culture

constant, becoming increasingly complex, and it was generally starting to move toward a civilized society, having entered the early stage of civilized society. The old order was being destroyed, a new order was being established, and the trends of differentiation and integration coexisted, becoming the biggest characteristic of the time.

1. The Upper and Middle Reaches of the Yellow River as the Main Body

At this time, the core area of early China relatively declined, and the main area, i.e., the area of Yangshao culture distribution other than the core area, was seriously diversified. Except for the Guanzhong area, other areas had increasingly strong local characteristics, but most could still be included in Yangshao culture. As for the culture of the Gansu–Qinghai area, it had differentiated and evolved into Majiayao culture and influenced the upper reaches of the Yangtze River and the eastern part of the Xizang Plateau to form the Shaopengzui culture phase II, Karuo culture, etc. It generally belonged to the jar–earthen bowl–basin–bottle cultural system.

1.1 The Relative Culture Decline in Southern Shanxi and Western Henan

Xiwang Type of Yangshao Culture
Around 3500 BCE, the Miaodigou type of Yangshao culture in the Central Plain core area changed to the Xiwang type, represented by archaeological sites such as Xiwang Village H4 in Ruicheng County, Shanxi Province,[2] and H143[3] and M27 in Lingbao City, Henan Province.[4] Its main pottery continues the lineage of the Miaodigou type. The double-lipped mouth of the small-mouth pointed-bottom bottle gradually degenerates into a trumpet mouth, and the bottom of the bottle becomes increasingly blunt; deep-belly jars and urns are getting taller and thinner, and the shoulder and belly are often encircled with several added relief decorations; the rim of basins and earthen bowls are nearly folded; new double-belly basins, jars with spouts, and cauldron-shaped *dings* with added relief decorations on feet are emerging. The basket pattern increases while the marked cord decreases, and gray-black pottery increases while painted pottery greatly declines. It was dominated by red net patterns, claw patterns, overlapping-scale patterns, etc., and still shadows of polka dots, hook leaves, and triangle patterns of painted pottery. The Xiwang type can be regarded as the most determined successor of the Miaodigou type. Of course, influences from the eastern regions

can be seen, such as the converging-mouth folded-rim high-foot plate, the open double-belly high-foot plate, the back pot,* the high-neck cauldron, etc., should be related to the influence of Dawenkou culture, the overlapping-scale pattern should be Hongshan culture factor, folded-shoulder pots, high-neck pots, painted pottery bowls, etc., are the factors of the Qinwangzhai type, and the earliest source of vessels with spouts is in the lower reaches of the Yangtze River. The *yue* and large-mouth vat can, of course, be inherited from the Miaodigou type, and it is not excluded that they were influenced by the culture of the lower reaches of the Yangtze River. It is worth noting that the range of the Xiwang type has expanded to the western edge of the Luoyang Basin, including the Yangshao phase II of Mianchi, Henan Province,[5] and Yangshao culture I and II phases of Xin'an Mahe.[6] It is just that there are slightly more Qinwangzhai type factors in it.

Adult burials remain in the form of rectangular vertical pit tombs, primarily extended supine, the previous multi-person secondary joint burial tombs have already disappeared. Tomb differentiation is obvious. The most striking is the Lingbao Xipo Cemetery. All tombs have two-layer platforms. The overall size is large, the mouth area of large tombs reaches 12 to 17 square meters, the tomb chamber is covered with wooden boards, specially equipped with foot pits, the burial includes exquisite jade *yues*, paired large-mouth vats, *gui*[†]-shaped utensils, and other potteries, highlighting the tomb owner's lofty status. However, most buried items in a tomb are no more than about ten flakes, and most are crude grave goods, showing the characteristics of measured life and death, valuing nobility over wealth, being orderly and courteous, and being modest and balanced (fig. 4.1).[7] Compared with surrounding areas, the degree of social complexity is relatively low, indicating that the Central Plain core area has become relatively weak. Generally, there is no second layer of the platform in the cemetery, most of them are small tombs with a mouth area of about one square meter that can barely accommodate the body, and there are rarely burial objects.

The condition of production tools is basically the same as the Miaodigou type, and single-hole stone knives and side-notched pottery knives are common agricultural harvesting tools. The economic method should also be basically the same as before. A rectangular pottery trowel with a handle, one of the earliest building decoration tools, was found at the Yuanqu Shanghao site.

---

* An ancient Chinese water vessel. It can hold water or be used to draw water, fixed on the back, for walking without worrying about the water inside the pot spilling or tipping over.—Trans.

† The "*gui*" here refers to an ancient Chinese container used for holding cooked rice or food, which also served as a ritual vessel, rather than the "*gui*" referring to cooking utensils. Both have the same pronunciation in Chinese. The "*gui*" in figure 35 is the same as the one here.—Trans.

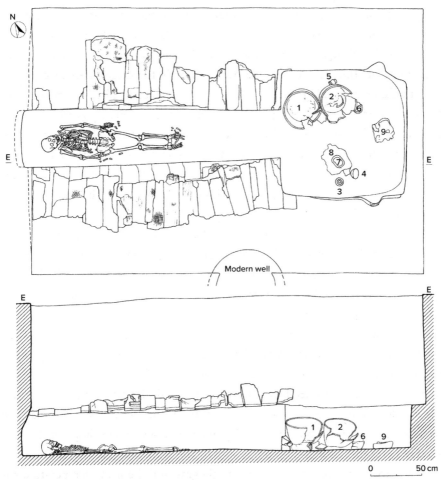

Figure 4.1 Plan and section of the M27 Xipo cemetery

1, 2. Large-mouth pottery vat	5, 6, 9. *Gui*-shaped pottery vessel	8. Pottery range
3. Pottery pot		
4. Pottery earthen bowl	7. Pottery cauldron	

Miaodigou Phase II Type of Yangshao Culture

Around 3000 BCE, the Xiwang type evolved into the Miaodigou phase II type, represented by the early "Miaodigou phase II cultural remains" in Dongguan site, Yuanqu County, Shanxi Province,[8] the II and III phases of Guzhen Village, Hejin City, Shanxi Province,[9] Miaodigou phase II in Shan County, Henan Province, and the Yangshao phase III remains in Mianchi. Most of the potteries have an inheritance relationship with the Xiwang type, only with slight differences in shape, such as the deep-belly jar is slimmer and straighter, with more added relief decorations, the *ding* is a basin-shaped *ding* with added-relief-decorated feet, the neck of the small-mouth pointed-bottom bottle changes from arc to straight, the bottom is blunter. It evolves into a small-mouth flat-bottom bottle based on the small-mouth pointed-bottom bottle, which further evolves into a small-mouth high-neck jar. The most noticeable new pottery is the cauldron-shaped *jia* (an ancient Chinese drinking vessel)—it is considered to be inspired by the *gui* from the Central Henan region (fig. 4.2).[10] The rest of the painted potteries in small amounts of thin-wall slanted-belly cups, *yu*-shaped cups, wide-rim straight-belly cups, high-neck pots, and painted pottery wide-flare-mouth jars, etc., are all spread from Central Henan or through Central Henan. In addition, wide-rim straight-belly cup, *gu*-shaped cup, high-neck cauldron, high-neck folded-shoulder *zun*, blunt pointed-bottom pottery *zun* (vat), etc., should be factors of Dawenkou culture, *yu*-shaped short round-foot cup, high-handle cup, painted pottery slanted-belly cup, double-belly high-foot plate, etc., should be factors of Qujialing culture. Dongguan also found a piece of jade *cong* (a jade cylinder used for rituals in ancient China) (IIH22: 72), which may be related to the influence of the early Liangzhu culture.

Houses are only seen as small circular semi-subterranean structures with white ash ground and dado. Fewer tombs have been found, and those in the Miaodigou site are all small rectangular vertical pit tombs, usually without burial objects, and only a few are accompanied by a small pottery cup. Both houses and tombs reflect the simple and moderate customs of the Central Plain core area, but this may also be a sign that its development is at a low point, although there should be higher-level remains that have not been discovered. The pottery kiln is a vertical pit kiln with a narrowing top, the pottery is mostly gray, and the firing temperature has increased. Production tools, economic forms, and decorations should be similar to those of the Xiwang type.

1.2 Stable Development of Culture in the Guanzhong Region

Late Banpo Type of Yangshao Culture

After 3500 BCE, the least influenced area by surrounding cultures was Guanzhong, where the Quanhu type of Yangshao culture evolved steadily into the late Banpo type, represented by the late Banpo in Xi'an City and phase III of the Fulinbao in Baoji City. Pottery has evolved toward gray and black, and most of the pottery such as flat-lipped or flared-mouth blunt-bottom pointed-bottom bottle, shallow-belly plate (often double-belly), wide-rim shallow or deep-belly basin, double-handle converging or open deep-belly basin, converging flat-bottom

THE ARCHAIC STATE STAGE OF EARLY CHINA 135

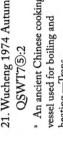

Figure 4.2 Spatial expansion of pottery *jia* and *li*[a] before the late Shang Dynasty

1. Laohushan F27: 1
2. Xueshan H66: 7
3. Youyao H248: 1
4. Guzhen H2: 1
5. Zhukaigou W2004: 2
6. Taosi IIIH303: 12
7. Liuwan M1103: 13
8. Qinweijia M36: 1
9. Shizhaocun T317②:10
10. Qinglongquan T2⑤C: 6
11, 12. Wangwan T58④: 1, H166.158
13. Dadianzi M726: 17
14. Baijinbao F3028: 3
15. Ping'anbao H1012: 1
16. Yinjiacheng H728: 1
17. Zhoubeidun H10: 25
18. Erligang H17: 119
19. Yangcheng YT39H29: 9
20. Panlongcheng PYWT23④: 1
21. Wucheng 1974 Autumn QSWT7⑤.2

[a] An ancient Chinese cooking vessel used for boiling and heating.—Trans.

earthen bowl or bowl, large-mouth deep-belly jar, high-neck jar (high-neck pot), converging urn, stove, etc., are all inherited from Quanhu type. Few new earthen bowl-shaped *zengs*, basins, or cauldrons with spouts appeared. A small amount of white color, imprint basket pattern, and grid pattern are seen, which should be related to its interaction with the Xiwang type. An arc line vortex pattern pot was found at places like Fulinbao in the middle reaches of the Wei River, which could be a factor of the Shilingxia type. The southern boundary of the late Banpo type has reached the area of Zhong County in northern Chongqing.[11]

The differentiation of settlements is becoming evident, with the largest Anban site covering an area of 700,000 square meters. Most of them are rounded square or rectangular semi-subterranean structures; the vast majority are of medium and small size. However, large ground-type houses like Anban F3 reach 165 square meters with a front porch and back hall. In the nearby ash pits, pottery dustpan-shaped vessels similar to those in Dadiwan were found, as well as red-painted pig mandibles, pig skulls wrapped in plant-woven materials, and eight pottery figurines, which might be related to some kind of ritual behavior. At the Nanzuo site in the Jing River Basin, a large, rammed earth wall ground-type building with a front hall and a back hall was found, covering an area of 680 square meters. The walls and floors were smeared with white ash, and an apron had been roasted outside the room.[12] The other nearby rammed earth ground-type buildings are also quite meticulous. The appearance of the "palace" type building in Nanzuo shows that the differentiation of settlements and society in the Jing River Basin is significant and has already moved toward a civilized society. However, the Yanggua site in the Jing River Basin consists of small semi-subterranean and cave-type houses,[13] also the earliest cave-type buildings in the northwest region. Tombs are still mainly rectangular vertical pit tombs, most are extended supine, and burial objects are rarely seen. Some tombs in the Yanggua site were accompanied by pig mandibles, and a unique circular tri-person joint burial pit was found where a whole pig was buried.

Production tools and economic forms are largely the same as the Quanhu type. Most knives (claw sickles) used as harvesting tools are still made of pottery, but the number of stone knives has slightly increased, indicating that grain harvesting efficiency has improved.

Quanhu Phase II Type of Yangshao Culture
Around 3000 BCE, the late Banpo type evolved into the Quanhu type phase II, represented by the II and III phases of *Quanhu Village in Hua County*, which also

includes phase III of Anban in Fufeng, phase II of Huxizhuang in Wugong, and the early Zhaojialai,[14] etc. The basic type of vessels continued the previous lineage, with basket patterns and added relief decorations prevailing. New tri-legged vessels such as *jia* and *he*, basin-shaped mortar and pestle, and common *ding* have emerged, all resulting from the influence of the Miaodigou phase II type. Flat-belly red-colored pots, large round-foot plates, round-foot bowls, open-mouth round-foot (false-round-foot) cups, and other early Qujialing culture or Qinwangzhai type factors. In the Quanhu site, pottery made by fast-wheel-throwing has clearly appeared, an advanced technology that must have been introduced from the East. In addition, in the upper reaches of the Jing River in the eastern part of Gansu Province, there is the Changshan type, represented by the lower Changshan site in Zhenyuan County, Guizhou Province,[15] which is similar to the Quanhu phase II overall, except for the lack of tri-legged vessels. The "Longshan culture remains" in the Lijia Village site in Xixiang County, Shaanxi Province in Hanzhong region, and Longgangsi, Nanzheng District, Shaanxi Province, with shoulder-folded jars, marked-cord deep-belly jars, and high-foot plates, etc., are also similar to Quanhu phase II type, and the complex imprinted patterns are very characteristic.

Houses are either semi-subterranean- or cave-type, with the floors and walls often laid with a white ash surface on grass-mixed mud. Some are painted with red lines, and some firepits have red and black painted circles around the fireplace. This practice of decorating the interior with colored lines gradually increased, probably related to the popularity of the clean white ash surface. Tombs still popularly use rectangular vertical pit tombs, which are often only large enough to hold a body; the vast majority are extended supine, burial objects are rarely seen, and many skeletons show limb loss.

The production tools and economic forms are basically the same as before. In sites such as Xiaweiluo and Anban, concentrated pottery kiln areas have been found. The pottery kilns are still horizontal cave type, gradually narrowing upward into a steamed bun shape, and traces of sealed mud at the top of the firebox have been found, indicating that a reducing atmosphere pottery kiln with a sealed top has appeared to fire gray pottery.

1.3 Cultural Variation in the Northern Region

Haishengbulang and Yijing Type of Yangshao Culture
As early as the end of the Miaodigou era, there were early remains of the Haishengbulang type in the Northern region, such as on the G1 of the Hongtaipo

site in Liangcheng County, Inner Mongolia the Wangmushan Pozhong.[16] It was formed based on the Bainiyaozi type under the profound influence of eastern culture: marked-cord jars, plain jars, earthen bowls, and basins inherited the Bainiyaozi tradition; cylindrical jars came from Hongshan culture, and small-mouth double-handle bulbous-belly jars were variants of the small-mouth double-handle high-neck jars of Xueshan culture phase I; deep folded-belly earthen bowls were similar to those of the Dasikong type in Yangshao culture. In terms of painted pottery, the newly emerged tricolor of black, purplish-red, and brown, relative double-hooked patterns, scale patterns, chessboard patterns, etc., came from Hongshan culture, and the inverted triangles, diamond shapes, and diamond grid patterns should have come from Xueshan culture phase I. In addition, a round-cornered square serpentine *bi* of the typical Hongshan cultural system was found in the remains of the Wangmushan Pozhong site, and polished serpentine jade material was found on the Hongtaipo site, indicating that Hongshan culture craftsmen carried jade material to the Daihai area.

By around 3500 BCE, the Haishengbulang type had spread to the Central and Southern of Inner Mongolia and most of the Northern Shaanxi region, represented by the remains of Haishengbulang in Tuoketuo County, Inner Mongolia,[17] Miaozigou in Chayouqian Banner,[18] and Wangmushan Poshang in Liangcheng County.[19] The overall trend is continued development based on the early stage, such as the change in the mid-abdomen of the small-mouth bulbous-belly jar from square-folded to round-drummed to slightly folded, the gradual decline of painted pottery, and the gradual increase of basket patterns. In addition, a painted pottery basin from the Baicaota site in Jungar, decorated with four groups of large circular patterns, should have been influenced by the Shilingxia type of Majiayao culture.[20] This type also shows regional differences, the most obvious of which is the popularity of the trumpet-mouth small-mouth pointed-bottom bottle in the areas on both sides of the Yellow River in Ordos. Still, it is not seen in the Daihai–Huangqihai area. At this time, the Northern Jinzhong area was already the Yijing type, represented by the Yijing T1⑥ in Taiyuan City, Shanxi Province,[21] Baiyan H99 in Taigu District,[22] and Xinghuacun H11 in Fenyang City, Shanxi Province.[23] The pottery as a whole is a continuation of the development of the Bainiyaozi type, the degree of variation is much smaller than that of the Haishengbulang type, but vertical band patterns, butterfly antenna patterns, grid patterns, chessboard patterns, diagonal triangle patterns, and other painted pottery still reflect influences from the Dasikong type and Xueshan culture phase I.

There are multiple settlement clusters of the Haishengbulang type. Houses in Wangmushanpo and Miaozigou settlements are rectangular semi-subterranean types, with one or two ranges inside, and the living surface is often padded with white clay. Some even have rectangular door stoops. Houses are distributed in groups, possibly reflecting the prominence of clan organizations. Overall there is no significant difference in size and function, reflecting what should be a basically equal social scene. The feature of houses with door stoops may come from the Shilingxia type of Majiayao culture. In Baiyan and other settlements of the Yijing type, cave-style buildings appeared—these are among the earliest cave-style buildings in China, with the living surface whitewashed on grass-mixed mud. The Miaozigou settlement has wide, short rectangular vertical pit graves with single, double, or multiple joint burials. The occupants are mostly flexed on the (left or right) side, and burial objects vary from a few to more than ten. The flexed burial custom should result from the influence of Xueshan culture phase I.

The production tools and economic forms are largely the same as before. The number of microlithic arrowheads, scraping tools, and compound tool bone-handle stone-blade knives suddenly increased at sites such as Wangmushanpo and Miaozigou, indicating an increase in the proportion of hunting and gathering economies.

Ashan Phase III Type and Baiyan Type of Yangshao Culture

Around 3000 BCE, the culture of the Northern region developed steadily on the original basis, with the Haishengbulang type transitioning to the Ashan phase III type and the Yijing type transitioning to the Baiyan type. The former is represented by the Ashan phase III in Baotou City, Inner Mongolia,[24] the Xiaoshawan site in Jungar Banner,[25] and Xiaoguandao site in Suide, Shaanxi Province.[26] Baiyan H538 and F2 represent the latter. Various types of jars, urns, basins, earthen bowls, straight-wall vats, high-foot plates, earthen bowl-shaped *zengs*, and other pottery are all further developments on the previous basis. However, the Ashan phase III type has a trumpet-mouth or shallow cup-mouth small-mouth pointed-bottom bottle, which continues the local tradition. The Baiyan type also has a small number of basin-shaped *dings*, folded-belly *jias*, stoves, cauldrons, plain high-neck folded-shoulder pots, etc., which is obviously the result of its proximity to southern Shanxi Province and the influence of the Miaodigou phase II type. Bovine bone scapulae used for divination were also found at the Baicaota site in Jungar Banner, which belongs to the Ashan phase III type.

The Ashan phase III type has many "stone city" settlements, including Baicaota, Xiaoshawan, Zhaizita, Maluta, Zhaizigedan, Ashan, Xiyuan, Shamujia, Heimaban, Weijun in the Jungar area, and Shiluoluoshan, Houzhaizimao in northern Shaanxi Province, etc. These settlements are located in perilous terrain, with popular stone walls around the main body of the settlement. There are large public places such as "altars" and "big houses" inside, as well as stone wall houses. Stone walls or "stone cities" are obviously for strengthening the defense of settlements, and "altars" and "big houses" are effective facilities for maintaining kinship and strengthening community unity. There are noticeable differences in the size of the houses, indicating that there may be a certain degree of wealth differentiation in society. All of these may be rooted in unprecedentedly tense relationships between populations. In addition, there are cave-type houses in northern Shaanxi, some of which have whitewashed living surfaces and wall dado, some have red parallel lines painted on the lower surface of the cave walls, and some have a black band painted around the firepit. The houses of the Baiyan type are basically cave-type. The burials of the two types are generally simple rectangular vertical pit graves with extended supine burials. There are no significant changes in production tools and economic forms from before.

1.4 Cultural Variation in Central and Southern Henan Province

Qinwangzhai and Baligang Type of Yangshao Culture
Due to the strong influence of Eastern and Southern cultures, central and southern Henan began the process of cultural variation by the end of the Miaodigou era and became more pronounced after 3500 BCE. Yangshao culture Yancun type in central Henan then transitioned into the Qinwangzhai type, represented by the Dahecun phase III in Zhengzhou City, Henan Province, and the Wangwan phase II sections I and II in Luoyang City;[27] Yangshao culture Xiawanggang type in southern Henan transitioned into the Baligang type, represented by the late Yangshao Baligang in Dengzhou, Henan,[28] and the Xiawanggang Yangshao phase III remains in Xichuan. As for the area along the Sui–Zao Corridor in northern Hubei that was previously part of Yangshao culture, it now essentially falls within the range of Daxi culture.

Overall, the Qinwangzhai type and Baligang type were quite similar. Both were dominated by pottery inherited from the local Yangshao culture, such as *dings*, deep-belly jars, basins, earthen bowls, urns, high-neck jars, small-mouth pointed-bottom bottles, large-mouth pointed-bottom bottles, and painted pottery with leaf contouring technique, circles, triangles, and their variants. Among them, the plain high-neck jars with round shoulders and large bellies are similar in shape but different in spirit to the high-neck jars that evolved from the small-mouth pointed-bottom bottle in the areas west of the Central Plain. But there are also many elements deeply influenced by Eastern and Southern cultures. Slender-neck pots, double-connected pots, large-mouth protruding-shoulder jars, and painted pottery with hexagonal star patterns and circle patterns, reflecting the influence of Dawenkou culture; curved-belly cups, round-foot bowls, short round-foot pots, short round-foot convergent-mouth cups, and engraved patterned pottery balls, reflecting the influence of Daxi culture Youziling type; pots with a turn at the shoulder and belly reflecting the impact of the Songze culture; perforated round-foot high-foot plates are common elements in the culture of the eastern region; other things like jars with spouts and eyelash patterns, X patterns, S pattern painted pottery are new. The difference between the Qinwangzhai type and the Baligang type is mainly manifested in the fact that the former had more folded-shoulder jars, folded-belly *dings*, deep-curved-belly earthen bowls, commonly decorated with horizontal grid pattern painted pottery jars, and more Dawenkou cultural elements. In contrast, jars, *dings*, and earthen bowls of the Baligang type are round-shoulder and curve-belly, common high-neck pot-shaped *dings*, curved-belly cups, and more Daxi cultural elements.

The Qinwangzhai type reveals the Xishan ancient city in Zhengzhou City—the earliest discovered city site in the Central Plain. The city was nearly circular in plan, with an area of about 35,000 square meters, built in sections, with city moats and gates, and sizable rammed earth buildings within the city, practicing the custom of infant sacrifice for foundation laying.[29] The appearance of this city was primarily for military defense purposes, perhaps an important facility for the Central Plain region to resist eastern populations,[30] and also one of the markers of progress toward a civilized society. Many settlements were found rows of mud-wall houses with wooden skeletons, some with several rooms, some with more than ten or even more than 20 rooms. For example, in Dahecun, each row had three or four rooms, there is a primary and secondary distinction between the rooms, and the door directions of the rooms are not necessarily identical. Each row probably belonged to a single family, so the entire settlement was made up of several families living communally.[31] At Xiawanggang, each row had more than 20 rooms, composed of several pairs of rooms and single-room suites. Each pair of rooms could be for a small family, and the whole row of houses could be for a large family or several families living communally. The prominence of a family organization is a major event of this era.

Adult burials were vertical pit graves, generally without grave goods. Several large rectangular vertical pit tombs with two-tier (or even triple-tiered) platforms were discovered in Yiquecheng, Yichuan, Henan. The tombs have coffins and outer coffins, with a tomb opening area of 6 to 11 square meters. However, each tomb only has one or two grave goods, including stone *yues* or *yue*-shaped tools, jade *huangs*, pottery jars, earthen bowls, etc.[32] The large tombs and two-tier platforms indicate that the tomb owner held a high social status. Still, the overall modesty and solidity were similar to the social features of Lingbao Xipo burials.

Production tools and economic forms were basically the same as before, still co-existing with dry and paddy farming. It is worth noting that at this time, rough stone knives with notches on both sides were often seen, while the previously popular ground perforated stone knives declined.

Guanshuihe Type of Yangshao Culture

Around 3000 BCE, the Qinwangzhai type in central Henan had developed into the Gushuihe type, while most of the southern part of Henan was under Qujialing culture. The Gushuihe type is represented by the Gushuihe phase III in Yuzhou, Henan Province,[33] the "early Longshan culture" in Yangcheng, Dengfeng City,[34] the Dahecun phase IV in Zhengzhou, and the Zhouli II and III phases remain in Mengjin District.[35] The main pottery followed the tradition of the previous era, with jars that had slightly bulging upper bodies and the white-coated painted pottery essentially disappeared, leaving behind a small amount of red-coated painted pottery. New additions include *jias*, basket patterns, and added relief decorations significantly increased, showing the increased influence of the Miaodigou phase II type. Straight-belly *dings*, back pots, and round-foot *dings* are elements of Dawenkou culture; double-belly high-foot plates and *yu*-shaped cups are elements of Qujialing culture; overlapping-scale patterns are elements of Hongshan culture; individual stone *bis*, jade bracelets, and jade *huangs* are elements of the Songze culture and Liangzhu culture. In addition, the *nao**-shaped vessels with large mouths and curved bodies found at the Zhouli site are very distinctive.

The Xishan ancient city in Zhengzhou was still in use during the early Gushuihe type. Settlements in the eastern part of Zhengzhou City area were mostly rows of mud-wall ground-level houses with wooden frames. In contrast, circular semi-subterranean houses were often seen in western Luoyang City, some with white ash surfaces. At the Zhouli Cemetery in Mengjin, a stone tool production area was

---

* An ancient ritual vessel used by Zhouli People in China. It is cylindrical at the top and trumpet-shaped at the bottom, with different sizes and comparable proportions.—Trans.

discovered, containing many stone materials, semi-finished stone tools, and stone tools. The burial situation is similar to the previous one. The graves in the Mengjin Zhouli Cemetery were neatly arranged. All are rectangular vertical pit graves, a few have two-tier platforms and coffins, and did not have grave goods. The largest grave, with an opening area of more than 20 square meters (M50), had a two-tier platform, the tomb chamber was covered with round wood, and the tomb owner's arm wore an ivory cuff, who apparently was an influential leader. However, there are no other burial goods, still showing the characteristic of valuing nobility over wealth. At the Dahecun site, there are phenomena of burying human bones and pig skeletons in ash pits. Production tools and economic forms were basically the same as before, but shoulder-equipped stone spades had significantly increased.

1.5 The Rise of Culture in the East of the Taihang Mountains Regions

Dasikong Type and Xueshan Culture Phase I of Yangshao Culture

Around 3500 BCE, the culture east of the Taihang Mountains rose again. Yangshao culture Dasikong type emerged in southern Hebei and Xueshan culture phase I emerged in central and northern Hebei.

The Dasikong type, represented by Yangshao culture, remains in Dasikong, Anyang City, Henan Province,[36] the Baojiatang remains,[37] and the Luositan phases I and II remains in Xinxiang,[38] developed from the Diaoyutai type.[39] The pottery is mainly gray, and the main types of pottery are converging-mouth or curved-belly earthen bowls, painted pottery bulbous-belly basins, protruding-shoulder deep-belly jars, high-neck jars, painted pottery jars, urns, etc. Some painted pottery bowls and chisel-shaped foot *dings* are likely elements of the Qinwangzhai type. The pottery is mainly plain, with several basket patterns and floral bordered-mouth jars. The painted pottery is red or black, and the most important arc edge hooked leaf triangle pattern and multiple vertical wave patterns are obviously developed from the Diaoyutai type painted pottery decoration. Other patterns include butterfly antenna pattern, concentric circle pattern, grid pattern, S pattern, eyelash pattern, floating ribbon pattern, etc. The last few likely were to be elements of the Qinwangzhai type. In addition, individual overlapping-scale patterns are elements of Hongshan culture. At Baojiatang, a steamed bun-shaped pottery kiln was found with the upper part of the kiln chamber narrowed and a cellar containing four pig skeletons.

Xueshan culture phase I can be divided into early and late stages, with the Zhongjiabi remains in Pingshan, Hebei representing the early stage,[40] and the

Xueshan phase I in Changping, Beijing,[41] the second layer of Wufang in Rongcheng, Hebei Province,[42] and the Jiangjialiang Cemetery in Yangyuan representing the late stage.[43] The main pottery of the early stage Zhongjiabi remains includes cylindrical jars, slanted-belly converging-mouth earthen bowls, basins, wide-flare-mouth jars, high-neck jars, pots, *zengs*, etc. The painted pottery has horizontal band patterns, vertical band patterns, triangle patterns, diamond patterns, grid patterns, polka dot patterns, wide-scale patterns, ladder patterns, etc. The most popular are composite patterns composed of diamond and grid patterns and triangle and vertical line patterns. Its main elements are close to the Hougang type of Yangshao culture in the Zhending Nanyangzhuang region in central Hebei. Still, there is a large gap between the two, while the cylindrical jars and wide-scale patterns are elements of Hongshan culture. In the late period, elements emerged as folded-belly basins, flat-bottom basins, and high-foot plates, which are elements of Dawenkou culture.

The houses of Xueshan culture phase I are mostly square semi-subterranean. The Jiangjialiang Cemetery is divided into zones for burial, probably a communal family cemetery composed of several families. Most are relatively wide and short pit vertical shaft tombs, popular with wooden coffins and "ripe soil second layer platform," all supine with flexed supine, and many have several burial objects. The refined stone arrowheads and double-holed stone knives among the production tools reflect the influence of Hongshan culture. It probably still mainly relied on dry millet grain and sorghum farming, but the proportion of hunting and gathering increased.

Taikou Type of Yangshao Culture

Around 3000 BCE, the culture east of the Taihang Mountains was relatively low, with few remains found. The area from central and northern Hebei to the Xiliao River probably still belonged to Xueshan culture phase I. In contrast, the area from southern Hebei to northern Henan was represented by Yangshao culture Taikou type, as exemplified by the Taikou site phase I remains in Yongnian District, Hebei Province,[44] and the "Yangshao culture remains" in Mengzhuang Town, Hui County City.[45] Pottery popularly featured vertical basket patterns and added relief decorations, with individual red, brown, or black grid patterns and broken-line patterns on painted pottery. Deep-belly jars with basket weave patterns and floral edges, plain jars, high-neck jars, double-belly basins, and cups are all main vessels developed from the Dasikong type. In contrast, high-foot plates, round-foot *zuns*, and high-neck pots are likely elements of Dawenkou culture.

Houses were often connected rectangular ground style, with timber-framed earthen walls or adobe walls, and living surfaces and wall dado were smeared with white ash, some of which were also coated with red on the white ash surface. In Xiaomintun, Anyang, a pottery production site, clay pits and a well-preserved steamed bun-shaped pottery kiln were found.[46] Production tools included stone shovels, stone axes, clay or shell knives, etc., still likely for millet grain farming.

1.6 The Variation and Expansion of the Culture in the Western Region

Shilingxia Type of Majiayao Culture
As early as the end of the Quanhu type, the painted pottery in the Gansu–Qinghai area in the west had become more complex, starting to diverge from regions such as Guanzhong. After about 3500 BCE, the degree of variation increased even more and finally developed into Majiayao culture Shilingxia type based on the Quanhu type with specific local characteristics.[47] Of course, from a more macro perspective, it still has many common points with the late Banpo type of Yangshao culture, and they undoubtedly still belong to a large cultural system.[48]

The Shilingxia type is mainly distributed in the upper reaches of the Wei River in the southeast of Gansu Province, represented by the Shilingxia remains in Wushan County,[49] including the late Yangshao remains in Dadiwan, Qin'an County,[50] phase IV of Shizhaocun, Tianshui City, phase IV of Xishanping site,[51] and the "Shilingxia type" remains in Fujiamen site.[52] The clay pottery still popularly featured painted pottery, mainly black, with painted pottery patterns such as arc triangle patterns, round cake patterns, wave patterns, and arc line patterns. Among them, variant bird patterns, variant frog patterns, and double continuous swirl patterns are very characteristic, and their patterns are mainly the complication and deformation of the Quanhu type painted pottery. The objects have either flat or pointed bottoms, including flat-mouth straight-neck flat-bottom pots, flat-mouth straight-neck pointed-bottom bottles, convergent-mouth flat-bottom earthen bowls, wide folded-rim deep-belly basins, convergent mouth arc-belly or open-mouth folded-belly plates (basins), deep-belly jars, bulbous-belly painted pottery jars, basin-shaped *zengs*, etc. The number of perforated stone *yue* increased. Fujiamen discovered divination bones with simple inscriptions, with traces of burning, which are the earliest divination bones found in China so far (fig. 4.3).

The Shilingxia type exhibits clusters of settlements, and the differentiation between and within settlements is quite severe. Taking the central settlement Dadiwan site B as an example, it spans an area of 500,000 square meters, and some

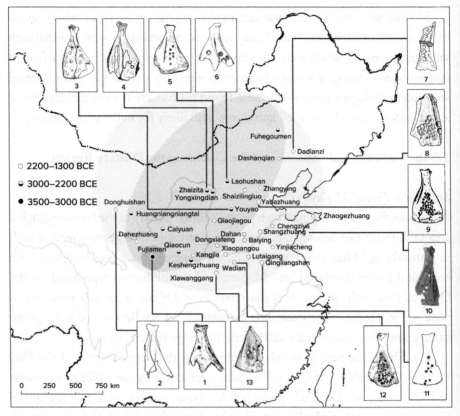

Figure 4.3 Distribution of divination bones before the late Shang Dynasty

1. Fujiamen 92KWF25H1: 25
2. Donghuishan 022
3. Youyao H194: 6
4. Zhaizita H47: 9
5. Yongxingdian H31: 12
6. Laohushan T510④4: 4
7. Dadianzi T5A: 2
8. Dashanqian 96KDIH145②: 1
9. Yabazhuang H106: 2
10. Shangzhuang H75: 63
11. Qingliangshan H18: 5
12. Wadian V T1H17: 3
13. Xiawanggang T15③: 42

of the houses in the settlement are very large and quite special. For instance, the F405 building was built on a flat ground with an area of 270 square meters and an interior area of 150 square meters. It has eaves and evidence of water dispersal, and the interior floor, walls, columns, and range surfaces are all plastered with grass-mixed mud and then topped with a layer of white ash. On its west side, there is a marble scepter head. F411 is a horizontally rectangular ground style building with a gate. There are murals of people and animals painted with black paint behind the range, which the excavators believe belong to the family's "ancestral god" worship, and some scholars believe that it is related to witchcraft rituals.[53] The most notable is F901, which is mainly composed of a main room, a back room, and east and west side rooms. In front of the main room, there are also auxiliary buildings and a wide-open area based on rows of blue stone columns. The main room has an area of 131 square meters, with a ground style range of about 2.5 meters in diameter in the center. In the middle and slightly rear of the room, there are two top beam-columns with nearly one-meter diameters, each with a blue stone column base. The ground is layered with loess, red-burned soil, and artificial lightweight aggregates, and the top is covered with a paste mainly made of Liaojiang stone (a stone shaped like ginger), similar to modern cement in properties. This house covers an area of 290 square meters, and together with the front auxiliary buildings, it reaches 420 square meters (fig. 4.4). It is one of the largest and highest-standard houses

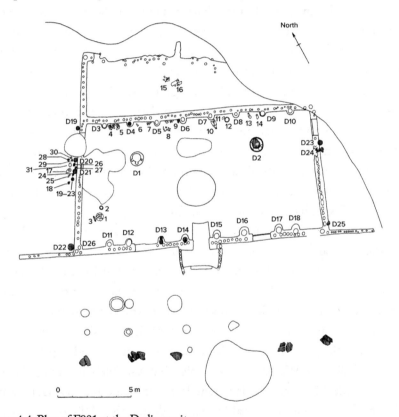

Figure 4.4 Plan of F901 at the Dadiwan site

1. Pottery tri-legged basin
2, 30. Pottery trumpet-shaped vessel
2. Pottery stripe-shaped plate
4, 12, 29, 31. Pottery jar
5. Pottery lid
5. Stone knife
7, 19–28. Pottery converging-mouth earthen bowl
8, 16, 18. Pottery urn
9, 10. Pottery dustpan-shaped vessel
11. Grinding stone
13, 14. Whetstone
15. Pottery vat
17. Grinding plate
D1–D27. Posthole[a]

[a] In archaeology, the term refers to the remnants of pillars found in archaeological sites, left behind due to the construction of buildings and houses. These remnants are often referred to as "postholes."—Trans.

in the late Yangshao in the northwest region. It initially exhibits basic Chinese classical architecture layout features, such as the clear differentiation between the front hall and back rooms, the symmetrical east and west wings, and the clear hierarchy of the left, middle, and right doors. It is considered a hall-style building. The house also unearthed special pottery such as four-foot plates, stripe-shaped plates, open jars, and dustpan-shaped vessels, indicating that special activities had occurred. The discovery of Dadiwan site B shows that there was already inequality within the settlement then, and some wealthy families gradually rose above other families. There were also rank differences between settlements, and central settlements like Dadiwan site B might have had more privileges than surrounding settlements. Notably, five divination bones were found on the ground of the F11 site in Fujiamen, perhaps suggesting that divination activities had been conducted in this room. The site also discovered a sacrificial pit containing buried pig bones.

Burial discoveries are rare, typically rectangular vertical pit tombs, single burials in extended supine, and a few accompanying pottery and decorations. All tombs from phase IV in Shizhaocun are either single or double "secondary burials." In addition to accompanying stone tools, animal teeth, and arranged stones, there are also numerous pottery shards at the bottom of the graves. If these "secondary burials" were intentionally disturbed to form "secondary disturbed burials," it would be the first of its kind in the Gansu–Qinghai region.[54]

The economic form is basically the same as the Quanhu type. In addition to millet grain and sorghum, evidence shows that cultivated rice was also discovered in the remains of this period in Qingyang City, Gansu Province, and Xishanping, Tianshui City.[55] Most of the knives (sickle claws) used as harvesting tools are still made of pottery, but the number of stone knives has slightly increased, indicating an improvement in grain harvesting efficiency. A sheep's lower jawbone was buried with grave M5 in Shizhaocun, and livestock made up 80% of the animals in Fujiamen, Wushan,[56] mainly pigs, but also likely including domestic sheep and cattle. Sheep and cattle require large grasslands for grazing, indicating significant development in animal husbandry during the Shilingxia type period in the Gansu–Qinghai region. Domestic sheep and cattle were first domesticated in Western Asia, and other Western elements likely entered the Gansu–Qinghai region with them.

Majiayao Type of Majiayao Culture

After 3000 BCE, Majiayao culture formed the Majiayao and Zongri types in the Gansu–Qinghai–Ningxia provinces region.

The Majiayao type, with its distribution center in the upper reaches of the Wei River in Gansu Province, is represented by the Majiayao site in Lintao, Gansu.[57] This includes phase V remains in Shizhaocun, Tianshui, Gansu and Xishanping, the "Majiayao type" remains in Fujiamen, and the Linjia remains in Dongxiang.[58] It extends north to southern Ningxia,[59] west to northeastern Qinghai[60] and the eastern part of the Hexi Corridor,[61] and south to the upper reaches of the Bailong River,[62] even reaching the northwestern part of Sichuan. It developed further based on the Shilingxia type[63] and can be divided into four consecutive minor stages: the Xipowa group, the Yanerwan group, the Wangbaobao group, and the Xiaopingzi group.[64]

Most fine clay pottery is decorated with black paint, accounting for about half of all pottery shards, with a few painted in white and red. The painted areas are large, applied inside and out, with complex compositions and smooth lines. There are patterns such as concentric circles, waves, spirals, and nets, as well as more representational designs such as frogs, lizards, tadpoles, and human faces. The main designs are largely circular or elliptical, and pottery decorated with multiple dancing figures has also been found at sites such as Shangsunjiazhai. The artifacts are generally flat bottom, inheriting the tradition of the Shilingxia type. Particularly noteworthy is a bronze arched-back knife, cast from two molds, found inside a Linjia house. This is the earliest bronze artifact in Northwest China and even in China. Copper slag was also found in the gray pit. According to research, this knife may have been smelted from co-existing copper and tin ores, representing a product of metallurgical technology still in its primitive stage.[65] Its shape is similar to a bone-handle stone-blade knife from the Guantaoyuan site in Baoji City, which belongs to the Baijia culture, suggesting that its predecessor may have been such bone-handle stone-blade knives. However, the emergence of bronze technology still cannot exclude the possibility of western cultural influence.

Most houses are square with rounded corners and half-underground, often with a square porch. Shizhaocun also contains some houses in the shape of the Chinese character "吕" (*lü*) with interconnected front and back rooms and stone circle sacrificial sites where pottery shards, pig mandibles, pig skulls, and limb bones have been found. Burials are rare, generally rectangular vertical pit graves, with single, one-time extended supine. Burials are usually accompanied by painted pottery.

The technology for making production tools has obviously improved, and labor efficiency should have increased. The biggest change is that stone knives have become noticeably more common than pottery knives, and beautifully ground rectangular perforated stone knives have increased, indicating significant progress in harvesting efficiency. The Linjia site found new types of stone knives, such as the concaved-backed stone knife and the crescent-shaped stone knife. Many carbonized millets were found in the cellar of the Linjia site, and carbonized millet grain, sorghum, and hemp seeds were also found in pottery,[66] suggesting that agriculture was still dominated by millet grain. At the same time, they were raising pigs, sheep, and cattle.[67] The presence of more refined stone tools and bone-handle stone-blade knives indicates that animal husbandry and hunting and gathering continued to develop.

Zongri Type of Majiayao Culture

The Zongri type is distributed in the eastern part of Qinghai Province, centered on the Gonghe Basin, and is represented by phase I of the Zongri site (M291 type) in Tongde.[68] Pottery can mainly be divided into two categories. The first is fine clay red pottery with exquisite black decorations, whose vessel types, painted pottery designs, and style are the same as the Majiayao type. At the Zongri site, basins decorated with dancing figures and two people carrying objects were also discovered. The second type is coarse sandy brown pottery, with some having rigid purple-red line decorations on the upper part. They feature bird patterns, bent-tipped triangle patterns, and broken-line patterns, all extremely rich in local characteristics. Most potteries have a fake round-foot shape at the bottom, and only three types of vessels are found: high-neck urns (pots), single or double-handle jars, and open earthen bowls (bowls). As Chen Honghai speculated, this type may be a product of the Majiayao type extending to Qinghai and merging with the local non-pottery culture. Notably, its rigid broken-line patterns seem to resemble geometric patterns on cylindrical jar-shaped vessels from the Eurasian steppe (fig. 4.5).

Zongri Cemetery can be divided into graveyards, grave groups, and grave clusters, representing at least four levels of social organization. Most of the tombs are rectangular vertical pit tombs with a two-layer platform, and on the two-layer platform, coffins made of timber or stone slabs were built. Most of the burials are for single individuals, primarily in extended prone. Many of these are secondary disturbed burials, often buried with practical "Majiayao style pottery." There are also individual instances of cremation. The economy is basically the same as the Majiayao type, but the components of animal husbandry and hunting and gathering are greater.

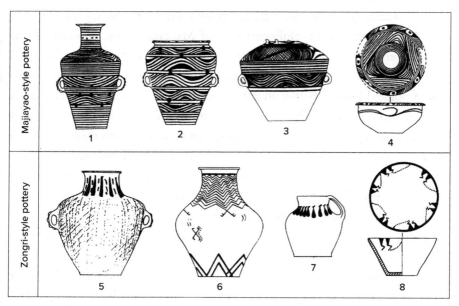

Figure 4.5 Two types of pottery from the Zongri type of Majiayao culture
1. Pot (M295: 1)
2, 3, 5, 6. Urn (M324: 1, M159: 12, M270: 5, M222: 3)
4. Basin (M294: 3)
7. Jar (M69: 3)
8. Earthen bowl (M12: 6)

1.7 The Rise of Neolithic Culture in the Upper Reaches of the Yangtze River

Around 3500 BCE or slightly earlier, remnants of the early stage of phase I of the Shaopengzui site appeared in the northeastern area of the upper reaches of the Yangtze River in Zhong County, Chongqing.[69] Judging only from the discovered degenerate forms of small-mouth pointed-bottom bottles and cord-mark jars, it could still be forcibly categorized as the late Banpo of Yangshao culture. Around 3000 BCE, it developed into remnants of the late phase I and phase II type of the Shaopengzui site, overall inheriting from the early phase I, such as the small-mouth pointed-bottom bottles evolving into small-mouth flat-bottom jars or small-mouth high-neck pots. They still have deep cord-mark jars, flat-bottom earthen bowls with converging mouths, etc., and added relief decorations are becoming increasingly popular, just like in the Guanzhong area. However, the plate mouth, floral-edge-mouth rim, interlaced marked cords, and other local features have significantly strengthened. Therefore, it can be named a separate archaeological culture, namely Shaopengzui culture phase II or Yuxiping culture.[70] Among these, painted pottery round-foot pots, high-handle cups, *zuns*, and vats belong to the Qujialing cultural elements.

Coincidentally, around 3500 BCE, remains similar to the Quanhu type of Yangshao culture and the Shilingxia type of Majiayao culture appeared in the northwestern mountainous region of the upper reaches of the Yangtze River and even in the northern part of the Chengdu Plain. The degenerate form of small-mouth pointed-bottom bottles found in Guiyuanqiao in Shifang is particularly striking. Around 3000 BCE, they evolved into a type of remains represented by Guiyuanqiao H20.[71] This type of remains features coarse marked cords and added relief decorations and even the mouths and bottoms of the vessels are cord-mark. Vessel types include cord-mark, floral-rim deep-belly jars, earthen bowls, basins, etc., and the overall appearance resembles phase II of the Shaopengzui culture.

As for the remains of the Maiping type in the Hanyuan area of Sichuan Province along the Dadu River,[72] the main vessel types are also deep-belly jars, small-mouth jars, and converging-mouth flat-bottom earthen bowls and marked cords and added relief decorations are popular. The overall appearance is similar to the early stage remains of Guiyuanqiao. The main source is still Majiayao culture, but its grid patterns, bead patterns, fine-tooth comb patterns with clustered dot patterns, and other geometric patterns are more distinctive. The Maiping site also discovered houses with timber-framed earthen walls and clay floors.

Under the southward expansion and influence of the Yangshao cultural system (including Majiayao culture), the upper reaches of the Yangtze River finally developed a Neolithic culture with more local characteristics.

The houses of phase II of the Shaopengzui culture are plastered with white lime, and tools such as stone axes, stone adzes, stone chisels, shell knives, and pottery spinning wheels were found. However, more are chipping stone tools such as chopping and scraping tools, suggesting extensive agriculture, and livestock such as pigs and dogs were also raised, with a considerable proportion of fishing, hunting, and gathering. The discovery of shell knives reflects the characteristics of the Yangtze River Basin. Moreover, the Three Gorges area is known for its stone tool industry, with many stone tool processing sites.

1.8 Karuo Culture of the Xizang Plateau

The earliest Neolithic culture on the Xizang Plateau is represented by the Karuo site in Chamdo County in the Xizang Autonomous Region, known as Karuo culture,[73] which dates to around 3000 BCE at the earliest. The main types of vessels in its early stage, such as high-neck jars and open-mouth basins, are relatively close in form to the early Zongri-style pottery of Majiayao culture Zongri type, such as the common use of the false-round foot, a small amount of black painting, and commonly seen incised folded line patterns, grid patterns, and added relief decorations that are similar to the latter's painted pottery designs. Other items, such as hole knives (some with concave backs), long-bodied adzes, chisels, and other ground stone tools, as well as stone *huangs*, stone beads, perforated shells, etc., are also similar. The aforementioned cultural characteristics are also associated with the Majiayao type of Majiayao culture in northwestern Sichuan. Karuo culture could be the result of the westward push of Majiayao culture in eastern Qinghai and northwestern Sichuan and its integration with the local pottery-free culture. It is worth noting that Karuo culture or similar remains may already be distributed to southeastern Xizang, centered on Lhasa and even to Sikkim.

In early Karuo culture, semi-subterranean or surface-level houses were found, mostly rectangular or square, with wooden columns supporting the roof. The semi-subterranean houses have a platform outside, and the inner side of the wall is smeared with grass and mud mixed and covered with wooden boards. In addition to the ground stone tools such as axes, adzes, chisels, and knives common in Majiayao culture, many pebble stone tools made by chipping were found, some of which have obvious use marks on the edges of the chipped spades, hoes, and knives, indicating that they are not semi-finished products. There are also many microliths, such as stone flakes, stone cores, scrapers, and perforated weights. Bone awls, bone needles, sawtooth bone flakes, pottery spinning wheels, and others are similar to those in Majiayao culture. Remains of domestic pigs, millet grain, and sorghum crops have been found in this culture, indicating the presence of dry farming. However, hunting and gathering likely held a more critical position.

2. Middle and Lower Reaches of the Yangtze River and Lower Reaches of the Yellow River

The middle and lower reaches of the Yangtze River and lower reaches of the Yellow River belong to the *ding*–high-foot plate–pot–cup cultural system.

2.1 The Strength and Expansion of Dawenkou Culture in Haidai Region

After around 3500 BCE, Dawenkou culture entered its middle period, represented by early Dawenkou burial site in Tai'an City, Shandong Province,[74] excavated in 1959, and including early Dawenkou culture remains in early Jianxin, Zaozhuang,[75] Yanzhou Liulijing,[76] Pizhou Liangwangcheng,[77] and others. Its main pottery includes *dings*, high-foot plates, back pots, high-handle cups, and deep-belly jars, which continue the tradition from its early stage. New items, such as chisel-shaped-foot *yans*, round-foot *zuns*, and vessels with spouts, such as *guis*, flat-bottom or tri-legged *hes*, and *yis* became popular. Red pottery decreased, while gray pottery increased, and wheel-made pottery appeared. A few painted pottery earthen bowls of Dawenkou culture with broken-line patterns, grid patterns, and overlapping-scale patterns may be related to influences from Hongshan culture or Xueshan culture phase I. The stone *bis*[78] and double-cylindrical-penetrating handles pot are seen in Weifang, Pingyin,[79] and other places are likely elements of Liangzhu culture. The graves in the north area of Huating in Xinyi City have many Liangzhu cultural elements, including jade artifacts. Due to interactions with the Qinwangzhai type, Xiwang type, and others of Yangshao culture, the southwestern Shandong area often sees deep-belly pots decorated with red band grid patterns and hanging beard patterns, or they may be stamped with marked cords and added relief decorations. Painted pottery high-neck jars, cord-mark double-handle earthen bowls, and other types also appear.

Around 3000 BCE, Dawenkou culture entered its late period, represented by mid-to-late finds at the Dawenkou burial site excavated in 1959, and including Dawenkou culture remains in mid-to-late Zaozhuang Jianxin, Qufu Xixiahou M26,[80] Ju County Lingyanghe,[81] and Mengcheng Yuchisi in Anhui Province.[82] Notably, many Dawenkou culture sites suddenly emerged during this period in the southeastern Shandong region. Pottery was mainly black-gray, and wheel-throwing technology became increasingly mature, with black thin-wall high-handle pottery cups being the most representative. The shapes of the vessels mostly developed in a tall and slender direction, with bag-foot *guis** being the most common. Double-belly high-foot plates might have evolved from the folded-rim high-foot plates of the middle period, and the earliest cojoined *yans* with chiseled-shaped feet also appeared at sites such as the Yuchisi—considered to be the earliest of its kind in China. Artifacts such as *bis* with protruding teeth, deer antler hook-shaped tools, and double-holed clam knives also appeared. While the impact on other regions was significant, elements from surrounding cultures also entered, such as the frequent appearance of basket weave and added relief decorations in the western regions, which might be related to influences from the Miaodigou phase II type and others. The fish fin-shaped *ding* feet and high-foot plates seen in phase I of the Yangjiaquan in Qixia City belong to the Liangzhu cultural elements.

The central settlements of over 100,000 square meters include Wulian Dantu in Shandong Province, Guzhen Gaixia in Anhui Province, Nancheng Zicheng

---

* A type of ancient Chinese wine or water vessel. It has a trumpet-shaped mouth with a folded rim, and the spout is nearly tubular with both sides curling inwards. The three spindle-shaped bag feet are directly connected to the neck, and a rope-shaped handle is attached to the upper part of the rear bag foot.—Trans.

THE ARCHAIC STATE STAGE OF EARLY CHINA   155

site, and Yuchisi moated settlements. The Yuchisi moated settlement includes more than ten rows and over 70 houses (figs. 4.6 and 4.7). The houses were mainly surface type with timber-framed earthen walls. There were group houses with 2 to 6 rooms, with doors uniformly located on one side of the group house, probably representing large families or clan organizations. Burials were all vertical pit graves, some with two-layer platforms or wooden burial equipment all were extended supine. The burial items and daily necessities differed, the phenomenon

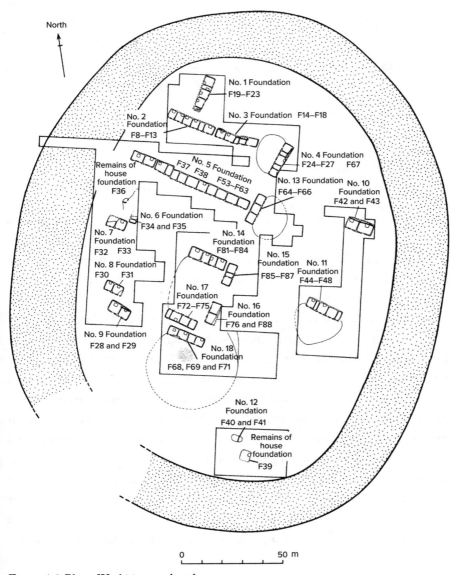

Figure 4.6 Plan of Yuchisi moated settlement

Figure 4.7 Plan and reconstruction of building No. 2 at Yuchisi (F8–F13)
Top: Plan of the foundation   Bottom: Reconstruction of the row of rooms[a]

[a] *Source:* Institute of Archaeology, Chinese Academy of Social Sciences, *Excavation and Research of Neolithic Settlement Remains at Mengcheng Weichisi, Northern Anhui* (Beijing: Science Press, 2001), figures 57–58.

of grave goods mimicking daily-use items was evident, and burial items were generally plain and small. The Dawenkou burial site excavated in 1959 is one of the highest-level burial sites of Dawenkou culture, with significant wealth and social status differentiation among different grave areas. For example, large tombs not only have many exquisite burial objects such as high-handle cups but also often contain stone or jade *yues* that might symbolize military power.[83] Cemetery M10, for instance, has an area of over 13 square meters at its entrance, with more than 180 burial items, including bone tubes, ivory tubes, ivory combs, crocodile scale plates (also known as alligator drums),* high-handle cups, and the only jade *yue* in the cemetery. The tomb owner might have been the community leader represented by the cemetery or even a wider group of people (fig. 4.8). A large number of high-handle cups were buried in tombs at sites such as Lingyang River in southeast Shandong, and the pottery *zuns* have clan emblem-like symbols, which is different from the areas near Dawenkou, indicating that Dawenkou culture likely had more than one center. The large tomb 79M17 at Lingyang River has an entrance area

---

* A kind of ancient drum made with hides of Chinese alligators.—Trans.

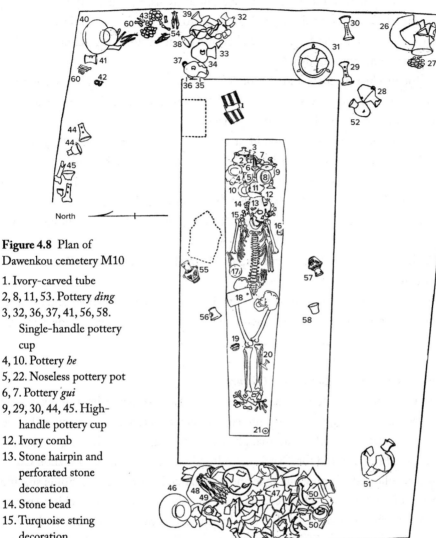

Figure 4.8 Plan of Dawenkou cemetery M10

1. Ivory-carved tube
2, 8, 11, 53. Pottery *ding*
3, 32, 36, 37, 41, 56, 58. Single-handle pottery cup
4, 10. Pottery *he*
5, 22. Noseless pottery pot
6, 7. Pottery *gui*
9, 29, 30, 44, 45. High-handle pottery cup
12. Ivory comb
13. Stone hairpin and perforated stone decoration
14. Stone bead
15. Turquoise string decoration
16. Stone axe
17. Jade bracelet
18. Jade spatula
19. Bone-carved tube (decorating the handle end of the *yue*)
20, 21. Pottery lid
23, 25. Stone hairpin
24. Ivory tube
26, 40, 46, 51. Wide-shoulder pottery pot
27, 43. Crocodile scale board
28, 33–35, 52. Back pottery pot
31, 48. Pottery jar
38, 39, 47. Thin-handle pottery high-foot plate
42. Jade finger ring
49, 54. Pig skull
50. Pottery bottle
55, 57. Back pottery pot
59. Ivory piece
60. Pig bone
61. Double-nosed pottery pot

(Some items are not shown in the figure as they were beneath other items or bodies.)

of 15 square meters and more than 192 burial items, including 33 flakes of pig mandibles. Dawenkou culture still had the custom of burying water deer teeth and tortoise shells, and the Sanlihe burial even had the custom of placing jade wares in mouths and burying fish.[84]

The production tools and economic forms of the middle and late Dawenkou culture are basically the same as before. The appearance of double-holed stone knives and stone sickles shows significant progress in harvesting technology. Grains of millet grain were found at the sites in Zaozhuang Jianxin, Jiaozhou Sanlihe, Guangrao Fujia, and Laiyang Yujiadian. At the Yuchisi site, the ratio of millet grain to rice is roughly equal. Pig farming was developed, and more than 160 pig mandibles were found in 25 graves at the Lingyang River Cemetery. However, fishing for shellfish should also have held an important position in coastal areas.

2.2 The Extreme Prosperity and Expansion of the Lower Yangtze River Culture

The culture of the lower Yangtze River region is extremely prosperous and expands outwards, exerting a strong influence on the surrounding areas, especially the South and Southeast coastal areas.

Songze Culture and Xuejiagang Culture

Around 3500 BCE, the culture of the lower Yangtze River became extremely prosperous. The Songze culture entered a developed late stage, represented by the Songze phase III in Qingpu, Shanghai, the late stage of Nanhebang in Jiaxing, Zhejiang Province, and the "Neolithic cultural remains" in Pishan, Huzhou City.[85] Pottery followed the previous style and popularized wheel making. Some specific forms of pottery had changed, such as the shovel-shaped and chisel-shaped *ding* feet, the emergence of fish fin-shaped feet, converging-mouth folded-rim bamboo joint-handle high-foot plates, false-belly round-foot plates, false-belly cups, tower-shaped pots with pipe-shaped flows, and so on are very representative of the era. Some high-foot plate spouts had perforated noses. The Beiyinyangying culture developed into Xuejiagang culture, represented by the main remains of Xuejiagang in Qianshan, Anhui Province,[86] and Lingjiatan in Hanshan.[87] It even reached eastern Hubei and northern Jiangxi, leaving behind late Saidun in Huangmei, Hubei Province, Gushan site in Wuexun,[88] and Zhengjiaao in Jing'an, Jiangxi Province.[89] The newly emerged single-handle solid-foot *gui*, goblet-shaped cup, high-handle cup, and other pottery and weaving pattern should have been influenced by the Songze culture and Dawenkou culture. The newly emerged round-foot pot, round-foot jar, hollow clay ball, curved-belly cup, *gui* (an ancient Chinese container or a ritual vessel here), and others in the Hubei–Anhui border area should have been elements of Daxi culture. The source of the imprinted round-foot pot should have been in the southeastern coastal region. Xuejiagang culture has newly appeared folded-belly *dings*, the feet of which are often shovel-shaped, chisel-shaped, duckbill-shaped, or upside-down trapezoid-shape, and often have complex engraved and stamped patterns on the feet. The duckbill-shaped feet of the *zikou ding* in the Northern Jiangxi region are exaggerated. Its multi-holed stone knives and stone *yues* are very distinctive, with 3 to 13 holes in the multi-holed stone knives, mostly odd numbers, and there are also double-holed ones. Some stone *yues* and stone knives had vermilion-painted peduncle-like decorations. Both cultures had jade artifacts, such as *yues*, jade *jues*, jade *huangs*, bracelets, *bis*, spoons, etc., as well as jade figures, jade dragons, jade tortoises, jade plaques, jade eagles, etc., among which a small number of double (tri-) connected *bis*, square *bis* with rounded corners, hoop-shaped ornaments, Y-shaped utensils, jade dragons, jade people, and other jade articles should be related to the southward influence of Hongshan culture.[90]

These cultures demonstrate examples of buildings with timber-framed earthen walls in both ground and semi-underground styles. Cemeteries are distributed into areas and groups. The graves continue to be rectangular vertical pit graves, some of which have coffin-like burial utensils, and the tomb owners are basically single individuals buried in extended supine, often with several burial objects. In some larger graves, each was accompanied by a stone *yue*, mainly found in male graves, indicating that the stone *yue* was indeed a weapon and may symbolize military power. Other adzes, chisels, multi-holed knives, and arrowheads were more prevalent in male graves. Decorative items such as jade *jue* and jade *huang* were more prevalent in female graves, while both genders wore bracelets. There are still burial customs of accompanying pig mandibles and dog bones. Graves M197 and M193 in the Saidun site each accompanied 50 and 34 pairs of pig mandibles, respectively. Wealth inequality had become very severe. The 07M23 burial site in Lingjiatan, Hanshan, Anhui Province, seems to have had a coffin-like burial, with 330 burial objects, most of which are jade and stone artifacts like *yues*, rings, bracelets, and jade *huangs*, jade *jues*, *bis*, and so on filling layers inside and outside the grave chamber, demonstrating stunning opulence.[91]

The tools made of stone are mainly adzes (including segmental adzes), followed by axes, chisels, sickles, knives, plow-shaped tools, etc., all finely ground, and cutting and tube-drilling technologies are prevalent. The prevalence of adzes is probably related to the advancement of its woodworking handicraft industry. There are various types of knives, among which the common single-hole stone knives might have a harvesting function, the stone knives with a convex button on the back (some of which have perforations at the button part, previously known as "weeders"), and multi-holed stone knives might have various possibilities like cutting, scraping, etc. The exquisite stone sickle is a highly efficient harvesting tool, and the stone plow-shaped tool is likely a highly efficient digging tool,[92] showing that the agricultural development of the late Songze culture has made a qualitative leap. The existence of many net pendants and stone arrowheads indicates that the fishing and hunting economy still occupied an important position.

Liangzhu Culture
Around 3300 BCE, the area around Tai Lake developed from Songze culture into Liangzhu culture, represented by Fanshan in Yuhang, Zhejiang Province,[93] Yaoshan graves,[94] and Fuquanshan Liangzhu culture graves in Qingpu, Shanghai.[95] Its main types of artifacts continued the tradition of the Songze culture, with developed wheel making, popular fish fin-shaped or T-shaped-foot *ding*, shallow folded-belly high-foot plate, wide-handle cup with spouts, round-foot plate, round-foot pot (*zun*), round-foot jar, *ding*-style *yan*, *gui*, and *he*, flat-bottom *yi* developed into round-foot or tri-legged *yi*, and new double-nosed pot, pot with cylindrical-penetrating handles, filters with trumpet-shaped flows, etc. Some pottery is shiny black, and some are engraved with intricate and delicate snake, bird, and cloud patterns and painted, extremely exquisite. Foreign influences are rare, with several back pots from Dawenkou culture in Jiangbei and a small number of *zikou dings* and marked-cord patterns from Fanchengdui culture in the south of the lower reaches of the Yangtze River. There are engraved character-like symbols on pottery from many places, such as Liangzhu in Yuhang, Zhuangqiaofen in Pinghu, Chenghu in Wu County, Maqiao in Shanghai, and Tinglin.

Jade and stone artifacts are inherited from the traditions of the Songze culture and Xuejiagang cultures. The primary jade artifacts, bracelets, *bis*, jade *huangs*, and jade *jues*, as well as the primary stone artifacts like axe, *yue*, adze, chisel, knife, etc., are all so. New items include jade *congs*, crown-shaped ornaments, semi-circular ornaments, trident-shaped tools, cone-shaped tools, column-shaped tools, jade *cong*-shaped tubes, hooks, tablet ornaments, spoons, etc., and there are also bird, turtle, fish, and other animal carvings. The jade artifacts are diverse in shape and intricately carved, unparalleled in ancient and modern times. God-human-animal-face patterns, bird patterns, accompanied by cloud-thunder patterns, etc., are often seen on jade *congs* and other jade artifacts, some of which belong to micro-carvings, as fine as a hair strand, astonishing. There were also exquisitely carved ivories, inlaid jade lacquerware, lacquer *gus*, lacquer plates, lacquer high-foot plates, and silk.

Liangzhu culture boasts a Liangzhu ancient city, spanning an area of more than 2.9 million square meters.[96] The city center, which is artificially built, consists of the Mojiaoshan Palace[97] and the storage area, both of which occupy an area of about 300,000 square meters and feature elaborate architecture (fig. 4.9). To the northwest of the city lies Fanshan, a noble Cemetery of Liangzhu culture,[98] where the highest-ranked M12 grave houses as many as 647 flakes of jade artifacts. Large jade *congs* (fig. 4.10), jade *yues* (fig. 4.11), painted lacquer plates, and cups inlaid with jade flakes were found in this grave, showcasing complete god-human-animal-face patterns, "indicating that the tomb owner was a leader who held military and religious authority."[99] Around 130 altar sites, cemeteries, settlements, and workshops are scattered in an area of approximately 50 square kilometers surrounding Liangzhu ancient city, and they can be divided into at least three levels.[100] The highest-ranked altars are the Yaoshan altar to the northeast of the city and the Huiguanshan altar to the west.[101] Next to the Fanshan Cemetery is the Yaoshan Cemetery, where complete god-human-animal-face patterns are also found on unearthed jade artifacts, followed by the Huiguanshan Cemetery, where complete patterns are not found. However, there are still jade ritual artifacts like jade *cong*, *yue*, and *bi*. In contrast, many smaller graves, with scarce or no jade artifacts, are also found, with about 20 to 30 burials per cemetery, corresponding to familial organizations. Moreover, there is a grand water control and flood protection system composed of multiple dams to the west and north of Liangzhu ancient city,[102] and to the south lies the Bianjiashan pier site.[103] Overall, the Mojiaoshan palace area is the core of Liangzhu ancient city, which likely served as the political, military, and religious center of the Liangzhu settlements. Liangzhu ancient city and its settlements were vast, strictly arranged, complexly structured, distinctly hierarchized, functionally explicit, and quite highly regulated, with complete ritualistic symbols not seen in other regions. The construction of the enormous architectural complex in Mojiaoshan required mobilizing resources far beyond a single settlement group. In the Fanshan, Yaoshan, and other cemeteries buried numerous exquisite jade artifacts were buried, which may have been produced within a strict organization, often monopolized by the noble class, with a high degree of specialization. Such a high degree of social organization required

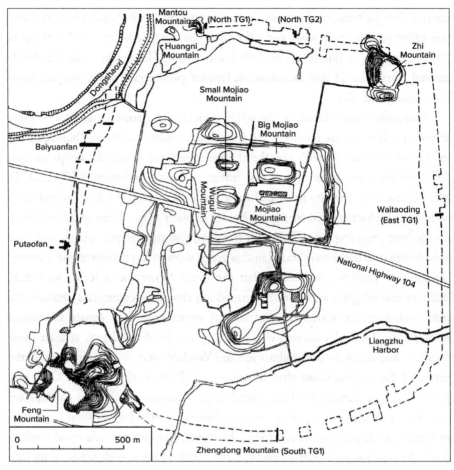

Figure 4.9 Plan of Liangzhu ancient city

Figure 4.10 Large jade *cong* from tomb M12 in Liangzhu Fanshan cemetery (M12: 98)

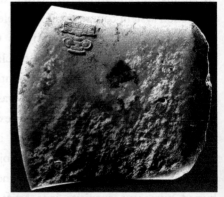

Figure 4.11 Large jade *yue* from tomb M12 in Liangzhu Fanshan cemetery (M12: 100)

both the inspiration of a strong religious atmosphere and the enforcement of armed personnel. Fanshan, Yaoshan, and Huiguanshan cemeteries all had buried *yues* symbolizing military power, and jade *congs* or *bis* symbolizing divine power. The Yaoshan and Huiguanshan cemeteries were even built on top of former altars, suggesting that these nobles were likely both headed shamans who could communicate with deities and generals commanding "armies,"[104] fitting the profile of the highest rulers of the Liangzhu settlements. The widespread discoveries of god-human-animal-face patterns, bird patterns, and dragon-shaped patterns may suggest the emergence of a unified power[105] and a highly consistent religious belief system throughout the Liangzhu cultural area, indicating a control network over the entire society.[106] As the largest and highest-ranked of all, the Liangzhu settlements, especially with complete god-human-animal-face patterns found only at Fanshan and Yaoshan, and the engraved jade artifacts, likely distributed from Liangzhu settlements outward during its peak,[107] were possibly the political core of the entire Liangzhu culture,[108] making it an early civilization. However, Liangzhu culture rarely absorbed elements from other cultures, showing a conservative and closed nature, which may have sowed the seeds of its eventual decline.

Houses were mostly ground style and stilt buildings, with some comprising multiple rooms with long corridors and beginning to use rammed earth for walls. There were square wooden wells. Wood structures often used mortise and tenon joints and popularized square wooden columns. The form and customs of burials were similar to the Songze culture, with larger graves having both coffins and outer coffins, some of which were painted with red patterns or inlaid with jade flakes inside and out. Jade *bis* and *yues* were placed on either side of or over the body, and some tomb occupants had jade wares in their mouths. The Fuquanshan Cemetery in Qingpu, Shanghai, had sacrificial pits and piles before and after the graves or on the graves, and some graves had human sacrifices inside or next to them.

The stone tools of Liangzhu culture were similar to the late Songze culture, with stone plow-shaped implements being common. The stone knives (weeders) with convex knobs on their backs, the ends of which were raised in a V shape, and new double-holed stone knives, slanted-handle stone knives, and segmental stone chisels were found. Large quantities of carbonized rice remain from Liangzhu culture period were discovered at the Shuitianfan site in Hangzhou, the Qianshanyang site in Huzhou, and the Chenghu site in Wu County. Most of the rice was japonica rice, with a small amount of indica rice, indicating the presence of a developed rice-based agricultural economy. They raised domestic animals such as pigs and dogs, and it is unclear whether water buffalos were domesticated.

Fanchengdui Culture and Shixia Culture

Around 3000 BCE, Fanchengdui culture, represented by lower Zhangshu Fanchengdui[109] and lower Zhuweicheng,[110] the phase III of Xinyu Shinianshan,[111] and the upper Jing'an Laohudun,[112] appeared in the northern and western regions of Jiangxi. This was also called the Zhuweicheng culture. At roughly the same time, Shixia culture, represented by the phase II of Qujiang Shixia, appeared in the northwest part of Guangdong from Shaoguan to Fengkai.[113]

Fanchengdui culture developed from Xuejiagang culture, which had certain local characteristics. Main pottery forms, such as *ding*, high-foot plate, pot, jar, *gui* (ancient Chinese containers or ritual vessels here), and cup, all inherited the line of Xuejiagang culture, only with some morphological changes. For instance, the belly of the *zikou* cauldron-shaped *ding* became shallow, turning it into a plate-shaped *ding*, and the *zikou* high-foot plate had wider ridges. High-handle pots and high-handle *gu*-shaped cups appeared, and *ding* feet varied in styles, including tile-shaped feet, duck-billed feet, conical feet, flat column feet, and unusual tubular feet, all complex in decoration. Besides, the jade *cong*, T-shaped feet, or fin-shaped feet *ding* should be influenced by Liangzhu culture. The double-belly high-foot plates, basket patterns, and square patterns were related to the influence of Qujialing culture. At the same time, the marked cords reflected exchanges with Tanshishan culture. Shixia culture, with its *zikou* shallow plate-shaped tile-foot *ding*, *zikou* high-foot plate, round-foot pot, round-foot jar, *gui*, and other main pottery, were similar to Fanchengdui culture. Its formation was likely related to the southward expansion of Fanchengdui culture. Still, local characteristics were also apparent, such as cauldron-shaped *dings*, cauldrons, and tri-legged plates. The base of the *ding* feet is noticeably wider than the tip, and small perforations are often seen on the *ding* feet and handles of vessels like high-foot plates.[114] Other influences included more pots and cord-mark pottery elements from the South China cultures.

Round ground style houses were found at the Shinianshan site, with larger ones having two rings of column holes. Both cultures mainly featured rectangular vertical pit graves, and many showed signs of scorching on the grave walls. There were occasional signs of carbonized wooden coffins, and human bones were often secondarily buried and burned, indicating the existence of cremation customs in these cultures. Shixia culture burials had two sets of grave goods, one set being broken pottery moved from the original grave along with the bones, and the other set being pottery placed in the grave at the time of reburial. Large tombs had hundreds of grave goods, revealing a significant wealth disparity.

The main production tools included axes, adzes (including segmental adzes), chisels, hoes, double-holed stone knives, pottery pads, pottery files, spinning wheels, etc. Shixia culture's long-bodied bow-backed double-edge stone *jue* (an ancient Chinese farming tool for digging in the earth) was distinctive. There were also many net pendants, arrowheads, distinctive perforated spinning wheel-shaped stone tools, shuttle-shaped stone tools (meteors*), etc. Both cultures discovered numerous carbonized rice grains, husks, stems, cultivated indica, and japonica rice, suggesting that rice farming played an important role in their economy.

Niubishan Culture and Tanshishan Culture

Around 3000 BCE or earlier, cultural remains represented by the lower Niubishan in Pucheng County, Fujian Province, appeared in the northwest of Fujian Province, the southwest of Zhejiang Province, and the southeast of Jiangxi Province,[115] which could be called Niubishan culture.[116] Their plain round-bottom cauldrons and jars, round-bottom pots, round-foot jars, and conical-foot cauldron-shaped *dings* were quite characteristic. However, a large number of high-foot plates and round-foot pots, as well as cylindrical-penetrating handles, were very similar to those of the Fanchengdui culture. A small number of upside-down trapezoid-shaped plates-shaped *dings* were more similar to the same category of instruments in Xuejiagang culture. This culture was assumed to result from the southward movement of Fanchengdui culture combined with the local indigenous culture. A bit later, Tanshishan culture arose along the southeast coast of Fujian, represented by the early phase II of Tanshishan in Minhou[117] and the lower phase I of Zhuangbianshan.[118] The main pottery included round-bottom cauldrons, round-bottom jars, round-foot pots, high-foot plates, round-foot plates, round-foot cups, *guis*, etc. The difference from Niubishan culture mainly lay in the fact that the pots and jars were generally decorated with marked cords, and there were no *dings* or cylindrical-penetrating handles features. Tanshishan culture mainly developed based on the local culture. Still, the popularity of high-foot and round-foot plates should also be related to the influence of the lower reaches of the Yangtze River.

Elliptical semi-subterranean house sites were found in Tanshishan culture. Both cultures featured rectangular vertical pit graves, often filled with clam shells, and the main burial position was extended supine. Grave goods included pottery, stone tools, and jade *jues*, with no obvious wealth disparity. The Niubishan culture

---

* A type of flexible weapon made by attaching a metal hammer head to one or both ends of a long rope, composed of three parts: the hammer head, the soft rope, and the handle. The hammer heads vary, with round, gourd-shaped, and shuttle-shaped forms, none of which have points or sharp edges.—Trans.

was a hill and basin site. The main production tools were stone axes, adzes, chisels, arrowheads, etc., perhaps indicating the existence of rice farming. The Tanshishan culture was mainly a shell mound site, with stone adzes, stone chisels, shell spades, stone arrowheads, bone arrowheads, pottery net pendants, pottery spinning wheels, pottery beaters, etc. The main economic mode was fishing, hunting, and gathering, but they also raised pigs and dogs as livestock.

2.3 Daxi Culture and Qujialing Culture in the Middle Reaches of the Yangtze River

Daxi Culture

Around 3500 BCE, the most significant change in the middle reaches of the Yangtze River was the extreme expansion of the late Youziling type of Daxi culture. Mainly distributed in the Jianghan Plain, the late Youziling type is represented by phase II of Youziling, "phase III of the Qujialing remains,"[119] and phase III of the Tanjialing remains. The pottery was mainly black, popularly wheel-made, and regularly shaped. Most vessels were just a continuation of the early Youziling type, with an increase in the high-handle high-foot plates, low round-foot jars, and low round-foot urns. In the later stage, new items appeared, such as high-neck jars, round-foot basin-shaped *zengs*, round-foot bowls, painted pottery round-foot high-neck pots, painted pottery basins, tower-shaped knob lids, etc. High-foot plates and basins changed from having converging mouths to open ones.

The late Youziling type was strong and powerfully expanded and significantly impacted surrounding areas. It greatly influenced the Liyang Plain to the south, causing a major shift in local cultural development. As a result, remains similar to the phase IV of Daxi culture were found at Chengtoushan in Li County.[120] A large number of low-foot *dings*, inward-folded-rim bamboo joint-handle high-foot plates, low round-foot *guis*, low round-foot basin-shaped *zengs*, slender high-neck pots, curved-belly cups, cylindrical cups, and small-mouth bottles appeared. There were also more small-mouth bottles and pots that were local features. It influenced the Yuan River Basin in the southwest from a great distance, leading to the appearance of phases I and II type remains at Gaokanlong in Huaihua,[121] with very few *dings* that were local features. It influenced the Xiajiang area to the west, with the emergence of the "Neolithic III period" at Zhongbaodao in Yichang and H117-type remains at Nanmuyuan in Badong. However, the small-mouth pointed-bottom bottles and cord-mark jars were elements of the late Banpo type of Yangshao culture. It expanded to the north to northern Hubei Province, leading to the appearance of phase III of the Diaolongbei site in Zaoyang, Hubei Province, and phase I type remains at the Yejiamiao site in Xiaogan City.[122] There was pottery with interlaced patterns, petal round-dot patterns, checkerboard patterns, and lattice patterns, round-foot jar-shaped *dings*, round-foot basin-shaped mortar-and-pestle earthen bowls with spouts. Round-bottom or pointed-bottom pottery vats had their unique features. There were many flat-bottom earthen bowls, deep-belly jars, low round-foot jars, low round-foot urns, and many horizontal basket patterns. Individual folded-shoulder urns and trumpet-shaped small-mouth pointed-bottom bottles should be elements of the Qinwangzhai type of Yangshao culture and the late Banpo type. It expanded to the east to the area of Ezhou–Huanggang, represented by M2 at Luoshishan in Huanggang (excavated in 1985), with multi-holed stone knives with cinnabar and converging-mouth folded-rim high-foot plates that belong to elements of Xuejiagang culture. In addition, the late Youziling type often saw perforated stone *yue*, jade *huang*, jade *jue*, jade bracelet, etc., which should be related to the influence of Xuejiagang culture.

Rectangular ground buildings were found at sites such as the Diaolongbei site, with wooden skeletons and mud walls, and the doors were of a horizontal sliding type. They are mostly 2 to 7 connected buildings, and some are single rooms. Connected buildings generally have separate ranges and doorways, and some adjacent rooms are connected by doorways to form suites, which should have been gradually added with the population increase. Burials are rectangular vertical pit tombs, some of which have two-tiered platforms and wooden burial objects. The flexed burial basically gave way to extended supine, and there were also secondary burials. In the northern Hubei area, it was popular to bury pig mandibles with the dead, with as many as 72 pairs in Diaolongbei M16, but there were no other grave goods. There were also burial customs of the tomb owner having a stone in his mouth and burial of fish bones, turtles, and terrapins. There was a rather obvious differentiation of wealth, such as Qujialing M2, accompanied by over 70 flakes of pottery, mostly small-sized grave goods. Yicheng Gujiapo M27 was accompanied by four jade and stone *yues*, bone arrowheads, pottery *guis* (an ancient Chinese container or a ritual vessel here), and about 30 pig mandibles, and the tomb owner might have been a military leader. In the Gujiapo Cemetery, the proportion of jade and stone *yues* to the total number of jade and stone artifacts was 82%, many bone arrowheads were buried, and secondary burials were common, reflecting a strong military atmosphere.[123]

Stone tools include axes, adzes, chisels, shovels, sickles, etc., with axes still being the most common and shoulder stone adzes being a characteristic feature. Carbonized rice grains, rice straws, rice husks, and other rice remains were commonly found. Dozens of centimeters thick layers of rice husk ash were found at the Guihuashu site in Songzi. Traces of rice fields were also found at the Chengtoushan site, indicating that rice agriculture had made considerable progress. They were mainly identified as japonica rice. Both millet grain and rice remains were found at the Diaolongbei site, indicating that it was a mixed area of dryland and paddy farming. The appearance of stone sickles, a harvesting tool in the northern Hubei area, indicates a significant change in how crops were harvested. The popularity of burials with pig mandibles reflects that pig farming was quite developed. Stone arrowheads, bone arrowheads, bone spears, stone balls, stone net pendants, etc., reflect that fishing and hunting still had a certain economic status. The popularity of pottery spinning wheels reflects the development of textile handicrafts. The Xinjiang area was still the main stone tool production center in the middle reaches of the Yangtze River.

Qujialing Culture

Around 3000 BCE, Daxi culture in the Jianghan Plain, northwest Hubei, and southwest Henan first transformed into Qujialing culture. Qujialing culture in the Jianghan Plain was represented by the late Jingshan Qujialing,[124] phase IV of Tianmen Tanjialing, and the "Qujialing cultural remains" in Dengjiawan and Xiaojiawuji.[125] The Qujialing cultural remains in northwest Hubei and southwest Henan were represented by the Qujialing cultural remains in Qinglongquan, Yun County, Hubei Province,[126] and the "Qujialing culture phase I" remains in Xiawanggang, Xichuan, Henan Province. It then expanded to surrounding areas, with its southern and southwestern influence forming the Qujialing cultural remains represented by sites, such as Li County Chengtoushan, Anxiang Huachenggang,[127] and Huaihua Gaokanlou phase III in the Liyang Plain and the Yuan River Basin. The westward influence formed the "Neolithic IV" and "Neolithic V" types remains in the Xiangjiang region of Yichang's Zhongbaodao. It expanded northeastward to the southeastern Henan region, forming Lishangwan Luoshan phase I.[128] It expanded eastward to eastern Hubei Province, forming the Huanggang Luosishan 90HLM1 type remains.

Qujialing culture mainly featured gray pottery. Painted pottery was often decorated in black, and in addition to the common grid pattern and square dot pattern of the Youziling type, a new checkerboard pattern, *Taiji* pattern, and dyed-style colorful pottery emerged. Among the pottery, short-legged *dings*, high-neck jars, flared-foot jars, vats, round-foot basin-shaped *zengs*, round-foot basins, round-foot bowls, painted pottery round-foot high-neck pots, painted slanted-belly pottery cups, tower-shaped knob lids, painted hollow pottery balls, etc., all followed the late Youziling type. A newly emerged set of characteristic double-belly *dings*, double-belly high-foot plates, double-belly round-foot bowls, and other double-belly vessels, while certainly seen as the development of similar vessels of the late Youziling type, could also be inspired by Dawenkou culture and Yangshao culture, as double-belly vessels such as high-foot plates and plates were already seen in the Yellow River Basin. As for high-handle cups, round-foot *zuns*, and folded-belly *gu*-shaped cups, they are more clearly related to the influence of Dawenkou culture, while basket patterns, added relief patterns, and other factors come from Yangshao culture, suggesting that the Dawenkou and Yangshao cultures played a significant role in the formation and development of Qujialing culture.[129] The southwestern Henan and northwestern Hubei regions, where the Yellow River and Yangtze River basins intersect, also have pottery double-belly plates from Yangshao culture, the tooth extraction customs of Dawenkou culture, etc., in their Qujialing cultural remains, making this area a key region for the formation of Qujialing culture through the fusion of various cultural factors. Qujialing culture *dings* are complex and diverse in their feet, rich in decoration, especially the wide, flat shovel-shaped feet, which are likely related to the influence of Xuejiagang culture. Painted pottery spinning wheels are popular, some decorated with spiral or *Taiji* patterns, rich in rotational dynamics. Similar engraved patterns were seen earlier in the Beiyinyangying culture Saidun type. Individual stone jade *congs*, stone *bis*, and slanted-handle stone knives seen in sites like Yun County's Qinglongquan reflect the influence of Liangzhu culture.

Qujialing culture itself had early and late stages. In the early stage, the slanted-belly cup had a large bottom and straight belly, the painted pottery round-foot pot had a large round belly, and the double-belly vessel had obvious transitions between the two bellies. In the late stage, the slanted-belly cup had a small bottom, slanted belly, and concave. The painted pottery round-foot pot had a flat folded-belly, and the double-belly vessel degenerated. This culture also had regional differences and can be divided into several local types. For example, small-mouth bottles and small-mouth folded-belly pots were still common in the Liyang Plain. In the

Xiangjiang region, deep-belly pots, high-neck pots, and converging-mouth urns decorated with crossed rope patterns, engraved grid patterns, stamped patterns, added relief decorations, etc., are distinctive. The deep-belly pot often had floral-edge rims, similar to the contemporary remains in the Hanzhong region. It is influenced by the type of the Quanshu phase II of Yangshao culture. The chisel-shaped-foot *dings* with basket patterns in eastern Hubei belongs to Dawenkou culture, and the double-spouted pot belongs to Liangzhu culture.

Qujialing culture has been discovered, including those in Shijiahe and Longzuicheng in Tianmen City, Hubei Province; Taojiahu and Jimingcheng in Gong'an County; Yejiamiao in Xiaogan City; Chenghe Village in Shayang; Majiayuan in Jingmen City; Yinxiangcheng in Jiangling County; Menbanwan in Yingcheng City; Zoumaling in Shishou City; and Jijiaocheng and Chengtoushan in Li County, Hunan Province. Among these, the largest one, Shijiahe, covers an area of 1.2 million square meters, with different functional planning areas, such as palace, burial, and sacrificial areas, occupying a very special status. The surrounding city sites range from tens of thousands to over 600,000 square meters. Together with general settlements, they form a multi-level settlement system centered on Shijiahe ancient city. The complexity of the social structure of Qujialing culture was quite severe. The houses were mostly rectangular and on-ground, and there were also circular single-room on-ground ones, with mud-brick walls or timber-framed mud walls, and whitewashing had begun to be applied on the living surface. The highest existing connected-room-style house in the Menbanwan site in Yingcheng, Hubei, is two meters high, with a corridor and courtyard in front. Both the doors and windows were sliding style, with the windows reaching the floor. The walls were built with mud bricks, similar to Liangzhu culture (fig. 4.12).[130] The row houses in Huanglianshu in Xichuan, Henan, were built with timber-framed mud walls.[131] The burial situation was basically the same as the Youziling type of Daxi culture. Some burials in Dengjiawan and Xiaojiawuji in the Jianghan Plain were placed on a second-level platform with dozens of high-neck jars, perhaps symbolizing storage items. Pottery cups and small *dings* at the feet or head of the skeleton may symbolize common utensils. However, burials in the Xiajiang region, such as Yangjiawan, were accompanied by a large number of food and drink utensils, such as high-handle cups, slanted-belly cups, and high-foot plates around the skeleton. Still, high-neck jars were rarely seen, which differed from the burial customs on the Jianghan Plain.[132] Qujialing culture burials were mainly accompanied only by pottery, starkly contrasting with the contemporary

Liangzhu culture. In the burial sites such as Huanglianshu in southwest Henan, there were also customs of burying infants in waist pits.*

The production tools were basically the same as the Youziling type of Daxi culture. The concaved-edge stone chisels unearthed from sites like Qinglongquan are quite characteristic and can process round mortise and tenon joints. Many sites, such as Qujialing, found that straw-mixed mud contains many rice husks, stems, etc. The rice mainly belongs to japonica rice, indicating that there should have been developed rice farming at that time; the discovery of carbonized rice and millet grain at the Huanglianshu site shows that the northern region of Qujialing culture belonged to a mixed distribution area of rice farming and dry farming.

Figure 4.12 The mud-brick wall connected-room house at the Menbanwan site

3. Southern and Western Regions of Northeast China
The southern and western regions of Northeast China belong to the cylindrical jar–painted pottery jar–earthen bowl cultural system.

---

* In the context of burial practices in ancient China, a waist pit typically refers to a small pit deliberately dug under the waist of the main tomb occupant. Sacrificial offerings or burial items are usually placed in this pit. In higher-ranking tombs, human sacrifices can often be found in these waist pits.—Trans.

3.1 Hongshan and Hamin Mangha Culture

Hongshan Culture

After 3500 BCE, Hongshan culture of the Xiliao River Basin entered its late stage, represented by the late remnants of the Niuheliang site 5, the most prosperous and developed period. Painted pottery was popular, with patterns such as triangles, broken-line Z-shaped patterns, parallel lines with hooked whorls, large overlapping scales, etc. New painted pottery urns with covers appeared, and pottery objects related to religious rituals, such as cylindrical vessels painted potteries, tower-shaped vessels, incense burner lids, and tri-legged cups. A number of pottery or stone figurines were found, some of which are vivid and expressive. Jade artifacts were prevalent, including bracelets, rings, square *bis* with rounded corners, connected *bis*, slanted-mouth cylindrical vessels, hook-cloud-shaped vessels, tri-holed ornaments with double human or animal heads, double animal-(eagle-owl-) headed ornaments, animal-face plaque ornaments, dragon-and-phoenix pendants, as well as jade figures, jade dragons (fig. 4.13), jade phoenixes (fig. 4.14), jade turtles, jade turtles, jade shells, etc. The jade artifacts are mainly made of serpentine rocks such as actinolite,[133] and the concave parts were often rounded and smooth, giving a strong natural and gentle texture. Its main source may be in its vast Northeastern region because as early as the lower Zuojiashan culture, the middle Zuojiashan culture, and Yabuli culture, jade artifacts such as axe, adze, chisel, arrowhead, *bi*, connected *bi*, tube, and stone dragon were common. A few perforated stone *yues* might have come from the Jianghuai region, and turtle-

Figure 4.13 Jade dragon from Hongshan culture at the Niuheliang site (N2Z1M4: 2)

Figure 4.14 Jade phoenix from Hongshan culture at the Niuheliang site (N16M4: 1)

shaped jade artifacts might have been influenced by the Jianghuai region's culture. Copper earrings were also discovered.

The Niuheliang site group includes at least 20 locations, distributed along the mountain ridges, with a grand atmosphere, and the main remains belong to the late Hongshan culture. The most important were the "temples, altars, and tombs" of the first and second locations. The "Goddess Temple" at the first location may be the core of the entire site group, with imitation wood structures and colored murals. The murals often show ocher triangles and connected lines patterns. Many fragments of female body statues were found, some of which are two to three times life-size. One of them, a human head inlaid with jade eyes, is a masterpiece. There are also fragments of bird-head pottery sculptures, tower-shaped vessels, incense burner lids, etc. Nearby, there are auxiliary facilities such as pits burying hundreds of pottery cylindrical vessels. The second location has "five tombs and one altar" built with stacked stones, covering nearly 6,000 square meters (fig. 4.15). The tombs have different shapes, including square, rectangular, circular, and a combination of square and circular. The inner side of the tomb boundary wall is surrounded by upright painted pottery cylindrical vessels, and pottery tower-shaped vessels are placed at the center and the four cardinal directions of the tomb top. Among them, tomb No. 2, with a large central tomb, is the main tomb, and near the main tomb, there is a circular altar with three layers of steps. The tombs at Niuheliang show a clear hierarchical division. The tomb walls and outer tomb boundaries of the large central tomb in tomb No. 2 have three layers of steps, indicating the highest noble standard; the two large tombs in the middle of tomb No. 1 are earthen pits with stone steps on one side, with slightly lower standards; the tombs on the south side of tomb No. 1 are of an even lower standard. The tombs of the above three levels generally have only a few to about 20 exquisite jade artifacts as burial objects. In addition, there are small tombs without jade burial objects. Outside of Niuheliang, altars piled stone tombs, and tombs with jade burial objects have also been discovered at many places in the Dalin River Basin, such as Dongshanzui in Kazuo,[134] Tianjiagou in Lingyuan, Hutougou in Fuxin,[135] Laohushan in Aohan, and Kangjiayingzi in Beipiao. However, none of them can compare with Niuheliang in terms of level. The Niuheliang site group may have been the holy land and ritual center of the entire Hongshan culture, and the owner of the large central tomb in tomb No. 2 may have been the leader of the religious or secular community of the entire Hongshan culture.

Figure 4.15 Panorama of the second location at Niuheliang site (west–east)

Religion always reflects the reality of society to varying degrees. The grand scenes, high standards, and pyramid-like hierarchical structure of Hongshan culture's religious remains were likely a reflection of the highly complex nature of contemporary society. Moreover, constructing such large-scale religious buildings would have required mobilizing many people, which would have been difficult to accomplish without a high social organization. The exquisite jade artifacts and meticulous design of painted pottery from Hongshan culture required a high-level craftsmanship, suggesting that there were professional jade and pottery artisans in this society. These factors indicate that the late Hongshan culture might have evolved into what Su Bingqi called an "archaic state," a "stable independent political entity higher than a tribe,"[136] and that it had already entered the realm of initial civilization. Unfortunately, our knowledge of the general settlements of the same period is still very limited. The production tools and economic forms should be roughly the same as in the middle period.

Hamin Mangha Culture

During the peak of the late Hongshan culture, it had a significant influence on the heartland of the Keerqin Grassland in the Tongliao–Baicheng area, leaving behind remains of the Hamin Mangha culture, represented by the Hamin Mangha in Inner Mongolia's Kezuozhong Banner[137] and phase II of Shuangta in Liaoning's Baicheng. Its double-handle pots, painted pottery jars, Z-shaped-pattern cylindrical jars, and slanted-mouth vats are similar to the typical Hongshan culture. Still, its plain or pitted pattern cylindrical jars show strong local characteristics. The jade artifacts, such as connected *bis* and square *bis* with rounded corners, might be local traditions. The Hamin Mangha settlement includes dozens of square or rectangular semi-subterranean houses, with a range in the front of the entrance and postholes on the inner walls and platforms, resembling the structures of Yangshao culture houses. Many human bones were found in some of the houses, with as many as 97 individuals found in house F40, mostly women and children, believed to have been dumped collectively after dying from disasters. The graves at Hamin Mangha and Shuangta are short rectangular vertical pit graves, with the body of the grave owner severely flexed supine, showing different funeral customs from Hongshan culture. Tools include stone axes, adzes, chisels, hoes, grinding stones, grinding rods, perforated mussel knives, bone awls, etc. There may have been agriculture, but hunting and fishing were still the main economic activities.

3.2 Xueshan Culture Phase I, Nanbaoligaotu Culture, Middle Xiaozhushan Culture, and Pianbuzi Culture

Xueshan Culture Phase I
Around 3300 BCE, Xueshan culture phase I moved north from the south of the Yan Mountains to the Xiliao River Basin, replacing the once glorious Hongshan culture. Xueshan culture phase I sites are small and few, far from comparable to Hongshan culture, represented by the remnants of the Nantai site in Aohan Banner, Inner Mongolia,[138] and the Da'nangou Cemetery in Wengniute Banner.[139] Painted pottery was predominantly black, with some red and some white clay coating. Cylindrical jars have a noticeably higher ratio than those of the Wufang type in the Hai River Basin, likely due to the influence of Hongshan culture tradition. At the same time, the *zun* seems to have been inherited from the Zhaobaogou culture. Earthen bowls, basins, plain wide-flare-mouth jars, high-neck jars, etc., originated south of the Yan Mountains. Eagle-owl-shaped slanted-mouth pots, high-neck pots, double-mouth pots, irregular pots, octagonal star patterns on pottery, stone *bis*, stone rings, stone bracelets, etc., likely originated from Dawenkou culture. In contrast, bone hairpins, swastika patterns, *Hui*-shaped patterns, cloud-thunder patterns, and dog-shaped animal patterns are unique to Xueshan culture phase I. The swastika pattern has long been seen in Western Asia and other places and might be related to influences from the West. These remnants can be called the Xiaoheyan type of Xueshan culture phase I.[140]

Nanbaoligaotu Culture
Around 3000 BCE, Xueshan culture phase I, the Xiaoheyan type, continued to expand eastward to the heartland of the Keerqin Grassland, blending with Pianbuzi culture in the Xialiao River Basin. The Xiaolaha culture phase I in the Nen River Basin and its northern region, forming the Nanbaoligaotu culture represented by the Nanbaoligaotu Cemetery in Zhalute Banner, Inner Mongolia.[141] Its plain wide-flare-mouth jars, high-neck jars, earthen bowls, basins, *zun*-shaped vessels, high-neck pots, double-mouth pots, and some cylindrical jars are elements of the Xiaoheyan type of Xueshan culture phase I. Eagle-owl-shaped slanted-mouth pots may have inspired turtle-shaped slanted-mouth pots, and there are also bone hairpins. Cylindrical jars with engraved parallel lines, basket patterns, and hoop patterns with added clay on the rim are elements of the Xiaolaha culture phase I. Double-handle overlapping-mouth jars with vertically added clay strips

on edge are elements of Pianbuzi culture. There are also jade artifacts such as *bi* with protruding teeth, axe, adze, ring, jade *huang*, tube, and pendant, which may be connected to the lower Zuojiashan culture. The engraved or painted geometric patterns such as triangles, diamonds, and cloud-thunder are quite characteristic. Deep-belly round-bottom pots with added relief decorations on the rim had already been popular in the Outer Baikal region. Some vessels with bearded band decorations on their shoulders had already been seen in the western part of the Eurasian continent. There are also pentagonal stone "buddhas," which should be scepter heads, which are widely seen in the western regions of the Eurasian continent.

Middle Xiaozhushan Culture and Pianbuzi Culture

After about 3500 BCE, the Liaodong region entered the late middle Xiaozhushan culture, with elements of the middle Dawenkou culture such as *gui* and *he* emerging. Around 3000 BCE, Pianbuzi culture, represented by phase I of Santangcun in Wafangdian, Liaoning Province,[142] and phase I of Zhaogongjie in Shenyang City, Liaodong region,[143] appeared. Pianbuzi culture was characterized by double-handle overlapping-lipped jars decorated with vertically added clay strips (snake patterns) and fine-tooth comb patterns with fine parallel stripes. There were also high-neck pots, slanted-belly, or folded-belly earthen bowls, round-foot bowls, and plain deep-belly jars, etc. The latter several types of pottery and jade *huangs* are mostly elements of Dawenkou culture, and *bis* with protruding teeth might be a northern element.

Apart from the Nanbaoligaotu culture, semi-subterranean houses have been found in other cultures. In the Xiaoheyan type sites such as Da'nangou, in addition to the common vertical pit graves, there are also side chamber graves—the earliest chamber graves in China, with burial practices being flexed burials. In contrast, in the Nanbaoligaotu culture and Pianbuzi culture, side chamber graves are not seen, and extended supine burials are popular. Both the Xiaoheyan type and Nanbaoligaotu culture have practices of burning the gravel pit and the body, which is also a burial custom commonly seen in the northern grassland area. The Xiaoheyan type also has instances of covering the body with birch bark.

All cultures have ground stone tools such as axes, adzes, chisels, *yues*, and chipped narrow-waist stone hoes, as well as bone darts, bone awls, etc., but there are differences. The middle Xiaozhushan culture and Pianbuzi culture in the southeast have ground stone knives and ground stone arrowheads. In contrast, Xueshan culture phase I, Xiaoheyan type, and Nanbaoligaotu culture in the northwest have stone grinding plates, stone grinding rods, and microlith arrowheads, scrapers, stone leaves, bone-stemmed stone-blade knives, etc., showing that agriculture is dominant in the south while hunting and gathering are dominant in the north. The bone-stemmed stone-blade knife is not seen in the middle Xiaozhushan culture but is seen in Pianbuzi culture, which is also a noteworthy phenomenon.

4. Cultures in Early China Outer Margin Zone

As mentioned above, the "early China" range in the late Yangshao culture has significantly expanded. However, some places in South China, Southwest China, Northeast China, and Northwest China are still not covered.

In the southern part of Fujian Province, southern Guangdong Province, and most of Guangxi Province in South China, the tradition of cord-mark cauldrons with round-foot plates persists, and the same is true for the Dabenkeng culture in Taiwan. For instance, in southern Fujian Province (including Taiwan), there are Dongshan Damaoshan-type remains distributed, which some people call Damaoshan culture.[144] In Southwest China's Guizhou Province and most of Yunnan Province, as well as the central and western parts of Xizang Province, and in northwest China's western Qinghai to Xinjiang provinces, the situation is even less clear, suggesting that even if there were Neolithic cultures, they would certainly not be developed. The major economy would still be hunting and gathering.

In the Northeast, the cultures approximately outside "early China" include the Xiaolaha culture phase I in the Nen River Basin, the upper Zuojiashan culture in the second Songhua River Basin, the lower Yinggeling culture in the Mudan River Basin, and the Jingu culture in the Tumen River Basin. The so-called Group A pottery, represented by cylindrical jars with engraved parallel lines and mat patterns, and the so-called Group B pottery with multiple added relief decorations, in the Xiaolaha phase I in Zhaoyuan County, Heilongjiang Province,[145] should just be parts of one archaeological culture, the Xiaolaha culture, without a distinction of early or late. Its distant origin may be in Xinglongwa culture rich in local characteristics northeast of the Xar Moron River.[146] Many microlith arrowheads, scrapers, bone darts, bone spearheads, etc., show that its economy is predominately fishing and hunting, with no signs of agriculture. The upper Zuojiashan culture, represented by the upper Zuojiashan in Nong'an County, Jilin Province, and the upper Xiduanliangshan in Dongfeng County,[147] with cylindrical jars decorated with chevron and meander patterns, semi-subterranean houses, chipped or slightly ground stone shovels, stone axes, stone grinding plates, stone grinding rods, etc. Strangely, the arrowheads are ground rather than pressed. There are also bone darts, net pendants, etc., which should be an economy where agriculture and fishing, and hunting coexist. The lower Yinggeling culture is basically close to the upper Zuojiashan culture. The Jingu culture, also known as the Xingcheng culture, mainly uses cylindrical jars, and its *Hui* and scroll patterns filled with fine-tooth comb patterns with clustered dot patterns are very distinctive.[148]

5. Cultural Exchanges during the Late Yangshao

In the late Yangshao or the early Chalcolithic, due to the weakening of the cultural power in the Central Plain core area, it was difficult to exert strong influence and radiation on the surrounding areas, so the main theme of cultural exchange became a mutual exchange between various local cultures. Especially, the culture of the eastern region had a greater impact on the cultures of the Central Plain and the western regions, while the western culture was pushed further west.

5.1 Cultural Exchanges of Yangshao Phase III

In Yangshao phase III or the late Yangshao, although the core area of Yangshao culture declined, it still had a visible influence on its surroundings. Among them, the Qinwangzhai type influenced the southwestern Shandong region. It resulted in red-banded grid-pattern or imprinted cord-mark deep-belly jars with added relief decorations to appear more of local Dawenkou culture. The late Banpo type even expanded south to the northern Chongqing region, where the upper and middle reaches of the Yangtze River meet. Xueshan culture phase I, mainly rooted in Yangshao culture, expanded northward to the Xiliao River Basin, replacing the once prosperous Hongshan culture.

The influence of the middle Dawenkou culture on the surrounding cultures significantly increased: it had profound interaction and exchange with Yangshao culture in the west, leading to the formation of the Qinwangzhai type. Its typical elements such as converging-mouth folded-rim high-foot plates, open-mouth double-belly high-foot plates, back pots, high-neck pots, round-foot *zuns*, etc., penetrated the Xiwang type at a long distance. Its influence extended northward to the central and northern Hebei, Xiliao River Basin, and Liaodong region, resulting in the appearance of folded-belly basins, flat-bottom basins, high-foot plates, multi-mouth pots, eagle-owl-shaped jars, octagram patterns, etc., in the late Xueshan culture phase I, and the appearance of pottery such as *gui* and *he* in the middle Xiaozhushan culture. It confronted and exchanged with Liangzhu culture in the northern Jiangsu region in the south, and typical elements such as back pots penetrated the hinterland of Liangzhu culture.

The late Hongshan culture also had a strong impact on the outside, not only influencing the formation of the Hamin Mangha culture similar to it in the east but also its chevron-pattern pottery cylindrical jars, scale patterns, filled diagonal triangles, relative double hooks, checkerboard patterns, continuous diamond block patterns, strip patterns, and other painted pottery elements influenced the central and southern Inner Mongolia Autonomous Region, Shanxi Province, Hebei Province, central Henan Province, and even Shandong Province, playing an important role in promoting the formation of the Haishengbulang type and Yijing type in Yangshao culture and Xueshan culture phase I. The serpentine *bis* and jade materials of the early Haishengbulang type in central and southern Inner Mongolia should be directly imported from the Xiliao River Basin; the round-corner square *bis*, connected *bis*, etc.; made of serpentine jades are also found in Dawenkou culture sites such as Yedian;[149] and the round-corner square *bis*, connected *bis*, hoop-shaped ornaments, Y-shaped utensils, jade dragons, and other Hongshan-style jades also influenced the Songze culture, Xuejiagang culture, etc., in the Jianghuai region.[150] Based on the distance and depth of the influence, we can roughly divide the southward influence of Hongshan culture into three levels. The influence process should be accompanied by the migration of a certain number of people, at least for the neighboring areas in central and southern Inner Mongolia, Shanxi, and Hebei (fig. 4.16).[151]

The Songze culture and Xuejiagang culture in the lower reaches of the Yangtze River had a wide-ranging influence, and the appearance of *gui, he,* and *yi* commonly seen in the Yellow River Basin during this period should be related to them. The jade *huang*, jade *jue*, stone *yue*, multi-holed stone knife, and converging-mouth folded-rim high-handle high-foot plate from Daxi culture of the middle Yangtze River are definitely influenced by Xuejiagang culture. Some people have proposed that the jade artifacts in the middle Yangtze River at that time belonged to the system of the lower Yangtze River.[152]

5.2 Cultural Exchanges of Yangshao Phase IV

In the Yangshao phase IV or the late Yangshao, the extent of cultural exchanges and clashes increased, and a number of common elements began to emerge. In early China, pottery across most of the country developed toward a gray-black color, and wheel-made pottery gradually increased.

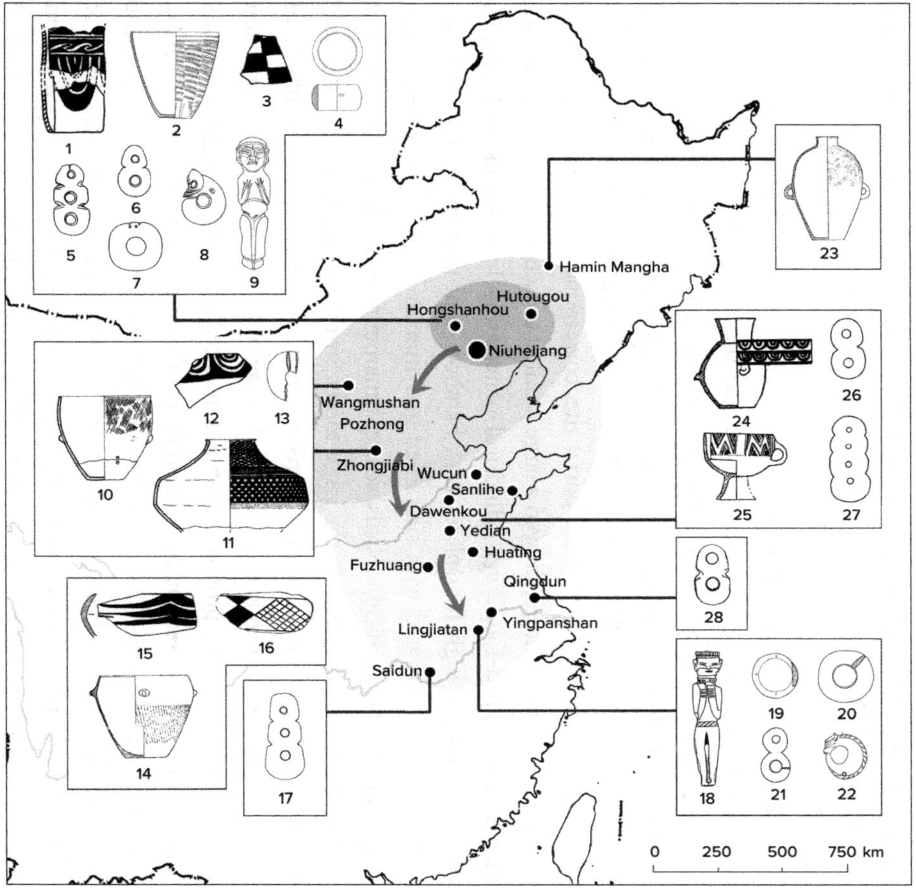

THE ARCHAIC STATE STAGE OF EARLY CHINA 181

Figure 4.16 Three levels of the southern influence of late Hongshan culture

1. Pottery cylindrical vessel (Cylinder No. 5 of Hutougou)
2, 10, 14. Pottery cylindrical jar (Niuheliang N5H14: 1, Hongtaipo Shang F5: 6, Zhongjiabi 0: 18)
3, 12, 16. Painted pottery shard (Chengzishan T1②: 5, Wangmushan Poxia IT1224③: 3, Zhongjiabi H32: 10)
4, 19. Jade bracelet (Niuheliang N5Z1M1: 3, Lingjiatan 87M4: 53)
5, 6, 17, 21, 26–28. Jade connected *bi* (Hutougou M3-4: 1, N2, Saidun M123: 4, Lingjiatan 85M15: 107-2, Yedian M22: 8, 4, Qingdun T10: 20)
7, 13, 20. Jade *bi* (Niuheliang N2Z1M15: 4, Wangmushan Pozhong T2②: 1, Lingjiatan 87M7: 42)
8, 22. Jade dragon (Niuheliang N2Z1M4: 2, Lingjiatan 98M16: 2)
9, 18. Jade figure (Niuheliang N16M4: 4, Lingjiatan 87M1: 3)
11. Pottery small-mouth bulbous-belly jar (Hongtaipo Shang F2: 1)
15. Pottery earthen bowl (Zhongjiabi 0: 1)
23, 24. Pottery pot (Hamin Mangha F8: 4, Jiaojia ZJ: 594)
25. Pottery high-foot plate (Wucun M90: 3)

At this time, although Yangshao culture was in a disadvantaged position, it still exerted an influence externally. For example, the basket weave patterns and added piled patterns in the late Dawenkou culture in western Shandong, eastern Henan, and northern Anhui are related to the influence of the Miaodigou phase II type, and the formation of Qujialing culture should also have a certain relationship with the southward influence of the Miaodigou phase II type.

Dawenkou culture significantly expanded externally, extending westward to eastern Henan and northwestern Anhui, forming the Yuchisi type. Its typical elements, such as chisel-shaped-foot *dings*, high-foot plates, bag-foot *guis*, and straight-belly vats penetrated the majority of Shanxi and Henan, and even some burial artifacts were essentially typical Dawenkou culture artifacts, suggesting the existence of population migration. High-handle cups, round-foot *zuns*, and even the tooth extraction had a long-distance impact on the southwest into the Jianghan region, playing a significant role in the transformation from Daxi culture to Qujialing culture. In addition, the advanced wheel-made black pottery technology of Dawenkou culture produced a radiating influence in a wave-like pattern.

Liangzhu culture expanded strongly, most importantly in the north and southwest. Its expansion to the north once reached the eastern part of the Jianghuai region,[153] and it had a strong influence on the northern Jiangsu region. The southern part of the Huating burial site in Xinyi, Jiangsu Province, belongs to the middle Dawenkou culture burials, without any Liangzhu cultural elements. In contrast, the northern part of the burial site, corresponding to the early stage of the late Dawenkou culture, showed a large number of Liangzhu cultural elements, including T-shaped-foot *dings*, cylindrical-penetrating-handle pots, wide-handle cups with spouts, high-foot plates with bamboo joint patterns, round-foot jars, and jade *congs* decorated with simplified god-human-animal-face patterns, jade *cong*-shaped tubes, conical utensils, strung ornaments, etc.[154] Equally noteworthy is that the main occupants of the large tombs in the northern area are all middle-aged men, consistent with a warrior status. Almost all large tombs have human sacrifices, a phenomenon seen in Liangzhu culture but not in Dawenkou culture. Yan Wenming proposed that this resulted from the Liangzhu people's expedition to the Dawenkou people and their subsequent clash and fusion.[155] Also, Liangzhu cultural elements like cylindrical-penetrating-handle pot and stone *bi* even infiltrated the heartland of Dawenkou culture. As for the discovery of Liangzhu culture T-shaped-foot *ding*, high-foot plate, and *ding*-shaped *yan* in the Yangjiaquan phase I of Qixia on the Shandong Peninsula,[156] it is estimated to be more likely the result of the maritime exchange. Liangzhu culture exerted influence to the west on southern and western Anhui Province, eastern Hubei Province, and Ningzhen area,[157] leading to elements of Liangzhu culture such as cylindrical-penetrating-handle pots, fish fin-shaped feet or T-shaped-foot *dings*, *guis*, slanted-handle stone knives, triangular stone plows, jade *congs*, *bis*, etc., to appear in Xuejiagang culture and others. It even influenced as far as Qujialing culture at Qinglongquan, Yun County and the Miaodigou phase II type at Dongguan, Yuanqu ancient city, causing the appearance of stone jade *congs*, *bis*, and slanted-handle knives. Its southward influence was strong on the Ningbo–Shaoxing Plain in eastern Zhejiang Province, making the upper culture at sites like Fenghua Mingshanhou and others look similar to Liangzhu culture,[158] and Liangzhu cultural elements were even found in the Zhoushan Archipelago. It affected the southwest of Zhejiang, the south of Anhui, and the north of Jiangxi, with cylindrical-penetrating handled pots of Liangzhu style being visible in phase I of Daiziping in Xiangxiang, Hunan Province.[159]

Qujialing culture also had a strong external influence. It influenced the central and western parts of Henan to the north, leading to the appearance of slanted-belly cups, double-belly high-foot plates, and pointed-bottom pots in Yangshao culture Miaodigou phase II type and Qinwangzhai type, and even red slanted-belly pottery cups appeared in the Dawenkou culture in northern Jiangsu.[160] It also influenced eastern Hubei,[161] southwestern Anhui, and northwestern Jiangxi to the east, leading to the appearance of pottery such as round-foot basin-shaped *zeng* in these areas.

In addition, the influence of Fanchengdui culture and others to the south led to the creation of Shixia culture in the northern part of Guangdong Province, arguably the earliest "Hakka culture." The *bi* with protruding teeth seen in Dawenkou culture, the middle Xiaozhushan culture, and the Nanbaoligaotu culture may have originated in the central and northern parts of the northeast or even in the Outer Baikal region. Seashells are occasionally found in the western Majiayao and Karuo cultures, indicating a connection with coastal regions.

5.3 The Westward Expansion of Majiayao Culture and the "Painted Pottery Road"

In the Yangshao phase IV, Majiayao culture of the Majiayao type spread to the west over a long distance, forming a "painted pottery road"—a path of east-to-west expansion and dissemination of early Chinese culture represented by painted pottery based on the Shaanxi and Gansu regions, over 3,000 years earlier than the

"Silk Road."[162] This also includes the reverse infiltration of western culture along this corridor.[162] The "painted pottery road" began around 3500 BCE with the end of the Quanhu type and the transition of the Shilingxia type. After the formation of the Majiayao type around 3000 BCE, communication became even more apparent, generally dividing into a southern and northern route, with the southern route further divided into two branches. The expansion of the Majiayao type from central Gansu to northeastern Qinghai[163] and the Hexi Corridor is the northern route; the expansion to the Gonghe Basin in eastern Qinghai forming Majiayao culture Zongri type is the northern branch of the southern route; the expansion to the Mao County, Wenchuan, Li County in northwestern Sichuan and even the Dali region in Yunnan[164] is the southern branch of the southern route. The most notable aspect of the westward expansion process of Majiayao culture is its penetration into the Xizang Plateau via the southern route and the formation of Karuo culture (fig. 4.17).

Interestingly, phase I section B remain at Burzahom in the Kashmir region also has many similarities with Karuo culture. They both mainly use coarse gray pottery made by the clay strip coiling, with brown pottery second; both have small-mouth high-neck jars and flat-bottom basins; both have similar features such as an outward rim, a hoop with added relief decorations on the neck and body, a false-round foot, and a woven pattern imprint on the bottom; both have similarly shaped double-holed or single-hole stone knives (claw sickles), polished long-bodied stone axes, adzes, chisels, etc., especially the concaved-backed stone knives; both live in semi-underground houses with roofs supported by wooden columns. So many commonalities can only be explained by a connection between them. Since these factors suddenly appeared in phase I of site in the Kashmir Valley, India and their absolute dates (2850–2550 BCE) are no earlier than Karuo culture,[165] it is speculated that they are related to the long-distance westward infiltration of Karuo culture tradition along the southern edge of the Himalayas.

Although the dominant direction of the above-mentioned early cultural exchange southern route is westward, cultural factors can spread eastward along this corridor. For example, dancing patterns similar to the Majiayao and Zongri types (fig. 4.18) have long been widespread in the Near East and Southeastern Europe between 9000 BCE to 6000 BCE.[166] The bronze knives of the Linjia Majiayao type in Dongxiang, Gansu Province, the Shilingxia type, the Majiayao type domestic sheep, etc., may also be related to the West. One of the possible routes of eastward spread is the early Chinese and Western cultural exchange southern route.

THE ARCHAIC STATE STAGE OF EARLY CHINA　　　　185

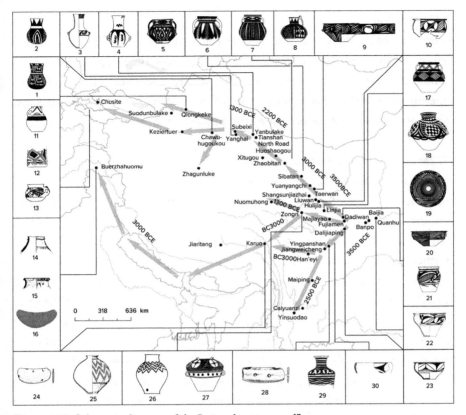

Figure 4.17 Schematic diagram of the "painted pottery road"

1–4, 8, 11, 29. Pottery jar (Qiongkeke M46A: 1, Chawuhugou cemetery No. 4 M156: 16, Yanghai cemetery No. 2 M242: 2, Yanbulake M2: 3, Yuanyangchi M72: 2, Shulabashate, Yingpanshan H12: 5)
5–7, 13–15, 17, 18, 21, 25–27. Pottery jar (urn) (Tianshan North Road, Ganguya M84: 1, Zhuanshawo JZH-A003, Shulabashate, Burzahom, Xiahaishi M10: 5, Tugutai M66: 1, Dadiwan F401: 2, Karuo F9: 126, Zongri M43: 2, M222: 1)
9, 10, 19, 22, 23. Pottery basin (Taerwan F10: 22, Hulijia H14: 2, Yanerwan H1: 36, Quanhu H224: 501, Dalijiaping H16: 1)
12. Pottery cup (Shulabashate)
16, 24, 28. Stone knife (Burzahom, Karuo F8: 69, Yingpanshan T11①: 3)
20, 30. Pottery earthen bowl (Dadiwan T703②: 95, Boxi G1: 4)

Figure 4.18 Majiayao culture painted pottery dancing-pattern basin
1. Shangsunjiazhai M384: 1　　2. Zongri M157: 1

6. Conclusion

After 3500 BCE, the scope of early China in a cultural sense further expanded. Internal collisions and exchanges became unprecedentedly active, features of "Chinese" culture further stood out, and society underwent drastic changes, entering the initial civilized society stage of early China—the archaic state stage, which also accelerated the pace of early Chinese and Western cultural exchanges.

(1) The integration and complementation of two major agricultural systems and the strengthening of diversified economic trends in the Northern region

The scope of the two major agricultural systems, millet grain farming and rice farming, significantly expanded. Millet grain farming extended to the eastern part of the Hexi Corridor, the eastern part of the Xizang Plateau, most of the northeastern region, even the Korean Peninsula and the East and West Siberia, while rice farming extended to northern Guangdong and the Shandong Peninsula, with the upper reaches of the Yangtze River possibly a mixed area of millet grain and rice farming (fig. 2.3). Both agricultural systems developed substantially. In the millet grain farming areas, agricultural tools such as stone knives and stone shovels were more finely polished, and the efficient harvesting tool, the stone sickle, gradually became popular. Liangzhu culture in the rice farming areas not only had a large number of exquisite stone sickles but also stone plow-shaped tools, showing a qualitative improvement in the level of productivity, consistent with the advanced degree of the Liangzhu civilization. However, it cannot be determined whether it had developed to the plowing stage like the civilizations of Mesopotamia and Egypt. The trend of integration and complementation of the two major agricultural systems significantly strengthened. Rice farming not only existed in the Huai River Basin and most of the lower reaches of the Yellow River but also in the upper and middle reaches of the Yellow River. Millet grain farming penetrated southward into the Han River Basin. The pattern of rice farming in the south and millet grain farming in the north still dominated. At this time, the proportion of hunting and gathering economy in the millet grain farming area significantly increased, with the proportion of microliths such as arrowheads, scrapers, and bone-handle stone-blade knives clearly increasing. After about 3000 BCE, domesticated sheep appeared in the Gansu and Qinghai regions, indicating the emergence of the earliest form of animal husbandry. The development and integration of the two major agricultural systems and the trend toward a diversified economy in the Northern regions ensured the stability of food sources in a wide range of areas.

(2) Wide exchange and innovative integration of "Chinese" characteristic artifacts

The types of "Chinese" characteristic artifacts, such as pottery, jade, lacquerware, and silk textiles, became more diverse, and their craftsmanship became more refined. The polished black pottery of Dawenkou culture and Liangzhu culture, the painted pottery of Majiayao culture, as well as the jade of Hongshan culture, Xuejiagang culture, and Liangzhu culture, were all exquisitely superior, standing out for the time. Polished black pottery and exquisite jade generally came from large tombs and were probably already preliminary "ritual vessels." The sharp- and round-bottom pottery *zuns* (vats) and jade *yues* were commonly found in large and medium-sized tombs in the Yellow River and Yangtze River basins and were probably ritual vessels with certain universal significance.[167] It is worth mentioning that jade was extraordinarily developed at the time, becoming the most representative material cultural remains in the eastern part of early China. Some even proposed the concept of a "Jade Age."[168]

Possibly influenced by the lower Yangtze River region, around 3500 BCE, most parts of early China began to see the appearance of pottery with spouts, which should represent the formation of a common lifestyle. Perhaps inspired by the *gui* in the lower Yellow River region, around 3000 BCE, the *jia* was innovatively formed in southern Shanxi Province and quickly spread to surrounding areas, marking the emergence of a highly efficient cooking method with distinct northern Central Plain characteristics. The distribution range of pottery *dings* continued to expand, and jade articles from different cultures in the east were exchanged. Bracelets, spinning wheels, and the like were almost seen in all cultures; pottery bells were still seen in the Yellow River and Yangtze River basins, and a few slender pottery drums were also found in Jinzhong.[169] The wooden muji, similar to the Dutch wooden clog but used in China thousands of years earlier of Liangzhu culture, the ivory combs of Dawenkou culture, and Qujialing culture were also distinctive. In addition, sporadic discoveries of bronze knives, copper rings, and the like were made in Majiayao culture, Hongshan culture, and others.

(3) Diverse development of the civil engineering techniques

The basic structure of houses was still pit-style in the Northern regions, ground style, and stilt beam-framed architectural houses in the middle and lower reaches of the Yangtze River. However, connected houses started to become popular in the middle and lower reaches of the Yangtze River and extended to the Huai River region. Cave-type structures began to appear in the Northern regions.

Architectural technology improved significantly. Super-large city settlements of two to three million square meters, such as those of the Liangzhu and Shijiahe cultures, emerged, along with many more small and medium-sized ancient cities. The city wall construction technology improved noticeably, with Liangzhu culture being the most impressive. Large high-platform buildings, palace-like structures with a "front hall, back room, east and west wings," and large "temples, altars, and tombs" appeared at sites like the Liangzhu ancient city, Dadiwan site B, Nanzuo, and Niuheliang. Rammed earth technology began to be popular, supporting the construction of numerous city walls and used in house construction. The rammed earth wall of Liangzhu culture was clearly compacted, with distinct layers, showing that the rammed earth technology was relatively mature. Applying lime to the ground and skirting of houses, a practice seen not only in Yangshao culture but also spread to Qujialing culture, made the houses brighter and more sanitary than ever before. Additionally, the Taikou type of Yangshao culture, Qujialing culture, and Liangzhu culture started using mud bricks for house construction; the Ashan type of Yangshao culture and Karuo culture had stone wall houses, and Qujialing culture had sliding doors and windows. There should have been dedicated lighting facilities in the houses, such as ceramic multiporous utensils found in Diaolongbei phase III of Daixi culture, which might have been used for inserting burning branches for lighting or for fire-starting tools.

(4) The decline of painted pottery and rise of character symbols
Painted pottery began to decline in the core areas of early China, but it did not decline comprehensively and never disappeared. Painted pottery from the Qinwangzhai type, Dasikong type, Haishengbulang type of Yangshao culture, phase I of Xueshan culture, and Hongshan culture was derived from the painted pottery of the Miaodigou period of Yangshao culture and incorporated elements of the Northern regions. They mutually integrate, and each excels in their respective fields. The dyed-style painted pottery of Qujialing culture and the colored painted pottery of Liangzhu culture were unique. Particularly, the painted pottery of Majiayao culture became dominant unexpectedly, with its complex patterns, smooth lines, and widespread use achieving an unparalleled level. The main colors of the painted pottery remained red and black. Additionally, there was a tradition of vermilion coating in the houses in Xipo and Dadiwan, indicating a tradition of redness.

As painted pottery declined, character-like symbols became more developed. Especially after 3000 BCE, the pottery tokens of Dawenkou culture and Liangzhu culture had stable shapes and complex structures. Some even combined multiple symbols, similar to the oracle bone inscriptions of later ages, likely already being a form of a character.[170] Both painted pottery images and character symbols had the function of expressing people's ideas. Still, the images are abstract and broad, while the characters are specific, so they are different. The emergence of characters just as painted pottery declined is more than a coincidence. The late Yangshao should be a critical time for the emergence of Chinese characters. Of course, previously popular patterns such as the octagram and the sun pattern still existed and were even more widespread. In Liangzhu culture, the prevalent animal-face patterns or god-human-animal-face patterns may represent the common cognition of the cultural and spiritual level of the Liangzhu society, becoming a cultural emblem. In the northeast region, symbols such as the swastika pattern from the Eurasian grasslands also appeared.

(5) Ancestor worship system
The burials were generally vertical pit graves, and the period still featured a secularized religious belief system centered on ancestor worship. However, partial cremation graves appeared in Xueshan culture phase I of the north, Nanbaoligaotu culture, Majiayao culture, and Fanchengdui culture of the south. Some even burned bones, at least implying that these deceased were not arranging a "permanent home" underground. The large tomb at the Xipo site in the Central Plain emphasized the difference between life and death and highlighted the family or clan. There were few pottery figurines and human images, lacking idol worship or ghost worship. Particularly noteworthy is the pottery grave goods of a Xipo large tomb showing a lag, intentionally imitating the late forms of the Miaodigou type of Yangshao culture, which should reflect the ideas of ancestor worship and "retro." The Hongshan culture's "temple," "altar," "tomb," female sculptures, "only jade for burial," the altars, jade *congs*, and *bis* jade artifacts of Daixi culture, Xuejiagang culture, and Liangzhu culture, and the animal bone sacrificial pits of buried pigs and dogs, all seem to have some content of idol worship and worship of heaven and earth.[171] However, the core is still the tradition of ancestor worship.

Eastern cultures continued to worship the sun and bird, often seeing bird patterns, octagram patterns, sun patterns, etc. Some pottery texts and bottle-shaped pottery of Dawenkou culture should also be related.[172] At the same time, images of turtles and tortoises were also common. The octagram pattern spread from Dawenkou culture to Xueshan culture phase I. The Hongshan culture had a tradition of dragon worship, with numerous jade dragons and many bird themes. A rectangular jade plate unearthed at Lingjiatan is engraved with two concentric circles, with four arrowheads outside the large circle and eight inside. The core is an octagram pattern, which some believe relates to concepts of the "round heaven and square earth," the "four dimensions and eight extremes."[73] The jade eagle's wings are two pig heads, and the center is an octagram pattern. It is evident that the octagram pattern held a very special position in their social consciousness.

Distinct religious customs were present in various regions. Daixi culture, Xuejiagang culture, and Dawenkou culture in the east frequently buried pigs and dogs in sacrificial pits, and pig mandibles were popular as burial items, especially in the Northern Hubei region, where many graves only included pig mandibles, likely symbolizing wealth. Daixi culture also often buried fish. At the Qinglongquan site of Qujialing culture, there were instances of pig and dog sacrifices beneath the foundations of houses, and two bowls were found placed face-to-face beneath the ridge of the Xiaojiawuji. Qujialing culture commonly had interlocking porcelain with a lid mouth and cylindrical pottery, either plain or with multi-row added relief decorations. Dense hair-like decorations adorned the spherical protrusions, and the long, thin ends were sealed, indicating these were not ceramic water pipes. There were also potentially related vessels with four trumpet-shaped outlets. At the Yuchisi site of Dawenkou culture, a sacrificial pit was found with 12 pottery *zuns* connected. Bone divination practices first appeared in the Shilingxia type of Majiayao culture and the Ashan phase III type of Yangshao culture.

The contents of religious worship were more complex, especially in the east and the Yangtze River region where the levels of sacrificial facilities were distinct, and large-scale religious facilities appeared.

(6) The formation of initial civilization and three modes

The trend of social change and complexity intensified in the early Chalcolithic, and the characteristics of the three social development modes became more prominent.

In the Central Plain's core region and nearby Zhengzhou Xishan, city wall sites emerged, and the number of stone *yue* and stone arrowhead increased, showing that war was becoming a regular occurrence. Mass graves of humans and the use of human sacrifices in foundations indirectly reflected the frequency of wars. In graveyards like Lingbao Xipo, Yichuan Yiquecheng, and Mengjin Zhuoli in Henan Province, graves were sectioned and grouped. Multi-room houses gradually became popular at sites like Dahecun, indicating the prominence of family organization and the increasingly clear situation of male superiority and female inferiority. However, despite their scale, large graves like those at Xipo had simple and sparse burial items, reflecting a regulated understanding of life and death, the importance of nobility over wealth, orderliness, and simplicity, emphasizing social status differences but limited wealth differentiation. Besides the existence of exquisite jade and stone *yue* reflecting possible specialization in jade and stone craftsmanship, there were no signs of other craft specialization.

In the eastern region, Dawenkou culture, Songze culture–Liangzhu culture, Xuejiagang culture, Hongshan culture in the northeast, and Daixi culture–Qujialing culture in the middle reaches of the Yangtze River all commonly had city walls, developed jade and stone *yues*, and stone arrowheads, and practiced human sacrifices, fostering tense interpersonal relationships and an atmosphere of war. The graves of these cultures were typically grouped and sectioned. Liangzhu culture and Dawenkou culture also often had independent family burial sites comprised of about 20 graves, further illustrating the prominence of the family as the most important social organization and the presence of male superiority.[74] The common multi-room architecture was likely gradually built up with the expansion of families, with each building likely corresponding to one large patriarchal family. Unlike the Central Plain, these cultures had severe wealth disparity, social status differentiation, and craft specialization. Settlements could be divided into three to four levels, with large-scale central settlements like the city of Liangzhu and Shijiahe and large-scale religious centers like Niuheliang site clusters. The internal structures of the settlement clusters and the settlements themselves were complex, with clear functional divisions, including large palace-like buildings and high-level religious structures. The graves clearly demonstrated class distinctions. Liangzhu culture had specific noble "tomb hills," and large graves were accompanied by hundreds of exquisite jade objects. Although the large stone cairn graves of Hongshan culture only had 10 to 20 jade objects, these were also exquisite works of art. The jade artifacts, black pottery, and painted pottery of these cultures were all exceptionally exquisite, likely the product of specialized craftwork.

In the Northern region, stone cities with a belt-like distribution appeared in types like Yangshao culture Ashan type, with mass graves and such, likely related to a backdrop of frequent brutal wars. The separation and grouping of houses also related to family organizations, which are similar to the Central Plain and Eastern regions. However, wealth and social status differentiation in the late Yangshao culture types and Majiayao culture of the Northern region was limited. The discovery of central settlements like Qin'an Dadiwan and Qingyang Nanzuo and palace-like structures indicated the existence of differentiation among settlements and some social status differentiation. Still, wealth differentiation did not appear particularly prominent. Painted pottery production in Majiayao culture might have already specialized, but there is essentially no evidence of other craft specialization.

In conclusion, although the early Chalcolithic had three different social development modes—"Central Plain Mode," "Eastern Mode," and "Northern Mode"—they generally shared trends of social differentiation, emphasis on family, and prominence of patriarchy and militarism. The "Eastern Mode," such as Liangzhu culture, Qujialing culture, and Dawenkou culture, should have developed initial state organizations around 3000 BCE, capable of exerting a certain degree of control and management over a large area, thus entering the initial stage of civilization. Although the wealth differentiation in the "Central Plain Mode" and "Northern Mode" is not very prominent, they too could potentially exert a certain level of control and management over larger areas, with their stages of social development roughly aligning with the "Eastern Mode."

(7) The archaic state stage of early China in the cultural sense
In the early Chalcolithic, the Central Plain's core area weakened, making it difficult to exert strong influence and radiation on surrounding cultures. Consequently, surrounding cultures each developed in their direction. For the culture of the Central Plain at that time, it was an opportunity to absorb more elements from surrounding cultures. Still, its maintenance of traditions was more tenacious than any other region. The surrounding cultures finally had more opportunities for change and innovation but were still based on their original foundations. Overall, early China formed in the previous cultural sense continued to develop and did not disintegrate due to the weakening of the central core area. Moreover, due to the substantial expansion of surrounding cultures to the outer edges, the scope of early China also expanded significantly (fig. 4.19). This is a significant difference between China in a cultural sense and China in a political sense.

At that time, many regional centers appeared in China, many of which already had the nature of initial states, such as Liangzhu culture centered around the Liangzhu site cluster, Qujialing culture centered around the Shijiahe site cluster, Dawenkou culture represented by the Dawenkou Cemetery and Dantu city site, Hongshan culture centered around the Niuheliang site cluster, Yangshao culture Xiwang type represented by the Xipo large tomb, Yangshao culture Qinwangzhai type represented by the Xishan ancient city, and Majiayao culture Shilingxia type

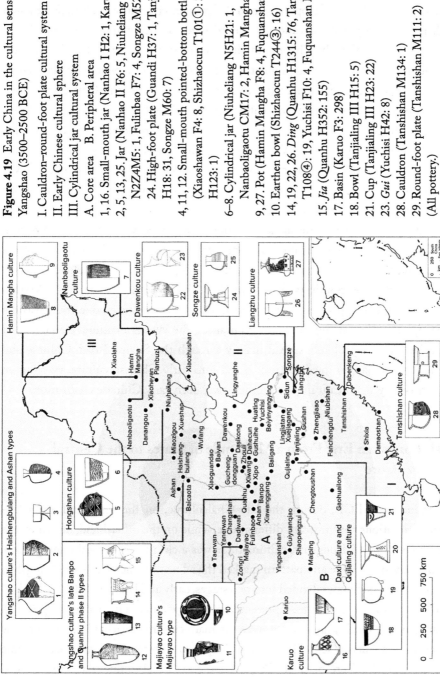

Figure 4.19 Early China in the cultural sense of the late Yangshao (3500–2500 BCE)

I. Cauldron-round-foot plate cultural system
II. Early Chinese cultural sphere
III. Cylindrical jar cultural system
A. Core area   B. Peripheral area

1, 16. Small-mouth jar (Nanhao I H2: 1, Karuo F17: 89)
2, 5, 13, 25. Jar (Nanhao II F6: 5, Niuheliang N2Z4M5: 1, Fulinbao F7: 4, Songze M52: 8) 3, 20, 24. High-foot plate (Guandi H37: 1, Tanjialing IV H18: 31, Songze M60: 7)
4, 11, 12. Small-mouth pointed-bottom bottle (Xiaoshawan F4: 8, Shizhaocun T101①: 39, Fulinbao H123: 1)
6–8. Cylindrical jar (Niuheliang N5H21: 1, Nanbaoligaotu CM17: 2, Hamin Mangha F2: 18)
9, 27. Pot (Hamin Mangha F8: 4, Fuquanshan M74: 166)
10. Earthen bowl (Shizhaocun T244③: 16)
14, 19, 22, 26. *Ding* (Quanhu H1315: 76, Tanjialing III T108④: 19, Yuchisi F10: 4, Fuquanshan M126: 7)
15. *Jia* (Quanhu H352: 155)
17. Basin (Karuo F3: 298)
18. Bowl (Tanjialing III H15: 5)
21. Cup (Tanjialing III H23: 22)
23. *Gui* (Yuchisi H42: 8)
28. Cauldron (Tanshishan M134: 1)
29. Round-foot plate (Tanshishan M111: 2)
(All pottery.)

represented by Dadiwan site B. The level of civilization and spatial range of only Liangzhu culture can be mentioned in the same breath as the contemporary West Asian and Egyptian civilizations! Its era is around 3500 BCE to 3000 BCE, roughly coinciding with the Mesopotamian and Egyptian civilizations. Overall, although there was no explicit indication of the existence of a core and sovereignty based on the whole of early China, and these small states had no clear hierarchical relationship with each other, similar to the small states or city-states controlled by priests in Western civilizations like Sumer, these small states in China were based on a previously triple-tiered large cultural circle, differentiating them from the West.

Su Bingqi proposed the path of "archaic state–regional state–empire" for civilization evolution.[175] Yan Wenming called it "archaic state–dynastic state–empire,"[176] and Wang Zhenzhong revised it to "state–dynastic state–empire."[177] We can call this era of the coexistence of these small independent states the archaic state stage or state era of early China.

Particularly worth noting is that the trend of early Chinese and Western cultural exchanges has become quite apparent. One route was the "painted pottery road" on the south and north sides of the Xizang Plateau. For instance, Majiayao culture influenced South Asia's Kashmir through the southern route, while Western elements like sheep spread to the Gansu–Qinghai area. The second route was the Steppe Road traversing the northern prairies; the Western cultural elements east of the Great Wall likely spread mainly through the Steppe Road. Chinese and Western exchanges injected fresh blood into early Chinese culture, exerting an increasingly significant impact on the newly born early Chinese civilization.

II. Longshan Era: From a Multitude of States to the Central Plain's Core

Around 2500 BCE, during the late Chalcolithic, on the one hand, some ancient traditions continued to differentiate, while on the other hand, driven by the emerging Haidai Longshan culture, there was a clear trend toward reintegration. This new appearance and pattern marked the advent of a new era—the Longshan era.[178] It can be further divided into two stages, early and late, around 2200 BCE.[179] The Longshan era cultures, represented by tri-legged vessels such as *ding*, *jia* (*li*), and *gui*, and black-gray pottery, were the main culture of early China in the new period in a cultural sense. In contrast, Majiayao culture in the west had become the marginal culture of early China (table 4.2). Social differentiation continued

Table 4.2 Cultural regions of the late Chalcolithic in China (2500–1800 BCE)

		Early stage (2500–2200 BCE)	Later stage (2200–1800 BCE)
Early Chinese cultural sphere	Most of the Yellow River and Yangtze River Basins and southern Liaodong	*Ding-jia* (*li*)–*gui* cultural system: Longshan era (Taoji culture, Miaodigou end phase II type, end Gushuihe type, Wangwan early phase III type, end Yuchisi type, Hougang early phase II type, early Laohushan culture, Keshengzhuang culture early phase II, Caiyuan culture, early Qijia culture, early Longshan culture, upper Xiaozhushan culture, Shijiahe culture, early Baodun culture, early Zhongba culture, end Liangzhu culture, Shanbei culture, and Haochuan culture)	*Ding-jia* (*li*)–*gui* cultural system: Longshan era (Late Taosi culture, Wangwan culture late phase III, Zaolütai culture, Hougang culture late phase II, Xueshan culture phase II, late Laohushan culture, Keshengzhuang culture late phase II, middle Qijia culture, late Longshan culture, upper Xiaozushan culture, Xiaojiawuji culture, late Baodun culture, late Zhongba culture, Guangfulin culture, Shanbei culture, and Haochuan culture)
	Upper reaches of the Yellow River and eastern Xizang Plateau	Jar–pot–earthen bowl–basin cultural system (Banshan type of Majiayao culture and Zongri type)	Jar–pot–earthen bowl–basin cultural system (Machang type of Majiayao culture)
	South China	Cauldron–*ding*–round-foot plate–high-foot plate cultural system (Tanshishan culture, Shixia culture, Hutoupu culture, Houshawan culture phase II, and Gantuoyan culture phase I)	Cauldron–*ding*–round-foot plate–high-foot plate cultural system (Hutoupu culture, Houshawan culture phase II, and Gantuoyan culture phase I)
	Yunnan Province	Xinguang culture	Xinguang culture
Early Chinese outer margin zone	North part of the Northeast China	Cylindrical jar cultural system	Cylindrical jar cultural system
	Other regions	Mesolithic culture	Mesolithic culture

to intensify, forming multiple regional centers and regional civilized societies, but ultimately the Central Plain were the most powerful. This was the era when the central position of the Central Plain culture gradually returned after a millennium.

1. Most of the Yellow River and Yangtze River Basins

Most Yellow and Yangtze River basins belonged to the *ding–jia* (*li*)–*gui* cultural system.

1.1 The Rise of Longshan Culture in Haidai

Around 2500 BCE, Dawenkou culture along the eastern coast of Shandong and the Wei River (one of the main rivers in Weifang City, Shandong Province) Basin was the first to develop into Longshan culture,[180] represented by early Longshan culture remains such as the Sanli River in Jiaozhou City,[181] Donghaiyu in Rizhao City,[182] Dafanzhuang in Linyi City,[183] and Lujiakou in Weifang City.[184] It later extended to the central and southern parts of Shandong, represented by the remains of Longshan culture sections I to III in Yinjiacheng, Sishui,[185] Longshan culture sections I to IV in Xiwusi, Yanzhou,[186] and Longshan culture sections I to III in Dinggong, Zouping.[187] It later expanded to the whole of Shandong and even northern Jiangsu. Its main pottery types, including *ding*, *gui*, high-foot plate, deep-belly pot, eggshell high-handle cup (fig. 4.20), cylindrical-belly cup, folded-belly pot, flat-bottom basin, *yi*, etc., are inherited from Dawenkou culture, just with more refined production and slight changes in shape. In contrast, Dawenkou culture's back pot, bottle, and *zun* basically disappeared. *Ding* has both pot and basin shapes, with the feet changing from chisel-shaped or spade-shaped to bird-head. The feet of the *yan* changed from bird-head to bag-shaped. The neck and belly of the *guis* are quite distinct; the widest part of the pot is often at the upper belly. Flat-bottom basins are often shallowly slanted-belly. High-handle cups have larger mouths, cylindrical-penetrating handles became more popular, and bird-head-foot *yans*, tri-looped-legged plates, round-foot plates, tile-foot or

Figure 4.20 Longshan culture eggshell black pottery cups from the Sanlihe site
Left: M2113: 3   Right: M203: 2

round-foot basins, *leis*,* boxes, cloud-thunder patterns, animal-face patterns, etc., appeared. Around 2200 BCE, entering the late Longshan period, represented by the remains of Longshan culture sections IV to VI in Yinjiacheng, Sishui, and Longshan culture section V in Xiwusi, Yanzhou, the feet of the *ding* gradually changed to side-mounted triangular; the bag feet of the *yan* became more and more apparent; the neck and belly of *gui* were not very distinct, the widest part of the pot was often in the middle belly; flat-bottom basins were often nearly straight and deeper, the appearance of folded-wall vessel lids, the mouths of porcelain with lids vessels, and false-round-foot vessels increased significantly; *Li* influenced by the Central Plain Longshan culture appeared. It also expanded to the northwestern part of Shandong, represented by Longshan culture remains in Shangzhuang, Chiping,[188] influenced by phase II of Hougang culture with double-belly basins, jar-shaped *jias*, and common basket patterns, square patterns, rope patterns, etc. Longshan culture jade artifacts include *yue*, knife, jade *zhang* (an ancient Chinese jade used for rituals), *bi* with protruding teeth (tooth-shaped *bi*), connected *bi*, bracelet, crown decoration, bird, etc. Jade *zhangs* were new, some inlaid with turquoise or engraved with animal-face patterns. There were stone *yues* and double-holed stone knives. Copper awls, copper bars, copper lumps, etc., were found at sites such as Sanlihe, Yangjiaquan, Yaowangcheng, and Dafanzhuang. Longshan culture can be divided into five or six local types.[189]

Longshan culture exhibits significant settlement differentiation, believed to have at least four levels. Many rammed earth city wall sites or central settlements, such as Chengziya in Zhangqiu, Tonglin in Linzi, Dinggong in Zouping, Bianxianwang in Shouguang, Jingyanggang in Yanggu, Jiaochangpu in Chiping, Dantu in Wulian, Yaowangcheng in Rizhao, and Liangchengzhen and Tenghualuo in Lianyungang, have been found, forming several settlement groups around them. Notably, the special-status Tonglin in northern Shandong found various sizes of "*lieyan*" in its ash pits, surrounded by eight "satellite" settlements. In southeastern Shandong, Liangchengzhen[190] and Yaowangcheng[191] were two central settlements, with exquisite jade artifacts found in Liangchengzhen.[192] Yaowangcheng's city wall base was padded with stone blocks, and rammed earth bases for 8 to 9 square meters of religious buildings were discovered. Houses were of three types: semi-subterranean, ground-level, and platform-based, square or round, usually single-room, but some had connected rooms. Walls were typically wooden frames with

---

* *Lei* is a kind of wine container in ancient China. It has a small mouth, wide shoulders, a deep belly, and round feet. It is usually covered and mostly made of bronze or pottery. It can also be used as a washing utensil.—Trans.

mud but rammed earth, and adobe walls also existed. The practice of smearing white lime on the ground and the wall skirt might have been borrowed from Hougang culture phase II. Cemeteries were typically small, with ten to twenty burials, with vertical pit burials and extended supine being the norm, with pottery as the main burial goods. The custom of burying with deer teeth and pig mandibles continued. There were significant status differences in scale, burial quality, and quantity. The highest-level burials, such as those at Xizhufeng in Linqu[193] and Yinjiacheng in Sishui, had two-tier platforms, painted coffins and caskets, side and foot boxes for placing burial goods, and were accompanied by numerous exquisite pottery items, including eggshell black pottery cups, jade crown decorations inlaid with turquoise, four-hole jade knives, jade hairpins, and crocodile scale plates (alligator drum) (figs. 4.21 and 4.22).

The tools of Longshan culture are essentially the same as those of the late Dawenkou culture. Stone tools include polished axes, adzes, chisels, *jues* (ancient Chinese farming tools for digging in the earth here), shovels, sickles, knives, arrowheads, etc. The proportion of farming tools such as *jues*, shovels, sickles, and knives is higher than that of Dawenkou culture, and there are quite a few clam knives. Carbonized rice grains have been excavated from the Sanlihe, Yaowangcheng, and Zhuanglixi sites. Rice imprints were found at the Yangjiaquan site, while carbonized wheat was found at the Liangchengzhen, Jiaochangpu, and Zhaojiazhuang in Jiaozhou sites.[194] These findings suggest the coexistence of millet grain, rice, and wheat agriculture in Longshan culture. Livestock was mostly pigs, followed by dogs, and domestic sheep were found at the Yaoguanzhuang and Jingyanggang sites. The types and quantities of ground stone and bone arrowheads increased significantly, with various types including horizontal cross section triangles, diamonds, etc. The late Longshan period saw the emergence of microlith arrowheads. There were also fish spears, fishhooks, spears, net pendants, spindle whorls, etc., indicating that hunting and fishing still played a significant role. A new building tool, the stone trowel, appeared. The pottery-making technology of Longshan culture, especially the eggshell pottery, reached an unprecedented and unsurpassed level, and the jade carving was intricate.

1.2 The Formation of Longshan Culture Subsystem in Central Plain

Around the same time as the formation of Longshan culture, the culture of the Central Plain also underwent transformation and reintegration. Since the reintegrated cultural remains in each region of the Central Plain cannot be accom-

THE ARCHAIC STATE STAGE OF EARLY CHINA 199

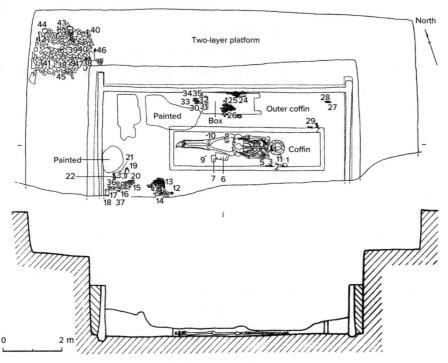

Figure 4.21 Plan and section of Xizhufeng cemetery M202

1, 2. Jade head (crown) decoration
3. Jade hairpin
4, 5, 9, 10. Turquoise decoration
6. Jade knife
7, 8. Jade *yue*
11. Turquoise lithic flake
12, 26. Crocodile bone plate
13, 15, 22, 25. Pottery eggshell cup
14, 20, 40. Pottery jar
16, 18, 19, 21. Pottery single-handle cup
17, 38, 47. Pottery *lei*
23. Bone dagger
24. Sharpening stone
27, 28. Bone arrowhead
29. Ivory slice decoration
30–35. Stone arrowhead
36, 37. Pottery lid
39. Pottery *ding*
41, 42. Pottery basin
43–46. Pottery *gui*

Figure 4.22 Jade hairpin from Xizhufeng burial (M202: 1, 2)

modated in a typical archaeological culture, they have been divided into several different "cultures." However, the ancient foundation of Central Plain culture still exists, and internal regional exchanges remain relatively close, so they can still be encompassed by the concept of "Longshan culture in Central Plain." Central Plain Longshan culture also has early and late stages.

Taosi and Late Taosi Culture

Around 2500 BCE, entering the early Longshan period, the cultural appearance of southern Shanxi changed, giving birth to the brand-new Taosi culture.[195] The early Taosi culture, represented by the remains of the Taosi site in Xiangfen, Shanxi,[196] is primarily limited to the Linfen Basin in the north. The areas of Yuncheng and Yuanqu in the south still have the remains of end Miaodigou II type culture, represented by the Dongguan of the ancient Yuanqu ancient city. The Taosi culture is actually formed on the basis of the Miaodigou II type of Yangshao culture, incorporating many eastern cultural elements.[197] Its stove, *jia*, basin-shaped *ding*, *zeng*, wide-flare-mouth jar, slanted-belly basin, folded-belly basin, flat pot, etc., belong to the traditional artifacts of the Miaodigou II type. Still, there are also many influences from the late Liangzhu or Dawenkou culture. These include frequently painted high-neck folded-shoulder *zun*, folded-belly *zun*, *gui*, and high-foot plate, with red as the base color and white, yellow, black, blue, green, and other colors in the decorative patterns, including *Hui* patterns, spiral patterns, linked patterns, coiling dragon patterns, etc. Painted wooden or lacquerwares, such as wooden board, chopping block, plate, high-foot plate, basin, spoon, bowl, cup, *gu*, and granary-shaped vessel, as well as the curved ruler-shaped kitchen knife, multi-holed knife, *yue*, shovel, *qi* (battle-axe, a name for an ancient Chinese weapon), jade *cong*, *bi*, jade *huang*, and *bi* with protruding teeth (tooth-shaped *bi*), jade or stone tools, are also included. The late Taosi culture, represented by the "middle" of the Taosi site and the Xiajin Cemetery in Linfen,[198] expanded southward to the Yuncheng Basin and even to the Ruicheng area along the Yellow River.[199] This period saw the emergence of painted deep-belly *gui* (an ancient Chinese container or a ritual vessel here), long-neck bottles, with high-neck folded-shoulder bottles becoming slenderer. A few *jia*-style *lis* from Laohushan culture, cylindrical-penetrating handles style and some animal-face crown-shaped ornaments belong to Longshan culture influences.

Taosi ancient city is divided into two periods, with the smaller city from the earlier period covering an area of about 560,000 square meters[200] and the larger city from the later period covering about 2.8 million square meters.[201] In the larger city, large, rammed earth architectural foundations covering tens of thousands of square meters have been discovered, with the main palace covering more than 280 square meters, which includes sacrifices made during foundation laying. Nearby, remains of arsenic-copper containers, stone kitchen knives, and painted pottery have been excavated.[202] A semi-circular architectural foundation covering about 1,740 square meters has also been found, with a concentric circle of rammed earth observation points at the center, and more than ten radiating observation crevices constructed on the southeast side, which may have functioned as an astronomical observatory[203] or also served as a site for rituals. Additionally, a large storage area with cellars was discovered in the eastern part of the city, where exquisitely carved white wall plaster was unearthed. Common houses included cave, half-underground, and rammed earth surface styles, with white ash ground and dado commonly seen.[204] Ceramic kiln[205] and lime kiln sites were also discovered.

Taosi culture has a large-scale cemetery with a clear division and orderly arrangement. All graves are vertical pit graves, some with wall niches, and corpses were laid on their backs with extended supine. Six large graves from the early Taosi period contained cinnabar in the coffins. They were accompanied by precious ritual vessels such as jade *yues*, jade *congs*, jade *bis*, alligator drums, chime stones, stone kitchen knives, wooden boards, wooden boxes, lacquer highfoot plate vessels, painted coiling dragon pattern pottery plates (fig. 4.23), painted pottery pots, and pig skeletons.[206] The occupants of the large graves were likely the rulers of the early city, with their graves significantly different in scale from the many other medium and small graves, indicating a clear class distinction and departing from the previously modest and simple style of the Miaodigou II type. Late-period graves like II M22 were highly ornate, with decorations of grass-mixed mud on the interior walls, wall niches at the bottom of all four walls, and red-painted wooden coffins. There were more than 100 remaining burial items, including jade *yue*, jade *qi*, jade *cong*, *bi*, jade animal-face crownshaped ornament, jade *huang*, painted pottery *gui* (an ancient Chinese container or a ritual vessel here), lacquer high-foot plate, and other valuable items, as well as neatly arranged sets of stone kitchen knives, wooden boards, and split pig sacrifices.[207]

Figure 4.23 Painted coiling dragon-pattern pottery plate from the Taosi site (M3072: 6)

This grave was extremely grand, suggesting that the occupant may have been one of the highest rulers of Taosi ancient city. In phase III of the Qingliangsi site, half of the graves contained one to three sacrificial victims, and M146 even had four, which not only serves as evidence of class differentiation but also is likely related to influences from cultures like Liangzhu.

Around 2200 BCE, the southward migration of Laohushan culture had a significant impact on Taosi culture,[208] which transitioned into the late Taosi culture, represented by Taosi IIIH303.[209] This also included the primary remains in Quwo Dongxu,[210] Fangcheng,[211] and Yicheng Nanshi.[212] A large number of double-handle *lis* of Laohushan culture appeared, as well as single-handle *lis*, *yans*, *jias*, deep-belly *guis*, folded-shoulder jars, round-foot jars, wide-flare-mouth jars, folded-belly basins, slanted-belly basins, *zengs*, single-handle jars, single-handle or double-handle flat-bottom or tri-legged cups, thick-handle or thin-handle high-foot plates. Cauldron-ranges and cylindrical jars gradually disappeared. Influenced by Laohushan culture, scorch-mark divination bones appeared, and individual *gui* and *he* belonged to Wangwan culture phase III. Curved chopper-shaped stone kitchen knives and ring-handle pottery mats were still popular.

The transition from Taosi culture to late Taosi culture is clearly reflected in settlement forms. For instance, the large city of Taosi was suddenly abandoned, and many killed and discarded human bones, especially those of mutilated females,[213] were found in the early late Taosi period in the ash trench IHG8. The larger graves of Taosi, Xiajincun, and Qingliangsi were almost all disturbed and looted. Interestingly, a large bag-foot *li* was found in the disturbance hole of Qingliangsi M269, which can be seen as compelling evidence that northern groups disturbed and destroyed the graves of Taosi culture. The housing situation was similar to the early period. Adult graves returned to the previous simple vertical pit form, most without burial goods, some with individual stone knives, jade *yuans* (ancient Chinese *bis* with large holes and small sides), *bi* with protruding teeth, bronze bells, and bronze gear-shaped artifacts.

The production tools of Taosi culture and the late Taosi culture were roughly the same, mainly still the axes, adzes, chisels, shovels, knives, and other stone tools seen early in the Miaodigou II type. As agricultural tools, stone shovels with or without shoulders were carefully ground; knives (sickle claws) were mainly rectangular perforated stone knives, with fewer pottery and shell ones. Carbonized millet grains as well as rice grains and wheat were found in the cellars, and human bone tests showed that the residents mainly consumed millet grains.[214] Livestock included pigs, dogs, cattle, and sheep. Various stone arrowheads, including diamond-shaped and triangular cross-sections, appeared, and microlith arrowheads appeared in the late period.

Wangwan Culture Phase III

At the beginning of the early Longshan period, the Sanmenxia region in the western part of western Henan was still characterized by the end remains of Yangshao culture. The Miaodigou II type in the area near Luoyang was still represented by the end remains of the Gu River type of Yangshao culture, represented by Xinan Xiwo[215] and Jiyuan Changquan[216] "Miaodigou culture phase II." There were transitions from horizontal to slanted basket patterns; the mouth of the *jia* became larger, and the feet moved outward; and elements of Shijiahe culture appeared, such as red slanted-belly pottery cups. At the same time or slightly later, in the central part of Henan, Wangwan culture phase III Haojiatai type[217] was formed, represented by Yancheng Haojiatai phases I and II[218] and Shangcai Shilipu phases II and III.[219] In the western part of Henan, Wangwan culture phase III Zhongziping type was formed, represented by Xin'an Zhongziping "Longshan culture remains."[220] Their deep-belly jars, high-neck jars, earthen bowls, basins, and flat-bottom bowls all developed from the local Gu River type. The two types differed mainly in that the Haojiatai type had many *dings*—with conical feet, wide-flat feet, and a few short-foot *dings*, bird-head-foot *dings*, common bag-foot *guis*, flat-bottom solid-foot *guis*, funnel-shaped mortars and pestles, folded-rim high-foot plates, round-foot plates, *gus*, *gu*-shaped cups, folded-belly pots. In contrast, the Zhongziping type had fewer *dings* and more *jias*, with many double-belly basins, plain jars, and a few *lis*, *yans*, and stoves. Among them, the bag-foot *gui*, flat-bottom solid-foot *gui*, bird-head-foot *ding*, folded-rim high-foot plate, round-foot plate, *gu*-shaped cup, and folded-belly pot are closely related to Longshan culture. The *gu* may be a legacy of Liangzhu culture. Funnel-shaped mortars and pestles, wide-flat-foot *dings*, and red slanted-belly pottery cups, which are common in both types, belong to Shijiahe culture elements. The *li* and *yan* reflect the influence of Taosi culture, while the double-belly basin and plain jar are common to the Zhongziping type and Hougang culture phase II.

In the late Longshan period, Wangwan culture phase III—Haojiatai type, in the southern side of Songshan, develop into the Meishan type, represented by Ruzhou Meishan[221] and Dengfeng Wangchenggang[222] Longshan remains. The northern side of Songshan saw Wangwan culture phase III Zhongziping type develop into the Wangwan type, spreading to the Zhengzhou area, represented by the Luoyang Wangwan III remains. The Meishan type saw a surge in short-foot *ding*, and the Wangwan type introduced the *he*, with the two types exchanging features. In the late Wangwan culture phase III, there was a strong outward expansion and influence, with the Wangwan type having a strong northwestward influence on the Sanmenxia, Yuncheng, and Yuanqu regions, leading to the appearance of remains represented by the late Longshan period in Shan County Sanliqiao,[223] Xia County Dongxiafeng,[224] and Yuanqu ancient city Dongguan, which can be termed Wangwan culture phase III Sanliqiao type.[225] Among them, jar-shaped *jias*, handless or singe-handle *lis*, single-handle or double-handle jars, and *guis* (ancient Chinese containers or ritual vessels here) belong to the phase II of Keshengzhuang culture or the late Taosi culture elements. The Meishan type expanded southward on a large scale, replacing Shijiahe culture in southern Henan, northern Hubei, and western Hubei, forming Wangwan culture phase III represented by the phase II of Zhumadian Yangzhuang in southeastern Henan and northern Hubei,[226] Wangwan culture phase III represented by the Longshan remains of Xichuan Xiawanggang in southwestern Henan and northwestern Hubei, and the Shibanxiangzi type represented by the Yidu Shibanxiangzi remains[227] in the Xiajiang area of western Hubei. Among them, the single-handle, double-handle, or triple-handle jars of the Xiawanggang type belong to phase II of Keshengzhuang culture elements, and the cauldrons of the Shibanxiangzi type are due to local traditional elements. By the late Longshan period, there emerged in the east of Songshan, represented by Xinmi Xinzhai phase II,[228] Wangwan culture phase III Xinzhai type, the pottery of which, including the mouths of porcelains with lids vessels (including jars, *dings*, urns, earthen bowls in the mouths of porcelains with lids, respectively, etc.), high-foot jar-shaped *dings*, folded-wall lid vessels, flat-bottom basins, and *yans*, reflected a strong influence from Zaolütai culture of eastern Henan.

The settlement differentiation of Wangwan culture phase III is quite significant.[229] In the early stage, city sites such as Yancheng Haojiatai have already appeared. In the later stage, there are more city sites such as Dengfeng Wangchenggang, Pingdingshan Puchengdian, and Xinmi Xinzhai. Among them, the Wangchenggang site consists of two small cities and one large city. The large city covers an area of 350,000 square meters and contains human and animal foundation pits. There are also high-level central settlements such as Yuzhou Wadian, where exquisite black pottery and jades such as *bi*, *yue*, and bird have been unearthed (fig. 4.24).[230] The Meishan house construction is mainly continuous ground style, with timber-framed earthen walls, rammed earth walls, or earthen walls. The Wangwan type and Sanliqiao type are mainly semi-subterranean and cave style, all commonly using white ash to smear the ground and skirt of the wall.

In the Zhaicheng site of Xinmi ancient city, a rammed earth platform palace-style building covering more than 380 square meters was discovered.[231] Adult graves are all rectangular vertical pit graves with extended prone, most without burial goods. There are a few potteries accompanying the burial and a number of infant urn burials. In many sites such as Wangwan, Meishan, Wadian, Xinzhai, Cuoli, and Xiaopangou, disordered human burial pits were found, with bodies decapitated or incomplete, or even co-existing with animal bones, showing that social contradictions had intensified to a considerable degree, consistent with the social complexity reflected by city walls and palace-style buildings.

Production tools are close to the Gu River type of Yangshao culture and Miaodigou II type, mainly still axes, adzes, chisels, shovels, knives, sickles, and arrowheads, but they are more finely ground, and the number of stone sickles has increased. The number of ground stone arrowheads has greatly increased, with many types such as triangular, diamond, and round cross-sections, and also a type of round-head arrow-shaped tool. Microlith arrowheads appeared in the late Longshan period. There were weapons such as *yues* and spears. There were also many bone arrowheads, bone shovels, and shell knives. Many sites found carbonized millet grains and rice remains, with millet agriculture being the main agricultural crop and rice agriculture being secondary. Wheat was also found in sites like Yuzhou Wadian, and domestic animals such as pigs, dogs, and sheep were raised. A piece of tin-lead bronze container fragment was found at Wangchenggang, a piece of copper smelting crucible fragment and copper slag was found at the Meishan site, and a small copper piece was found at Zhengzhou Dongzhai, indicating that the late Wangwan culture phase III was already capable of casting bronze and even copper vessels.

Figure 4.24 Black *gu*-shaped pottery cup from the Wadian site (IT3H12: 11)

Zaolütai Culture

In the early Longshan period, the eastern Henan Province and northern Anhui Province regions were still primarily characterized by the end Dawenkou culture Yuchisi type, with a small infiltration of Longshan cultural elements like egg-shelled black pottery cups, *guis*, etc. There were also signs of Shijiahe culture, such as red pottery cups. In the later the early Longshan period and up until the late Longshan period, the Yuchisi type evolved into Zaolütai culture,[232] represented by Longshan sites in Yongcheng Zaolütai,[233] Wangyoufang,[234] and Bengbu Yuhui in Henan.[235] Its main pottery types include tri-legged pot-shaped *dings* with triangular or chiseled-shaped feet, deep-belly pots, wide-mouth pots, high-neck jars, high-neck pots, high-foot plates, flat-bottom basins, flat-bottom bowls, cylindrical-belly cups, *gu*-shaped cups, and *zuns* (vats), which inherit from the Yuchisi type. *Gui* vessels, bird head-legged tri-legged pots, false-round-foot vats, urns, round-foot plates, and false-round-foot vessel lids reflect a strong influence from Longshan culture, so much so that some people include them within Longshan culture.[236] Meanwhile, short-neck urns, basket-pattern deep-belly jars, basin-shaped mortars and pestles, etc., reflect the influence of Wangwan culture phase III. The *yan* is likely influenced by Hougang culture phase II, folded-belly basins or double-belly basins by Wangwan culture phase III or Hougang culture phase II. Long-neck pots, *zengs*, etc., belong to Shijiahe culture. The long-neck *he* is similar to the vessel of Shijiahe culture and final Liangzhu culture. Zaolütai culture also presents local variations. In the eastern Henan region, the characteristic round-belly tri-legged pots with triangular side feet, common short-neck urns, false-round-foot knob lids often with folded walls, and many *yans* can be classified as the Wangyoufang type. In the northern Anhui region, *dings* with drooping bellies are common, high-neck jars are often seen, false-round-foot knob lids often have curved walls, and there are characteristic vessels like false-belly high round-foot *guis*, long-neck pots, and shallow plates, which can be called the Yuhui type.[237] In the late Zaolütai culture, there was a temporary southeastward expansion to the Jianghuai area, leaving behind sites such as Xinghua Nandang[238] and Gaoyou Zhoubeidun in Jiangsu Province,[239] which can be called the Nandang type. The side triangular-foot *ding* is rarely seen with basket patterns or square patterns and mostly has marked-cord patterns or plain surfaces. The *yan* has a shallow belly; some columnar-foot *dings* are local traditions.

A 50,000-square-meter square city site built with rammed earth was found at Huaiyang Pingliangtai. The layout is regular, with gatehouses (塾, *shu*)* on both sides of the south gate. Under the central road, there is a "品" (*pin*) shaped drain made of ceramic pipes. Inside the city, there are rectangular row houses with walls

---

* Ancient Chinese places used to teach and study.—Trans.

made of earth bricks.[240] Other sites mostly have square or round ground buildings, either in rows or single rooms, with walls made of earth bricks or timber-framed earthen, and white ash is popularly used for the surface. There are lime pits and wells. Graves are all rectangular vertical pit graves with extended supine. Zaolütai culture has a strong religious color. A large strip-shaped sacrificial site of 2,000 square meters was found at the Yuhui site, with layers of the earth of different colors padded and long rows of postholes on top. A sacrificial platform was found at the Lutaigang site in Qi County, a cattle sacrifice pit at the Pingliangtai site, and a chaotic burial pit at the Yuchisi site in Mengcheng. There are cases of children or adults being used as sacrificial foundations at the Pingliangtai, Wangyoufang, and other sites, with some male skulls being decapitated.

Stone tools mainly include axes, adzes, chisels, shovels, knives, arrowheads, and *yues*. Polished stone arrowheads are numerous and varied, similar to those found in Wangwan culture phase III. There also appeared microlith arrowheads. Bone tools include arrowheads, darts, and more. Shell tools, such as knives, sickles, arrowheads, etc., are common. There are also pottery plasterers for wall smoothing and pottery mats for pottery making. Carbonized seeds of crops such as wheat, rice, and millet were found at the Yuhui site. A knife-shaped copper relic was unearthed at the Lutaigang site, a small copper chunk at the Luantai site, and copper slag at the Pingliangtai site, indicating the emergence of a copper tool manufacturing technology.

Hougang Culture Phase II and Xueshan Culture Phase II

During the Longshan period, northern Henan Province and southern Hebei Province were characterized by Hougang culture phase II, while central and north Hebei and the Beijing–Tianjin area were characterized by Xueshan culture phase II. The overall appearances of these two cultures are very similar.

Hougang culture phase II is represented by Longshan sites at Anyang Hougang II,[241] Tangyin Baiying,[242] and Hui County Mengzhuang in Henan Procince. Xueshan culture phase II is represented by Beijing Changping Xueshan phase II,[243] Fangshan Zhenjiangying Neolithic phase IV,[244] and Renqiu Yabazhuang phase I in Hebei Province.[245] The main pottery types of both cultures include *yans*, *jias*, deep-belly jars, short-neck urns, large-mouth urns, flat-bottom basins, tile-foot basins, *zengs*, high-foot plates, round-foot plates, pots, flat-bottom bowls, and cylindrical-belly cups, among others. Especially distinctive are the plain deep-belly jars made of clamped-shell pottery. The former culture has a greater variety of double-belly basins, slanted-belly earthen bowls, cauldron-shaped *jias*, and mortars and pestles, common to Wangwan culture phase III, and *dings* were similar to those of Zaolütai culture, with mainly gray pottery. The latter culture has a greater variety of double-handle bag-foot *lis* and elements of Laohushan culture, with a significant number of red-brown pottery flakes.

Hougang culture phase II can be divided into two stages: the early stage represented by the early to middle Longshan sites at Hougang and the early Longshan site at Mengzhuang, where *yans* have plain feet without solid foot roots, the widest part of the deep-belly pot is close to the upper belly, and the flat-bottom basins have shallow bellies slanting straight; and the later stage represented by the late Longshan sites at Hougang and Mengzhuang, where *yans* have corded foot decoration with solid foot roots, the widest part of the deep-belly pot is lowered to the middle belly, and the flat-bottom basins have deeply curved bellies. Xueshan culture phase II is roughly equivalent to the later Hougang culture phase II and should result from the northern expansion of Hougang culture phase II. The deep-belly jars, short-neck urns, large-mouth urns, flat-bottom basins, flat-bottom bowls, and cylindrical cups of the early Hougang culture phase II all have a heritage relationship with the Taikou type of Yangshao culture. The jar-shaped *jia* should be a variant of the cauldron-shaped *jia* from southern Shanxi, and the bag-foot *yan* may be an invention based on the solid-foot *yan* and *jia* of the Yuchisi type. The double-belly basin should be a joint creation with Wangwan culture phase III. The bird-head-foot *ding*, *gui*, *lei*, round-foot plate, tile-foot basin, basin in the mouth of porcelain with a lid, urn in the mouth of porcelain with a lid, false-round-foot folded-wall lid, and basin-shaped lid with cylindrical-penetrating handles, etc., appearing in the early stage of Hougang culture phase II and Xueshan culture phase II, should be related to the strong influence from Longshan culture.

During the Mengzhuang site excavation, the cultural remains of the Hougang phase II city site were discovered, covering an area of approximately 140,000 square meters and surrounded by outer moats. The rammed earth walls at the Hougang site may also be part of the city walls. Hougang culture phase II houses were predominantly circular ground-level structures with wooden beams, mud walls, or adobe walls. White plaster was commonly used, and some houses had wooden floors. Water wells were frequently found, with the square wooden structure water well at the Baiying site being the most representative. There were also white-plastered pit dwellings. Adult burials were primarily rectangular vertical pit graves without accompanying burial goods and infant urn burials were also found. Random burial pits and instances of foundation ceremonies involving children were discovered. Xueshan culture phase II revealed the presence of round semi-subterranean structures and square wooden structure water wells. The tools of these two cultures were similar to those of Wangwan culture phase III and Zaolütai culture, with more polished stone tools such as arrowheads, scrapers, and blades later. Agriculture focused on millet cultivation, and animals such as pigs, dogs, and sheep were raised.

Laohushan Culture

The Laohushan culture was prevalent in the southern part of Inner Mongolia, central and northern Shanxi, northern Shaanxi, and northwestern Hebei, corresponding to the narrow definition of the "Northern region."[246] It is represented by the Laohushan site in Liangcheng, Inner Mongolia. It includes other Laohushan sites such as Yuanzigou in Liangcheng[247] and Yongxingdian, Jungar, Inner Mongolia,[248] Xinghuacun in Fenyang[249] and Youyao in Xinzhou, Shanxi,[250] Shenmu Shimao in Shaanxi,[251] and Shaizilingluo in Yu County, Hebei.[252] Common pottery shapes in this culture included double-handle or ring-shaped handled vessels, such as *jias* or *jia*-shaped *lis*, *yans*, *hes*, deep-belly jars, high-neck jars, short-neck urns, straight-wall vats, high-neck *zuns*, wide-mouth *zuns*, wide-mouth urns, converging-mouth urns, single or double-handle jars, slanted-belly basins, folded-belly basins, high-foot plates, earthen bowls, bowls, pots, and *zengs*. A few red copper bracelets were also found. The Laohushan culture can be divided into two phases. The early phase featured horizontal basket patterns and had cauldron-shaped *jia* and introduced *jia*-shaped *li* based on it. Based on regional differences, it can be further classified into Laohushan, Yongxingdian, and Youyao types. The later phase featured diagonal basket patterns, and the *jia*-shaped *li* evolved into *li*. Tri-legged urns already appeared in northern Shaanxi. This phase can be further classified into Baicaota, Youyao, and Shaizilingluo types.[253] The Laohushan culture primarily developed from the Ashan III type of Yangshao culture, specifically the Ashan phase III type. However, the origin of the newly emerged cauldron-shaped *jia* is believed to be in the Southern Shanxi regions. Other pottery vessels such as *yan* and *he* may have connections with Hougang culture phase II.

The Laohushan culture typically features clusters of settlements, many of which are stone cities surrounded by stone walls, with some serving as central settlements. The situations of the Yuanzigou and Laohushan settlements in the settlement clusters on the north shore of the Daihai are the clearest during the early Longshan period. The houses in the Yuanzigou settlement are combined to form courtyards, clusters, and rows (fig. 4.25), which may represent different

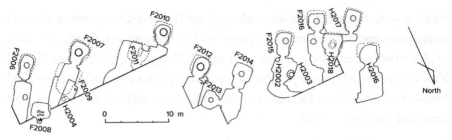

Figure 4.25 Plans of cave-style houses of part Laohushan culture in Yuanzigou site section II

levels of social organization such as families, extended families, and clans, and the three districts maybe three large clans, forming a clan commune for the entire settlement. The overall layout of the Laohushan settlement is similar to that of Yuanzigou, except that the main body of the settlement is surrounded by a stone wall. Special facilities include small square stone circles, stone wall houses, stone piles on the top of the mountain, and concentrated kiln sites outside the "city." The most representative of the late Longshan period is the stone city of Shenmu Shimao in Shaanxi, which is divided into inner and outer cities, covering a total area of up to four million square meters, with large-scale facilities such as city gates.[254] It should at least have been the central settlement of the northern Shaanxi region at the time. The houses of Laohushan culture are mainly cave style houses composed of protruding main rooms and rectangular outer rooms, as well as stone wall ground style and semi-underground houses, with floors and wall dado smeared with grass-mixed mud and white lime, and some have black or red lines painted around the firepits or on the walls. The burials are all vertical pit graves that can only accommodate the body, mainly in extended supine with few burial objects and accompanying objects. A rare sight is a tomb in Jungar Erliban where the tomb owner wore stone-bead decorations and a copper bracelet, and several flakes of pottery were buried with him. Pottery-making sites composed of kilns, workrooms, worktables, storage rooms, etc., were found at sites like Laohushan. The volume of pottery kilns has significantly increased, with a diameter of more than two meters.

Ground stone tools include ordinary axes, *yues*, shovels, adzes, chisels, knives, etc., and exquisite stone spinning wheels and lime-smeared stone plasterers. In addition, there are also microlith arrowheads and mushroom-shaped pottery mats. The economy was probably based on millet farming, with hunting and gathering also playing an important role.

Furthermore, in the early Longshan period, there were also Ganquan Shijiawan-type remains in the southern part of northern Shaanxi.[255] The pottery is coarse, and small-mouth high-neck jars (pots), double-handle jars, stoves, double-handle curved-belly basins, etc., clearly inherit the Xiaoguandao type or Miaodigou II type of Yangshao culture, indicating that it mainly developed based on local culture. However, the large-mouth folded-belly *jia* is a product influenced by the Taosi type,[256] and the red pottery cup is a typical element of Shijiahe culture in the Jianghan region. The Shijiawan settlement also has cave-style houses, with the ground and walls covered in white lime.

Keshengzhuang Culture Phase II, Qijia Culture, and Caiyuan Culture

During the Longshan era, Keshengzhuang culture phase II, Qijia culture, and Caiyuan culture were distributed in places like Guanzhong, Longdong, and southern Ningxia, represented by the Keshengzhuang phase II in Xi'an, Shaanxi,[257] the phases VII of the Shizhaocun and Xishanping in Tianshui,[258] and the Caiyuan Linziliang remains in Haiyuan, Ningxia.[259] Their overall characteristics are mainly similar.[260] Keshengzhuang culture early phase II, the early Qijia culture, and Caiyuan culture belong to the early Longshan period. The Keshengzhuang culture late phase II and the middle Qijia culture belong to the late Longshan period.

In the early Longshan period, all three cultures popularized baskets, marked cords, and other piled patterns. The main types of vessels are *jias* or *jia*-shaped *lis*, small-mouth high-neck jars, neck-bundled jars, single-handle or double-handle jars, floral-rim jars, slanted-belly basins, folded-belly or curved-belly basins, high-foot plates, flat-bottom bowls, *zengs*, and mortars and pestles. Only the *jia*-shaped *lis* of Keshengzhuang culture phase II is slender and tall, with tower-shaped knob lids, converging-mouth urns, *guis*, etc. The *jia*-shaped *li* of Qijia culture is shorter and also has a tower-shaped knob lid, converging-mouth urn, *gui*, etc. The Caiyuan culture has a small amount of painted pottery, mainly in black or composed of multi-colors with red (brown) or purple, with sawtooth, grid, diamond, checkerboard, overlapping arc, scale, and circle patterns. In the belly of the pot, it is often divided into several large units with circles, triangles, diamonds, etc., filled with various patterns and even human-like painted pottery pots. Keshengzhuang culture phase II and Caiyuan culture were respectively developed from the Quanhu II and Changshan types of Yangshao culture. Qijia culture is a local variant of Keshengzhuang culture phase II. The *gui* of Keshengzhuang culture phase II and Qijia culture newly emerged from the Central Plain region, but the earlier source is in Longshan culture. The multicolored painted pottery, oblique-mouth pots, and double-holed knives of Caiyuan culture should come from the Haishengbulang type of the eastern Yangshao culture and Xueshan culture phase I, etc.[261] In the late Longshan period, Caiyuan culture disappeared, and the *jia*-shaped *li* of Keshengzhuang culture phase II and Qijia culture became *li*. Of note is that at this time, Qijia culture expanded from eastern Gansu to central and western Gansu, eastern Qinghai, and southern Ningxia. Jade artifacts like *bis*, jade *congs*, multi-holed knives, etc., should be related to the influence of Taosi culture, and many "jade *huangs*" may be connected to form *bis* or rings. In the western part of Qinghai Ledu Liuwan[262] and Wuwei Huangniangniangtai[263] sites, a small amount of painted pottery was found, mainly a legacy of Majiayao culture Majiayao type. A pointed-crown pattern (some call it a variant frog pattern) should be an element from the Central Asian Bronze Age. All three cultures have discovered many scapula bones of sheep, pigs, and cows used for divination.

The housing in all three cultures is basically cave-style construction with walls tapering upward, mostly square or rectangular, with some circular ones. White ash surface floors and wall dado are popular, and some white ash surfaces are painted with red lines. Building components such as red pottery cylinder tiles and slab tiles, which may belong to Qijia culture, have been found in Qiaozhen, Baoji,[264] and Qiaocun, Lingtai (fig. 4.26). There are many wedge-shaped small holes for inserting illuminating objects on the walls of houses in Linziliang. Houses are combined into courtyards, groups, rows, etc., and the social organization method is similar to Laohushan culture. Some bag-shaped pits are padded with wooden boards or bark, which are grain pits or artifact storage. There are pottery kilns and lime-burning kilns. The Caiyuan culture cemetery can be divided into cemetery areas and cemetery groups. The tombs are mostly irregular-shaped chamber tombs, most of which are single-person flexed burials and secondary disturbed burials. There are several to dozens of everyday pottery buried with them. The customs of chamber tombs and flexed burials come from the eastern Xueshan culture phase I,

Figure 4.26 Cylindrical tiles from Qijia culture at the Qiaozhen site
Left: Front side   Right: Back side

etc. The graves of Keshengzhuang culture phase II and Qijia culture are mostly rectangular vertical pit tombs that can only accommodate one person. They are extended supine and have few burial objects. Liuwan has a few tomb burials that are chamber tombs blocked by stones at the entrance. Coffin burials are common, with two to five people in the same tomb. Adult double-joint burials often see males with coffins and females without coffins. Some males extended, and females flexed. There are also high-level tomb burials. For example, a tomb of Qijia culture at Shizuitou in Baoji was accompanied by *bis*, spinning wheels, adzes, and other jade artifacts, as well as turquoise ornaments. There were also red and black lacquer skin marks, and the bottom of the tomb was covered with cinnabar.[265] The central tomb of the "altar" in Lajia was accompanied by 15 jade artifacts, including *bis* connected with three jade *huangs* (rings) and pig jawbones outside the coffin.[266] In a joint burial of one man and two women in Huangniangniangtai, the man lay in the center with extended supine, and the women lay on their sides flexed, facing the man. Just placing stone *bis* on the man's body, there were as many as 83 flakes, reflecting the concept of a patriarchal society where men are superior to women. In addition, there are infant urn burials, chaotic burial pits, and sacrificial remains of buried cow heads, pig bones, jade artifacts, etc.

The main production tools are still ground axes, adzes, chisels, shovels, knives, arrowheads, and other stone tools. Especially notable are the exquisite long-bodied stone axes and long-bodied stone adzes. Individual gear-shaped stone tools may be scepter heads. Many concaved-bottom arrowheads, stone cores, stone leaves, scrapers, and other microliths exist, especially in Qijia culture. The Qijia culture also discovered red copper knives, awls, chisels, rings, drill bits, strip tools, bone *bis*, tri-pronged bone forks, etc. The more frequent appearance of copper tools should be related to the influence of Central Asian Bronze culture. Agriculture is still mainly based on millet, and Lajia even discovered the world's earliest foxtail millet noodles. What is particularly noteworthy is that wheat should have been grown then. The plant impressions in the wall straw-clay mix of Zhaojialai F11 might be wheat straw. The crops found in Xishanping, Tianshui, Gansu included millet grain, sorghum, rice, wheat, oats, highland barley, soybeans, and buckwheat—as many as eight kinds.[267] The crops in Wangjiazui, Zhouyuan, consisted mostly of millet grain, followed by sorghum and soybean, as well as individual wheat and rice, which exactly match the "five grains" of "rice, sorghum, millet, wheat, and *shu* (菽, a general term for beans)."[268] The main livestock are pigs, sheep, dogs, and cattle. Sheep farming is more common in Gansu and Qinghai. Hunting still plays a certain role, especially in the Hexi Corridor area where hunting is more prevalent.

1.3 Shijiahe Culture and Xiaojiawuji Culture in the Middle Reaches of the Yangtze River

During the early Longshan era, Shijiahe culture was dominant in the middle reach of the Yangtze River and the southern Henan region. The core region, Jianghan Plain, represented by phase I and II of Shijiahe culture in Dengjiawan, Shijiahe Town, Tianmen, Hubei Province, and the early remains of Shijiahe culture in Xiaojiawuji. The peripheral regions include the late Lishangang in Macheng, in eastern Hubei,[269] the Yaojialin in Tongcheng, in southeastern Hubei,[270] Shijiahe culture remains in Chengtoushan in Li County, northern Hunan, phase III of Qinglongquan in southwestern Henan, phase I of Yangzhuang in Zhumadian, southeastern Henan, and even Zhangsidun types in Anqing, southern Anhui.[271] These can roughly be divided into several local types. Around 2200 BCE, the culture entered the late Longshan period, with Wangwan phase III culture strongly expanding southward and influencing areas like southeastern and southwestern Henan and western Hubei and northern Hubei, all occupied by Wangwan culture phase III. Even the cultural landscape of the Jianghan Plain and nearby areas resembled Wangwan culture phase III,[272] which some call Xiaojiawuji culture.[273]

Shijiahe culture developed from Qujialing culture, with its broad and flat-foot *dings*, chisel-shaped-foot *dings*, high-neck jars, waist drum-shaped jars, floral border-foot jars, *zengs*, *zuns* (vats), high-foot plates, round-foot bowls, round-foot plates, arc-belly basins, folded-belly pots, long-neck pots, red slanted-belly pottery cups, high-handle cups, folded-belly cups, painted pottery spinning wheels and more—all evolved from similar Qujialing culture implements. They created funnel-shaped mortars and pestles based on basin-shaped ones. A large number of red pottery plates were kneaded red pottery for small animals and small people. Animal pottery shapes include various domestic animals, beasts, birds, turtles, fish, etc. Small human pottery shapes include those holding fish, dogs, or carrying items; the posture is lively (fig. 4.27). There are also new appearances of chicken and duck-shaped oblique-mouth pots. In addition, the emergence of *gui* and inscribed pottery vases may be related to the influence of the Yuchisi type from Dawenkou culture. A few *jias* may belong to the factors of the late period of the Miaodigou phase II type of Yangshao culture. The cauldrons seen in the west are of native tradition, and the *gu*-shaped cups, long-neck *guis*, and *hes* seen in southern Anhui are distinctive. By Xiaojiawuji culture, most of the typical items of Shijiahe culture had disappeared, with only a small number of arc-belly basins, red pottery plates, and tri-legged cups remaining. The main items were low-neck urns, thin high-handle high-foot plates, and side-mounted-foot *dings*, similar to the same class of items in Wangwan culture phase III. *Gui* and *he* belong to Longshan culture or Zaolütai cultural elements. At the same time, flat-foot jars, convex-bottom jars, bottomless *zengs*, other items, and leaf vein patterns reflect local characteristics. Notably, the jade of Xiaojiawuji culture was rather developed, with types such as cicadas, human heads, tiger heads, flying eagles, coiled dragons, deer or sheep heads, hairpins, handle-shaped ornaments, jade *huangs*, and tubes. Their origins are likely in Longshan culture or Wangwan culture phase III.[274]

The more than ten walled settlements built during Qujialing culture period were mainly still in use during Shijiahe culture period. The core Shijiahe settlements further expanded, with building and burial conditions similar to those of Qujialing culture. A large house was found at the Tanjialing site north of Shijiahe ancient city. The multiple secondary joint burials in Qilihe are distinctive.[275] Some burials at Xiaojiawuji (M7) had over 100 pottery burial objects, as well as a stone *yue*, likely belonging to a leader. Many sacrificial remains were found at sites such as Dengjiawan and Xiaojiawuji, composed of *zun* sets, inverted *zuns* and bowls, clearly inheriting the Yuchisi type of Dawenkou culture. The accumulation of many small pottery animals and figures is also likely related to sacrifices. However, in Xiaojiawuji culture, all the city sites of Shijiahe culture had been destroyed, and sacrificial remains of Shijiahe culture style disappeared. There were still contiguous ground houses and simple round ground houses.[276] Jade burial objects in urn burials became popular.

The production tools of Shijiahe culture were similar to those of Qujialing culture. Rice farming was still the main agricultural activity, but there was also a small amount of millet.[277] They raised pigs, dogs, sheep, and chickens, as seen in the pottery figures. *Yues*, spears, and adzes were weapons, especially polished stone arrowheads with diverse forms. The tools of Xiaojiawuji culture were similar to

Figure 4.27 Pottery figures of Shijiahe culture at Dengjiawan site

those of Shijiahe culture, but there were more types and quantities of polished stone arrowheads.

1.4 Baodun Culture and Zhongba Culture in the Upper Reaches of the Yangtze River

During the Longshan era, the Baodun and Zhongba cultures were dominant in the Chengdu Plain and Chongqing areas, respectively. The Baodun culture, represented by the Baodun remains in Xinjin, Sichuan,[278] includes the Longshan remains of Mangcheng in Dujiangyan,[279] Gucheng Village in Pi County,[280] Yufu in Wenjiang,[281] and Shuanghe in Chongzhou.[282] The Zhongba culture is represented by the I and II phases of the Neolithic remains in Zhongba, Zhong County, Chongqing,[283] which includes phase III of the Shaopengzui in Zhong County.[284]

Both cultures were similar overall. The common main pottery types, including floral-rim cord-mark deep-belly jars, trumpet-mouth pots, and high-neck jars, were directly related to the previous pottery in the upper reaches of the Yangtze River. The common flat-bottom *zuns*, high-foot plates, and round-foot plates were either remnants of the Qujialing cultural elements from the middle reach of the Yangtze River or influenced by the contemporary Shijiahe culture and Wangwan culture phase III, especially the Wujia Liangzi remains in Wushan in the west,[285] which had more short-neck urns, round-foot plates, etc., of later Wangwan phase III cultural elements. However, Baodun culture had more flat- or wide-round-foot *zuns*, more popular swirl patterns, and engraved, stamped wave patterns, net patterns, and grouped parallel lines. Similar elements were seen earlier in Maiping types in Hanyuan and were also related to the Xinguang culture in Yunnan. At the same time, the Zhongba culture had more flat-mouth jars, round-foot or false-round-foot earthen bowls, folded-belly bowls, etc. Some pottery items had distinctive rope-cut concaved and convex floral edges.

Baodun culture has discovered city wall ruins such as Xinjin Baodun, Dujiangyan Mangcheng, Pi County Gucheng Village, Wenjiang Yufu, Chongzhou Shuanghe, and Chongzhou Zizhu, most of which are inner and outer city structures. The largest, Baodun ancient city, has an outer city area of 2.68 million square meters. Houses are generally rectangular, built with timber-framed earthen wall construction. The Gucheng Village has a large, rectangular building that covers an area of 550 square meters, with five rectangular piles of cobblestones inside, which might be religious buildings. This indicates that the Chengdu Plain society had entered the initial stage of civilization, while Zhongba culture settlements are generally smaller and not highly complex. Burials are usually rectangular vertical pit graves, mostly without burial goods and a few with several flakes of pottery or stone artifacts. Baodun culture usually employs extended supine, while Zhongba culture tends to use flexed burials, possibly inherited distantly from Daxi culture.

Both cultures primarily used polished stone tools such as axes, adzes, chisels, shovels, hoes, and knives, some of which had both top and bottom blades. There were stone weapons such as *yues* and spears. Some stone *yues* had distinctive double or triple holes at the top. The majority of crops found at the Baodun site were rice, with a small amount of millet,[286] suggesting that Baodun culture was primarily based on rice farming. In contrast, sites like Zhongba were primarily based on dry farming of millets. In addition, in the Three Gorges area, there seems to have been technology for concentrating and producing salt using pits.

Furthermore, in the northwestern plateau of Sichuan, there are remains similar to Baodun culture, such as those at Xiaguanzi in Mao County,[287] which also has deep ties with Majiayao culture.

1.5 Cultures in the Lower Reaches of the Yangtze River and Nearby Regions

Liangzhu Culture and Guangfulin Culture
In the Ningzhen region, during the early Longshan period, large Dawenkou culture Yuchisi type remains were discovered, such as those at Beiyinyangying H2, which include pottery such as *guis* and engraved *zuns*. In the Jiangsu–Zhejiang region, the slightly earlier part of the early Longshan period represented by Liangzhu culture remains of Fuquanshan phase V in Qingpu, Shanghai. This later developed into the late Liangzhu culture represented by Guangfulin phase II in Songjiang, Shanghai.[288] The fish fin-shaped-foot *dings* were large and exaggerated. There were long-neck round-foot pots, long-neck *guis*, etc. The former is similar to tools in the Tanshishan and Shijiahe cultures, and new artifacts such as the side-mounted flat-foot *ding*, spiral-broken marked-cord pattern, spiral-broken basket pattern jar, etc., are likely influenced by Shijiahe culture type remains in southeastern Henan, eastern Hubei, and southern Anhui. The late Longshan period was represented by the Guangfulin culture represented by Guangfulin phase III in Songjiang, Shanghai. Its main artifacts, such as side-mounted flat-foot *dings*, concaved-rim jars, short-neck jars, short-neck urns, thin high-handle high-foot plates, flat-bottom bowls, etc., are quite similar to those of Zaolütai

culture Nandang type and Wangwan culture phase III Yangzhuang type. The *yan*, white pottery *gui*, vertical-striped straight-belly cup, etc., should also be related to Zaolütai culture. Decorated with cloud-thunder patterns, square patterns, leaf vein patterns, etc., the stamped-pattern short-neck concaved-bottom jars, round-foot jars, and round-bottom bowls show strong local characteristics, probably having some inheritance relationship with Liangzhu culture, and related to Tanshishan culture in South China. Stone plow-shaped artifacts, segmental stone adzes, etc., should be remnants of Liangzhu culture. The Guangfulin culture is likely formed on the basis of the late Liangzhu culture, strongly influenced by the Central Plain Longshan culture, and incorporated elements of the South China culture moving northward.

Shanbei Culture and Haochuan Culture

In the early Longshan period, the north and central part of Jiangxi Province was represented by the Shanbei culture, as evidenced by the ruins at Paomaling in Xiushui,[289] while the southern part of Zhejiang Province was represented by Haochuan culture, as represented by the graves at Suichang Haochuan.[290]

Both cultures are primarily characterized by the *ding*, high-foot plate, plain high-neck jar, high-neck round-foot pot (*zun*), and *gui*. They both have plain or stamped-pattern cauldrons related to local traditions such as Fanchengdui culture. The main difference is that the Shanbei culture has deeper-belly *dings* with many chiseled-shaped feet, high-foot plates with more mouths of porcelain with lids, and commonly seen high-neck flat-belly round-foot pots and red clay small animals similar to Shijiahe culture. On the other hand, Haochuan culture has shallower-belly *dings* with more side-mounted flat feet, high-foot plate plates with edges protruding below, and more commonly seen single-handle round-foot *hes*, as well as wide-handle cups with spouts, double-nosed pots, single-handle round-foot cups, tri-nosed *guis* (ancient Chinese containers or ritual vessels here), etc., belonging to the Liangzhu cultural elements, as well as Liangzhu style artifacts such as jade *yues*, jade cone-shaped tools, lacquerware inlaid with jade and lithic flakes. They should be related to the influences of Shijiahe culture and Liangzhu culture, respectively. Among them, the influence of Liangzhu culture on Haochuan culture is greater. Still, Haochuan culture does not see jade *cong* or *bi*, double-holed stone *yue*, and triple-tiered jade ornament are distinctive. The shape of the jade flakes and the engraved symbols on the pottery of Dawenkou culture such as Lingyang River, Yuchisi, etc., are similar. In addition, Haochuan culture has more Tanshishan cultural elements such as imprinted-pattern round-foot jars. Both cultures are popular with segmental axes, shoulder axes, segmental adzes, *yues*, arc-backed double-holed knives, stone chisels, and other polished stone tools.

Wood-bone mud-wall ground-type suite buildings were discovered at Paomaling in Shanbei. The differences in the size of the graves in the Haochuan Cemetery are quite noticeable, with large graves located in the center, all of which are distinctive, nearly rectangular vertical pit graves with rectangular coffin-type wooden burial utensils. They are mainly accompanied by pottery, with the custom of painting pottery with vermilion being popular, and a small number of jade artifacts, red lacquerware, etc., are also buried with them.

2. The Upper Reaches of the Yellow River and the Eastern Xizang Plateau

While the significant parts of the Yangtze and Yellow River basins were integrating and forming the Longshan era, represented by gray-black pottery and tri-legged vessels, the upper Yellow River in the central and western part of Gansu and most of Qinghai were following a different path featuring colorful pottery, retaining more of the ancient Yangshao culture foundation. It belongs to the jar–pot–earthen bowl–basin cultural system and plays a more significant role in the early cultural exchange between the East and the West.

2.1 Banshan Type of Majiayao Culture

In the early Longshan period, the Banshan type of Majiayao culture was distributed in the central and western parts of Gansu, centered around Lanzhou, and the eastern part of Qinghai. It is represented by the Banshan Cemetery in Guanghe, Gansu,[291] including the Qinggangcha residential site in Lanzhou, Gansu,[292] the early graves at Tugutai,[293] and the Bianjialin graves in Kangle,[294] as well as the "Banshan type graves" in Liuwan, Qinghai,[295] and the "Banshan culture graves" in Suhusa, Xunhua.[296] Black and red polychrome pottery is prevalent, with elements such as straight lines, arcs, triangles, forming patterns such as sawtooth, horizontal stripes, grids, multiple arc lines, swirls, waves, broken lines, circles, gourd, shells, chessboards, rhombus, squares, opposing triangles, scale patterns, etc. These various patterns are combined, filled with each other, and are complex and varied. Most artifacts have a single handle or double handles. Typical types include small-mouth high-neck pots (jars), single- or double-handle long-neck bottles, wide-flare-mouth bulbous-belly urns, small-mouth high-neck urns, arc- or bulbous-belly basins, single-handle jars, double-handle jars, and converging-mouth earthen bowls, earthen bowls or basins with spouts or unsealed spouts, eagle-owl-shaped pots, double-mouth pots, single-handle cups, etc. Decorations include beaded necklaces, turquoise earrings, bone piece arm ornaments, stone bracelets, bone combs, etc. The Banshan type is developed based on the Xiaopingzi group of the Majiayao type while also receiving a large number of influences from Caiyuan culture, including offset chamber graves, flexed burials, black and red polychrome, and developed inner coloring, as well as double-mouth pots, eagle-owl-shaped pots, swastika patterns, etc. Its earlier sources are the eastern Xueshan culture phase I and the Haishengbulang type.[297] The source of the stone (jade) *bi* should be in southern Shanxi, while the prevalence of sawtooth patterns should be related to the influence of the Chalcolithic—Bronze Age culture from central Asia.

Centered around the Gonghe Basin in the eastern part of Qinghai Province, there are late remains of the Zongri type of Majiayao culture, represented by the Zongri M172 type three remains in Tongde.[298] Pottery is still clearly divided into two major categories. The first category of fine-textured clay red pottery turns into black and red polychrome, with the types of polychrome pottery patterns and style essentially the same as the Banshan type and can be called "Banshan-style pottery." The second category of coarse-sand, "Zongri-style pottery," has significantly increased in number, and its shape is slightly different from the early period. The local characteristics of the Zongri type in this period have been further developed.

Rectangular semi-subterranean houses were found in the Banshan type remains of Qinggangcha, some with two or three connected firepits. Graves in the same cemetery can be divided into various levels, such as zones, groups, and sets. The graves are mainly rectangular vertical pit graves and nearly round chamber graves; in some places, stone coffin graves predominate. A considerable number of vertical pit graves have rectangular wooden coffins, some with two-tiered platforms, or "foot pits" for burying pottery and wall niches; chamber graves are in the shape of "日" (*yue*) or "凸" (*tu*) and are often sealed with stone slabs or wooden sticks. Most are single burials, but there are also two to seven people in joint burials and many second-time disturbed graves. The area near Lanzhou in the east practices burials in flexed on the (left or right) side; meanwhile, the area near Xining in the west in incomplete skeleton secondary disturbed burials, with individual cremation graves where the bones of the graves have been burned. Most Banshan type graves have burial objects, mostly pottery, ranging from one or two pieces to a dozen pieces, as well as production tools and decorations, with the overall disparity in burial objects not significant. Zongri type cemeteries also distinguish between zones, groups, and sets. Most graves are rectangular vertical pit graves, with a few having two-tiered platforms. Most do not have burial objects, with a few having wooden or stone coffins. The majority are single burials, with a few double graves, and the most common posture is prone with extended prone, a considerable number of which are second-time disturbed burials. Most are accompanied by practical "Banshan-style pottery."

Stone tools are more finely ground, especially long-bodied stone spades, and axes are the most representative. The economic form is basically the same as the Majiayao type period, still mainly planting millet grains and sorghums, and grains and their straw (millet grains) were found in Qinggangcha F1. But it should have already begun to plant wheat. Livestock farming and animal husbandry are nearly the same as before, with the main livestock being pigs, and sheep rearing is more common in the Gansu–Qinghai region. Tools related to hunting include stone (bone) arrowheads, stone balls, chopping tools, scrapers, stone cores, bone-handle stone-blade knives, etc., and the closer to the Gansu–Qinghai–Ningxia border area, the more microlithic components. The Banshan type has a long-perforated whetstone, which should be for the convenience of carrying, reflecting an increase in the mobility of the population.

2.2 Machang Type of Majiayao Culture

During the late Longshan period, the Machang type was distributed in central and western Gansu and eastern Qinghai, represented by the Machangyuan Cemetery in Qinghai Minhe,[299] including late Tugutai in Lanzhou, Gansu,[300] Yangshan,[301] and Liuwan in Minhe, Qinghai, etc. Pottery is basically similar to the Banshan type; the polychrome pottery painting gradually becomes careless, single-color black is prevalent, and there is also single-color red and black-red polychrome. Most polychrome pottery patterns inherit the Banshan type with slight changes. X-shaped patterns, horizontal individual word patterns, vertical broken-line patterns, stringed shell patterns, *Hui* patterns, swastika patterns, concentric circle patterns, star patterns, etc., are new or mainly seen in the Machang type, human frog patterns (frog limb patterns) increase greatly, and types are complex. The pattern of four large circles is prevalent. Most vessels inherit the Banshan type, converging-mouth urn, high-foot plate pot, four-handle basin, handless slanted-belly basin, tower-shaped knob lid, etc., are influenced by Qijia culture and are new. In addition, its swastika pattern and pointed-topped crown pattern were seen earlier in Central and Western Asia, indicating cultural connections between China and Central and Western Asia as early as before the second millennium

BCE. Individual human figures or human-face polychrome small-mouth pots and square straight-belly cups are quite unique. Over time, the Machang type gradually extended to the Hexi Corridor, reaching as far west as the Hami area in Xinjiang. The Zongri type in central Qinghai basically disappeared.

The Machang type has square and round semi-subterranean houses. The basic situation of graves is the same as the Banshan type. It can be divided into two major categories. The first category of graves represented by Liuwan near Xining has slightly more rounded rectangular vertical pit graves, followed by chamber graves with tomb passages, which can be divided into zones, groups, and sets, representing different levels of social organizations. Most graves have wooden coffin burial objects. Single burials account for the vast majority. A few are joint burials of two to six people; prevalent extended supine, second disturbed burials are second; and a few flexed limb burials. Most burials are accompanied by one or two dozen daily-use pottery, production tools, and decorations. The few have only one or two pieces, and the many have dozens to hundreds of pieces, reflecting the trend of "rich burials" and significant wealth differentiation. Individual burials are also accompanied by pig mandibles or sheep bones. The second category of graves represented by Tugutai near Lanzhou still maintains the traditional customs of chamber graves and flexed burials. The main type of single burial in Yangshan Cemetery is extended prone, followed by flexed on the (left or right) side. There are sacrificial pits for burying livestock, such as cattle and sheep.

The economic form is roughly the same as the Banshan type. The Machang type pottery urn in Yuanyangchi was filled with millet. Li Fan and others collected carbonized barley, rye, great millet, millet, and millet grains from the Donghuishan site[302] before 2000 BCE. This shows that during the Machang type period, wheat cultivation had spread eastward to the Gansu–Qinghai region.[303] Harvesting tools are mainly rectangular perforated stone knives, basically, no pottery knives, indicating improved harvesting efficiency. The number of sheep in the Gansu–Qinghai region is second only to pigs. The Machang type also has perforated whetstones that are convenient to carry.

3. Cultures in Western Northeastern and Southern China

During the Longshan period, the western part of northeastern China, including the Xiliao River region and the grasslands of Keerqin, was mainly occupied by Xueshan culture phase I and the late Nanbaoligaotu cultures. The Xialiao River Basin retained remnants of Pianbuzi culture or similar cultural elements. At the same time, the southern part of Liaodong was associated with the upper Xiaozhushan culture, and the lower Yalu River region was associated with the Beigou culture.

The upper Xiaozhushan culture, represented by the remains at Xiaozhushan, actually belongs to the early Longshan culture, while the remains at Shuangtuozi in Dalian[304] belong to the later Longshan culture. This culture was formed under the strong influence of Longshan culture, building upon the foundations of the middle Xiaozhushan culture and Pianbuzi culture. Pottery vessels, such as protruding-shoulder jar, urn, basin-shaped *ding*, *gui*, high-foot plate, tri-looped-legged plate, tri-legged cup, single-handle cup, *yu*, flat-bottom bowl, and vessel lid, generally exhibit characteristics of Longshan culture. However, the region-specific features include incised or stamped geometric patterns on jars and urns and polychrome geometric patterns. Cylindrical jars, overlapping-lipped jars, and jade artifacts such as rings and *bis* with protruding teeth are unique to the local tradition. Weapons such as stone *yue* and stone spear have also been discovered. The architectural styles of houses include semi-subterranean and surface-level structures, with some featuring walls made of mud and wood. Burials are characterized by mound-like structures, often containing multiple rectangular burial chambers. Tools primarily consist of polished stone implements such as axes, adzes, chisels, and knives. There are also polished or microlith arrowheads and a significant number of net pendants and fish dart points, indicating a relatively greater emphasis on fishing, hunting, and gathering alongside agriculture.

The Beigou culture, represented by the remains at Beigou in Xiuyan County, Liaoning Province,[305] is characterized by pottery vessels with decorative engraved geometric patterns, vertically attached clay strip patterns, and added relief decorations. Notably, the distinctive shape of the pot with a straight neck and bulbous-belly sets it apart. This culture shows some connections with Pianbuzi culture, but artifacts such as tri-looped-legged plates and high-foot plates clearly belong to the Longshan cultural elements. The Beigou culture features semi-subterranean houses and exhibits similar production tools and economic patterns to the upper Xiaozhushan culture.

4. Culture in South China

During the Longshan era, the late Tanshishan culture represented by the middle and late phase II in Fujian Minhou Tanshishan and phases II and III in lower Zhuangbianshan developed along the southeast coast of Fujian. New pottery items similar in form to Haochuan culture emerged, including the folded-belly *dings* with imprint cord-mark patterns and the long-neck round-foot pots, which were common in the lower reaches of the Yangtze River and most of the southeast coastal areas. The high-foot and round-foot plates also had ridges on their bellies, similar to Haochuan culture, suggesting a close exchange with cultures such as Haochuan. Other items continued to develop from their early stages, with increased stone *yues* and spearheads. Settlements, tombs, and economic forms remained largely the same. The Tanshishan culture expanded northwest of Fujian, represented by the upper Niubishan type in Pucheng. However, the *gui* and *yan* did not appear in the coastal areas of Fujian, and the existence of *yan* may be related to the influence of Zaolütai culture. The square-shaped tombs at the Niubishan site are also similar to Haochuan culture.

The northwest part of Guangdong is marked by the late period of Shixia culture, with new pottery such as round-foot *zeng* and *gui*. Common ground stone tools like shoulder adzes, segmental adzes, chisels, *yues*, chisels, etc. The jade objects such as jade *cong*, *bi*, *yuan*, bracelet, *huang*, and *jue* (an ancient Chinese farming tool for digging in the earth here) are related to Liangzhu culture, suggesting the possibility of Liangzhu people migrating here. The differentiation between large and small tombs became more severe, with large tombs often accompanied by hundreds of burial items, including Liangzhu style jade wares.

Hutoupu culture, represented by the Puning Hutoupu site, is spread across southern Fujian and eastern Guangdong.[306] Phase II of Zhuhai Houshawan,[307] phase II of Zhuhai Baojingwan,[308] the first and second groups of Dongguan Yuanzhou,[309] and the late Hong Kong Yonglang[310] are distributed in the central and southern part of Guangdong (including Hong Kong and Macau [China]), temporarily named phase II of Houshawan culture. These sites generally resemble each other. They developed from the base of the cauldron–round-foot plate, mainly pottery such as stamped cauldrons, stamped round-foot jars, stamped round-bottom earthen bowls, high-foot plates (or *guis*—ancient Chinese containers or ritual vessels here), and stilted objects. The stamps include marked cords, basket marks, broken lines, checkerboard patterns, leaf vein patterns, cloud-thunder patterns, double circle patterns, etc. There are also ground stone tools such as axes, shoulder adezs, segmental adezs, *jues* (ancient Chinese farming tools for digging in the earth here), *yues*, spearheads, stone *jues*, stone rings, etc., which are related to the long-standing jade tradition in eastern China. They had stilt or ground style houses, rectangular vertical pit graves, and close relations with Tanshishan culture. Of course, there are some regional differences. For example, shell mound and sand mound sites are more common along the coast, with few conical-foot *dings* and tile-foot *dings* with notches at the bases from the root of Shixia culture. Complicated geometric patterns with imprint patterns likely relate to the earlier Xiantouling culture tradition. More net pendants, stone grinding plates, stone grinding sticks, and perforated heavy stones are found,[311] which are likely related to the fishing, hunting, and gathering economy. In contrast, in the central part of Guangdong, there are generally hillside sites with more conical-foot and tile-foot *dings*, suggesting the possibility of agriculture.

The majority of Guangxi is marked by phase IV of Yongning Dingsishan, Pingnan Shijiaoshan,[312] Napo Gantuoyan phase I,[313] and Wuming Bawang, Nongshan type of sites,[314] or can be temporarily named Gantuoyan culture phase I. The foundation of this culture is still the cord-mark round-bottom cauldron tradition. Pottery such as round-bottom cauldrons, round-bottom earthen bowls, tri-legged jars, round-foot pots, round-foot bowls, and round-foot cups, mostly decorated with marked cords, grouped wave-shaped, horizontal, and vertical S-shaped, and floating ribbon-shaped incised patterns are very distinctive, with band-like red-painted decoration. The conical-foot *dings* and high-foot plates in the eastern part are related to Shixia culture. Ground stone tools include shoulder adzes, shoulder choppers, shouldered-large stone spades, arrowheads, etc., with the shouldered-large stone spade being the most distinctive. There are also a lot of stone grinding plates and grinding sticks, as well as jade *jues*, jade pendants, and shell decorations. There are rectangular vertical pit graves and special cave burials. The phenomenon of concentrated burials of large stone spades has often been found, possibly related to special religious customs. This culture should have agriculture, but the hunting and gathering economy is still heavily present.

5. Xinguang Culture in Yunnan

In the northwest part of Yunnan, we see sites such as Yongping's Xinguang,[315] Yongren's Caiyuanzi, and the Mopandi.[316] This might be referred to as Xinguang culture. The early Binchuan's Baiyangcun[317] and Yuanmou's Dadunzi[318] also fall into this category. The pottery consists mainly of various jar types, also pots, earthen bowls, flat-bottom bowls, and round-foot plates. There are often floral-rim lips, and a prevalence of geometric decorations engraved, imprinted, or stamped, including grid patterns, diagonal lines, wave patterns, fine-tooth comb patterns with clustered dot patterns, bead-chain patterns, triangular patterns, *Hui* patterns, Z-shaped patterns, S-shaped patterns, corded patterns, and drape patterns. These are divided into primary and secondary decorations, forming complex designs. The most distinctive are those decorated with corded or drape patterns around the edge with circular patterns. There are also added relief decorations and red and white painted designs. This culture can also be divided into phases. The Caiyuanzi remains with marked-cord pottery are earlier than those of the Mopandi and Xinguang. The origins of this culture may be related to Majiayao culture in western Sichuan and its subsequent traditions, as in the earlier Sichuan Hanyuan Maiping type remains, there are jars and earthen bowls decorated with corded or similar circular or grid patterns. It may also have a connection with the geometrically decorated Karuo culture. Its round-foot plates should be related to the influence of Baodun culture. The tools of the Xinguang culture mainly include axes, adzes, chisels, knives, and arrowheads of ground stone, as well as spinning wheels, stone grinding plates, and stone grinding rods. The double-holed stone knives continue the tradition of Majiayao culture, and there is mixed farming of millet grain, sorghum, and rice.[319]

6. The Outer Margin Zone Culture of Early China

During the Longshan era, the cultural area of "early China" expanded further. Only the northeastern and northwestern fringe areas remained outside its reach. For instance, the Zhenxing phase I type B remains in Hailin, Heilongjiang, in the northern Northeast, still belonging to the cylindrical jar cultural system. The situation in areas such as Xinjiang in the northwest is still unclear.

7. Cultural Exchanges in the Longshan Era

Cultural exchanges during the Longshan era became increasingly frequent and profound, especially in the Yellow and Yangtze River basins.

Longshan culture was the most active and characteristic. The unique wheel-thrown black pottery technology radiated from the core areas of eastern Shandong along the coast and the Wei River (the main river in Weifang City here) Basin to surrounding areas. The closer to its core, the more black pottery found, and the more advanced the wheel-throwing technique. Its early westward influence made an essential contribution to the rise of Wangwan culture phase III and later had a significant impact on Hougang culture phase II. Its northward influence led to the formation of the upper Xiaozhushan culture, even influencing Beigou culture, bringing rice farming to the Northeast and spreading it to the Korean Peninsula. Later, the strong westward influence significantly affected the areas of eastern Henan and northwestern Anhui, leading to the transformation of the Yuchisi type into Zaolütai culture. In contrast, the northward influence contributed to the emergence of Xueshan culture phase II. Elements like *guis* can be seen in most

Yellow and Yangtze River basins. It can be said that Longshan culture played a crucial role in the formation and development of the Longshan era. Of course, regardless of the intensity, exchanges are generally a mutual process. For instance, central elements such as basket patterns and white-gray surfaces are common in the western part of Longshan culture. At the same time, the Jiaodong Peninsula has small cylindrical-shaped jars, *bis* with protruding teeth, etc., from the Liaodong Peninsula.[320]

The Central Plain Longshan culture came later but increasingly influenced the wider area. During the early Longshan period, Taosi culture had a wide influence. Its jade ware, lacquerware, and other elements spread westward to northern Shaanxi and even infiltrated the early Qijia and Caiyuan cultures. Shijiahe culture expanded eastward as far as southern Anhui, profoundly influencing the surrounding cultures. The most characteristic red slanted-belly pottery cup was not only common in the early Wangwan culture phase III in central Henan but also appeared in the Miaodigou phase II type of Yangshao culture in western Henan and southern Shanxi and in the late Gushuihe type, the Yuchisi type of Dawenkou culture in northwestern Anhui, and even made its way as far north as the Shijiawan site in Gansu, northern Shaanxi.[321] Of course, the early Wangwan culture phase III, most deeply influenced by it, also includes funnel-shaped mortars and pestles, wide and flat-foot *dings*, and small red pottery animals. Shijiahe culture also influenced the Zhongba and Baodun cultures.

In the late Longshan period, Laohushan culture, represented by the Youyao type, exerted a massive southward influence, constructing a four million square meter Shimao stony city in northern Shaanxi, leading to the replacement of the late Taosi type in the Linfen Basin by the Taosi type, spreading the double-handle *lis* into the Sanliqiao type and Wangwan culture phase III in the Central Plain, and spreading divination bones and microlith arrowheads to vast areas along the middle and lower reaches of the Yellow River.[322] The spread of domestic sheep to the southeast was likely mainly through this route. Perhaps as part of a chain reaction, Wangwan culture phase III had an even greater influence on its surroundings later on, extending its range northward to the western part of Henan and southern Shanxi, eastward influencing the formation of Zaolütai culture, and southward replacing Shijiahe culture in southeastern Henan, southwestern Henan, and western Hubei, profoundly impacting the vast areas along the middle reaches of the Yangtze River, turning the once prosperous Shijiahe culture in these areas into the Xiaojiawuji culture similar to Wangwan culture phase III, and even influencing the lower reaches of the Yangtze River. Zaolütai culture massively expanded to the Jianghuai region, profoundly influencing the formation of the Guangfulin culture, and the most distant influence of factors such as *yans* penetrated Tanshishan culture in northwestern Fujian (fig. 4.28). Hougang culture phase II extended northward to form Xueshan culture phase II. Of course, the late Taosi culture also influenced the Sanliqiao and Wangwan types of Wangwan culture phase III.

The middle Qijia culture, roughly part of the Central Plain Longshan culture, expanded forcefully from east to west, replacing the Caiyuanzi culture and gra-

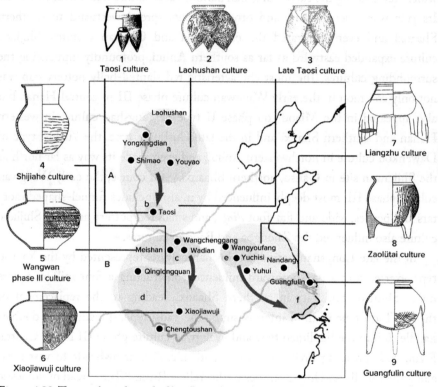

Figure 4.28 The southward trend of late Longshan culture

Early Longshan:
a. Laohushan culture
b. Taosi culture
c. Wangwan culture phase III
d. Shijiahe culture
e. Yuchisi type of Dawenkou culture
f. Liangzhu culture

Late Longshan:
A. Laohushan culture and late Taosi culture
B. Wangwan culture phase III and Xiaojiawuji culture
C. Zaolütai culture and Guangfulin culture
1. *Jia* (Taosi M3002: 32)
2, 3. *Li* (Youyao H186: 1, Taosi IIIH303: 12)

4. High-neck jar (Xiaojiawuji H80: 2)
5, 6. Short-neck urn (Wadian IV T3H30: 5, Xiaojiawuji H254: 8)
7–9. *Ding* (Guangfulin H128: 3, Wangyoufang H16: 1, Guangfulin TD9: 5)
(All pottery.)

dually pushing the Machang type out of central Gansu and eastern Qinghai. However, some indigenous Machang elements were inevitably retained. The Machang type expanded westward to the western Hexi Corridor and even the Hami region in the east of Xinjiang. The discovery of marine shells in Qijia culture indicates a connection with coastal regions.

The Tanshishan culture influenced the Guangfulin culture in Jiangsu and Zhejiang, and the conical-foot and tile-foot *ding* of Shixia culture had a widespread influence on the southeastern coastal region and affected the eastern part of Guangxi to the southwest. Due to cultural exchanges, concaved-bottom vessels frequently appeared in the Huai River and the middle and lower reaches of the Yangtze River.

At this time, cultural exchanges between China and foreign countries further developed. The pointed-crown pattern possibly originated from central Asia and appeared on the pottery of Qijia culture in the Hexi region. Meanwhile, wheat, which originated from Western Asia, is found almost throughout the Yellow River Basin. In contrast, the cultural system of South China extended to northern Vietnam and even Thailand.[323]

8. Conclusion

(1) Further expansion of the scope of two agricultural systems and further strengthening of the diversified economic trend in the Northern regions of the Central Plain

The scope of the millet and rice agricultural systems continued to expand. Millet agriculture had extended westward to the western part of the Hexi Corridor and even to eastern Xinjiang. In contrast, rice agriculture may have extended northward to the Liaodong Peninsula and southwest to Yunnan Province (fig. 2.3). Of course, the basic pattern of "rice in the south and millet grain in the north" and the mutual integration and complementarity have not changed. The upper and middle Yangtze River, the Yellow River Basin, and the Huai River Basin should still be areas where millet and rice are mixed. Still, the proportion of the south and north is different. Overall, millet is the main crop in the upper and middle reaches of the Yellow River, and rice is the main crop in the upper and middle reaches of the Yangtze River. The two agricultural systems continued to improve development by making tools such as stone knives, shovels, and sickles more refined and efficient.

The trend toward a diversified economy in the Northern regions of the Central Plain was further strengthened, primarily manifested by the appearance and spread of wheat. Before 2000 years BCE, wheat was not only found in the Machang type of Majiayao culture, Qijia culture, and Keshengzhuang culture phase II in the northwest region but also Longshan culture of the Central Plain and Haidai Longshan culture. Wheat has been cultivated in West Asia for tens of thousands of years, and it is generally believed that wheat in China was introduced from the West, which differs from native Chinese crops such as millet grain and sorghum in terms of growing conditions. The appearance of wheat has, to some extent, changed the structure of dryland agriculture in the Northern regions of the Central Plain, further enhancing the stability of food supply in the dryland agricultural economy. A surprising number of eight different crops have been discovered at Xishanping in Tianshui, Gansu, including millet grain, sorghum, rice, wheat, oats, highland barley, soybeans, and buckwheat. The crops discovered at Wangjiazui in Zhouyuan exactly meet the so-called "five grains" number of "rice, sorghum, millet, wheat, and *shu*." Of course, wheat's share in agriculture was still small during the Longshan era, and millet and sorghum dominated in the upper and middle reaches of the Yellow River. Moreover, the number of domestic animals in the Northern regions of the Central Plain also increased at this time, with the widespread breeding of pigs, dogs, sheep, and goats. In comparison, in the Yangtze River Basin, especially in the middle and lower reaches, the main crops were rice, and the main livestock were pigs and dogs. The monotony of the crops may have resulted in a less stable food source than in the Northern regions of the Central Plain, which may be one reason the culture in the middle and lower reaches of the Yangtze River declined while the culture in the Northern regions of the Central Plain developed rapidly.

(2) Expansion of black and gray pottery and tri-legged vessels and the emergence of bronze containers

During the Longshan era, a different-level gray-black pottery culture circle, with eastern Shandong as its core, was formed: black pottery developed in the Haidai and adjacent areas, gray pottery dominated in most of the Central Plain and the Yangtze River Basin, Qijia culture was mostly reddish-brown pottery, and Majiayao culture in the western frontier still favored reddish-brown and painted pottery. Due to the interaction and strong external influence of cultures such as Longshan, Wangwan phase III, Hougang phase II, Zaolütai, Laohushan, Keshengzhuang phase II, etc., typical "Chinese" style tri-legged vessels like the *ding, gui, he, li, yan,* and *jia* widely spread. *Ding, gui,* and *he,* popular in the east, extended north to the southern part of the northeast, south to the northern part of

Guangdong, and west to the Three Gorges area; *li* and *yan*, originated in the north, extended west to the eastern part of the Hexi Corridor, south to the northern part of Anhui, east to the Shandong coast. The wide expansion of these tri-legged vessels represents the maturation and gradual universalization of the "Chinese" style of cooking and eating.

The two main jade centers in the lower Yangtze River and western Liaoning had declined. Still, new centers such as Jianghan, southern Shanxi, and Gansu–Qinghai, linked to the previous two centers, have emerged with new types of jade artifacts, like jade *zhangs*. The jade of Shandong, southern Shanxi, and Jianghan was intricately carved, showing new developments in craftsmanship. Other lacquerware and silk fabrics continued to develop, bracelets, hairpins, spinning wheels, etc., were still almost seen in all cultures. In the Central Plain Longshan culture, Shijiahe culture, Xiaojiawuji culture, etc., there were blunt arrow-shaped tools. Musical instruments such as pottery *xun* and bell were still common in the Yellow and Yangtze River basins. Taosi culture and late Taosi culture musical instruments include alligator drums, clay drums,* chime stones, pottery or bronze bells, pottery *xuns*, etc. Wangwan culture phase III and Qijia culture have chime stones, pottery bells, pottery *xuns*, etc., showing that the Central Plain and even the northwest region had initially formed a drum, chime, and bell musical instrument combination. These musical instruments, together with tri-legged pottery vessels like the *ding*, *gui*, etc., and jade and stone tools like the *yue*, jade *zhang*, etc., formed the ritual vessels of the new period, laying the early foundation for the unique ritual and music system of "China."

Unlike the sporadic discovery of bronze ware in the late Yangshao, bronze ware was generally discovered in most areas of the Yellow and Yangtze River basins in the Longshan era, entering the late Chalcolithic. For example, in Qijia culture of Huangniangniangtai, red copper knives, cones, chisels, rings, drill bits, strip tools, etc., were found; copper bracelets were found in Laohushan culture remains of Erlitou; Dengjiawan, Luojiabailing and many other places belonging to Shijiahe culture and Xiaojiawuji culture have discovered copper ores, fragments of copper knives; artifacts such as knife-shaped remnants of copperware, small copper blocks, copper slag were unearthed at Lutaigang, Luantai, Pingliangtai, etc., belonging to Zaolütai culture; yellow copper-like cast copper cones were found in Longshan culture remains of Sanlihe; Meishan, Guchengzhai, Niuzhai remains belonging to Wangwan culture phase III discovered fragments of copper refining crucibles,

---

* A Chinese primitive percussion instrument that has a frame made of clay and is covered with skin on both sides.—Trans

fragments of copper containers were unearthed from Wangchenggang, Xinzhai sites;[324] red copper bells,[325] arsenical copper container fragments, copper cog-shaped tools, copper rings, etc., were found in Taosi culture and late Taosi culture. Most of these bronze wares are red copper; some with bronze or brass characteristics should be obtained by refining symbiotic ores containing copper, zinc, tin, etc.[326] Of particular note is the discovery of bronze containers in the Central Plain at that time, indicating that they already possessed the clay composite mold casting technology, which differs from the long-standing stone mold technology in the West. It can be seen that during the Longshan era, the tradition of bronze casting with Chinese characteristics was basically formed.

(3) Maturation of civil engineering techniques
The spatial distribution pattern of housing types in the Longshan era continued the legacy of previous periods, with the Northern regions predominantly featuring semi-subterranean and cave style, and the Yangtze River Basin, South China, and Southwest China mainly featuring ground-level and stilted houses. Due to frequent exchanges, many construction techniques were shared across vast areas, such as the widespread use of rammed earth for building cities and walls, mud-brick wall construction technology, and the technique of finishing floor skirting with lime plaster in the Yellow River and Yangtze River basins. Of course, local characteristics still existed, such as stone wall houses in the Northern regions and wood frame mud-wall houses in the Southern regions. Most notable is the emergence of brick and tile, a construction material with "Chinese" characteristics. The smooth, patterned ceramic slabs of Taosi culture may have been used as wall tiles, while Qijia culture produced a full range of flat and tubular tiles, similar to later generations. This suggests that "Chinese" civil engineering techniques gradually matured. The simultaneous use of rammed earth, timber, mud bricks, and tiles in Chinese civilization's architecture contrasted with the monotony of contemporaneous Egyptian buildings using stone, Mesopotamian civilization using sun-dried mud bricks, and Indus Basin civilization using fired bricks.

City walls, settlements, and large palace-like structures were found in most areas of the Yellow River and Yangtze River basins. There were enormous city wall settlements nearly three million square meters in size, such as Taosi ancient city, as well as palace-like structures seen at Guchengzhai in Xinmi City, Gucheng Village in Pi County, and others. Special buildings with astronomical observation functions also appeared at the Taosi site.

(4) Coexistence of multiple character systems

The Longshan era not only had a definite presence of character but at least three systems can be discerned. One is the Central Plain Longshan cultural system, similar to the oracle bone script. Two red characters written in vermilion were found on a flat pot from the late Taosi culture, which resembles the oracle bone script. One character is interpreted as "文" (*wen*), and the other as "易"[327] (*yang*), "尧"[328] (*yao*), or "邑"[329] (*yi*). This suggests that a writing system similar to the oracle bone script had already formed in the Central Plain, was widely used, and played an important role in society. However, such writing may have been primarily inscribed on perishable organic materials such as silk, bamboo, or wood, hence its scarcity. The second is the Longshan cultural system. On the bottom of a discarded flat-bottom basin from the Dinggong site, 11 inscriptions were engraved,[330] likely forming a sentence that recorded specific content, undeniably qualifying as writing. However, it does not seem to belong to the same system as oracle bone or bronze script, and its relationship with Dawenkou culture pottery script is unclear. Some believe it to be an ancient script of the Dongyi,[*] which was later phased out,[331] and some have even attempted to decipher it by comparing it with the modern *Yi* script.[332] The third is the Dawenkou culture–Shijiahe cultural system. The pottery script found in Shijiahe culture includes *yue*-shaped, bird and sun combined shapes, bent angle shapes, slanted-belly cup shapes, high-handle cup shapes, diamond shapes, spinning wheel shapes, etc. Among them, *yue*-shaped and bird and sun combined shapes are similar to those of Dawenkou culture, indicating that they belong to the same writing system as that of Dawenkou culture at the Yuchisi.

In addition to writing, painted pottery of Majiayao culture in the northwest still prevailed, including symbols with profound implications and long-standing traditions, such as the swastika and octagram. Following Liangzhu culture, animal-face patterns were gradually accepted by Longshan culture in the middle and lower reaches of the Yellow River and the Central Plain Longshan culture. In addition, clear images of the *gui* (an ancient Chinese cooking utensil here) character was found on the pottery from the Zhangsidun site, which largely belongs to Shijiahe culture. The Haochuan culture featured a carved symbol similar to the oracle bone script character for "五" (*wu*) with an extra horizontal stroke. Patterns resembling a dog and a square hole round coin were engraved on stone *yues*.

---

[*] A collective term for ancient peoples in Chinese records. In most cases, it referred to inhabitants of eastern China.—Trans.

(5) The unity and diversity of ancestor worship

A secular religious belief system centered on ancestor worship remained fundamental in early China. The vast majority of tombs are essentially earth pit tombs with the nature of "underground homes," only with a smaller scale and a more emphasized family focus. However, cremation graves are still present in cultures like the Majiayao culture semi-mountain type.

Regional differences are mainly manifested between the south and north. With the decline of Hongshan culture, the idol worship tradition that previously held a certain position in the Northern region basically disappeared, overall tending toward simplicity, "secularism,"[333] and "cruelty." A new religious custom of bone divination by scorching, used to predict fortune, widely spread in the Central Plain region in the north.[334] A similar bone-burning divination custom was widespread in the vast Northern Hemisphere, which some believe is related to fire worship.[335] In Longshan culture, Wangwan culture phase III, Hougang culture phase II, Qijia culture, etc., common chaotic human burial pits, sacrificial pits burying pigs, dogs, cows, and other animals, or animal or human sacrifices for foundation laying were observed. In the Hougang II culture remains in Jiangou, Handan, even the customs of making human skull cups and skinning human heads were discovered.[336] At sites such as Pingliangtai and Wangyoufang, some foundation-laying male sacrifices had the tops of the heads cut off. In addition, special sacrificial facilities have been found in the northern Central Plain, such as a large linear sacrificial relic found at the Yuhui site, a sacrificial platform discovered at the Lutaigang site in Qi County, and a structure akin to an ancestral hall built on tomb M2 in Daxincun, which belongs to phase II of Keshengzhuang culture.[337] In comparison, the religious customs conveyed by clay sculptures of small animals, small people, and grouped pottery statues in Shijiahe culture in Central China appear quite different.

(6) The development of initial civilizations and three patterns

The trend of social change further intensifies in the late Chalcolithic, allowing three patterns to continue and intermingle.

In the Central Plain, ancient cities such as Taosi, covering nearly three million square meters, and others like Wangchenggang and Pingliangtai ancient city emerged, forming several regional centers. The city walls were often built from rammed earth, quite steep and sturdy, improving defensive capabilities. In addition to *yues*, spears were added to the specialized weapons. Stone arrowheads are well-made, numerous, and varied in shape, reflecting frequent wars, unprecedented specialization, and intensity of warfare. Large palace-like buildings and luxurious tombs have been discovered in Taosi, which carry diverse cultural factors. Qingliangsi tombs even have human sacrifice, heavily influenced by eastern traditions, leading to severe social stratification. Cultures like Wangwan III, Zaolütai, and Hougang II feature palace-like structures in ancient walled cities and large sacrificial buildings at Yuhui. However, their tombs seldom contain grave goods, maintaining a certain simplicity. The production of jade artifacts, high-grade pottery, lacquerware, and bronze ware in Taosi culture was specialized, with specific stone tool-making sites already discovered. Beautiful pottery, jade ware, bronze ware, etc., in Wangwan culture phase III and others, should also be such, showing significant developments in the social division of labor in the Central Plain region.

In the Eastern region, many city walls have also appeared in Longshan culture and Baodun culture in the upper reaches of the Yangtze River. The ancient cities built during Qujialing culture period in the middle reaches of the Yangtze River were often reused until Shijiahe culture. However, their construction is less refined than in the Central Plain. In addition to jade and stone *yue*, there are spears and numerous stone arrowheads, but these are fewer in number and simpler in shape. In terms of war preparation, these cultures seem to lag behind the Central Plain. Each Longshan culture cemetery generally only has ten to twenty tombs, highlighting the importance of familial organization. On a waist drum-shaped jar from Shijiahe culture at Xiaojiawuji, there is a carved image of a figure holding a *yue* and wearing a headdress, perhaps a military leader of the Shijiahe ancient city. These cultures exhibit serious wealth, social status differentiation, and craft industry specialization. At least four levels can be identified in settlements, with large-scale central settlements such as Tonglin ancient city, Shijiahe ancient city, and Sanxingdui ancient city at their core. These cities feature large palace-like buildings and high-level religious structures. Graves are clearly hierarchical, especially the large tombs of Longshan culture at Xizhufeng and Yinjiacheng, which contain multiple coffin layers, exquisite pottery, and jade ware, revealing the noble status of the tomb owners. Naturally, the jade artifacts, high-grade pottery, lacquerware, etc., of these cultures must be the products of specialized craft industry divisions.

In the Northern region, many stone cities have been discovered in Laohushan culture, with the Shimao stone city even covering a massive four million square meters, showing the extreme importance of war defense in society. However, the city wall thickness is generally no more than one to two meters, and construction techniques are relatively simple. Laohushan culture, Keshengzhuang culture phase II and Qijia culture rarely show specialized weapons like *yues* or spears, and stone arrowheads are simple in shape, with weaponry equipment far inferior to the Central Plain. Houses are clearly grouped, with the family-level organization being the most important. These are areas similar to the Central and Eastern regions. However, wealth and social status differentiation in these northern cultures is quite limited. Higher-level structures may have been found in Shimao stone city, indicating the existence of differentiation between settlements and certain social status differentiation. Still, there is no evidence of significant wealth differentiation. Some jade and stone artifacts and bronze ware of Laohushan culture in northern Shaanxi and Qijia may be professionally made. In general settlements, almost all items can find raw materials in the surrounding area, and many are made within each family, showing a clear characteristic of self-sufficiency.

In conclusion, the three different patterns of societal development, namely the "Central Plain Mode," "Eastern Mode," and "Northern Mode," still existed in the late Chalcolithic. These patterns intermingled with each other, with the Eastern pattern significantly impacting the other two, causing social division of labor and social status differentiation to start appearing in the Central Plain and the Northern regions. The pace of social development accelerated, leading to the further development of the initial civilization society.

(7) The archaic state stage with multiple powers
In the late Chalcolithic, multiple regional centers formed, each with large walled settlements at their core. Many of these entered the stage of initial states or civilized societies. Each archaeological culture had at least one or two such centers. Although these centers had mutual influence, they were generally not in a hierarchical relationship but present an era characterized by the simultaneous rise of multiple powers, each leading in its way. Hence, it is still called the "archaic state stage." The regions along the middle and lower reaches of the Yangtze River were trending toward decline. The once splendid Liangzhu culture no longer possessed ultra-large ancient cities and many exquisite jades; Shijiahe culture was also declining, with no new city walls being built, and pottery and stone tools production was increasingly crude. The Central Plain core area rose again, and its external influence gradually strengthened: The development of Taosi culture in the early Longshan period was unmatched, and its cultural influence at least covered most of the Central Plain Longshan period is unmatched, and its cultural influence

at least covers most of the Central Plain Longshan culture area. It seems like a core culture, perhaps already entering the stage of a formative dynastic state.[338] In the late Longshan period, Wangwan culture phase III expanded and strongly influenced its surroundings, causing the decline of Shijiahe culture and an unprecedented expansion of the Central Plain culture range. The Central Plain culture had deep local traditions and integrated excellent elements from surrounding cultures. It is the culmination of long-term cultural development in most parts of China, co-created by the ancestors of all regions. Changes and innovations also occurred in surrounding cultures but are still based on their original foundations. On the whole, early China, in a cultural sense, had further developed, forming different levels of cultural circles with the Central Plain at their core. At the same time, due to the push of Central Plain culture and the expansion of peripheral cultures, the range of early China was further expanded (fig. 4.29).

At that time, Mesopotamian civilization, Minoan civilization, and especially Egyptian civilization were in their prime. The Indus Basin also entered the stage of a civilized society, with the emergence of several "empires" ruled by kings—similar to the dynastic state stage in China, but with a lower degree of identification with the central culture. Early cultural exchanges between China and the West further developed. The introduction of western wheat significantly impacted the economic and social development of the Northern and Central Plain of early China. Symbols like the swastika pattern and the pointed-crown pattern on pottery in the Northern regions reflect exchanges with Central and Western Asia in spiritual aesthetics.

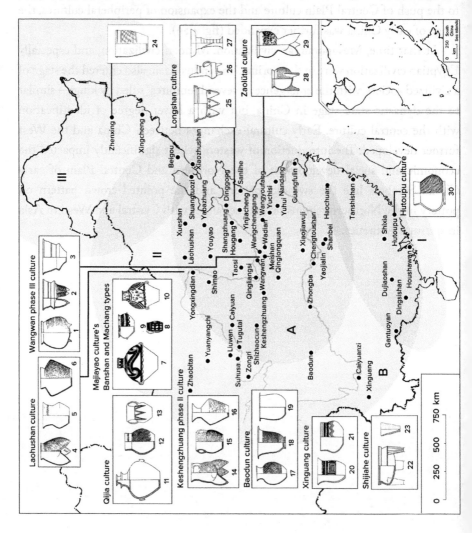

Figure 4.29 Early China in a cultural sense during the Longshan era (2500–1800 BCE)
I. Cauldron–round-foot plate cultural system
II. Early Chinese cultural sphere
III. Cylindrical jar cultural system
A. Core area   B. Peripheral area
1, 22, 25, 28. *Ding* (Wangchenggang H433: 5, Xiaojiawuji H32: 1, Yinjiacheng T192⑧: 13, Wangyoufang H27: 25)
2. *Jia* (Wangwan T58④: 1)
3, 9. Basin (Wangwan H212: 4, Suhusa M24: 2)
4, 14. *Li* (Yongxingdian H14: 2, Zhaojialai H2: 3)
5–7, 10–13, 15–17, 20, 21, 30. Jar (urn) (Yongxingdian H66: 1, H17: 1, Suhusa M55: 4, Liuwan [publicly-sourced] 01, M1103: 36, M366: 5, M977: 5, Zhaojialai H20: 2, 1, Mangcheng G4: 265, Xinguang T1104⑩: 56, T1106⑨: 21, Hutoupu III T0202④: 3)
8, 23 27. Cup (Liuwan M1250: 6, Xiaojiawuji H497: 36, Sanlihe M2100: 5)
18, 19. *Zun* (Baodun T1929⑦: 128, H16: 57)
24. Cylindrical jar (Zhenxing H161: 4)
26. *Gui* (Sanlihe M134: 1)
29. *Yan* (Wangyoufang H5: 4)
(All pottery.)

CHAPTER 5

The Dynastic State Stage of Early China

(1800–1300 BCE)

AROUND 2000 BCE, WITH THE ADVENT of the Bronze Age, significant changes occurred in technology, economic structure, cultural patterns, and social forms throughout most of China, a phenomenon aptly termed the "Bronze Age Revolution."[1] During this significant social transformation, while the infiltration of Western cultural elements was indeed noteworthy, the dominant influence of the Erlitou and Erligang cultures from the Central Plain core area after approximately 1800 BCE is more deserving of attention. Because these two cultures have a certain lineage relationship and roughly the same interaction with surrounding cultures, spanning only about 500 years, it is necessary to consider them as a whole, termed the "Erlitou–Erligang era." With around 1550 BCE as the boundary, it can be divided into two stages: Erlitou and Erligang cultures. At this time, the tri-legged vessels and black and gray pottery from the Longshan period, such as *ding, li, yan,* and *gui,* continued to be the main cultural elements of early China in a cultural sense, and their range expanded further. The traditional Majiayao culture in the west, with its painted pottery, combined with Western bronze cultural elements, formed a distinctive early China peripheral culture (table 5.1). Social differentiation significantly increased, with the Central Plain exhibiting unprecedented dominance and exclusivity.

Table 5.1 Cultural regions of the early Bronze Age in China (1800–1300 BCE)

		Erlitou period (1800–1550 BCE)	Erligang period (1550–1300 BCE)
Early Chinese cultural sphere	Most of the Yellow River and Yangtze River and Liaoning River basins	*Ding–li–yan* cultural system (Erlitou culture, Xiaqiyuan culture, Yueshi culture, Doujitai culture, lower Dianjiangtai culture, Maqiao culture, Zhukaigou culture, lower Xiajiadian culture, Gaotaishan culture, Xiaolaha culture)	*Ding–li–yan* cultural system (Erligang culture, Yueshi culture, Hushu culture, Maqiao culture, Wucheng culture, Zhukaigou culture, lower Xiajiadian culture, Gaotaishan culture, Xiaolaha culture)
	Upper reaches of the Yellow River to eastern Xinjiang	Jar–pot cultural system (Qijia culture, Siba culture, Hami Tianshan North Road culture)	Jar–pot cultural system (Xindian culture, Siwa culture, Kayue culture, Hami Tianshan North Road culture)
	Upper reaches of the Yangtze River	Sanxingdui culture	Sanxingdui culture
	South China regions	Cauldron–concaved-bottom jar–high-foot plate cultural system (Huangguashan culture and Houshan culture)	Cauldron–concaved-bottom jar–high-foot plate cultural system (Huangguashan culture and Houshan culture)
Early China outer margin zone	Central and western Xinjiang	Jar cultural system (Gumugou culture, Keermuqi culture and Andronovo culture)	Jar cultural system (Keermuqi culture and Andronovo culture)
	Southern Xizang	Qugong culture	Qugong culture

I. The Majority of the Yellow River, Yangtze River, and Liao River Basins

The majority of the Yellow River, Yangtze River, and Liao River basins belong to the *ding-li-yan* cultural system.

1. Erlitou Culture and Xiaqiyuan Culture in the Central Plain

Erlitou Culture

Around 1750 BCE, the Wangwan phase III culture's Xinzhai type moved east into the Luoyang Basin. It was influenced by Qijia culture to form Erlitou culture.[2] The Erlitou culture, represented by the Erlitou phases I to IV relics in Yanshi, Henan Province,[3] gradually transitioned from flat-bottom deep-belly jars to round-bottom jars, and the large-mouth *zun* gradually enlarged. The main pottery of Erlitou culture such as jar-shaped *ding*, deep-belly jar, deep-belly vat, basin-shaped *zeng*, arc-belly basin, flat-bottom basin, basin-shaped mortar and pestle, straight-neck urn, *zun*-shaped urn, folded-belly high-foot plate, tile-shaped-foot plate, folded-belly lid, flat-bottom bowl, *gu*, *gui*, and others, all evolved from the Xinzhai type. The rudimentary form of pottery *jue* (an ancient China drinking vessel here) was already present in the Wangwan phase III culture.[4] The cloud-thunder pattern, *Hui* pattern, cloud pattern, overlapping ring pattern, and other imprinted patterns, as well as the duck-shaped *ding*, originated from Maqiao culture and others in the Southeast region.[5] The *li*, which appeared later, came from Xiaqiyuan culture, along with new four-ear pots and others. Meanwhile, many neck-bundled round-belly pottery jars are likely to have originated from Qijia culture, and the four-foot small square cup was also early found in Qijia culture remains at Dahezhuang. Similarly, due to the bridge role of Qijia culture, Western elements such as bronze ring-pommel swords and axes were introduced.[6] The impact of Western bronze smelting technology on Erlitou culture led to the creation of bronze ritual vessels such as *jue*, *jia*, *he*, *gu*, and *ding* on the basis of Central Plain pottery and Central Plain clay composite casting technology (fig. 5.1). The Central Plain region finally

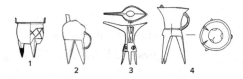

Figure 5.1 Bronze vessels from Erlitou culture[a]

1. *Ding* (87VM1: 1) 3. *Jue* (80IIIM2: 2) (All from the Erlitou site.)
2. *He* (86IIM1: 1) 4. *Jia* (84VIM9: 1)

[a] *Source:* Erlitou Team, Institute of Archaeology, Chinese Academy of Social Sciences, "A Brief Report on the Excavation of the Erlitou Site in Yanshi, Henan in the Autumn of 1980," *Archaeology*, no. 3 (1983): 199–205; Erlitou Team, Institute of Archaeology, Chinese Academy of Social Sciences, "Several Tombs Found in the Erlitou Site in Yanshi, Henan in the Autumn of 1984," *Archaeology*, no. 4 (1986): 318–323; Institute of Archaeology, Chinese Academy of Social Sciences, *Chinese Archaeology: Xia-Shang Volume* (Beijing: Encyclopedia of China Publishing House, 2003), 105.

entered the Bronze Age more than two hundred years later than Xinjiang and other regions. The Erlitou culture also introduced a new specialized weapon similar to the Western axe with a short cylindrical tube attached, the copper *ge*,[*] and turquoise-inlaid animal-face patterned copper plate ornaments (fig. 5.2), Proto-East Asian round plate (or round bubble-shaped plate). The jade tools such as *yue*, *qi*, *ge*, multi-holed knife, jade *ya zhang*,[†] *gui*,[‡] and handle-shaped tools are exquisitely made, except for the *ge*, the rest can find their source in the Longshan era, and the frequent presence of decorative ridge becomes a characteristic of the era. In addition, the appearance of vehicles in this culture is also likely to be related to influence from the West.[7]

After the formation of Erlitou culture, it immediately began to expand outward, reaching its peak during phase III. During the expansion process, it combined with local cultures to form several local types.[8] The core region of the Central Plain, including Zhengzhou and Luoyang and its nearby regions, represents the Erlitou type. The aforementioned bronze containers, jade articles, and other important artifacts are mainly found in this type. The southern part of Shanxi is represented by the Dongxiafeng type, exemplified by the contemporary remains of Xia County's Dongxiafeng.[9] This type has fewer *dings* but more *lis*, *yans*, and handled jars. Tri-legged urns and *lis* and *jias* with foot heels and vertical grooves are influenced by Zhukaigou culture of Jinzhong City. Southeastern Henan is represented by the Yangzhuang type, exemplified by phase III of Yangzhuang in Zhumadian City,[10] where drooping-belly *dings* and concaved-folded basket weave jars reflect local traditions. Southwestern Henan is represented by the Xiawanggang type, with phase III of Xiawanggang in Xichuan County as an example,[11] where round-bottom cauldrons and other artifacts reflect local traditions. Eastern Henan is represented by the Niujiaogang type, exemplified by

Figure 5.2 Turquoise-inlaid bronze plaque ornaments from Erlitou culture[a]

[a] *Source:* Erlitou Team, Institute of Archaeology, Chinese Academy of Social Sciences, "A Brief Report on the Excavation of the Erlitou Site in Yanshi, Henan in the Autumn of 1981," *Archaeology*, no. 1 (1984): 37–40.

---

* An ancient Chinese weapon with a long handle.—Trans.
† A type of edged implement used for rituals, with a blade at the upper end of the body, a rectangular shape at the lower end, and protruding teeth on both sides of the bottom.—Trans.
‡ An ancient Chinese jade vessel here used for rituals, was held by the highest-ranking official.—Trans.

the contemporary site at Niujiaogang in Qi County, characterized by distinctive pit-and-grid pattern and fine marked-cord *li*, olive-shaped jar, *yu*, and neck-bundled basin influenced by the Xiaqiyuan and Yueshi cultures. Shangluo and nearby regions are represented by the Donglongshan type, exemplified by the "late Xia" remains at Donglongshan in Shangluo City,[12] where double-handle round-belly jars and small-mouth folded-shoulder jars reflect local characteristics. In addition, the H23 site in Jingnansi in Jiangling of the middle reaches of the Yangtze River[13] and phase I of the Panlongcheng city site in Huangpi[14] are also generally considered part of Erlitou culture.

There is significant differentiation between the regions and settlements of Erlitou culture, with clear functional divisions and hierarchical distinctions in dwellings and tombs within central settlements. The ancient city of Erlitou is not only an unparalleled mega-settlement in the Luoyang Basin,[15] but it is also unrivaled within the entire Erlitou culture. The ancient city of Erlitou had an area of over one million square meters in phase I and expanded to over three million square meters after phase II. A palace area of over 100,000 square meters appeared in the center, where more than ten large palaces were built in succession; the total area of palace No. 1 was close to 10,000 square meters, with the main hall being 900 square meters (fig. 5.3). Surrounding the palace city are dozens of medium and

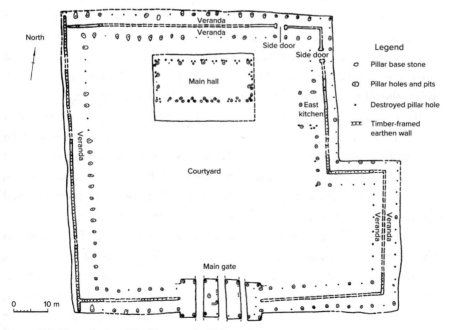

Figure 5.3 Plan of palace No. 1 base at the Erlitou site

small rammed earth architectural foundations, which should be the residential area for nobles, while the western and northern parts of the site are likely general residential areas; a bronze casting workshop was discovered south of the palace area, and there are sacrificial activity areas in the middle and east of the site, as well as pottery and bone processing workshops.[16] Although hundreds of scattered tombs have been discovered within the ancient city of Erlitou, they should not be the main body of the site's tombs; the medium-sized tombs found in the palace city with the accompanying turquoise dragon-shaped artifacts should also not be the highest-grade tombs of the ancient city of Erlitou. Large settlements outside the ancient city of Erlitou, such as Gongyi Shaochai, cover hundreds of thousands of square meters at most and have yielded valuable artifacts such as white pottery *gui* and are likely secondary centers. Huijü in Yanshi may have been a large stone tool manufacturing site primarily serving the ancient city of Erlitou.[17] Moreover, the production of valuable items, such as bronze ritual vessels, jade, lacquerware, etc., may also have been controlled by the ancient city of Erlitou. Other regions, such as the ancient city of Dashigu in Zhengzhou, with 510,000 square meters,[18] and the central settlement of Dongxiafeng, with an area of nearly 200,000 square meters, cannot be compared to the ancient city of Erlitou. Some people believe that the Erlitou state had already established a network for producing and distributing noble items, especially bronze ritual vessels, forming an "Erlitou world system."[19] This reflects a significant expansion in the scope and intensity of control and management by the ancient city of Erlitou. The palace foundations from phase II of Erlitou onwards are large and well-organized, numerous, and differentiated, indicating the formation of a fairly strict palace system at the time. Society should have already entered a mature, civilized stage by then.

The main architectural form of Erlitou culture was rectangular ground-level buildings with rammed earth walls, mud brick walls, or timber-framed earthen walls, with some semi-subterranean and cave style in the northern part. Graves were traditional rectangular vertical pit graves with extended supine burials. Larger graves contained lacquered coffins and caskets. Some graves were lined with cinnabar at the bottom and contained pottery and other grave goods.

The tools of Erlitou culture were similar to those of phase III of the Wangwan culture, mainly stone axes, adzes, chisels, and other woodworking tools, shovels, knives, sickles, and other agricultural implements, and stone or bone arrowheads as hunting tools or weapons. New copper tools appeared, such as adzes, chisels, arrowheads, knives, drills, and copper or bone saws. According to data from the

Erlitou, Zaojiaoshu,[20] and Yangzhuang sites, the main crops were millet grain, sorghum, rice, wheat, and soybeans, the "five grains," with rice predominating in the south and millet grain and wheat in the north. Domestic animals included cattle, pigs, dogs, and sheep, with a significant increase in the proportion of cattle and sheep, likely due to influences from western pastoral cultures. Arrowheads, fishhooks, fish spears, and net pendants indicate the existence of a fishing and hunting-gathering economy.

Xiaqiyuan Culture

Xiaqiyuan culture emerged in the southern Hebei region around phase II of Erlitou culture, represented by the third and fourth layers remains of the Xiaqiyuan site in Ci County,[21] which includes the "pre-Shang culture" remains such as Anyang Zhangdeng[22] and Hebi Liuzhuang.[23] Its typical vessels, like deep-belly jars with rolled rims, segmental *yans* with waists, and basins, inherited the types from phase II of Hougang and Xueshan cultures. At the same time, the rolled-rim *li* and tri-legged urn originated from the Baiyan type of Zhukaigou culture in Jinzhong City.[24] The *ding, jue, gui,* high-foot plate, large-mouth *zun*, egg-shaped urn, and four-ear pot, as well as the cloud pattern, cloud-thunder pattern, overlapping ring pattern, and *Hui* pattern, are primarily influenced by the Erlitou and Dongxiafeng types of Erlitou culture. The emergence of *gui* and inner-arced high-foot plate suggests that it is a product of the fusion of multiple cultural elements. Xiaqiyuan culture also had early and late stages,[25] and regional differences: in southern Hebei, the third and fourth layers remains of the Xiaqiyuan site represent the Zhanghe type;[26] in central Hebei, phase I of the Xiayuegezhuang site in Yi County[27] represents the Xiayuegezhuang type, with some protruding-shoulder *li* and footless *li* influenced by the Datuotou type of the lower Xiajiadian culture; in eastern Henan, the "pre-Shang culture" remains of Lutaigang in Qi County represent the Lutaigang type, with a few *zun*-shaped vessels belonging to Yueshi culture; in northern Henan, the Songyao site in Qi County[28] represents the Songyao type, which shows more influences from the Erlitou and Dongxiafeng types of Erlitou culture, with more *dings*, floral-rim round-belly jars, large-mouth *zuns*, egg-shaped urns, and jars.

Xiaqiyuan culture features semi-subterranean caves, caves, and timber-framed earthen wall houses. Graves are grouped by region, primarily small rectangular vertical pit graves with extended supine burials, occasionally featuring two-layer platforms and wooden or stone coffins. The tools are similar to those found in phase II of Hougang culture, so the economic form should also be similar.

Microlith arrowheads continue to be found, and new Western elements such as bronze knives, arrowheads, earrings, and bronze hairpins have appeared.

2. Erligang Culture in the Central Plain and Surrounding Regions

Erligang culture emerged around 1550 BCE and can be divided into at least phase III, represented by the lower and upper Erligang site in Zhengzhou[29] and the second layer remains of the Baijiazhuang site.[30] The transition from fine to coarse marked cords, from rolled to folded *li* rims, and from thick, short to thin, tall *zun* show a clear evolutionary trajectory. Typical vessels such as the *li*, *yan*, and basin are inherited from Xiaqiyuan culture. In contrast, the *jue* (an ancient China drinking vessel here), *jia*, *gu*, deep-belly round-bottom jar, large-mouth *zun*, pot, pinched-mouth round-belly jar, mortar and pestle, *zeng*, and high-foot plate are mainly influenced by Erlitou culture. Hard pottery or primitive porcelain *zuns* and jars likely originate from Jiangnan.[31] New forms such as *li*-shaped *jia* and *gui* (an ancient Chinese container or a ritual vessel here) suggest that Erligang culture was formed when Xiaqiyuan culture moved westward into Zhengzhou and incorporated many Erlitou cultural elements. The lower Zhengzhou Nanguanwai shows clear influences from Yueshi culture besides the Xiaqiyuan and Erlitou cultures, reflecting the early presence of Xiaqiyuan culture in eastern Henan. Erligang culture inherited the bronze tradition of Erlitou culture, with bronze types including *ding*, *li*, *yan*, *jue*, *he*, *jia*, *gu*, *gui*, plate, *zun*, *lei*, *you*,* and weapons or tools such as *yue*, *ge*, axe, adze, chisel, knife, arrowhead, and saw. The large square *ding* decorated with nipple-nail and animal-face patterns is the most representative (fig. 5.4). There are also jade objects such as *yue*, *ge*, *bi*, jade *huang*, and handle-shaped objects.

After its formation, Erligang culture quickly expanded westward to the core area of Erlitou culture in Luoyang City. It then rapidly spread around, forming the Erligang type in the Central Plain with Zhengzhou and Luoyang as its core,[32] where many bronze ritual vessels have been unearthed. In northern Henan, it is represented by the Liulige type, with representative relics in Hui County Liulige Shang Dynasty site,[33] characterized by slightly bulbous-belly *li*s and deep-belly basins with shoulders.[34] In southern Hebei, it is represented by the Taixi type, with the early habitation site relics in Gaocheng Taixi[35] as its representative, lacking round-bottom vessels but with plain *li*s and other elements of the lower Xiajiadian culture Datuotou. In southern Shanxi, it is represented by the

---

* An ancient Chinese wine vessel. Most of them are round or oval in appearance, with feet at the bottom.—Trans.

Dongxiafeng type, with representative relics in the V and VI phases of Dongxiafeng in Xia County, characterized by the tri-legged urns, *jia*-styled *yans*, and handled jars. In Guanzhong, it is represented by the Beicun type, with representative relics in Yaozhou Beicun phase I,[36] characterized by numerous floral-rim round-belly jars. In most of Hubei and northern Hunan, it is represented by the Panlongcheng type, with the main relics in Huangpi Panlongcheng as its representative, characterized by flat-crotch *li*, flat-crotch *jia*, bamboo joint-handle high-foot plate, long-neck pot, large-mouth vat, and numerous hard pottery or primitive porcelain and with cauldron, cauldron-shaped *ding*, convex-shoulder jar, convex-shoulder cup, fine-handle high-foot plate, deep-belly *zeng* and other Sanxingdui culture and indigenous culture elements in the west, Jingzhou, and Shimen areas.[37]

Figure 5.4 The bronze square *ding* of Erligang culture
(Duling No. 1 in the South Street of Zhangzai Village, Zhengzhou City)[a]

[a] *Source:* Henan Provincial Institute of Cultural Relics and Archaeology, Zhengzhou Municipal Institute of Cultural Relics and Archaeology, *Zhengzhou Shang Dynasty Bronze Wares Hoard* (Beijing: Science Press, 1999).

In Anhui Province, it is represented by the Dachengdun type, with the phase IV relics from the second excavation of Hanshan Dachengdun[38] as its representative, characterized by plain jars with added relief decorations on the neck, bowl-shaped high-foot plate, and other Yueshi culture elements. In central and western Shandong, it is represented by the Daxinzhuang type, with the Shang Dynasty cultural relics in Jinan Daxinzhuang[39] as its representative, characterized by red-brown pottery *li*, *yan*, small-mouth urn, deep-belly basin, and other Yueshi culture style artifacts.

Erligang culture features super urban centers such as the Zhengzhou Shangcheng, Yanshi Shangcheng, and Zhengzhou Xiaoshuangqiao, as well as regional urban centers such as Huangpi Panlongcheng, Yuanqu Shangcheng,[40] Jiaozuo Fucheng Shangcheng, and Huixian Mengzhuang Shangcheng. There are also many general settlements. The Zhengzhou Shangcheng has two walls, inner and outer, and the rectangular inner city alone covers an area of over three million square meters, making it the largest city site of the time. The northeastern part of the inner city is the palace district, with workshops for casting bronze, making pottery, and manufacturing bone tools between the inner and outer city.[41] There are also water supply and drainage systems, including wells. The tombs are mostly medium and small-sized rectangular vertical pit graves. There is a custom of waist pits and dog sacrifices. Slightly larger graves are accompanied by a dozen or so bronze wares. No large graves matching the status of the city site have been found yet.[42] The Yanshi Shangcheng also has inner and outer cities built at different periods. The inner city covers an area of 810,000 square meters, and the outer city nearly two million square meters. The center of the inner city is a square palace city, with many palaces composed of courtyards and colonnades, which should be the core of the ancient city. There are also several other important building foundation groups, some of which may belong to government treasuries (fig. 5.5). There are also general residences with timber-framed mud walls or semi-subterranean dwellings, workshops for casting bronze, making pottery, manufacturing bone tools, gardens, water supply and drainage systems, small tombs, etc.[43] The Xiaoshuangqiao settlement discovered palaces, palace-style buildings, large sacrificial sites, pits, etc.[44] The Panlongcheng covers an area of more than 70,000 square meters inside the city (maybe this is just the inner city), with the palace district in the northeastern part; outside the city, there are medium and small-sized dwellings as well as workshops for casting bronze and making pottery. More importantly, tombs of

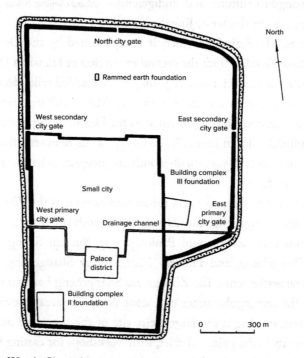

Figure 5.5 Plan of Yanshi Shangcheng

different levels were found, and medium-sized noble tombs had coffins, waist pits, and human sacrifices, accompanied by dozens of bronze, jade, and pottery artifacts. The cave-like tombs discovered by Dongxiafeng, along with the circular "十" (*shi*) character grid layout of the warehouse-like buildings, possess distinctive characteristics. In addition, the production tools and economic forms are similar to those of Erlitou culture.

3. Yueshi Culture in Haidai Region

During the Erlitou–Erligang period, Yueshi culture prevailed in Shandong and neighboring areas such as northern Jiangsu, northern Anhui, and eastern Henan,[45] represented by the early remains of Dongyueshi in Pingdu, Shandong,[46] including the contemporary remains of Haojiazhuang in Qingzhou,[47] Yinjiacheng in Sishui, Zhaogezhuang in Muping,[48] and Anqiugudui in Heze.[49] It extended north to the Liaodong Peninsula, leaving the phase II remains in Shuangtuozi, Dalian, and reached as far south as the middle reaches of the Yangtze and Huai Rivers, represented by the second type of cultural remains in Zhoubeidun, Gaoyou. Yueshi culture is a successor to Longshan culture. With the eastward expansion of Erligang culture, Yueshi culture gradually retreated eastward, and by the late Erligang culture, the boundary between the two had reached central Shandong.

Most pottery items in Yueshi culture, such as *dings*, high-foot plates, *zun*-shaped vessels, deep-belly jars, jars in the mouths of porcelains with lids, basins, boxes, and lids, as well as the wheel-made style, are inherited from Longshan culture. Many red, white, and yellow painted pottery may also have originated from Longshan culture. A few cord-mark *lis*, cord-mark deep-belly jars, large-mouth *zuns*, *jues*, *jias*, cloud-thunder patterns, *Hui* patterns, etc., are elements of Erlitou culture, Xiaqiyuan culture, and Erligang culture. A few Z-shaped patterns and boat-shaped vessels probably originated from the upper Xiaozhushan culture. At the same time, some hard pottery and primitive porcelain have their roots in the Jiangnan region. New tri-legged jars in the mouths of porcelains with lids and a small number of bronze weapons such as arrowheads, knives, chisels, awls, and bracelets have also been found. This culture can also be divided into several local types.[50] In the northwestern region, a few cord-mark *li* and cord-mark deep-belly jars belong to the Xiaqiyuan–Erligang culture. In the eastern Henan region, a small number of large-mouth *zuns*, olive-shaped jars, round-belly jars, cockscomb-handle basins, *jues*, and *jias* belong to the Erlitou and Xiaqiyuan cultures. In central Jiangsu, a small number of basket-pattern high-neck jars and basins are the local Zaolütai culture tradition. At the same time, the bag-foot *li* may have been produced under the influence of Erligang culture.

The settlements of Yueshi culture also show differentiation, with central settlements such as the ancient city of Chengziya in Licheng, Shandong Province. The houses have three types: semi-subterranean, ground, and platform-based, which can be single or multi-roomed. In the Shijia site in Huantai County, storage or sacrificial pits with wooden structures have been discovered.[51] The tombs are rectangular vertical pit graves with extended supine burials. The tools are mostly similar to those of Longshan culture, but its crescent-shaped double-holed stone knife and large perforated tri-blade stone hoe-shaped tool are pretty distinctive. The economy is generally similar to that of Longshan culture. Still, as the remains at sites such as Tonglin in Linzi, Shandong, and Zhaogezhuang in Muping show, the proportion of millet grain cultivation has increased. In contrast, the proportion of rice cultivation has decreased.[52]

4. Culture in the Huai River, Yellow River, and Lower Yangtze River Regions

Doujitai Culture

During the Erlitou period, Doujitai culture was present in the Anhui region, represented by phases II to IV of Doujitai in Shou County[53] and the early Shigudun in Tongling.[54] The Dachengdun type of Erligang culture later replaced it. Doujitai culture mainly developed from the local Wangwan phase III culture. Its drooping-belly *dings*, concaved-bottom pots, and cockscomb-handle basins belong to the Wangwan phase III Yangzhuang type tradition. The *ding* with press-fingered pattern feet, floral-rim round-belly jar, curved-handle arc-belly high-foot plate, tile-foot plate, and *gu* are elements of Erlitou culture. The *zun*-shaped vessels, pots in mouths of porcelains with lids, inward concaved-belly high-foot plates, deep-belly jars with added relief decorations on the neck, and the crescent-shaped perforated stone knives are elements of Yueshi culture. The *yan* with added relief decoration on the waist and crotch part and imprinted with rope pattern is a variant of Yueshi culture. The source of imprinted patterns like cloud-thunder patterns, concentric circle patterns, and diamond patterns should be Maqiao culture.

Lower Dianjiangtai Culture and Hushu Culture

In the Ningzhen region, lower Dianjiangtai culture[55] and Hushu culture[56] existed roughly at the same time as the Erlitou and Erligang cultures. Both can be found in successive early and late stratigraphic relations at sites like Dianjiangtai in Jiangning[57] and Tuanshan in Dantu.[58] Hushu culture also includes remains from the third layer remains of Beiyinyangying in Nanjing. Lower Dianjiangtai culture seems to have developed mainly on a cultural foundation similar to the southern wandering type of the Zaolütai culture. Its plain *yan*, plain *ding*, curved-handle high-foot plate, basin, single-handle cylindrical-belly cup, ring-foot plate, and urn are all inheritances from the Zaolütai and Longshan cultures with unique characteristics. The curved-handle high-foot plate and press-finger patterned *ding* feet reflect the influence of Erlitou culture, while the *zun*-shaped vessels are elements of Yueshi culture. Hushu culture inherits local traditions like plain *yan* and plain *ding* from Doujitai culture. Under the strong influence of Erligang culture, a large number of cord-mark or plain *li*, cord-mark *yan*, cord-mark jar, folded-rim high-foot plate, *gui*, and animal-face patterns have appeared, with the plain *li* showing strong local characteristics. Influenced by Maqiao culture or Jiantounong type remains, more pottery pots pottery with imprinted patterns have also appeared. The tools of Hushu culture are close to those of Maqiao culture but also include slanted-handle stone knives, double-holed near-backed crescent-shaped arc-edge stone knives, stone sickles, and bronze weapons such as knives and arrowheads.

Maqiao Culture and Jiantounong Type Remains

During the Erlitou period, Maqiao culture was found around Tai Lake and in the northeastern part of Zhejiang Province,[59] represented by the remains of this period at Maqiao in Minhang District, Shanghai,[60] including the "Shang–Zhou period" remains at Xiangshan Tashan,[61] and possibly continuing to the Erligang period. Maqiao culture developed based on the local Guangfulin culture and was influenced by Erlitou culture. Its typical cord-mark *ding* and cord-mark *yan* are inherited from Guangfulin culture, except that their feet are not side-mounted but tongue-shaped, concave arc-shaped, or conical; the folded-rim or high-neck concaved-bottom jars, earthen bowls, high-foot plates, *guis*, mortar and pestle bowls, and single-handle cups can all trace their origin back to Guangfulin culture, but the imprinted patterns on the handle belly part is very characteristic of the era; a large number of cloud-thunder patterns, *Hui* patterns, stripe-grid patterns, vein patterns, mat patterns, etc., were already seen in Guangfulin culture; the newly appeared duck-shaped pots may have a heritage relationship with the high-neck pots that were popular in the late Liangzhu culture, Haochuan culture, and Tanshishan culture; the newly appeared reddish-brown pottery, and the earliest black-glazed or greenish-glazed high-foot plate and jar types of primitive porcelain, may be influenced by Jiantounong type remains;[62] the *gu*, *zhi* (an ancient

Chinese ritual vessel to serve wine), basin, tile-foot plate, *he*, *gui* (an ancient Chinese cooking utensil here), and mushroom knob lid belong to Erlitou culture factors, and the deep-folded-belly style of the high-foot plate and *gui* also relates to the influence of Erlitou culture; a few tri-legged jar in the mouth of porcelain with a lid, *yu* in mouth of porcelain with a lid (like the *zun*-shaped vessel), etc., belong to Yueshi culture factors. Maqiao culture also has regional differences. For example, the northeastern Zhejiang region has a long local tradition of cauldrons.

Roughly at the same time, at the junction of Jiangxi, Zhejiang, and Fujian provinces, there are Jiantounong type remains closely related to Maqiao culture, represented by the second and third units of Jiantounong in Jiangshan, Zhejiang.[63] Its folded-shoulder *zuns*, folded-shoulder high-neck jars, folded-shoulder urns are mainly based on the first unit of Jiantounong type remains, and their earlier origin lies in the local Shanbei culture and Haochuan culture; concaved-bottom deep-belly jar, basin, tile-foot plate, curved-handle high-foot plate, *he*, *gui*, and flat-bottom *gui*-shaped vessel reflect the influence from Maqiao culture and even Erlitou culture; the absence of *ding*, *yan*, and *gu* is a main distinction from Maqiao culture, and the widespread popularity of pottery with imprinted patterns, especially black-glazed pottery with imprinted patterns, is one of its major features.

Maqiao culture has mud-wall constructions with wooden frames, stilted buildings, and many wells. The tombs are rectangular vertical pit graves with extended supine. Tools are mainly ground stone tools such as axes, adzes, chisels, hoes, knives, sickles, arrowheads, etc. There are sectioned stone adzes, slanted-handle stone knives, horizontal-handle stone knives, stone sickles, etc., all of which were already popular in Liangzhu culture. Half-moon-shaped arc-edge knives with two holes near the back and concaved-backed arc-edge knives are distinctive. There are also bronze adze, knife, chisel, etc., stone or bronze *yue*, *ge*, spear, and other weapons. *Yue* has an internal fence, and the arc edge turns upward. The economy should be similar to Liangzhu culture, with rice agriculture occupying an important position as well as raising pigs, dogs, and other livestock.

Wucheng Culture

In the late Erligang culture, Wucheng culture is distributed in most parts of Jiangxi Province,[64] represented by phase I of the Wucheng remains in Zhangshu City.[65] This culture should have formed based on the Jiantounong type remains under the strong influence of Erligang culture (including the Panlongcheng type). Its separate-crotched *li*, *yan*, large-mouth *zun*, large-mouth vat, deep-belly basin, deep-belly jar, straight-belly jar, false-belly high-foot plate, *jia*, *jue*, mushroom knob vessel lid and most other pottery, as well as marked-cord pattern, basically belong to Erligang culture factors; decorated with marked-cord patterns, or linked bead patterns, square grid patterns, cloud-thunder patterns, etc., features such as hard pottery, glazed pottery, primitive porcelain, etc., belong to the local tradition; later, *yan*-shaped vessels without bag-shaped feet appeared; folded-shoulder jar, folded-shoulder *zun*, folded-shoulder urn are similar to the same kind of vessels in Erligang culture, but in fact, these types of vessels already existed in part in the Jiantounong type; side flat-foot basin-shaped *ding*, drooping-belly concaved-bottom jar, bird head-shaped handle, etc., basically belong to the local tradition. Bronze vessels such as the *ding* and *jia* were discovered, as well as bronze tools or weapons such as knives, axes, adzes, chisels, spears, *ges*, and stone molds for casting these tools and weapons.

Wucheng culture includes the ancient Wucheng city covering more than 600,000 square meters, which includes living areas, pottery making areas, bronze smelting areas, sacrificial areas, and burial areas. The tombs are rectangular vertical pit graves. Stone tools or weapons include axes, adzes, chisels, shovels, knives, sickles, arrowheads, *ges*, spears, spinning wheels, net pendants, etc. There are features like sectioned stone adzes, concaved-backed arc-edge knives with two holes near the back, and also a good number of ceramic concaved-backed arc-edge knives. The economy should have been based mainly on rice farming, with a considerable component of fishing and hunting.

5. Zhukaigou Culture in the Northern Region

During the Erlitou–Erligang period, the narrowly defined northern region was distributed with Zhukaigou culture,[66] represented by the Zhukaigou site in Ejin Horo Banner, Inner Mongolia,[67] including the Xinhua site in Shenmu, northern Shaanxi,[68] phases IV and V of the Baiyan site in Taigu, Jinzhong,[69] and phases V and VI of the Xinghuacun site in Fenyang,[70] among others. Zhukaigou culture primarily developed based on Laohushan culture. Most pottery, such as the double-handle *li*, single-handle *li*, converging-mouth *yan*, *he*, *jia*, buttoned jar, basket-pattern folded-shoulder jar, double-handle jar, single-handle jar, long-neck pot, large-mouth *zun*, high-collared *zun*, slanted-belly basin, straight-handle high-foot plate, etc., are inherited from Laohushan culture, and tri-legged urn may have expanded from northern Shaanxi to the entire territory; large-fat bag-foot *li*, round-foot jar, ring-foot plate, deep-belly *gui*, tri-legged cup, single-handle cup, *gui*-shaped vessel, plain or pressed-decorated folded-shoulder jar, etc., should have come from late Taosi culture; double (triple) large-handle jar belongs to

Qijia culture elements; early to middle curved-handle high-foot plate, late pottery folded-rim divided-crotch *li*, single-handle converging-mouth *jia*, high-foot plate, bowl-shaped *gui*, as well as large triangular patterns, large cross-shaped hollowed-out pattern, cloud-thunder pattern, animal-face pattern, etc., belong to Erlitou and Erligang culture elements, bronze *ge* and *ding* also belong to Erligang culture elements, showing that it was greatly influenced by Erligang culture in the late period. In addition, the "snake patterns" of the snake-pattern *lis* in this culture, as well as the short swords, ring-pommel swords, and protectors that appeared in the late period, which are "Ordos-style bronzes," should have come from the bronze culture in the northwest of China or even the western grassland region.

Zhukaigou culture also has regional differences. For example, the early floral-rim *li*, buttoned pots, etc., in the central and southern parts of Inner Mongolia are not seen in northern Shaanxi and Jinzhong. In contrast, the high-collared *li* in Jinzhong is almost connected at the crotch. The spade, *yue*, knife, jade *ya zhang*, connected *bi*, *bi* with protruding teeth, *gui*, jade *jue*, jade *huang*, human face-shaped carving, and other jades found in northern Shaanxi are unique and should be related to Taosi culture. In the middle and late periods, the *li* in the central and southern parts of Inner Mongolia are short and plump, with not very obvious solid feet. Tri-legged urns have hollow feet, with more snake-pattern *li*, snake-pattern *yan*, buttoned pots, etc.; the *li* in Jinzhong are slender and tall, with pointed and long solid feet. The early ones have more vertical grooves and horizontal binding marks at the foot end. Tri-legged urns have mostly solid feet, with more *dings*, *jues*, *jias*, and other Erlitou–Erligang culture elements.

The early Zhukaigou culture settlements are most notable in the northern Shaanxi Shimao stone city, with its vast size of more than four million square meters, the "shadow walls" with regularly inserted jade knives, grand and complex city gates, pits with female heads, multicolored geometric mural paintings, etc., all of which reveal the status of this archaeological site as a super central settlement. The settlements such as Shimao, Xinhua, and Zhukaigou have ground-based and semi-subterranean houses. The walls are constructed using three methods: earthen, a mix of earth, stone, and pottery shards, and mud walls with wooden frames; white plaster surfaces are not as popular as before. Graves can be divided into different areas. Adult graves are rectangular vertical shaft earthen pits, with a few having wooden coffins and double-layer platforms; the common burial practice is a single person with extended supine, a few mixed-gender joint burials generally have the male with extended supine, and the female with one or two bodies in flexed on the side, or the male has a coffin while the female does not, reflecting a clear male-dominated mindset, which has some connections to Qijia culture. The graves contain a small amount of pottery or lower jawbones of pigs, sheep, dog skeletons, etc. The wealth difference is not very significant. Popular side chamber tombs characterize the Baiaobao Cemetery.[71] In the late period of Zhukaigou, some graves contained bronze weapons and ornaments such as the *ges*, short swords, ring-pommel swords, earrings, neck ornaments, and bronze plaques, indicating the status of the tomb owners as "farmers in peacetime, warriors in wartime." Some graves in Xinghuacun have sacrificial dog pits. Xinhua also discovered a special pit that may have been used for rituals, with more than 30 jade artifacts such as *yues*, knives, *guis*, jade jues, jade huangs, spades, and axes arranged at the bottom of the pit.

The production tools of Zhukaigou culture are similar to those of Laohushan culture, with the most common harvesting tools being stone knives and sickles, especially thick-backed curved stone knives which are quite distinctive, reflecting an agriculture-based economy. On the other hand, there are also a certain number of ring-pommel copper swords, bone-handle stone-blade knives, scraping tools, perforated whetstones, short-tooth bone combs, microlith arrowheads, bone (copper) arrowheads, etc. The proportion of sheep and cattle was also increasing, and there was even a custom of sacrificing sheep, indicating that the importance of animal husbandry and hunting had increased.

6. Lower Xiajiadian Culture and Gaotaishan Culture in the Liao River Basin and North and South of Yan Mountains

Lower Xiajiadian Culture

During the Erlitou–Erligang period, the Xiliao River Basin, the Ling River Basin, and the north and south of the Yan Mountains region were characterized by the lower Xiajiadian culture,[72] represented by the lower remains of Xiajiadian in Chifeng, Inner Mongolia,[73] including the Yaowangmiao type represented by the Chifeng Yaowangmiao in Inner Mongolia and Dadianzi remains in Aohan Banner,[74] the Datuotou type represented by the H2 of Datuotou in Dachang, Hebei,[75] and phase II of Zhangying in Changping, Beijing,[76] and the Huliu River type represented by the M2008 of the Sanguan in Yu County, Hebei, and the Qianbao F1 remains.[77]

The lower Xiajiadian culture mainly developed based on phase II of Xueshan culture and was greatly influenced by phase II of Hougang culture, and later expanded to the Xiliao River and the Huliu River basins. Typical pottery there such as the bulbous-belly or arc-belly *li*, wide-flare-mouth *yan*, deep-belly jar, protruding-shoulder urn, folded-belly *zun*, round-foot plate, tri-legged plate, flat-bottom basin, double-handle arc-belly basin, shallow high-foot plate, flat-bottom bowl, high-neck pot, etc., are all closely related to the above two cultures, even the most representative cylindrical-belly *li* was seen early in the Yabazhuang site in Renqiu City. Only a few elements, such as the geometric-pattern painted pottery and folded-belly *zun*, may have some connection with the Xiaoheyan type of phase I of Xueshan culture, especially the red, white, or yellow painted hooks and complex combinations, mainly similar to the animal-face pattern theme. Pottery snake-pattern *lis*, floral-rim *lis*, and thick-backed curved stone knives are elements of Zhukaigou culture. A small number of plain pots in the east are elements of Gaotaishan culture, and bronze trumpet-mouth earrings, bronze rings, gold earrings, etc., reflect the influence of the West.[78] The early stage *jue*, *gui*, *he*, etc., from the Dadianzi and other cemeteries belong to Erlitou culture elements. In contrast, the solid-foot *li* and false-belly high-foot plate (and their cross-shaped hollowed-out decorations) from the south of Yan Mountains in the later stage belong to Erligang culture elements. This culture also has bronze *ge* with connected handles, bronze comb, jade *bi*, jade *jue*, jade ring, lead cane head, lacquer *gu*, etc. In addition, the Yaowangmiao type is popular with cylindrical-belly *li*, the Datuotou type often has fat-bag-foot *li* and protruding-shoulder *li*, and the Huliu River type sees tri-legged urns from Jinzhong, reflecting certain local differences.

The lower Xiajiadian culture is best represented by stone cities that are distributed in bands on the hillsides along the rivers and grouped together,[79] possibly serving the function of an initial Great Wall.[80] These stone cities vary in size; for instance, the Chifeng Chijiayingzi stone city, covering 100,000 square meters, may be one of the central settlements. The Sanzuodian stone city in Chifeng has a pair of large and small cities side by side, with horse faces on the city walls, indicating strong military defense characteristics.[81] In addition to the stone cities, rammed earth cities are built on the mountains' front slopes, such as Dadianzi and Erdaojingzi[82] in Chifeng. Houses are mostly semi-subterranean but include ground-level houses with rammed earth walls, mud brick or stone walls, round or square with rounded corners, often with attached corridors or side rooms, and whitewashed surfaces (fig. 5.6). Other than the distinctive stone walls, they resemble phase II of Hougang culture. The tombs are generally vertical pit graves, with extended on the side or extended supine. There are large-scale cemeteries where tombs are grouped, which may reflect family distinctions and indicate a certain degree of wealth disparity. For example, the larger tombs at the Dadianzi

Cemetery have two-tier platforms and wooden coffins with exquisitely painted pottery and special burial objects such as *jue*, *gui*, and *he*.

Production tools and weapons mainly include ground stone tools such as axes, adzes, chisels, shovels, *yues*, knives, and sickles, as well as microliths or chipped stone tools such as stone hoes, concaved-bottom triangular arrowheads, scrapers, pounding tools, and stone leaves, as well as bronze tools like ring-pommel swords, winged arrowheads, carved knives, awls, chisels, hooks with barbs, and pottery tools such as spinning wheels, pottery cushions, pottery beaters, net pendants, bag-foot molds, and bone tools such as arrowheads, awls, needles, needle tubes, darts, and knives. The economy was primarily based on dry millet grain and sorghum farming, supplemented by hunting, fishing, and animal husbandry. Livestock included pigs, sheep, cattle, and dogs. The discovery of bronze ring-pommel swords, perforated whetstones, and the phenomenon of burial of cattle and sheep in tombs indicates significant development in animal husbandry. The biggest change in handicraft technology from the Longshan era was the initial rise of bronze casting. Many bronze smelting sites were found in the Chifeng area, and there were copper casting workshop areas in the Zhangying site in Changping. Most of the bronzeware is tin bronze, with a few being lead-tin bronze. Craftsmen at the time not only knew that adding tin could improve the mechanical properties of bronze but also were able to adjust the tin content according to different uses.[83] The prevalence of simple stone mold casting, supplemented by forging and the popularity of tin bronze, shows that it belonged to the early metallurgical technology circle facing the northwest inland. The technology of adjusting tin content according to different

Figure 5.6 Courtyard group at the Erdaojingzi site (west–east)

uses is close to that of the Central Plain area, perhaps due to the influence of the Central Plain.

Gaotaishan Culture

Gaotaishan culture (early stage), which existed concurrently with the lower Xiajiadian culture in the Xialiao River Basin,[84] is primarily represented by the remains found at the Gaotaishan site in Xinmin, Liaoning Province,[85] and the phases II and III of the Ping'anbao site in Zhangwu.[86] Gaotaishan culture likely emerged from Pianbuzi culture or similar remains, influenced by Yueshi culture. Its high-collared jar, double-handle jar (urn), double-lipped jar, double-handle basin, single-handle cup, high-foot plate, earthen bowl, flat-bottom bowl, and *zeng* have an inherited relationship with Pianbuzi culture or the upper Xiaozhushan culture. Earlier examples of plain non-solid-foot *yan* with added relief decorations in the pelvis section, and jar in the mouth of porcelain with a lid likely incorporate elements of Yueshi culture, whereas later *yan* with the solid foot, as well as solid-foot straight-belly *li*, protruding-shoulder *li*, and arc-belly *li*, are probably influenced by the lower Xiajiadian culture. Gaotaishan culture, with the Liaoxi Plain as its center, extended east to the northeastern part of Liaodong[87] and was also known as Miaohoushan culture or Machengzi culture,[88] featuring many conical-foot *dings* and vessels with cylindrical-penetrating handles. In the later stage, it expanded westward to the Liaoxi mountainous region, replacing the original lower Xiajiadian culture there and incorporating elements like the folded-belly *zun* from the lower Xiajiadian culture.[89] In addition, individual bronze trumpet-mouth earrings, ring-pommel swords, etc., belong to the Western cultural elements. There are abacus-shaped stick heads (scepter heads).

Gaotaishan culture consists of rectangular semi-subterranean houses and round ground-level buildings, with instances of using mud bricks as building materials, which is likely a result of influence from the lower Xiajiadian culture. In the Liaoxi Plain, graves are rectangular vertical pit graves, with a few having a two-tiered platform and wooden coffin. They mainly contain single individuals flexed on the side. In the northeastern part of Liaodong there are cave and stone coffin tombs, with primary burials in extended supine or flexed burials, secondary burials, and cremation is common. Few grave goods include pottery and stone tools, and pig mandible bones are often buried in the eastern part. Tools are similar to those of the lower Xiajiadian culture, mainly including ground stone tools such as axes, adzes, chisels, sickles, knives, chipped stone hoes, microlithic arrowheads, ground stone arrowheads, as well as bone shovels, bone arrowheads, spinning wheels, net pendants, etc. Double-holed stone knives have various shapes, such as arched-backed flat blade, flat-backed arched blade, concaved-backed arched blade, and rectangle. The economy was predominantly agricultural, with significant fishing, hunting, and gathering components.

Xiaolaha Culture and Xingcheng Culture

Xiaolaha culture in the Nen River Basin of northeastern China is represented by phase II of the Xiaolaha site in Zhaoyuan, Heilongjiang,[90] and phase I of the Baijinbao site.[91] Pottery is mainly plain, with its cylindrical jars, high-neck pots, small-mouth urns, single-handle cups, false round-foot bowls, and earthen bowls showing a certain inheritance relationship with the earlier local Nanbaoligoutu culture. It was greatly influenced by Gaotaishan culture, and individual arc-belly *li* belonged to the influence of the lower Xiajiadian culture. A small number of fine-tooth comb patterns with clustered dot patterns are very characteristic. There are rectangular semi-subterranean houses and rectangular vertical pit graves. In addition to ground stone tools such as axes, adzes, and chisels, clam knives, and bone awls are common, as well as bronze knives, but no agricultural stone knives are seen, which suggests that the economy may have been mainly based on fishing and hunting.

In addition, Xingcheng culture (early stage), represented by the Bronze Age remains in Xingcheng, Helong, Jilin Province in the Tumen River Basin,[92] is characterized by pottery with floral rims and plain surfaces, and deep-belly jars and urns, as well as basins, bowls, and cups. It is quite different from the Neolithic cylindrical jar cultural system and may have formed under the significant influence of phase II of the Shuangtuozi type of Yueshi culture. However, no *ding*-, *li*-, or *yan*-type vessels have been found. There are rectangular semi-subterranean houses. The main production tools include chipped stone hoes, stone shovels, ground axes, adzes, chisels, spades, knives, and arrowheads. Microlithic tools such as spears, arrowheads, and scrapers are developed, as well as spinning wheels, net pendants, bone sickles, bone awls, etc. Double-holed stone knives reflect its connection with the Shuangtuozi type phase II. The economy was predominantly agricultural, with a substantial proportion of fishing and hunting.

II. From the Upper Reaches of the Yellow River to Eastern Xinjiang

From the upper reaches of the Yellow River to eastern Xinjiang, it belongs to the jar–pot cultural system.

Late Qijia Culture

Around 1900 BCE to 1500 BCE, which is the same or slightly earlier period than Erlitou culture, the Gansu–Qinghai–Ningxia provinces area (excluding the Hexi Corridor) was marked by the late Qijia culture remains,[93] which also extended eastward to the middle and lower reaches of the Wei River in Shaanxi. The culture is represented by the Qijiaping site in Guanghe, Gansu, including the Mogou site in Lintan, Gansu,[94] the Qinweijia site in Yongjing,[95] the Dahezhuang site,[96] and the contemporary Laoniupo site in Xi'an, Shaanxi.[97] The late Qijia culture only has a few *li* and *he* and is essentially no longer part of the *ding–li–yan* cultural system. The differentiation trend is obvious and can be divided into at least three local types. The Qijiaping, Qinweijia, and Dahezhuang type sites in central Gansu, eastern Qinghai, and southern Ningxia belong to the Qijiaping type, where jar vessels overall develop toward slim and tall shapes, floral-rim pots have long bellies, and new painted pottery pots, snake-pattern pots, large-mouth folded-shoulder *zuns*, and small square cups emerge as unique vessel shapes. The Mogou type sites in southern Gansu belong to the Mogou type, where jar vessels overall develop toward short and chubby shapes, with newly painted pottery pots, some of which have double-handle jars already slightly concave at the mouth resembling a saddle. The Laoniupo and Nanshacun type sites in the Guanzhong region belong to the Laoniupo type, where floral-rim pots have round bellies and more plain wheel-made round-belly jars are seen. The late Qijia culture was greatly influenced by the West. At this time, new double-handle or single-handle axe with a hole in the axe for attaching the handle, spear, knife, human-face dagger, awl, mirror, crescent-shaped ornament, ring, trumpet-mouth earring, bracelet, *chuan*,* hollow bead, other tin bronze or red copper utensil were found, as well as pottery with color painted, added fine clay strips (snake patterns), stamped broken line patterns, beard-like hanging band patterns, sheep head-shaped patterns, bead patterns, etc., which were all seen earlier in Southern Siberia, central Asia, etc., belonging to the Western cultural elements. In addition, the pottery *hes* and flat-bottom *he*-shaped

---

* An ancient Chinese bracelet made of beads or jade threaded together.—Trans.

vessels from Qijiaping in Guanghe County and the bronze plaques inlaid with turquoise from Tianshui City[98] should belong to the influence of Erlitou culture.

The housing and burial conditions of the late Qijia culture are basically the same as those of the middle period. The burial grounds at Qinweijia, Mogou, etc., are neatly arranged, with distinctions between sections, rows, and groups, representing different levels of social organization. Vertical pit-side chamber tombs were prevalent at the Mogou burials, with some having multiple side chambers or multiple burials. There were both single and joint burials, with primary burials mainly being extended supine, and secondary burials were also present. Adult joint burials often took the form of the male in extended supine and the female in flexed on the side, and there are also adult and children's joint burials, reflecting a male-dominant and family-oriented society. Some bones in tomb passages may be sacrificial. Wall niches are common, and usually, a small number of pottery and other burial goods were present, and the custom of burying pig mandibles continued. The difference between rich and poor is not very apparent.

The production tools remained largely the same as in the previous era, with agriculture remaining the main economy. Carbonized millet grains and husks are often found, but animal husbandry and hunting proportions increased further. The number of sheep increased, and there was a custom of burying sheep horns, indicating that sheep farming played a significant role in the animal husbandry industry while cattle were also raised. Copper knives and axes are also common tools in pastoral cultures.

Xindian Culture, Siwa Culture, and Kayue Culture

Around 1500 BCE to 1300 BCE, which is the period of Erligang culture, the Gansu–Qinghai–Ningxia area (excluding the Hexi Corridor) was marked by the early Xindian culture, Kayue culture, and Siwa culture. They are represented by the early burials at Shanjiatou in Minhe, Qinghai,[99] Panjialiang in Xiaxi River in Huangzhong, Qinghai,[100] and the late burials at Mogou in Lintan, Gansu.

All three cultures originated from Qijia culture, with their main types of vessels such as the double large-handle jar, double small-handle jar, floral-rim cord-mark jar, painted pottery jar, and high-foot plate, all inheriting the lineage of Qijia culture. Specifically, Xindian culture and Kayue culture both originate from the Qijiaping type of Qijia culture, both having double large-handle jars, double small-handle cord-mark jars, floral-rim cord-mark jars, and other main types of vessels. However, the former commonly have round bottoms while the latter all have flat or round feet, and the former has more painted pottery and marked-cord patterns. The Siwa culture specifically comes from the Mogou type of Qijia culture, with fewer double large-handle jars but popular small saddle-mouth double-handle jars and fewer painted pottery. The pottery decoration of these three cultures not only inherits Qijia culture and the Machang type but also incorporates new cultural elements related to the West, such as beard patterns, hanging band patterns, sheep head-shaped patterns, and animal-shaped patterns such as sheep, dogs, and deer.

Compared to Qijia culture, the types of bronze tools increased, which also primarily belonged to Western cultural elements. These include curved-backed knives, holes in axes for attaching the handles or axes with short cylindrical tubes attached, spears, mirrors, bells, earrings, rings, buckles, and hollow beads. The copper cooking *li* in Kayue culture at Baojiazhai in Xining is basically consistent with those in the upper Erligang culture in Zhangzhai, Zhengzhou,[101] indicating the influence of Erligang culture has reached this area.[102] Several chunky iron artifacts were found in the early Siwa culture remains at Mogou, dating to around the 15th century BCE. These are the earliest man-made iron products in China,[103] and their origin should be in West Asia.

The houses and tombs are similar to those of Qijia culture. There are rectangular semi-subterranean houses with living surfaces smeared with white ash. There are larger cemeteries, with many graves marked with stones or burial mounds. Mainly rectangular vertical pit tombs are used, with a few side chamber tombs, often with wall niches, and many have been disturbed twice, followed by single instances of extended supine burials. Animal sacrifice customs include cattle, sheep, dogs, and cremation. Some graves in Kayue culture at Panjialiang have more than 500 burial objects, with over 20 copper tools such as *yue*, axe, and spear, and there is also evidence of human sacrifice, indicating a significant disparity between the rich and the poor.

The production tools are similar to those of Qijia culture, with stone knives and other agricultural tools being common, suggesting that agriculture still held the overall advantage. The main grain crops were millet grain, wheat, and barley. Animal husbandry was quite developed, with cattle and sheep likely being raised and other livestock such as pigs and dogs. Many graves have animal sacrifice customs, with bones of cattle, sheep, and dogs found, but pig bones are rare. Accordingly, many portable tools appear, such as ring-pommel and animal-head bronze swords, whetstones with holes or grooves at both ends, and long-bodied short-tooth bone combs for grooming livestock.

Siba Culture and Hami Tianshan North Road Culture

From 2000 BCE to 1300 BCE, or slightly earlier during the Erlitou–Erligang era, Siba culture[104] and Hami Tianshan North Road culture existed in the Hexi Corridor and eastern Xinjiang. The former is represented by the remains at Sibatan in Shandan, Gansu,[105] and Donghuishan in Minle.[106] The Hami Tianshan North Road (or Yalinban) Cemetery represents the latter.[107]

The two cultures are similar, both primarily based on the Machang type of Majiayao culture and strongly influenced by Western culture. Their primary pottery includes double-handle jars, single-handle jars, pots, four-handle jars, high-foot plates, single-handle cups, basins, earthen bowls, and cylindrical cups. The parallel horizontal band pattern, broken line pattern, rhombus pattern, checkerboard pattern, triangle pattern, grid pattern, and vertical band painted pottery all have a legacy relationship with the Machang type. The sheep head-shaped pattern and the human image with the upper body in an inverted triangle shape should belong to Western elements. The main difference between the two cultures is that the double-pierced cylindrical jar decorated with horizontal broken lines or vertical broken lines in the Hami Tianshan North Road culture is not found in Siba culture, which should have more connections with the cylindrical jar cultural system of the Eurasian grassland.[108] Siba culture also has four-foot square plates, multi-sub-boxes, lidded cylindrical jars, human-shaped jars, etc. The two cultures have bronze tools such as knives, swords, spears, axes with holes in axes for attaching the handles, adzes, chisels, awls, sickles, arrowheads, spears, mirrors, earrings, bracelets, bells, plaques, hollow beads, buckles, beads, tubes, pins, etc., which belong to Western cultural elements. Western elements include gold and silver earrings, jade and stone scepter heads, and copper sheep head-shaped scepter heads.

Siba culture has discovered rammed earth walls, stone walls, and sun-dried brick buildings, different from the popular semi-subterranean and cave styles in the Yellow River Basin. Large-scale clan public cemeteries are prevalent, arranged in dense rows, with rectangular pit vertical graves, side-room graves, or vertical earthen-brick chamber graves, some with wall niches and a few with wooden burial equipment. Siba culture practices extended supine burials, while the Hami Tianshan North Road culture practices flexed on the side with secondary and joint burials. The practice of burying the horns and bones of livestock, such as sheep, dogs, pigs, cattle, and horses, with sheep being the most common, is widespread. Overall, the wealth gap is limited, but some graves in the Huoshaogou Siba culture cemetery are accompanied by more than ten pieces of pottery, as well as copper, gold, silver, and jade utensils, and there are human sacrifices, reflecting the high status of the tomb owner.

The two cultures should have a semi-agricultural and semi-pastoral economy. On the one hand, crops such as wheat and millet grain have been found in both cultures and food processing tools such as stone grinding plates and rods. In Siba culture, there are also stone knives, copper sickles, and pigs, indicating the presence of dry farming. On the other hand, the bones of sheep, cattle, and horses are commonly found, and many tombs are buried with their heads, horns, and hooves. Many tools such as copper knives, bows and arrowheads, and perforated whetstones indicate that the livestock and hunting economy was relatively developed.

III. Sanxingdui Culture in the Upper Reaches of the Yangtze River Region

During the Erlitou–Erligang era, the upper Yangtze River was Sanxingdui culture, including the Sanxingdui type in the Chengdu Plain and its nearby areas and the Chaotianzui type in the Xiajiang region of eastern Sichuan. The former is represented by the second to fourth layers remains excavated in Sanxingdui, Guanghan, Sichuan from 1980 to 1981,[109] and the latter is represented by the "Xia and Shang dynasties cultural remains" in Chaotianzui, Zigui, Hubei Province.

The convex-shoulder jar, high-neck jar, large-mouth *zun*, low-handle high-foot plate, and thin high-handle high-foot plate in Sanxingdui culture all have certain connections with the Baodun culture. *He* and *gui* and the curved-handle high-foot plate are Erlitou culture elements. Individual round-foot embossed pots are South China elements, and there are new high-foot plate-shaped utensils, *gu*-shaped cups, elongated pots, bottles, shallow-belly round-foot plates, open-mouth shallow-belly earthen bowls, bird head-handle spoons, etc. Among them, the Chaotianzui type also has Erlitou culture elements such as floral-rim round-belly jars, cockscomb-handle basins, large-mouth urns, and *gus*, as well as local traditional elements such as cauldrons and large-mouth vats.

The Sanxingdui culture has a super central settlement of the ancient Sanxingdui city, covering an area of three to four million square meters. Inside the city are sizable rectangular palace buildings built on the ground. There are also altars, and rectangular vertical pit graves, with buried spiral jade objects possibly related to the influence of Erlitou culture.[110] The tools are similar to Baodun culture.

IV. Culture in South China

During the Erlitou–Erligang period, most parts of South China still largely belonged to the cauldron–round-foot plate–high-foot plate cultural system, only with a significant increase in concaved-bottom jar and pot types, and it may be necessary to call it the cauldron–concaved-bottom jar–high-foot plate cultural system. Hard pottery with imprinted patterns is popular, with pottery mainly including cauldron, small-mouth concaved-bottom jar (*zun*), short round-foot jar (pot), pot with spout, round-foot plate, and high-foot plate. They also commonly contain *ges*, jade *ya zhangs*, sectioned or shouldered adzes, grooved stone beaters, and other jade stone implements. *Ge* and jade *ya zhang* are elements of Erlitou culture, and some of the *zun* and jar types with folded shoulders may be related to the influence of Erligang culture. There are often shell or sand mounds sites, ground or stilt-style buildings with wood and bone mud walls, and rectangular vertical pit graves. The economy is primarily based on fishing, hunting, and gathering, but there should also be rice and even wheat farming.[111]

There are quite noticeable regional differences. Huangguashan culture, represented by the Huangguashan site in Xiapu in the lower reaches and the eastern coastal area of the Min River,[112] even spread to Taiwan region. It has glazed pottery and a considerable amount of ocher color painted pottery. Its *yan*-shaped utensils, single long-handle pots, round-foot cups, and earthen bowls are distinctive and have a certain inheritance relationship with Hutoupu culture. The *yan*-shaped utensils are influenced by Maqiao culture, etc. Houshan culture[113] in eastern Guangdong and southern Fujian, represented by Puning Houshan[114] and Zhangzhou Niaolunwei,[115] features rhombus and square patterns and has duck-shaped pots, single-handle pots, round-foot cups, and other pottery. The middle layer of the Shixia culture in northern Guangdong is reflected in a small number of jars with cylindrical-penetrating handles. The Tangxiahuan in Zhuhai[116] and the Cuntou type remains in Dongguan in the Pearl River Delta have many cord-mark, leaf-veined, and cloud-thunder patterns, with drooping-belly pots, etc. Moreover, in the southwestern mountains of Guangxi, there are Gengsayan in Longzhou,[117] and the early phase II remains like Gantuoyan in Napo, featuring marked cords and grouped engraved patterns, with cauldrons, round-foot jars, round-foot bowls, cups, and other utensils that are inherited from phase I of Gantuoyan culture. There are cave burials, adzes, chisels, jade *jues*, grooved stone beaters, etc.

V. Culture of Early China Outer Margin Zone

During the Erlitou–Erligang period, the range of "early China" in the cultural sense expanded unprecedentedly. Only in peripheral areas, such as central and western Xinjiang and southern Xizang, were still unexplored places.

The vast Xinjiang region was inhabited by humans as early as the late Paleolithic Age. Still, the overall cultural landscape was not clear until around 2000 BCE when it entered the Bronze Age, with only some microlithic remains discovered, suggesting a long period of Mesolithic economy based on hunting and gathering. Around 2000 BCE, eastern and western cultures entered this region almost simultaneously, blending in the Hami Basin in eastern Xinjiang to form the Hami Tianshan North Road culture. Meanwhile, in central and western Xinjiang, the Andronovo culture, Keermuqi culture, and Gumugou culture, mainly belonged to the Western cultural system. We used to call it the "cylindrical jar cultural system"[118] to differentiate it from the Northeast China region, also called the "jar cultural system."

The Andronovo culture is mainly distributed in a vast area of western Xinjiang, represented by phase I of burials at Taxkorgan Xiabandi,[119] the Adunqiaolu site in Wenquan,[120] and the Kalasu site in Nileke,[121] mainly being the localized production of the Andronovo culture's expansion from South Siberia and central Asia. The pottery mainly comprises large-mouth curved or folded-belly cylindrical jars, slanted curved-belly bowls, and cup types with stamped or engraved geometric patterns such as triangles and broken lines. There are bronze axes, sickles, adzes, chisels, spears, bronze or silver bell-mouth earrings, etc. There are rectangular stonewall semi-underground houses. The graves on the ground are marked with stone piles and stone enclosures, divided into vertical pit graves, stone chamber graves, and stone coffin graves, with most of the inhumations being flexed on the side, and there are also cremations. Stone sickles, microliths, etc., belong to a semi-agricultural and semi-pastoral economy.

The Keermuqi culture is distributed around Altay to the northern foothills of the central Tianshan, represented by the early burials of Keermuqi in Altay,[122] and its appearance is similar to the Afanasyevo culture–Oksunev culture in the south of Siberia.[123] The most distinctive pottery is a pointed-bottom olive-shaped jar, and there are also flat-bottom cylindrical jars and high-foot plate-shaped vessels, with the outer surface showing imprinted or engraved geometric decorations such as scale patterns, horizontal fine-tooth comb patterns, diagonal triangle patterns, grid patterns, pearl patterns, etc. The area around the tombs often uses large stones to build rectangular tombs. Most of the graves are vertical pit stone coffin tombs, with stone carvings of human figures or standing stones in front of the tombs. The burial style is often flexed on the side, with substandard grave goods. Tools or weapons include microlithic arrowheads, bone arrowheads, copper arrowheads, copper knives, copper spears, and copper axes. Still, no clear settlements, crops, or agricultural tools have been found, mainly belonging to a pastoral economy.

The Gumugou culture, or Xiaohe culture, is distributed near Lop Nur at the lower reaches of the Kongque River, represented by Gumugou[124] and Xiaohe[125] cemeteries, with the source probably related to the Afanasyevo culture and the Keermuqi culture. All the tombs are vertical pit sand chambers with boat-shaped bottomless wooden coffins, usually a single supine extended burial. The burial goods are mainly personal items and decorations, mostly made of hair, skin, and wood. Each tomb has a round-bottom grass woven basket placed on the right side of the cloak outside, with ladder patterns, triangle patterns, etc. There are also jade beads, microlithic arrowheads, small copper coils, small copper pieces, etc. Wheat, millet grain, and other crops have been found, with the raising of cattle, sheep, etc., thus belonging to a semi-agricultural and semi-pastoral economy.

After 2000 BCE, Qugong culture appeared in the Lhasa area of Xizang,[126] with distinctive polished pottery and imprinted and engraved rhombus patterns, round-bottom jars, small round-foot jars, small round-foot pots, round-bottom earthen bowls, round-foot cups, triangular openwork-handle high-foot plates, and other pottery, as well as monkey-face pottery sculptures, bone hairpins, etc. The origins and influences of this culture are not yet clear. The culture has rectangular vertical pit earth graves, grave walls stacked with stone blocks, and flexed burials. The stone tools are mostly chipped chopping and scraping tools, arrowheads, a small number of ground short-tooth combs, adzes, knives, as well as microliths, perforated weights, stone grinding plates, stone grinding rods, etc., and individual copper arrowheads, and with domestic animals such as yaks, sheep, dogs, etc. The economic form is mainly agriculture, but animal husbandry also plays an important role.

VI. Cultural Exchange in the Erlitou–Erligang Era

Erlitou culture and Erligang culture of the Central Plain core area during the Erlitou–Erligang era were powerful and had a significant radiative impact on surrounding cultures. The western bronze culture and South China's imprinted pottery culture also had a nearly global influence.

After phase II of Erlitou culture, it rapidly expanded its cultural scope to most parts of Henan and southern Shanxi and greatly influenced its surroundings. Its typical elements, such as the deep-belly jar with marked-cord patterns, floral-rim round-belly jar, *ding*, large-mouth *zun*, curved-handle folded- or arc-belly high-foot plate, tile-foot plate, *jue, jia, gui, gu*, mushroom-button utensil lid, etc., can be seen more or less in the surrounding Xiaqiyuan culture, Yueshi culture, Doujitai culture, Dianjiangtai culture, Maqiao culture, Sanxingdui culture, Qijia culture, Zhukaigou culture, etc. The *jue, gui*, etc., even reach the lower Xiajiadian culture in the Xiliao River Basin. The *ge* and *ya zhang* can be widely seen in South China.

The influence of Erligang culture on its surroundings was even greater, especially during the upper Erligang period. The conical-foot *li* and *yan* of Xiaqiyuan culture, which preceded it, had a southward influence on Erlitou culture and an eastward influence on Yueshi culture. After the formation of Erligang culture, its cultural scope expanded to the central and southern Hebei in the north, the central and western Shandong in the east, the Jianghuai and the middle reaches of the Yangtze River in the south, and the vast areas of Guanzhong in the west. Its marked-cord *li*, marked-cord *yan*, marked-cord deep-belly jar, large-mouth *zun*, deep-belly basin, false-belly high-foot plate, *jue, jia, gui*, mushroom-button utensil lid, and other pottery infiltrated into the surrounding cultures, including lower Xiajiadian culture, Yueshi culture, Hushu culture, Wucheng culture, Zhukaigou culture, especially the *ding, jia*, knife, axe, adze, chisel, spear, and *ge* of Wucheng culture, which are basically elements of Erligang culture. In addition, some folded-shoulder *yan*-shaped vessel, *zun*, and jar types in South China are also related to the influence of Erligang culture, and individual Erligang-style copper *li* even spread westward to Kayue culture.

In South China, the imprinted pottery and proto-porcelain culture represented by Maqiao culture and Wucheng culture have influenced the vast areas of the Yellow River Basin. Their imprinted patterns, like cloud-thunder patterns, *Hui* patterns, circle patterns, and leaf vein patterns, have permeated into Erlitou culture, Erligang culture, Yueshi culture, and Sanxingdui culture. The duck-shaped *ding* is also seen in Erlitou culture, and primitive porcelain *zuns* and jars are found in Erligang culture.

Other cultures also had more or less exchanges with surrounding cultures. Yueshi culture influenced Erligang culture in Zhengzhou to the west, reached Xiaqiyuan culture to the northwest, expanded northward up to the southern part of Liaodong, and influenced Gaotaishan culture and Xincheng culture. It also expanded southward up to northern Jiangsu, influencing Doujitai culture, Maqiao culture, and others. The lower Xiajiadian culture expanded eastward to the Liaoxi mountainous region, marked-cord and folded-belly *zun* infiltrated Gaotaishan culture, and the arc-belly *li* even infiltrated northeastward into Xiaolaha culture in the Nen River Basin. Gaotaishan culture strongly influenced Xiaolaha culture in the Nen River Basin northward, affected the lower Xiajiadian culture westward, and occupied the distribution area of the lower Xiajiadian culture in the Liaoxi mountainous region at a later stage. The snake-pattern *li*, tri-legged urn, and thick-backed curved stone knife of Zhukaigou culture influenced Erlitou culture Dongxiafeng type, Erligang culture, and the lower Xiajiadian culture. In addition, the discovery of seashells in the northern region indicates the possibility of long-distance exchanges with coastal areas.

The exchange between Chinese and Western cultures was unprecedentedly strengthened at this time. The Xinjiang Hami Tianshan North Road, Gumugou, Keermuqi, and Andronovo cultures, which entered the Bronze Age before the Erlitou–Erligang era, had a far-reaching eastward influence. The main sources were the Western bronze types of knives, axes, adzes, awls, arrowheads, mirrors, earrings, rings, bracelets, hollow beads, and buckles, which almost constituted the main body of the bronze artifacts in the Gansu–Qinghai–Ningxia regions, including Siba culture, the late Qijia culture, Xindian culture, and Kayue culture, which further penetrated eastward into Zhukaigou culture and the lower Xiajiadian culture. They even influenced the appearance of bronze artifacts such as the ring-pommel sword and axe in Erlitou culture (fig. 5.7). Meanwhile, the painted pottery of the Xinjiang region has also influenced central Asia.

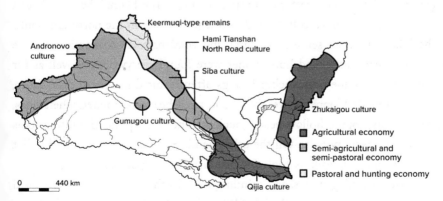

Figure 5.7 Map of the distribution of early Bronze Age cultures in Northwest China (2000–1500 BCE)

VII. Conclusion

(1) The expansion of millet grain agriculture and the rapid development of the pastoral economy in the northwest region

The two major systems of millet grain farming and rice farming continued to develop, especially the expanded scope of millet grain farming. In areas such as the middle and lower reaches of the Yellow River, the proportion of millet grain increased while the proportion of rice decreased. Stone knives used for harvesting millet grain crops were not only popular in the northern Central Plain. Still, they were also commonly seen in Doujitai culture, Maqiao culture, Dianjiangtai culture, Hushu culture, and Wucheng culture in the south of the Yangtze River, indicating that millet grain farming may have expanded southeastward to the lower reaches of the Yangtze River. In addition, millet grain farming also extended westward to Hami in eastern Xinjiang and even to the Lop Nor region and northeastward, possibly to the Nen River Basin. At this time, the northern part of the Yangtze River Basin, the southern part of the Yellow River Basin, and the Huai River Basin were all mixed zones of millet grain and rice farming. Wheat had become one of the main crops in the northern Central Plain, even penetrating southward into the Yangtze River Basin and the southeast coastal area. The so-called "five grains" agriculture of "rice, sorghum, millet, wheat, and *shu*" in the Central Plain developed steadily.

The biggest change was the rapid development of the pastoral economy in the northwest region.[127] Around 2000 BCE, a series of Bronze Age cultures with varying degrees of pastoralism emerged in the early China margin zone, most of which were in Xinjiang. The Keermuqi culture in the Altay region of northern Xinjiang was based on a pastoral hunting economy. The Hami Tianshan North Road culture, Andronovo culture, and Gumugou culture in the north and south of the Tianshan were semi-agricultural and semi-pastoral economies: on the one hand, sheep, cattle, and horse bones were found everywhere, as well as fur products. At the same time, rock paintings often featured images of deer, sheep, and other animals. Copper knives, bows and arrowheads, perforated whetstones, copper mirrors, copper hollow beads (buckles), and other pastoral hunting tools or decorations were popular. On the other hand, crops such as wheat and millet grain were found, as well as tools for dry farming or grain processing such as stone sickles, grinding stones, and grinding rods. In the eastern part of the Hexi Corridor and areas to its east, the late Qijia culture, Zhukaigou culture, the lower Xiajiadian culture, Xindian culture, Kayue culture, and Siwa culture, etc., although often found millet grain, wheat, domestic pigs, stone knives (claw sickles), stone sickles, etc., indicating that they were still mainly agricultural economies, but the proportion of pastoral hunting significantly increased. The proportion of sheep in the sites has significantly increased, and there are customs of burying sheep horns or sacrificing sheep and domestic pigs. Tools for pastoral hunting, such as bone-handle stone-blade knives, bone-handle copper knives, copper knives, scrapers, perforated whetstones, short-tooth combs, etc., are often seen, indicating that sheep-farming-based pastoralism occupies an important position.

Pastoral, semi-agricultural and semi-pastoral, and agricultural economies with a significant pastoral component have a strong adaptability in arid and semi-arid areas, especially the various forms of semi-agricultural and semi-pastoral economies complement each other, making them even more adaptable. This led to the rapid emergence of a series of cultures in areas such as Xinjiang, central and western Qinghai, the Xilingol area in Inner Mongolia, and the Xiliao River Basin, where culture had been previously depressed. The vast northwest inland arid areas and Inner Mongolia's semi-arid grassland areas finally welcomed the first peak of human development, and the culture of the Xiliao River Basin flourished once again. This was an unprecedented major change in the cultural pattern of China since the "Neolithic Revolution."

(2) The further expansion of tri-legged vessels, the northward movement of imprinted pottery primitive porcelain, and the rise of bronzeware

Due to the strong influence of the Erlitou and Erligang cultures, a multi-layered tri-legged vessels cultural circle centered on the Central Plain was formed: the core of the Central Plain was the Erlitou type of Erlitou culture and the Erligang type of Erligang culture, whose *ding, li, yan, jue, gui, jia,* and *he* were the most developed and the most finely crafted and elegant. The surrounding Erlitou culture and Erligang culture were secondary, and the outer ring of Yueshi culture, Doujitai culture, Dianjiangtai culture, Hushu culture, Maqiao culture, Wucheng culture, Sanxingdui culture, Qijia culture, and others all included tri-legged vessels to varying degrees. Zhukaigou culture and the lower Xiajiadian culture were the source areas of *li* and *yan*. The prevalence of *li* and *yan* here was certainly not mainly influenced by the Central Plain, but indeed also included factors such as *jue, gui, jia, he,* and Central Plain style *li* and *yan* types. The further expansion of these tri-legged vessels meant that the "Chinese" style of cooking and eating had spread to most of early China. Although the wheel-thrown pottery technology of the Longshan era was at a low point, the standardization degree of pottery making in Erligang culture and others was quite high, showing that at least the specialization of pottery production in the core area of the Central Plain had increased.

In South and Southeast China, geometric stamped pottery with cloud-thunder patterns, *Hui* patterns, circle patterns, leaf vein patterns, and square patterns had become mainstream. They were widely popular in Maqiao culture, Wucheng culture, Dianjiangtai culture, Hushu culture, Huangguashan culture, Houshan culture, etc. Maqiao culture and Wucheng culture also produced the earliest porcelain—primitive porcelain. Both geometric stamped pottery and primitive porcelain had penetrated northward into Erlitou culture, Erligang culture, Yueshi culture, Doujitai culture, etc., to varying degrees. Interestingly, the area at the junction of Jiangxi, Zhejiang, and Fujian, where the earliest primitive porcelain appeared, was also the first place pottery appeared in the world. Primitive porcelain is the culmination of nearly 20,000 years of pottery development in southeast China, adding a new type of utensil to early China and even the ancient world. Its dense texture and smooth surface were unprecedented, and it was destined to play an increasingly important role in the social life of the Chinese people.

Around 2000 BCE, first in the northwest of China, then in the north, northeast, and Central Plain, and finally in the eastern regions along the rivers and the sea, a wave of bronze culture swept from west to east, ushering these regions into the Bronze Age one after another. These bronze artifacts can be roughly divided into two major traditions. The first is the western or northern tradition, which mainly includes tools, weapons, and decorations,[128] and has its primary origins in the western regions of the Eurasian continent.[129] It includes bronze artifacts such as knives, axes, adzes, awls, arrowheads, mirrors, earrings, rings, bracelets, hollow beads, and buckles made of copper-tin or copper-arsenic alloys. They are seen in the cultures of the Tianshan North Road in Hami, Gumugou, Keermuqi, Andronovo, Siba, Qijia, Xindian, Kayue, Siwa, Zhukaigou, and the lower Xiajiadian culture. Then is the Central Plain tradition, which mainly includes vessels and weapons, which is thought to have originated based on Central Plain culture and been influenced by Western bronze culture. It includes bronze vessels such as the *ding*, *li*, *yan*, *jue*, *he*, *jia*, *gu*, *gui* (an ancient Chinese container or a ritual vessel here), plate, *zun*, *lei*, and *you*, and bronze weapons or tools such as the *yue*, *ge*, axe, adze, chisel, knife, arrowhead, and saw. Apart from copper-tin alloys, the most unique are copper-lead or copper-lead-tin alloys. They are mainly seen in Erlitou, Erligang, and Yueshi cultures and have influenced Wucheng culture, etc (fig. 5.8). The western (northern) tradition of bronze tools and weapons significantly improved

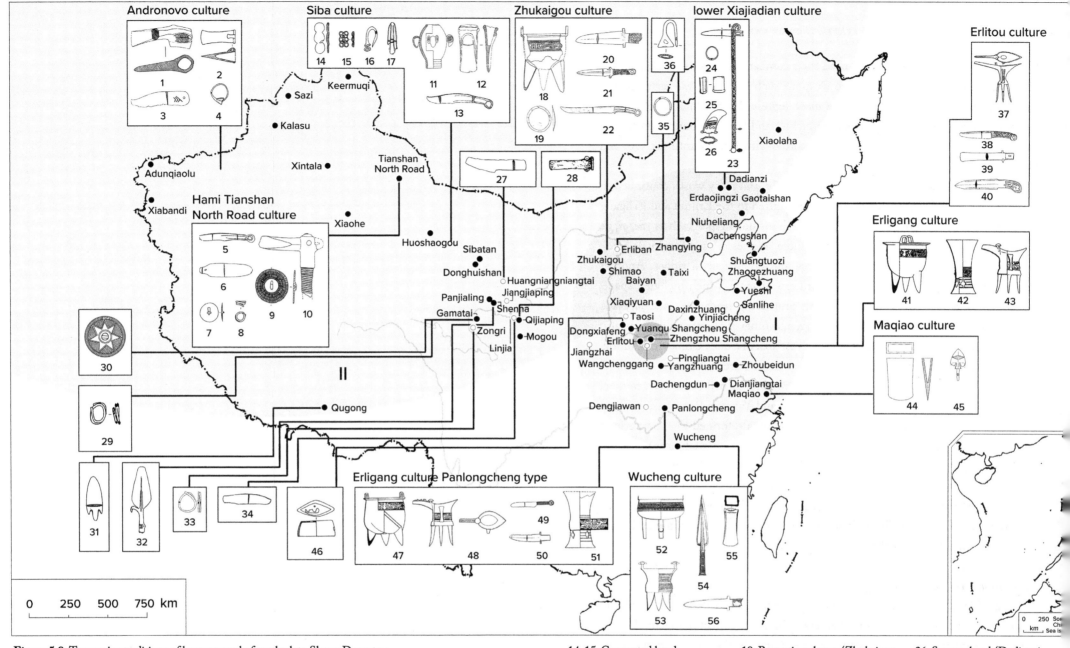

Figure 5.8 Two major traditions of bronzeware before the late Shang Dynasty

I. Central Plain tradition

II. Western (northern) tradition

1, 2, 10, 12, 28, 39, 44, 55. Axe (Gongliu A: 3, Tekesi 91TR: 1, Nanwan, Ganguya, Qijiaping, Erlitou IV KM3: 1, Maqiao II T1032③A: 1, Wucheng 1974QSW [publicly-sourced]: 36)

3. Sickle (Gongliu A: 6)

4, 8, 16, 24, 29, 33, 35, 36. Earring (Xiabandi II M4:2 [1], Nanwan, Caiji, Dadianzi M453: 9, Gamatai, Zongri M122: 2-1, Erliban M1:4, Zhangying T12⑤: 4)

5, 13, 22, 27, 34, 38, 49. Knife (Tianshan North Road, Caiji, Zhukaigou M1040: 3, Huangniangniangtai T17: 5, Linjia F20: 18, Erlitou III M2: 3, Panlongcheng PLZ M2: 6)

6, 32, 54. Spear (Tianshan North Road, Shenna, Wucheng 1976QSW [publicly-sourced]: 2)

7. Buckle (Tianshan North Road)

9, 30. Mirror (Tianshan North Road, Gamatai)

11. Scepter head (Huoshaogou)

14, 15. Connected bead decorations (Yingshuwo, Caiji)

17, 31, 45. Arrowhead (Ganguya, Qugong H12: 33, Maqiao II T1033③B: 3)

18, 41, 47, 52. *Ding* (Zhukaigou H5028: 4, Minggonglu M2: 2, Panlongcheng PLZM2: 38, Wucheng 1974QSW [publicly-sourced]: 31)

19. Protective plaque (Zhukaigou M1040: 5)

20, 23, 40, 50, 56. *Ge* (Zhukaigou M2012: 1, Shuishouyingzi, Erlitou IV KM3: 2, Panlongcheng PLZM2: 25, Wucheng 1976QSW [publicly-sourced]: 3)

21. Sword (Zhukaigou M1040: 2)

25. *Dun*[a] (Dadianzi M715: 15)

26. Scepter head (Dadianzi M43: 12)

37, 43, 48. *Jue* (Erlitou 75 VII M1: 1, Minggonglu M2: 21, Panlongcheng PLZM2: 12)

42, 51. *Gu* (Minggonglu M2: 8, Panlongcheng PLZM2: 5)

46. Bell (Taosi M3296: 1)

53. *Jia* (Wucheng 1973QSW [Zhengtangshan] M3: 5)

[a] The flat-bottom metal sleeve at the end of the spear or halberd handle.—Trans.

local productivity and greatly enhanced their combat and expansion capabilities. The Central Plain traditional bronze weapons such as *ge* and *yue* certainly also enhanced combat capabilities, but the more representative ritual vessels played a significant role in stabilizing social hierarchies and laid the foundation for the subsequent focus on bronze vessels as the core of ritual items until the Qin and Han dynasties.

The early traditional Chinese jade, lacquer, silk, and ivory works continued to develop. The core of high-grade exquisite jade shifted to the Erlitou and Erligang cultures at the heart of the Central Plain, which included types such as *yue, qi, ge*, multi-hole knife, *zhang, gui* (an ancient Chinese jade vessel used for rituals here), and handle-shaped utensil. They were large and popular, with ridges. Another jade center was Zhukaigou culture in northern Shaanxi, which included spade, *yue*, knife, *ya zhang*, connected *bi*, *bi* with protruding teeth, *gui*, jade *jue*, jade *huang*, and human-face sculpture. *Zhang, ge*, and other jade (stone) artifacts also influenced the Yangtze River Basin and the vast area of South China. In addition, bracelets, hairpins, spinning wheels, and other items were still almost seen in all cultures. Stone chimes, pottery *xuns*, pottery bells, bronze bells, and other musical instruments were common in the Yellow River and Yangtze River basins. These musical instruments, along with bronze and jade rituals, formed the new period's combination of ritual objects and the material basis of the early Chinese ritual and music system. The appearance of carts in Erlitou culture and Erligang culture is a noteworthy event. China had spinning wheels 8,000 years ago and pottery wheels 7,000 years ago, but no wheels or carts. The cart in China was likely introduced from the West. Cowrie shells or clam shells were discovered in Erlitou and other cultures and may have served as primitive currency.

(3) Maturation of civil engineering technology

The spatial layout and building technology of the house types in the Erlitou–Erligang era are close to the Longshan era. Still, the architectural technology of the central settlements is more mature, as exemplified by the construction of large city walls and groups of large palaces.

The Zhengzhou Shangcheng and Yanshi Shangcheng used segmented rammed earth technology, and the walls were relatively steep with dense, uniform rammed layers. The city walls covered a vast area, especially the inner city of Zhengzhou, which alone had an area of three million square meters, a massive undertaking. Settlements like Erlitou and Yanshi Shangcheng had specialized palace cities, with multiple large palaces within the palace city, as well as pools, gardens, and drainage systems. The main palaces were generally laid out from south to north, sequentially featuring doors (one or three doorways) and gatehouses (*shu*), courtyards, and main halls, surrounded by covered walkways and wing rooms, laying the foundation for the layout of later Chinese palaces with the palace facing south, having a front hall and a back room, and east–west wings. The total area of the No. 1 palace at Erlitou is close to 10,000 square meters, with the main hall at 900 square meters; the No. 5 palace in Yanshi Shangcheng has a total area of over 9,000 square meters, with the main hall at over 800 square meters. The construction of such vast city walls and palaces reflects advanced architectural technology and strong organizational ability.

In addition, well-preserved settlements from the lower Xiajiadian culture, such as Sanzuodian and Erdaojingzi, have door sockets with single or double doors, which perhaps represent the situation in most of the Central Plain in the north, and differ from the push-pull doors and windows of Qujialing culture in the middle reaches of the Yangtze River.

(4) Formation and influence of the oracle bone script system
Pottery inscriptions found in Gaocheng Taixi, Zhengzhou Shangcheng, and Zhengzhou Xiaoshuangqiao are very similar in shape and structure to the oracle bone script, marking the formal formation of the oracle bone script system—an ancient Chinese character system. Some of these inscriptions were written with cinnabar, mainly found on small pottery *zuns*, like the pottery inscriptions of the Dawenkou culture on large-mouth *zuns*, which may indicate a close relationship with eastern writing systems.

Outside the Central Plain, two pottery inscriptions similar to oracle bone script were found in the settlements of the lower Xiajiadian culture at Sanzuodian, and Wucheng culture also has pottery inscriptions similar to oracle bone script, which may suggest that the oracle bone script, centered in the Central Plain, had been spread to surrounding vast areas. This would have greatly promoted information exchange, cultural transmission, and social management in a large territory in early China. Of course, Wucheng culture, Maqiao culture, Xiaolaha culture, etc., have more engraved symbols.

Besides texts and symbols, some complex patterns also contain rich information. Animal-face patterns were popular in most of the Yellow River, Yangtze River, and Xiliao River basins, as seen in Erlitou culture, Erligang culture, Wucheng culture, and lower Xiajiadian culture, which means that the range of this more abstract cognitive tradition further expanded. The sheep head-shaped patterns, drooping band patterns, and images of sheep, dogs, deer, and people on pottery (mainly painted pottery) of various cultures in the Northwest region express a more concrete cognitive tradition based on pastoral culture.

(5) Differences between east and west China in ancestor worship
Most regions of China still use vertical pit graves, which reflect the funerary concept of "rest in peace" and are part of a secularized religious belief system centered on ancestor worship. The major regional differences shifted from north and south to east and west. The eastern regions centered around the Yellow River and Yangtze River basins are primarily earth burials, mainly with extended supine. Cemetery sites typically contain only twenty to thirty graves, emphasizing family organization. However, in Xinjiang, in addition to earth burials, there are many cremations, possibly reflecting a mentality that places less value on the "physical body" and more on the "soul." These are typically flexed burials, and large cemeteries with hundreds of graves densely arranged are common, emphasizing the clan concept even more. The cultures in Gansu and Qinghai regions, the Gaotaishan culture, and other northern cultures also have a small number of cremation graves, and the scale of cemeteries is larger, falling between the aforementioned two.

Other religious customs also show east-west differences. East of the Hexi Corridor in China, idol worship is rare, and it is common to practice divination by burning the scapula bones of animals such as cows, sheep, pigs, and deer. In the lower Xiajiadian culture sites of Dadianzi in Aohan Banner, Erdaojingzi, and Dashanqian in Kalaqin Banner,[130] a new form of divination first appeared, which involved carving before burning, and later became popular in Erligang culture, Yueshi culture, etc. This new form might serve to control the divination results. Many cultures also commonly sacrifice animals such as cows, sheep, pigs, dogs, and even humans in rituals or foundation laying. The sacrificial sites and pits found in Zhengzhou Shangcheng and Xiaoshuangqiao are particularly noteworthy. In contrast, cultures in Xinjiang have stone carvings of human figures in front of their graves or human figurines and human heads buried with the dead, indicating idol worship. Bone divination and foundation laying are not seen. Most animal bones in graves are likely seen as "food" for the deceased to enjoy in the underworld.

(6) Formation of mature civilization and two major patterns
Significant social changes took place in the Erlitou–Erligang era, represented by two societal development models in the Central Plain and the west.

The vast area of eastern and central China—the early main region of China—is represented by the social development of Erlitou culture and Erligang culture. Super-large central settlements such as Erlitou, Zhengzhou Shangcheng, Yanshi Shangcheng, and Xiaoshuangqiao appeared in the core area of the Central Plain. Surrounding regions saw the emergence of super-large or large central settlements such as Dongxiafeng, Yuanqu Shangcheng, Chengziya, Panlongcheng, Wucheng, Sanxingdui, and Shimao, forming several regional centers. The city walls were mostly rammed earth construction, with some made of stone, providing steeper and more robust defenses. Weapons specialized for warfare expanded beyond the *yue* and spear to include the *ge*, signifying more specialized warfare. Ritual human sacrifice and the use of human bones as tools were observed. Large palace complexes and grouped palaces were discovered in Erlitou and Yanshi Shangcheng, indicating the preliminary formation of a palace system with imposing large-scale palaces of tens of thousands of square meters and towering city gates. The smaller scale of cemeteries reflected a more pronounced family organization, with serious differentiation in tombs. High-quality grave goods, such as turquoise dragons and exquisite jade artifacts, were found in large and medium-sized tombs, but a considerable number of tombs had few or no grave goods. The crafting techniques of Erlitou culture and Erligang culture for bronze, jade, pottery, lacquer, and bone artifacts were superior. They became more specialized, indicating a significant development in the social division of labor. Overall, the societies in eastern and central China underwent significant changes, entering the stage of mature, civilized society; palaces, tombs, and artifacts all displayed a high degree of secularism, hierarchy, and order, which likely reflected the increasing maturity of rites and rituals. Sovereignty had emerged, and divine authority was subordinate to sovereignty. The three previous models of social development gradually merged, forming a new "Central Plain Mode" that encompassed almost all of the eastern and central regions. Of course, the differentiation of wealth and social labor in Zhukaigou culture and the lower Xiajiadian culture in the north was still not as pronounced as in the Central Plain and the east, and the previous "Northern Mode" was still somewhat continued.

The situation in the western Xinjiang region is quite different. Various cultures generally have large-scale public cemeteries, and there are no significant differences in the size of tombs or the number of grave goods. Except for bronze artifacts, the crafting of other pottery and stone artifacts showed no signs of specialization, overall displaying a more egalitarian clan society. These cultures also practiced idol worship, and their development of tools and weapons was advanced. However, they lacked ritual vessels, which was entirely different from the Central Plain. In general, they represent the emergence of a new social development mode, which can be called the "Western Mode."

Particularly noteworthy is the significant difference in the symbols of power between the east and the west. The symbol of power in most of early China to the east of the Hexi Corridor was the *yue*, while in Xinjiang to the west of the Hexi Corridor, it was the scepter. The former emphasized secular military power and was seen in the eastern and central regions from the formation of early China; the latter emphasized divine authority and was widely popular in the western regions of the Eurasian continent around the same time.[131] The east–west difference within China can be seen as a concentrated reflection of the east–west difference in the spiritual aspect of societies across the Eurasian continent.

(7) The dynastic state stage centered on the Central Plain
Finally, the glorious era of the Central Plain has returned! After 1800 BCE, the cultural landscape underwent significant adjustments due to the strong influence of Erlitou culture and Erligang culture from the core area of the Central Plain. The cultures in most parts of China once again intermingled and connected to form a larger relative cultural community. Its spatial structure can be divided into at least four levels from the inside out: The first level is the core area of Zhengzhou and Luoyang, with super-large central settlements such as Erlitou, Zhengzhou Shangcheng, and Yanshi Shangcheng, and groups of large palaces. They have many tall and exquisite bronze and jade ritual vessels, such as *ding, li*, and *yan*. The second level mainly includes the middle reaches of the Yellow River and the Huai River Basin. It later extends to the Yellow River's upper reaches and the Yangtze River's middle reaches. This is the distribution area of Erlitou culture and Erligang culture outside the core area, with regional differences. Large central settlements such as Dongxiafeng, Yuanqu Shangcheng, Taixi, and Panlongcheng and several regional centers exist. The number of cities is not large, and the bronze and jade ritual vessels are small, low in quantity, and not as refined as those in the core area. The third level includes the surrounding areas of the lower Yellow River, the lower Yangtze River, the upper Yangtze River, the Northern region, and the northeastern region. It includes cultures such as Yueshi, Doujitai, Dianjiangtai, Hushu, Maqiao, Wucheng, Sanxingdui, Zhukaigou, lower Xiajiadian, and Gaotaishan. Super-large or large central settlements such as Chengziya, Wucheng, Sanxingdui, and Shimao form several local centers. There are a small number of bronze and jade ritual vessels and some tri-legged pottery items such as the *li, yan, ding, jue*,

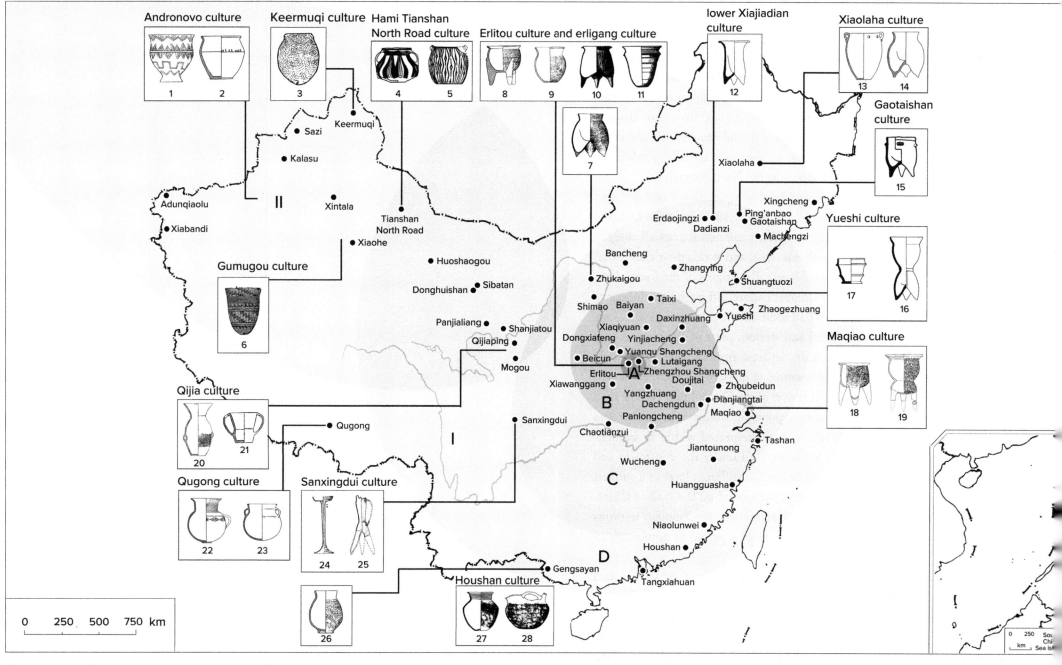

Figure 5.9 Early China in a cultural sense during the Erlitou–Erligang era (1800–1300 BCE)

I. Early Chinese cultural sphere
II. Jar cultural system
A. Core area
B. Main area
C. Peripheral area I
D. Peripheral area II

1–5, 9, 13, 20, 22, 23, 26, 27. Jar (Sazi M3: 2, Xiabandi AII M042: 1, Keermuqi M16: 1, Tianshan North Road, Tianshan North Road, Erlitou II·VT104⑤: 18, Baijinbao F3032: 2, Qinweijia M96: 2, Qugong M111: 1, H17: 7, Gengsayan 07LG: 08, Houshan M4: 1)

6. Deep basket (Xiaohe MC: 24)
7, 10, 12, 14, 15. Ge (Zhukaigou W2007: 1, Erligang H17: 119, Dadianzi M612: 14, Baijinbao F3028: 3, Ping'anbao H1012: 1)
8, 18. Ding (Erlitou II·VT104⑥: 51, Maqiao II TD101: 11)
11. Large-mouth zun (Nanguanwai T87: 46)
16, 19. Yan (Underwater collection in the south of Miaodao, Maqiao IIT1209③B: 9)
17. Zun (Zhaogezhuang H6: 14)
21. Double large-handle jar (Qinweijia M68: 3)
24. High-foot plate (Sanxingdui BaT1②: 36)
25. Gui (Sanxingdui DcT1②: 4
28. Duck-shaped pot (Houshan M1: 1)

(Except for 6 made of grass, the rest are all pottery.)

jia, and *gui*. The fourth level includes peripheral areas such as South China, the northwestern regions of Gansu, Qinghai, and Ningxia provinces, and the northern parts of Northeast China. This includes cultures like the Huangguashan, Houshan, Qijia, Siban, Hami Tianshan North Road, Xindian, Kayue, Siwa, and Xiaolaha cultures. These regions lack high-ranking settlements and ritual vessels and rarely have tri-legged vessels. Jade and stone *zhangs* are seen in South China, while the Northwestern regions favor tools and weapons in the Northern style.

Among the four cultural levels, the first level occupies a core position, and the second level forms and develops under the direct influence of the first. The cultures of the third level, despite their significant differences, can all roughly trace their origins to early China in a cultural sense, and at this time, they are all greatly influenced by the first and second levels. The origins of the fourth level cultures are closely related to the early Chinese culture, although their influence from the previous levels is relatively weak. In addition, the cultures of Andronovo, Keermuqi, and Gumugou in the central and western parts of Xinjiang, as well as Qugong culture in Xizang, have basically departed from the category of early China in a cultural sense. From the perspective of modern China, these would constitute a fifth level. Overall, the great revival of the Central Plain at this time was powerful and unparalleled, radiating a powerful influence around it and reaching a true dynastic state stage where it was respected within its borders. The surrounding cultures of various levels were all under the constraint and influence of the Central Plain to varying degrees. A different level of a cultural sphere centered on the Central Plain once again formed on the land of China, and early China, in a cultural sense, achieved significant development in terms of spatial scope and unity. From then on, it entered a period of dominance in unity (fig. 5.9).[132]

This era of splendid development of early China in a cultural sense coincided with the decline of ancient Western civilization. Massive invasions by Semites and Indo-European pastoral tribes led to the decline of Mesopotamian, Egyptian, and ancient Indus civilizations. Although the Hittite civilization and Mycenaean civilization arose in the Tigris-Euphrates River Basin and Greece afterward, and Egypt regained its glory, their cultural connotations and external influences underwent significant changes. In stark contrast, the Indo-European pastoral tribes only had a distant indirect influence on early China. Not only did they not cause the decline of early Chinese civilization, but the spread of their bronze technology and animal husbandry added fresh vitality to early Chinese civilization and promoted its development.

CHAPTER 6

Early China and Ancient Legends

"EARLY CHINA" IS A VERY "HISTORICAL" topic that requires interpretation in conjunction with documentary records. However, the time range of this book's research is before the late Shang Dynasty, before oracle bone inscriptions appeared in large quantities. Although writing had already occurred, the amount was too small to explain the main events of that time. Only in later documents were the legendary memories of that era preserved. In this sense, the "early China" in this book basically belongs to the category of the "age of legends,"[1] equivalent to what Westerners call the "Protohistoric."

Feng Youlan once mentioned the three stages or trends regarding ancient history: "Believing-the-Ancient – Doubting-the-Ancient – Interpreting-the-Ancient."[2] In fact, these three can be considered as indispensable scholarly attitudes that coexist: believing that the legends of ancient history have a real historical background, which is "believing"; acknowledging that the materials of the legends are complicated with a mixture of truth and falsehood, which is "doubting"; and trying to use scientific methods to distinguish the genuine from the false, which is "interpreting." The early interpretations of the ancient primarily started from sorting out the documentary materials themselves. In recent years, the interpretation the ancient has increasingly integrated archaeological materials. Xu Xusheng and Meng Wentong comprehensively sorted out the ancient historical literature, proposing three major groups in ancient China: Huaxia, Dongyi, and Miaoman,[3] or Heluo, Haidai, and Jianghan.[4] Zou Heng and others used the "inferring the unknown from the known" method to infer that Erligang culture belonged to the early Shang culture and Erlitou culture belonged to Xia culture.[5] Su Bingqi, Yu Weichao, Yan Wenming, and others explored the Sanmiao, Dongyi, and Emperors Yan and Yellow cultures and proposed a "Five-Emperor Period" before the Xia Dynasty.[6] These have become an important basis for the study of ancient Chinese history in early China. Of course, most Westerners still doubt the existence of the Xia Dynasty or think that Xia is just a myth conceived by the Shang people,[7] not to mention the Five-Emperor Period. The dialogue between China and Western academic circles on the issue of ancient Chinese history still has a long way to go.

The ancient legends of China are primarily centered around Huaxia, with limited or no records of matters outside the Central Plain of Huaxia. The recorded content is also quite limited, so do not expect ancient legends to provide a comprehensive and detailed interpretation of early China. I have conducted a more systematic observation of the ancient history of China during the Five-Emperor Period, proposing that the early Yangshao, late Yangshao, and early Longshan periods in archaeology correspond to the legendary Emperors Yan and Yellow, Zhuanxu and Emperor Ku, and Emperors Yao and Shun periods, respectively.[8] The discussion in this chapter is essentially based on this framework. As for the earlier "Three Sovereigns era," the academic community generally holds a negative attitude, and even if it existed, it should have been before the formation of early China,[9] so this book does not intend to focus on it.

I. The Yan Emperor and the Yellow Emperor Period

At the beginning of the discovery of Yangshao culture, Xu Zhongshu linked it to Xia culture,[10] and even Li Ji's excavation of the Xiyincun site in Xia County, Shanxi, in 1926, was to some extent aimed at exploring Xia culture.[11] However, with the later discovery of Erlitou culture, this view was gradually abandoned, and more people noticed the possible connection between Yangshao culture and the Yan Emperor and the Yellow Emperor.[12] Huang Huaixin explicitly proposed that the Banpo type of Yangshao culture was Yan Emperor culture, and the Miaodigou type was Yellow Emperor culture.[13] I not only further argued from near to far that the Banpo type and Miaodigou type of early Yangshao period may respectively be the Yan Emperor and Yellow Emperor clan lineage cultures of the Huaxia group, but also proposed that the Hougang type of Yangshao culture might be the

Chiyou clan lineage culture of the Miaoman group. The early Beixin culture and Dawenkou culture may be the Shaohao clan lineage culture of the Dongyi group.[14]

1. Emperors Yan and Yellow Clan Lineages and Their Culture

The Yan Emperor and the Yellow Emperor were early representatives of the Huaxia group, with the Yellow Emperor being the first of the "Five Emperors" listed in the *Records of the Grand Historian · Basic Annals of the Five Emperors*. In the *Discourses of the States · Discourses of Jin*, it says: "In ancient times, Shaodian married a woman from Youjiao *shi*,* giving birth to the Yellow Emperor and Yan Emperor. The Yellow Emperor was conceived by the Ji water, and the Yan Emperor was conceived by the Jiang water. Their virtues differed after they grew up. Hence the Yellow Emperor was named Ji, and the Yan Emperor was named Jiang." This is the most important record of the origins of the Yan Emperor and the Yellow Emperor. From this, it is known that they differentiated from the same origin. The location of Jiang water is the key to determining the homeland of the Yan Emperor. Xu Xusheng, based on the record in the *Commentary on the Water Classic · Wei River* that "Qi water flows eastward, passing south of Jiangshi city, becoming Jiang water," argued that the birthplace of the Yan Emperor is centered around Baoji in the upper reaches of the Wei River.[15] In addition, according to the *Commentary on the Water Classic · Wei River*, which quotes the *Chronicles of Emperors*: "Yan Emperor, Shennong, was of the Jiang surname, his mother was a girl named Deng, who roamed Huayang and conceived the Yan Emperor by divine intervention, raised by Jiang water," it is known that the central region of the Yan Emperor might also include Huayang, that is, near Hanzhong in the upper reaches of the Han River south of the Qinling Mountains. The location of Ji water is unclear, but in some respects, the origin of the Ji surname is probably near the southwest of Jin in the lower reaches of the Fen River. First, the southwest of Jin is the place of origin for the most famous Ji Zhou in later generations of the Ji surname.[16] Second, Ji Zhou often identified themselves as the Xia people,[17] and the southwest of Jin used to be the "Xia ruins."[18] Third, quite a few small Ji-named countries in the southwest of Jin presumably existed even before the Western

---

* *Shi* is a branch of ancient Chinese surnames. As the descendants of the same ancestor proliferated, the family would often divide into several branches scattered in different places. In addition to retaining their surname, the descendants of each branch would take an additional title as a marker, the "氏" or *shi*. The *shi* could change with fiefdoms or official positions, so a person's descendants might have several *shi*, or father and son could have different *shi* within two generations. Moreover, different surnames might adopt *shi* in the same way, resulting in instances where the surnames are different but the *shi* is the same.—Trans.

Zhou Dynasty.[19] In summary, the Emperors Yan and Yellow, two clan lineages, share the same origin and neighboring homelands, together constituting the main body of the early Huaxia group. However, it should be noted that Yan Emperor and Yellow Emperor were probably not entirely contemporary. At least their prosperous periods were with the Yan Emperor first and the Yellow Emperor later.

To explore the culture of the Yellow Emperor, it is necessary to base it on the identification of Xia culture. Erlitou culture, centered in western Henan, mainly belongs to the late Xia culture, while the late Wangwan culture phase III represents the early and middle Xia culture. Tracing back from this, the early Wangwan culture phase III and its precursors, the Gu River type and the Miaodigou phase II type, belong to the pre-Xia culture. Before the Miaodigou phase II type in the Southwestern Shanxi and the western part of Western Henan was the Xiwang type, and before that was the Dongzhuang–Miaodigou type. The Xiwang type is limited in strength, while the Dongzhuang–Miaodigou type is strong and glorious. The latter's distribution and level of development coincide with the records about the Yellow Emperor, suggesting that the Miaodigou era is the Yellow Emperor period. Since the heyday of the Yan Emperor preceded that of the Yellow Emperor, the culture of the early stage of the Yan Emperor should naturally precede the Dongzhuang–Miaodigou type. The central region of the Yan Emperor is around Baoji in the upper reaches of the Wei River (including the Han River), which is precisely the birthplace of the Banpo type. Thus, there should be a corresponding relationship between the Yan Emperor and the Banpo type.

There are other clues to the correspondence between Emperors Yan and Yellow and archaeological cultures. For example, in the list of twelve surnames of the Yellow Emperor in *Discourses of the States · Discourses of Jin*, the second is the surname "You," which Su Bingqi believes is the pictogram of the small-mouth pointed-bottom bottle, the most representative of the Dongzhuang–Miaodigou type and Banpo type in Yangshao culture.[20] Huang Huaixin, based on records in the *Classic of Mountains and Seas*, pointed out that descendants of the Yan Emperor had "human faces and fish bodies" and descendants of the Yellow Emperor had "human faces and bird bodies,"[21] which perfectly coincide with the worship of fish and birds in the Banpo type and Dongzhuang–Miaodigou type respectively.

Yan Wenming pointed out, "In the *Annals of the Five Emperors*, the Yan Emperor seems to be the last leader of the Shennong *shi*."[22] The most notable achievements of the Yan Emperor are the invention of agriculture. The *Chronicles of Emperors* even say that the Yan Emperor and "Lieshan *shi*" (列山氏) are the same person. The origin of millet grain farming in the northern region has a history of tens of thousands of years, so agriculture is certainly not the invention of the Yan Emperor. However, the Loess Plateau is suitable for large-scale planting of crops, and the Banpo type is developed in agriculture, so perhaps the Yan Emperor's clan lineage did play an important role in the development of dry farming. The Lieshan (列山) *shi*, also known as the Lianshan (连山), Lieshan (烈山), or Lishan (厉山) *shi*, may be related to slash-and-burn farming. Wang Xiantang proved that their initial region should be in Guanzhong (Li Mountain [骊山] in Shaanxi Province),[23] which is the core area of the Banpo type. Qian Mu proved that Lishan (厉山, Li Mountain) and Lieshan (烈山, Lie Mountain) are indeed Jieshan (介山, Jie Mountain) in Jinzhong,[24] and the Lujiapo type in Jinzhong is exactly the combination of the Banpo type and the Hougang type. As for the legend of Lishan (厉山) in Suizhou, Hubei should be a much later story.

The Yellow Emperor, who rose after the Yan Emperor, has many inventions and creations, which can roughly be divided into four categories: first, those that basically coincide with archaeological findings, such as the "Yellow Emperor made a range," as stated in the lost text of *Huainanzi*, and indeed, there are complete sets of stoves in the Dongzhuang–Miaodigou type. The *Yuejueshu · Spinoff · Record of Treasured Swords* says, "In the time of the Yellow Emperor, jade was used as a weapon," and indeed, jade *yue* became popular in the lower reaches of the Yangtze River during the Miaodigou era. The second category includes inventions similar to archaeological findings but not necessarily the inventions of the Yellow Emperor, such as drums, wells, fire food, arithmetic, and character (*Book of Origins · Inventors*). The third category includes inventions that might have existed at that time but may not have been preserved or proven, such as *mianliu* (ancient Chinese king's crown with tassels) and astronomy, including divination of the sun, moon, and stars (*Book of Origins · Inventors*). The fourth category includes things that were unlikely to have appeared at that time, such as chariots and cast *ding*, but it is a fact that pottery *ding* was popular in the Miaodigou type.

2. The Chiyou Clan Lineage and Its Culture

Chiyou, or the Limiao clan lineage, is an early representative of the Miaoman group. The *Book of Documents · Lü on Punishments*: "Chiyou was the first to rebel … The Miaomin did not use spirits but made laws with punishments, creating five cruel punishments, killing innocents … The emperor (Yellow Emperor) pitied the innocent victims, responded to the cruelty with awe, and suppressed the Miaomin, forbidding them to live on." The *Discourses of the States · Discourses of Zhou (Part Three)* mentions "the King of Limiao," and the *Discourses of the States · Discourses of Chu (Part Three)* states "Sanmiao is the descendant of Jiuli." All these indicate that Chiyou, Miaomin, and Jiuli originally referred to the same thing. Chiyou was the great leader of the Jiuli and the Miaomin and the ancestor of the Limiao, Limin, Youmiao, Sanmiao, and Miaoman.[25] The *Book of Zhou · Changmai* records: "Chiyou lived in Shaohao," which means Chiyou lived in Shaohao's territory or near Shaohao's old place in Shandong. In fact, legends or place names related to Chiyou and Jiuli are distributed in a vast area from western Shandong, Hebei, and northern Henan to southeastern Shanxi, especially in Zhuolu, Hebei, where there have been many legends about Chiyou since the Han and Wei dynasties.

According to the Battle of Zhuolu record in the *Book of Zhou · Changmai*, Chiyou should have lived at the same time as the Yan Emperor (Red Emperor). Therefore, the Hougang type of Yangshao culture, which coincides with the Banpo type and is distributed in Hebei and other places, could naturally be the cultural remains of the Chiyou clan lineage. In legends, Chiyou is a war god and the master of soldiers, capable of making advanced bronze weapons. The *Book of Origins · Inventors* says, "Chiyou made weapons with metal." However, the Hougang type of Yangshao culture does not have specific weapons, let alone metal weapons. The legend that Chiyou invented bronze weapons probably stems from speculation about his bravery and skill in battle.

3. The Shaohao Clan Lineage and Its Culture

The Shaohao clan lineage is an early representative of the Dongyi group. Shaohao (少昊), also known as Shaohao (少皞) and Xiaohao (小皞); Hao (昊) is sometimes written as hao (皓) or hao (颢). The *Classic of Mountains and Seas · Eastern Dahuang* states: "Outside the East Sea is a great gully, the country of Shaohao." Shaohao's successor, Xu, lived in Lu (now Qufu City, Shandong Province), and his descendants, small nations such as Tan, Ju, Xu, Fei, Ying, Liu, Jiang, and Huang, were all in the area from central and southern Shandong to southeastern Henan.[26] As Shaohao and Chiyou were roughly contemporary, Beixin culture, which coincides with the Hougang type and is distributed in Shandong and other places, should at least be the cultural remains of the Shaohao clan lineage. Yan Wenming has long pointed out from the traces of the Dongyi in the Shandong Peninsula in the Zhou Dynasty, through Zhenzhumen culture in the Shang Dynasty, Yueshi culture in the Xia Dynasty, and all the way back to the Neolithic, that "the entire period from Beixin culture, Dawenkou culture to Longshan culture, should belong to the system of the ancient culture of the Dongyi."[27] Wang Xun has a more detailed discussion on this and further speculates that the Shaohao clan lineage belongs to Dawenkou culture.[28] That is to say, both Beixin culture and early Dawenkou culture may belong to the culture of the Shaohao clan lineage at different periods. In addition, the Longqiuzhuang culture in the Jianghuai region may belong to the Taihao clan lineage culture, and the Longqiuzhuang culture is one of the important sources of Dawenkou culture.

The *Commentary of Zuo · Duke Zhao Seventeenth Year* records the words of Tanzi, who said that his ancestor Shaohaozhi "was the master of birds and named birds," and all the heads of the officials were named after birds. Hao (昊) and Hao (皞) are derived from the sun, and birds and the sun are often considered one. Therefore, it is known that, like Yellow Emperor, Shaohao also popularized the custom of worshipping birds and the sun. Dawenkou culture indeed discovered patterns of the sun and octagonal stars, etc. The *Classic of Mountains and Seas · Eastern Dahuang* records that "the son of Shaohao eats sorghum." Beixin culture and Dawenkou culture exist in dry millet grain and sorghum farming and cultivating rice. The *Classic of Mountains and Seas · Eastern Haiwai* says, "The country of the giant man is to its north, the people are big, and they shave the boat while sitting." This East Sea, giant man country, should belong to the Dongyi clan lineage. According to measurements of human bones unearthed from Dawenkou culture, the average height of males is 1.72 meters, which is higher than the average of 1.68 meters for males in Yangshao culture; Dawenkou culture had close interactions with the Liaodong Peninsula, so there is no doubt that its coastal people were skilled at boats.

4. Reflection of the Battle of Zhuolu in Archaeology

The "Battle of Zhuolu" was a significant historical event during the early Five-Emperor Period. The most detailed account of the "Battle of Zhuolu" is in the *Book of Zhou · Changmai*.

> Once upon a time, when heaven and earth were initially separated, the heavens established two sovereigns for the people, namely the Red Emperor and Yellow Emperor mentioned below. They were tasked with setting up codes of conduct and laws to govern the world. The heavens also commanded the Red Emperor to appoint two officials to govern the world and ordered Chiyou to assist Shaohao. The heavens instructed them to govern the four directions and complete the assigned tasks. However, Chiyou desired to drive away the Red Emperor and fought a great battle with him at the land of Zhuolu, which affected all the people across the nine regions. The Red Emperor was afraid and asked the Yellow Emperor for help. Together, they

captured Chiyou and killed him in central Jizhou, using armor and weapons to release their anger. They acted in accordance with justice and in alignment with heavenly principles, paying tribute to the great emperor. The place where this occurred was named the Field of Severed Reins. The Red Emperor then commanded Shaohao to purge and reorganize the military and bird forces in order to rectify the offices of the Five Emperors, and this decree was named "Zhi." Heaven was greatly fulfilled by their actions, and there was order to this day.

The Red Emperor here refers to the Yan Emperor, and the "two emperors" should refer to the Yan Emperor and Chiyou.[29] From this paragraph, we can at least infer as follows:

1. The Yan Emperor, Yellow Emperor, Chiyou, and Shaohao coexisted for at least a period of time.
2. Initially, there was a conflict between the Yan Emperor and Chiyou, with the Yan Emperor at a disadvantage; later, the Yellow Emperor and Chiyou battled, and Chiyou was captured and killed.
3. The Yan Emperor and the Yellow Emperor had a close relationship and had successively dealt with their common enemy, Chiyou.
4. Chiyou lived in Shaohao's land, which seems to suggest that the two were close, but after Chiyou was killed and Shaohao was unharmed, it indicates that there is an important difference between them.[30]

As for the location of Zhuolu, it is generally believed to be around today's Zhuolu in northwest Hebei,[31] but there are other opinions.[32]

The so-called "Battle of Banquan" is also related to the Battle of Zhuolu. According to the *Commentary of Zuo*, in the 25th year of Xigong: "Encountered the Yellow Emperor to fight at the Banquan," one side of this battle was the Yellow Emperor. According to the *Book of Zhou · Shiji Jie*: "In the past, the Banquan *shi* used endless warfare, fought endlessly, and had no relatives. There was no established culture, which disheartened wise men. They moved to Dulu, and the feudal lords rebelled against it, and Banquan perished," we know that the Banquan *shi* perished in Dulu. Dulu should be Zhuolu. Banquan and Zhuolu are the same places.[33] Then we know that the Battle of Banquan should be the Battle of Zhuolu.[34] The *Records of the Grand Historian · Basic Annals of the Five Emperors* distinguishes the Battle of Banquan between the Yellow Emperor and the Yan Emperor from the Battle of Zhuolu between the Yellow Emperor and Chiyou, which is only based on the *Book of Rites of Dai the Elder · Five Emperors Virtues*, which may not be credible.[35] But this does not deny the possibility of conflicts between the Yan and the Yellow. Xu Xusheng said: "When the Yan Emperor *shi* was not declining, the Yellow Emperor's clan had already begun to prosper, and it is common for two strong clans to be jealous of each other and fight."[36]

From the perspective of archaeological culture, in the beginning, the Banpo type and the Hougang type confronted each other from west to east, each with distinct characteristics consistent with the record of conflicts between the Yan Emperor and Chiyou. Slightly later, the Dongzhuang type rose and strongly influenced the expansion northward and westward. However, it could never cross the Taihang Mountains to the east, which shows that the Yellow Emperor clan lineage had a stalemate with the Chiyou clan lineage for a period of time when it first rose. After the rise of the Miaodigou type, the situation underwent a fundamental change. Bainiyaozi and Diaoyutai types, similar to the Miaodigou types, appeared in the northwest and central Hebei, respectively. Still, the overall appearance of the east of the Taihang Mountains was a scene of desolation, which should be the specific manifestation after the Battle of Zhuolu.

As for the possible conflict between the Yan and the Yellow, it is reflected in the strong influence of the Dongzhuang–Miaodigou type on Guanzhong. Obviously, the Yellow Emperor had the upper hand. The "water bird catching fish" theme of the Shijia type, and the slightly later *Stork Fish and Stone Axe* (or *Stork Fish and* Yue) in Ruzhou City, Henan Province, may all be evidence of the bird-worshipping clan lineage defeating the fish-worshipping clan lineage.[37]

5. The Yellow Emperor Period and Early China

There are many deeds of the Yellow Emperor, the most important of which are to pacify the world and govern all countries. According to the *Records of the Grand Historian · Basic Annals of the Five Emperors*, "Those who are not obedient in the world, the Yellow Emperor will conquer them. He left after pacifying a place. He cleaved mountains on the way to pacify the world and never settled down to live anywhere." After defeating the Yan Emperor and Chiyou in the Battles of Banquan and Zhuolu, "All the feudal lords revered Xuanyuan as the son of heaven." The Yellow Emperor not only "went east to the sea, climbed Wan Mountain and Tai Mountain; went west to Kongtong, and climbed Jitou; south to the Yangtze, climbed Xiong Mountain and Xiang Mountain. He chased Xunyu to the north, held a grand assembly at Fushan where the various lords paid homage to themselves, and established the capital in the basin at the foot of Zhuolu

Mountain" but also tried to manage all the countries in the world to a certain extent." "Set up large supervisors on the left and right to oversee all countries." "Appointed Fenghou, Limu, Changxian, and Dahong to govern the people." According to the record of the *Commentary of Zuo · Duke Zhao Seventeenth Year*, there were various officials named after birds in the time of Shaohao, including Li Zheng, Si Fen, Si Zhi, Si Qi, Si Bi, Si Tu, Si Ma, Si Kong, Si Kou, Si Shi, Wu Jiu (Five Pigeons), and Wu Gongzheng (Five Just Officials).*

The archaeologically dominant Dongzhuang–Miaodigou type has a significant expansion externally. Its distribution and influence range east to the Bohai Sea and Tai Mountain, west to Gansu and Qinghai, south to the Yangtze and Xiang, and north to Yan Mountain. It is similar to the places where the Yellow Emperor went, as recorded in the *Records of the Grand Historian*. In the ancient history system represented by the *Records of the Grand Historian · Basic Annals of the Five Emperors* as well as the *Emperor System* and *Five Emperors Virtues* in the *Book of Rites of Dai the Elder*, the Five Emperors are one line and take the Yellow Emperor as their ancestor. In legends, even the Beidi is part of the Yellow Emperor clan lineage,[38] which is consistent with the far-reaching influence of the Dongzhuang–Miaodigou type. It was in this process that early China, with the Central Plain as its core in a cultural sense, was formally formed on the land of China. No matter how the cultures of early China changed later, the thought of the Yellow Emperor as their common ancestor has been deeply ingrained in people's hearts and has become a lasting national memory. The status of the Yellow Emperor as the ancestor of the Chinese nation is not a fabrication of people since the Warring States period, as claimed by the doubting ancients.

The expansion of the Yellow Emperor may indicate that the real background of the expansion of the Dongzhuang–Miaodigou type was based on warfare. At that time, specialized weapons such as stone *yue* began appearing frequently. Although there were three different modes in early China at this time, overall, it had embarked on the path of evolution toward a civilized society. Among them, large palace-like houses appeared in the core area of the Central Plain, and the differentiation between rich and poor in the graves in the eastern region was signi-

---

* Li Zheng was an official responsible for astronomy and the calendar. The following were subordinate officials under Li Zheng: Si Fen, Si Zhi, Si Qi, and Si Bi.

Si Tu, Si Ma, Si Kong, Si Kou, and Si Shi were all administrative officials in ancient China, responsible for managing various aspects of the populace. They respectively used "Five Pigeons" ("*Wu Jiu*" in Chinese) for correspondence. The reason why "*Wu Jiu*" (five pigeons) is used to name these five official positions that manage the populace is that "*jiu*" (pigeon) means to gather or assemble in Chinese.

Wu Gongzheng refers to a group of officials who were responsible for ensuring fairness and equality among the populace in ancient China.—Trans.

ficant, which are all consistent with the records of the Yellow Emperor ruling the world and Shaohao setting up a hundred officials. What needs to be particularly noted is that the Yellow Emperor's "supervision of all countries" probably only involves surveillance of the surrounding areas, making them conform to certain orders and norms, rather than appointing officials to directly manage the local areas; Fenghou might be the leader of the Feng surname Taihao clan lineage, Fenghou, Limu, Changxian, Dahong might just be local leaders recognized by the Yellow Emperor. The early China of that time was perhaps only a central core with the Yellow Emperor as the nominal leader.

In addition, the historical records of the Yellow Emperor's deeds mostly belong to secular content, which is consistent with the characteristics of the Dongzhuang-Miaodigou type of being stable and introverted, valuing the noble and lightening the rich, orderly, plain and moderate, valuing the people, not admiring ghosts and gods, and resonates with the cultural temperament of the Jizhou culture, the descendants of the Yellow Emperor.

II. Zhuanxu and Emperor Ku Period

The Zhuanxu and Emperor Ku period roughly corresponds to the late Yangshao period.

1. Zhuanxu and Emperor Ku's Clan Lineages and Their Culture

Zhuanxu and Emperor Ku are the two emperors listed in succession after the Yellow Emperor in the *Records of the Grand Historian · Basic Annals of the Five Emperors*. Their activity areas are located at the junction of the Huaxia and Dongyi groups in the eastern part of Henan and the western part of Shandong, which is actually the result of the mutual integration of the two groups. One can say that they both belong to the Dongyi and Huaxia groups.

Zhuanxu has a deep relationship with both Huaxia and Dongyi. On the one hand, as recorded in the *Discourses of the States · Discourses of Lu (Part One)*, "The Youyu *shi* reveres the Yellow Emperor and acknowledges Zhuanxu as their ancestor, and they offer sacrifices in the suburbs to Yao and honor Shun as their forebear. The Xia *shi* reveres the Yellow Emperor and acknowledges Zhuanxu as their ancestor. They offer sacrifices in the suburbs to Gun and honor Yu as their forebear," Youyu and Xiahou clans of Huaxia all regarded him as their ancestor for worship. The *Classic of Mountains and Seas · The Inner Seas* states, "The Yellow

Emperor gave birth to Changyi, Changyi gave birth to Hanliu, Hanliu gave birth to Zhuanxu." However, the *Book of Rites of Dai the Younger · Emperor System* and the *Records of the Grand Historian · Basic Annals of the Five Emperors* say that he is the grandson of the Yellow Emperor, with one generation missing from Hanliu. On the other hand, the *Classic of Mountains and Seas · Eastern Dahuang* also says that he is the "Shaohao's raised emperor," belonging to the descendants of the Dongyi ancestor Shaohao. As for Emperor Ku Gaoxin, the *Records of the Grand Historian · Basic Annals of the Five Emperors* records him as the great-grandson of the Yellow Emperor and the son of the Zhuanxu clan lineage. Wang Guowei has verified that he is Emperor Jun in the *Classic of Mountains and Seas*.[39] The *Commentary of Zuo · Duke Zhao Seventeenth Year* states: "The Wey is the ancient ruins of Zhuanxu." The Wey during the Spring and Autumn period is in Puyang, Henan Province. *Master Lü's Spring and Autumn Annals · Ancient Music* says that Zhuanxu lived in Kongsang, in Qufu, Shandong Province, originally the ruins of Shaohao. Regarding the residence of Emperor Ku, Wang Guowei verified that Ku's residence Bo is in today's Cao County, Shandong Province, based on the statement of *Shu · Shangshuxu*, "Tang began to live in Hao, followed the residence of the former king, and made an ode to Emperor Gao" and *Book of Documents · Preface of Book Shang*: "Qi's father Emperor Ku lived in Bo, Tang moved from Shangqiu, so it is said to follow the residence of the former king" from Kongchuan. The *Chronicles of Emperors* says that Zhuanxu and Emperor Ku were both buried in "Dunqiu Guangyangli in Dongjun," which is in Neihuang, Qingfeng, Henan Province. There are still "Two Emperor Mausoleums" here. In summary, the activity areas of Zhuanxu and Emperor Ku should be similar to those of Shaohao, roughly in the eastern Henan, western Shandong, and central and southern Shandong areas, which is exactly the junction of the Huaxia and Dongyi groups.

Zhuanxu of the Gaoyang *shi*, the name Gaoyang is related to the sun. The *Classic of Mountains and Seas* mentions many times that Emperor Jun drove "four birds," saying that there are colorful birds always accompanying Emperor Jun, and it also says that Emperor Jun gave birth to "ten *ri*" (ten suns) and "twelve *yue*" (twelve moons). The *Discourses of the States · Discourses of Lu (Part One)* says, "Emperor Ku could sequence the three stars to solidify the people," the *Book of Rites of Dai the Elder · Five Emperors Virtues* says he "calculated the sun and moon and welcomed them." Like the Yellow Emperor and Shaohao, Zhuanxu and Emperor Ku also paid great attention to observing the sun, moon, and stars so that they may have made further contributions to astronomy and the lunar calendar or have a long history of the sun and bird worship. The late Dawenkou culture has sun patterns, octagram patterns, bird-sun combination pottery patterns with a circle above and a double triangle below, and standing bird pottery ancestor shapes, which match the textual records.[40] Since the early Dawenkou culture belonged to the Shaohao clan lineage culture, then the remains of the mid-to-late Dawenkou culture distributed at least in the eastern Henan, western Shandong, and central and southern Shandong areas should be the culture of Zhuanxu of the Gaoyang *shi* and Emperor Ku of the Gaoxin *shi*, respectively. This area's Dawenkou culture indeed integrates many elements of Yangshao culture.

Discourses of the States · Discourses of Zhou (Part Three) says, "The positions of the stars and the sun are all in the constellations of the North, which Zhuanxu established, and Emperor Ku received it." Some documents from the Warring States to the Western Han Dynasty regarded Zhuanxu as the emperor of the north. The *Zhuangzi: The Great and Venerable Teacher* has the saying, "Zhuanxu got it and stayed in Xuan Palace"; the *Book of Rites of Dai the Elder · Five Emperors Virtues* says Zhuanxu "went north to Youling," Youling is Youzhou. The Hebei Plain, where Jiuli lived, has many place names and people's names with the prefix "Xuan." Xuan is black, which is close to the "You" of "Youzhou," the scope of Xuan Palace and Youzhou is roughly in the northern part of Hebei to the southwestern part of Liaoning and the southeastern part of Inner Mongolia. This region's Xueshan culture phase I incorporates many elements of Dawenkou culture, which may be related to the northward movement of part of the Zhuanxu clan lineage population.

Furthermore, the overall Huaxia group at this time may still be a continuation of the Yan Emperor and the Yellow Emperor clan lineages, and the two are generally still divided by the southward-flowing Yellow River. The late Banpo type of Yangshao culture in the middle and lower reaches of the Wei River, Majiayao culture (Shilingxia type, Majiayao type) in the Gansu–Qinghai–Ningxia region may still belong to the Jiangrong clan lineage related to the Yan Emperor,[41] the Xiwang type–Miaodigou phase II type in the southern Shanxi and western Henan region, the Yijing type–Baiyan type in the central part of Shanxi, the Haishengbulang type–Ashan phase III type in the central and southern parts of Inner Mongolia, all may belong to the clan lineages related to the Yellow Emperor.

2. Zhuanxu and Gonggong: Incompatible Rivals

According to legend, Zhuanxu once waged war with Gonggong. The *Songs of Chu · Tian Wen* contains the sentence, "Kanghui is enraged. Why does the earth tilt toward the southeast?" Wang Yi's "Chu Ci Zhangju" says: "Kanghui is the name of Gonggong." The *Section and Sentence Commentary to Songs of Chu* records more clearly: "Gonggong competed with Zhuanxu for the title of emperor, angrily and hit the Buzhou Mountain." *Huainanzi* provides a detailed description of this war, as seen in *On Military Strategy, Patterns of Heaven*, and other chapters.[42] *Discourses of the States · Discourses of Zhou (Part Three)* says: "In the past, Gonggong abandoned this way ... wanted to block and flood the rivers, to destroy the high and fill the low, to harm the world." It seems that the cause of the war was due to Gonggong, who was upstream, causing a flood that brought disaster to the Zhuanxu clan lineage downstream.

According to Xu Xusheng's research, there were three rivers called Gong in ancient times, and two countries called Gong, of which Gong County of Henei Commandery in the *Book of Han · Treatise on Geography* is most likely to be the original residence of Gonggong. This Gong County is called "Gong Shou" in *Zhuangzi · Rang Wang* and "Gong Tou" in *Xunzi · Ru Xiao*, which is actually the area of today's Hui County in Henan. Hui County has unearthed many Shang and Zhou bronzes with the *shi* emblem "Gong," showing that this was the hometown of the "Gong" *shi*, i.e., the Gong *shi* during the Shang and Zhou periods.[43] Gonggong is famous for developing water conservancies. The *Commentary of Zuo · Duke Zhao Seventeenth Year* says, "The Gonggong *shi* used water to record matters. Therefore, they named all the heads of departments using characters related to water." The ancient term for "Hong River" is "Gong River," named after Gonggong. According to Xu Xusheng's research, "Hong River" was not a general term in the early days but a proper noun, specifically referring to the river flowing through Gonggong's old land, Hui County, and its neighboring eastern counties, which is the Jiang (降) River or Jiang (洚) River, roughly equivalent to the current Wei River (Shandong and Henan). It merges with the Qi River and flows into the Yellow River. Hui County is close to "the ancient ruins of Zhuanxu," Puyang, so Zhuanxu and Gonggong could have possibly waged war.[44] *Huainanzi · Forms of Earth* has the words "the northwest direction is called Buzhou Mountain, the gate of Youdu," then the Buzhou Mountain that Gonggong hit should be near Youdu, Youzhou, or Hui County. Hui County and Puyang may have often been threatened by floods. Gonggong once tried to control the water, but it was impossible to fundamentally solve the problem. The flooding brought severe disaster to the Zhuanxu clan lineage downstream. However, the Zhuanxu people could not truly understand the cause of the flooding, and they thought it was caused by the upstream Gonggong "shaking the flood."

As mentioned earlier, Zhuanxu culture may have been the remains of the middle Dawenkou culture. Therefore, Yangshao culture of the Dasikong type, which was distributed in the northern Henan and southern Hebei areas at the same time, may have belonged to the culture of Gonggong. Although these two cultures are closely adjacent in terms of geography, they are quite different in culture. Dawenkou culture was characterized by tri-legged and round-foot pottery such as the *ding*, high-foot plate, pot, and *gui*,[45] while flat-bottom jar and earthen bowl characterize the Dasikong type. Dawenkou culture was simple and elegant with a little color, while the Dasikong type popularized painted pottery with patterns such as hooked leaf triangles, double hooks, S patterns, zigzag lines, scale patterns, diagonal lines, and grid patterns. Elements such as high-foot plate, pot, and octagonal star pattern in the middle Dawenkou culture can follow the eastern edge of the Dasikong type to the north to the Xueshan phase I culture in the central and northern Hebei and even the Xiliao River Basin. Still, there is no trace in the nearby Dasikong type, indicating the degree of opposition between the two cultures. This cultural opposition may well reflect the poor relationship between Gonggong and Zhuanxu. Later, the local Yangshao culture of the Taikou type obviously contains more components of Dawenkou culture, forming a stark contrast with the previous cultural opposition, which coincides with the documented situation of Gonggong's defeat.

3. Zhurong's Southward Migration and the Miaoman's Revival

Zhurong is also closely related to Zhuanxu. Zhurong held a special position in religion, was Zhuanxu's main assistant in severing the heaven-earth connection, and also had many connections with the Dongyi, Huaxia, and Miaoman groups, and represents the integration of the three major groups in ancient China.

The *Commentary of Zuo · Duke Zhao Twenty-Ninth Year* says: "Zhuanxu had a son named Li, who is Zhurong." *Classic of Mountains and Seas · Western Dahuang* says: "Zhuanxu gave birth to Laotong, Laotong gave birth to Chong and Li, the Emperor ordered Chong to present to the heavens, and ordered Li to mound the earth." The *Records of the Grand Historian · Chu Hereditary Houses* is more complex: "The ancestors of Chu originated from the Gaoyang of Emperor Zhuanxu. Gaoyang, the grandson of the Yellow Emperor, was the son of Changyi. Gaoyang gave birth to Chen, Chen gave birth to Juanzhang, and Juanzhang gave birth to Chong and Li."[46] Juanzhang should be Laotong; the two characters are similar in form. Li (犁) and Li (黎) are interchangeable, probably names, and Zhurong is a job title. In summary, there should be no doubt that Chong and Li came from the Zhuanxu system. What is very interesting is that in the late Shang tomb M8 in Subutun, Qingzhou, Shandong, there are 13 bronzes with the *shi* emblem "Rong." The *shi* emblem has two *lis*, buckled up and down, which is "double *li*" ("重鬲"), that is, "Chong and Li" (重黎).⁴⁷

Why did Chong and Li become Zhurong? According to the *Records of the Grand Historian · Chu Hereditary Houses*, Chong and Li were the Fire Officers of Emperor Ku's Gaoxin *shi*, made significant contributions, and could illuminate the world, so they were appointed as Zhurong by Emperor Ku. The *Commentary of Zuo · Duke Zhao Twenty-Ninth Year* also states, "The Fire Officer is called Zhurong." Zhurong's ancestor Zhuanxu Gaoyang *shi* worshipped the sun or was itself the embodiment of the sun, Zhurong could illuminate the world and shine all over the world. Isn't this also the image of the sun god? The sun is the essence of *Yang* fire, and it is only natural for the sun god to evolve into the Fire Officer and Fire God. "Zhu" means shaman and priest, or the actual Zhurong was just a high priest who presided over the worship of the sun. One of the biggest functions of fire for humans is to cook food, and the *li* is a typical cooking utensil. *Rong* and *li* themselves have the meaning of cooking with fire; no wonder Zhurong is also regarded as the god of the kitchen.

The *Commentary of Zuo · Duke Zhao Seventeenth Year* says: "Zheng is the ruins of Zhurong," these ruins of Zhurong, "Zheng," are generally believed to be in Xinzheng, Henan today. However, the hometown of Zhurong's ancestor Zhuanxu is in the eastern part of Henan to Shandong's central and southern parts. The range of residences of the descendants of Zhurong is even wider. *Discourses of the States · Discourses of Zheng* says that there are eight surnames for the descendants of Zhurong. Wei Zhao annotates them as Ji, Dong, Peng, Tu, Yun, Cao, Zhen, and Mi. According to the research by Xu Xusheng, these surnames are distributed in Puyang, Wen County, Yanshi, Xinmi, Xuchang in Henan Province, Fan County, Dingtao, Zoucheng, Juxian in Shandong Province, Tongshan in Jiangsu, Huanggang, Zigui in Hubei Province, etc., covering the middle and lower reaches of the Yellow River, the middle reaches of the Huai River and the middle reaches of the Yangtze River. Henan and Shandong are all in or near the hometown of Zhuanxu and Zhurong. It should be natural for their descendants to live in these places. The strange thing is how the descendants of Zhurong could be as far away as the middle reaches of the Yangtze River. This can probably only be explained by the southward migration of the Zhurong tribe.

According to legend, the Miaoman who live in the middle reaches of the Yangtze River all have a deep connection with Zhurong. The *Classic of Mountains and Seas · Southern Dahuang* mentions, "Yanrong gave birth to Huandou," while *Northern Dahuang* says, "Huandou gave birth to Miaomin." This shows that the origin of Miaomin is Yanrong. Yanrong only appears once in the *Classic of Mountains and Seas*, while Zhurong is mentioned seven times. It is very likely that Yanrong is Zhurong. Of course, if we trace back further, the ancestor of the Miaomin is Zhuanxu, so the *Classic of Mountains and Seas · Northern Dahuang* says, "Zhuanxu gave birth to Huandou, Huandou gave birth to Miaomin," omitting the generation of Zhurong. Of course, the main root of the Miaomin is still in the Jiuli of Chiyou. The *Classic of Mountains and Seas · Northern Dahuang* says, "The Miaomin is of Li (厘) surname." Li (厘) is the same as Li (黎). This "Li" (黎) is probably both the "Li" of Chiyou's Jiuli and the "Li" of Zhurong's Chong and Li. Probably Zhurong was originally a product of the integration of the Limiao and Zhuanxu clans.

The areas of the Yellow River middle and lower reaches, Huai River middle reaches, and Yangtze River middle reaches where the eight surnames of Zhurong are found are distributed with Dawenkou culture, Yangshao culture Qinwangzhai type, and Daxi culture Youziling type-Qujialing culture in the late Yangshao period. These cultures may all have some relationship with Zhurong. And the ancient city of Xishan in Zhengzhou, which belongs to the Qinwangzhai type of Yangshao culture, maybe the "ruins of Zhurong."[48] From the rise and outward expansion of Qujialing culture, it can be seen that the Miaoman group related to Zhurong entered a revival stage at this time.

4. Severing the Heaven-Earth Connection and the Origin of Civilization

Zhuanxu's greatest achievement is severing the heaven-earth connection. The *Discourses of the States · Discourses of Chu (Part Three)* records: "In ancient times, there was a clear distinction between the people and the gods ... By the end of the Shaohao period, the Jiuli tribe had fallen into moral disarray. Each person among them could freely offer sacrifices to the deities, and every household had its own shamans and historians. This led to a mingling of humans and gods, with no distinction between them. As a result, humans began to place themselves on an equal footing with the gods and lost their reverence for the divine. This caused heaven and earth to lose their original order and principles, leading to crop failures and incessant disasters in the human world ... Seeing this situation, Emperor

Zhuanxu ordered Nan Zheng Chong to take charge of heaven and Huo Zheng* Li to take charge of the earth, thereby severing the connection between heaven and earth. This separated humans from gods, each in their respective places, and restored the order of heaven and earth, cutting off direct communication between humans and gods." The *Book of Documents · Lü on Punishments* also says, "Chong and Li were then ordered to sever the heaven-earth connection. This allowed heaven and earth to each have their proper place, and humans established a fixed order and system of norms between them."

Actually, everyone worshipped gods, and every family had a shaman. This should have been a general situation of the previous stage of society, not the result of the disturbance of Chiyou Jiuli. The essence of severing the heaven-earth connection may have been Zhuanxu's monopoly on religious power. As Xu Xusheng said, Zhuanxu ordered Chong to monopolize the right to communicate with the heavenly spirits, blocking the freedom of ordinary people to communicate with heaven and earth at will.[49] Chong and Li were in charge of religious affairs, also known as Zhurong. If Zhurong was a headed shaman, then Zhuanxu should have been the chief of the great shamans. The *Book of Rites of Dai the Elder · Five Emperors Virtues* says that he "steps in time to resemble heaven, follows ghosts and gods to set righteousness," Zhuanxu's achievements are mainly in religion and astronomy, which are interrelated.

The monopoly on religious affairs and interpretation of celestial phenomena means that a major change had taken place in the entire society. The appearance of joint burials of adult men and women in the middle and late Dawenkou culture, and the arrangement of men on the left and women on the right, should be a clear sign of the emergence of a patrilineal *shi* society, with male superiority and female inferiority becoming more and more common. This is so consistent with the "law of Zhuanxu" mentioned in *Huainanzi · Placing Customs on a Par* that women should give way to men on the road! The difference in size and accompanying objects in these burials is very large. The owner of the large tomb holds the stone *yue*, symbolizing military power, and is buried with bone-carved tubes, alligator drums, high-handle cups, and other precious objects, revealing the image of a wealthy noble leader who holds military and divine power in one

---

* Nan Zheng and Huo Zheng were official titles in ancient China. Nan Zheng was in charge of matters concerning the heavens and was responsible for serving the gods, while Huo Zheng was in charge of matters on Earth and was responsible for managing the populace.—Trans.

hand. It can be seen that although the separation of heaven and earth seems to be a major religious change on the surface, behind it was the emergence of classes and patrilineal *shi* society, and the initial civilization society was initially formed at this point.

III. Emperors Yao and Shun Period

The Emperors Yao and Shun period roughly corresponds to the Longshan period.

1. The Conquest of Western Xia by Tang and Tangtao *Shi* Culture

The "Conquest of Western Xia by Tang" first appears in the *Book of Zhou · Records of the Grand Historian Explanations*: "In the past, the ruler of the Western Xia was inherently benevolent and opposed to using military force. He never repaired the city walls or prepared military defenses; warriors held no status in the country. The ruler of Western Xia was kind and generous, granting rewards to such an extent that the national treasury was depleted. When the Tang *shi* attacked, Western Xia's city defenses were inadequate, and the warriors were useless. Consequently, Western Xia fell." *Records of Diverse Matters · Miscellaneous Sayings (Part One)* has similar statements.[50] The sequence of this Xia before Tang is also consistent with the records in the *Commentary of Zuo · Duke Zhao First Year*.[51]

The "Western Xia" and "Tang *shi*" mentioned here refer to the Xia and Taotang tribes often seen in historical records, and there have been different opinions about their dwellings. Regarding the main residence of Xia, it cannot have been beyond southern Shanxi and western Henan in general,[52] and it should have moved from southern Shanxi to Henan.[53] Southern Shanxi is the real ancient home of the Xia people, so there is a place called "Xia ruins."[54] The situation of the residence of Taotang is much more complicated, with theories pointing to Shandong, Hebei, and Shanxi. The Shanxi theory is important because it appears in pre-Qin classics such as the *Commentary of Zuo*. Still, there are divergences, including the "Pingyang" theory in southern Shanxi, Linfen, and the "Jinyang" theory in Taiyuan, central Shanxi.[55] It might be closest to the truth that Huangfu Mi advocated moving from Jinyang to Pingyang.[56] Although the Shandong and Hebei theories explicitly appeared in the Han Dynasty, they should not be overlooked. Ying Shao believes that both Tang County and Pingyang were residences of Yao, which might have an earlier source, so there is a possibility that Taotang *shi* moved from Hebei to Shanxi.[57] Further connecting Yao as the son of Ku[58] and the argument that the Gaoxin *shi* lived in the east, it is possible that the initial residence of the Taotang *shi* was indeed in the east. Thus, from near Shandong at the beginning, through Hebei and central Shanxi, to finally arriving in southern Shanxi, this could form a possible route for the Taotang *shi* moving from east to west.

The westward and southward movements of the Taotang *shi* should have involved conflicts and integration with the local inhabitants, especially when they finally intended to occupy the Xia people's base in southern Shanxi. Perhaps the two sides went through a fierce war, which might be the origin of the "Conquest of Western Xia by Tang." Reflected in archaeology, it should be the replacement of the Miaodigou phase II type of Yangshao culture by Taosi culture in the early Longshan period: the Taosi culture was formed based on the Miaodigou phase II type by adopting many elements from the eastern cultures such as Dawenkou culture and Liangzhu culture. This further proves that the Miaodigou phase II type should be the earliest pre-Xia culture, and Taosi culture is the Taotang *shi* culture.[59]

The large city of nearly three million square meters in the Taosi central settlement, the luxurious "royal tomb," and advanced handicraft techniques were unsurpassed in the early Longshan period. This is both a result of the Taotang *shi*'s inclusiveness and absorption of all good aspects and a clear proof of their powerful strength. The cultures of Jiangrong, early Xia, early pre-Zhou (1046–256 BCE), and Gonggong *shi* were all distributed around the Linfen Basin, with the Taotang *shi* at the center. They may have been somewhat regulated by the Taotang *shi* (Yao). Perhaps at that time, as recorded in the *Book of Documents · Canon of Yao*, there was already a prototype of a kingdom centered on the Taotang *shi*. However, this Yao might have been, at most, the unanimously elected leader of "all countries in the world" and had not yet established a hereditary monarchy. The legends of Emperors Yao and Shun's abdication recorded in the *Book of Documents · Canon of Yao*, *Mozi · Promoting the Worthy*, and *Mengzi · Wan Zhang* might simply reflect the decline of the Taotang *shi* that Yao belonged to and the rise of the Youyu *shi* that Shun belonged to.[60]

Furthermore, the *Book of Documents · Canon of Yao* also records that Yao ordered Xihe to "observe the images of the sun, moon, stars, and celestial bodies and respectfully teach the people about time." Evidence of astronomical observation and time teaching has indeed been found at the Taosi site. The *Analects · Tai Bo* highly praises Yao for his "great achievements are like towering mountains, and the etiquette system he established is truly splendid and beautiful." Indeed, the Taosi site has uncovered red inscriptions on pottery with the characters *"yang"* (昜) and *"wen"* (文), which are mature in form and very similar to oracle bone inscriptions and inscriptions on bronze.

2. The Strength and Expansion of the Youyu *Shi*

The *Discourses of the States · Discourses of Lu (Part One)* states: "The Youyu *shi* reveres the Yellow Emperor and acknowledges Zhuanxu as their ancestor, and they offer sacrifices in the outskirts to Yao and honor Shun as their forebear." The *Records of the Grand Historian · Basic Annals of the Five Emperors* records: "Yu Shun, named Chonghua. Chonghua's father was Gusou, Gusou's father was Qiaoniu, Qiaoniu's father was Juwang, Juwang's father was Jingkang, Jingkang's father was Qiongchan, Qiongchan's father was Emperor Zhuanxu, and Zhuanxu's father was Changyi." It can be seen that the Youyu *shi* were descendants of the Yellow Emperor and Zhuanxu, with Shun as their representative figure. *Mengzi* says, "Shun was born in Zhufeng, moved to Fuxia, and died in Mingtiao. He was a person from the Dongyi." The *Records of the Grand Historian · Basic Annals of the Five Emperors* records: "Shun was a man from Jizhou. Shun plowed Li Mountain, fished in Leize, made pottery on the banks of the river, made all kinds of utensils in Shouqiu, and resided in Fuxia." There are different views on the dwelling places of the Youyu *shi* and Shun, mainly concentrated in southern Shanxi, eastern Henan, and western Shandong. There are also theories that the Gui River, where the Youyu *shi* lived, was in Yanqing, Beijing.

From an archaeological perspective, the Eastern Henan and Northwestern Anhui region still belonged to the distribution area of Dawenkou culture Yuchisi type in the early Longshan period. By the late Longshan period, it was strongly influenced by Longshan culture and Wangwan culture phase III, evolving into Zaolütai culture. This culture was distributed in the land where Shun's descendants lived[61] during the Longshan era, and it might be the remains of the Youyu *shi* (Shun),[62] actually having a deep connection with the Taihao clan lineage. The Zaolütai culture may be considered part of the Central Plain Longshan culture or classified under Hai–Dai Longshan culture, reflecting its transitional nature between the two, which coincides with the situation that Shun may belong to the

Dongyi or the Huaxia. From the perspective of the ancient city of Pingliangtai in Huaiyang, its advanced building technology, regular form, and rigorous layout reflect the high level of development of the Youyu *shi*. At one time, they may even have replaced the Taotang *shi* as the leaders of the Central Plain Huaxia, as recorded in the *Book of Documents · Canon of Yao*.

Book of Documents · Canon of Yao records that Shun, on the orders of Yao, "banished Gonggong to Youzhou, cast Huandou onto Chong Mountain, expelled the Sanmiao to Sanwei, and executed Gun at Yu Mountain" and "with these four punishments, all under heaven submitted." The *Records of the Grand Historian · Basic Annals of the Five Emperors* has similar records. From an archaeological perspective, after the late Dawenkou culture, Zaolütai culture indeed experienced a large-scale outward expansion, especially to the south, which profoundly influenced the formation of Guangfulin culture and Doujitai culture. Influences such as *yan* penetrated as far as the Tanshishan culture in the northwest of Fujian, and its impact even reached the Jianghan Basin for a time. This may be the origin of legends like Yu Shun's southern expedition and his burial in the fields of Cangwu.[63] Even the beginnings of Gouwu culture may also be related to this.[64]

3. Pre-Xia Culture

The pre-Xia culture refers to the culture of the Xia people before the establishment of the Xia Dynasty. The *Discourses of the States · Discourses of Lu (Part One)* states that "the Xia *shi* reveres the Yellow Emperor and acknowledges Zhuanxu as their ancestor," and *Book of Rites of Dai the Younger · Emperor System* states "Zhuanxu gave birth to Gun," who was the father of Yu, the founder of the Xia Dynasty. It can be seen that, like the Youyu *shi*, the Xiahou *shi* and their descendant Gun are also descendants of the Yellow Emperor and Zhuanxu. As mentioned earlier, "Xia ruins" wwere originally located in southern Shanxi, and the Xia people were actually likely to have originated in southern Shanxi and then moved to Henan. Archaeologically, the Miaodigou culture phase II is probably the earliest pre-Xia culture, which had a strong southward influence on the Gu River type and significantly contributed to the formation of Wangwan culture phase III. The early Wangwan culture phase III should be considered the late stage of the pre-Xia culture.

In addition, Hougang culture phase II in northern Henan and southern Hebei during the early Longshan period might be the late remnants of the Gonggong *shi*,[65] Laohushan culture Youyao type in central Shanxi might represent the early pre-Zhou culture (Ji), the Keshezhuang culture phase II in Guanzhong might be the remnants of the Jiangrong (Four Mountains). Majiayao culture Banshan type, Caiyuan culture, and Qijia culture in the Gansu–Qinghai–Ningxia regions should also be classified under Jiangrong or the Diqiang clan lineages.

IV. Xia Dynasty

The Xia Dynasty roughly corresponds to the late Longshan period and Erlitou culture period.

1. "Ji Expels Danzhu" and Early Pre-Zhou Culture

The "Ji Expels Danzhu" incident is recorded in the *Ancient Bamboo Annals*: "Houji expelled Emperor Zhu to the Dan River."[66] There are also those who connect Danzhu's exile with Shun, probably because Shun was the leader of the Central Plain at the time. Therefore, such significant events were conducted under his name. The residence of Houji and his mother, Jiangyuan of Tai *shi*, was traditionally thought to be around the Jing and Wei Rivers. Still, Qian Mu proposed the theory of origin in southern Shanxi.[67] Since Danzhu was the son of Yao,[68] his original residence should naturally be in the Linfen Basin. As for the residence in the Dan River in the southwest of Henan, it may be the result of exile.[69]

In terms of archaeology, around the transition between the early and late Longshan periods, the Linfen Basin underwent another major cultural change. This was manifested by the once prosperous Taosi culture being replaced by the late Taosi culture and the occurrence of noteworthy events such as the abandonment of city walls, the destruction of tombs, and violence against women. The cause of the change was the southward movement of the Laohushan culture Youyao type, and the appearance of many double-handle *yis* is clear evidence. This may be the reflection of "Ji Expels Danzhu," and its essence is nothing more than the conquest of the Taotang by the northern Ji Zhou ancestors. This also proves that the late Taosi culture and Laohushan culture Youyao type represent the earliest pre-Zhou culture represented by Houji.[70] Interestingly, the pottery human feet found at the Laohushan, Liangcheng, Wutai, Yangbai, and other sites that belong to Laohushan culture coincide with the legend in the *Book of Songs · Major Court Hymns · Decade of Sheng Min* where Jiangyuan stepped on the big toe of the emperor and gave birth to Houji.[71] The Youyao type and the area of southern Shanxi where the late Taosi culture is distributed had an excellent natural environment suitable for the development of agriculture, consistent with the record of Houji's proficiency in farming.

2. "Yu Conquers the Sanmiao" and Early Xia Culture

The event of Yu conquering the Sanmiao is most detailed in the record of *Mozi · Condemning Aggression (Part Three)* "In ancient times, the Sanmiao tribes were in great chaos, and the heavens decreed their punishment. The sun, being malicious, appeared at night, and blood rain fell for three days. Dragons were seen in ancestral temples, and dogs cried in the market. In summer, water froze, the ground cracked open to reveal springs, and the crops could not ripen. The people were greatly alarmed. The ancient Emperor Gaoyang, in the Xuan Palace, bestowed a command to Yu. Yu, holding the jade token granted by the heavens, personally went to fight against Youmiao. At that time, thunder and lightning shook the earth. A deity with a human face and bird body respectfully stood by, shooting and killing the leader of the Youmiao with an arrow. The Miao army was thrown into chaos and later declined. After Yu's victory over the Sanmiao, he divided the mountains and rivers, categorized the hierarchy of things, regulated the four directions, and brought harmony between gods and humans, bringing peace to the world. This is the story of Yu's campaign against the Youmiao." It seems that Yu suddenly invaded when the Sanmiao were suffering from natural disasters and internal chaos. The Sanmiao were defeated and completely conquered. Their ancestral temples were destroyed, "descendants became slaves,"[72] and the Sanmiao withdrew from the historical stage. The *Strategies of the Warring States · Strategies of Wei* also recorded: "In the past, the dwelling of the Sanmiao, on the left was the wave of Pengli, on the right was the Dongting Lake, Wen Mountain was in the south, and Heng Mountain was in the north. Relying on this danger, they ruled poorly, and Yu banished them."

The Xia people originated in southern Shanxi and migrated to Henan. By the time Yu was the leader of the Xiahou *shi*, their main activity area was already in the central and western parts of Henan. Xu Xusheng, based on the above record of the *Strategies of the Warring States · Strategies of Wei*, inferred that the main habitat of the Sanmiao was in the Jianghan Plain.[73] In the early Longshan period, Henan's central and western part was successively occupied by the Miaodigou type phase II, the Gu River type, and the early Wangwan culture phase III, which are all pre-Xia cultural remains. At the same time, the Jianghan Plain was the possible Sanmiao culture of Shijiahe culture. From the relatively large number of red slanted-belly pottery cups and other Shijiahe culture found in the central and western parts of Henan, it can be seen that Sanmiao culture was dominant.[74] At the beginning of the late Longshan period, the central and western parts of Henan entered the late Wangwan culture phase III, among which the Meishan type expanded southward on a large scale and replaced the Shijiahe culture in southern Henan, northern Hubei, and western Hubei, even forming the Xiaojiawuji culture that is close to the third culture of Wangwan in the Jianghan Plain and nearby areas. This huge cultural change is the true reflection of the "Yu Conquers the Sanmiao" event in archaeology.[75]

Since Yu was the actual founder of the Xia Dynasty,[76] his conquest of the Sanmiao should be the most important war event around the founding of the Xia Dynasty. From this, it can be confirmed that the Xia Dynasty basically entered the late Longshan period, and the late Wangwan culture phase III represents early Xia culture.[77] The late Wangwan culture phase III expanded forcefully, not only reaching the Jianghan region to the south and affecting the Dongting Lake region but also had a significant influence on Zaolütai culture to the east, the Sanliqiao type and the phase II of Keshengzhuang culture to the northwest, and the phase II of Hougang culture to the north. In *Xunzi · Discourse on the Use of Soldiers*, there is a saying that "Yu fought against Gonggong," and the *Classic of Mountains and Seas* also records "Yu attacked the mountain of Gonggong's country," and Yu killed Gonggong's servant "Xiangyao" or "Xiangliu *shi*."[78] This may reflect the influence of Wangwan culture phase III on Hougang culture phase II. The *Book of Documents · Speech at Gan* records that Qi (or Yu) attacked Youhu, which may be related to the influence of Wangwan culture phase III in the northwest direction. In fact, after the Taotang and Youyu *shi*, the Xiahou *shi* not only became the core force of the Central Plain Huaxia but also controlled a larger range and had a more far-reaching influence. As recorded in *Commentary of Zuo · Duke Ai Seventh Year*: "Yu summoned various lords to a grand assembly at Tu Mountain, where, in front of the lords, he held jade and silk in his hands and offered sacrifices to the heavens." *Discourses of the States · Discourses of Lu (Part Three)*: "In the past, Yu summoned all gods to the mountains of Kuaiji, Fangfeng *shi* came late, and Yu killed him."[79] It can be seen that it not only had a great appeal to the surrounding small countries but also possibly held the power of life and death. Moreover, after Yu, hereditary monarchical power was implemented, establishing the institutional basis for the Xia people to occupy the Central Plain for a long time and control China. This familial rule continued to the Shang and Zhou dynasties and beyond.

3. Shaokang's Revival and the Middle and Late Xia Culture

According to the literature, there were political changes in the early Xia Dynasty, such as "Taikang losing the kingdom," "Houyi replacing Xia," and "Shaokang's revival." The "loss of the country by Taikang" was due to the invasion of the Dongyi people. Afterward, through Zhongkang, Houyi became the king,[80] and he "used the Xia people to replace Xia's politics" (*Commentary of Zuo · Duke Xiang Fourth Year*). King Xiang's wife, Houmin, fled to Youreng and gave birth to Shaokang. Later, Shaokang attacked and killed Zhuo and Jiao with the help of the Youyu *shi* and the Youge *shi*, restored the Xia regime, and achieved a "revival" situation.[81]

Around 1900 BCE, the late period of Wangwan culture phase III, the core area of the Dengfeng and Yuzhou Meishan type culture declined, which may be related to the changes of "Taikang lost the state" and "Houyi replacing Xia." However, a little later, the Xinzhai type in Zhengzhou and Xinmi east of Song Mountain rose strongly. In other words, at this time, only the cultural pattern and focus of the Central Plain region were adjusted and transferred, and there was no widespread cultural decline. The Xinzhai type contains many eastern elements, such as Zaolütai culture, which may be the middle Xia culture formed after the Shaokang's revival and the integration of many eastern Zaolütai culture elements.[82]

Around 1800 BCE, Wangwan culture phase III Xinzhai type moved east into the Luoyang Basin and was influenced by Qijia culture to form Erlitou culture. This should be the late Xia culture developed by a Xia king who moved west to the Luoyang Basin several generations after Shaokang.[83] The late Xia culture represented by Erlitou culture had large cities and palaces. Under its strong influence, the cultures of most parts of China blended and connected to form a wider cultural significance of early China, truly entering the period of the supreme kingdom.[84]

4. Pre-Shang Culture

Pre-Shang culture refers to the Shang people's culture before the Shang Dynasty's establishment. Pre-Shang from the Qi to Tang's extermination of the Xia coincided with the Xia Dynasty. According to the *Book of Documents* and *Records of the Grand Historian* and other records, Qi and Yu were contemporaries. According to the *Current Bamboo Annals*, Shang Xian Gong had important activities or significant events that occurred before the Shang during the reigns of the Xia King Xiang, Shaokang, Zhu, Mang, Xie, Bujiang, Kongjia, and Lügui.[85] The *Book of Songs · Eulogies of Shang · Long-Term Development* states: "When the Yousong *shi* tribe was on the rise, King Yu established the Yousong *shi* as his consort, and she gave birth to Qi." The *Songs of Chu · Tian Wen* says: "Jiandi resides deep within the nine-tiered Yaotai; how could Emperor Ku take a liking and admire her?" It can be seen that the ancestor of Shang was Emperor Ku, and he married the Yousong *shi* or Jiandi. The *Records of the Grand Historian · Basic Annals of Yin* synthesizes it as "Yin Qi, his mother was called Jiandi, a daughter of the Yousong *shi*, who was the second concubine of Emperor Ku." Tang Lan believed that Yousong was Rong[86] (the minority group in western China in ancient times), and together with the Di (a people in the north of China in ancient times) of Jiandi, it formed Rongdi, which should have been a large tribal group in the northern region of China. Qi was the first ruler of Shang clan. The *Book of Origins · Residences (of Rulers)* states: "Qi lives in Bo"[87] (蕃). Ding Shan doubted this Bo was a phonetic surrogate for Bo (亳) between the Yongding River and the Kou River today.[88] Zhao Tiehan believes that Qi initially lived in Qi, or Ji, in today's Beijing area.[89] The two theories are similar. *Xunzi · Chengxiang* states: "Qi Xuan King gave birth to Zhaoming, lived in Dishi, and moved to Shang." Ding Shan verified that Dishi is today's Di River Basin, and Shang is along the Zhang River. Later, King Hai moved to Yin, the land near Anyang Yin Ruins today,[90] which is also very close to Zhang. King Hai, Shangjia Wei's two generations are the most drastic period in pre-Shang history, during which two major interconnected events occurred. King Hai was killed by the Youyi *shi* when driving an ox cart to do business elsewhere. Then Shangjia Wei borrowed the master of the Hebo to kill the Lord of the Youyi *shi*, Mian Chen, to avenge King Hai. These two incidents are recorded in books such as the *Songs of Chu · Tian Wen*, the *Book of Changes*, the *Classic of Mountains and Seas · Eastern Dahuang, Current Bamboo Annals*, etc., and have been thoroughly examined by Wang Guowei, Gu Jiegang, Wu Qichang, and others.[91]

The era when the Qi lived until the Ming should be the late Longshan period. At that time, the late Hougang culture phase II Jiangou type and Xueshan culture phase II were distributed in Hebei and Beijing. The pottery was most typically represented by the rolled-rim olive-shaped jar and the rolled-rim *yan* with waist separation, which may be the early pre-Shang culture.[92] The late Hougang culture phase II Jiangou type and Xueshan culture phase II were greatly influenced by Longshan culture or Zaolütai culture, and there were also northern cultural elements such as double-handle fat-bagged-foot *li*, which exactly matched the record of Emperor Ku and Jiandi. Around the time of Erlitou culture phase II, Xiaqiyuan culture was formed in the southern Hebei region. The most important change was the emergence of many rolled-rim arc-belly *li* from central Shanxi. This may correspond to Shangjia Wei borrowing the Hebo's master,[93] indicating that Xiaqiyuan culture might be the late pre-Shang culture after Shangjia Wei.[94] In addition, as the late Xia culture, Erlitou culture once strongly influenced Xiaqiyuan culture, which was the late pre-Shang culture.

5. "Nine Provinces and Five *Fu*" and Early China

The *Book of Documents · Tribute of Yu* records in detail how Yu divided the land into nine provinces—Ji, Yan, Qing, Xu, Yang, Jing, Yu, Liang, Yong, and implemented the system of Five *Fu**—*Dian, Hou, Sui, Yao*, and *Huang*.[95] As for the formation of the "Nine Provinces" in the "Tribute of Yu," there are theories of the Western Zhou, Spring and Autumn, Warring States, and Western Han periods, with the Warring States theory advocated by Gu Jiegang having the greatest impact.[96] However, some research combined with archaeological analysis believes that the "Tribute of Yu" reflects the general situation of Yu or the Longshan era.[97] As for the Five *Fu* in the "Tribute of Yu," Gu Jiegang believes it is an ideal description of a system that was practiced during the Western Zhou period.[98] There are also views that it has a real historical background in the Xia Dynasty,[99] and Zhao Chunqing further demonstrated from archaeology that it basically matches the situation of the Longshan era.[100]

From an archaeological point of view, the relative rise of Wangwan culture phase III in the core area of the Central Plain in the late Longshan period and the establishment of the Xia Dynasty should be the historical background of the legend of Yu defining the Nine Provinces and implementing the Five *Fu*. The *Commentary of Zuo · Duke Ai Seventh Year* states: "Yu summoned various lords to a grand assembly at Tu Mountain, where, in front of the lords, he held jade and silk in his hands and offered sacrifices to the heavens." It can be seen that the hinterland of the Central Plain had a certain core status at the beginning of Xia. However, the legend of the Nine Provinces and Five *Fu* matches the situation during the Erlitou culture period more closely. The Erlitou type in the core area of Erlitou culture is exceptionally strong. Under its strong influence, the cultures of most parts of China merged and connected into four relatively cultural communities, forming a larger range of early China in the cultural sense with the Central Plain at the core. Its first level is the Zhengzhou–Luoyang core area or the Wangji area, and the second level is the Erlitou culture distribution area outside the core area or the *Dian Fu* and *Hou Fu* area. The third level is the cultures of the surrounding lower Yellow River, lower Yangtze River, upper Yangtze River, northern region, and northeastern part or the *Sui Fu* area. The fourth level is the cultures of peripheral

---

* Five *Fu* refers to the creation of five concentric circles centered around the emperor, based on distance and the degree of closeness.—Trans

South China, Northwestern Gansu–Qinghai–Ningxia region, and northeastern, northern region or the *Yao Fu* and *Huang Fu* area. In this, the distribution area of Erlitou culture, or Xia culture, is roughly equivalent to Yu Province, and the rest of the surrounding cultures roughly correspond to the provinces of Ji, Yan, Qing, Xu, Yang, Jing, Liang, and Yong. The Yueshi, or the Dongyi culture, distribution area roughly corresponds to Qing and Yan provinces, and the Doujitai culture, or the Huaiyi culture, distribution area roughly corresponds to Xu province. Perhaps the system of Nine Provinces and Five *Fu* originated in the early Xia Dynasty, formed in the late Xia Dynasty, continued to the Shang Dynasty, and matured in the Western Zhou Dynasty. As for the records in the *Book of Documents · Tribute of Yu*, there may have been content added later, even during the Warring States period, but it cannot be denied that its main core had already existed.

There is also a famous legend about casting nine *dings* during the Xia Dynasty. The *Commentary of Zuo · Duke Xuan Third Year* records: "In ancient times when the Xia Dynasty was implementing a benevolent government, various regions from afar drew pictures of all kinds of exotic things. The nine provinces contributed metals to cast nine *dings*, and the images of various things that were drawn were cast onto the tripods." *Mozi · Gengzhu* explicitly says that Xia Qi cast nine *dings*, while the *Records of the Grand Historian · Treatises of Feng Shan* says, "Yu collected gold from the nine shepherds and cast nine *dings*." From an archaeological point of view, there is some evidence that the late Wangwan culture phase III at the beginning of the Xia Dynasty could cast bronze containers. The possibility of casting *dings* cannot be ruled out. In contrast, Erlitou culture of the late Xia Dynasty clearly had bronze *dings*, indicating that the casting of nine *dings* in Xia, like the Nine Provinces and Five *Fu*, has a real historical background. More interestingly, in the legend, the nine *dings* were passed down as national treasures from the Xia to the Shang and Zhou dynasties, disappearing exactly at the end of the three dynasties. It can be seen that the nine *dings* were the most important symbols of the three dynasties of Xia, Shang, and Zhou and are unmistakable evidence of the continuous development of their cultural inheritance and political structure with the Central Plain as the core.

V. Early Shang Dynasty

The early Shang Dynasty corresponds to the period of Erligang culture.

1. Revolution of Tang and Wu and Early Shang Culture
The *Book of Changes · Ge · Tuan* says: "The revolution of Tang and Wu conforms to heaven and responds to people." In the late Xia Dynasty, the people of the Shang arose and started a series of wars to overthrow the Xia Dynasty under the leadership of Tang (also known as Dayi or Gaozu Yi in oracle bone script). *Mengzi · King Hui of Liang (Part Two)* says: "Tang launched a campaign, starting from Ge." The *Book of Songs · Eulogies of Shang · Long-Term Development* says: "The two states of Wei and Gu have been subdued, and now moving on to conquer Kunwu and Xia Jie." Finally, "... battled Jie at the field of Mingtiao, made the oath of Tang" (*Preface of the Book of Documents*), "Jie fled to Nanchao" (*Discourses of the States · Discourses of Lu [Part One]*), the Xia Dynasty fell, and the Shang Dynasty was established.

The residence of Ge, Wei, Gu, Kunwu, and Xia Jie,[101] like Zhenxun, Mingtiao, and Nanchao, have been the subject of many different theories over the years, mainly distributed in a narrow band from southern Shanxi, northern Henan, eastern Henan, western Shandong to Zhengzhou–Luoyang, roughly belonging to the distribution area of the pre-Shang culture and Xia culture.[102] From an archaeological perspective, the late pre-Shang culture expanded to the area of eastern Henan, intermingling with Yueshi culture of the Dongyi.[103] The Zhengzhou lower Nanguanwai remains contain obvious Yueshi cultural elements in addition to the Xiaqiyuan and Erlitou cultures, which may reflect that the Shang people moved into the Zhengzhou area from eastern Henan. The defeat of the Xia by the Shang would have followed a detour route through northern Henan, eastern Henan, Zhengzhou, and Yanshi. Zou Heng has argued in detail that Erligang culture is the early Shang culture. Its typical potteries such as the *li* and *yan* have a lineage relationship with the pre-Shang culture, and it differs from Erlitou culture of the Xia people, which is characterized by pottery *ding*.[104] However, Erligang culture also inherited many aspects of Erlitou culture, including bronze wares, large-mouth *zuns*, other potteries, and the palace system.

2. Early Shang's "Wangji and Sizhi" and Early China
In the *Preface of the Book of Documents*, Kong Yingda quoted Ban Gu as saying, "The people of Yin moved repeatedly, eight times before and five times after,"

indicating that there were eight and five relocations, respectively before and after the establishment of the Shang Dynasty. According to records such as the *Preface of the Book of Documents*, the *Book of Origins*, and the *Ancient Bamboo Annals*, Tang first lived in Bo, Zhong Ding moved to Ao (隞) or Ao (囂), He Dan Jia lived in Xiang, Zu Yi moved to Xing (Geng, Bi), Nan Geng moved to Yan, and Pan Geng moved to Yin, making a total of five relocations. The locations of these five relocations, apart from Yin in Anyang and Xing in Xingtai, are clear; the others have many different theories[105] but generally concentrate between eastern Henan and western Shandong to western Henan. Among them, there are several theories about the location of Bo, including Xibo in Yanshi, Beibo in Cao County, and Zhengbo in Zhengzhou. However, Sun Miao, based on the saying in the *Preface of the Book of Documents* that "Tang first lived in Bo, following the previous kings," proposes that Bo is near Puyang.[106]

The time when Tang lived in Bo to the time before Pan Geng moved to Yin is considered the early Shang period. The *Book of Songs · Eulogies of Shang · Yin Wu* says: "In ancient times, when Cheng Tang established the Yin-Shang Dynasty, the distant ethnic groups such as Di and Qiang, none dared not to come and offer tributes, none dared not to come and pay homage to the king. The King of Yin was truly the leader of the world." The *Current Bamboo Annals* also records that during the time of Da Wu, "the nine eastern Yi tribes came to visit," during the time of Zhong Ding, "he campaigned against the Lanyi" (*Ancient Bamboo Annals* also records "he campaigned against the Lanyi"), during the time of He Dan Jia "he campaigned against the Lanyi," "he attacked the Banfang," during the time of Yang Jia "he campaigned west against the Danshan Rong." This indicates that during the early Shang period, they exercised royal power over various tribes, including the Di, Qiang, and nine Yi, or carried out campaigns against them. The *Book of Documents · Announcement about Drunkenness* says: "Those who cross the outer *Fu* are marquis, *Hou, Dian, Nan, Wei*, and *Bangbo*; those who cross the inner *Fu* are Bailiao, Shuyin, Weiya, Weifu, and Zonggong." The Shang people's inner *Fu* mainly managed the Wangji, and the outer *Fu* was similar to the Five *Fu* system of the "Tribute of Yu," probably an inheritance and development of the Xia Five *Fu* system.

Currently discovered early Shang period city settlements include Zhengzhou Shangcheng, Yanshi Shangcheng, and Zhengzhou Xiaoshuangqiao settlements. The nature of these city settlements has been debated since their discovery. Xu Xusheng proposed that the Erlitou site was Tang's capital Xibo. Later others proposed, based on new discoveries, that Yanshi Shangcheng was Xibo, known as the "Xibo" theory. What is related to this is the theory proposed by An Jinhui that Zhengzhou Shangcheng was Aodu.[107] Zou Heng proposed that Zhengzhou Shangcheng was Tang's capital Bo,[108] and Yanshi Shangcheng was Tai Jia's Tong Palace,[109] known as the "Zhengbo" theory, related to this is the Xiaoshuangqiao Aodu theory.[110] Regardless, both Zhengzhou Shangcheng and Yanshi Shangcheng were established at the beginning of the Shang. Both have the possibility of being Tang's capital, and the Zheng–Luo region was indeed the Wangji during the early Shang period. Under the strong influence of the Erligang type of Erligang culture in the Wangji, following Erlitou culture, once again, an early China with four levels centered on the Central Plain was formed, only the degree of consensus was deeper, and the coverage was wider. The aforementioned Shang campaigns against the nine Yi and Di and Qiang can also correspond to the strong oppression of Erligang culture to the east against Yueshi culture and the strong influence on the west against the Zhukaigou culture, etc. After entering the late Shang, due to the pressure of the northern ethnic groups, Shang culture generally tended to retreat to the southeast, and the cultural unity was not as strong as before. Many people, because the cultural unity of late Shang China was not very strong, speculate that the cultural unity of China was weaker before, and the earlier, the weaker it was. Seemingly reasonable, but it is conjecture.

VI. Conclusion

In sum, we find that the two largely coincide in many aspects through the comparative analysis of ancient historical legends and archaeology. The distribution of groups and leading figures in the legends, their existence in different eras, and their major events generally correspond to the spatiotemporal and inherent characteristics of the archaeological cultures in the Yellow River and Yangtze River basins. Significant events in the legends, such as wars, can generally be traced to the drastic changes in archaeological cultures. From the time of the Yellow Emperor onwards, ancient legends basically revolve around Huaxia culture, which coincides with the archaeological findings that the Central Plain became the center of early China multiple times after the Miaodigou period. Following the "archaic state–regional state–empire" or "archaic state–dynastic state–empire" model of state evolution proposed by Su Bingqi, Yan Wenming, and others, the archaic state and dynastic state stages fall within the scope of early China in a cultural sense.

The archaic state stage corresponds to the late Neolithic and the Chalcolithic, specifically, the early stage of late Yangshao culture Miaodigou period, late Yangshao, and the early Longshan culture, which coincides with the Five-Emperor Period. The archaic state stage, or the Five-Emperor Period, can be divided into three periods. The early period, or the Yellow Emperor period, or the Miaodigou period, saw the rapid expansion and influence of the Miaodigou type, leading to cultural integration in most parts of Central and Eastern China with Central Plain at the core, forming early China in a cultural sense. Despite the steps taken toward civilization in Central and Eastern regions, other regions were still at a relatively simple stage, with the Central Plain being dominant, far from a situation of "all kingdoms under heaven" or "all countries under heaven." Calling it the ancient state era is more appropriate than the era of the countries. The middle period, the era of Zhuanxu and Emperor Ku, or the late Yangshao culture, saw the Central Plain relatively weak, with the east and the south flourishing and the core region in the ancient legends shifting to Eastern Henan and Western Shandong. Social complexity accelerated, and three patterns emerged in the north, the Central Plain, and the east. The Central Plain became a melting pot absorbing cultural elements from its surroundings, and cultural clashes and integration in other regions became more intense, indicating a situation of "all countries under heaven," yet in reality, it was merely an evolution based on the previous stage and still more appropriately classified as the archaic state era. The late period, or the era of Emperors Yao and Shun, or the early Longshan culture, saw the Central Plain gradually rising to a certain core position. The overall situation was still an archaic state stage with "all kingdoms under heaven."

The dynastic state stage corresponds to the Bronze Age and the early Iron Age, specifically the Xia, Shang, and Zhou dynasties. Within the scope of this study, it refers to the early dynastic state stage from the Xia to the early Shang. Due to the vigorous expansion of the Xia and Shang core areas, the pattern of early China with the Central Plain as the cultural core reemerged. Society became more complex and entered a mature stage of civilization. The Xia and Shang kingdoms in the Central Plain had a significant subordinate relationship with the surrounding regional states, gradually forming the Nine Provinces and Five *Fu* system, which continued into the late Shang and Western Zhou periods. Some call this the "composite dynasty" stage.[III]

In reality, in the process of integrating ancient history and archaeology, we still encounter some issues, namely, the issue of the attribution of the late Longshan culture. In the archaeology section of Chapter Four, we discuss the late Longshan period within the larger framework of the "archaic state stage of early China." The reason is that archaeologically, the late and early Longshan periods are closely related; apart from major changes in the Central Plain and the Jianghan area, other regions did not undergo fundamental changes. In the ancient history section of chapter 6, we place the late Longshan period and Erlitou culture, which clearly entered the dynastic state stage, in the same section. The reason is that in ancient history, the late Longshan period has already entered the early to middle Xia Dynasty. Thus, it should be placed together with the late Xia culture—Erlitou culture. In the late Longshan period, the Central Plain did have a certain core position but to a limited extent. The early to middle Xia Dynasty had a certain royal authority, but it was merely a nascent royal authority. It can be seen that the late Longshan period indeed has a transitional nature from the archaic state era to the dynastic state stage, and there is some justification for attributing it to either the archaic state or dynastic state stage from different archaeological and historical perspectives.

CHAPTER 7

The Geographical Environmental Basis of Early China

THE GUANZI · WATER AND LAND says, "Land is the origin of all things and the root of life." Humans are the product of the land or the natural environment. The spatial pattern, intrinsic characteristics, and development evolution of early China in a cultural sense all have a specific geographical environmental basis and are all restricted by the natural environment. This is not to say that the natural environment determines everything about humans. Humans have selectivity and initiative in the face of the natural environment and its changes. The development and evolution of early China are imbued with the experience and wisdom of countless Chinese ancestors adapting to nature over thousands of years.

I. The Geographical Environmental Basis of Early China

1. Relatively Independent and Vast and Diverse Geographical Environment

In the 1980s, Yan Wenming discussed the unity and diversity of China's prehistoric culture, starting from its specific geographical background. He said, "China itself is a huge geographical unit, which is in a state of relative isolation or semi-isolation from the outside world. This determines the indigeneity of the origin of China's prehistoric culture and determines that it has basically followed an independent path of development for a long time. Meanwhile, the contact with prehistoric cultures in neighboring areas can only be maintained at a lower level." "The complex and variable natural geographical conditions in different parts of

China should be an important reason for the various forms and complex lineages of prehistoric culture."[1] We may use "relatively independent, vast and diverse" to summarize his view of China's geography.

There are certainly many geographical units on the earth that are more independent than China. For example, North and South America, which have long been separated from the Eurasian continent, could only develop slowly within their cultural circles. Australia, isolated overseas, remained in the Paleolithic Age. The secret of civilization lies in the "accessibility" to other civilizations and learning from each other,[2] not self-appreciation. There are also places on earth that are more "accessible" than China, such as the Mediterranean region, where land and water routes connect Europe, Asia, and Africa. However, this is also why its civilization is easily impacted by many forces and is difficult to develop stably.

The uniqueness of China lies in its "relative independence." The independent aspect in geography is manifested in its southeast facing the ocean, the southwest being the world's rooftop Xizang Plateau, the northwest having deserts and high mountains, and the northeast adjacent to the sparsely populated East and West Siberia. This not only determined the indigeneity and unity of early Chinese culture but also ensured that it had the opportunity for long-term stable and continuous development. The "accessibility" in geography is reflected in the fact that the southeast sea route can reach the Pacific Islands, the west and north can communicate with central Asia and West Asia through oases, grasslands, and mountain passes, and the southwest can communicate with South Asia over the Himalayas. This provided conditions for early China to draw on the essence of civilizations in surrounding areas, especially West Asia, ensuring that early Chinese civilization was an important part of Eurasian civilization.

Great and enduring civilizations must have a sufficiently large geographical space. Mesopotamian and Egyptian civilizations had a high level of development, but they are significantly limited in space. The Tigris and Euphrates rivers are relatively narrow, and the world's longest river, the Nile, is merely a green corridor running through the desert. When these civilizations were invaded by nomadic pastoralists from outside, they had limited room to maneuver, and therefore they all fell in turn. China has a relatively vast geographical space, and early on formed an early Chinese cultural circle dominated by the Yellow River and Yangtze River areas. The volume and population of this cultural circle were incomparable to other early civilizations. The invasions by northern pastoralists could, at most, cause a shift in its cultural or political center but could not shake its fundamentals, and the new elements brought by the pastoralists instead provided fresh blood for its development.

The key to the persistence of civilization also lies in its diversity, rooted in the diversity of the geographical environment. The Egyptian civilization and the Indus civilization were each primarily built on the material basis of a river. Through the management and control of the Nile and the Indus, they could achieve extremely high levels of civilization and establish highly unified state power in an abbreviated period. However, their cultural connotations were monotonous and uniform, lacking many potential factors for change. When faced with severe external attacks, they had difficulty finding more choices, and the result was sadly to withdraw from the historical stage. The early Chinese geographical environment was diverse, with numerous rivers, and its agricultural development itself mainly did not rely on river irrigation.[3] It is hard to imagine that controlling a river could control the economic lifeline of the entire river basin, and it is hard to imagine that controlling a region could directly restrict the overall situation. This determined early Chinese culture's diversity,[4] development models' diversity,[5] and the possibilities of change. It determined the persistence, gradualism, and strong risk resistance of early Chinese civilization, and it also determined that the formation of early China relied more on common cultural cognition rather than political control.

2. Two Major River Basins and Two Agricultural Systems

Hunters move with animal herds; pastoralists reside, according to water and grass, migrate, expand outward, and search new resource areas, which are common in hunting and pastoral societies and an effective way for them to survive over the long term. Over time, this can potentially form an outwardly expansive societal temperament, even after settling down. Agricultural societies, however, are different. Agricultural production requires a lengthy cycle: the selection of seeds, maintenance of soil fertility, preparation of production tools and facilities, and the inheritance of production experience all require long-term stability of the dwelling place and society. Over time, this can accumulate a stable and introverted societal character. The development of early great civilizations is invariably built on the foundation of agriculture.

The natural factors that restrict agricultural development are mainly soil, water, and temperature. The development of Mesopotamian civilization, Egyptian civilization, and Indus civilization were all based on agriculture, with the

Tigris, Euphrates, Nile, and Indus rivers providing abundant water sources for the development of agricultural civilization, river sediments providing fertile soil for agriculture, and the moderate temperatures of mid-latitudes suitable for the growth of most cereal crops. The birth of these civilizations was inevitable. Compared to high and low latitudes, these civilizations are "moderate" cultures nurtured in a "moderate" environment. However, these civilizations mostly rely on one or two rivers, and the main crops are wheat, which is quite monotonous. Although these civilizations are interconnected, their geographical distances are too far apart to form a long-term, stable, close cultural circle.[6]

Early Chinese civilization was also located in mid-latitude areas. Still, the two major rivers it possessed, the Yellow River and the Yangtze River, and the vast loess region it occupied significantly differed from other early civilizations. The Yellow River and the Yangtze River basins, covering nearly three million square kilometers, have a vast regional range and an even wider range of influence. The monsoon climate in East Asia coincides with the rainy and hot season, providing good conditions for the growth of cereal plants. This forms the largest agricultural cultural community in the ancient world, which has long nourished the world's largest population. The Yellow River and the Yangtze River basins were the main bodies of the two major agricultural systems of millet grain and rice cultivation. In adjacent areas of two, grain millet and rice were cultivated. After the fifth millennium BCE, wheat farming entered, complementing each other, and forming an agricultural cultural community with a super-stable structure in the ancient world. Thus, the Yellow River and Yangtze River basins became the main body of early Chinese culture.

Early agricultural development in China also had the unique advantage of the loess base.[7] Loess mainly consists of wind-deposited loess and ancient soils formed during the Pleistocene and Holocene epochs. It is primarily distributed in the Loess Plateau and its peripheral areas, reaching the lower reaches of the Yellow River, the middle and lower reaches of the Yangtze River, and even the basins of the Heilongjiang and Liao Rivers and the regions of Southern China, essentially covering more than half of China.[8] The main part of the loess closely related to early Chinese agriculture is the Holocene loess, which mainly includes the Potou loess in the main area of the Loess Plateau[9] and the Zhouyuan loess in the southeast edge area.[10] Loess and ancient soils are primarily composed of silt, with a loose texture and abundant pores. The vertical jointing is well-developed, the soil layer is thick and uniform, and the fertility is strong. Loess, widely distributed across the Chinese land, provided a good incubator for the development of early

Chinese agricultural culture, offering people a relatively consistent production base, facilitating the formation of a relatively consistent production mode and more convenient communication channels, thus forming a relatively common cultural accumulation and value standards. This forms the foundation of the unity of early Chinese culture.

As the largest agricultural cultural community with a super-stable structure in the ancient world, the early Chinese people had an unparalleled persistence in long-term agricultural management on fixed land, inevitably tending to form a super-stable, super-large-scale society. Such a society is long-term committed to maintaining the stability of internal social order, gradually forming complex rituals and a stable, introverted character.

3. Central Plain: The Center of the World

Early China also had a cultural and geographical center—the Central Plain, also known as "China," "Central Land," or "Central China." Unlike the Mediterranean, which has many civilizations but no place that can serve as a cultural and geographical center in a dual sense. In a narrow sense, the Central Plain primarily refers to the area of Henan Province centered on Zhengzhou and Luoyang cities; in a broad sense, it extends to the vast areas of the middle and lower reaches of the Yellow River.

The Central Plain is in the core position of early China, situated in the "center of the world." Its average annual temperature, precipitation, and sensitivity to climate change are all moderate, and the Holocene Zhouyuan loess under these moderate climate conditions can be fully utilized.[11] Therefore, most regions of the Central Plain could simultaneously develop rice, millet, and wheat farming. The fluctuations in temperature and humidity due to climate change had limited impacts, ensuring that the Central Plain culture could develop relatively stable over the long term and become the center of early China culture.

II. Environmental Evolution and Cultural Changes

The environment in China is complex and diverse, and the development of regional cultures is deeply constrained by the natural environment and its evolutionary process. The most direct manifestations are in resource utilization and economic forms, further influencing the rise and fall, development, and migration of cultures, settlement patterns, and even the formation of cultural and societal models, and constraining societal development. Conversely, human development behavior can also have varying degrees of impact on the natural environment of the region. The natural environment will give feedback on its impact on humans, which can be observed from the "unnatural" environmental changes and the abnormal reflections of human culture caused by this.

1. The Evolution of China's Quaternary Period Environmental

The collision of the Indian Plate and the Eurasian Plate that began in the early Tertiary period, and the subsequent continuous uplift of the Xizang Plateau, changed the atmospheric circulation and geographical pattern in Asia. For 22 million years, it has formed the basic pattern of China's climate. It formed and strengthened the southwest and southeast monsoon, causing east and west differentiation in north China, with the east being humid and the west arid. The arid environment in central Asia provided a source of material for dust storms. At the same time, the Asian winter winds provided the power conditions for dust transportation, forming vast areas of the Gobi and desert and accumulating loess hundreds of meters thick in areas south of them. Since the Quaternary period, the amplitude of climate fluctuation has been large, with dozens of major temperature and humidity changes, the most notable features being periodicity, instability, and increased aridity. The Last Glacial Maximum from 20,000 to 14,000 years ago and the Holocene Optimum (the Great Warm Period) from 8,500 to 3,000 years ago represented the most inferior and optimal climate and ecological environment extremes in recent times. The modern climate falls between these two climate types, closer to the Holocene Optimum. During the Last Glacial Maximum, the temperature was 5°C to 8°C lower than today, the overall precipitation was less than today, the forest belt massively migrated south, and the desert area expanded. During the Holocene Optimum, the temperature was about 2°C to 3°C higher than today, and precipitation in most areas was greater. The forest belt migrated north, the desert shrank, and a thin layer of soil and grassland landscape formed on the surface of the desert in the semi-arid region east of Helan Mountain.[12]

The Holocene climate in China still experienced multiple fluctuations, showing relative instability. The Holocene Optimum or Suitable Period is a relatively stable period of warmth and humidity.[13] Some researchers have also identified several cold periods[14] or believe there exist quasi-periods of 2,000 years[15] or periods of different scales of 500, 1,000, and 1,300 years.[16] These periodic changes also have global characteristics,[17] showing that the temperature change at the millennium scale is mainly constrained by global factors, and the locality of precipitation changes is far greater than temperature changes.[18]

I once divided the northwest region of China into three regions: the Loess Plateau, the Inner Mongolia semi-arid grassland, and the northwestern inland arid region. I sorted out the geoscientific research results of these regions' Holocene environmental evolution. Overall, the Holocene northwest region has experienced three major climate evolution periods: the Early Holocene warming period, the middle Holocene suitable period, and the late Holocene cooling and drying period. Within each major period, there are also minor fluctuations with considerable consistency, with several cold periods around 8,200, 7,000, 5,000, 4,200, and 3,100 years ago and several warm periods around 4,500 and 3,800 years ago, almost occurring in all regions.[19] Fang Xiuqi and others, through the integrated reconstruction of more than 1,100 ancient temperature records, believed that the warming period of the early Holocene temperature fluctuation was 11,500 to 8,900 years ago; the mid-Holocene great warm period was 8,900 to 4,000 years ago. Starting 4,000 years ago, it has been the relatively cold late Holocene.[20]

2. China's Natural Environment and Cultural Development before Early China

The natural environment deeply constrained the development of China's Paleolithic Age culture. First, environmental changes during climate transition periods were likely the main drivers of two waves of human migration. According to Wu Wenxiang and Liu Dongsheng's research, there might have been two waves of human migration in the early Pleistocene: 1.8 million to 1.6 million years ago, as the birthplace of humans, Africa, became more arid, stimulating ancient humans to evolve into Homo erectus and begin leaving Africa, migrating to other tropical-subtropical regions in mid-to-low latitudes. The early Homo erectus and its culture in China likely appeared during this time. About one million years ago, the climate was generally colder during glacial periods and warmer during interglacial periods. Homo erectus had the conditions to start occupying temperate and arid-semiarid regions in mid-to-high latitudes, also spreading to a larger area in China.[21] Second, the formation and long-term development of China's two Paleolithic Age cultural systems were directly based on different natural environments. The tradition of large pebble tools likely existed in the warmer and more humid forest environment of the south. Pebble tools were suitable for chopping trees or digging plant roots and stems, representing the type of gathering-hunting economy; the tradition of small stone tools-microliths likely existed in the grassland zones of the north, small stone tools-microliths were more used as hunting tools and prey processing tools, representing a "specialized" hunting economy.[22] Third, different regions in China had different degrees of climate fluctuation, resulting in diverse cultural development and change. South China was in a low-latitude region with a generally warm and humid climate, limited climate fluctuations and environmental changes, and the long-term prevalence of the large pebble tool tradition, with more continuity in cultural development. At the same time, the Yellow River and Yangtze River basins and areas along the Great Wall were in mid-latitude regions with significant climate fluctuations and environmental changes, significant cultural changes, especially in the late Paleolithic Age, different industrial traditions such as small stone tools, microliths, and stone leaves appeared.

Around 18000 BCE, we entered the Last Glacial Maximum, and around 13000 to 12000 BCE, the climate shifted toward warmth and humidity, gradually entering the deglacial period.[23] This dramatic environmental change posed many challenges to human survival, stimulating late Homo sapiens to undergo significant cultural changes. At this time, stone grinding plates, grinding rods, and shovels began to appear in northern regions, indicating the possibility of concentrated collection and processing of drought-resistant Gramineae and perhaps even efforts to protect and cultivate them. In the junction between the Yangtze River Basin and Southern China, pottery and primitive rice agriculture clearly emerged, entering the early stage of the Neolithic. It is speculated that the arrival of the Last Glacial Maximum severely deteriorated the survival environment for humans in most of China, causing a crisis in the traditional hunting model in Northern China, and people began to seek a broadening of food sources, leading to the concentrated collection and use of Gramineae; and causing a crisis in the economic mode of gathering plant roots and stems in the junction between the Yangtze River Basin and Southern China, and people began to try to protect and cultivate the limited wild rice locally, collect shellfish to supplement their livelihood, and invent pottery for cooking rice and shellfish. As for most of Southern China, due to its warm and humid climate, the impact of the Last Glacial Maximum on plant resources was limited, and there was no need to develop agriculture.[24]

Around 10000 BCE, the Younger Dryas event characterized by rapid cooling occurred,[25] which must have significantly impacted the newly-born agriculture and semi-settled lifestyle, further stimulating people's desire to develop agriculture. After around 9000 BCE, we entered the Holocene, with temperature and precipitation fully rebounding, flora and fauna becoming increasingly abundant, providing new and favorable conditions for developing agricultural culture. Under this backdrop, we developed to the late stage of the early Neolithic, with agriculture, pottery, and ground stone tools coexisting, and expanding from the junction of the Yangtze River Basin and Southern China to the lower reaches of the Yangtze River, the Central Plain, the lower reaches of the Yellow River, and Northern China, forming five major cultural systems. After around 7000 BCE, the natural environment became even warmer and more humid. The culture in most parts of China generally developed into the middle stage of the Neolithic period, gradually forming a complementary dual grain agriculture system with South rice and North dryland, with the appearance of abundant pottery and sophisticated tool life, early mature woodworking craftsmanship and beam-framed architectural houses, colorful pottery, symbols, and more complex spiritual life. After the cold period in 6200 BCE, the environment further improved, entering the Holocene Optimum or Great Warm Period. Cultural exchange and integration formed four cultural systems, especially the rapid development of Peiligang culture in the Central Plain, under its strong expansion influence forming the prototype of the early Chinese cultural sphere. After the brief cold period in 5000 BCE, the climate became even warmer and more humid, and most parts of China developed into the late Neolithic. The two agricultural systems further developed. Pottery, jade, lacquerware, silk, etc., were abundant and colorful, especially the colorful pottery was brilliant, the order of settlements was well-ordered, and cultural exchanges became more frequent, forming three major cultural systems.

In addition, the time each region in China entered the Neolithic period was uneven. Generally, the south was earlier than the north, and the east was earlier than the west. Regarding the natural environment, the southeast was indeed more humid than the northwest, and the time to enter the Holocene Optimum was also earlier in the southeast than in the northwest. This shows that the natural environment has a significant impact on agricultural culture.

3. Early China: Environmental Formation in Cultural Context

Around 4200 BCE to 3500 BCE, the climate tended toward the warmest and most humid period of the Holocene. The culture in the middle reaches of the Yellow River, especially the western culture of southern Shanxi and western Henan, developed unprecedentedly, forming the distinctive Dongzhuang–Miaodigou type. This type stimulated its vigorous innovation, initiative, and pioneering spirit, possibly also leading to a population boom and rapid expansion and influence. Under its influence, the Quanhuhu type massively expanded westward to eastern

Qinghai and southern Ningxia, and the Baimuyao type expanded northward to Guyang, Shangdu, Huade, and even Sonid Right Banner and Abag Banner in the Inner Mongolia semi-arid grassland area. The modern natural environment in these areas is relatively harsh, especially in Shangdu, Huade, Sonid Right Banner, Abag Banner, and other places on the edge of the Hunshandake Sandy Land, which are now mainly areas interspersed with grasslands and sandy lands, unsuitable for developing agriculture. However, during the most suitable climate period, the annual precipitation in these places could reach 500 to 600 millimeters, and the highest annual average temperature could reach 6°C. At the same time, there were needle-broadleaf mixed forests distributed, which could fully meet the needs of grain growth.

Indeed, it was under such highly suitable climatic conditions that the two agricultural systems matured, characteristic Chinese utensils flourished, civil engineering matured, painted pottery entered its heyday, settlements and society began to differentiate, officially forming three levels of early China in the cultural sense under the influence of the Dongzhuang–Miaodigou type, and had taken steps toward a civilized society, initially forming three models of social development.

4. The Natural Environment and Cultural Development of Early China in the Ancient State Era

From around 3500 BCE, the climate began to cool, reaching a low point around 3000 BCE. This reduced natural resources in the vast areas of the North and increased survival pressures. However, the South was able to escape the problems of swamps and floods, welcoming good development opportunities. Five significant changes occurred as a result:

First, the development of agriculture in the Central Plain was limited, leading to a temporary decline in culture. The external influence of the Central Plain core area culture significantly weakened, and the influence of surrounding areas on the Central Plain culture strengthened, weakening the unity of early China in a cultural sense. However, the basic structure of early China in a cultural sense was still continuing, marking the ancient state era of early China.

Second, the seas receded, and the marshes disappeared in the middle and lower reaches of the Yangtze River and the lower reaches of the Yellow River, revealing large fertile plains. These gave birth to the splendid Liangzhu civilization, Qujialing civilization, Dawenkou civilization, and others. The rise of the Liangzhu settlements with an ancient city of three million square meters, and the appearance of the late Dawenkou culture settlements in southeast Shandong are related to the drop in sea level.

Third, the further north you go, the worse the living conditions. Places like Daihai–Huangqihai experienced a cultural "interruption" after the natural disasters shown by the Miaozigou settlement, leading to multiple chain reactions of people moving south. North Asian Proto-East Asians began to infiltrate the northern areas in small amounts. During this time, many groups of people may have moved from central and southern Inner Mongolia to the Gansu–Qinghai area, and the Majiayao type expanded significantly to the southwest and west from Gansu, with Western culture also infiltrating the Gansu–Qinghai area, forming an early "Painted Pottery Road" for East and West exchanges.

Fourth, the intense collision and blending of cultures in different regions deeply affected the originally relatively stable social structure, allowing significant adjustment and reform. War became a major issue that people face daily with fortifications and weapon improvements necessary for defense.[26] Furthermore, the emphasis on the patriarchal family, the prominence of military leaders, and the common appearance of settlement groups and central settlements were necessary changes in social structure and organization to face these challenges. Even the increasingly strong religious color shown by altars and oracle bones may have been necessary for organizing military forces or as a means of releasing pressure. Ultimately, this led to the Chalcolithic, with most parts of China entering the initial stage of civilization.[27]

Fifth, the changes led to the development of animal husbandry in the northern regions, an increase in the hunting economy, as shown by the raising of sheep and goats, and the sudden increase in bone-handle stone-blade knives and microlith arrowheads. Additionally, the appearance of cave-style architecture and stone wall buildings may also be related to the degradation of forest resources.

Around 2500 BCE, temperature and precipitation rose again, but it was no longer comparable to the warm and humid conditions around 4000 BCE. Against this backdrop, culture, after reorganization, flourished once more, entering the Longshan era or the late Chalcolithic. Even the Daihai area, with its poorer environmental conditions, welcomed another climax of cultural development from a cultural "blank," even the semi-arid grassland area of Inner Mongolia had remnants of Laohushan culture. Central Plain culture was rejuvenated, with the emergence of the nearly three million square meter Taosi ancient city, while the Liangzhu ancient city and its settlements were in decline. According to surveys, the late Liangzhu culture deposits are generally covered by a layer of light-yellow silt, indicating that a flood may have occurred here at the end of Liangzhu culture.[28] However, even without sudden disasters, the Liangzhu people had to choose to migrate as the water level gradually rose.

Around 2200 BCE to 2100 BCE, the climate deteriorated significantly. Affected by this, the cultural pattern of the late Longshan period became turbulent, with northern culture showing a significant trend of moving south, and wheat originating from the west was introduced into the Yellow River Basin. The climate-sensitive Daihai area culture experienced a "gap." The northern Laoxigushan culture moved south on a large scale again, and Taosi culture was extinguished, and the late Taosi culture was formed, corresponding to the "Ji Expels Danzhu" incident. Its chain reaction also included the large-scale replacement of Shijiahe culture by Wangwan culture phase III, corresponding to the "Yu Conquers the Sanmiao," which marked the birth of the Xia Dynasty. As the climate became drier and colder, vegetation was increasingly reduced, soil and water loss became more serious, rivers were silted up, and floods prevailed.[29] Floods were evident at many sites, including Laohushan and Lajia.[30] However, the floods naturally reduced significantly when precipitation decreased to a certain extent. This might be why Gonggong, Gun, and Yu all worked on water control, but Yu, who was the latest, ultimately succeeded in water control.

5. Environment and Cultural Development of Early China in the Dynastic State Stage

Around 2000 BCE, the climate entered a cold and dry trough, or "Little Ice Age,"[31] and a trend of large-scale movement from northwest to southeast appeared in the cultures of the Eurasian continent. This "Little Ice Age" had the greatest impact on the southern region of the Ural Mountains, prompting the formation of a pastoral economy represented by horses and horse-drawn chariots, giving rise to the Sintashta–Petrovka culture. Under the same climatic background, and with the promotion of the Sintashta–Petrovka culture, a trend toward pastoralization emerged widely in Siberia and central Asia. To pursue fertile pastures and arable land resources, these semi-agricultural and semi-nomadic groups who spoke Indo-Iranian languages expanded on a large scale to the south and southeast,[32] forming powerful shockwaves that spread various Western elements to all places along the way and played a vital role in promoting the rise of the northern Eurasian steppe pastoral economy belt. The emergence of various bronze cultures in the Xinjiang region and the Hexi Corridor, the sudden increase of Western cultural elements in Qijia culture, Zhukaigou culture, and the lower Xiajiadian culture are all related to this background. This led to the emergence of a series of cultures in a brief period in areas such as Xinjiang, the central and western parts of Qinghai, the Xilingol area of Inner Mongolia, and the Xiliao River Basin, where the culture had previously been depressed. The vast northwestern inland arid area and the semi-arid grassland area of Inner Mongolia finally welcomed the first climax of human development, and the culture in the Xiliao River Basin flourished again. This was an unprecedented major change in the cultural pattern of China since the "Neolithic Revolution" around 10,000 years ago. In the northwest region, the traditional dichotomy between the agricultural and hunting economies was changed, and animal husbandry became increasingly important. This was not only related to the eastward trend of Western culture, but more importantly, it was a product of adaptation to local environmental changes.[33]

After 1800 BCE, the climate shifted again toward warmer and wetter conditions.[34] In this context, the Erlitou bronze civilization in Central China was formed and developed rapidly, exerting a profound influence on surrounding areas and forming a four-level structure of early China culture. It marked the mature state stage represented by the late Xia Dynasty[35] or the Kingdom stage. Around 1500 BCE, the climate developed in the direction of cold and dry, but the extent was limited. Central Plain culture developed to the early Shang kingdom stage represented by Erligang culture and unprecedentedly influenced the surroundings. Meanwhile, the culture of the northwest region continued to differentiate, and the degree of pastoralism deepened further. After 1300 BCE, the climate became significantly colder and drier. Xinjiang had entered the early Iron Age, where nomadic culture dominated, and the pastoral tribes along the Great Wall moved southward forcefully, putting immense pressure on the Shang Dynasty. Shang King Wuding was hailed as a revivalist leader because of his ability to wage war, but most of his wars against the northern tribes were merely defensive. The unity of early China was once again challenged during the late Shang period.

III. Conclusion

To sum up, China's relatively independent, diverse, and predominantly two major river basins geography, centered on the Central Plain, largely determines the multi-faceted unity, stable and introspective characteristics, and continuous development process of early Chinese culture. The origin, formation, and early development of early China in the cultural sense are all closely related to changes in the natural environment. It is noteworthy that the warm and humid climate around 4000 BCE led to the vigorous development of Central Plain culture and the formation of early China, the cooling climate around 3500 BCE resulted in the comprehensive rise of initial civilizations and the cold period around 2000 BCE triggered China's "Bronze Age Revolution" and the emergence of mature civilizations. The reason is that whether the climate warms or cools, it does not become entirely suitable or deteriorate for the vast and diverse early China. Climate change did cause the prosperity or decline of early Chinese culture but only provided opportunities for cultural changes.

CHAPTER 8

Conclusion

We can now make some conclusions about early China before the late Shang period in the cultural sense.

Culturally, early China is rooted in the distant Paleolithic Age and the early to middle Neolithic. During the approximately two million years of the Chinese Paleolithic Age, features of later Proto-East Asian races such as shovel-shaped incisors were widespread, and the tradition of the gravel-lithic flake industry was consistent throughout. The difference between gravel tools in the south and small stone tools in the north persisted for a long time, showing significant continuity, unity, and diversity in human evolution and cultural development. Around 18000 BCE, the border area between South China and the Yangtze River Basin entered the earliest Neolithic; around 9000 BCE, Neolithic culture expanded to the central and eastern parts of China, forming five major cultural systems, while other areas still remained in the late Paleolithic or Mesolithic Age. The economic and cultural diversity is apparent at this time, and the tripartite unity of agriculture, pottery (pottery vessels), and ground stone tools also reflects considerable unity, let alone the possibility of a single origin of pottery cannot be ruled out.

Early China emerged culturally during the middle of the Neolithic around 6000 BCE. The middle of the Neolithic period began around 7000 BCE. Agriculture developed significantly, especially after 6200 BCE, and communication between various cultural areas became noticeably frequent, influenced by the strong expansion of Central Plain cultures such as Peiligang culture, integrating into four cultural systems, forming the fledgling early Chinese culture sphere or culturally early China. After entering the late Neolithic around 5000 BCE, it finally integrated into three major cultural systems, and the fledgling "early Chinese cultural sphere" continued to develop. In any case, the early Chinese society at that time was still in a relatively simple, equal stage. The early stage of the late Neolithic period might correspond to the era of the legendary Yan Emperor and Chiyou.

Early China was formed in a cultural sense during the Miaodigou era around 4000 BCE. In the late stage of the late Neolithic period, due to the strong outward expansion and influence of the Yangshao culture of the type Dongzhuang–Miaodigou in the Central Plain core area, from the south of Shanxi and west of Henan core area, the pattern of the three major cultural areas or systems greatly changed. The culture of most parts of China merged and connected into a cultural community with three levels, and early China in the cultural sense was officially formed. The Miaodigou era is also a time when society began to differentiate, and three modes of social development formed, heralding early Chinese civilization's origin. The Miaodigou era may correspond to the era of the legendary Yellow Emperor.

The period from about 3500 BCE to 1800 BCE is the archaic state stage of early China in the cultural sense. Around 3500 BCE, during the early period of the Chalcolithic, the influence of Central Plain culture weakened, and the regional characteristics of local cultures greatly enhanced. However, the basic pattern of early China still existed. The intensity of cultural exchanges and collisions was unprecedented, social differentiation significantly strengthened, generally began to move toward a civilized society, and basically entered the stage of an initial civilized society. Around 2500 BCE, during the late Chalcolithic or the early Longshan period, the Central Plain core area rose again, and its influence gradually strengthened, but overall it still belonged to the era of many competing leaders, with numerous ancient cities, myriad countries, and the initial civilization society further developed. This stage may correspond to the era of the legendary Zhuanxu, Zhurong, Emperor Ku, Yao, and Shun. Around 2200 BCE, during the late Longshan period, Central Plain cultures such as the Wangwan culture phase III expanded strongly toward the middle reaches of the Yangtze River, and the Central Plain culture regained its core position, which is roughly equivalent to the early to middle Xia Dynasty. The Longshan period actually has a transitional nature from the archaic state stage to the dynastic state stage and can be called the fledgling dynastic state stage.

The period from around 1800 BCE to 1300 BCE marks the dynastic state stage in the cultural sense in early China. After 1800 BCE, Erlitou and Erligang cultures strongly influenced outward from the core area of the Central Plain, resulting in a major adjustment in the cultural pattern and reintegration of culture in most parts of China into a cultural community of four levels within a larger scope. Large cities and palace systems formed during this time, and the ritual bronze vessels and ceremonial systems became more refined. The appearance of royal cities like Erlitou, which dominated the world and held an unchallenged position, marked the transition into a mature civilization and a real dynastic state stage, forming two major social development models in the east and west. This phase should correspond to the legendary Xia Dynasty and the early Shang Dynasty.

It can be seen that "China" is neither ancient and unchanging nor an "imagined community" of the Chinese people as some claim. Early China has a tumultuous, rise and fall of origin, formation, and development process. Only by understanding this process can the truth within be perceived. Rather than endlessly arguing whether China is chauvinistic, it is better to first explore how China became China.

In the origin, formation, and development of early China, distinctive features and characteristics were gradually formed that differentiated it from other civilizations in the world.[1]

First, agriculture-based, stability and introversion, and ceremonial bronzes.

For the people, food is supreme.[2] The way to obtain food can be hunting, gathering, and animal husbandry, but agriculture is undoubtedly the method with the most developmental potential. Early China was located in the moderate climate of the mid-latitude region, with the Yellow River and Yangtze River, occupying a vast loess belt suitable for cultivation. Over 10,000 years ago, it invented rice farming and millet grain farming, forming two complementary agricultural systems and a collective concept based on farming. On this basis, early China has long been committed to maintaining the stability of the social internal order, gradually forming a complex system of rites and introverted characteristics. Although early China has thousands of years of development, its main range has always been restricted to the eastern part of the Hexi Corridor in present-day China, with no large-scale external expansion. "It is not that they do not do it, but they do not want to" (*Mengzi · King Hui of Liang [Part One]*).

The system of rites is the social and moral norms rooted within the society. "The vessels serve as repositories for rituals." The system of rites eventually needs to be expressed, emphasized, and maintained in the form of ritual vessels or physical forms, and ritual vessels also have thousands of years of development and evolution. The invention of pottery on the land of China 20,000 years ago was for cooking needs. The primary function of the especially developed pottery during early China was still cooking, and cooking based on an agricultural society.

A combination of ritual vessels with a special cooking vessel poetry *ding* at the core appeared 6,000 years ago. For the next 4,000 years until the Spring and Autumn and Warring States periods, the *ding* remained the primary ritual vessel in China. Food and drink vessels, wine vessels, and musical instruments were also accompanying. At least 8,000 years ago, jade artifacts appeared in the land of China, and the multi-element jade culture added much gentleness and peace to early China. Similarly, about 6,000 years later, *yue* and other jade artifacts became important to ritual vessels. Lacquerware and silk with Chinese characteristics should also be included as ritual vessels. About 4,000 years ago, they entered the Bronze Age, and precious and durable bronze vessels quickly became the main body of the ritual vessels. Regardless, although the form of the ritual vessels and the connotation of the ceremonial system changed over time, the system of rites was handed down as one of the cultural characteristics of China until the Qin and Han dynasties.[3] The system of rites certainly has class attributes, but its characteristics of moderation and self-restraint are clearly different from Western civilization. In addition, the enclosed courtyard layout represented by the Erlitou palace city also reflects the characteristics of the system of rites.

Second, holistic thinking, secular concepts, and ancestor worship.

Early Chinese culture emphasizes holistic thinking, emphasizing a comprehensive, holistic, systematic, and organic view of things. Zhang Guangzhi stated: "One of the most notable characteristics of ancient Chinese civilization is, ideologically speaking, that it was created within the framework of a holistic cosmogony."[4] He also cited Peter T. Furst's view, describing this holistic cosmogony as a shamanistic or sorcerous cosmos.[5] This holistic cosmology may be rooted in the special experience and understanding of circles during China's Paleolithic Age, as shown in the possible divination, music, medicine, and astronomy of Peiligang culture's shamans, and characterized by octagonal patterns, *Taiji* patterns, animal-face jade *congs*, and animal-face bronze vessels after the formation of early China. Additionally, the painted pottery of early China mostly had geometric patterns, expressing certain abstract holistic concepts.

The culture of early China overall focuses on the secular world. Its primitive religious beliefs are mainly contained in daily production and life, with rare altar statues inside house buildings, few instances of idol worship, and ancestor worship should be the core of this belief system.[6] Burial in the ground was prevalent, arranging permanent underground dwellings for ancestors. Graveyards were divided and grouped, orderly, and their spatial division should be mainly based on blood relationships, reflecting respect for ancestors and the importance of social order, emphasizing clans and families. Other altars, sacrificial pits, and other sacrificial sites were only secondary.

Third, a multi-elemental cultural structure with a subject and a center.

The tradition of gravel-lithic flake industries ran through the Paleolithic Age in China, and there were different systems of southern gravel tools and northern small stone tools, showing significant characteristics of unity and diversity in cultural development. The Neolithic integrated five cultural systems into three cultural systems, where the core position of the Yellow River and Yangtze River basins, especially the Central Plain area, during the middle Neolithic period was already highlighted. The Miaodigou period formally formed early China with a three-tier structure with the Yellow River and Yangtze River basins as the main body, and the Central Plain area as the core. Early China during the Erlitou–Erligang era even developed a four-tier structure. Although there were times when the Central Plain culture in the core area was relatively weak, the basic structure was still maintained. This "multi-petaled flower" multi-elemental cultural structure continued until the late Shang and Western Zhou dynasties, and even after the Qin and Han dynasties.

The origin, formation, and development of Chinese civilization also embody the characteristics of diversity and unity. Starting from the Miaodigou period, the "Eastern Mode," "Northern Mode," and "Central Plain Mode" of civilization origin and social development gradually formed. The characteristics of the "Central Plain Mode," such as well-regulated life and death, emphasis on nobility over wealth, orderly manners, and simple adherence to moderation, actually became the core qualities of later Chinese civilization. In terms of each region, 5,500 years ago, many local civilizations such as the Liangzhu, Dawenkou, and Qujialing emerged, representing the "diverse" aspect. At the same time, early China generally showed trends such as social differentiation, prominence of family clans, and prominence of patriarchy and militarism. The real early China civilization must focus on the overall situation, which occurred after the Xia Dynasty about 4,000 years ago, representing the "unified" aspect.

The characteristic of diversity and unity with a subject and a center in early China culture is the source of the infinite vitality and continuous development of Chinese civilization.[7] And this cultural feature is closely related to China's relatively independent, vast and diverse geographical environment, and the suitable agricultural development environment of the two major river basins.

Fourth, a roller coaster-like process of culture continues development.

Early China culture, with the Central Plain culture as its core, is largely related to the rise and fall of the Central Plain culture and the merging and division process of early China. The Central Plain possesses special conditions that allow it to influence the overall situation in prosperous times and draw on the strengths of others in low times. During the peak periods of Central Plain cultural development, such as the Miaodigou period and the Erlitou–Erligang era, the unity within the Central Plain significantly strengthened, and its external influence also significantly increased, which is referred to as "merging." In the gradual preparation process or low stage, the unity of Central Plain culture was significantly weakened, and external influence significantly increased, which is referred to as "dividing." The significant role of Central Plain culture in its peak period is undoubtedly important. Still, during transitional or low periods, Central Plain culture had the opportunity to draw on the strengths of others and brew improvements, the significance of which should not be underestimated. These two stages are clearly complementary and causal. It is in this dialectical process of inhaling and exhaling, tension and relaxation, and division and merging, that Central Plain culture could develop and grow in a spiral; the range of the "early Chinese cultural sphere" grew from small to large; internal connections became increasingly close; and the sense of identity strengthened. The historically significant "early China" originated, formed, and continuously developed.[8] This trend of "long united, must divide; long divided, must unite" continues after the Shang, Zhou, Qin, and Han periods.[9]

The roller-coaster-like continuous cultural development process of early China has cultivated the collective character of Chinese people who cherish traditions exceptionally. The fundamental reason for this is related to the cyclical changes in the climate environment.

The issues of race and language in early China also need to be mentioned. After the Qin and Han dynasties, China was mainly composed of the Han nationality, speaking mainly Mandarin. The primary source of the Han ethnicity comes from the East Asian Proto-East Asian race that lived in the Yellow River and Yangtze River basins during the Shang and Zhou periods, and the main language at that time might have been Old Chinese. Before the Shang and Zhou periods, in addition to the East Asian Proto-East Asian race, early China also included South Asian, Northeast Asian, and North Asian Proto-East Asian races, which in many cases were mixed types of several Proto-East Asian subtypes. From an ancient perspective, they can be referred to as the "ancient Central Plain type," "ancient North China type," "ancient Northwest type," "ancient Northeast type," "ancient South China type," etc.,[10] and they might have spoken different dialects.[11] However, regardless, they generally belonged to the Proto-East Asian race, and the main area of the Yellow River and Yangtze River basins was mainly composed of East Asian Proto-East Asians. The main language probably did not go beyond the scope of the ancient Sino-Xizang language family, and like culture, it may have had a diverse unity with a main body. Of course, it is true that around 4,000 years ago, Europeans who possibly spoke Indo-European languages entered most of Xinjiang. Still, it is also common to show phenomena of mixed blood with the Proto-East Asian race.[12] Culturally, they also had exchanges with places like Hexi, laying the foundation for integration into the larger early Chinese cultural sphere about 3,300 years ago. The same racial type might have a greater sense of identity, but different racial types can also have genetic and cultural exchanges. The so-called "Huaxia race" or "Han nationality" is mainly based on culture rather than bloodline.

Examining the past and observing the present, we can see that early China, in cultural terms, has had a profound impact on the continuous development of China in both cultural and political senses. Its diverse unity with a subject and a center in cultural structure became the foundation for the *Ji* and *Fu* system of the Shang and Zhou dynasties, the multi-ethnic and unified political culture of China from the Qin and Han dynasties to modern times. It directly influenced the formation of the Chinese civilization model within the world civilization system, influenced the choice of the "Chinese path" after the establishment of the People's Republic of China, and influenced the establishment of the ancient "tribute system" and the independent and self-reliant foreign policy of New China. Its roller-coaster-like continuous cultural development process laid the foundation for the continuous development of China in a cultural sense and the long-term pursuit and maintenance of unity in a political sense. The characteristics or traits of early China such as agriculture-based, stability, introversion, emphasis on ritual systems, holistic thinking, and reverence for secular matters and ancestor worship have influenced the formation of important thoughts such as Confucianism and Taoism in the pre-Qin period, emphasizing concepts of benevolence, harmony, righteousness, filial piety, and ritual, as well as the unity of *Tao** and nature and the harmony between heaven and humanity. These characteristics have endured

---

* *Tao* is a fundamental concept in Chinese philosophy. It is a term that signifies "the way," "path," or "principle," and is central to both philosophical and religious Taoism. In a broader sense, it can refer to the natural order of the universe and is seen as a force that flows through all living things.—Trans.

to the present day, almost like inherited genes. We can gain more insights from early China's development path for China's future development. For example, we should uphold the principle of diverse unity in culture and embrace reform and opening up; adhere to the strategy of cultural strength and guide China's healthy development based on traditional, inclusive, and diverse cultures; uphold mutual respect, peaceful coexistence, and common development among diverse cultures internationally, and oppose expansionism, colonial systems, and cultural discrimination, and so on. At the same time, we should also be aware that early Chinese culture emphasized maintaining social order internally and was somewhat conservative in terms of cultural exchanges with the outside world. Early China culture, focused on agriculture and family, limited the development of cities, commerce, and public affairs. We should firmly inherit the excellent aspects, be critical of the flaws, and be open to learning what is lacking. Only by actively absorbing all outstanding cultures from the West and around the world based on traditional culture can our country and nation maintain enduring cultural vitality.

Postscript

THIS BOOK IS BASED ON THE results of the National Social Science Foundation of China Funded Project—Formation and Development of the Early Chinese cultural sphere, funded by the National Social Science Foundation, and the Beijing Municipal Higher Education Institution Innovation Team Construction Project also supported the research of this project.

In 1999, something happened. It was during the final year of my doctoral studies at Peking University at the School of Archaeology and Museology. I don't remember who assigned me the task. Still, I was asked to translate an article by Chinese American scholar Professor Wu Hung, a response to the strong criticisms of Professor Bagley, an American scholar of Wu Hung's book *Monumentality in Early Chinese Art and Architecture*, published in 1996. The exchange of views between Bagley and Wu Hung was eventually translated and published in the second issue of the *Journal of Chinese Scholarship* in 2000. My translation, perhaps due to my inadequate skills, was not adopted. However, this experience sparked my deep interest in the issues of early China in a cultural sense. I thought that Bagley's remarks might have been too extreme. Still, he pointed out a significant academic issue we must face: labeling many prehistoric cultures as "Chinese" is inappropriate without proper evidence. Whether it is Chinese culture or civilization, there should always be a relatively clear temporal and spatial definition.

As early as the 1980s, Mr. Yan Wenming and Mr. Zhang Guangzhi had already paid attention to and studied this issue. Mr. Yan Wenming proposed that prehistoric China had a "multi-elemental" pattern with the "multi-petaled flower" structure, which laid the foundation for unified and multi-ethnic modern China. Mr. Zhang Guangzhi suggested that an "interaction circle of China" had formed around 4000 BCE. I had read their relevant works as an undergraduate student at Peking University, but at that time, I needed to grasp their true significance fully. Of course, the research of these two scholars laid the foundation, and many details still need further exploration, especially considering the abundant archaeological data in recent years. Inspired by these two scholars and the event involving Wu Hung, I officially began my research in this field in 2000. The papers I have published since 2004 propose that the "Early Chinese cultural sphere" or culturally significant "Early China" emerged in the mid-Neolithic period around 6000 BCE and formally formed in the late Neolithic period around 4000 BCE, with a particular emphasis on the special status of Central Plain culture. By 2010, I felt the need to sort out the issues of early China comprehensively and deeply and thus applied for a research project funded by the National Social Science Foundation of China Funded Project.

My research covers the extensive period from the early Paleolithic era to the early Shang Dynasty in China, involving various aspects such as cultural lineages, settlement archaeology, environmental archaeology, ancient history, legends, and more. The workload has been quite substantial. The most demanding task was categorizing hundreds of representative sites nationwide into chronological stages and merging them into smaller and larger regional steps, ultimately forming the temporal and spatial framework of early China's culture before the late Shang Dynasty. Of course, archaeological surveys across the country were also essential. In addition, in August 2011, an academic symposium on the formation and development of culturally significant "early China" was held at the Beijing International Convention Center. The conference papers were published as *Research on Early China (Volume One)* in 2013. Despite the increasingly demanding responsibilities of teaching and service work, which occupied most of my time, I achieved preliminary results in this research project according to the plan, which is something to be proud of. I believe that if my research can draw attention from the academic community to the issues of early China, I have achieved my goal. Any mistakes and omissions are unavoidable, and I hope readers will understand.

Professor Yan Wenming, my advisor and a professor at the School of Archaeology and Museology at Peking University, has always been my academic guide. To a certain extent, my research can be seen as an interpretation of his concept of the "multi-petaled flower" structure in prehistoric China. Throughout the research process, I have received continuous guidance and encouragement from him, and he also kindly wrote the preface for this book. I express my deep gratitude to him!

I would also like to express my gratitude to Mr. Zhou Kunshu, a researcher at the Institute of Geology and Geophysics of the Chinese Academy of Sciences, Professor Zhao Hui of the School of Archaeology and Museology at Peking University, and Mr. Chen Xingcan, a researcher at the Institute of Archaeology of the Chinese Academy of Social Sciences, as well as other colleagues who attended the conference in 2011. They have shown great interest in this research and have discussed related issues. I would like to thank them! I also thank my friends in archaeology and museology, who have assisted me and my graduate students in conducting investigations and excavations.

The introduction of this book was translated by Professor Zhang Liangren from the Department of History at Nanjing University, with proofreading by Professor Wang Yudong from the School of Art and Humanities at the Guangzhou Academy of Fine Arts. Both of them are my classmates from university, with doctoral degrees from the United States. I express my gratitude for their excellent translation work!

Director Wu Changqing and editor Jia Limin from the Eighth Editing Office of Shanghai Ancient Books Publishing House provided valuable suggestions and meticulous editing for the publication of this book. I express my gratitude to them!

The leaders of Beijing Union University, where I teach, including Professor Xu Yongli, Zhang Liancheng, Zhou Zhicheng, and Zhang Baoxiu, have given great attention and support to my research. In particular, Professor Xu Yongli has emphasized the importance of this research on multiple occasions, which has deeply moved me. I thank them and other leaders, colleagues, and students who have always cared for and supported me!

November 2, 2014
At Rongyu Jiayuan

Notes

Preface

1. Yan Wenming, "The Unity and Diversity of Chinese Prehistoric Culture," *Wenwu*, no. 3 (1987), 38–50.
2. Zhang Guangzhi, "The Interaction Sphere in China and the Formation of Civilization," in *Collected Papers Celebrating Su Bingqi's Fifty-Five Years in Archaeology* (Beijing: Cultural Relics Press, 1989), 6.
    Translation of Kwang-chih Chang, *The Archaeology of Ancient China*, 4th ed., rev. and enlarged (London: Yale University Press, 1987).
3. Su Bingqi and Yin Weizhang, "On the Typological Problem of Archaeological Culture," *Wenwu*, no. 5 (1981): 10–17.
4. The fact that both Mr. Yan and Mr. Zhang were able to reach similar important conclusions from their respective research fields is both a result of the accumulation of archaeological materials to a certain stage and related to their extraordinary academic vision and research level.
    According to Yan Wenming *Footprints: Impressions of Archaeology*, Zhang Guangzhi, who commented on his speech on the morning of June 22, 1986, "completely supported" his views and mentioned, "the possibility that archaeological cultures began to form a network around 4000 BCE." See Yan Wenming, *Footprints: Impressions of Archaeology* (Beijing: Cultural Relics Press, 2011), 142–143.
5. Xia Nai, "The Origin of Chinese Civilization," in *Xia Nai Collection*, vol. 1 (Beijing: Social Sciences Academic Press, 2000), 413.
6. Wu Hung, *Monumentality in Early Chinese Art and Architecture* (California: Stanford University Press, 1995).
7. Robert Bagley, *Review of Wu Hong's Monumentality in Early Chinese Art and Architecture*, *Chinese Scholarship*, vol. 2 (Beijing: The Commercial Press, 2000), 161–229. Translation of Robert Bagley, "Reviewed Work(s): Monumentality in Early Chinese Art and Architecture by Wu Hong," *Harvard Journal of Asiatic Studies* 58, no. 1 (June 1998): 231–232.

8. Bagley Robert, "Reviewed Work(s): Monumentality in Early Chinese Art and Architecture by Wu Hong," *Harvard Journal of Asiatic Studies* 58, no. 1 (June 1998): 256.
9. Bagley states, "Increasing archaeological discoveries prove that the essence of the traditional interpretation model, that is, the centrality and cultural unity of the Shang Dynasty, does not actually exist in the archaeological materials of the Anyang (Yin Ruins) period." See Bagley Robert, "Shang Archaeology," in *Cambridge History of Ancient China: From the Origins of Civilization to 221 BCE*, ed. Michael Loewe and Edward L. Shaughnessy (Cambridge: Cambridge University Press, 1999), 124–231.
10. Wu Hung, "Response to Robert Bagley's Review of My Book Monumentality in Early Chinese Art and Architecture, *Chinese Scholarship*, vol. 2 (Beijing: The Commercial Press, 2000). Translation of Wu Hung, "A Response to Robert Bagley's Review of My Book, Monumentality in Early Chinese Art and Architecture (California: Stanford University Press, 1995)," *Archives of Asian Art* 51 (1998/1999): 92–102.
11. Li Ling, "Academic 'Kosovo'—A Discussion Around Wu Hong's New Work," in *Chinese Studies*, vol. 2 (Beijing: The Commercial Press, 2000), 202–216.
12. Li Feng, "Early China Studies and Its Archaeological Foundation—New Observations in the Age of Globalization." In *North American Sinology—Research Overview and Literature Resources*, trans. Hu Baohua (Beijing: Zhonghua Book Company, 2010), 51–69.

Chapter 1   Introduction

1. Ma Chengyuan, "Preliminary Interpretation of *He Zun* Inscription," *Wenwu*, no. 1 (1976): 64–65.
2. *Book of Zhou · Zuoluo* states: "When (Duke of Zhou) was about to govern, he built the great city of Chengzhou in the central land." This "central land" should be the "middle land" mentioned in *Rites of Zhou · Dasitu*.

   According to Zhao Yongheng's research, the summer solstice shadow length recorded in *Rites of Zhou · Dasitu* is the measurement data at the time of "Duke of Zhou's divination of Luo," with a geographical latitude of 34.32 degrees, which is very close to today's Dengfeng Gaocheng, which is the "middle land" sought by the Zhou people. See Zhao Yongheng, "*Zhoubi · Suanjing* and Yangcheng," *Journal of the History of Chinese Science and Technology*, no. 1 (2009): 107.
3. Li Dalong, "The Overlap of 'China' and 'The World': The Historical Trajectory of the Formation of Ancient Chinese Territory," *Chinese Border History and Geography Research* 17, no. 3 (2007): 1–15.
4. Ouyang Xiu once said that the Western Xia "wants to compare itself with Khitan and confront China to form a tripod stance" ("First Statement on Western Affairs," in *Wenzhong Ji [Volume 114] · Zouyi [Volume 18]*), the "China" mentioned here actually refers to the Song Dynasty, and does not include the Liao, Western Xia and other regimes, but this does not mean that the contemporary view of "the world" is only limited to the Song Dynasty mainland.
5. Chen Jibing once used the two terms "Cultural China" and "Political China" to summarize the above two meanings of China, but did not emphasize its geographical range and

pattern (Chen Jibing, "Political Concept and Cultural Concept of 'China,'" *China Economic Times* [October 17, 2005].)

The term "Cultural China" actually appeared in the late 1970s and gradually became popular after the 1980s, and its connotations are not completely consistent (Zhang Hongmin, "The Concept of 'Cultural China': A Retrospective," *Journal of Shenzhen University* [Humanities and Social Sciences] 28, no. 3 (2011): 56–59).

6. Xing Yulin, "A Review of the Study on the Theoretical Issues of Ancient Chinese Territory 1989–1998," *Chinese Border History and Geography Research* 10, no. 1 (2001): 88–101.
7. Tan Qixiang, "China in History and the Boundaries of Chinese Dynasties," *Chinese Border History and Geography Research*, no. 1 (1991): 59–64.
8. David N. Keightley, "Editorial Statement," *Early China* 1 (Fall 1975): i.
9. Han Jianye, "On the 'Division' and 'Integration' Phenomena in the Early Chinese Cultural Cycle," supplement, *Shilin* (2005): 65–71.
10. Gu Jiegang et al., ed., *Doubting Antiquity* (Shanghai: Shanghai Ancient Books Press, 1982).
11. Wang Guowei, "A Study of the Ancestors and Kings Seen in the Oracle Bones of Yin," in *Guantang Jilin*, vol. 9 (Beijing: Zhonghua Book Company, 1959): 409–436.
12. Xu Xusheng, *The Mythical Era of Ancient Chinese History*, new ed. (Beijing: Cultural Relics Press, 1985).
13. Meng Wentong, *Gushi Zhenwei* (Shanghai: Shanghai Commercial Press, 1933).
14. Li Ji, *Anyang* (Hebei: Hebei Education Press, 2000).
15. The *Book of Document · Announcement about Drunkenness*: "Beyond the outer *Fu*, the lords of varying ranks—*Hou, Dian, Nan, Wei*, and *Bangbo* should abide by the law; within the inner *Fu, Bailiao, Shuyin, Weiya, Weifu*, and *Zonggong*, as well as the common people living in the capital, should all respect the legal system and maintain order."
16. Yang Shengnan, "The Subject-Subordinate Relationship of the Princes to the Shang Royal Family Seen from the Oracle Bones," in *Oracle Bones and Yin Shang History* (Shanghai: Shanghai Ancient Books Press, 1983): 128–169.
17. *Discourses of the States · Discourses of Zhou*: "The system of the ancient kings: the area within 500 *li* [an ancient Chinese unit of length measurement. 1 *li*=500 m] of the royal domain was called "*Dian Fu*"; the area beyond 500 *li* from the royal domain up to the "*Hou Fu*" was called "*Bin Fu*"; the area beyond "*Bin Fu*" but within "*Wei Fu*" was inhabited by the barbarians and was called "*Yao Fu*"; beyond the "*Yao Fu*," the lands of the Rong and Di tribes were known as "*Huang Fu*." *Xunzi · Discussion of Justice* also has similar records.
18. Some scholars advocate that the enfeoffment system already existed in the Shang Dynasty, such as Dong Zuobin, "Five Ranks in Yin Shang," in *Collection of the Institute of History and Philology, Academia Sinica* 6, no. 3 (1936): 413–429; Hu Houxuan, "Discussion on the Feudal System of the Yin Dynasty," in *Oracle Bone Study and History of Yin Dynasty* (Chengdu: Institute of Guoxue Research, Qilu University, Chengdu, 1944), 2–21; Li Xueshan, *Study on the Feudal System of the Shang Dynasty* (Beijing: China Social Sciences Press, 2004).

Some scholars believe that it only existed in the Western Zhou Dynasty, such as Huang Zhongye, "Questioning the 'Feudal' Theory of the Shang Dynasty," *Academic Monthly*, no. 5 (1986): 76–79.

19. Xu Hong, *The Earliest China* (Beijing: Science Press, 2009).
20. Ai Lan, "Erlitou and the Formation of Chinese Civilization: A New Way of Thinking," in *Multidimensional Perspective—The Shang Dynasty and the Study of Early Chinese Civilization* (Beijing: Science Press, 2009), 27.
21. Su Bingqi, *New Exploration of the Origins of Chinese Civilization* (Beijing: SDX Joint Publishing Company, 1999), 161–162.
22. Yan Wenming, "Reconstructing the History of Early China," in *Early China—The Origin of Chinese Civilization* (Beijing: Cultural Relics Press, 2009), 15–23.
23. Zhao Hui, "The Formation of the Historical Trend Centered on the Central Plain," *Wenwu*, no. 1 (2000): 41–47.
24. Zhao Hui, "The Prehistoric Foundation of China—Re-discussing the Historical Trend Centered on the Central Plain," *Wenwu*, no. 8 (2006): 50–54.
25. Han Jianye, "On the Historical Position of the Neolithic Central Plain Culture," *Jianghan Archaeology*, no. 1 (2004): 59–64.
26. Han Jianye, "On the 'Division' and 'Combination' Phenomenon of Early Chinese Culture," supplement, *Shilin* (2005): 65–71.
27. Han Jianye, "The Migration Influence of Peiligang Culture and the Embryo of the Early Chinese Culture Circle," *Cultural Relics of Central China*, no. 2 (2009): 11–15.
28. Song Xinchao, *A Regional Study of Yin Shang Culture* (Xi'an: Shaanxi People's Press, 1991).
29. Ge Zhaoguang, *Dwelling in China: Reconstructing the Historical Discourse on "China"* (Beijing: Zhonghua Book Company, 2011), 3–33.

CHAPTER 2   CHINA BEFORE EARLY CHINA

1. Wu Rukang, Wu Xinzhi, and Zhang Senshui, *Chinese Ancient Humans* (Beijing: Science Press, 1989). Alternatively, some scholars argue that the early and middle phases of the Chinese Paleolithic show greater similarities and are significantly different from the late phase. Therefore, they can be combined into two major phases. See Gao Xing, "A Study on the 'Middle Palaeolithic' in China," *Acta Anthropologica Sinica* 18, no. 1 (1999): 1–16.
2. Dai Erjian, "The Paleolithic of Guo Wangling and Its Vicinity in Lantian, Shaanxi," *Vertebrate Paleontology and Paleoanthropology* 10, no. 1 (1966): 30–32; Dai Erjian and Xu Chunhua. "New Materials of Lantian Paleolithic and Lantian Ape-Man Culture," *Acta Archaeologica Sinica*, no. 2 (1973): 1–12.
3. Wang Youping, *The Origins of Ancient Human Culture in China* (Beijing: Cultural Relics Press, 2005), 19.
4. Wu Rukang and Wu Xinzhi, eds., *Chinese Ancient Human Sites* (Shanghai: Shanghai Science and Technology Education Publishing House, 1999).
5. Wu Liu et al., "Human remains from Zhirendong, South China, and modern human emergence in East Asia," *PNAS* 107, no. 45 (2010): 19201–19206.
6. Gao Xing, "Who Are the Direct Ancestors of the Chinese People?" *Chinese Cultural Relics News*, 5th ed. (January 21, 2011).
7. Wu Xinzhi, "The Origin of Modern Humans in China: Insights from Cranio to Dental Features of Late Pleistocene Homo sapiens," *Journal of Anthropology* 17, no. 4 (1998): 276–282.

8. J. G. D. Clark, *World Prehistory: A new outline*, 2nd ed. (Cambridge: Cambridge University Press, 1968), 24–47.
9. Wang Youping, *The Origins of Ancient Human Culture in China* (Beijing: Cultural Relics Press, 2005), 33–34, 305.
10. Wang Youping, *The Origins of Ancient Human Culture in China* (Beijing: Cultural Relics Press, 2005), 51, 306–307.
11. Tang Huisheng, "Archaeological Culture and Economic Formations from the Late Paleolithic to the Early Neolithic Period in the Xizang Plateau," *Archaeology*, no. 4 (2011): 443–466.
12. Li Yongxian, "A Brief Discussion on the Microlithic Remains in Xizang," *Xizang Studies*, no. 1 (1992): 126–132; Yuan Baoyin, Huang Weiwen, and Zhang Dian, "New Evidence of Late Pleistocene Human Activities in Northern Xizang." *Chinese Science Bulletin* 52, no. 13 (2007): 1567–1571.
13. Fang Yingsan, Wang Fubao, and Tang Huisheng, "New Materials on Lithic Flake Stone Tools in Xizang," in *Proceedings of the 9th Annual Conference of Chinese Vertebrate Paleontology* (Beijing: Marine Publishing House, 2004), 211–222.
14. Represented by the Luotuoshi site in Hoboksar Mongol Autonomous County. See Gao Xing and Pei Shuwen, "Paleolithic Sites in Xinjiang," in *Archaeology in China · 2005* (Beijing: Cultural Relics Press, 2006), 376–377.
15. Zhang Senshui, *Chinese Paleolithic Culture* (Tianjin: Tianjin Science and Technology Press, 1987).
16. Wang Youping, *The Origins of Ancient Chinese Human Culture* (Beijing: Cultural Relics Press, 2005), 313–316.
17. Gao Xing et al., "Ancient Human Fossils and Ivory Engravings from Xinglong Cave in the Three Gorges Dating from 120,000 to 150,000 Years Ago," in *Collection of Papers on the Paleolithic Age: Celebrating the 80th Anniversary of the Discovery of the Shuidonggou Site* (Beijing: Cultural Relics Press, 2005), 202–213.
18. Wu Rukang, *Ancient Anthropology* (Beijing: Cultural Relics Press, 1989); Yan Wenming, "Unity and Diversity of Prehistoric Chinese Culture," *Wenwu*, no. 3 (1987): 38–50.
19. Su Bingqi, "Reflections on Reconstructing the Prehistoric History of China," in *Chinese · Descendants of the Dragon · Chinese People: Archaeological Quests for Roots* (Shenyang: Liaoning University Press, 1994), 114–123.
20. China also has handaxes, and there may be a connection with handaxes in the western Eurasian continent. However, there are significant differences, and they mainly belong to the gravel culture tradition. See Gao Xing, "Characteristics and Significance of Handaxes in the Chinese Paleolithic Age," *Acta Anthropologica Sinica* 32, no. 2 (2012): 97–112.
21. At the Malta site near Lake Baikal in East Siberia, female figurines dating back over 20,000 years have been discovered, indicating the existence of "Venus" in the eastern part of Eurasia and its close connection with the west. However, their numbers are limited, and no discoveries have been made in the Paleolithic sites within present-day China.
22. Zhang Guangzhi proposed the concept of the "Maya-Chinese cultural continuum," speculating that "when most Native Americans, about 20,000 to 30,000 years ago, mi-

grated from Asia to the Americas via the Bering Strait, the cultural content they brought from Asia to the Americas might be unexpectedly rich. This is the extension of the Maya-Chinese cultural continuum to the New World," primarily involving witchcraft and shamanic culture. See Zhang Guangzhi, *Lectures on Archaeology* (Beijing: Cultural Relics Press, 1986), 20–22.

23. V. Gordon Childe, *A History of Ancient Culture*, chapter 5 (Beijing: Zhonghua Book Company, 1958), 60–96.

24. Jiangxi Provincial Cultural Relics Management Committee, "Excavation at Daxianren Cave Site in Wannian, Jiangxi," *Archaeology*, no. 1 (1963): 1–16; Jiangxi Provincial Museum, "Second Excavation Report of Daxianren Cave Site in Wannian, Jiangxi," *Wenwu*, no. 12 (1976): 23–35; School of Archaeology and Museology, Peking University, and Jiangxi Provincial Institute of Cultural Relics and Archaeology, *Daxianren Cave and Diaotonghuan* (Beijing: Cultural Relics Press, 2014).

25. Institute of Archaeology, Chinese Academy of Social Sciences et al., *Zengpiyan in Guilin* (Beijing: Cultural Relics Press, 2003).

26. Yuan Jiarong, *Hunan Paleolithic Culture and the Yuchanyan Site* (Changsha: Hunan Yuelu Publishing House Co., Ltd., 2013), 181–299.

27. Yang Hu and Liu Guoxiang, "Discussion on Residential Burial Customs of the Xinglongwa Culture and Related Issues," *Archaeology*, no. 1 (1997): 29.

28. Han Jianye, "Combing the Lineage of the Ancient Chinese Flexed Burial," *Wenwu*, no. 1 (2006): 53–60.

29. Zhang Chi, "Early Pottery in Southern China," *Ancient Civilization*, vol. 5 (Beijing: Cultural Relics Press, 2006), 1–16.

30. The age of the Yuchanyan deposits is concentrated between 18,500 and 17,500 years ago. See Wu Xiaohong, "The Age of Early Pottery in Southern China and the Problem of Neolithic Markers," in *Archaeological Research Collected Paper of Celebrating the 80th Birthday of Mr. Yan Wenming*, vol. 9 (Beijing: Cultural Relics Press, 2012), 49–68.

The earliest pottery in Xianren Cave is believed to date back to 20,000 to 19,000 years ago. See Wu Xiaohong et al., "Early Pottery at 20,000 Years Ago in Xianren Cave, China," *Science* 336 (2012), no. 6089: 1696–1700.

31. Zhao Zhijun, "The Middle Yangtze Region in China Is One Place Where Rice Was Domesticated: Phytolith Evidence from the Diaotonghuan Cave, Northern Jiangxi," *Antiquity* 278 (1998): 885–897.

32. Li Youheng and Han Defen, "Animal Assemblage from Zengpiyan Site in Guilin, Guangxi," *Vertebrate Paleontology and Paleoanthropology* 16, no. 4 (1978): 244–254.

33. During the Zengpiyan phase I, starch granules from yam plants were found on the surfaces of some lithic flaked stone tools.

Lü Liedan, "Preliminary Analysis of Residues on Stone Tools from Zengpiyan Site," in *Guilin Zengpiyan* (Beijing: Cultural Relics Press, 2003), 646–651.

34. K. V. Flannery, "Origins and Ecological Effects of Early Domestication in Iran and the Near East," in *Domestication and Exploitation of Plants and Animals*, ed. Peter J. Ucko and G. W. Dimbleby (Chicago: Aldine Publishing Co., 1969), 73–100.

35. Han Jianye, "A Study on the Cultural Affinities of Early and Middle Neolithic Periods in China," in *Archaeological Research* (Beijing: Cultural Relics Press, 2012): 24–36.
36. Archaeological Team of Guangxi Workgroup, Chinese Academy of Social Sciences, "Excavation of Dingsishan Site in Yingning County, Guangxi," *Archaeology*, no. 11 (1998): 11–33.
37. Fujian Museum, "Brief Report on the Excavation of Qihe Cave Prehistoric Site in Zhangping City, Fujian," *Archaeology*, no. 5 (2013): 7–19.
38. Zhejiang Provincial Institute of Cultural Relics and Archaeology and Pujiang Museum, "Brief Report on the Excavation of Shangshan Site in Pujiang County, Zhejiang," *Archaeology*, no. 9 (2007): 7–18; Jiang Leping, "Discovery and Consideration of Neolithic Sites in the Puyang River Basin," *Journal of Zhejiang Provincial Institute of Cultural Relics and Archaeology* 8 (2006): 439–461.
39. Zhang Heng, Wang Haiming, and Yang Wei, "Discovery of Early Neolithic Deposits at Xiaohuangshan Site in Shengzhou, Zhejiang," *Chinese Cultural Relics News*, 1st ed. (September 30, 2005).
40. Jiang Leping et al., "New Discovery of Longyou Hehuashan Site in the Upper Reaches of the Qiantang River," *Chinese Cultural Relics News*, 5th ed. (October 25, 2013).
41. Zheng Yunfei and Jiang Leping, "Discovery and Significance of Ancient Rice Remains from the Shangshan Site," *Archaeology*, no. 9 (2007): 19–25.
42. School of Archaeology and Museology, Peking University and Zhengzhou Institute of Cultural Relics and Archaeology, "Brief Report on the Excavation of Lijiagou Site in Xinmi City, Henan," *Archaeology*, no. 4 (2011): 3–9; Zhengzhou Institute of Cultural Relics and Archaeology, Center for Chinese Archaeology and Peking University, "Report on the 2009 Excavation of the Northern Area of Lijiagou Site in Xinmi, Henan," *Ancient Civilizations* 9 (2013): 177–207; Center for Chinese Archaeology, Peking University, Zhengzhou Institute of Cultural Relics and Archaeology, "Report on the 2009 Excavation of the Southern Area of Lijiagou Site in Xinmi, Henan," *Ancient Civilizations* 9 (2013): 208–239.
43. Sun Bo, "Introduction to the Bianbian Cave," *Cultural Relics Research* 16 (2009): 51–60.
44. Baoding District Cultural Relics Management Office et al., "Brief Report on the Trial Excavation of Nanzhuangtou Site in Xushui County, Hebei," *Archaeology*, no. 11 (1992): 961–970; Guo Ruihai and Li Jun, "Examining the Origin of Agriculture and Pottery in the North China Region Based on the Nanzhuangtou Site," in *Origin of Rice, Pottery, and Urbanization* (Beijing: Cultural Relics Press, 2000), 51–64.
45. Li Jun and Wang Youping, "Late Paleolithic Sites at Yujiagou, Yangyuan," in *Annual Archaeology (1996)* (Beijing: Cultural Relics Press), 96.
46. Zhou Guoxing and You Yuzhu, "Neolithic Tombs in Beijing's Donghulin Village," *Archaeology*, no. 6 (1972): 12–15; School of Archaeology and Museology, Peking University, Center for Chinese Archaeology, Peking University, Beijing Municipal Institute of Cultural Relics, "Prehistoric Sites in Donghulin, Mentougou District, Beijing," *Archaeology*, no. 7 (2006): 3–8.
47. Yu Jincheng et al., "Discovery of Early Neolithic Sites in Beijing's Transitional Years," *Beijing Cultural Relics*, no. 3 (1998): 36; Li Chaorong, "New Discoveries in Paleolithic Archaeology in the Beijing Area," in *A Century Review of Chinese Archaeological Research (Paleolithic Archaeology Volume)* (Beijing: Science Press, 2004), 77–79.

48. Border Archaeological Research Center, Jilin University and Jilin Provincial Institute of Cultural Relics and Archaeology, "Neolithic Remains at Shuangta Site, Baicheng, Jilin," *Acta Archaeologica Sinica*, no. 4 (2013): 501–533.
49. "Women ... at the age of fifteen, have their hairpins inserted." (*Book of Rites · Neize*).
50. Zhao Zhijun, "The Formation Process of Ancient Chinese Agriculture: Evidence from Flotation-recovered Plant Remains," *Quaternary Sciences* 34, no. 1 (2014): 73–84.
51. Qin Ling, "Plant Archaeological Research on the Origin of Chinese Agriculture: Current State and Future Perspectives," in *Archaeological Research Collected Paper of Celebrating the 80th Birthday of Mr. Yan Wenming*, vol. 9 (Beijing: Cultural Relics Press, 2012), 291–294.
52. Qian Yaopeng, "A Brief Discussion on the Origin and Basic Types of Ground Stone Tools," *Archaeology* 12 (2004): 66–75.
53. Zhang Chi, "Early Pottery in Southern China," in *Ancient Civilizations*, vol. 5 (Beijing: Cultural Relics Press, 2006), 16.
54. Institute of Archaeology, Chinese Academy of Social Sciences and Shaanxi Provincial Institute of Archaeology, "Longwangchan Paleolithic Site in Yichuan County, Shaanxi," *Archaeology* 7 (2007): 3–8.
55. Cultural Bureau of Linfen Administrative Office, Shanxi Province, "Shizitan Middle Paleolithic Cultural Site in Ji County, Shanxi," *Acta Archaeologica Sinica* 3 (1989): 305–324; "Shizitan Paleolithic Site Cluster in Ji County, Shanxi," in *2003 Important Archaeological Discoveries in China* (Beijing: Cultural Relics Press, 2004), 5–9; Shizitan Archaeological Team, "Excavation Report of Site S12G at Shizitan in Ji County, Shanxi," *Archaeology and Cultural Relics* 3 (2013): 3–8.
56. Wang Jian, Wang Xiangqian, and Chen Zheyin, *Acta Archaeologica Sinica* 3 (1978): 259–288.
57. Gao Xing, Zhou Zhenyu, and Guan Ying, "Late Pleistocene Human Remains and Subsistence Patterns in the Marginal Region of the Xizang Plateau," *Quaternary Sciences* 28, no. 6 (2008): 969–977; Yi Mingjie et al., "Investigation and Excavation Report of Prehistoric Sites in the Marginal Region of the Xizang Plateau in 2009," *Acta Anthropologica Sinica* 30, no. 2 (2011): 124–136.
58. Liu Li et al., "Plant Exploitation of the Last Foragers at Shizitan in the Middle Yellow River Valley China: Evidence from Grinding Stones," *Journal of Archaeological Science* 38, no. 12 (2011): 3524–3532.
59. An Zhimin and Wu Ruzuo, "The Stone Age Remains in the Daliushayuan Area of Chaoyi, Shaanxi," *Acta Archaeologica Sinica* 3 (1957), 1–12.
60. Graham Clarke, *Mesolithic Prelude: The Paleolithic–Neolithic Transition in Old World Prehistory* (Edinburgh: Edinburgh University Press, 1980).
61. There is considerable debate regarding the existence of "Mesolithic" in China. Classifying Late Pleistocene assemblages with abundant microliths as belonging to the Mesolithic is inappropriate. However, this should not negate the possibility of the existence of Mesolithic culture in China during the Holocene (Huang Qixu, "A Discussion on the Concept of 'Mesolithic,'" *Prehistoric Research* 3 [1987]: 14–20; Chen Xingcan, "Several Issues Concerning the Mesolithic," *Archaeology* 2 [1990]: 135–142).
62. Bruce D. Smith, "Low-level Food Production," *Journal of Archaeological Research* 9, no. 1 (2001):1–43.

63. Henan Provincial Institute of Cultural Relics and Archaeology, *Wuyang Jiahu* (Beijing: Science Press, 1999), 465–519.
64. Jiqing Highway Cultural Relics and Archaeology Team, "Preliminary and Second Excavation Report of Houli Site in Linzi, Shandong," *Archaeology* 11 (1992): 987–996; Jiqing Highway Cultural Relics Work Team, "Third and Fourth Excavation Report of Houli Site in Linzi, Shandong," *Archaeology* 2 (1994): 97–112.
65. Shandong Provincial Institute of Cultural Relics and Archaeology and Zhanqiu City Museum, "Investigation and Excavation Report of Xiaojingshan Site in Zhanqiu City, Shandong," *Huaxia Archaeology* 2 (1996): 1–28.
66. For example, such as the urn burials at Jiahu site. See Henan Provincial Institute of Cultural Relics and Archaeology, *Wuyang Jiahu* (Beijing: Science Press, 1999), 198–199.
67. Qin Ling, "Archaeobotanical Research and Prospect on the Origin of Agriculture in China," in *Archaeological Research Collected Paper of Celebrating the 80th Birthday of Mr. Yan Wenming*, vol. 9 (Beijing: Cultural Relics Press, 2012), 264–266.
68. The early horn-handle jars at Jiahu show similarities to the earlier straight-bellied cauldrons in Zengpiyan and Yuchanyan. In fact, the early Jiahu also had pottery vessels that is cauldron with rounded bottoms. From this, it can be inferred that the straight-bellied jars of the Lijiagou culture may have a connection with the early stage of the early Neolithic in South China.
69. Gary W. Crawford, Chen Xuexiang, and Wang Jianhua, "Discovery of Carbonized Rice from the Houli Period at Yuezhuang Site, Changqing District, Jinan, Shandong," *Eastern Archaeology*, vol. 3 (Beijing: Science Press, 2006), 247–251.
70. Hunan Provincial Institute of Cultural Relics and Archaeology, *Pengtoushan and Bashidang* (Beijing: Science Press, 2006).
71. Han Jianye, "An Overview of Ancient Chinese Flexed Burials," *Wenwu*, no. 1 (2006): 53–60.
72. The early remains discovered in 2007 at Huadang in Lili County and Songjiagang in Li County, Hunan Province, with an absolute dating of before 7000 BCE. They had crude brown pottery with marked-cords decorations, which may belong to the "South China cord-mark round-bottom cauldron cultural system" or serve as a direct predecessor of Pengtoushan culture.

    See Guo Weimin, *Cultures and Societies in the Liyang Plain and the Handong Region during the Neolithic* (Beijing: Beijing: Cultural Relics Press, 2010), 44.
73. Kaifeng Cultural Management Committee and Xinzheng County Cultural Management Committee, "Xinzheng Peiligang Neolithic Site," *Archaeology*, no. 2 (1978): 73–79; Institute of Archaeology, Chinese Academy of Social Sciences, Henan Team 1, "Excavation Report of the Peiligang Site in 1979," *Acta Archaeologica Sinica*, no. 1 (1984): 23–52.
74. Institute of Archaeology, Chinese Academy of Social Sciences, *Baijiacun in Lintong* (Chengdu: Bashu Press, 1994); Gansu Provincial Institute of Cultural Relics and Archaeology, *Dadiwan in Qin'an: Excavation Report of the Neolithic Site* (Beijing: Cultural Relics Press, 2006).
75. Zhang Yonghui et al., "Identification and Analysis of Starch Grains on the Surface of Grinding Stones from the Peiligang Site," *Quaternary Sciences* 31, no. 5 (2011): 891–899; Liuli

et al., "What Did Grinding Stones Grind? New Light on Early Neolithic Subsistence Economy in the Middle Yellow River Valley, China," *Antiquity* 84 (2010): 816–833.

76. For example, the urn burial of Baijia culture at the Ruanjiaba Site in Hanyin, Shaanxi. See Shaanxi Provincial Institute of Archaeology et al., *Collection of Archaeological Reports in Southern Shaanxi* (Xi'an: Sanqin Press, 1994), 211–212.

77. Liu Changjiang, Kong Zhaochen, and Lang Shude, "Discussion on Agricultural Plant Remains and Human Survival Environment at Dadiwan Site," *Cultural Relics of Central China*, no. 4 (2004): 26–30.

78. Han Jianye, "Migration Influence of Peiligang culture and the Prototype of Chinese Cultural Sphere in Early China," *Cultural Relics of Central China*, no. 2 (2009): 11–15.

79. Hubei Provincial Institute of Cultural Relics and Archaeology, *Chengbeixi in Yidu* (Beijing: Cultural Relics Press, 2001).

80. Institute of Archaeology, Chinese Academy of Social Sciences, Anhui Team, "Excavation Briefing of Xiaoshankou and Gutaisi Sites in Su County, Anhui," *Archaeology*, no. 12 (1993): 1062–1075.

81. Nanjing Museum Institute of Archaeology et al., "Shunshanji Neolithic Site in Sihong County, Jiangsu," *Archaeology*, no. 7 (2013): 3–14.

82. Luan Fengshi, "A Preliminary Study on the Later Li Culture," *Archaeological Research in Haidai Region* (Jinan: Shandong University Press, 1997), 1–26.

83. Institute of Archaeology, Chinese Academy of Social Sciences, Guangxi Team et al., "Excavation of the Leopard-Head Shell Mound Site in Nanning City, Guangxi," *Archaeology*, no. 10 (2003): 22–34.

84. Zhejiang Provincial Institute of Cultural Relics and Archaeology and Xiaoshan Museum, *Kuahuqiao* (Beijing: Cultural Relics Press, 2004).

85. Han Jianye, "On the Origin and External Influence of Kuahuqiao Culture—A Discussion on Cultural Exchange in the Middle and Lower Reaches of the Yangtze River during the Middle Neolithic Period," *Southeast Culture*, no. 6 (2010): 62–66.

86. Hebei Provincial Administration of Cultural Relics and Handan Cultural Relics Storage Institute, "Cishan Site in Wu'an, Hebei," *Acta Archaeologica Sinica*, no. 3 (1981): 303–339.

87. Hebei Provincial Institute of Cultural Relics Research, *Beifu: Prehistoric Sites in the Yishui River Basin* (Beijing: Cultural Relics Press, 2007).

88. Institute of Archaeology, Chinese Academy of Social Sciences, Inner Mongolia Team, "Excavation Briefing of the Xinglongwa Site in Aohan Banner, Inner Mongolia," *Archaeology*, no. 10 (1985): 865–874; Institute of Archaeology, Chinese Academy of Social Sciences, Inner Mongolia Team, "Excavation Briefing of the Xinglongwa Settlement Site in Aohan Banner, Inner Mongolia in 1992," *Archaeology*, no. 1 (1997): 1–26.

89. Inner Mongolia Autonomous Region Institute of Cultural Relics and Archaeology, *Baiyinchanghan: Excavation Report of a Neolithic Site* (Beijing: Science Press, 2004).

90. Liaoning Provincial Institute of Cultural Relics and Archaeology, "Excavation of the Chahai Site in Fuxin County, Liaoning, 1987–1990," *Wenwu*, no. 11 (1994): 4–19.

91. Institute of Archaeology, Chinese Academy of Social Sciences et al., *Hake Site: Archaeological Excavation Report, 2003–2008* (Beijing: Cultural Relics Press, 2010).

92. Qin Mountains, "Archaeobotanical Research and Prospects on the Origins of Agriculture in China," in *Archaeological Research Collected Paper of Celebrating the 80th Birthday of Mr. Yan Wenming*, vol. 9 (Beijing: Cultural Relics Press, 2012), 297–298.
93. Zhijun Zhao, "New Archaeobotanic Data for the Study of the Origins of Agriculture in China," *Current Anthropology* 52, no. S4 (October 2011): S295–S306.
94. Dawei Tao et al., "Starch Grain Analysis for Groundstone Tools from the Neolithic Baiyinchanghan Site: Implications for Their Function in Northeast China," *Journal of Archaeological Science* 38, no. 12 (2011): 3577–3583.
95. Represented by the Xiaohexi site in Aohan, Inner Mongolia, and phase I site of Baiyinchanghan in Linxi, it is referred to as the "Xiaohexi culture" by some.
96. Gongyi Cultural Relics Management Office, "Excavation Brief Report of the Wayaozui Neolithic Site in Gongyi City, Henan Province," *Archaeology*, no. 7 (1996): 12–16; Zhengzhou Cultural Relics Work Team and Gongyi Cultural Relics Management Office, "Excavation of the Wayaozui Neolithic Site in Gongyi City, Henan Province," *Archaeology*, no. 11 (1999): 13–20.
97. Henan Provincial Bureau of Cultural Relics, *Archaeological Report of the Yellow River Xiaolangdi Reservoir*, vol. 2 (Zhengzhou: Zhongzhou Ancient Books Publishing House, 2006), 157–211.
98. Institute of Archaeology, Chinese Academy of Social Sciences, *Shizhaocun and Xishanping* (Beijing: Encyclopedia of China Publishing House, 1999).
99. Anhui Provincial Institute of Cultural Relics and Archaeology and Bengbu Museum, *Bengbu Shuangdun: Excavation Report of the Neolithic Site* (Beijing: Science Press, 2008).
100. Jining City Cultural Relics and Archaeology Research Office, "Excavation of the Zhangshan Site in Jining City, Shandong Province," *Archaeology*, no. 4 (1996): 1–7.
101. Han Jianye, "The Northward Expansion of the Shuangdun Culture and the Formation of Beixin culture: Starting from the 'Beixin Culture Remains' in Zhangshan, Jining, Shandong Province," *Jianghan Archaeology*, no. 2 (2012): 46–50.
102. Hunan Provincial Museum, "Lower-Level Neolithic Remains in Zaoshi, Shimen County, Hunan Province," *Archaeology*, no. 1 (1986): 1–11.
103. Hunan Provincial Institute of Cultural Relics and Archaeology, "Hujiawuchang Neolithic Site in Linyin County, Hunan Province," *Acta Archaeologica Sinica*, no. 2 (1993): 171–206.
104. Hunan Provincial Institute of Cultural Relics and Archaeology, "Excavation Brief Report of the Gaomiao Site in Hunan Province," *Wenwu*, no. 4 (2000): 4–23; Hunan Provincial Institute of Cultural Relics and Archaeology, "Gaomiao Neolithic Site in Hongjiang City, Hunan Province," *Archaeology*, no. 7 (2006): 9–15.
105. Hubei Provincial Institute of Cultural Relics and Archaeology, *Yidu Chengbeixi* (Beijing: Cultural Relics Press, 2001).
106. The Badong area belongs to the transitional zone between the upper and middle reaches of the Yangtze River. Its cultural system is similar to that of the middle reaches of the Yangtze River, so it is still classified as part of the middle reaches of the Yangtze River cultural area. See the Office of the State Council Three Gorges Project Construction Committee and National Cultural Relics Administration, *Badong Nanmu Garden* (Beijing: Science Press, 2006).

107. Yin Jianshun, "An Analysis of the Periodization and Cultural Attributes of the Zaoshi Lower-Level Culture in Dongting Lake Area, Hunan," in *Prehistoric Culture in the Middle Reaches of the Yangtze River and Proceedings of the Second Asian Civilization Symposium* (Changsha: Hunan Yuelu Publishing House Co., Ltd., 1996), 105–125; He Jiejun, *Neolithic Cultures in the Middle Reaches of the Yangtze River* (Wuhan: Hubei Education Press, 2004).
108. Institute of Archaeology, Chinese Academy of Social Sciences, *Aohan Zhaobaogou: Neolithic Settlement* (Beijing: Encyclopedia of China Publishing House, 1997).
109. Shenyang Cultural Relics Management Office and Shenyang Imperial Palace Museum, "Second Excavation Report of the Xinle Site in Shenyang," *Acta Archaeologica Sinica*, no. 2 (1985): 209–222; Xinle Site Museum and Shenyang Cultural Relics Management Office, "Rescue and Clearance Excavation Brief Report of the Xinle Site in Shenyang, Liaoning," *Archaeology*, no. 11 (1990): 969–980.
110. Archaeology Teaching and Research Office, Jilin University, "Zuojiashan Neolithic Site in Nongan," *Acta Archaeologica Sinica*, no. 2 (1989): 187–212.
111. Heilongjiang Provincial Cultural Relics and Archaeology Work Team, "Xinkailiu Site in Mishan County," *Acta Archaeologica Sinica*, no. 4 (1979): 491–518; Zhu Yanping, "Ornamentation and Chronology of Pottery from the Xinkailiu Culture," in *Qingguo Collection: Memorial Collection for the 10th Anniversary of the Archaeology Department of Jilin University* (Beijing: Knowledge Press, 1998), 11–17.
112. Han Jianye, "The Migration Influence of Peiligang Culture and the Prototype of Early Chinese cultural sphere," *Cultural Relics of the Central Plain*, no. 2 (2009): 11–15.
113. Yang Xiaoyan et al., "Functional Analysis of Grinding Slabs and Pestles from the Shangzhai Site in Pinggu, Beijing: Evidence from Plant Starch Grains," *Chinese Science D: Earth Sciences* 39, no. 9 (2009): 1266–1273.
114. Jiamusi Cultural Relics Management Station et al., "Neolithic Tombs in Xiaonanshan, Raohe County, Heilongjiang," *Archaeology*, no. 2 (1996): 1–8; Liu Guoxiang, "Research on Prehistoric Jade Artifacts in Heilongjiang," *Journal of the Chinese History Museum*, no. 1 (2000): 72–86; Zhao Binfu, Sun Mingming, and Du Zhanwei, "Chronology and Nature of Jade Artifacts Unearthed from the Xiaonanshan Tombs in Raohe," in *Frontier Archaeological Research*, vol. 14 (Beijing: Science Press, 2013): 69–78.
115. Gai Pei and Wang Guodao, "Excavation Report of the La Yihai Site in the Upper Yellow River," *Acta Anthropologica Sinica* 2, no. 1 (1983): 49–59.
116. Qinghai Provincial Cultural Relics and Archaeology Team, "Lithic Flaked Stone Tools from the Dayutai Site in Longyangxia, Qinghai," *Archaeology*, no. 7 (1984): 577–581.
117. D. B. Madsen et al., "Settlement Patterns Reflected in Assemblages from the Pleistocene/Holocene Transition of North Central China," *Journal of Archaeological Science* 23, no. 2 (1996): 217–231.
118. Yan Wenming, "The Three Systems Theory of Ancient Chinese Culture: On the Position of Chifeng Region in the Development of Ancient Chinese Culture," in *Proceedings of the International Symposium on Ancient Culture in North China* (Beijing: Chinese Literature and History Press, 1995), 17–18.
119. Yan Wenming, "The Cradle of Oriental Civilization," in *Origin of Agriculture and the Rise of Civilization* (Beijing: Science Press, 2000), 155.

120. Yan Wenming, "The Dawn of Yangtze River Civilization: A Dialogue with Mei Yuanmeng," in *Dawn of Yangtze River Civilization* (Wuhan: Hubei Education Press, 2004), 104.
121. Analysis of residue on Jiahu pottery suggests the presence of fermented beverages made from rice, honey, and fruits. See Patrick E. McGovern et al., "Fermented Beverages of Pre- and Proto-Historic China," *Proceedings of the National Academy of Sciences of the United States of America* 101, no. 51 (2004): 17593–17598.
122. Wang Hui, "Research on the Origin of Chinese Writing," *Journal of Shaanxi Normal University*, Philosophy and Social Sciences ed. 40, no. 3 (2011): 5–23.
123. He Gang, *Prehistoric Remains in Xiangxi and the Legends of Ancient Chinese History* (Changsha: Hunan Yuelu Publishing House Co., Ltd., 2013).
124. Institute of Archaeology, Chinese Academy of Social Sciences, Inner Mongolia First Working Team, "Excavations at the Xinglonggou Colony Site, Chifeng City, Inner Mongolia, 2002–2003," *Archaeology*, no. 7 (2004): 3–8.
125. Hebei Provincial Institute of Cultural Relics, "Excavation Brief of Dongzhai Site, Qianxi County, Hebei Province," supplement, *Wenwu Chunqiu* (1992): 128–143.
126. Deng Cong, "The Origin and Spread of Jade Decoration in East Asia," in *Dongfang Archaeology*, vol. 1 (Beijing: Science Press, 2004), 23–35.
127. Chen Jiling and Chen Shengqian, "An Analysis of Decorative Art on Tubular Jars of the Xinglongwa Culture," in *Bianjing Archaeology Study*, vol. 11 (Beijing: Science Press, 2012), 313–327.
128. Zhang Guangzhi, *Six Lectures of Archaeology* (Beijing: Cultural Relics Press, 1986), 20–22.
129. Han Jianye, "The Northward Expansion of Shuangdun Culture and the Formation of Beixin Culture: A Study Based on 'Beixin Culture Remains' in Zhangshan, Jining," *Jianghan Archaeology*, no. 2 (2012), 47–51.
130. The excavators of the Beixin site have long noticed significant differences between the early, middle, and late periods of the remains. "Through the analysis of unearthed artifacts from these three periods, it is evident that the relationship between the middle and late periods is relatively close, while the relationship between the early and middle periods is not as close due to the scarcity of early-period artifacts, suggesting a possible missing link."

    See Institute of Archaeology, Chinese Academy of Social Sciences, Shandong Team et al., "Shandong Teng County Beixin Site Excavation Report," *Acta Archaeologica Sinica*, no. 2 (1986): 190.
131. Shandong Provincial Institute of Cultural Relics and Archaeology, *Dawenkou Continuation: Reports on the Second and Third Excavations of the Dawenkou Site* (Beijing: Science Press, 1997).
132. Institute of Archaeology, Chinese Academy of Social Sciences, *Shandong Wangyin: Report on the Excavation of a Neolithic Site* (Beijing: Science Press, 2000).
133. Shandong Team, Institute of Archaeology, Chinese Academy of Social Sciences, Brief Report on the Excavation of Dongjiabaicun Neolithic Site in Wenshang County, Shandong Province, *Archaeology*, no. 6 (1993): 481–487.
134. Hebei Provincial Cultural Relics Management Office, "Excavation Report of the Xia Panwang Site in Ci County," *Acta Archaeologica Sinica*, no. 1 (1975): 73–116.

135. Nanyang Area Cultural Relics Team et al., "Neolithic Site of Dazhangzhuang in Fangcheng County, Henan," *Archaeology*, no. 5 (1983): 398–403.
136. Shanxi Provincial Institute of Archaeology, *Yicheng Zaoyuan* (Beijing: Science and Technology Literature Publishing House, 2004).
137. Han Jianye, "Studies on Early Yangshao Culture," in *Ancient Civilization*, vol. 8 (Beijing: Cultural Relics Press, 2010), 16–35.
138. Shaanxi Provincial Institute of Archaeology, *Lintong Lingkou Village* (Xi'an: Sanqin Press, 2004).
139. Yan Wenming, "Preliminary Discussion on the Origins and Development Stages of Yangshao Culture," in *Yangshao Culture Research* (Beijing: Cultural Relics Press, 1989), 122–165.
140. Dai Xiangming, "The Evolution of Neolithic Cultural Patterns in the Yellow River Basin," *Acta Archaeologica Sinica*, no. 4 (1998): 389–418.
141. Sun Zuchu, "Transition from the Middle to Late Neolithic in the Central Plain," *Huaxia Archaeology*, no. 4 (1997): 47–59.
142. Baoji City Archaeological Team and Shaanxi Provincial Institute of Archaeology Baoji Team, *Excavation Report of the Fulinbao Neolithic Site in Baoji City* (Beijing: Cultural Relics Press, 1993).
143. Hebei Provincial Institute of Cultural Relics Research, *Excavation Report of the Nanyangzhuang Site in Zhengding County* (Beijing: Science Press, 2003).
144. Yan Wenming, "A Brief Discussion on the Origin and Development Stages of Yangshao Culture," in *Yangshao Culture Research* (Beijing: Cultural Relics Press, 1989), 122–165.
145. Specifically, the early Banpo culture as classified by Yan Wenming. See Yan Wenming, "Stages and Typology of Yangshao Culture at Banpo," *Archaeology*, no. 3 (1977): 182–188; Institute of Archaeology, Chinese Academy of Sciences and Xi'an Banpo Museum, *Xi'an Banpo: Settlement Site of the Primitive Clan Community* (Beijing: Cultural Relics Press, 1963).
146. Wang Zhihao and Yang Zemeng, "Preliminary Exploration of the Chronology and Genealogy of Yangshao Period Remains in Ordos Region," in *Collected Works on Primitive Culture in Central and Southern Inner Mongolia* (Beijing: Ocean Press, 1991), 86–112.
147. Archaeological Team of the Institute of Archaeology, Chinese Academy of Sciences, Anyang Excavation Team, "Brief Report on the 1971 Excavation at Hougang, Anyang," *Archaeology*, no. 3 (1972): 14–25; Anyang Team of the Institute of Archaeology, Chinese Academy of Social Sciences, "Excavation of the Neolithic Site at Hougang, Anyang," *Archaeology*, no. 6 (1982): 565–583.
148. Some have even referred to the two as separate cultures, namely, Banpo culture and Hougang culture phase I. See Zhao Binfu, "Banpo Culture Research," *Huaxia Archaeology*, no. 2 (1992): 34–55; Zhang Zhongpei and Qiao Liang, "Research on the Hougang Culture Phase I," *Acta Archaeologica Sinica*, no. 3 (1992): 261–280.
149. Han Jianye, *Research on Neolithic Cultures in North China* (Beijing: Cultural Relics Press, 2003).
150. Inner Mongolia Institute of Cultural Relics and Archaeology and Japan Kyoto Society of Chinese Archaeology Daihai Regional Investigation Team, "Excavation Report of

the Shihuoshan Site" in *Daihai Archaeology (II)—Research Report Collection on Sino-Japanese Investigations in the Daihai Region* (Beijing: Science Press, 2001), 18–145.
151. Inner Mongolia Institute of Cultural Relics and Archaeology, "Lujiapo Site in Jungar Banner" in *Collection of Cultural Relics and Archaeology in Inner Mongolia*, vol. 2 (Beijing: Encyclopedia of China Publishing House, 1997), 120–136.
152. Zhengzhou Municipal Institute of Cultural Relics and Archaeology, *Dahecun in Zhengzhou* (Beijing: Science Press, 2005).
153. Banpo Museum etc., *Jiangzhai: Excavation Report of the Neolithic Site* (Beijing: Cultural Relics Press, 1988).
154. Yan Wenming, "An Important Achievement in Prehistoric Settlement Archaeology: A Review of Jiangzhai," *Wenwu*, no. 12 (1990): 22–26.
155. Gong Qiming and Yan Wenming, "Exploring the Social Organizational Structure of Jiangzhai's Inhabitants from the Early Village Layout," *Archaeology and Cultural Relics*, no. 1 (1981): 63–71.
156. Li Runquan, "Multiple Interactions among Cultural Structure, Social Media, and Architectural Environment: On the Subjective Initiative of Yangshao Ancestors," in *Archaeology in the New Century: Multiple Interactions among Culture, Location, and Ecology* (Beijing: Forbidden City Publishing House, 2006), 26–60.
157. Zhang Zhongpei, "Reflections on Social Organization Reflected in the Yuanjunmiao Cemetery," in *Collection of Archaeology in North China* (Beijing: Cultural Relics Press, 1990), 34–50; Yan Wenming, "Analysis of the Hengzhen Cemetery," in *Yangshao Culture Research* (Beijing: Cultural Relics Press, 1989), 248–261.
158. Henan Institute of Cultural Relics and Archaeology and Puyang City Cultural Relics Protection and Management Office, *Xishuipo in Puyang* (Zhengzhou: Zhongzhou Ancient Books Publishing House and Beijing: Cultural Relics Press, 2012).
159. Wang Weilin and Wang Zhankui, "A Preliminary Discussion on the Function of 'Round Potsherds' in Banpo Culture," *Archaeology*, no. 12 (1999): 54–60.
160. Hunan Institute of Cultural Relics and Archaeology, *Tangjiagang in Anxiang: Excavation Report of the Neolithic Site* (Beijing: Science Press, 2013).
161. Hunan Institute of Cultural Relics and Archaeology et al., "The Second Excavation Report of Huachenggang Site in Anxiang, Hunan," *Acta Archaeologica Sinica*, no. 1 (2005): 55–108.
162. Hunan Institute of Cultural Relics and Archaeology, *Chengtoushan in Li County: Excavation Report of the Neolithic Site* (Beijing: Cultural Relics Press, 2007).
163. He Gang and Chen Liwen, "Gaomiao Culture and Its External Transmission and Influence," *Nanfang Wenwu*, no. 2 (2007): 51–60.
164. Guo Weimin, "Re-Study of Gaomiao in the Dongting Lake Region," in *Archaeological Research Collected Paper of Celebrating the 80th Birthday of Mr. Yan Wenming*, vol. 9 (Beijing: Cultural Relics Press, 2012), 166–196.
165. The Wushan area belongs to the transitional zone between the upper and middle reaches of the Yangtze River. The cultural system is the same as that of the middle reaches of the Yangtze River, so it should still be classified as part of the cultural area of the middle reaches of the Yangtze River. Sichuan Provincial Museum, "The Third Excavation of Daxi Site in Wushan," *Acta Archaeologica Sinica*, no. 4 (1981): 461–490.

166. Chinese Academy of Social Sciences Institute of Archaeology Hubei Work Team, "Excavation Brief of Guanmiaoshan Neolithic Site in Zhijiang County, Hubei," *Archaeology*, no. 4 (1981): 289–297; Chinese Academy of Social Sciences Institute of Archaeology Hubei Work Team, "The Second Excavation of Guanmiaoshan Site in Zhijiang County, Hubei," *Archaeology*, no. 1 (1983): 17–29.
167. Guo Weimin, *Cultures and Society of Liyang Plain and Handong Region in the Neolithic* (Beijing: Cultural Relics Press, 2010), 52–57; Guo Weimin, "Re-Study of Gaomiao in the Dongting Lake Region," in *Archaeological Research Collected Paper of Celebrating the 80th Birthday of Mr. Yan Wenming*, vol. 9 (Beijing: Cultural Relics Press, 2012), 166–196.
168. Shenzhen Museum and Department of Anthropology, Sun Yat-sen University, "Excavation Brief of Xiantouling Sand Dune Site in Dapeng, Shenzhen," *Wenwu*, no. 11 (1990): 1–11; Shenzhen Cultural Relics and Archaeological Appraisal Institute, *Shenzhen Xiantouling: 2006 Excavation Report* (Beijing: Cultural Relics Press, 2013).
169. Phase I of Shixia in Qujiang may belong to Xiantouling culture. See Guangdong Provincial Museum and Qujiang County Cultural Bureau Shixia Excavation Team, "Excavation Brief of Shixia Burials in Qujiang, Guangdong," *Wenwu*, no. 7 (1978): 1–15.
170. Qu Jiafa, "A Discussion on the Transmission and Disappearance of Various Primitive Cultures in the Middle and Lower Reaches of the Yangtze River to Guangdong Region," in *Collection of Papers on Lingnan Ancient Yue Culture* (Hong Kong: Urban Council Publications, 1993), 24–33; He Gang and Chen Liwen, "Gaomiao Culture and Its External Transmission and Influence," *Nanfang Wenwu*, no. 2 (2007): 51–60.
171. Guangxi Zhuang Autonomous Region Cultural Relics Work Team et al., "Excavation Brief of Xiaojin Neolithic Site in Ziyuan County, Guangxi," *Archaeology*, no. 3 (2004): 7–30.
172. Guo Weimin, *Cultures and Society of Liyang Plain and Handong Region in the Neolithic* (Beijing: Cultural Relics Press, 2010), 144–147.
173. Zhejiang Provincial Institute of Cultural Relics and Archaeology, *Hemudu: Archaeological Excavation Report of a Neolithic Site* (Beijing: Cultural Relics Press, 2003).
174. Zhejiang Provincial Institute of Cultural Relics and Archaeology, "Excavation Brief of Tianluoshan Neolithic Site in Yuyao, Zhejiang in 2004," *Wenwu*, no. 11 (2007): 4–24.
175. Majiabang culture was found at the Majiabang site in Jiaxing, Zhejiang. Zhejiang Provincial Cultural Relics Administration, "Excavation of the Majiabang Neolithic Site in Jiaxing, Zhejiang," *Archaeology*, no. 7 (1961): 345–351.
176. Luo Jiajiao Archaeological Team, "Excavation Report of the Luojiajiao Site in Tongxiang County, Zhejiang," *Journal of Zhejiang Provincial Institute of Cultural Relics and Archaeology* (Beijing: Cultural Relics Press, 1981), 1–42.
177. Suzhou Museum and Zhangjiagang Cultural Relics Administration, "Excavation Brief of the Dongshan Village Site in Zhangjiagang City," *Wenwu*, no. 10 (2000): 45–57.
178. Nanjing Museum, Institute of Archaeology, "Excavation of the Luotuodun Neolithic Site in Yixing City, Jiangsu," *Archaeology*, no. 7 (2003): 3–7.
179. Nanjing Museum, "Trial Excavation and Drilling Brief of the Dingshadi Site in Jurong, Jiangsu," *Southeast Culture*, no. 1, 2 (1990): 241–254.
180. Zhejiang Provincial Institute of Cultural Relics and Archaeology et al., *Loujiaqiao, Buzhi Tangshanbei, and Jianshanwan* (Beijing: Cultural Relics Press, 2010).

181. Longqiuzhuang Site Archaeological Team, *Longqiuzhuang: Excavation Report of the Neolithic Site in Eastern Jianghuai* (Beijing: Science Press, 1999).
182. Nanjing Museum, Lianyungang Museum et al., "Excavation of the Dayishan Site in Guanyun, Jiangsu, in 1986," *Wenwu*, no. 7 (1991): 10–27.
183. Suzhou Archaeological Institute, *Chuodun Site in Kunshan* (Beijing: Cultural Relics Press, 2011), 34.
184. Suzhou Archaeological Research Institute et al., "Excavation Brief of the Jiangli Neolithic Site in Kunshan, Jiangsu, in 2011," *Wenwu*, no. 1 (2013): 4–24.
185. Dorian Q. Fuller et al., "The Domestication Process and Domestication Rate in Rice: Spikelet Bases from the Lower Yangtze," *Science* 323, no. 5921 (2009): 1607–1610.
186. Qin Ling et al., "Livelihood Patterns at the Hemudu Site: Discussion of Some Issues in Rice Agriculture Research," *Dongfang Archaeology*, no. 3 (Beijing: Science Press, 2006), 307–350; Liu Li et al., "Discussion and Debate on Evidence of the Origin of Rice Agriculture in China," *Southern Cultural Relics*, no. 3 (2009): 25–37.
187. Inner Mongolia Autonomous Region Institute of Cultural Relics and Archaeology, *Baiyinchanghan: Excavation Report of the Neolithic Site* (Beijing: Science Press, 2004).
188. Inner Mongolia Working Team of the Institute of Archaeology, Chinese Academy of Social Sciences, "Xiaoshan Site in Aohan Banner, Inner Mongolia," *Archaeology*, no. 6 (1987): 481–503.
189. Tala et al., "Excavation Results of the Weijiawopu Site in Chifeng, Inner Mongolia, in 2011," *Chinese Cultural Relics News* (February 10, 2012), 4th ed.
190. Inner Mongolia Working Team of the Institute of Archaeology, Chinese Academy of Social Sciences, "Xishuiquan Hongshan Culture Site in Chifeng," *Acta Archaeologica Sinica*, no. 2 (1982):183–198.
191. Beijing Institute of Cultural Relics et al., "Excavation Brief of the Shangzhai Neolithic Site in Pinggu, Beijing," *Wenwu*, no. 8 (1989): 1–8.
192. Hebei Provincial Institute of Cultural Relics and Archaeology et al., "Excavation Report of the Xizhai Site in Qianxi County in 1988," supplement, *Weneu Chunqiu* (1992): 144–177.
193. Han Jianye, *Archaeology of Pre-Qin Period in Beijing* (Beijing: Cultural Relics Press, 2011).
194. Phase I of the Xiaozhushan site, divided by excavators since 2006, includes the lower Houwa, and cylindrical jars with straight mouths. The "lower Xiaozhushan culture" defined by excavators in 1978 actually includes two types of cylindrical jars: those with straight mouths and those with inverted rims, with the latter dating to a later period. This book still retains the name "lower Xiaozhushan culture," but the content has changed.

    See Liaoning Provincial Museum et al., "Dachangshan Shell Mound Site on Guanglu Island in Changhai County," *Acta Archaeologica Sinica*, no. 1 (1981): 63–110; Institute of Archaeology, Chinese Academy of Social Sciences and Liaoning Provincial Institute of Cultural Relics and Archaeology et al., "Excavation Brief of the Xiaozhushan Neolithic Site in Changhai County, Liaoning, in 2009," *Archaeology*, no. 5 (2009): 16–25; Xu Yulin, Fu Renyi, and Wang Chuanpu, "Summary of Excavation at Houwa Site in Donggou County, Liaoning," *Wenwu*, no. 12 (1989): 1–23.
195. Heilongjiang Provincial Institute of Cultural Relics and Archaeology, "Xinkailiu Site in Mishan County," *Archaeology*, no. 4 (1979): 491–518.

196. Represented by phase I class A remains of the Zhenxing site in Hailin, Heilongjiang. See Heilongjiang Provincial Institute of Cultural Relics and Archaeology and Jilin University Department of Archaeology, *Hekou and Zhenxing: Report on the Excavation of Lianhua Reservoir in Mudan River, Heilongjiang* (Beijing: Science Press, 2009).
197. Heilongjiang Provincial Institute of Cultural Relics and Archaeology, "Cleaning Brief of the Yabuli Neolithic Site in Shangzhi County, Heilongjiang," *Northern Cultural Relics*, no. 1 (1988): 2–7.
198. Jilin Provincial Institute of Cultural Relics and Archaeology et al., "Yaojingzi Neolithic Site in Changling County, Jilin," *Archaeology*, no. 8 (1992): 673–688.
199. Nanjing Museum et al., "Excavation Brief of the Shendun Neolithic Site in Liyang, Jiangsu," *Southeast Culture*, no. 5 (2009): 45–58.
200. Zhang Xuqiu, "Preliminary Study on the Neolithic Cultures in the Eastern Han River Region," *Archaeology and Cultural Relics*, no. 4 (1987): 56–66.
201. Shanxi Provincial Institute of Archaeology, "Trial Excavation Brief of the Chucun Site in Houma, Shanxi," *Cultural Relics Quarterly*, no. 2 (1993): 1–10.
202. Shaanxi Provincial Institute of Archaeology, *Longgangsi: Report on the Excavation of a Neolithic Site* (Beijing: Cultural Relics Press, 1990).
203. Jinan Municipal Cultural Relics and Archaeology Research Office et al., "Excavation Brief of the Yuhuangding Site in Jining, Shandong," *Archaeology*, no. 4 (2005): 3–11.
204. Nanjing Museum, "Exploration Report on the Dadunzi Site in Sihu Town, Pi County, Jiangsu," *Acta Archaeologica Sinica*, no. 2 (1964): 9–50.
205. Jilin Provincial Institute of Cultural Relics and Archaeology, "Excavation of the Yuanbaogou Neolithic Site in Nongan County, Jilin," *Archaeology*, no. 12 (1989): 1067–1075.
206. Peking University Archaeological Field School et al., "Excavation Brief of the Beizhuang Site in Changdao, Shandong," *Archaeology*, no. 5 (1987): 385–394; Zhang Jiangkai, "On the Beizhuang Type," in *Archaeological Studies*, vol. 3 (Beijing: Science Press, 1997), 37–51.
207. Nanjing Museum et al., "Neolithic Sites in Dongshan Village, Zhangjiagang City, Jiangsu," *Archaeology*, no. 8 (2010): 3–12.
208. Longquzhuang Site Archaeological Team, *Longqiuzhuang: Report on the Excavation of a Neolithic Site in Eastern Jianghuai* (Beijing: Science Press, 1999).
209. Shaanxi Provincial Institute of Archaeology, *Longgangsi: Report on the Excavation of a Neolithic Site* (Beijing: Cultural Relics Press, 1990), 18, 158.
210. Henan Provincial Institute of Cultural Relics Research et al., *Xiawanggang in Lichuan* (Beijing: Cultural Relics Press, 1989), 40.
211. Rice agriculture in southern China, appearing around 4000 BCE, was previously believed to have been preceded by the so-called primitive agriculture of tuber crops or garden agriculture. See Zhao Zhijun, "Reconsidering Primitive Agriculture in Southern China," in *Prehistoric Archaeology in South China and Southeast Asia: Proceedings of the International Symposium Commemorating the 30th Anniversary of the Excavation at Zengpiyan Site* (Beijing: Cultural Relics Press, 2006), 145–156.
212. Yang Hongxun, "Investigation of Early Wood Construction Techniques at the Hemudu Site," in *Collected Papers on Architectural Archaeology* (Beijing: Cultural Relics Press, 1987), 145–156.

213. Guo Moruo, "The Dialectical Development of Ancient Writing," *Acta Archaeologica Sinica*, no. 1 (1972): 1–13.
214. Hubei Provincial Institute of Cultural Relics and Archaeology, *Yangjiawan in Yichang City* (Beijing: Science Press, 2013).
215. Chengde Regional Cultural Relics Preservation Office et al., "Excavation Brief of the Houtaizi Site in Luanping County, Hebei," *Wenwu*, no. 3 (1994): 53–74.
216. Shaanxi Provincial Institute of Archaeology, *Longgangsi: Report on the Excavation of a Neolithic Site* (Beijing: Cultural Relics Press, 1990), 118, figure 83.
217. Li Yangsong, "On the Wenguan Burials of the Yangshao Culture," *Archaeology*, no. 6 (1976): 356–360.
218. Zhang Guangzhi, "The Tri-legged *Jue* Vessel of Puyang and the Human-Animal Patterns in Ancient Chinese Art," *Wenwu*, no. 11 (1988): 36–39; Feng Shi, "Astronomical Studies of Tomb No. 45 at Xishuipo, Puyang, Henan," *Wenwu*, no. 3 (1990): 52–60.
219. Song Zhaolin, "The Shamanistic Meaning in the Sculptures of the Houwa Site," *Wenwu*, no. 12 (1989): 23–28; Guo Dashun, "Reconsideration of the 'Exclusive Use of Jade for Burials' and the Origin of the Liaohe Civilization in the Hongshan Culture," *Wenwu*, no. 8 (1997): 20–26; Cao Nan, "Analysis of Jade Shaman Figures in the Hongshan Culture," in *Studies on the Hongshan Culture* (Beijing: Cultural Relics Press, 2006), 322–328.
220. Sun Shoudao and Guo Dashun, "Discovery and Study of the Female Deity Head from Niuheliang in the Hongshan Culture," *Wenwu*, no. 8 (1986): 18–24; Tang Chi, "On the Stone-Carved Female Deity Unearthed from the Lower Stratum of the Houtaizi Site in Luanping," *Wenwu*, no. 3 (1994): 46–51; Liu Guoxiang, "On the Remains of the Lower Stratum at Houtaizi in Luanping and Related Issues," in *Collection of Archaeological Knowledge* (Beijing: China Social Sciences Press, 1997), 194–212.

CHAPTER 3   THE MIAODIGOU ERA AND THE FORMATION OF EARLY CHINA

1. "Miaodigou era" is a concept corresponding to the "Longshan era." See Yan Wenming, "Longshan Culture and the Longshan Era," *Wenwu*, no. 6 (1981): 41–48; Han Jianye, "The Miaodigou Era and 'Early China,'" *Archaeology*, no. 3 (2012): 59–69.
2. Su Bingqi, "Several Issues on Yangshao Culture," *Acta Archaeologica Sinica*, no. 1 (1965): 51–82.
3. Yan Wenming, "A Brief Discussion on the Origin and Development Stages of Yangshao Culture," in *Yangshao Culture Studies* (Beijing: Cultural Relics Press, 1989), 122–165.
4. Zhang Zhongpei, "Several Issues on Archaeology in Eastern Inner Mongolia," in *Collection of Archaeological and Cultural Studies in Eastern Inner Mongolia* (Beijing: Marine Press, 1991), 3–8.
5. Zhang Zhongpei, "The Yangshao Period: Prosperity of Prehistoric Society and Transition to a Civilized Era," *Wenwu Jikan*, no. 1 (1997): 1–47.
6. Wang Renxiang, *Artistic Waves in Prehistoric China: A Study of Painted Pottery from Miaodigou Culture* (Beijing: Cultural Relics Press, 2011).
7. Yan Wenming, "A Brief Discussion on the Origin and Development Stages of Yangshao Culture," in *Yangshao Culture Studies* (Beijing: Cultural Relics Press, 1989), 122–165.

8. Shanxi Work Team of the Institute of Archaeology, Chinese Academy of Sciences, "Excavation of Dongzhuangcun and Xiwangcun Sites in Ruicheng, Shanxi," *Acta Archaeologica Sinica*, no. 1 (1973): 1–63.
9. Shanxi Provincial Institute of Archaeology, "Excavation Report on the Beigan Site in Yicheng, Shanxi," *Wenwu Jikan*, no. 4 (1993): 1–51.
10. Zhang Zhongpei and Yan Wenming, "Cultural Nature and Dating of the Yangshao Remains at Sanliqiao," *Archaeology*, no. 6 (1964): 301–305.
11. Tian Jianwen, Xue Xinmin, and Yang Linzhong, "A New Understanding of Neolithic Archaeological Cultures in Southern Shanxi," *Wenwu Jikan*, no. 2 (1992): 35–44; Shanxi Provincial Institute of Archaeology, "Excavation Report on the Beigan Site in Yicheng, Shanxi," *Wenwu Jikan*, no. 4 (1993): 1–51.
12. Yan Wenming, "On the Banpo and Miaodigou Types," *Archaeology and Cultural Relics*, no. 1 (1980): 64–72; Dai Xiangming, "On the Origin of Miaodigou Culture," in *Qingguoji: Jilin University Department of Archaeology's 10th Anniversary Collection* (Beijing: Knowledge Press, 1998), 18–26.
13. Institute of Archaeology, Chinese Academy of Sciences, *Miaodigou and Sanliqiao* (Beijing: Science Press, 1959).
14. Henan Provincial Institute of Cultural Relics and Archaeology, *Nanjiaokou in Sanmenxia* (Beijing: Science Press, 2009).
15. Institute of Archaeology, Chinese Academy of Sciences, *Miaodigou and Sanliqiao* (Beijing: Science Press, 1959).
16. Li Ji, "Prehistoric Remains in Xiyin Village," in *Tsinghua Research Institute Series 3* (Beijing: Tsinghua Research Institute, 1927); Shanxi Provincial Institute of Archaeology, "Second Excavation of Prehistoric Remains in Xiyin Village," *Sanjin Archaeology*, vol. 2 (Taiyuan: Shanxi People's Press, 1996), 1–62.
17. Henan Provincial Institute of Cultural Relics and Archaeology et al., "Brief Report on the Spring 2001 Excavation at Xipo Site, Lingbao, Henan," *Huaxia Archaeology*, no. 2 (2002): 31–52.
18. Henan Provincial Institute of Cultural Relics and Archaeology, Institute of Archaeology et al., "Brief Report on the Spring 2001 Excavation at Xipo Site, Lingbao, Henan," *Huaxia Archaeology*, no. 2 (2002): 31–52; Henan Provincial Institute of Cultural Relics and Archaeology et al., "Room Site of Yangshao Culture, No. 105, at Xipo Site, Lingbao, Henan," *Wenwu*, no. 8 (2003): 4–17; Institute of Archaeology, Chinese Academy of Social Sciences, Henan Team et al., "Discovery of a Large-Scale Mid-Yangshao Culture Room Site at Xipo Site, Lingbao, Henan," *Archaeology*, no. 3 (2005): 3–6.
19. Wang Xiaoqing, "On the Typology of Yaoshao Culture Historians," *Acta Archaeologica Sinica*, no. 4 (1993): 415–434.
20. Xi'an Banpo Museum et al., "Prehistoric Sites in Weinan, Shaanxi," *Archaeology*, no. 1 (1978): 41–53.
21. Banpo Museum et al., *Jiangzhai: Excavation Report of a Neolithic Site* (Beijing: Cultural Relics Press, 1988).
22. Zhao Chunqing, "From Battle to Integration: An Analysis of Fish and Bird Painted Pottery in Yaoshao Culture," *Cultural Relics of Central China*, no. 2 (2000): 13–15.

23. Baoji City Archaeological Team and Shaanxi Provincial Institute of Archaeology, *Yuanzitou in Long County* (Beijing: Cultural Relics Press, 2005).
24. Gansu Provincial Institute of Cultural Relics and Archaeology, *Dadiwan in Qin'an: Excavation Report of a Neolithic Site* (Beijing: Cultural Relics Press, 2006).
25. A finely painted round-bottom earthen bowl of the historian type was collected from the Sanjiaocheng Site in Gulang, Gansu Province. See Gansu Provincial Institute of Cultural Relics and Archaeology, School of Archaeology and Museology and Peking University, *Prehistoric Archaeological Survey Report of the Hexi Corridor* (Beijing: Cultural Relics Press, 2011), 65, figure 35, 1.
26. Peking University Department of Archaeology, *Quanhu Village in Hua County* (Beijing: Science Press, 2003).
27. Wang Weilin and Zhang Pengcheng, "Baishui Xiahe Neolithic Site in Shaanxi," in *Important Archaeological Discoveries in China* (Beijing: Cultural Relics Press, 2011), 18–20.
28. Northwest University School of Cultural Relics, Archaeology Department, *Excavation Report of the Fufeng Anban Site* (Beijing: Science Press, 2002).
29. Baoji City Archaeological Team and Shaanxi Provincial Institute of Archaeology Baoji Team, *Fulinbao in Baoji: Excavation Report of a Neolithic Site* (Beijing: Cultural Relics Press, 1993).
30. Qinghai Provincial Institute of Cultural Relics and Archaeology, "Trial Excavation Report of Yangwapo Site in Minhe, Qinghai," *Archaeology*, no. 1 (1984): 15–20; Chinese Academy of Social Sciences Institute of Archaeology Gansu and Qinghai Team and Qinghai Provincial Institute of Cultural Relics and Archaeology, "Excavation of Hulijia Site in Minhe County, Qinghai," *Archaeology*, no. 1 (2001): 40–58.
31. Peking University Archaeology Fieldwork Team et al., Excavation Report of Yehezi Site in Longde, in *Archaeological Research* (Beijing: Science Press, 1997), 158–195.
32. Peking University Department of Archaeology and Gansu Provincial Institute of Cultural Relics and Archaeology, "Excavation Report of Dali Jiaoping Neolithic Site in Wudu County, Gansu," Collected Papers of Archaeology, vol. 13 (Beijing: Encyclopedia of China Publishing House, 2000), 1–36; Chengdu Institute of Cultural Relics and Archaeology et al., "Trial Excavation of Boxi Site in Mao County, Sichuan in 2002," in *Archaeological Discoveries in Chengdu (2004)* (Beijing: Science Press, 2006), 1–12.
33. Shaanxi Provincial Institute of Archaeology et al., *Archaeological Reports in Southern Shaanxi* (Xi'an: Sanqin Press, 1994).
34. Gao Qiang and Yun Kuen Lee, "A Biological Perspective on Yangshao Kinship," *Journal of Anthropological Archaeology* 12, no. 3 (1993): 266–298.
35. Yan Wenming, "Significant Achievements of Prehistoric Settlement Archaeology: A Review of Jiangzhai," *Wenwu*, no. 12 (1990): 22–26.
36. Han Jianye, *Research on Neolithic Cultures in Northern China* (Beijing: Cultural Relics Press, 2003).
37. Cui Xuan and Siqin, "Excavation Report on Points C and J of Qingshuihe Bainiyaozi, Inner Mongolia," *Archaeology*, no. 2 (1988): 97–108.
38. Inner Mongolia Institute of Cultural Relics and Archaeology etc., *Excavation Report Collection of Daihai Archaeology 3: Yangshao Culture Sites* (Beijing: Science Press, 2003).

39. Shanxi Provincial Institute of Archaeology and Datong Museum, "Majiaxiao Village Neolithic Site in Datong, Shanxi," *Wenwu Jikan*, no. 3 (1992): 7–16.
40. For example, Duanjiazhuang H3 and Liulin Yangjiaping F1 in Fenyang, Shanxi (National Cultural Relics Administration, Shanxi Provincial Institute of Archaeology, and Jilin University Department of Archaeology, *Archaeology in Jinzhong*, Beijing: Cultural Relics Press, 1999); Sanguan F3 in Weixian, Hebei (Zhangjiakou Archaeological Team, "Major Achievements in Weixian Neolithic Archaeology in 1979," *Archaeology*, no. 2 [1981]: 97–105), etc. However, *ding* remains rare.
41. *Zhengzhou Dahecun* classifies it as the type M jar.
42. Nanyang Cultural Relics Team et al., "Dazhangzhuang Neolithic Site in Fangcheng County, Henan," *Archaeology*, no. 5 (1983): 398–403.
43. Henan Provincial Institute of Cultural Relics Research et al., *Xiawanggang in Xichuan* (Beijing: Cultural Relics Press).
44. Peking University Archaeology Field School and Nanyang Institute of Cultural Relics Research, "Excavation Report of Baligang Site in Dengzhou, Henan," *Wenwu*, no. 9 (1998): 31–45.
45. Zhengzhou Museum, "Excavation Report of Dianjuntai Site in Xingyang in 1980," *Cultural Relics of Central China*, no. 4 (1982): 1–21.
46. Zhang Songlin, Liu Yanfeng, and Liu Hongmiao, "Excavation Report of Shuidihe Site in Gongyi, Henan," in *Archaeology and Research on Zhengzhou Cultural Relics*, vol. 1 (Beijing: Science Press, 2003), 220–254.
47. Yan Wenming, "A Brief Discussion on the Origin and Development Stages of Yangshao Culture," in *Research on Yangshao Culture* (Beijing: Cultural Relics Press, 1989), 122–165; Yuan Guangkuo, "A Study on the Yan Village Type," *Acta Archaeologica Sinica*, no. 3 (1996): 307–324.
48. Represented by Dasi H98 in Yun County and the Phase I in Zaoyang, see Hubei Provincial Institute of Cultural Relics and Nanshui–Beitiao Office of Hubei Provincial Cultural Relics Bureau, "Excavation Report of Dasi Site in Yun County in 2006," *Archaeology*, no. 4 (2008): 3–13; Institute of Archaeology, Chinese Academy of Social Sciences, *Zaoyang Carved Dragon Tablet* (Beijing: Science Press, 2006).
49. Henan Provincial Institute of Cultural Relics Archaeology and Nanyang Institute of Cultural Relics Archaeology, "Excavation Report of Laofengang Yangshao Culture Site in Xixia, Henan," *Acta Archaeologica Sinica*, no. 2 (2012): 217–268.
50. Henan Provincial Institute of Cultural Relics Archaeology, *Hongshan Temple in Ruzhou City* (Zhengzhou: Zhongzhou Ancient Books Press, 1995).
51. Yan Wenming, *Stork Fish and Stone Axe*, postscript, *Wenwu*, no. 12 (1981): 79–82.
52. Hebei Provincial Institute of Cultural Relics Research and Handan District Cultural Relics Management Office, "Excavation Report of Shibeikou Site in Yongnian County," in *Collected Archaeological Works of Hebei Province* (Beijing: Dongfang Press, 1998), 46–105.
53. Yan Wenming, "A Brief Discussion on the Origin and Development Stages of Yangshao Culture," in *Research on Yangshao Culture* (Beijing: Cultural Relics Press, 1989), 122–165.

54. Represented by Sanguan F4 in Yu County, Hebei. See Zhangjiakou Archaeological Team, "Major Achievements in the Archaeology of the Neolithic Age in Yu County in 1979," *Archaeology*, no. 2 (1981): 97–105.
55. Liaoning Provincial Institute of Cultural Relics Archaeology, *Niuheliang—Excavation Report of Hongshan Culture Site (1983–2003)* (Beijing: Cultural Relics Press, 2012).
56. Liaoning Provincial Museum et al., "Discovery of Three Primitive Cultures in Xiaoheyan, Aohan Banner, Liaoning," *Wenwu*, no. 12 (1977): 1–22.
57. Su Bingqi, "The New Dawn of Chinese Civilization," *Southeast Culture*, no. 5 (1988): 1–7.
58. Lin Xiuzhen and Yang Hu, "Discovery and Research on Xitai Type of Hongshan Culture," in *Collection of Archaeology* 19 (Beijing: Science Press), 59–99.
59. Liaoning Provincial Museum et al., "Discovery of Three Primitive Cultures in Xiaoheyan, Aohan Banner, Liaoning," *Wenwu*, no. 12 (1977): 1–22.
60. Chinese Academy of Social Sciences Institute of Archaeology Inner Mongolia Working Team et al., "Investigation of Tuanjie Site in Hailaer City, Inner Mongolia," *Archaeology*, no. 5 (2001): 3–17.
61. Including the remains of middle and lower flipped-rimmed cylindrical jars excavated in 1978 at Xiaozhushan and the remains of Xiaozhushan Phases II and III excavated since 2006.
62. Liaoning Provincial Museum and Lvshun Museum, "Guojiacun Neolithic Site in Dalian City," *Acta Archaeologica Sinica*, no. 3 (1984): 287–330.
63. Shandong Provincial Institute of Cultural Relics and Archaeology, *Continuation of Dawenkou—Second and Third Excavation Reports of Dawenkou Site* (Beijing: Science Press, 1997); Chinese Academy of Social Sciences Institute of Archaeology, *Wangyin, Shandong—Excavation Report of Neolithic Site* (Beijing: Science Press, 2000); Han Jianye, "The Northward Migration of Longqiuzhuang Culture and the Formation of Dawenkou Culture," *Jianghan Archaeology*, no. 1 (2011): 59–64.
64. Shandong Provincial Institute of Cultural Relics and Archaeology et al., "Excavation Report of Qianbuxia Site in Weifang, Shandong," in *Archaeological Reports of Shandong Provincial Highways (1997)* (Beijing: Science Press, 2000), 1–108.
65. Peking University Archaeological Internship Team et al., "Brief Report on the Excavation of Beizhuang Site in Changdao, Shandong," *Archaeology*, no. 5 (1987): 385–394.
66. Wu Shichi, "An Overview of Agricultural Archaeology in Shandong Neolithic Period," *Agricultural Archaeology*, no. 2 (1983): 165–171.
67. Han Kangxin and Pan Qifeng, "The Origin and Significance of Tooth Extraction Customs in China," *Archaeology*, no. 1 (1981): 64–76.
68. Shanghai Municipal Administration of Cultural Relics, *Songze—Excavation Report of Neolithic Site* (Beijing: Cultural Relics Press, 1987).
69. Zhejiang Provincial Institute of Cultural Relics and Archaeology, *Nanhebang—Excavation Report of Songze Culture Site* (Beijing: Cultural Relics Press, 2005).
70. The northern boundary of Beiyinyangying culture extends to the northwest of Jiangxi, such as the lower remains of Laohudun in Jing'an. See Jiangxi Provincial Institute of

Cultural Relics and Archaeology et al., "Brief Report on the Prehistoric Site of Laohudun, Jing'an, Jiangxi," *Wenwu*, no. 10 (2011): 4–21.

71. Nanjing Museum, *Beiyinyangying—Excavation Report of Neolithic and Shang and Zhou Period Site* (Beijing: Cultural Relics Press, 1993).
72. Anhui Provincial Institute of Cultural Relics and Archaeology, "Huangshanzui Site in Susong, Anhui," *Acta Archaeologica Sinica*, no. 4 (1987): 451–469.
73. Chinese Academy of Social Sciences Institute of Archaeology, *Saidun Site in Huangmei* (Beijing: Cultural Relics Press, 2010).
74. Anhui Provincial Institute of Cultural Relics and Archaeology, "Gugeng Site in Feixi County, Anhui," *Archaeology*, no. 7 (1985): 577–583.
75. Nanjing Museum, "Qingdun Site in Haian, Jiangsu," *Acta Archaeologica Sinica*, no. 2 (1983): 147–190.
76. Nanjing Museum, "Caoxieshan Site in Wuxian, Jiangsu," in *Collected Materials on Cultural Relics*, vol. 3 (Beijing: Cultural Relics Press, 1980), 1–24.
77. Jiangsu Sanxing Village Joint Archaeological Team, "Sanxing Village Neolithic Site in Jintan, Jiangsu," *Wenwu*, no. 2 (2004): 4–26, figure 53, 5, 10.
78. Due to special soil conditions and excavation techniques, the early excavated tombs belonging to these cultures were often described as "buried on the ground," but they were actually vertical pit graves. This applies to all tombs at the Saidun Site, and similar vertical pit graves have also been found at the Songze and Longqiuzhuang sites.
79. Nanjing Museum et al., "Neolithic Site in Dongshan Village, Zhangjiagang City, Jiangsu," *Archaeology*, no. 8 (2010): 3–12.
80. Nanjing Museum et al., "Excavation of Ancient Well Group in Chenghu, Wuxian City, Jiangsu Province," in *Collected Materials on Cultural Relics*, vol. 9 (Beijing: Cultural Relics Press, 1985), 1–22.
81. Hubei Jingzhou Regional Museum, "Trial Excavation of Xishan Youziling Neolithic Site, Hubei Province," *Archaeology*, no. 10 (1994): 865–876.
82. Hubei Jingzhou Regional Museum, Peking University Department of Archaeology, and Hubei Provincial Institute of Cultural Relics and Archaeology, *Tanjialing* (Beijing: Cultural Relics Press, 2011).
83. Zhang Xuqiu, *An Introduction to the Neolithic Cultures in the Middle Reaches of the Yangtze River* (Wuhan: Hubei Science and Technology Press, 1992).
84. State Administration of Cultural Relics Three Gorges Archaeological Team, *Chaotianzui and Zhongbaodao* (Beijing: Cultural Relics Press, 2001).
85. Hubei Yichang Regional Museum and Archaeology Major in the Department of History, Sichuan University, "Excavation of Qingshuitan Neolithic Site in Yichang County, Hubei," *Archaeology and Cultural Relics*, no. 2 (1983): 1–17.
86. Sichuan Provincial Museum, "The Third Excavation of Daxi Site in Wushan," *Acta Archaeologica Sinica*, no. 4 (1981): 461–490.
87. Hubei Excavation Team, Institute of Archaeology, Chinese Academy of Sciences, "Excavation of Luoshishan Site in Huanggang, Hubei," *Archaeology*, no. 7 (1962): 339–344.
88. Guo Weimin, *Cultures and Society in the Liyang Plain and Handong Region during the Neolithic Age* (Beijing: Cultural Relics Press, 2010), 76–86.

89. Zhang Chi, "Stone and Jade Industry in Daxi, Beiyinyangying, and Xuejiagang," in *Archaeological Research*, vol. 4 (Beijing: Science Press, 2000), 55–76.
90. Fujian Museum, *The Eighth Excavation Report of Tanshishan Site in Minhou* (Beijing: Science Press, 2004).
91. Fujian Provincial Museum, "Brief Report on the Excavation of Keqiutou Site in Pingtan, Fujian," *Archaeology*, no. 7 (1991): 587–599.
92. Chang Kwang-chih, *Fengpitou, Tapenkeng, and the Prehistory of Taiwan* (New Haven: Department of Anthropology of Yale University, 1969), 166–168.
93. Zhengzhou Institute of Cultural Relics and Archaeology, "Report on the Excavated Textiles from Qingtai Site in Xingyang," *Cultural Relics of Central China*, no. 3 (1999): 4–9.
94. Wu Hung, "The 'Retro' Mode in Chinese Art and Visual Culture," in *Art in Time and Space: Wu Hung's Collection of Chinese Art History Essays*, vol. 2 (Beijing: Joint Publishing, 2009), 3–30.
95. Su Bingqi pointed out that 6,000 years ago was a turning point from clan development to the nation-state's emergence. Su Bingqi, "Embracing the New Century of Chinese Archaeology," in *Chinese · Descendants of the Dragon · Chinese People: Archaeological Quests for Roots* (Shenyang: Liaoning University Press, 1994), 238.
96. The inscription on the Plate of Duke Xuan of Guo (Guoji Zibai) during the Western Zhou Dynasty states, "Tin is used for bows, and vermilion arrows are in the center; Tin is used for *yue*, for the expedition against the southern barbarians." [The tin bow is a low-level bow. Its only use is shooting arrows from a distance to damage enemies.]

    The *Book of Documents · Speech at Muye* says, "King Wu held the yellow *yue* in his left hand, and in his right hand, he held the military flag to command." Wu Qichang and Lin Yun believed that the character "王" (wang, which means the king) originally represented the shape of an axe or *yue*. See Lin Yun, "On the Meaning of '王,'" *Archaeology*, no. 6 (1965): 311–312.
97. Han Jianye, "A Brief Discussion on the General Trend and Different Patterns of Social Development during the Bronze and Stone Coexistence Period in China," in *Ancient Civilization* 2 (June 2003): 84–96.
98. Yan Wenming, "Unity and Diversity of Prehistoric Chinese Culture," *Wenwu*, no. 3 (1987): 38–50.
99. Song Xinchao, *Regional Study of Yin and Shang Cultures* (Xi'an: Shaanxi People's Press, 1991).

CHAPTER 4   THE ARCHAIC STATE STAGE OF EARLY CHINA

1. Yan Wenming, "On the Chalcolithic in China," *Prehistoric Research*, no. 1 (1984): 36–44; Yan Wenming, "An Investigation into the Settlement Patterns of China's Neolithic," in *A Collection of Papers Celebrating the 55th Anniversary of Su Bingqi's Archaeological Career* (Beijing: Cultural Relics Press, 1989), 24–37.
2. Shanxi Working Team of the Institute of Archaeology, Chinese Academy of Sciences, "Excavations of the Dongzhuang Village and Xiwang Village Sites in Ruicheng, Shanxi," *Acta Archaeologica Sinica*, no. 1 (1973): 1–63.
3. Henan Provincial Institute of Cultural Relics and Archaeology et al., "The 105 Yangshao Culture House Site at Lingbao Xipo in Henan," *Wenwu*, no. 8 (2003): 4–17.

4. Institute of Archaeology, Chinese Academy of Social Sciences and Henan Provincial Institute of Cultural Relics and Archaeology, *Lingbao Xipo Cemetery* (Beijing: Cultural Relics Press, 2010).
5. Henan Provincial Institute of Cultural Relics et al., "Excavation Report of Mianchi Yangshao Site in 1980–1981," *Prehistoric Research*, no. 3 (1985): 38–58.
6. Henan Provincial Administration of Cultural Heritage and Henan Provincial Institute of Cultural Relics and Archaeology, *Archaeological Report of the Yellow River Xiaolangdi Reservoir (I)* (Zhengzhou: Zhongzhou Ancient Books Publishing House, 1999), 225–272.
7. Han Jianye, "Xipo Tombs and the 'Central Plain Mode,'" in *Yangshao and Her Era—Collection of Papers from the International Symposium Commemorating the 90th Anniversary of the Discovery of Yangshao Culture* (Beijing: Cultural Relics Press, 2014), 153–164.
8. Archaeological Department of the Museum of Chinese History et al., *Yuanqu ancient city Dongguan* (Beijing: Science Press, 2001).
9. Shanxi Provincial Institute of Archaeology, "Excavation Report of the Guzhen Site in Hejin, Shanxi," in *Archaeology of the Sanjin*, vol. 2 (Taiyuan: Shanxi People's Publishing House, 1996), 63–126.
10. Bu Gong, "Several Issues on the Miaodigou II Culture," *Wenwu*, no. 2 (1990): 38–47; Chen Bingbai, "A New Exploration of the Origin of Hollow-Footed Tripod Vessels in the Neolithic," in *Proceedings of the 8th Annual Meeting of the Chinese Archaeological Society (1991)* (Beijing: Cultural Relics Press, 1996), 84–101; Zhang Zhongpei, "The Emergence of Hollow Tri-Legged Vessels in the Yellow River Basin," *Huaxia Archaeology*, no. 1 (1997): 30–48.
11. Archaeological Research Center of Peking University et al., "Excavation Report of the Shaopengzui Site in Zhong County," in *Chongqing Reservoir Area Archaeological Report Collection*, vol. 1999 (Beijing: Science Press, 2006), 530–643.
12. Zhao Xueye, "Large-Scale Architectural Site of Yangshao Culture in Nanzuo Gedaqu, Xifeng City," *Archaeological Annual (1995)* (Beijing: Cultural Relics Press, 1997), 251–252; Zhao Xueye, "Neolithic Site in Nanzuo, Xifeng City," *Archaeological Annual (1997)* (Beijing: Cultural Relics Press, 1999), 233–234.
13. Qingyang Regional Museum, "Trial Excavation Report of the Yanggua Site in Ning County, Gansu," *Archaeology*, no. 10 (1983): 869–876.
14. Institute of Archaeology, Chinese Academy of Social Sciences, *Excavation Report of Wugong—Huxizhuang and Zhaojialai Sites* (Beijing: Cultural Relics Press, 1988).
15. Jingwei Working Team, Institute of Archaeology, Chinese Academy of Social Sciences, "Excavation Report of Changshan Site in Longdong Zhenyuan," *Archaeology*, no. 3 (1981): 201–210.
16. Inner Mongolia Institute of Cultural Relics and Archaeology et al., *Archaeology of Daihai (III)—Collection of Excavation Reports of Yangshao Culture Sites* (Beijing: Science Press, 2003).
17. Department of Archaeology, Peking University et al., "Excavation Report of the Haishengbulang Site in Tuoketuo, Inner Mongolia," in *Archaeological Research*, vol. 3 (Beijing: Science Press, 1997), 196–239.

18. Inner Mongolia Institute of Cultural Relics and Archaeology, *Miaozigou and Dabagou* (Beijing: Encyclopedia of China Publishing House, 2003).
19. Inner Mongolia Institute of Cultural Relics and Archaeology and Japan Kyoto Chinese Archaeology Research Association Daihai Area Investigation Team, "Excavation Report of the Site on Wangmushan Poshang," in *Daihai Archaeology (II)—Collection of Sino-Japanese Daihai Area Investigation Research Reports* (Beijing: Science Press, 2001), 146–205.
20. Inner Mongolia Institute of Cultural Relics and Archaeology, "Baicaota Site in Jungar Banner," in *Collection of Cultural Relics and Archaeology Papers in Inner Mongolia*, vol. 1 (Beijing: Encyclopedia of China Publishing House, 1994), 183–204.
21. Shanxi Provincial Cultural Relics Administration Committee, "Brief Report on the Clearance of Yijing Village Site in Taiyuan," *Archaeology*, no. 4 (1961): 203–206.
22. Jinzhong Archaeological Team, "Brief Excavation Report of the First Site of Baiyan in Taigu, Shanxi," *Wenwu*, no. 3 (1989): 1–21; Jinzhong Archaeological Team, "Brief Excavation Report of the Second, Third, and Fourth Sites of Baiyan in Taigu, Shanxi," *Wenwu*, no. 3 (1989): 22–34.
23. State Administration of Cultural Heritage, Shanxi Institute of Archaeology, and Department of Archaeology, Jilin University, *Archaeology in Jinzhong* (Beijing: Cultural Relics Press, 1999).
24. Inner Mongolia Academy of Social Sciences Institute of Proto-East Asian History and Baotou Cultural Relics Administration Office, "Brief Report on the Excavation of the Ashan Site in Baotou City, Inner Mongolia," *Archaeology*, no. 2 (1984): 97–108.
25. Inner Mongolia Institute of Cultural Relics and Archaeology, "Xiaoshawan Site and Stone Coffin Tombs in Jungar Banner," in *Collection of Cultural Relics and Archaeology Papers in Inner Mongolia*, vol. 1 (Beijing: Encyclopedia of China Publishing House, 1994), 225–234.
26. Shaanxi Archaeological Team of the Shaanxi Institute of Archaeology, "Excavation of the Longshan Culture Site at Xiaoguandao in Suide, Shaanxi," *Archaeology and Cultural Relics*, no. 5 (1983): 10–19.
27. Yan Wenming, "Viewing the Yangshao Culture through Wangwan," in *Studies on the Yangshao Culture* (Beijing: Cultural Relics Press, 1989), 1–20; School of Archaeology and Museology of Peking University, *Excavation Report on Field Archaeology in Luoyang Wangwan* (Beijing: Peking University Press, 2002).
28. Fan Li, "The Development Sequence of Neolithic Culture in Southwestern Henan and Its Relationship with Neighboring Regions," *Acta Archaeologica Sinica*, no. 2 (2000): 147–182.
29. National Cultural Relics Bureau Archaeological Leadership Training Class, "Excavation of the Yangshao Period City Site in Xishan, Zhengzhou," *Wenwu*, no. 7 (1999): 4–15.
30. Han Jianye, "An Exploration into the Rise and Fall of the Ancient City of Xishan," *Cultural Relics of Central China*, no. 3 (1996): 59–62.
31. Yan Wenming, "Research on Yangshao Houses and Settlement Patterns," in *Studies on the Yangshao Culture* (Beijing: Cultural Relics Press, 1989), 180–242.
32. Luoyang City Second Cultural Relics Work Team, "Brief Report on the Excavation of Yangshao Culture Remains at the Yique City Site in Yichuan County, Henan," *Archaeology*, no. 12 (1997): 8–16.

33. Henan Provincial Museum, "Brief Report on the Excavation of the Gushui River Site in Yu County, Henan," *Archaeology*, no. 4 (1979): 300–307.
34. Henan Provincial Cultural Relics Research Institute and Archaeological Department of the National Museum of Chinese History, *Wangchenggang and Yangcheng in Dengfeng* (Beijing: Cultural Relics Press, 1989), 205–210.
35. Henan Provincial Cultural Relics Administration, *Xiaolangdi Reservoir on the Yellow River: Archaeological Report*, vol. 2 (Zhengzhou: Zhongzhou Ancient Books Publishing House, 2006), 6–156.
36. Archaeological Institute of the Chinese Academy of Sciences, Anyang Excavation Team, "Brief Report on the Excavation of Yin Ruins in 1958–1959," *Archaeology*, no. 2 (1961): 63–76.
37. Chinese Academy of Social Sciences, Institute of Archaeology, Anyang Team, "Anyang Baojiatang Yangshao Culture Site," *Acta Archaeologica Sinica*, no. 2 (1988): 169–188.
38. Xinxiang District Cultural Relics Management Committee et al., "Brief Report on the Trial Excavation of the Luositang Site in Xinxiang County, Henan," *Archaeology*, no. 2 (1985): 97–107.
39. Yan Wenming, "Analysis of the Types of Pottery from Dasikong," in *The Origins of Chinese Civilization* (Beijing: Cultural Relics Press, 2011), 127–156.
40. Hutuo River Archaeological Team, "Archaeological Survey and Trial Excavation in the Hutuo River Basin, Hebei," *Archaeology*, no. 4 (1993): 300–310.
41. Archaeology Specialized Senior Class of the History Department, Peking University, "Neolithic to Liao Dynasty Cultural Sites Discovered by the Archaeology Specialized Senior Class of the History Department, Peking University, during Field Practice in the Suburbs of Beijing," *Guangming Daily* (April 2, 1964).
42. Hebei Provincial Cultural Relics Research Institute, "Trial Excavation of the Neolithic Site in Wufang, Rongcheng County, Hebei," in *Archaeological Collection*, vol. 5 (Beijing: China Social Sciences Press, 1987), 61–78.
43. Hebei Provincial Cultural Relics Research Institute, "Excavation of the Neolithic Site in Jiangjiali, Yangyuan County, Hebei," *Archaeology*, no. 2 (2001): 13–27.
44. Hebei Provincial Cultural Bureau Cultural Relics Team, "Brief Report on the Excavation of the Taikoucun Site in Yongnian County, Hebei," *Archaeology*, no. 12 (1962): 635–640.
45. Henan Provincial Cultural Relics and Archaeology Research Institute, *Hui County Mengzhuang* (Zhengzhou: Zhongzhou Ancient Books Publishing House, 2003).
46. Xiaomintun Archaeological Team in Yin Ruins, "Brief Report on the Excavation of Neolithic Kiln Sites in Xiaomintun, Anyang City, Henan," *Archaeology*, no. 10 (2007): 3–13.
47. Yan Wenming, "Majiayao Type is the Continuation and Development of Yangshao Culture Miaodigou Type in Gansu–Qinghai Area," in *Collected Works on Prehistoric Archaeology* (Beijing: Science Press, 1998), 167–171; Xie Duanju, "On the Cultural Nature of Shilingxia Type," *Wenwu*, no. 4 (1981): 21–27.
48. Yan Wenming, "The Origins of Gansu Painted Pottery," *Wenwu*, no. 10 (1978): 62–76.
49. Gansu Provincial Cultural Relics Management Committee, "Archaeological Survey in Wei River Upper Stream Weiyuan, Longxi, and Wushan Counties, Gansu," *Archaeology Communications*, no. 7 (1958): 6–16.

50. Gansu Provincial Institute of Cultural Relics and Archaeology, *Qinan Dadiwan: Excavation Report of Neolithic Site* (Beijing: Cultural Relics Press, 2006).
51. Institute of Archaeology, Chinese Academy of Social Sciences, *Shizhaocn and Xishanping* (Beijing: Encyclopedia of China Publishing House, 1999), 50–71, 248–253.
52. Gansu–Qinghai Working Team, Institute of Archaeology, Chinese Academy of Social Sciences, "Brief Report on the Excavation of the Prehistoric Cultural Site at Fujiamen, Wushan, Gansu," *Archaeology*, no. 4 (1995): 289–296; Gansu–Qinghai Working Team, Institute of Archaeology, Chinese Academy of Social Sciences, "Excavation and Research of the Fujiamen Site in Wushan," in *Archaeological Collection*, vol. 16 (Beijing: Science Press, 2006), 380–454.
53. Li Yangsong, "Research on the Ground Paintings of the Yangshao Late Period at Dadiwan Site in Qinan," *Archaeology*, no. 11 (1986): 1000–1004.
54. Chen Honghai, "Analysis of Secondary Disturbed Burials in the Prehistoric Culture of the Gansu and Qinghai Regions," *Archaeology*, no. 1 (2006): 54–68.
55. Zhang Wenxu and Wang Hui, "Research on Ancient Cultivated Rice in Qingyang, Gansu," *Agricultural Archaeology*, no. 3 (2000): 80–85; Li Xiaoqiang et al., "Archaeological Biological Indicators of Rice Remains in Northwest China 5000 a BP," *Chinese Science Bulletin* 52, no. 6 (2007): 673–678.
56. Yuan Jing, "On the Ways of Acquiring Meat Resources by the Residents of China's Neolithic," *Acta Archaeologica Sinica*, no. 1 (1999): 1–22.
57. Gansu Provincial Cultural Relics Management Committee, "Brief Report on the Archaeological Survey in Lintao and Linxia Counties, Gansu," *Archaeological Communication*, no. 9 (1958): 36–48.
58. Gansu Provincial Cultural Relics Working Team et al., "Excavation Report of Linjia Site in Dongxiang, Gansu," in *Archaeological Collections*, vol. 4 (Beijing: China Social Sciences Press, 1984), 111–161.
59. Peking University Archaeological Practice Team et al., "Brief Report on the Excavation of the Caowa Site in Haiyuan, Ningxia," *Archaeology*, no. 3 (1990): 206–209; Peking University Archaeological Practice Team et al., "Excavation Report of the Neolithic Site in Yehezi, Longde," in *Archaeological Research*, vol. 3 (Beijing: Science Press, 1997), 158–195.
60. Qinghai Provincial Archaeological Team, "Majiayao-Type Tombs Discovered in Naozhuang, Ledu County, Qinghai," *Archaeology*, no. 6 (1981): 554–555; Qinghai Provincial Archaeological Team, "Majiayao-Type Tomb No. 1 in Hetaozhuang, Minhe, Qinghai," *Wenwu*, no. 9 (1979): 29–32.
61. Gansu Provincial Institute of Cultural Relics and Archaeology, "Brief Report on the Excavation of the Neolithic Site and Wubashan Tombs in Taerwan, Wuwei," *Archaeology and Cultural Relics*, no. 3 (2004): 8–11; Li Shuicheng, "Newly Discovered Majiayao Cultural Remains in the Hexi Region and Related Issues," in *Su Bingqi and Contemporary Chinese Archaeology* (Beijing: Science Press, 2001), 121–135.
62. Chengdu Institute of Cultural Relics and Archaeology et al., "Trial Excavation Report of Yingpanshan Site in Mao County, Sichuan," *Chengdu Archaeological Discoveries* (2000) (Beijing: Science Press, 2002), 1–77.

63. Zhang Xuezheng, Zhang Pengchuan, and Guo Deyong, "On the Phases and Interrelations of Majiayao, Banshan, and Machang Types," in *Proceedings of the First Annual Meeting of the Chinese Archaeological Society* (Beijing: Cultural Relics Press, 1979), 50–71.
64. Yan Wenming, "The Origins of Gansu Painted Pottery," *Wenwu*, no. 10 (1978): 62–76; Yan Wenming and Zhang Wancang, "Yanerwan and Xipowa," in *Collected Essays on Archaeology and Culture*, vol. 3 (Beijing: Cultural Relics Press, 1993), 12–31.
65. Sun Shuyun and Han Rubin, "The Discovery of Early Copperware in Gansu and the Study of Smelting and Manufacturing Techniques," *Wenwu*, no. 7 (1997): 75–84.
66. Northwest Normal University Institute of Botany and Gansu Provincial Museum, "Millet and Hemp Unearthed from the Majiayao Culture Site of Linjia in Dongxiang, Gansu," *Archaeology*, no. 7 (1984): 654–655.
67. Zhou Benxiong, "Animal Remains from the Shizhaocun and Xishanping Sites," in *Shizhaocun and Xishanping* (Beijing: Encyclopedia of China Publishing House, 1999), 335–339.
68. Qinghai Provincial Cultural Relics Management Office and Hainan State Ethnic Museum, "Brief Report on the Excavation of the Zongri Site in Tongde County, Qinghai," *Archaeology*, no. 5 (1998): 1–14; Gesangben and Chen Honghai, eds., *Selected Essays on the Cultural Relics of the Zongri Site* (Chengdu: Sichuan Science and Technology Press, 1999).
69. Archaeology Research Center at Peking University et al., "Excavation Report of the Shaopengkou Site in Zhong County," in *Chongqing Reservoir Area Archaeological Reports Collection 1999* (Beijing: Science Press, 2006), 530–643.
70. See Zou Houxi and Yuan Dongshan, "Neolithic Culture in the Xiajiang Region of Chongqing," in *Proceedings of Chongqing 2001 Three Gorges Cultural Relics Protection Symposium* (Beijing: Science Press, 2003), 17–40; Bai Jiujang, *Neolithic Culture in Chongqing: Focused on the Three Gorges Area* (Chengdu: Bashu Publishing House, 2010).
71. Sichuan Provincial Institute of Cultural Relics and Archaeology et al., "Brief Report on the Excavation of the Guiyuanqiao Neolithic Site in Shifang, Sichuan," *Wenwu*, no. 9 (2013): 4–12.
72. Sichuan Provincial Institute of Cultural Relics and Archaeology et al., "Excavation of the Maiping Neolithic Site in Hanyuan County, Sichuan in 2007," *Archaeology*, no. 7 (2008): 11–19.
73. Cultural Relics Management Committee of the Xizang Autonomous Region and History Department of Sichuan University, *Changdu Karuo* (Beijing: Cultural Relics Press, 1985).
74. Shandong Provincial Cultural Relics Administration and Jinan Museum, *Dawenkou: Excavation Report of Neolithic Tombs* (Beijing: Cultural Relics Press, 1974).
75. Shandong Provincial Institute of Cultural Relics and Archaeology et al., *Zaozhuang Jianxin: Excavation Report of Neolithic Site* (Beijing: Science Press, 1996).
76. National Cultural Relics Administration Archaeological Leadership Training Class, *Yanzhou Liulijing* (Beijing: Science Press, 1999).
77. Nanjing Museum et al., *Excavation Report of Liangwangcheng Site: Prehistoric Volume* (Beijing: Cultural Relics Press, 2013).
78. As in Qianbuxia, Phase II, H128:9. See Shandong Provincial Institute of Cultural Relics and Archaeology et al., "Excavation Report of Qianbuxia Site in Weifang, Shandong," in

Shandong Province Highway Archaeological Reports Collection (1997) (Beijing: Science Press, 2000), 1–108.

79. Pingyin Zhouhe Archaeological Team, "Excavation of Dawenkou Culture Tombs at Zhouhe Site in Pingyin County, Shandong," *Archaeology*, no. 3 (2014): 3–12.

80. Shandong Team of the Institute of Archaeology, Chinese Academy of Sciences, "First Excavation Report of the Xixiahou Site in Qufu, Shandong," *Acta Archaeologia Sinica*, no. 2 (1964): 57–106; Shandong Team of the Institute of Archaeology, Chinese Academy of Social Sciences, "Second Excavation Report of the Xixiahou Site," *Acta Archaeologia Sinica*, no. 3 (1986): 307–338.

81. Shandong Provincial Institute of Archaeology, Shandong Museum et al., "Brief Report on the Excavation of Dawenkou Culture Tombs at Lingyanghe in Ju County, Shandong," *Prehistoric Research*, no. 3 (1987): 62–82.

82. Institute of Archaeology, Chinese Academy of Social Sciences, *Excavation and Research of Neolithic Settlement Remains at Mengcheng Yuchisi, Northern Anhui* (Beijing: Science Press, 2001); Institute of Archaeology, Chinese Academy of Social Sciences et al., *Mengcheng Yuchisi*, vol. 2 (Beijing: Science Press, 2007).

83. Han Jianye, "Analysis of Dawenkou Cemetery," *Cultural Relics of Central China*, no. 2 (1994): 48–61.

84. Institute of Archaeology, Chinese Academy of Social Sciences, *Jiaoxian Sanlihe* (Beijing: Cultural Relics Press, 1988).

85. Zhejiang Provincial Institute of Cultural Relics and Archaeology and Huzhou Museum, *Pishan* (Beijing: Cultural Relics Press, 2006).

86. Anhui Provincial Institute of Cultural Relics and Archaeology, *Qianshan Xuejiagang* (Beijing: Cultural Relics Press, 2004).

87. Anhui Provincial Institute of Cultural Relics and Archaeology, *Lingjiatan—Field Archaeological Excavation Report I* (Beijing: Cultural Relics Press, 2006).

88. Hubei Province Jingjiu Railway Archaeological Team and Hubei Provincial Institute of Cultural Relics and Archaeology, *Wuxue Gushan—Excavation Report of Neolithic Cemetery* (Beijing: Science Press, 2001).

89. Jiangxi Provincial Institute of Cultural Relics and Archaeology et al., "The Second Excavation of Zhengjiaao Cemetery in Jing'an," *Archaeology and Cultural Relics*, no. 2 (1994): 12–26.

90. Tian Mingli, "Exploring the Origins of Jade Articles from Lingjiatan Cemetery," *Southeast Culture*, no. 5 (1999): 18–25; Tian Mingli, "The Lingjiatan Remains and Hongshan Culture," in *Cultural Relics Research*, vol. 15 (Hefei: Huangshan Book Society, 2007), 79–90.

91. Anhui Provincial Institute of Cultural Relics and Archaeology, "New Discoveries from the Fifth Excavation of the Lingjiatan Site in Hanshan County, Anhui," *Archaeology*, no. 3 (2008): 7–17.

92. Some believe that this kind of plow-shaped implement is the earliest plow and that it had already entered the plow farming stage (Mou Yongkang and Song Zhaolin, "Stone Plows and Soil-breaking Implements in Jiangsu and Zhejiang: A Preliminary Discussion on the Origin of Plow Farming in China," *Agricultural Archaeology*, no. 2 [1981]: 75–84), while others deny its function as a plow based on microwear analysis and experimental

archaeological results (Liu Li et al., "Is the Triangular Stone Implement from the Neolithic Period in the Lower Reaches of the Yangtze River a Stone Plow?—Microwear Analysis of the Triangular Stone Implement Excavated from Pishan Site," *Southeast Culture*, no. 2 [2013]: 36–45).

93. Zhejiang Provincial Institute of Cultural Relics and Archaeology, *Fanshan* (Beijing: Cultural Relics Press, 2003).
94. Zhejiang Provincial Institute of Cultural Relics and Archaeology, *Yaoshan* (Beijing: Cultural Relics Press, 2003).
95. Shanghai Cultural Relics Management Committee, *Fuquanshan—Excavation Report of Neolithic Site* (Beijing: Cultural Relics Press, 2000).
96. Zhejiang Provincial Institute of Cultural Relics and Archaeology, "Excavations at the Liangzhu Ancient City Site in Yuhang District, Hangzhou City, 2006–2007," *Archaeology*, no. 7 (2008): 3–10.
97. Zhejiang Provincial Institute of Cultural Relics and Archaeology, "Excavations at the Mojiaoshan Site in Yuhang, 1992–1993," *Wenwu*, no. 12 (2001): 4–19.
98. Zhejiang Provincial Institute of Cultural Relics and Archaeology, *Fanshan* (Beijing: Cultural Relics Press, 2003).
99. Yan Wenming, "An Excellent Archaeological Report—Fanshan," *China Cultural Relics News*, 4th ed. (July 12, 2006).
100. Zhejiang Provincial Institute of Cultural Relics and Archaeology, *Liangzhu Settlements* (Beijing: Cultural Relics Press, 2005).
101. Zhejiang Provincial Institute of Cultural Relics and Archaeology, *Yaoshan* (Beijing: Cultural Relics Press, 2003); Zhejiang Provincial Institute of Cultural Relics and Archaeology et al., "Brief Report on the Excavation of Liangzhu Culture Altar and Cemetery at Huiguanshan in Yuhang, Zhejiang," *Wenwu*, no. 7 (1997): 7–19; Zhejiang Provincial Institute of Cultural Relics and Archaeology, "Brief Report on the Second Excavation of the Huiguanshan Site of Liangzhu Culture," *Wenwu*, no. 12 (2001): 36–41.
102. Wang Ningyuan, "Exploration of the Peripheral Structures of the Liangzhu Ancient City—On the Application of GIS and RS in the Archaeology of Large Sites," in *Proceedings of the 14th Annual Conference of the Chinese Archaeological Society 2011* (Beijing: Cultural Relics Press, 2012), 60–68.
103. Zhejiang Provincial Institute of Cultural Relics and Archaeology, *Bianjiashan* (Beijing: Cultural Relics Press, 2014).
104. Zhang Zhongpei, "The Age of Liangzhu Culture and the Social Stage it Occupied," *Wenwu*, no. 5 (1995): 47–58.
105. Zhang Chi, "A Preliminary Analysis of the Large Tombs of Liangzhu Culture," in *Archaeological Studies*, vol. 3 (Beijing: Science Press, 1997), 57–67.
106. Zhao Hui, "Several Specific Aspects of Liangzhu Culture —On the Causes of the Decline of a Prehistoric Civilization in China," in *Liangzhu Culture Studies—Proceedings of the International Academic Conference Commemorating the 60th Anniversary of the Discovery of Liangzhu Culture* (Beijing: Science Press, 1999), 109–117.

107. Qin Ling, "Comparative Study of Liangzhu Jade Decorations—Viewing the Social Relationship Network of Liangzhu through Engraved Jade," in *Journal of Zhejiang Provincial Institute of Cultural Relics and Archaeology*, vol. 8 (Beijing: Science Press, 2006), 23–52.
108. Yan Wenming, "Random Notes on Liangzhu," *Wenwu*, no. 3 (1996): 28–35.
109. Jiangxi Provincial Cultural Relics Working Team et al., "Brief Report on the Excavation of Fanchengdui Site in Qingjiang, Jiangxi," *Archaeology and Cultural Relics*, no. 2 (1989): 20–40.
110. Jiangxi Provincial Museum et al., "Second Excavation of the Zhuweicheng Site in Qingjiang, Jiangxi," *Archaeology*, no. 2 (1982): 130–138.
111. Jiangxi Provincial Institute of Cultural Relics and Archaeology et al., "Shinianshan Site in Xinyu, Jiangxi," *Acta Archaeologica Sinica*, no. 3 (1991): 285–324.
112. Jiangxi Provincial Institute of Cultural Relics and Archaeology et al., "Brief Report on the Excavation of the Laohudun Prehistoric Site in Jing'an, Jiangxi," *Wenwu*, no. 10 (2011): 4–21.
113. Guangdong Provincial Museum and Qujiang County Culture Bureau Shixia Excavation Group, "Brief Report on the Excavation of Shixia Tombs in Qujiang, Guangdong," *Wenwu*, no. 7 (1978): 1–15; Su Bingqi, "Preliminary Discussion on Shixia Culture," *Wenwu*, no. 7 (1978): 16–22.
114. These features were seen around 4000 BCE in the early Huangmei Saidun culture similar to the Beiyinyangying culture at the junction of Hubei and Anhui. It is possible that similar remains existed in the area from northwestern Jiangxi to northwestern Guangdong at that time.
115. Fujian Provincial Museum, "First and Second Excavations of the Neolithic Site at Niubishan in Pucheng County, Fujian," *Acta Archaeologica Sinica*, no. 2 (1996): 165–197.
116. Huang Yunming and He Qi, "Reunderstanding of Niubishan Culture: A Discussion on the Exchange of Archaeological Cultures in the Late Neolithic Period in the Border Area of Fujian, Zhejiang and Jiangxi," in *Proceedings of the 14th Annual Conference of the Chinese Archaeological Society 2011* (Beijing: Cultural Relics Press, 2012), 181–207.
117. Fujian Museum, *The Eighth Excavation Report of the Minhou Tanshishan Site* (Beijing: Science Press, 2004).
118. Fujian Provincial Museum, "Excavation Report of the Zhuangbianshan Site in Minhou, Fujian," *Acta Archaeologica Sinica*, no. 2 (1998): 171–227.
119. Qujialing Archaeological Excavation Team, "Third Excavation of the Qujialing Site," *Acta Archaeologica Sinica*, no. 1 (1992): 63–96.
120. Including the division of "Qujialing culture" phase I remains in Li County Chengtoushan—Neolithic Site Excavation Report.
121. Hunan Provincial Institute of Cultural Relics and Archaeology et al., "Neolithic Site at Gaokanlou in Huaihua," *Acta Archaeologica Sinica*, no. 3 (1992): 301–328.
122. Hubei Provincial Institute of Cultural Relics and Archaeology et al., "Brief Report on the Excavation of the Neolithic City Site at Yejiamiao in Xiaogan City, Hubei," *Archaeology*, no. 8 (2012): 3–28.

123. Jia Hanqing, "Tribal Conflicts in the Cultural Intersection Zone during the Prehistoric Period as Seen from the Excavation of Gujiapo Cemetery," *Huaxia Archaeology*, no. 4 (2004): 77–86.
124. Institute of Archaeology, Chinese Academy of Sciences, *Jingshan Qujialing* (Beijing: Science Press, 1965).
125. Jingzhou Museum of Hubei Province, Hubei Provincial Institute of Cultural Relics and Archaeology, and Department of Archaeology, Peking University, *Xiaojiawuji* (Beijing: Cultural Relics Press, 1999); Hubei Provincial Institute of Cultural Relics and Archaeology, Department of Archaeology, Peking University, and Jingzhou Museum of Hubei Province, *Dengjiawan* (Beijing: Cultural Relics Press, 2003).
126. Institute of Archaeology, Chinese Academy of Social Sciences, *Qinglongquan and Dasi* (Beijing: Science Press, 1991).
127. Hunan Provincial Institute of Cultural Relics and Archaeology et al., "Second Excavation Report of the Huachenggang Site in Anxiang, Hunan," *Acta Archaeologica Sinica*, no. 1 (2005): 55–108.
128. Hunan Provincial Institute of Cultural Relics and Archaeology et al., "Neolithic Site at Lishangwan in Luoshan County, Henan," *Huaxia Archaeology*, no. 3 (2000): 3–16.
129. Han Jianye and Yang Xingai, "Exploration on the Origin and Formation of the Miaoman Group," *Cultural Relics of Central China*, no. 4 (1996): 44–49.
130. Li Taoyuan, "Large House Building at Menbanwan Site in Yingcheng," *Jianghan Archaeology*, no. 1 (2000): 96.
131. Changjiang Basin Planning Office Archaeological Team Henan Branch, "Excavation Report of Huanglianshu Site in Xichuan, Henan," *Huaxia Archaeology*, no. 3 (1990): 1–69.
132. Hubei Provincial Institute of Cultural Relics and Archaeology, *Yichang County Yangjiawan* (Beijing: Science Press, 2013).
133. Guo Dashun suggests the possibility of a relationship between Hongshan Culture jade artifacts and Lake Baikal jade material. See Guo Dashun, *Hongshan Culture* (Beijing: Cultural Relics Press, 2005), 137.
134. Guo Dashun and Zhang Keju, "A Brief Report on the Excavation of the Hongshan Culture Architectural Site at Dongshanzui, Kazuo County, Liaoning Province," *Wenwu*, no. 11 (1984): 1–11.
135. Fang Dianchun and Liu Baohua, "The Discovery of Hongshan Culture Jade Artifacts in Hutougou, Fuxin County, Liaoning Province," *Wenwu*, no. 11 (1984): 1–5.
136. Su Bingqi, "Ancient Culture, Ancient City, and Ancient Dynastic State in Western Liaoning: A Discussion on the Current Focus or Major Topics in Field Archaeology," *Wenwu*, no. 8 (1986): 41–44.
137. Inner Mongolia Institute of Cultural Relics and Archaeology et al., "Brief Report on the 2010 Excavation of the Hamin Mangha Neolithic Site in Kezuozhongqi, Inner Mongolia," *Archaeology*, no. 3 (2012): 3–19; Ji Ping, "The Hamin Prehistoric Settlement Site in Tongliao, Inner Mongolia," in *Major Archaeological Discoveries in China 2011* (Beijing: Cultural Relics Press), 29–34.

138. Liaoning Provincial Museum et al., "The Discovery of Three Kinds of Primitive Cultures at Xiaoheyuan, Aohan Banner, Liaoning Province," *Wenwu*, no. 12 (1977): 1–22.
139. Liaoning Provincial Institute of Cultural Relics and Archaeology and Chifeng Museum, *Da'nangou: Excavation Report of the Late Hongshan Culture Cemetery* (Beijing: Science Press, 1998).
140. Han Jianye, "On the Xueshan Culture Phase I," *Huaxia Archaeology*, no. 4 (2003): 46–54.
141. Inner Mongolia Institute of Cultural Relics and Archaeology et al., "The Neolithic Cemetery at Nanbaoligaotu, Zhalute Banner, Inner Mongolia," *Archaeology*, no. 7 (2008): 20–31; Inner Mongolia Institute of Cultural Relics and Archaeology et al., "Brief Report on the Excavation of the Neolithic Cemetery at Site C, Nanbaoligaotu, Zhalute Banner, Inner Mongolia," *Archaeology*, no. 11 (2011): 24–37; Zhu Yonggang and Ji Ping, "Some Thoughts on the Cultural Nature of the Nanbaoligaotu Cemetery," *Archaeology*, no. 11 (2011): 67–72.
142. Liaoning Provincial Institute of Cultural Relics and Archaeology, Department of Archaeology at Jilin University, and Lushun Museum, "The Neolithic Site at Santang Village, Changxing Island, Wafangdian City, Liaoning Province," *Archaeology*, no. 2 (1992): 107–121.
143. Northeastern Working Team of the Institute of Archaeology, Chinese Academy of Social Sciences, "Excavations at the Zhaogongjie and Zhengjiawazi Sites in Shenyang," *Archaeology*, no. 10 (1989): 885–892.
144. Fujian Museum and Department of Anthropology, Harvard University, "Excavation of the Damaoshan Shell Mound Site in Dongshan County, Fujian," *Archaeology*, no. 12 (2003): 19–31.
145. Heilongjiang Provincial Institute of Cultural Relics and Archaeology and Department of Archaeology, Jilin University, "Excavation Report of the Xiaolaha Site in Zhaoyuan County, Heilongjiang," *Acta Archaeologica Sinica*, no. 1 (1998): 61–101.
146. Department of Anthropology, Sun Yat-sen University and Inner Mongolia Institute of Cultural Relics and Archaeology, "Brief Report on the 2009 Excavation of the Neolithic Site at Tabuaobao in Balinyou Banner, Inner Mongolia," *Archaeology*, no. 5 (2011): 3–15.
147. Jilin Provincial Institute of Cultural Relics and Archaeology, "Excavation of the Neolithic Site at Xiduanliangshan in Dongfeng County, Jilin," *Archaeology*, no. 4 (1991): 300–312.
148. Yanbian Museum, "Brief Report on the Clearance of the Neolithic Site at Jingu in Longjing County, Jilin Province," *Northern Wenwu*, no. 1 (1991): 3–18; Jilin Provincial Institute of Cultural Relics and Archaeology and Yanbian Korean Autonomous Prefecture Museum, *Helong Xingcheng: Excavation Report of the Neolithic and Bronze Age Sites* (Beijing: Cultural Relics Press, 2001); Zhao Binfu, *Archaeology of the Stone Age in Northeast China* (Changchun: Jilin University Press, 2003); Yang Zhanfeng, *Research on Neolithic Cultures in the Yalu River, Tumen River, and Ussuri River Basins* (Beijing: Cultural Relics Press, 2013).
149. Zhao Chaohong et al., "The Relationship between Hongshan Culture and Dawenkou Culture as Seen from the Investigation of the Raw Materials of Jade Artifacts," in

Research on Hongshan Culture: Proceedings of the 2004 International Academic Symposium on Hongshan Culture (Beijing: Cultural Relics Press, 2006), 456–463.

150. Tian Mingli, "Exploration of the Origins of Jade Artifacts in Lingjiatan Cemetery," *Southeast Culture*, no. 5 (1999): 18–25; Tian Mingli, "The Lingjiatan Site Remains and Hongshan Culture," in *Cultural Relics Research*, vol. 15 (Hefei: Huangshan Book Society, 2007), 79–90.

151. Han Jianye, "Three Levels of the Southward Influence of Late Hongshan Culture," in *Cultural Relics Research*, vol. 16 (Hefei: Huangshan Book Society, 2009), 61–66.

152. Yang Jianfang, "Exploration of the Origins of Daxi Culture Jade—Also on the Research Methods of the Spread and Influence of Chinese Neolithic Culture," in *Southern Ethnology Archaeology*, vol. 1 (1987), 15–20; Zhang Chi, "Stone and Jade Industries of Daxi, Beiyinyangying and Xuejiagang," in *Archaeological Research*, vol. 4 (Beijing: Science Press, 2000), 55–76.

153. Archaeological Research Institute of the Nanjing Museum, "Luzhuang Site in Funing, Jiangsu," in *Light of Oriental Civilization—A Collection Commemorating the 60th Anniversary of the Discovery of Liangzhu Culture* (Haikou: Hainan International News Publishing Center, 1996), 130–146; Nanjing Museum et al., "Neolithic Site of Dongyuan in Funing County, Jiangsu," *Archaeology*, no. 6 (2004): 7–21.

154. Nanjing Museum, *Huating—Excavation Report of the Neolithic Cemetery* (Beijing: Cultural Relics Press, 2003).

155. Yan Wenming, "Collision and Fusion—Thoughts on the Burial Situation of the Huating Cemetery," *Cultural Relics World*, no. 6 (1990): 18–20.

156. Archaeological Internship Team of Peking University, Shandong Provincial Institute of Cultural Relics and Archaeology, "Excavation Report of Yangjiaquan Site in Qixia," *Jiaodong Archaeology* (Beijing: Cultural Relics Press, 2000), 151–206.

157. Shuo Zhi, "Preliminary Analysis of Liangzhu Culture," *Acta Archaeologica Sinica*, no. 4 (2000): 421–451.

158. Mingshanhou Archaeological Site Team, "Major Discoveries from the First Phase of Excavation at Fenghua Mingshanhou Site," in *Journal of Zhejiang Provincial Institute of Cultural Relics and Archaeology: 10th Anniversary of Institute Establishment (1980–1990)* (Beijing: Science Press, 1993), 119–123.

159. Hunan Provincial Museum, "Daiziping Neolithic Site in Xiangxiang," in *Hunan Archaeological Collection*, vol. 2 (Changsha: Yuelu Publishing House, 1984), 1–25.

160. Nanjing Museum et al., *Excavation Report of Liangwangcheng Site: Prehistoric Volume* (Beijing: Cultural Relics Press, 2013), 59.

161. Hubei Working Team, Institute of Archaeology, Chinese Academy of Social Sciences, "Neolithic Tombs at Ludun, Huangmei, Hubei," *Archaeology*, no. 6 (1991): 481–496.

162. Han Jianye, "'The Pottery Road' and Early Cultural Exchanges between East and West," *Archaeology and Cultural Relics*, no. 1 (2013): 28–38.

163. Archaeological Team of the Qinghai Provincial Cultural Relics Administration, "Dance-patterned Colored Pottery Basin Excavated from Shangsunjiazhai, Datong, Qinghai," *Wenwu*, no. 3 (1978): 48–49.

164. Yunnan Provincial Institute of Cultural Relics and Archaeology et al., "Excavation Briefing of Yinsuo Island Site in Haidong, Dali City, Yunnan," *Archaeology*, no. 8 (2009): 23–41; Wan Jiao, *Prehistoric Culture of the Cang'er Area* (Beijing: Cultural Relics Press, 2013).
165. V. M. Masong, ed., *History of Central Asian Civilization*, vol. 1 (Beijing: China Translation & Publishing House, 2002), 86–106.
166. Joseph Garfinkel (Israel), "An Attempt to Analyze the Dance Decorations on Prehistoric Polychrome Pottery in the Near East and Southeast Europe," *Archaeology and Cultural Relics*, no. 1 (2004): 83–95.
167. Pottery *zun* (vat) with a pointed round bottom are mostly considered as wine vessels. See Wang Shuming, "Pottery Vessels in Archaeological Discoveries and Ancient Wine Brewing in China," in *Haidai Archaeology*, vol. 1 (Jinan: Shandong University Press, 1989), 370–389.
168. Qu Shi, *The Era of Chinese Jade Ware* (Taiyuan: Shanxi People's Publishing House, 1991).
169. Shanxi Provincial Institute of Archaeology et al., "Excavation Briefing of Dugou Site in Qingxu," in *Sanjin Archaeology*, vol. 3 (Taiyuan: Shanxi People's Publishing House, 2006), 15–59.
170. Wang Hui, "On the Era of the Origin of Chinese Characters through the Comparison of Oracle Bone Scripts, Bronze Inscriptions, and Archaeological Materials," *Acta Archaeologica Sinica*, no. 3 (2013): 283–296.
171. Zhang Guangzhi believes that the round inside and square outside of the jade *cong* symbolizes heaven and earth, while the faces of deities, humans, and animals represent shamans and their assistants, whose primary function is to communicate between heaven and earth. See Zhang Guangzhi, "On the 'Cong' and Its Significance in Ancient Chinese History," in *Collection of Cultural Relics and Archaeology—30th Anniversary of the Cultural Relics Press* (Beijing: Cultural Relics Press, 1986), 252–260.
172. Han Jianye and Yang Xingai, "Standing Bird Pottery and Bottle-Shaped Pottery Patterns of Dawenkou Culture," *Jianghan Archaeology*, no. 3 (2008): 43–47.
173. Feng Shi, *Chinese Archaeoastronomy* (Beijing: Social Sciences Academic Press, 2001); Li Xinwei, "The Cosmology Reflected in China's Prehistoric Jade Wares—and the Discussion on the Upper-Level Exchange Network in East China's Prehistoric Complex Society," *Southeast Culture*, no. 3 (2004): 66–72.
174. Zhao Hui, based on his analysis of Daxi culture cemeteries and settlements in the middle reaches of the Yangtze River, posited a correspondence that: grave-group = a set of rooms = nuclear family; grave-cluster = a house = extended family; grave-area = a row of houses = large clan; and graveyard = settlement = clan. See Zhao Hui, "Research on Neolithic Cemeteries in the Middle Reaches of the Yangtze River," in *Archaeological Research*, vol. 4 (Beijing: Science Press, 2000), 23–54.
175. Su Bingqi, "Welcoming the New Century of Chinese Archaeology," in *The Chinese: Descendants of the Dragon—Archaeological Quest for Roots* (Shenyang: Liaoning University Press, 1994), 236–251.
176. Yan Wenming, "The Origins and Development of Civilization in the Yellow River Basin," *Huaxia Archaeology*, no. 1 (1997): 49–54.

177. Wang Zhenzhong, "States, Dynastic State, and Empires: The Evolution of State Forms in Pre-Qin China," *Journal of Henan University (Social Science Edition)*, no. 4 (2003): 28–32.
178. Yan Wenming, "Longshan Culture and the Longshan Era," *Wenwu*, no. 6 (1981): 41–48.
179. Han Jianye and Yang Xingai, "Research on Wangwan Phase III Culture," *Acta Archaeologica Sinica*, no. 1 (1997): 1–22; Han Jianye, "Phases and Lineages of Miaodigou II—Longshan Era Culture in Southwest Shanxi and West Henan," *Acta Archaeologica Sinica*, no. 2 (2006): 179–204.
180. In the late period of Dawenkou culture, many late Dawenkou cultural sites suddenly emerged in the southeastern Shandong area, such as Sanlihe in Jiaozhou, Donghaiyu in Rizhao, Chengzi in Zhucheng, Lingyang River in Ju County, Dazhujia Village in Ju County, etc. These newcomers were less bound by tradition and were rich in innovation, ultimately completing the transition from Dawenkou culture to Longshan culture at the earliest and influencing the formation of the Longshan era.

    See Sun Bo, "Re-discussion on the Transition from Dawenkou Culture to Longshan Culture," in *Ancient Civilization*, vol. 6 (Beijing: Cultural Relics Press, 2007), 12–33.
181. Institute of Archaeology, Chinese Academy of Social Sciences, *Sanlihe in Jiao County* (Beijing: Cultural Relics Press, 1988).
182. Shandong Provincial Museum et al., "Excavation of the Donghaiyu Site in 1975," *Archaeology*, no. 6 (1976): 378–382.
183. Linyi Cultural Relics Team, "Excavation of Neolithic Tombs in Dafanzhuang, Linyi, Shandong," *Archaeology*, no. 1 (1975): 13–22.
184. Shandong Working Team of the Institute of Archaeology, Chinese Academy of Social Sciences et al., "Lujiakou Neolithic Site in Wei County," *Acta Archaeologica Sinica*, no. 3 (1985): 313–351.
185. Shandong University, Department of History, Archaeology Major Teaching and Research Office, *Sishui Yinjiacheng* (Beijing: Cultural Relics Press, 1990).
186. National Cultural Relics Bureau Archaeological Team Leader Training Class, *Yanzhou Xiwusi* (Beijing: Cultural Relics Press, 1990).
187. Shandong University, Department of History, Archaeology Major et al., "Brief Report on the Trial Excavation of the Zouping Dinggong Site in Shandong," *Archaeology*, no. 5 (1989): 391–398; Shandong University, Department of History, Archaeology Major, "Brief Report on the Second and Third Excavations of the Zouping Dinggong Site in Shandong," *Archaeology*, no. 6 (1992): 496–504; Luan Fengshi, "Phases and Types of Haidai Longshan Culture," in *Archaeological Research in Haidai Region* (Jinan: Shandong University Press, 1997), 233.
188. Shandong Provincial Institute of Cultural Relics and Archaeology, "Chiping Shangzhuang Neolithic Site," *Acta Archaeologica Sinica*, no. 4 (1985): 465–506.
189. Zhao Hui, "Phases and Regional Types of Longshan Culture," in *Collection of Cultural Archaeological Essays*, vol. 3 (Beijing: Cultural Relics Press, 1993), 230–269; Luan Fengshi, *Archaeological Research in Haidai Region* (Jinan: Shandong University Press, 1997), 229–282.
190. Sino-American Liangcheng Regional Joint Archaeological Team, "Brief Report on the Excavation of the Liangchengzhen Site in Rizhao City, Shandong Province from

1998 to 2001," *Archaeology*, no. 9 (2004): 7–18; Sino-American Rizhao Regional Joint Archaeological Team, *Systematic Archaeological Survey Report of the Southeastern Shandong Coastal Region* (Beijing: Cultural Relics Press, 2012).

191. Linyi Regional Cultural Management Association et al., "Trial Excavation Brief Report of the Longshan Culture Site of Yaowangcheng in Rizhao," *Prehistoric Research*, no. 4 (1985): 51–64.

192. Liu Dunyuan, "Materials on Jade Pit and Jade Ware in Liangchengzhen, Rizhao," *Archaeology*, no. 2 (1988): 121–123.

193. Shandong Working Team of the Institute of Archaeology, Chinese Academy of Social Sciences, "Longshan Culture Tombs in Zhufeng, Linqu, Shandong," *Archaeology*, no. 7 (1990): 587–594.

194. Jin Guiyun et al., "Study on the Carbonized Plant Remains of Longshan Culture at Zhaojiazhuang Site in Jiaozhou, Shandong," in *Scientific Archaeology*, vol. 3 (Beijing: Science Press, 2011), 36–53.

195. Gao Tianlin, Zhang Daihai, and Gao Wei, "The Chronology and Phases of the Taosi Type in Longshan Culture," *Prehistoric Research*, no. 3 (1984): 22–31; Zhang Daihai, "Taosi Culture and Longshan Era," in *Festschrift in Honor of the 55 Years of Archaeology by Su Bingqi* (Beijing: Cultural Relics Press, 1989), 245–251; He Nu, "A Comprehensive Study on the Lineage of Taosi Culture," in *Ancient Civilization*, vol. 3 (Beijing: Cultural Relics Press, 2004), 54–86.

196. Shanxi Working Team of the Institute of Archaeology, Chinese Academy of Social Sciences, Linfen Regional Culture Bureau, "Brief Report on the Excavation of the Taosi Site in Xiangfen County, Shanxi Province," *Archaeology*, no. 1 (1980): 18–31; Shanxi Working Team of the Institute of Archaeology, Chinese Academy of Social Sciences, Linfen Regional Culture Bureau, "Brief Report on the Excavation of the Taosi Cemetery in Xiangfen, Shanxi from 1978 to 1980," *Archaeology*, no. 1 (1983): 30–42.

197. Han Jianye, "The Tang Dynasty's War against Xixia and the Jifang Danzhu," *Journal of Peking University (Philosophy and Social Sciences Edition)*, no. 3 (2001): 119–123; Han Jianye, "Division and Lineage of the Culture in Miaodigou Phase II to the Longshan Era in Southwest Shanxi and West Henan," *Acta Archaeologica Sinica*, no. 2 (2006): 179–204.

198. Cultural Bureau of Linfen, Shanxi Province, Shanxi Working Team of the Institute of Archaeology, Chinese Academy of Social Sciences, "Report on the Excavation of the Taosi Culture Cemetery in Xiajin Village, Linfen, Shanxi Province," *Acta Archaeologica Sinica*, no. 4 (1999): 459–486; Xiajin Archaeological Team, "Brief Report on the Excavation of the Cemetery in Xiajin, Linfen, Shanxi Province," *Wenwu*, no. 12 (1998): 4–13.

199. Represented by Qingliangsi phases II–IV. See Shanxi Provincial Institute of Archaeology et al., "Neolithic Cemetery in Qingliangsi, Ruicheng, Shanxi," *Wenwu*, no. 3 (2006): 4–16; Shanxi Provincial Institute of Archaeology et al., "Prehistoric Cemetery in Qingliangsi, Ruicheng, Shanxi," *Acta Archaeologica Sinica*, no. 4 (2011): 525–560.

200. Shanxi Team of the Institute of Archaeology, Chinese Academy of Social Sciences et al., "2002 Excavation Report of the Taosi Ancient City Site in Xiangfen, Shanxi," *Acta Archaeologica Sinica*, no. 3 (2005): 307–346.

201. Liang Xingpeng and Yan Zhibin, "The Discovery of the Taosi Ancient City Site and Its Academic Significance for the Study of the Origins of Ancient Chinese Civilization," *Newsletter of Ancient Civilization Studies, Chinese Academy of Social Sciences*, no. 3 (2002): 60–63; He Nu and Yan Zhibin, "Further Exploration of the Largest Prehistoric City Site in the Yellow River Basin," *China Cultural Relics News*, 1st ed. (February 8, 2002).
202. Shanxi Team of the Institute of Archaeology, Chinese Academy of Social Sciences et al., "Discovery of Large-scale Rammed Earth Building Foundations from the Middle Period of Taosi Culture at the Taosi Site in Xiangfen County, Shanxi," *Archaeology*, no. 3 (2008): 3–6.
203. Shanxi Team of the Institute of Archaeology, Chinese Academy of Social Sciences et al., "Brief Report on the Excavation of Large-Scale Building Foundations in the Ritual Area of the Taosi Ancient City Site in Xiangfen County, Shanxi in 2003," *Archaeology*, no. 7 (2004): 7–24; "Brief Report on the Excavation of Large Building IIFJT1 Foundations in the Middle Taosi Ancient City Site, Xiangfen County, Shanxi 2004–2005," *Archaeology*, no. 4 (2007): 3–25.
204. Shanxi Team of the Institute of Archaeology, Chinese Academy of Social Sciences et al., "Brief Report on the Excavation of Residential Sites in Area II of the Taosi Site in Xiangfen County, Shanxi 1999–2000," *Archaeology*, no. 3 (2003): 3–17.
205. Shanxi Provincial Institute of Archaeology, "Brief Report on the Excavation of the Taosi Kiln at the Taosi Site," *Wenwu Quarterly*, no. 2 (1999): 3–10.
206. Gao Wei, "Ritual System of the Longshan Era," in *Festschrift in Honor of the 55 Years of Archaeology by Su Bingqi* (Beijing: Cultural Relics Press, 1989), 235–244.
207. Shanxi Team of the Institute of Archaeology, Chinese Academy of Social Sciences et al., "Discovery of Mid-Taosi Culture Tombs at the Taosi Ancient City Site," *Archaeology*, no. 9 (2003): 3–6.
208. Zhang Yajun, He Nu, and Zhang Fan, "Lineage Analysis of Human Bones from the Middle and Late Taosi Periods," *Acta Anthropologica Sinica* 28, no. 2 (2009): 363–371.
209. Previously referred to by me [the author] as the late Taosi type, mainly referring to what the excavators call the Taosi type or late Taosi culture, including the IIIH321 type remains of the middle period. See Shanxi Working Team of the Institute of Archaeology, Chinese Academy of Social Sciences et al., "Major Achievements from the Excavation of Residential Sites in Area III of the Taosi Site, 1983–1984," *Archaeology*, no. 9 (1986): 773–781.
210. Shanxi Provincial Institute of Archaeology et al., "Investigation and Excavation Report of Dongxu Site in Quwo, Shanxi," in *Sanjin Archaeology*, vol. 2 (Taiyuan: Shanxi People's Publishing House, 1996), 220–244.
211. Shanxi Working Team of the Institute of Archaeology, Chinese Academy of Social Sciences et al., "Brief Report on the Excavation of the Fangcheng Site in Quwo County, Shanxi," *Archaeology*, no. 4 (1988): 289–294.
212. Shanxi Provincial Institute of Archaeology, "Investigation and Preliminary Excavation Report of the Nanshi Site in Yicheng, Shanxi," in *Archaeology of Sanjin*, vol. 2 (Taiyuan: Shanxi People's Publishing House, 1996), 245–258.

213. Shanxi Team of the Institute of Archaeology, Chinese Academy of Social Sciences et al., "Excavation Report of the Taosi Ancient City Site in Xiangfen, Shanxi in 2002," *Acta Archaeologica Sinica*, no. 3 (2005): 307–346.
214. Cai Lianzhen and Qiu Shihua, "Carbon-13 Dating and Ancient Diet Research," *Archaeology*, no. 10 (1984): 949–955.
215. Henan Provincial Bureau of Cultural Relics, Henan Provincial Institute of Cultural Relics and Archaeology, in *Archaeological Report of the Xiaolangdi Reservoir on the Yellow River*, vol. 1 (Zhengzhou: Zhongzhou Ancient Books Publishing House, 1999), 391–422.
216. Henan Provincial Bureau of Cultural Relics, Henan Provincial Institute of Cultural Relics and Archaeology, in *Archaeological Report of the Xiaolangdi Reservoir on the Yellow River*, vol. 1 (Zhengzhou: Zhongzhou Ancient Books Publishing House, 1999), 4–94.
217. Han Jianye and Yang Xingai, "Research on the Phase III Culture of Wangwan," *Acta Archaeologica Sinica*, no. 1 (1997): 1–22.
218. Henan Provincial Institute of Cultural Relics and Archaeology, *Yancheng Haojiatai* (Zhengzhou: Elephant Press, 2012).
219. Henan Zhumadian District Cultural Management Committee, "Neolithic Site of Shilipu in Shangcai, Henan," in *Archaeological Collections*, vol. 3 (Beijing: China Social Sciences Press, 1983), 69–80.
220. Henan Provincial Bureau of Cultural Relics, Henan Provincial Institute of Cultural Relics and Archaeology, in *Archaeological Report of the Xiaolangdi Reservoir on the Yellow River*, vol. 1 (Zhengzhou: Zhongzhou Ancient Books Publishing House, 1999), 337–390.
221. Chinese Academy of Social Sciences, Archaeological Research Institute, Henan Second Team, "Excavation Report of Meishan Site in Linru, Henan," *Acta Archaeologica Sinica*, no. 4 (1982): 427–476; Henan Provincial Institute of Cultural Relics, "Excavation Report of Linru Meishan Site in 1987–1988," *Huaxia Archaeology*, no. 3 (1991): 5–23.
222. Henan Provincial Institute of Cultural Relics and Archaeology Department of the Museum of Chinese History, *Dengfeng Wangchenggang and Yangcheng* (Beijing: Cultural Relics Press, 1992); School of Archaeology and Museology, Peking University and Henan Provincial Institute of Cultural Relics, *Archaeological Discoveries and Research of Dengfeng Wangchenggang (2002–2007)* (Zhengzhou: Elephant Press, 2007).
223. Institute of Archaeology, Chinese Academy of Sciences, *Miaodigou and Sanliqiao* (Beijing: Science Press, 1959).
224. Chinese Academy of Social Sciences, Archaeological Research Institute, Museum of Chinese History, and Archaeological Team of Dongxiafeng, Shanxi Provincial Cultural Relics Working Committee, "Dongxiafeng Longshan Culture Site in Xia County, Shanxi," *Acta Archaeologica Sinica*, no. 1 (1983): 55–92.
225. It was previously generally referred to as the Sanliqiao type of Longshan culture or Sanliqiao culture.
226. Department of Archaeology, Peking University and Zhumadian Municipal Cultural Relics Protection Management Office, *Zhumadian Yangzhuang: Mid-Holocene Cultural Relics and Environmental Information in the Upper Huai River* (Beijing: Science Press,

1998); Han Jianye, "Preliminary Discussion on the Archaeological Culture of the Longshan Period in Southeastern Henan," in *Archaeological Studies*, vol. 3 (Beijing: Science Press, 1997), 68–83.

227. Hubei Provincial Institute of Cultural Relics and Archaeology, *Yidu Chengbeixi* (Beijing: Cultural Relics Press, 2001).

228. Peking University, Center for Research on Chinese Ancient Civilization and Zhengzhou Municipal Institute of Cultural Relics and Archaeology, *Xinmi Xinzhai: Field Archaeological Excavation Report 1999–2000* (Beijing: Cultural Relics Press, 2008).

229. Zhao Chunqing, *The Evolution of Neolithic Settlements in the Zhengzhou–Luoyang Region* (Beijing: Peking University Press, 2001).

230. Henan Provincial Institute of Cultural Relics and Archaeology, *Yuzhou Wadian* (Beijing: World Publishing Corporation, 2004).

231. Henan Provincial Institute of Cultural Relics and Archaeology et al., "Excavation Report of Longshan Culture City Site in Guchengzhai, Xinmi Ancient City, Henan," *Huaxia Archaeology*, no. 2 (2002): 53–82.

232. It was previously generally referred to as Zaolütai type or Wangyoufang type. For example, those referring to it as Zaolütai type include Yan Wenming, "Longshan Culture and Longshan Period," *Wenwu*, no. 6 (1981): 41–48; Li Boqian, "On Zaolütai Type," *Wenwu*, no. 4 (1983): 50–59. Those referring to it as Wangyoufang type include Wu Ruzuo, "Preliminary Exploration on Xia Culture and its Source," *Wenwu*, no. 9 (1978): 70–73.

233. Li Jinglan, "Investigation of Shangqiu Yongcheng in Eastern Henan and Small Excavations at Zaolütai, Heigu Dui, Caoqiao and Other Sites," *Bulletin of the Chinese School of Archaeology* 2 (1947), 83–120.

234. Chinese Academy of Social Sciences, Archaeological Research Institute, Henan Second Team et al., "Excavation Report of Wangyoufang Site in Yongcheng, Henan," *Archaeological Collection* 5 (Beijing: Chinese Academy of Social Sciences Press, 1987), 9–119.

235. Chinese Academy of Social Sciences, Archaeological Research Institute and Bengbu Museum in Anhui Province, *Bengbu Yuhui Village* (Beijing: Science Press, 2013).

236. Luan Fengshi, "Preliminary Discussion on Wangyoufang Type of Longshan Culture," *Archaeology*, no. 10 (1992): 924–935.

237. Only from the perspective of the Yuhui Village site in Bengbu, the period should be around the transitional phase of early and late Longshan or the beginning of the late Longshan period.

238. Nanjing Museum Archaeological Research Institute et al., "Xinghua Daijiashe Nandang Site in Jiangsu," *Wenwu*, no. 4 (1995): 16–31.

239. Nanjing Museum Archaeological Research Institute et al., "Excavation Report of Zhoubeidun Site in Gaoyou, Jiangsu," *Acta Archaeologica Sinica*, no. 4 (1997): 481–514.

240. Henan Provincial Institute of Cultural Relics et al., "Preliminary Excavation Report of Longshan Culture City Site in Pingliangtai, Huaiyang, Henan," *Wenwu*, no. 3 (1983): 21–36.

241. Chinese Academy of Social Sciences, Archaeological Institute Anyang Working Team, "1979 Excavation Report of Anyang Hougang Site," *Acta Archaeologica Sinica*, no. 1 (1985): 33–88.

242. Anyang District Cultural Relics Management Committee of Henan Province, "Excavation Report of Longshan Culture Village Site in Baiying River, Tangyin, Henan," *Archaeological Collection*, vol. 3 (Beijing: Chinese Academy of Social Sciences Press, 1983), 1–47.
243. "Peking University History Department Archaeology Major 4th Year Practice in the Suburbs of Beijing—Excavation of Neolithic to Liao Dynasty Cultural Sites," *Guangming Daily* (April 2, 1964).
244. Beijing Municipal Institute of Cultural Relics, *Zhenjiangying and Tazhao—Types and Lineages of Pre-Qin Archaeological Cultures in the Juma River Basin* (Beijing: Encyclopedia of China Publishing House, 1999).
245. Hebei Provincial Institute of Cultural Relics and Cangzhou District Cultural Relics Management Office, "Excavation Report of Yabazhuang Site in Renqiu City, Hebei Province," supplement, *Wenwu Chunqiu* (1992): 178–219.
246. Tian Guangjin, "On the Prehistoric Archaeology of Central and Southern Inner Mongolia," *Acta Archaeologica Sinica*, no. 2 (1997): 121–146.
247. Inner Mongolia Institute of Cultural Relics and Archaeology, *Daihai Archaeology (I)—Collection of Excavation Reports of Laohushan Culture Sites* (Beijing: Science Press, 2000).
248. Inner Mongolia Institute of Cultural Relics and Archaeology, "Yongxingdian Site in Jungar Banner," in *Collection of Inner Mongolia Cultural Relics and Archaeology*, vol. 1 (Beijing: Encyclopedia of China Publishing House, 1994), 235–245.
249. State Administration of Cultural Heritage, Shanxi Provincial Institute of Archaeology, and Jilin University Department of Archaeology, *Archaeology in Jinzhong* (Beijing: Cultural Relics Press, 1999).
250. Frontier Archaeology Research Center of Jilin University et al., *Archaeology in Xinzhou Youyao* (Beijing: Science Press, 2004).
251. Xi'an Banpo Museum, "Brief Report on the Investigation and Trial Excavation of the Shimao Site in Shenmu, Shaanxi," *Prehistoric Research*, no. 2 (1983): 92–100.
252. Zhangjiakou Archaeological Team, "The Main Achievements of Neolithic Archaeology in Yu County in 1979," *Archaeology*, no. 2 (1981): 97–105; Zhangjiakou Archaeological Team, "A Brief Account of Yu County Archaeology," *Archaeology and Cultural Relics*, no. 4 (1982): 10–14.
253. Han Jianye, *Research on Neolithic Cultures in Northern China* (Beijing: Cultural Relics Press, 2003).
254. Shaanxi Provincial Institute of Archaeology et al., "Shimao Site in Shenmu County, Shaanxi," *Archaeology*, no. 7 (2013): 15–24.
255. Shaanxi Provincial Institute of Archaeology et al., "Shijiawan Site in Ganquan County, Northern Shaanxi," *Wenwu*, no. 11 (1992): 11–25.
256. Zhang Zhongpei and Sun Zuchu believe that the remains of the Shijiawan type are the result of the westward development of the Fen River Basin culture.

See Zhang Zhongpei, Sun Zuchu, "A Study on the Lineage of Prehistoric Culture in Shaanxi and the Formation of Zhou Civilization," in *Distant Views Collection—Anniversary Collection of the 40th Anniversary of the Shaanxi Provincial Institute of Archaeology* (Xi'an: Shaanxi People's Fine Arts Publishing House, 1998), 150.

257. Archaeological Research Institute of the Chinese Academy of Sciences, Fengxi Excavation Team, *Report on the Excavation in Fengxi* (Beijing: Cultural Relics Press, 1962).
258. Institute of Archaeology, Chinese Academy of Social Sciences, *Shizhaocun and Xishanping* (Beijing: Encyclopedia of China Publishing House, 1999).
259. Ningxia Institute of Cultural Relics, Archaeological Department of the Museum of Chinese History, *Ningxia Caiyuan—Excavation Report of Neolithic Sites and Tombs* (Beijing: Science Press, 2003).
260. Han Jianye, *Natural Environment and Cultural Development in Northwest China during the Pre-Qin Period* (Beijing: Cultural Relics Press, 2008), 142–196.
261. Han Jianye, "The Formation of the Banshan Type and the Westward Migration of Eastern Culture," *Archaeology and Cultural Relics*, no. 3 (2007): 33–38.
262. Institute of Archaeology, Chinese Academy of Social Sciences, *Qinghai Liuwan* (Beijing: Cultural Relics Press, 1984).
263. Gansu Provincial Museum, "Excavation Report of Huangniangniangtai Site in Wuwei, Gansu," *Acta Archaeologica Sinica*, no. 2 (1960): 53–72; Gansu Provincial Museum, "The Fourth Excavation of Huangniangniangtai Site in Wuwei," *Acta Archaeologica Sinica*, no. 4 (1978): 421–448.
264. Baoji City Institute of Archaeology, "Discovery of Architectural Components from the Longshan Culture Period in Baoji," *Wenwu*, no. 3 (2011): 44–45.
265. Archaeological Practice Team of the 1982 Class in History Department, Northwest University, "Excavation Report of the Eastern Area of Shizuikou in Baoji," *Acta Archaeologica Sinica*, no. 2 (1987): 209–226.
266. Institute of Archaeology, Chinese Academy of Social Sciences et al., "Excavation of the Prehistoric Site of Lajia in Minhe, Qinghai," *Archaeology*, no. 7 (2002): 3–5; Gansu and Qinghai Work Team of the Institute of Archaeology, Chinese Academy of Social Sciences et al., "Brief Report on the 2000 Excavation at Lajia Site in Minhe County, Qinghai," *Archaeology*, no. 12 (2002): 12–28; Gansu and Qinghai Work Team of the Institute of Archaeology, Chinese Academy of Social Sciences et al., "Discovery of the Qijia Culture Altar and Raised-Floor Buildings at Lajia Site in Minhe, Qinghai," *Archaeology*, no. 6 (2004): 3–6.
267. Li Xiaoqiang et al., "Bioindicator Records of the Earliest Agricultural Diversification in China from the Xishanping Site in Gansu," *Chinese Science Bulletin: Earth Sciences* 37, no. 7 (2007): 934–940.
268. Zhouyuan Archaeological Team, "Results and Preliminary Analysis of the Attempted Flotation at the Zhouyuan Site (Wangjiazui Location)," *Wenwu*, no. 10 (2004): 89–96.
269. Archaeological Teaching and Research Office of the History Department, Wuhan University et al., "Neolithic Site of Lishangang in Macheng, Hubei," *Acta Archaeologica Sinica*, no. 4 (1990): 439–474.
270. History Department specializing in Archaeology, Wuhan University et al., "Trial Excavation of Yaojialin Site in Tongcheng, Hubei," *Jianghan Archaeology*, no. 3 (1983): 1–12.
271. Department of Archaeology, Peking University and Anhui Provincial Institute of Cultural Relics and Archaeology, "Preliminary Excavation Report of Zhangsidun Site in Anqing, Anhui," *Archaeology*, no. 1 (2004): 20–31.

272. Yang Xingai and Han Jianye, "Exploration of Yu's Campaign Against the Sanmiao," *Cultural Relics of Central China*, no. 2 (1995): 46–55.
273. He Nu, "Discussion on Xiaojiawuji Culture and Related Issues," in *Three Generations Archaeology*, vol. 2 (Beijing: Science Press, 2006), 98–145.
274. Eagle-head hairpins like the ones unearthed at the Xiaojiawuji site have also been found at the Wadian site in Yuzhou, Henan, and coronet-shaped openwork jade ornaments similar to those from Zhongxiang, Liuhe, and other sites have also been seen in the large tomb of Zhufeng in Linqu, Shandong, and Taosi M22 in Xiangfen, Shanxi.
275. Hubei Provincial Institute of Cultural Relics and Archaeology, *Qilihe in Fang County* (Beijing: Cultural Relics Press, 2008).
276. Xiaogan City Museum, "Excavation of Wujiatan Site in Xiaogan, Hubei," *Acta Archaeologica Sinica*, no. 3 (1998): 331–360.
277. Deng Zhenhua, Liu Hui, and Meng Huaping, "Analysis of Plant Remains Unearthed from the Shijiahe Ancient City, Sanfangwan and Tanjialing Sites in Tianmen City, Hubei," *Archaeology*, no. 1 (2013): 91–99.
278. Sino-Japanese Joint Archaeological Survey Team, "Preliminary Report on the Excavation of Baodun Site in Xinjin County, Sichuan in 1996," *Archaeology*, no. 1 (1998): 29–50; Chengdu Cultural Relics and Archaeological Research Institute et al., *Baodun Site—Excavation and Research of Baodun Site in Xinjin* (Hadano: Japan Arupu Ltd., 2000); Chengdu Cultural Relics and Archaeological Research Institute et al., "Preliminary Report on the Survey and Excavation of Xinjin Baodun Site (2009–2010)," in *Discoveries in Chengdu Archaeology (2009)* (Beijing: Science Press, 2011), 1–67.
279. Chengdu Cultural Relics and Archaeological Work Team et al., "Investigation and Excavation of Mangcheng Site in Dujiangyan City, Sichuan," *Archaeology*, no. 7 (1999): 14–27.
280. Chengdu Cultural Relics and Archaeological Work Team et al., "Investigation and Excavation of the Ancient City Site in Pi County County, Sichuan," *Wenwu*, no. 1 (1999): 32–42.
281. Chengdu Cultural Relics and Archaeological Work Team et al., "Investigation and Excavation of Yufu Village Site in Wenjiang County, Sichuan," *Wenwu*, no. 12 (1998): 38–56.
282. Chengdu Cultural Relics and Archaeological Work Team, "Preliminary Report on the Excavation of Shuanghe Prehistoric City Site in Chongzhou City, Sichuan," *Archaeology*, no. 1 (2002): 3–19.
283. Sichuan Provincial Cultural Relics and Archaeological Research Institute et al., "Preliminary Report on the Excavation of Zone II of Zhongba Site in Zhong County," in *Collected Reports on Chongqing Reservoir Area Archaeology*, vol. 1998 (Beijing: Science Press, 2003), 607–648; Sichuan Provincial Cultural Relics and Archaeological Research Institute et al., "Preliminary Report on the 1999 Excavation of Zhongba Site in Zhong County," in *Collected Reports on Chongqing Reservoir Area Archaeology*, vol. 1998 (Beijing: Science Press, 2007), 964–1042; Sun Zhibin, "Preliminary Study on the Neolithic Remains of Zhongba Site," *Sichuan Cultural Relics*, no. 3 (2003): 32–40.
284. Center for Archaeological Research at Peking University et al., "Excavation Report of Shaopengzui Site in Zhong County," in *Collected Reports on Chongqing Reservoir Area Archaeology*, vol. 1999 (Beijing: Science Press, 2006), 530–643.

285. Changjiang Sanxia Work Team of the Institute of Archaeology, Chinese Academy of Social Sciences, "Excavation of the Weijialiangzi Site in Wushan County, Sichuan," *Archaeology*, no. 8 (1996): 1–18.
286. Jiang Ming et al., "Preliminary Analysis of the Flotation Results of the 2009 Archaeological Excavation at the Xinjin Baodun Site," in *Discoveries in Chengdu Archaeology (2009)* (Beijing: Science Press, 2011), 68–82.
287. Chengdu Cultural Relics and Archaeological Research Institute et al., "Preliminary Report on the Excavation of the Xiaguanzi Site in Mao County, Sichuan," in *Discoveries in Chengdu Archaeology (2006)* (Beijing: Science Press, 2008), 31–62.
288. Shanghai Museum Archaeological Research Department, "Preliminary Report on the Excavation of the Guangfulin Site in Songjiang District, Shanghai from 1999 to 2000," *Archaeology*, no. 10 (2002): 31–48; Shanghai Museum Archaeological Research Department, "Preliminary Report on the Excavation of the Guangfulin Site in Songjiang District, Shanghai from 2001 to 2005," *Archaeology*, no. 8 (2008): 3–21.
289. Jiangxi Provincial Cultural Relics Management Committee, "Archaeological Survey and Excavation in the Shanbei Area of Xiushui, Jiangxi," *Archaeology*, no. 7 (1962): 353–367.
290. Zhejiang Provincial Cultural Relics and Archaeological Research Institute et al., *Haochuan Cemetery* (Beijing: Cultural Relics Press, 2001).
291. Andersson, J. G. *Archaeological Research in Kansu* (Geological Bulletin, series A, no. 5, 1925). Banshan was part of Ningding County in Gansu at that time.
292. Gansu Provincial Museum, "Preliminary Report on the Excavation of the Qinggangcha Site in Lanzhou, Gansu," *Archaeology*, no. 3 (1972): 26–31; Cultural Relics Working Team of Gansu Provincial Museum, "The Second Excavation of the Banshan Site at Qinggangcha in Lanzhou, Gansu," in *Collected Papers on Archaeology*, vol. 2 (Beijing: China Social Sciences Press, 1982), 10–17.
293. Gansu Provincial Museum et al., "Tugutai Banshan—The Ma Factory Culture Cemetery in Lanzhou," *Acta Archaeologica Sinica*, no. 2 (1983): 191–222.
294. Linxia Hui Autonomous Prefecture Museum, "Preliminary Report on the Cleanup of the Neolithic Cemetery at Bianjialin in Kangle County, Gansu," *Wenwu*, no. 4 (1992): 63–76.
295. Archaeological Team of Qinghai Provincial Cultural Relics Administration Office and Institute of Archaeology, Chinese Academy of Social Sciences, *Qinghai Liwan—A Primitive Society Cemetery in Ledu Liwan* (Beijing: Cultural Relics Press, 1984).
296. Qinghai Provincial Institute of Archaeology, "Qinghai Xunhua Suhusa Cemetery," *Acta Archaeologica Sinica*, no. 4 (1994): 425–469.
297. Han Jianye, "The Formation of Banshan Types and the Westward Migration of Eastern Culture," *Archaeology and Cultural Relics*, no. 3 (2007): 33–38.
298. Cultural Relics Administration Office of Qinghai Province, Hainan Prefecture Ethnic Museum, "Preliminary Report on the Excavation of the Zongri Site in Tongde County, Qinghai," *Archaeology*, no. 5 (1998): 1–14; Gesangben and Chen Honghai, eds., *Selection of Essential Cultural Relics and Discussions on Zongri Site* (Sichuan: Sichuan Science and Technology Press, 1999).
299. Andersson, J. G. *Archaeological Research in Kansu* (Geological Bulletin, series A, no. 5, 1925). Machangyuan belonged to Nianbo County in Gansu at the time.

300. Gansu Provincial Museum et al., "Tugutaiban Banshan—The Ma Factory Culture Cemetery in Lanzhou," *Acta Archaeologica Sinica*, no. 2 (1983): 191–222.
301. Qinghai Provincial Institute of Cultural Relics Archaeology, *Minhe Yangshan* (Beijing: Cultural Relics Press, 1990).
302. Li Fan et al., "New Discoveries of Ancient Agricultural Remains at the Donghuishan Neolithic Site in Minle County, Gansu Province," *Agricultural Archaeology*, no. 1 (1989): 56–69.
303. Li Shuicheng, "The Collision and Exchange of Eastern and Western Cultures around 2000 BCE as Seen from Archaeological Discoveries," *Xinjiang Cultural Relics*, no. 1 (1999): 53–65; Li Shuicheng and Mo Duowen, "Chronological Study of Carbonized Wheat at Donghuishan Site," *Archaeology and Cultural Relics*, no. 6 (2004): 51–60.
304. Institute of Archaeology, Chinese Academy of Social Sciences, *Shuangtaizi and Gangshang—The Discovery and Study of Prehistoric Culture in Eastern Liaoning* (Beijing: Science Press, 1996).
305. Xu Yulin and Yang Yongfang, "Preliminary Report on the Excavation of the Beigou Xishan Site in Xiuyan, Liaoning," *Archaeology*, no. 5 (1992): 389–398.
306. Jieyang Archaeological Team et al., "Excavation Report of the Neolithic Site at Hutoupu in Puning City," in *Jieyang Archaeology (2003–2005)* (Beijing: Science Press, 2005), 3–50.
307. Li Ziwen, "Excavation of the Haishawan Site on Qi'ao Island," in *Zhuhai Archaeological Discoveries and Research* (Guangzhou: Guangdong People's Publishing House, 1991), 3–21.
308. Guangdong Provincial Institute of Cultural Relics and Archaeology and Zhuhai Museum, *Baojingwan in Zhuhai—Excavation Report of the Island-type Prehistoric Cultural Site* (Beijing: Science Press, 2004).
309. Guangdong Provincial Institute of Cultural Relics and Archaeology and Dongguan Museum, "Excavation of the Yuanzhou Shell Mound Site in Dongguan City, Guangdong," *Archaeology*, no. 6 (2000): 11–23.
310. Antiquities and Monuments Office, Hong Kong, "Preliminary Report on the Excavation of the Neolithic Site at Yonglang in Hong Kong," *Archaeology*, no. 6 (1997): 35–53.
311. The stone grinding slab is concave in the middle and round-bottom, while one end of the grinding rod is eroded into a pestle shape, possibly used for crushing and grinding edible plant roots and stems. This was common in South China, different from the stone grinding slabs and rods used for processing grains in the Northern region.
312. Guangxi Zhuang Autonomous Region Cultural Relics Working Team et al., "Preliminary Report on the Excavation of the Shijiaoshan Site in Pingnan County, Guangxi," *Archaeology*, no. 1 (2001): 15–21.
313. Guangxi Zhuang Autonomous Region Cultural Relics Working Team et al., "Preliminary Report on the Excavation of the Gantuoyan Site in Napo County, Guangxi," *Archaeology*, no. 10 (2003): 35–56.
314. Guangxi Institute of Cultural Relics and Archaeology and Nanning Museum, *Guangxi Pre-Qin Rock Cave Burials* (Beijing: Science Press, 2007).
315. Yunnan Provincial Institute of Cultural Relics and Archaeology et al., "Excavation Report of the Xinguang Site in Yongping, Yunnan," *Acta Archaeologica Sinica*, no. 2 (2002): 203–234.

316. Yunnan Provincial Institute of Cultural Relics and Archaeology et al., "Excavation Report of the Caiyuanzi and Mopandi Sites in Yongren, Yunnan in 2001," *Acta Archaeologica Sinica*, no. 2 (2003): 263–293.
317. Yunnan Provincial Museum, "The Baiyangcun Site in Binchuan, Yunnan," *Acta Archaeologica Sinica*, no. 4 (1981): 349–368.
318. Yunnan Provincial Museum, "The Dandunzi Neolithic Site in Yuanmou, Yunnan," *Acta Archaeologica Sinica*, no. 1 (1977): 43–72.
319. Jin Hetian et al., "Flotation Results and Analysis of the Dandunzi Site in Yuanmou, Yunnan," *Jianghan Archaeology*, no. 3 (2014): 109–114.
320. Okamura Hidenori, "Exchanges of Prehistoric Cultures between the Liaodong Peninsula and the Shandong Peninsula," in *Proceedings of the International Academic Conference on Archaeology around the Bohai Sea (Shijiazhuang, 1992)* (Beijing: Knowledge Press, 1996), 108–111.
321. Han Jianye, "Slanted-Bellied Cup and Sanmiao Culture," *Jianghan Archaeology*, no. 1 (2002): 67–72.
322. Han Jianye, "The Expansion and External Influence of Laohushan Culture," *Cultural Relics of Central China*, no. 1 (2007): 17–23.
323. Peter Bellwood and Hong Xiaochun, "The Spread of Early Rice Agriculture from South China to Southeast Asia," in *Proceedings of the Hemudu Culture International Academic Forum* (Beijing: China Time Economic Publishing House, 2013), 95–107.
324. Li Hongfei, "A Preliminary Analysis of the Role of Bronze Ware in Early Chinese Social Change," *Nanfang Cultural Relics*, no. 4 (2011): 67–73.
325. Institute of Archaeology, Chinese Academy of Social Sciences Shanxi Work Team and Linfen District Culture Bureau, "The First Discovery of Bronze Ware in Taosi Site, Xiangfen, Shanxi," *Archaeology*, no. 12 (1984): 1069–1071.
326. Metallurgical History Group, Beijing Institute of Iron and Steel, "Preliminary Study on Early Chinese Bronze Ware," *Acta Archaeologica Sinica*, no. 3 (1981): 287–302.
327. Luo Kun, "An Interpretation of Taosi Pottery Inscriptions," *Newsletter of the Center for Ancient Civilization Studies, Chinese Academy of Social Sciences*, no. 2 (2001): 13–18.
328. He Nu, "New Exploration of the Flat Pot Zhu Writing 'Characters' in the Taosi Site," *China Cultural Relics News*, 7th ed. (November 28, 2003); Ge Yinghui, "Deciphering the Title of Emperor Yao, Advancing the Study of Civilization," *Newsletter of the Research on Ancient Civilization*, no. 32 (2007): 1–6.
329. Feng Shi, "A Study of 'Wenyi,'" *Acta Archaeologica Sinica*, no. 3 (2008): 273–290.
330. Archaeology Major, History Department, Shandong University, "Brief Report on the Fourth and Fifth Excavations of the Dinggong Site in Zouping, Shandong," *Archaeology*, no. 4 (1993): 295–299.
331. Wang Entian, Tian Changwu, Liu Dunyuan, et al., "Experts Discuss the Pottery Texts Excavated from Dinggong Site," *Archaeology*, no. 4 (1993): 344–354.
332. Feng Shi, "Interpreting the Characters of Longshan Era at Dinggong, Shandong," *Archaeology*, no. 1 (1994): 37–54.

333. Sun Bo, "Revisiting the Transition from Dawenkou Culture to Longshan Culture—Also Discussing the Turning Point between Yangshao Period and Longshan Period," in *Early China Studies*, vol. 1 (Beijing: Cultural Relics Press, 2013), 143–162.
334. Zhang Zhongpei, "A Glimpse into the Lingjiatan Cemetery," *Wenwu*, no. 9 (2000): 55–63.
335. Araki Hiyoriko, "The Symbolic Significance of Oracle Bones," in *Proceedings of the International Academic Symposium Commemorating the 100th Anniversary of the Discovery of Oracle Bones in Yin Ruins* (Beijing: Social Sciences Academic Press, 2003), 335–351.
336. Yan Wenming, "Skull Cups and Scalping Customs in Jiangou," *Archaeology and Cultural Relics*, no. 2 (1982): 38–42.
337. Yongcheng Archaeological Team, "Brief Report on the Excavation of the Daxincun Site in Fengxiang County, Shaanxi," *Archaeology and Cultural Relics*, no. 1 (1985): 1–11.
338. Han Jianye, "Liangzhu, Taosi, and Erlitou—The Path of Early Chinese Civilization's Evolution," *Archaeology*, no. 11 (2010): 71–78.

Chapter 5 The Dynastic State Stage of Early China

1. Han Jianye, "A Brief Discussion on China's 'Bronze Age Revolution,'" *Western Region Studies*, no. 3 (2012): 66–70.
2. Han Jianye, "On the Rise of the Erlitou Bronze Civilization," *Chinese Historical Relics*, no. 1 (2009): 37–47.
3. Institute of Archaeology, Chinese Academy of Social Sciences, *Yanshi Erlitou—1959–1978 Archaeological Excavation Report* (Beijing: Encyclopedia of China Publishing House, 1999); Institute of Archaeology, Chinese Academy of Social Sciences, *Erlitou (1999–2006)* (Beijing: Cultural Relics Press, 2014).
4. The early stage of Wangwan Phase III culture is seen at the Shilipu site in Shangcai, Henan, and the later period is seen at the Xiaopangou site in Mengjin. See Cultural Relics Management Committee of Zhumadian Region, Henan Province, "Neolithic Site in Shangcai, Henan," in *Collection of Archaeology*, vol. 3 (Beijing: China Social Sciences Press, 1983), 69–80; Luoyang Museum, "Preliminary Excavation Report of the Xiaopangou Site in Mengjin," *Archaeology*, no. 4 (1978): 244–255.
5. The cloud-thunder pattern was first seen in the remains of the Majiabang culture in Sanxing Village, Jintan District, and later in various cultures in the eastern part.
6. As Lin Yun pointed out (Lin Yun, "Several Chronological Issues of Early Northern Bronze Ware," in *Collection of Cultural Relics and Archaeology in Inner Mongolia*, vol. 1 [Beijing: Encyclopedia of China Publishing House, 1994], 291–295), one of the bronze ring-pommel swords unearthed from the Erlitou site phase three clearly belongs to the northern system, and another copper qi is actually a variant of the northern battle axe.

In addition, the copper *yue* unearthed from the Erlitou site, its shape, and grid-like pattern are also similar to the axes commonly seen in the West (Erlitou Task Force, Institute of Archaeology, Chinese Academy of Social Sciences, "A Bronze *Yue* Found at the Erlitou Site in Yanshi, Henan," *Archaeology*, no. 11 [2002]: 31–34). These artifacts can find similar types in the late Qijia culture.

7. The Erlitou site phase three discovered double wheel rut marks, with a track width of about 1.2 meters (Institute of Archaeology, Chinese Academy of Social Sciences, *Chinese Archaeology: Xia Shang Volume* [Beijing: Encyclopedia of China Publishing House, 2003], 122–123); double-wheel horse carriages in the Sintashta tombs in the southern Urals Mountains from the early 2nd millennium BCE, with a track width of 1.25–1.3 meters, are similar to each other.
8. Institute of Archaeology, Chinese Academy of Social Sciences, *Chinese Archaeology: Xia and Shang Dynasties* (Beijing: Encyclopedia of China Publishing House, 2003), 61–139.
9. Institute of Archaeology, Chinese Academy of Social Sciences, Museum of Chinese History, and Shanxi Provincial Institute of Archaeology, *Xia County Dongxiafeng* (Beijing: Cultural Relics Press, 1988); Li Boqian, "A Preliminary Analysis of the Dongxiafeng Types," *Cultural Relics of Central China*, no. 1 (1981): 25–29.
10. Department of Archaeology, Peking University and Zhumadian Municipal Cultural Relics Conservation Management Office, *Zhumadian Yangzhuang: Middle Holocene Cultural Remains and Environmental Information in the Upper Huai River* (Beijing: Science Press, 1998).
11. Henan Provincial Institute of Cultural Relics and Henan Branch of the Archaeological Team, Changjiang River Basin Planning Office, *Xichuan Xiawanggang* (Beijing: Cultural Relics Press, 1989).
12. Shaanxi Provincial Institute of Archaeology and Shangluo Municipal Museum, *Shangluo Donglongshan* (Beijing: Science Press, 2011).
13. Jingzhou Museum, *Jingzhou Jingnansi* (Beijing: Cultural Relics Press, 2009).
14. Hubei Provincial Institute of Cultural Relics and Archaeology, *Panlongcheng: Archaeological Excavation Report 1963–1994* (Beijing: Cultural Relics Press, 2001).
15. Erlitou Working Team, Institute of Archaeology, Chinese Academy of Social Sciences, "Archaeological Survey Brief Report in Luoyang Basin, Henan, 2001–2003," *Archaeology*, no. 5 (2005): 18–37.
16. Xu Hong, Chen Guoliang, and Zhao Haitao, "Preliminary Investigation of the Settlement Morphology of the Erlitou Site," *Archaeology*, no. 11 (2004): 23–31.
17. Chen Xingcan et al., "The Process of Social Complexity in the Central Plain of Chinese Civilization: A Study of Settlement Morphology in the Yiluo River Area," *Acta Archaeologica Sinica*, no. 2 (2003): 161–218.
18. Zhengzhou Municipal Institute of Cultural Relics and Archaeology, *Zhengzhou Dashigou* (Beijing: Science Press, 2004).
19. Liu Li, *The Chinese Neolithic Period: On the Path to Early Statehood* (Beijing: Cultural Relics Press, 2007), 216–217.
20. Luoyang Municipal Cultural Relics Working Team, *Luoyang Zaojiaoshu: 1992–1993 Excavation Report of the Erlitou Culture Settlement Site at Luoyang Zaojiaoshu* (Beijing: Science Press, 2002).
21. Hebei Provincial Cultural Relics Management Office, "Excavation Report of the Ci County Xiaqiyuan Site," *Acta Archaeologica Sinica*, no. 2 (1979): 185–214.
22. Henan Provincial Institute of Cultural Relics and Archaeology, *Anyang Zhangdeng* (Zhengzhou: Elephant Press, 2012).

23. Henan Provincial Cultural Relics Bureau, *Hebi Liuzhuang: Excavation Report of the Xiaqiyuan Culture Cemetery* (Beijing: Science Press, 2012).
24. Zou Heng, "On the Attempt to Discuss Xia Culture," in *Collection of Archaeological Papers on Xia, Shang, and Zhou Dynasties* (Beijing: Cultural Relics Press, 1980), 95–182; Li Boqian, "Exploration of Pre-Shang Culture," in *Collection of Papers Celebrating 55 Years of Su Bingqi's Archaeology* (Beijing: Cultural Relics Press, 1989), 280–293; Wang Lixin and Zhu Yonggang, "Exploration of Xiaqiyuan Culture," *Huaxia Archaeology*, no. 4 (1995): 59–67; Han Jianye, "Exploration of Pre-Shang Culture," *Cultural Relics of Central China*, no. 2 (1998): 48–54.
25. Institute of Archaeology, Chinese Academy of Social Sciences, *Chinese Archaeology: Xia and Shang Dynasties* (Beijing: Encyclopedia of China Publishing House, 2003), 147–152.
26. Zou Heng was the first to propose the classification scheme of pre-Shang culture as Zhanghe type, Huiwei type, and Nanguanwai type, which he asserted to be essentially the same as the later proposed Xiaqiyuan culture. See Zou Heng, "On the Attempt to Discuss Xia Culture," in *Collection of Archaeological Papers on Xia, Shang, and Zhou Dynasties* (Beijing: Cultural Relics Press, 1980), 95–182.
27. Juma River Archaeological Team, "Preliminary Excavation Report of the Ancient Site at Laishui, Yi County, Hebei," *Acta Archaeologica Sinica*, no. 4 (1988): 421–454.
28. Shang and Zhou Group, Department of Archaeology, Peking University, "Excavation Report of the Songyao Site in Qi County, Henan," in *Archaeological Collection*, vol. 10 (Beijing: Geology Press), 89–160.
29. Henan Provincial Department of Culture, Cultural Relics Working Team, *Zhengzhou Erligang* (Beijing: Science Press, 1959).
30. First Team of the Cultural Relics Working Team, Henan Provincial Department of Culture, "Excavation Briefing of the Baijiazhuang Site in Zhengzhou," *Cultural Relics Reference Material*, no. 4 (1956): 3–8.
31. Some believe that the primitive ceramics unearthed in Zhengzhou were produced in southern areas such as Wucheng (Chen Tiemei et al., "Neutron Activation Analysis of the Origin of Primitive Ceramics from the Shang Period," *Archaeology*, no. 7 [1997]: 39–52), while others believe they are local products (Zhu Jian et al., "Reanalysis of the Origins of Shang and Zhou Primitive Ceramics," *Southern Cultural Relics*, no. 1 [2004]: 19–22). In any case, their cultural origins should be in the Jiangnan region.
32. Zou Heng was the first to propose dividing the Early Shang culture into Erligang type, Taixi type, Panlongcheng type, and Jingdang type, while Wang Lixin divided Early Shang culture into Erligang type, Beicun type, Dongxiafeng type, Taixi type, Daxinzhuang type, Dachengdun type, and Panlongcheng type. See Zou Heng, "On the Attempt to Discuss Xia Culture," in *Collection of Archaeological Papers on Xia, Shang, and Zhou Dynasties* (Beijing: Cultural Relics Press, 1980), 95–182; Wang Lixin, *Study on Early Shang Culture* (Beijing: Higher Education Press, 1998).
33. Institute of Archaeology, Chinese Academy of Sciences, *Huixian Excavation Report* (Beijing: Science Press, 1956).
34. Institute of Archaeology, Chinese Academy of Social Sciences, *Chinese Archaeology: Xia and Shang Dynasties* (Beijing: Encyclopedia of China Publishing House, 2003), 170–248.

35. Hebei Provincial Institute of Cultural Relics, *Shang Dynasty Site at Gaocheng Taixi* (Beijing: Cultural Relics Press, 1985).
36. Shang-Zhou Group, Department of Archaeology, Peking University and Shaanxi Provincial Institute of Archaeology, "Excavation Report of the Beicun Site in Yao County, Shaanxi, 1984," in *Archaeological Research*, vol. 2 (Beijing: Peking University Press, 1994), 283–342; Xu Tianjin, "On the Shang Culture in the Guanzhong Region," in *Collection of Papers Commemorating the 30th Anniversary of the Archaeology Major at Peking University* (Beijing: Cultural Relics Press, 1990), 211–242.
37. Jingzhou Museum, *Jingzhou Jingnansi* (Beijing: Cultural Relics Press, 2009); Hunan Provincial Institute of Cultural Relics and Archaeology, "Shang Dynasty Remains in Zaoshi, Shimen, Hunan," *Acta Archaeologica Sinica*, no. 2 (1992): 185–219.
38. Anhui Provincial Institute of Cultural Relics and Archaeology et al., "The Fourth Excavation Report of the Dachengdun Site in Hanshan, Anhui," *Archaeology*, no. 2 (1989): 101–117.
39. Department of History and Archaeology Major, Shandong University et al., "Preliminary Excavation Report of the Daxinzhuang Site in Jinan in the Autumn of 1984," *Wenwu*, no. 6 (1995): 12–27.
40. Archaeological Department of the Museum of Chinese History et al., *Yuanqu Shangcheng: 1985–1986 Survey Report* (Beijing: Science Press, 1996).
41. The production of bronze, pottery, and bone artifacts in Erligang culture was highly specialized. At the casting sites in Zhengzhou, such as Nanguanwai and Zijingshan, cast copper fields, workshops, sand storage pits, and copper smelting furnaces were discovered, along with a large amount of copper ore, lead ore, melted copper pottery crucibles, copper slag, various ceramic molds for artifacts, and remnants of bronze artifacts. These bronze artifacts were made of copper, lead, and tin or copper and lead alloys. The amount of sand contained in the ceramic molds varied depending on the type of artifact and the inner and outer molds. The mold clay was specifically chosen, indicating that bronze casting technology was relatively mature and had formed distinct Chinese characteristics.

    There was a large-scale pottery workshop to the west of Minggong Road in Zhengzhou, which included pottery kilns, pottery-making fields, workshops, storage pits, raw material pits, wells, as well as pottery clay, pottery blanks, pottery waste products, pottery paddles, pottery pads, pottery molds, and pottery funnels, reflecting the high degree of specialization in pottery-making. A large number of bone materials, semi-finished products, bone artifacts, and whetstones were unearthed in the Zijingshan and palace area workshops, especially over 100 human skulls with saw marks.
42. Henan Provincial Institute of Cultural Relics and Archaeology, *Zhengzhou Shangcheng: Archaeological Excavation Report 1953–1985* (Beijing: Cultural Relics Press, 2001).
43. Institute of Archaeology, Chinese Academy of Social Sciences, *Yanshi Shangcheng* (Beijing: Science Press, 2013).
44. Henan Provincial Institute of Cultural Relics and Archaeology, *Zhengzhou Xiaoshuangqiao: Archaeological Excavation Report 1990–2000* (Beijing: Cultural Relics Press, 2012).
45. Yan Wenming, "Longshan Culture and the Longshan Period," *Wenwu*, no. 6 (1981): 41–48.
46. Shandong Excavation Team of the Institute of Archaeology, Chinese Academy of Sciences,

"Neolithic Site and Warring States Tomb at Dongyue Shicun in Pingdu, Shandong," *Archaeology*, no. 10 (1962): 509–518.
47. Wu Yuxi, "A Preliminary Exploration of the Regional Types of Yueshi Culture: A Discussion Based on the Discovery of the Yueshi Remains at Haojiazhuang," in *A Collection of Archaeological and Cultural Essays*, vol. 3 (Beijing: Cultural Relics Press, 1993), 270–310.
48. Shandong Team of the Institute of Archaeology, Chinese Academy of Social Sciences et al., "The Zhaogezhuang Site in Muping, Shandong," *Acta Archaeologica Sinica*, no. 4 (1986): 447–478.
49. Wang Xun, *Research on the Dongyi Culture and Huaiyi Culture* (Beijing: Peking University Press, 1994), 7–13.
50. Yan Wenming, "The Exploration of the Dongyi Culture," *Wenwu*, no. 9 (1989): 1–12; Luan Fengshi, "Periodization and Types of Yueshi Culture," in *Archaeological Research in the Haidai Region* (Jinan: Shandong University Press, 1997), 318–347.
51. Zibo City Bureau of Cultural Relics et al., "The Excavation of the Yueshi Culture Wooden Structure Sacrificial Utensil Pit at the Shijia Site in Hantai County, Shandong," *Archaeology*, no. 11 (1997): 1–18.
52. Agricultural Research Group, "Agricultural Economic Characteristics during the Formation of Chinese Civilization," in *Scientific Archaeology*, vol. 3 (Beijing: Science Press, 2011), 1–35.
53. Shang-Zhou Group of the Department of Archaeology, Peking University and Anhui Provincial Cultural Relics Work Team, "Archaeological Survey and Preliminary Excavation Report of Huoqiu, Liu'an, and Shou County in Anhui Province," in *Archaeological Research*, vol. 3 (Beijing: Science Press, 1997), 240–299.
54. Anhui Provincial Institute of Cultural Relics and Archaeology, "A Brief Report on the Excavation of the Shigudun Site in Tongling County, Anhui," *Archaeology*, no. 6 (2013): 3–23.
55. Zhang Min, "A Preliminary Discussion on Dianjiangtai Culture," *Southeast Culture*, no. 3 (1989): 125–140.
56. Zeng Zhaoyu and Yin Huanzhang, "A Preliminary Discussion on the Hushu Culture," *Archaeology*, no. 4 (1959): 47–58.
57. Nanjing Museum, "The Dianjiangtai Site in Tangshan, Jiangning," *Southeast Culture*, no. 3 (1987): 38–50.
58. Tuanshan Archaeological Team, "The Tuanshan Site at Zhaojiayao in Dantu, Jiangsu," *Southeast Culture*, no. 1 (1989): 73–121.
59. Li Boqian, "The Origins of Maqiao Culture," in *A Collection of Essays on Chinese Primitive Culture: In Commemoration of the 80th Birthday of Yin Da* (Beijing: Cultural Relics Press 1989), 222–228.
60. Shanghai Cultural Relics Management Committee, *Maqiao: Excavation Report 1993–1997* (Shanghai: Shanghai Shuhua Publishing House, 2002).
61. Zhejiang Provincial Institute of Cultural Relics and Archaeology et al., "The Phases I and II of Excavation at the Tashan Site in Xiangshan County," *Journal of the Zhejiang Provincial Institute of Cultural Relics and Archaeology* (Beijing: Changzheng Publishing House, 1997), 22–73.

62. Chen Yaocheng et al., "A New Exploration into the Origins of High-Temperature Ceramic Glaze," *Fujian Wenbo*, no. 2 (1996): 11–17.
63. Zhejiang Provincial Institute of Cultural Relics and Archaeology et al., "Survey and Trial Excavation of Ancient Sites and Tombs in the Southern District of Jiangshan County," *Journal of the Zhejiang Provincial Institute of Cultural Relics and Archaeology* (Beijing: Cultural Relics Press, 1981), 57–84.
64. Li Boqian, "A Preliminary Discussion on the Wucheng Culture," in *Cultural Relics Collection*, vol. 3 (Beijing: Cultural Relics Press, 1981), 133–143.
65. Jiangxi Provincial Institute of Cultural Relics and Archaeology, and Zhangshu City Museum, *Wucheng: 1973–2002 Archaeological Excavation Report* (Beijing: Science Press, 2005).
66. Tian Guangjin and Han Jianye, "Study on the Zhukaigou Culture," in *Archaeological Research*, vol. 5 (Beijing: Cultural Relics Press, August 2003), 227–259.
67. Inner Mongolia Autonomous Region Institute of Cultural Relics and Archaeology, and Ordos Museum, Zhukaigou: Excavation Report of the Early Bronze Age Site (Beijing: Cultural Relics Press, 2000); Han Jianye, "Analysis of Relevant Issues of the Zhukaigou Site in Inner Mongolia," *Archaeology*, no. 3 (2005): 55–64.
68. Shaanxi Provincial Institute of Archaeology, and Yulin City Institute of Cultural Relics Protection, *Shenmu Xinhua* (Beijing: Science Press, 2005).
69. Jinzhong Archaeological Team, "A Brief Report on the Excavation of Site No. 1 at Baiyan in Taigu, Shanxi," *Wenwu*, no. 3 (1989): 1–21.
70. State Administration of Cultural Heritage, Shanxi Provincial Institute of Archaeology, and Jilin University Department of Archaeology, *Archaeology in Jinzhong* (Beijing: Cultural Relics Press, 1999).
71. Inner Mongolia Institute of Cultural Relics and Archaeology et al., "The Baiaobao Cemetery in Ejin Horo Banner," in *Anthology of Inner Mongolia Cultural Relics and Archaeology*, vol. 2 (Beijing: Encyclopedia of China Publishing House, 1997), 327–337.
72. Zou Heng, "Preliminary Discussion on the Cultures of the Northern Regions during the Xia and Shang Periods," in *Collection of Archaeological Papers on Xia, Shang, and Zhou Dynasties* (Beijing: Cultural Relics Press, 1980), 242–244; Zhang Zhongpei et al., "Study on Lower Xiajiadian Culture," in *Collection of Archaeological and Cultural Papers*, vol. 1 (Beijing: Cultural Relics Press, 1987), 58–78; Li Boqian, "On Lower Xiajiadian Culture," in *Research on the Structural System of Chinese Bronze Culture* (Beijing: Science Press, 1998), 124–142.
73. Chinese Academy of Sciences Institute of Archaeology Inner Mongolia Team, "Preliminary Excavation Report on Yaowangmiao and Xiajiadian Sites in Chifeng," *Acta Archaeologica Sinica*, no. 1 (1974): 111–144.
74. Chinese Academy of Social Sciences Institute of Archaeology, *Dadianzi—Excavation Report of Lower Xiajiadian Culture Site and Cemetery* (Beijing: Science Press, 1996).
75. Tianjin Municipal Bureau of Culture Archaeological Excavation Team, "Preliminary Excavation Report on Datuotou Site in Dachang Hui Autonomous County, Hebei," *Archaeology*, no. 1 (1966): 8–13.

76. Beijing Cultural Relics Research Institute and Beijing Changping District Culture Commission, *Excavation Report of Zhangying in Changping—Early Bronze Culture Sites in the Southern Foothills of the Yan Mountains* (Beijing: Cultural Relics Press, 2007).
77. Zhangjiakou Archaeological Team, "Brief Archaeological Notes of Yu County," *Archaeology and Cultural Relics*, no. 4 (1982): 10–14; Zhangjiakou Archaeological Team, "Major Achievements in Archaeology of Xia and Shang Dynasties in Yu County," *Archaeology and Cultural Relics*, no. 1 (1984): 40–48.
78. Lin Yun, "Bronze Wares of the Northern System in the Xia Dynasty," in *Frontier Archaeological Research*, vol. 1 (Beijing: Science Press, 2002), 1–12.
79. Xu Guangji, "Stone City Sites in Yingjin River and Yin River Basin of Chifeng," in *Research on Chinese Archaeology–Collection of Papers Commemorating Fifty Years of Archaeology by Mr. Xia Nai* (Beijing: Cultural Relics Press, 1986), 83–84.
80. Su Bingqi, "Significant Cultural Historical Sites in Liaoning That Symbolize China," in *The Chinese: Descendants of the Dragon, Seeking Roots through Archaeology* (Shenyang: Liaoning University Press, 1994), 92; Han Jianye, "Preliminary Discussion on the Early Northern Stone Cities as 'Prototypes' of the Great Wall," *Huaxia Archaeology*, no. 1 (2008): 48–53.
81. Inner Mongolia Institute of Cultural Relics and Archaeology, "Stone City Site of Lower Xiajiadian Culture at Sanzuodian in Chifeng City, Inner Mongolia," *Archaeology*, no. 7 (2007): 17–27.
82. Inner Mongolia Institute of Cultural Relics and Archaeology, "Excavation of the Erdaojingzi Site in Chifeng City, Inner Mongolia," *Archaeology*, no. 8 (2010): 13–26.
83. Li Yanxiang, Jia Haixin, and Zhu Yanping, "Preliminary Study on the Bronze Wares Unearthed from the Lower Xiajiadian Culture Tombs in Dadianzi, Aohan Banner," *Nonferrous Metals*, no. 4 (2002): 123–126; Cui Jianfeng, Yu Jincheng, Guo Jingning, et al., "Preliminary Scientific Analysis of the Bronze Wares Unearthed from the Zhangying Site in Changping, Beijing," in *Excavation Report of Zhangying in Changping—Early Bronze Culture Sites in the Southern Foothills of the Yan Mountains* (Beijing: Cultural Relics Press, 2007), 243–253.
84. Zhao Binfu, *Archaeological Culture Study of Northeast China from Xia to Warring States Period* (Beijing: Science Press, 2009).
85. Xinmin County Cultural Museum et al., "Brief Report on the Excavation of the Neolithic Site at Gaotaishan in Xinmin in 1976," in *Cultural Relics Materials Series*, vol. 7 (Beijing: Cultural Relics Press, 1983), 80–91.
86. Liaoning Provincial Institute of Cultural Relics and Archaeology and Jilin University Department of Archaeology, "Ping'anbao Site in Zhangwu, Liaoning," *Acta Archaeologica Sinica*, no. 4 (1992): 437–475.
87. Shenyang Cultural Relics Management Office, "Preliminary Excavation Report on the Xinle Site in Shenyang," *Acta Archaeologica Sinica*, no. 4 (1978): 209–222; Archaeological Teaching and Research Office of the History Department, Liaoning University, et al., "Excavation of the Liuwan Site in Faku County, Liaoning," *Archaeology*, no. 12 (1989): 1076–1086.

88. Liaoning Provincial Museum et al., "Brief Report on the Excavation of the Cave Cemetery at Miaohoushan in Benxi County, Liaoning," *Archaeology*, no. 6 (1985): 485–496; Liaoning Provincial Institute of Cultural Relics and Archaeology and Benxi City Museum, *Machengzi—Cave Remains in the Upper Reaches of the Taizi River* (Beijing: Cultural Relics Press, 1994).
89. Liaoning Provincial Institute of Cultural Relics and Archaeology and Jilin University Department of Archaeology, "Excavation Report of the Pingdingshan Stone City Site in Fuxin, Liaoning," *Archaeology*, no. 5 (1992): 399–417.
90. Heilongjiang Provincial Institute of Cultural Relics and Archaeology and Jilin University Department of Archaeology, "Excavation Report of the Xiaolaha Site in Zhaoyuan County, Heilongjiang," *Acta Archaeologica Sinica*, no. 1 (1998): 61–101.
91. Heilongjiang Provincial Institute of Cultural Relics and Archaeology and Jilin University Department of Archaeology, *Zhaoyuan Baijinbao—Revelations of a Bronze Age Site in the Lower Nen River* (Beijing: Science Press, 2009).
92. Jilin Provincial Institute of Cultural Relics and Archaeology and Yanbian Korean Autonomous Prefecture Museum, *Helong Xingcheng—Excavation Report of the Neolithic and Bronze Age Sites* (Beijing: Cultural Relics Press, 2001).
93. Han Jianye, *The Natural Environment and Cultural Development in Northwestern China during the Pre-Qin Period* (Beijing: Cultural Relics Press, 2008), 196–201.
94. Gansu Provincial Institute of Cultural Relics and Archaeology and Northwest University Center for Cultural Heritage and Archaeology, "Excavation Report of the Qijia Culture Cemetery in Mogou, Lintan, Gansu," *Wenwu*, no. 10 (2009): 4–24; Gansu Provincial Institute of Cultural Relics and Archaeology and Northwest University Center for Cultural Heritage and Archaeology, "Qijia Culture Cemetery in Mogou, Lintan, Gansu," *Archaeology*, no. 7 (2009): 10–17.
95. Chinese Academy of Sciences Institute of Archaeology Gansu Work Team, "Qijia Culture Cemetery of Qinweijia in Yongjing, Gansu," *Acta Archaeologica Sinica*, no. 2 (1975): 57–96.
96. Chinese Academy of Sciences Institute of Archaeology Gansu Work Team, "Excavation Report of the Dahezhuang Site in Yongjing, Gansu," *Acta Archaeologica Sinica*, no. 2 (1974): 29–62.
97. Liu Shi'e, *Laoniupo* (Xi'an: Shaanxi People's Publishing House, 2002).
98. Zhang Tianen, "Bronze Animal-Faced Plaques Excavated in Tianshui and Related Issues," *Cultural Relics of Central China*, no. 1 (2002): 43–46.
99. Qinghai Provincial Cultural Relics Administration, "Brief Report on the Cleanup of the Shanjiatou Cemetery in Hetaozhuang, Minhe, Qinghai," *Wenwu*, no. 11 (1992): 26–31.
100. Qinghai Provincial Institute of Cultural Relics and Archaeology, "Kayue Culture Cemetery at Panjialiang in Xiaxi River, Huangzhong, Qinghai," in *Collected Papers on Archaeology*, vol. 8 (Beijing: Science Press, 1994), 28–86.
101. Henan Provincial Institute of Cultural Relics and Archaeology, Zhengzhou Municipal Institute of Cultural Relics and Archaeology, *Shang Dynasty Bronze Ware Cellar in Zhengzhou* (Beijing: Science Press, 1999), 78.
102. Zhao Shengchen, "Discovery of Kayue Culture Bronze *Li* in Xining, Qinghai," *Archaeology*, no. 7 (1985): 635.

103. Chen Jianli et al., "Ironware Excavated from Siwa Culture Tombs in Mogou, Lintan, Gansu and the Origins of Iron Metallurgy in China," *Wenwu*, no. 8 (2012): 45–53.
104. Li Shuicheng, "Research on Siba Culture," in *Collection of Papers on Archaeological Cultures*, vol. 3 (Beijing: Cultural Relics Press, 1993), 80–121.
105. An Zhimin, "Ancient Culture in Gansu and Some Related Issues," *Archaeological Newsletter*, no. 6 (1956): 9–18; An Zhimin, "Neolithic Site of Sibatan in Shandan, Gansu," *Acta Archaeologica Sinica*, no. 3 (1959): 7–16.
106. Gansu Provincial Institute of Cultural Relics and Archaeology, Northern Archaeology Research Office of Jilin University, *Archaeology in Donghuishan, Minle: Revealing and Researching the Siba Culture Cemetery* (Beijing: Science Press, 1998).
107. Lü Enguo, Chang Xien, and Wang Binghua, "A Preliminary Discussion on the Archaeological Culture of the Bronze Age in Xinjiang," in *Su Bingqi and Contemporary Chinese Archaeology* (Beijing: Science Press, 2001), 179–184.
108. Li Shuicheng, "The Collision and Exchange of Eastern and Western Cultures in the Second Millennium BCE as Seen from Archaeological Discoveries," *Xinjiang Cultural Relics*, no. 1 (1999): 53–65.
109. Sichuan Provincial Cultural Relics Management Committee et al., "Sanxingdui Site in Guanghan, Sichuan," *Acta Archaeologica Sinica*, no. 2 (1987): 227–254.
110. Sanxingdui Site Work Station of Sichuan Provincial Institute of Cultural Relics and Archaeology, "Rensheng Village Pit Tombs at Sanxingdui Site in Guanghan City, Sichuan," *Archaeology*, no. 10 (2004): 14–22.
111. Wheat and barley remains were discovered at the Huangguashan site. See Fujian Provincial Museum, "Second Excavation of Huangguashan Site in Xiapu, Fujian," *Fujian Wenbo*, no. 3 (2004): 1–18.
112. Fujian Provincial Museum, "Excavation Report of Huangguashan Site in Xiapu, Fujian," *Fujian Wenbo*, no. 1 (1994): 3–37.
113. Wei Jun, "Periodization and Lineage of Pre-Qin Archaeological Cultures in Eastern Guangdong and Southern Fujian," in *Archaeological Research Collected Paper of Celebrating the 80th Birthday of Mr. Yan Wenming*, vol. 9 (Beijing: Cultural Relics Press, 2012), 140–165.
114. Guangdong Provincial Institute of Cultural Relics and Archaeology and Puning City Museum, "Excavation Report of Chiwei Haoshan Site in Puning City, Guangdong," *Archaeology*, no. 7 (1998): 1–10.
115. Fujian Museum Institute of Cultural Relics and Archaeology et al., *Niaolunwei and Goutoushan: Archaeological Excavation Report of Shang and Zhou Dynasty Sites in Fujian Province* (Beijing: Science Press, 2004).
116. Guangdong Provincial Institute of Cultural Relics and Archaeology et al., "Excavation Report of Tangxiahuan Site in Pingsha, Zhuhai," *Wenwu*, no. 7 (1998): 4–16.
117. Guangxi Institute of Cultural Relics and Archaeology and Nanning City Museum, *Pre-Qin Rock-Cave Tomb in Guangxi* (Beijing: Science Press, 2007).
118. Han Jianye, *The Bronze Age and Early Iron Age Cultures in Xinjiang* (Beijing: Cultural Relics Press, 2007).
119. Xinjiang Institute of Cultural Relics and Archaeology, *Xinjiang Xiabandi Cemetery* (Beijing: Cultural Relics Press, 2012).

120. Institute of Archaeology, Chinese Academy of Social Sciences et al., "Qiaolu Site and Cemetery in Wenquan County, Xinjiang," *Archaeology*, no. 7 (2013): 25–32.
121. Xinjiang Institute of Cultural Relics and Archaeology et al., "Archaeological Excavation Report of Kalasu Site in Nileke County," *Xinjiang Cultural Relics*, no. 3–4 (2008): 33–43.
122. Xinjiang Academy of Social Sciences Institute of Archaeology, "Excavation Report of Keermuqi Ancient Tomb Group in Xinjiang," *Wenwu*, no. 1 (1981): 23–32.
123. Wang Binghua, "Preliminary Analysis of Bronze Age Archaeological Cultures in Xinjiang," *Xinjiang Social Science*, no. 4 (1985): 50–60; Cong Dexin and Jia Weiming, "Preliminary Analysis of Qiemu'erqieke Cemetery and its Early Remains," in *Collection of Essays Celebrating the 80th Birthday of Mr. Zhang Zhongpei* (Beijing: Science Press, 2014), 275–308.
124. Xinjiang Academy of Social Sciences Institute of Archaeology, "Excavation and Preliminary Study of the Kongque River Gumugou," *Xinjiang Social Science*, no. 1 (1983): 125–126.
125. Bergman, *Archaeological Notes on Xinjiang*, trans. Wang Anhong (Urumqi: Xinjiang People's Publishing House, 1997), 75–183; Xinjiang Institute of Cultural Relics and Archaeology, "Archaeological Investigation and Excavation Report of Xiaohe Cemetery in 2002," *Xinjiang Cultural Relics*, no. 2 (2003): 8–64; Xinjiang Institute of Cultural Relics and Archaeology, "Excavation Report of Xiaohe Cemetery in Lop Nur, Xinjiang in 2003," *Wenwu*, no. 10 (2007): 4–42.
126. Institute of Archaeology, Chinese Academy of Social Sciences and Xizang Autonomous Region Cultural Relics Bureau, *Lhasa Qugong* (Beijing: Encyclopedia of China Press, 1999).
127. Yu Weichao noted that the transition from primitive hoe farming to a pastoral economy was a major advancement in human societal development. See Yu Weichao, "New Understandings of 'Kayue Culture' and 'Tangwang Culture,'" in *Collection of Essays on Archaeology of Pre-Qin and Han Dynasties* (Beijing: Cultural Relics Press, 1985), 193–210.
128. Lin Yun, "Study on the Relationship between Shang Culture Bronzes and Northern Bronzes," in *Collection of Essays on Archaeological Culture*, vol. 1 (Beijing: Cultural Relics Press, 1987), 129–155; Mei Jianjun, "'Northern Series Bronzes'—The 'Birth' and 'Growth' of a Term," in *French Sinology*, vol. 11 (Beijing: Zhonghua Book Company, 2006), 132–147.
129. E. N. Chernykh, *Ancient Metallurgy in the USSR—The Early Metal Age*, trans. Sarah Wright (Cambridge: Cambridge University Press, 1992).
130. Chifeng Archaeological Team, "A Brief Report on the Excavation of Dashanqian Site in Kalaqin Banner, Inner Mongolia in 1996," *Archaeology*, no. 9 (1998): 43–49.
131. School of Archaeology and Museology of Peking University and Gansu Provincial Institute of Cultural Relics and Archaeology, "Excavation and Achievements of the Ganguya Cemetery in Jiuquan, Gansu," *Acta Archaeologica Sinica*, no. 3 (2012): 351–368.
132. Kiyotaka Nishie et al. once pointed out that during the Erlitou period, there was a distinction between the Central Plain dynasty and regions outside its domain, and the Central Plain dynasty was composed of metropolitan areas and secondary regions. This essentially recognizes the existence of a three-level cultural structure centered on the Central Plain during the Erlitou period.

NOTES 403

Seiichi Nakano and Daisuke Kuji, "Viewing the Spatial Structure of the Central Plain Dynasty in the Erlitou Culture Period through Inter-regional Relationships," in *Erlitou Site and Erlitou Culture Studies* (Beijing: Science Press, 2006), 444–456.

CHAPTER 6 EARLY CHINA AND ANCIENT LEGENDS

1. Xu Xusheng, *The Mythical Era of Ancient Chinese History*, new ed. (Beijing: Cultural Relics Press, 1985).
2. Feng Youlan, "New Trends in Historical Studies in Recent Years in China," in *Sansongtang Academic Anthology* (Beijing: Peking University Press, 1984), 331–32.
3. Xu Xusheng, *The Mythical Era of Ancient Chinese History*, new ed. (Beijing: Cultural Relics Press, 1985). [Miaoman refers to the name of tribes in ancient Chinese, with a very broad scope that includes many ethnic minorities in the south, originating from the Yunnan-Xizang region.]
4. Meng Wentong, *The Delicate Examination of Ancient History* (Shanghai: The Commercial Press, 1933).
5. Zou Heng, *Collection of Archaeological Papers on Xia, Shang, and Zhou Dynasties* (Beijing: Cultural Relics Press, 1980).
6. Yu Weichao, "Archaeological Speculation on the Culture of Pre-Chu and the Sanmiao," *Wenwu*, no. 10 (1980): 1–12; Yan Wenming, "The Exploration of the Dongyi Culture," *Wenwu*, no. 9 (1989): 1–12; Yan Wenming and Zhang Zhongpei, preface to *A General History of China*, vol. 2, ed. Bai Shouyi and Su Bingqi (Shanghai: Shanghai People's Publishing House, 1994), 17–20.
7. Sarah Allan, "The Myth of the Xia Dynasty," *Journal of the Royal Asiatic Society of Great Britain and Ireland*, no. 2 (1984): 242–56.
8. Han Jianye and Yang Xingai, *The Era of the Five Emperors: An Archaeological Observation of the Ancient History System with Huaxia as the Core* (Beijing: Academy Press, 2006).
9. We once said, "The early Yangshao culture should belong to the culture of the Emperors Yan and Yellow period. Therefore, Peiligang culture and its branch, Baijia culture, may correspond to the culture of Fuxi and Nüwa, which is earlier than the Emperors Yan and Yellow. In fact, including the Songshan culture circle, a large part of Henan Province is the core area of Fuxi and Nüwa legends.

    At the same time, such legends are also popular in the eastern part of Gansu Province and the Guanzhong area of Shaanxi Province along the Wei River, which should not be a coincidence. The status of Fuxi and Nüwa as human ancestors in culture is also consistent with the core position of the Peiligang culture in the embryonic early Chinese cultural circle." (Han Jianye and Yang Xingai, "On the Core Position of the Songshan Culture Circle in the Early Chinese Cultural Circle," in *Research on Chinese Civilization and Songshan Civilization*, vol. 1 [Beijing: Science Press, 2009], 141–52).

    Moreover, the legends of Fuxi making nets, Fuxi creating the *Bagua*, and Nüwa making *sheng* [a type of free-reed musical instrument from China], etc., seem to be related to the net pendants, turtle shell inscriptions, and bone flutes of Peiligang culture. It can be seen that there may indeed exist a Three Sovereigns era earlier than the Five Emperors era, although there are no "Three Sovereigns" in the strict sense.

10. Xu Zhongshu, "Re-discussion on Xiaotun and Yangshao," *Anyang Excavation Report*, no. 3 (1931): 523–58.
11. Zhang Lidong, "Liji, Xiyincun, and Xia Culture," *Huaxia Archaeology*, no. 1 (2003): 95–99.
12. Tian Changwu, *New Theory on the Periodization of Ancient Society* (Beijing: People's Publishing House, 1982), 35–62; Yan Wenming, "The Legend of Emperors Yan and Yellow and Culture of Yan and Yellow," in *Yan–Yellow Culture and National Spirit* (Beijing: Renmin University of China Press, 1993), 45–60.
13. Huang Huaixin, "Yangshao Culture and the Primitive Huaxia Tribe—Yan and Yellow Tribes," *Archaeology and Cultural Relics*, no. 4 (1997): 33–37.
14. Han Jianye, "Exploration of the Battle of Zhuolu," *Cultural Relics of Central China*, no. 4 (2002): 20–27; Han Jianye, "Archaeological Observation of the Ancient Historical System of the Five Emperors Era with Huaxia as the Core," in *The Era of Five Emperors: An Archaeological Observation of the Ancient History System with Huaxia as the Core* (Beijing: Academy Press, 2006), 149–70.
15. Xu Xusheng, *The Mythical Era of Ancient Chinese History*, new ed. (Beijing: Cultural Relics Press 1985).
16. Regarding the place where the ancestors of Ji Zhou, Houji and his mother had the land of Tai *shi* Jiangyuan, the old saying was in the Jing and Wei rivers. Only Qian Mu proposed the origin theory of southern Jin ("Geographical Study of Early Zhou Dynasty," *Yanjing Journal*, no. 10 [1931]: 1955–2008).
17. For example, the *Book of Documents · Announcement to Kang*: "Therefore, it began to shape our little Xia"; the *Book of Documents · Lord Shi*: "Because King Wen valued those who could govern and harmonize our China"; the *Book of Documents · Establishment of Government*: "This led to our Zhou King replacing King Zhou of Shang in receiving the Mandate of Heaven, and pacifying and governing the common people of the world." and so on.
18. The *Commentary of Zuo · Duke Ding Fourth Year*: "Tangshu was granted major thoroughfares and the drums from Mixu, along with Quegong armor and Guxi bells, embracing nine lineages of his surname, and holding the five principal offices. He was entrusted with the *Decree of Tang* and enfeoffed in Xia ruins, where he began the governance in the manner of Xia, delineating its territory with the tributes of the Rong people." Tangshu's fief is undoubtedly in the south of Jin.

See Department of Archaeology of Peking University, Shang and Zhou Group and Shanxi Provincial Institute of Archaeology, *Tianma Qu Village (1980–1989)* (Beijing: Science Press, 2000).

19. Such as Yang, Wei, Xun, Jia, Geng, etc., see Xu Xusheng, *The Mythical Era of Ancient Chinese History*, new ed. (Beijing: Cultural Relics Press, 1985), 45.
20. Su Bingqi, "Issues on Jin Culture—Speech at the Jin Culture Research Conference," in *Chinese: Descendants of the Dragon—An Archaeological Quest for Roots* (Shenyang: Liaoning University Press, 1994), 17–21.

21. Huang Huaixin, "Yangshao Culture and the Primitive Huaxia Tribe – Yan and Yellow Tribes," *Archaeology and Cultural Relics*, no. 4 (1997): 33–37.
22. Yan Wenming, "The Legend of Emperors Yan and Yellow and Yan–Yellow Culture," in *Yan–Yellow Culture and National Spirit* (Beijing: Renmin University of China Press, 1993), 45–60.
23. Wang Xiantang, "A Study on the Yan and Huang Clan Culture," (Jinan: Qilu Book Society, 1985), 404–14.
24. Qian Mu, "Geographical Study of Early Zhou Dynasty," *Yanjing Journal*, no. 10 (1931): 1955–2008.
25. The modern Miao people often regard Chiyou as their ancestor and call him by different names in various dialects, such as "Jiuli Chiyou," "Pouyou," "Chiyelao," "Bangxiangyou," "Yougong," "Xiangyougong," etc. Some directly call them Meng Chiyou or Chiyou.
26. Xu Xusheng, *The Mythical Era of Ancient Chinese History*, new ed. (Beijing: Cultural Relics Press, 1985).
27. Yan Wenming, "Exploration of the Dongyi Culture," *Wenwu*, no. 9 (1989): 1–12.
28. Wang Xun, *Study on Dongyi Culture and Huaiyi Culture* (Beijing: Peking University Press, 1994).
29. Xu Xusheng, *The Mythical Era of Ancient Chinese History*, new ed. (Beijing: Cultural Relics Press, 1985), 50.
30. *Discourses on Salt and Iron · Marriage Alliances*: "Xuanyuan fought at Zhuolu, killing Liang Yi and Chiyou to become the Emperor," which obviously refers to the Battle of Zhuolu. Xuanyuan refers to the Yellow Emperor, "Liang Yi" is also known as "Liang Hao," meaning Shaohao and Taihao (Xu Xusheng, *The Mythical Era of Ancient Chinese History*, new ed. [Beijing: Cultural Relics Press, 1985], 53).

    In this instance, Liang Hao and Chiyou were killed, which is inconsistent with the *Book of Zhou*, and must have a different source.
31. Yang Shoujing's note under "Zhuo River originates from Zhuolu Mountain" in the *Commentary on the Water Classic · Lei River* states: "*Records of the Grand Historian · Annals of the Five Emperors*'s collected commentaries cite Fu Qian saying, Zhuolu (涿鹿) is a mountain name, in Zhuo County. Zhang Yan says Zhuolu is in Shanggu. *Suo Yin* says Zhuolu (浊鹿), the characters are different between ancient and modern times. According to the *Treatise on Geography*, Shanggu has Zhuolu County, so Fu Qian's statement that it is in Zhuo County is incorrect."

    See *Commentaries on Commentary on the Water Classic*, 1183–1184 (Nanjing: Jiangsu Ancient Books Publishing House, 1989).
32. The annotation by Fu Qian mentions Zhuo County (modern-day Zhuo County, Hebei), while the *Chronicles of Emperors* cites the *Book of Origins* mentioning Pengcheng (modern-day Ci County, Hebei). Xu Xusheng speculates that it might be in Julu, Hebei (*The Mythical Era of Ancient Chinese History*, new ed. [Beijing: Cultural Relics Press, 1985]).
33. The *Commentary on the Water Classic · Lei River*: "Zhuo River originates from Zhuolu Mountain ... The water further northeast merges with Banquan, the watercourse is to the east of Yuan County ..." Citing *Earth in Wei*: "Sixty *li* southeast of Xialuo City, there

is Zhuolu City, and 1 *li* east of the city there is Banquan, and above the spring there is a temple to the Yellow Emperor."
34. Liang Yusheng had already pointed this out in the *Doubts on the Records of the Historian*.
35. *Records of the Grand Historian · Annals of the Five Emperors*: "Xuanyuan then cultivated virtue and rallied troops ... to fight against Yan Emperor in the fields of Banquan. They fought three times before he achieved his ambition." In *Five Emperors Virtues*, Yan Emperor is referred to as "Red Emperor."
36. Xu Xusheng, *The Mythical Era of Ancient Chinese History*, new ed. (Beijing: Cultural Relics Press, 1985), 100.
37. Yan Wenming, Colophon on the *Stork Fish and Stone Axe, Cultural Relics*, no. 12 (1981): 79–82; Zhao Chunqing, "From the Battle to the Fusion of Fish and Birds—An Analysis of the Fish and Bird Pottery Patterns of Yangshao Culture," *Cultural Relics of the Central Plain*, no. 2 (2000): 13–15.
38. The *Classic of Mountains and Seas · Western Dahuang* states: "The grandson of the Yellow Emperor is called Shijun, who gave birth to the Beidi people." In archaeology, the Baoniyaozi type of Yangshao Culture, which is similar to the Miaodigou type, has extended northward to the regions north of Yinshan and Daqingshan. Beidi culture that later appeared in this area should have some connections with the Baoniyaozi type.
39. Wang Guowei, "A Study of the Ancestral Kings in the Oracle Bone Inscriptions of the Yin Dynasty," in *Guantang Jilin*, vol. 9 (Beijing: Zhonghua Book Company, 1959), 409–436.
40. Han Jianye and Yang Xingai, "The Standing Bird Pottery and Bottle-shaped Pottery Patterns of Dawenkou Culture," *Jianghan Archaeology*, no. 3 (2008): 43–47.
41. Xie Duanju, *Prehistoric Archaeology in Gansu and Qinghai* (Beijing: Cultural Relics Press, 2002).
42. The *Huainanzi · Searching out Dao*: "Long ago, Gonggong's force struck the Buzhou Mountain, causing the earth to tilt towards the southeast. He fought with Gaoxin for the throne and then submerged in the abyss, his clan was destroyed and his lineage was cut off." This mentions that Gonggong had a war with Gaoxin. Since the event is exactly the same as the records in *On Military Strategy* and *Patterns of Heaven*, except for the opponent in the war, it is suspected that "Gaoxin" is likely a mistake for "Gaoyang."
43. Cao Shuqin and Yin Weizhang, "Bronze Vessels with Dragon and Gong Inscriptions and Related Issues during the Shang and Zhou Dynasties," in *Archaeological and Cultural Collection*, vol. 3 (Beijing: Cultural Relics Press, 1993), 395–410.
44. Xu Xusheng, *The Mythical Era of Ancient Chinese History*, new ed. (Beijing: Cultural Relics Press, 1985), 48.
45. In the late Yangshao period remains at Puyang Gaocheng, there are pottery *ding*, high-footed plate, and pot, which belong to Dawenkou culture rather than Yangshao culture. See Henan Provincial Institute of Cultural Relics and Archaeology et al., "Excavation Report of Gaocheng Site in Puyang County, Henan," *Archaeology*, no. 3 (2008): 18–30.
46. The tomb No. 2 at Baoshan contains Chu bamboo slips with records of "Chu Xian, Lao Tong (僮 or 童), Zhu Rong, Chi Yan." See Hubei Jingsha Railway Archaeological Team, *Chu Bamboo Slips from Tomb No. 2 at Baoshan* (Beijing: Cultural Relics Press, 1991), 2–217, 2–237, 34, 36.

47. Wang Xun, *A Study on Dongyi Culture and Huaiyi Culture* (Beijing: Peking University Press, 1994), 133–138.
48. Han Jianye, "A Tentative Exploration of the Rise and Fall of the Xishan Ancient City," *Cultural Relics of the Central Plain*, no. 3 (1996): 59–62.
49. Xu Xusheng, *The Mythical Era of Ancient Chinese History*, new ed. (Beijing: Cultural Relics Press, 1985), 74–87.
50. The *Records of Diverse Matters · Miscellaneous Sayings (Part One)*: "In the past, the ruler of the Western Xia was inherently benevolent and opposed to using military force. He never repaired the city walls or prepared military defenses; warriors held no status in the country. The Tang *shi* attacked, and Western Xia fell."
51. The *Commentary of Zuo · Duke Zhao First Year*: "Once upon a time, the Gao Xin *shi* had two sons. The elder was called Ebo, and the younger was called Shichen. They lived in the vast forest, and they could not get along with each other. They looked for weapons every day to fight against each other. Emperor Hou thought that if this went on, there would be problems. He moved Ebo to Shangqiu to rule over Chen, and the people of Shang followed suit. Therefore, the Chen star is the Shang star ... In ancient times, the Jintian *shi* had a descendant named Mei, who served as the head of the water officials and had sons Yun Ge and Tai Dai. Tai Dai was able to inherit his father's profession, dredging the Fen and Tao Rivers, building embankments to hold back the great marshes, and allowing people to live on the vast plateau. The emperor thus commended him and enfeoffed him in the Fen River Basin. The four states of Shen, Si, Ru, and Huang are all his descendants."
52. Xu Xusheng, "Preliminary Report on the Investigation of 'Xia Ruins' in Western Henan in the Summer of 1959," *Archaeology*, no. 11 (1959): 592–600.
53. Liu Qiyu, "A Discussion on the Origin of Xia Culture in Southern Shanxi Based on the Original Habitat of the Xia Ruins," in *Huaxia Civilization*, vol. 1 (Beijing: Peking University Press, 1987), 18–52.
54. The *Commentary of Zuo · Duke Ding Fourth Year*: "Tangshu was granted major thoroughfares and the drums from Mixu, along with Quegong armor and Guxi bells, embracing nine lineages of his surname, and holding the five principal offices. He was entrusted with the *Decree of Tang* and enfeoffed in Xia ruins, where he began the governance in the manner of Xia, delineating its territory with the tributes of the Rong people." Tangshu's fief is undoubtedly in the south of Jin.
55. Xu Xusheng, "Yao, Shun, Yu (Part One)," in *Wen Shi*, vol. 39 (Beijing: Zhonghua Book Company, 1994), 1–26.
56. *Chronicles of Emperors* states: "Emperor Yao was initially enfeoffed in Tang, and later moved to Jinyang. When he became emperor, his capital was Pingyang."
57. The *Book of Han · Treatise on Geography (Part One)* under the section of Hedong County, Pingyang, Yingshao said: "This was Yao's capital, located on the north side of the Ping River." In the *Book of Han · Treatise on Geography (Part Two)* under the section of Zhongshan State, Tang, there is a mention of "Yao Mountain was in the south," and Yingshao said: "This was the ancient state of Yao."
58. *Records of the Grand Historian · Annals of the Five Emperors*: "Emperor Ku married a lady from the Chen Feng *shi*, and she gave birth to Fang Xun ... who became Emperor Yao."

59. Wang Wenqing, "The Relics of Taosi May Be the Cultural Remains of the Taotang *Shi*," in *Huaxia Civilization*, vol. 1 (Beijing: Peking University Press, 1987), 106–123.
60. The text *Han Feizi · Shuo Yi*: "Shun forced Yao, Yu forced Shun, and Tang deposed Jie."
61. The *Commentary of Zuo · Duke Zhao Eighth Year*: "Chen is the clan of Zhuanxu." Chen is descended from Shun of Youyu *shi*, and its territory is located in Huaiyang, east of Henan.
62. Li Boqian, "On the Types of Zaolütai," *Wenwu*, no. 4 (1983): 50–59.
63. The *Book of Rites · Tan Gong (Part One)*: "Shun was buried in the fields of Cangwu." The *Records of the Grand Historian · Annals of the Five Emperors*: "(Shun) during his southern hunting expedition, died in the fields of Cangwu. He was buried in Jiuyi, south of the Yangtze River, which is Lingling."
64. Zhang Min and Han Mingfang, "Emperor Shun's Southern Hunting Expedition and the Beginning of Gouwu," *Journal of Nanjing University* (Philosophy, Humanities, and Social Sciences), no. 3 (1999): 105–113.
65. Zou Heng, "Preliminary Discussion on the Cultures of Neighboring Regions in the Northern Area during the Xia and Shang Periods," in *Collection of Archaeological Papers on Xia, Shang, and Zhou Dynasties* (Beijing: Cultural Relics Press, 1980), 253–294.
66. Annotation in the *Classic of Mountains and Seas · Southern Hainei*. In addition, commentary in *Records of the Grand Historian · Annals of the Gaozu* cites "Houji banished the emperor's son Danzhu to Dan River"; *Records of the Grand Historian · Annals of the Five Emperors* cites "Houji banished the Emperor's son Danzhu."
67. Qian Mu, "Geographical Study of Early Zhou," *Yanjing Journal*, no. 10 (1931): 1955–2008.
68. The *Records of the Grand Historian · Annals of the Five Emperors* quotes the *Chronicles of Emperor*: "Yao married a lady from the San Yi *shi*, named Nü Huang, who bore Danzhu."
69. The *Records of the Grand Historian · Annals of the Five Emperors* quotes Fan Wang's *Jingzhou* as saying: "Danshui County is in Danchuan, where Yao's son Zhu was enfeoffed." The *Description Encompassing the Earth* states: "The ancient city of Danshui is located 130 *li* southwest of Neixiang County in Dengzhou."
70. Han Jianye, "Origins and Developmental Stages of Pre-Zhou Culture," in "Pre-Qin Archaeology," supplement, *Archaeology and Cultural Relics* (2002): 212–218.
71. The *Book of Songs*: "Originally, the ancient ancestors were born because Jiang Yuan was able to give birth. How were the ancient ancestors born? By praying to the divine and sacrificing to the Heavenly Emperor, they sought to have children and avoid being without heirs. By stepping on the imprint of the Heavenly Emperor's thumb, they received the blessings and protection of the divine. The fetus would sometimes move and sometimes remain still, and when it was born, it would be diligently nurtured. The child would become the ancestor Zhou Houji." According to *Er Ya*, "Wu means footprints; Min means big toes."
72. The *Discourses of the States · Discourses of Zhou (Part Three)*: "The king should also compare yourself to the kings of Jiuli and Sanmiao, as well as the rulers of the Xia and Shang dynasties at their decline ... As a result, their ancestral temples were destroyed by others, sacrificial vessels were burned, their descendants became slaves, and even the common people suffered calamities."

73. Xu Xusheng, *The Mythical Era of Ancient Chinese History*, new ed. (Beijing: Cultural Relics Press, 1985), 57–59.
74. Han Jianye, "Slanted-Bellied Cups and Sanmiao Culture," *Jianghan Archaeology*, no. 1 (2002): 67–72.
75. Yang Xingai and Han Jianye, "Exploration of Yu's Campaign against the Sanmiao," *Cultural Relics of the Central Plain*, no. 2 (1995): 46–55.
76. The *Ancient Bamboo Annals*: "From Yu to Jie there were seventeen generations, with and without kings, in 471 years" (*Imperial Reader*, vol. 82); "From Yu to Jie, there were seventeen kings of Xia Dynasty" (annotation in *Selections of Refined Literature · Treatises of Six Dynasties*). The *Discourses in the Balance · Listing the Shortcomings*: "Xia began with Yu, Yin originated with Tang, and Zhou's ancestor was Houji."
77. Han Jianye, "Origins and Developmental Stages of Xia Culture," *Journal of Peking University* (Philosophy and Social Sciences), no. 4 (1997): 120–125.
78. The *Classic of Mountains and Seas · Western Dahuang*: "Beyond the Northwestern Sea, in the corner of the Dahuang, there is a mountain that does not converge, named Buzhou Fuzi ... Yu attacked Gonggong's mountains." The *Classic of Mountains and Seas · Northern Dahuang*: "Gonggong's servant was named Xiang Yao ... Yu controlled the floodwaters and killed Xiang Yao." *Classic of Mountains and Seas · Northern Dahuang*: "Gonggong's servant was from the Xiangliu *shi* ... Yu used stones to fill marshy streams."
79. Sacrificial relics from the transitional period of Longshan Culture were discovered at the Yuhui site in Bengbu, Anhui. The excavators et al. speculated that it might be related to the legend of Yu meeting the lords. See Institute of Archaeology, Chinese Academy of Social Sciences, and Bengbu Museum of Anhui Province, *Bengbu Yuhui Village* (Beijing: Science Press, 2013), 421–425.
80. Annotation in the *Lopi · Second Chronicle*, vol. 13, quotes the *Bamboo Annals*: "Taikang resided in Zhenxun and lost his state." The *Imperial Reader*, vol. 82, quotes the *Chronicles of Emperors*: "Taikang was unprincipled, ruled for twenty-nine years, lost governance, and died." The *Records of the Grand Historian · Basic Annals of Xia*: "King Taikang lost his kingdom," and the *Collected Commentaries* quotes Kong Anguo: "He was chased by Yi and couldn't return to his state."
81. See the *Commentary of Zuo · Duke Xiang Fourth Year, Commentary of Zuo · Duke Ai First Year, Qianfu Lun · Five Virtues, Bamboo Annals, Songs of Chu · Tian Wen, Li Sao*, etc.
82. Han Jianye, "On the Rise of Erlitou Bronze Civilization," *Chinese Historical Relics*, no. 1 (2009): 37–47.
83. Zou Heng proposed and elaborated the view that Erlitou culture is Xia culture. See Zou Heng, "On Xia Culture," in *Collection of Archaeological Papers on Xia, Shang, and Zhou Dynasties* (Beijing: Cultural Relics Press, 1980), 95–182.
84. Han Jianye, "Liangzhu, Taosi and Erlitou—The Evolutionary Path of Early Chinese Civilization," *Archaeology*, no. 11 (2010): 71–78.
85. The *Current f Bamboo Annals* (Annotated by Wang Guowei), "In the fifteenth year of Emperor Xiang, Lord of Shang made a chariot." "In the eleventh year of Emperor Shaokang, he ordered Lord Ming of Shang to manage the river." "In the thirteenth year of Emperor

Zhu, Lord Ming of Shang died in the river." "In the thirty-third year of Emperor Mang, Lord of Shang moved to Yin." (Annotated by Wang Guowei: "This is based on 'King Zihai of Yin' in the *Bamboo Annals* quoted in the *Classic of Mountains and Seas*. Hence the establishment of moving to Yin.")

"In the twelfth year of Emperor Xie, Lord Zihai of Yin was a guest at Youyi, Youyi killed and released him. In the sixteenth year, Lord Wei of Yin attacked Youyi with the Hebo troops, killing its lord, Lord Mian." "In the ninth year of Emperor Kongjia, ascent to the throne. Lord of Yin returned to Shangqiu." "In the thirty-first year of Emperor Gui, there was heavy thunder and rain, and a battle took place at Mingtiao."

86. Tang Lan, "Using Bronze Inscriptions to Study the History of Western Zhou—A General Discussion on the Important Historical Value of a Batch of Bronzes Discovered in Baoji in Recent Years," *Wenwu*, no. 6 (1976): 31–39.
87. *Commentary on the Water Classic · Wei River* quotes, and *Comprehensive Explanation of Historical Geography* cites it as "Bo" (番).
88. Ding Shan, *Study of Shang and Zhou Historical Materials* (Beijing: Zhonghua Book Company, 1988).
89. Zhao Tiehan, "New Verification of the Eight Migrations before Tang," *Mainland Magazine* 27, no. 6 (1963).
90. Zou Heng, "On Tang's Capital Zhenghao and Its Preceding and Following Migrations," in *Collection of Archaeological Papers on Xia, Shang, and Zhou Dynasties* (Beijing: Cultural Relics Press, 1980), 183–218.
91. Wang Guowei, "A Study of the Ancestors of Yin Seen in Oracle Bone Inscriptions," in *Guantang Collection*, vol. 9 (Beijing: Zhonghua Book Company, 1959), 409–436; Gu Jiegang, "Stories in the Hexagrams and Lines of Zhouyi," in *Doubting Antiquity*, vol. 3 (Shanghai: Shanghai Ancient Books Publishing House, 1982), 1–44; Wu Qichang, "Three Continued Studies on the Ancestors of Yin Seen in Oracle Bone Inscriptions," in *Doubting Antiquity*, vol. 7 (Shanghai: Shanghai Ancient Books Publishing House, 1982), 333–359.
92. Han Jianye, "Exploring the Origins of Pre-Shang Culture," *Cultural Relics of Central China*, no. 2 (1998): 48–54.
93. According to Zou Heng's verification, the Jinzhong region may have been the original habitat of the Hebo. See Zou Heng, "On Xia Culture," in *Collection of Archaeological Papers on Xia, Shang, and Zhou Dynasties* (Beijing: Cultural Relics Press, 1980), 95–182.
94. Zou Heng was the first to clearly propose and prove the issue of pre-Shang culture. See Zou Heng, "On Tang's Capital Zhenghao and Its Preceding and Following Migrations," in *Collection of Archaeological Papers on Xia, Shang, and Zhou Dynasties* (Beijing: Cultural Relics Press, 1980), 183–218.
95. The legend of Yu dividing the land into nine provinces was widely spread before the Spring and Autumn period. For example, in the "Bell of Marquis Qi" it says, "All nine provinces are the earth divided by Yu." In the *Commentary of Zuo · Duke Xiang Fourth Year*, it says: "Vast are the traces of Yu, drawn into nine provinces."
96. Gu Jiegang, "The 'Tribute of Yu' (Fully Annotated)," in *Selected Readings of Ancient Chinese Geographic Works*, vol. 1 (Beijing: Science Press, 1959), 1–44.

NOTES   411

97. Li Min, "The 'Tribute of Yu' and the History of Xia," in *Research on the Book of Documents and Ancient History*, suppl. and rev. ed. (Zhengzhou: Zhongzhou Calligraphy and Painting Society, 1981), 45–64; Shao Wangping, "Archaeological Study on the 'Nine Provinces' in the 'Tribute of Yu,'" in *Collection of Cultural Archaeology*, vol. 2 (Beijing: Cultural Relics Press, 1989), 11–30.

98. Gu Jiegang, "The 'Tribute of Yu' (Fully Annotated)," in *Selected Readings of Ancient Chinese Geographic Works*, vol. 1 (Beijing: Science Press, 1959), 1–44.

99. Liu Ti, "On the Metropolitan and Regional System in the 'Tribute of Yu'—A Tentative Exploration of the Oldest Border Theory in China," *Research on Chinese Border History and Geography*, no. 1 (1991): 43–55.

100. Zhao Chunqing, "Archaeological Observations on the Five *Fu* of the 'Tribute of Yu,'" *Cultural Relics of Central China*, no. 5 (2006): 10–22.

101. The *Records of the Grand Historian · Basic Annals of Xia*, citing Chen Zan in the commentary, "According to the *Ji Tomb Ancient Texts*: 'Taikang resided in Zhenxun, Yi also resided there, and Jie resided there as well.'"

102. Zou Heng, "Investigation on the Geographical Aspects of Legends Related to the Xia People within the Distribution Area of Xia Culture," in *Collection of Archaeological Papers on Xia, Shang, and Zhou Dynasties* (Beijing: Cultural Relics Press, 1980), 219–252; Sun Miao, *History of Xia and Shang* (Beijing: Cultural Relics Press, 1987), 285–319.

103. Song Yuqin, "A Preliminary Discussion on the Confluence of Archaeological Cultures of Yi, Xia, and Shang," *Cultural Relics of Central China*, no. 1 (1992): 11–19.

104. Zou Heng, "On Xia Culture," in *Collection of Archaeological Papers on Xia, Shang, and Zhou Dynasties* (Beijing: Cultural Relics Press, 1980), 95–182.

105. Sun Miao, *History of Xia and Shang* (Beijing: Cultural Relics Press, 1987), 345–369.

106. Sun Miao, *History of Xia and Shang* (Beijing: Cultural Relics Press, 1987), 285–319.

107. An Jinhuai, "A Preliminary Study on the Shang Dynasty City Site in Zhengzhou—Aodu," *Wenwu*, no. 4–5 (1961): 73–80.

108. Zou Heng, "On the Capital of Tang in Zhengbo and its Subsequent Migrations," in *Collection of Archaeological Papers on Xia, Shang, and Zhou Dynasties* (Beijing: Cultural Relics Press, 1980), 183–218.

109. Zou Heng, "The Hypothesis That Yanshi Shangcheng Is Tai Jia's Tong Palace," *Journal of Peking University* (Philosophy and Social Sciences), no. 4 (1984): 17–19.

110. Chen Xu, "The Theory that the Shang Dynasty Site at Xiaoshuangqiao, Zhengzhou is Aodu," *Cultural Relics of Central China*, no. 2 (1997): 45–50.

111. Wang Zhenzhong, *The Origin of Ancient Chinese States and the Formation of Monarchy* (Beijing: China Social Sciences Press, 2013), 391–518.

CHAPTER 7   THE GEOGRAPHICAL ENVIRONMENTAL BASIS OF EARLY CHINA

1. Yan Wenming, "The Unity and Diversity of China's Prehistoric Culture," *Wenwu*, no. 3 (1987): 38–50.

2. Leften Stavros Stavrianos, quoting Franz Boas in *Global History*: "The history of mankind has shown that the progress of a society often depends on whether it has the opportunity

to absorb the experiences of neighboring social groups." He then stated: "If other geographical factors are the same, then the key to human progress lies in the accessibility between various ethnic groups."

See Leften Stavros Stavrianos, *Global History: The World before 1500*, trans. Wu Xiangying and Liang Chimin (Shanghai: Shanghai Academy of Social Sciences Press, 1999), 57.

3. Wang Zhenzhong, *Comparative Study on the Origins of Chinese Civilization*, suppl. and rev. ed. (Beijing: China Social Sciences Press, 2013), 476.

4. Su Bingqi categorized early China culture into six major systems and two large blocks facing the southeast coast and northwest inland, respectively; Yan Wenming divided early Chinese culture into hunting and gathering culture, dry farming culture, and rice farming culture, with hundreds of archaeological cultures involved in early China.

See Su Bingqi and Yin Weizhang, "On the Types of Archaeological Cultural Systems," *Wenwu*, no. 5 (1981): 10–17; Yan Wenming, "The Unity and Diversity of China's Prehistoric Culture," *Wenwu*, no. 3 (1987): 38–50.

5. Han Jianye, "A Brief Discussion on the General Trends and Different Modes of Social Development during China's Chalcolithic," *Ancient Civilizations* 2 (June 2003): 84–96.

6. Yan Wenming, "The Cradle of Eastern Civilization," in *The Origin of Agriculture and Civilization* (Beijing: Science Press, 2000), 148–174.

7. He Bingdi, *Loess and the Origins of Chinese Agriculture* (Hong Kong: Chinese University of Hong Kong Press, 1969).

8. Liu Dongsheng et al., *Loess and Environment* (Beijing: Science Press, 1985); Zhou Kunshu, *Environmental Archaeology* (Beijing: Cultural Relics Press, 2007), 179–181.

9. Liu Tungsheng and Yuan Baoyin, "Paleoclimatic Cycles in Northern China: Luochuan Loess Section and Its Environmental Implication," in *Aspects of Loess Research* (Beijing: China Ocean Press, 1987), 3–26.

10. Zhou Kunshu, "Loess of Zhouyuan and Its Relationship with Cultural Layers," *Quaternary Period Research*, no. 2 (1995): 174–181.

11. Zhou Kunshu, Zhang Guangru, and Cao Bingwu, "Ancient Cultures and Environment in Central Plain," in *Research on the Historical Evolution of China's Living Environment*, vol. 1 (Beijing: Ocean Press, 1993), 111–122.

12. Shi Yafeng et al., "Climate and Environment during the Climax of the Holocene Megathermal in China," *Science in China* (Series B) 23, no. 8 (1993): 865–873; Liu Dongsheng, ed., *Research on Water Resource Allocation, Ecological Environment Construction, and Sustainable Development Strategy in the Northwest Region*, vol. Natural History (Beijing: Science Press, 2004), 109.

13. Shi Yafeng et al., "The Basic Characteristics of Climate and Environment during the Holocene Megathermal in China," in *Climate and Environment during the Holocene Megathermal in China* (Beijing: Ocean Press, 1992), 1–18.

14. Wang Shaowu et al., "Research on Climate Change in China," *Climate and Environment Research* 7, no. 2 (2002): 137.

15. Shi Peijun, *Theory and Practice of Geographic Environment Evolution Research—Research on Geographic Environment Evolution in the Ordos Region Since the Late Quaternary* (Beijing: Science Press, 1991); Shi Peijun et al., "Precipitation Changes in the Hetao and Adjacent

Areas on Several Time Scales over the Past 10,000 Years," in *Collection of Research on the Evolution of Environment and the Rule of Water and Sand Operation in the Yellow River Basin*, vol. 2 (Beijing: Geological Publishing House, 1991), 57–63; Zhang Lansheng, Shi Peijun, and Fang Xiuqi, "Holocene Environmental Evolution and Prediction for the Next Century in the Northern Farm-Pastoral Ecotone (Ordos Area)," in *Holocene Environmental Evolution and Prediction in the Northern Farm-Pastoral Ecotone* (Beijing: Geological Publishing House, 1992), 1–15.

16. Fang Xiuqi et al., "Holocene Cold Events and Millennial-Scale Climate Changes," *Advances in Natural Sciences* 14, no. 4 (2004): 456–461.
17. Bond, G. et al., "A Pervasive Millennial-Scale Cycle in North Atlantic Holocene and Glacial Climates," *Science* 278, no. 5341 (1997): 1257–1266.
18. Shi Peijun and Fang Xiuqi, "Comparative Study on Holocene Environmental Evolution of the Agricultural-Pastoral Transitional Zone in North China and Sahel Zone in Africa," in *Holocene Environmental Evolution and Prediction in the Northern Farm-Pastoral Ecotone* (Beijing: Geological Publishing House, 1992), 87–92; Zhou Shangzhe et al., "Preliminary Study on Millennial-Scale Environmental Changes in Western China during the Holocene," in *Environmental Archaeological Research*, vol. 1 (Beijing: Science Press, 1991), 230–236; Wang Shaowu and Zhu Jinhong, "Chronological Study on Millennial-Scale Climate Oscillations during the Holocene," *Progress in Climate Change Research* 1, no. 4 (2005): 157–160.
19. Han Jianye, "Natural Environment and Cultural Development in Northwest China during the Pre-Qin Period," in *Natural Environment and Cultural Development in Northwest China during the Pre-Qin Period* (Beijing: Cultural Relics Press, 2008), 18–39.
20. Fang Xiuqi and Hou Guangliang, "Integrated Reconstruction of Holocene Temperature Series in China," *Geographical Science* 31, no. 4 (2011): 385–393.
21. Wu Wenxiang and Liu Dongsheng, "Climate Transition and Early Human Migration," *Marine Geology and Quaternary Geology* 21, no. 4 (2001): 103–109.
22. Wang Youping, *The Origins of Ancient Human Culture in China* (Beijing: Science Press, 2005).
23. Wu Naiqin et al., "Phytoliths—Conversion Function of Climate Factors and Its Application in the Study of Paleoenvironment in Weinan Since the Late Ice Age," *Quaternary Sciences*, no. 3 (1994): 270–279.
24. Yan Wenming proposed that the middle and lower reaches of the Yangtze River are the origins of rice farming because places with rich plant resources such as South China, Southeast Asia, and India can sustain livelihoods through gathering, lacking the impetus for agricultural development. In contrast, the Yangtze River Basin, despite having wild rice, is already on the periphery. When climate fluctuations cause food shortages, it is most likely to develop initial rice agriculture. This theory is known as the "Marginal Theory" of the origin of rice cultivation.

    See Yan Wenming, "Revisiting the Origins of Rice Farming in China," *Agricultural Archaeology*, no. 2 (1989): 72–83.
25. Yang Zhihong et al., "Younger Dryas Event Records in the Guliya Ice Core," *Chinese Science Bulletin* 42, no. 18 (1997): 1975–1978.

26. The stone cities from Yangshao Culture's phase IV in the central–southern part of Inner Mongolia and northern Shaanxi may be regarded as the "prototype" of the Great Wall, and their function might be related to resisting the northern hunter-gatherer tribes.

    See Han Jianye, "On the Early Northern Stone Cities as the 'Prototype' of the Great Wall," *Huaxia Archaeology*, no. 1 (2008): 48–53.

27. Han Jianye, *Research on the Neolithic Culture in Northern China* (Beijing: Cultural Relics Press, 2003); Wu Wenxiang and Liu Dongsheng, "The Role of the 5500-Year Climate Event in the Evolution of Ancient Civilizations and Cultures in the Three Ancient Civilized Countries," *Earth Science Frontiers* 9, no. 1 (2002): 155–160; Wu Wenxiang and Ge Quansheng, "Holocene Climate Events and Their Impact on the Development of Ancient Cultures," *Huaxia Archaeology*, no. 3 (2005): 60–67; Han Jianye, "The Impact of the 5000-Year and 4000-Year Climate Events on the Culture of the Northern Region of China," in *Environmental Archaeological Research*, vol. 3 (Beijing: Peking University Press, 2006), 159–163.

28. Zhejiang Provincial Institute of Cultural Relics and Archaeology, "Excavations of the Liangzhu Ancient City Site in Yuhang District, Hangzhou City, 2006–2007," *Archaeology*, no. 7 (2008): 3–10.

29. Cui Jianxin and Liu Shangzhe, "Discussion on Floods and Culture in China before 4,000 Years Ago," *Journal of Lanzhou University*, ed. Natural Science 39, no. 3 (2003): 94–97.

30. Xia Zhengkai, Yang Xiaoyan, and Ye Maolin, "Prehistoric Disaster Events at the Lajia Site in Qinghai," *Science Bulletin* 48, no. 11 (2003): 1020–1024.

31. V. A. Demkin and T. S. Demkina, "Paleoecological Crisis and Optima in the Eurasian Steppes in Ancient Times and the Middle Ages," in *Complex Societies of Central Eurasia from the 3rd to the 1st Millennium BC*, eds. Karlene Jones-Bley and D. G. Zdanovich (Washington: Institute for the Study of Man, 2002), 389–399.

32. E. E. Kuzmina, "The First Migration Wave of Indo-Iranians to the South," ed. James P. Mallory, *Journal of Indo-European Studies* 29, no. 1–2 (2001): 1–40.

33. Shui Tao, "The Relationship between Human and Land in the Rise and Fall of Early Civilizations in the Gansu and Qinghai Region," in *Bronze Age in Northwestern China* (Beijing: Science Press, 2001), 168–186.

34. Department of Archaeology of Peking University and Zhumadian City Cultural Relics Preservation and Management Office, *Cultural Relics of the Middle Holocene in the Upper Reaches of the Huai River—Zhumadian Yangzhuang* (Beijing: Science Press, 1998); Luoyang City Cultural Relics Working Team, *Excavation Report of Erlitou Culture Settlement Site at Luoyang Zaojiaoshu—1992–1993* (Beijing: Science Press, 2002).

35. Many people have noticed the significant impact of climate events around 4,000 years ago on ancient civilizations in the Old World. See Wu Wenxiang and Liu Dongsheng, "Cooling Event around 4000a B.P. and the Birth of Chinese Civilization," *Quaternary Sciences* 21, no. 5 (2001): 443–451; Wang Wei, "Exploration of the Causes of Large-Scale Cultural Changes in China around 2000 BCE," *Archaeology*, no. 1 (2004): 67–77; Wang Shaowu, "Climate Change from 2200 BCE to 2000 BCE and the Decline of Ancient Civilizations," *Progress in Natural Science* 15, no. 9 (2005): 1094–1099.

Chapter 8 Conclusion

1. Xu Pingfang and Zhang Guangzhi have discussed the characteristics of Chinese civilization and its position in the history of world civilizations: "Chinese civilization, whether in terms of crop cultivation (grain millet in the north and rice in the south), livestock rearing (primarily pigs and dogs), the invention of silk, the creation of porcelain, architectural forms of earth and wood structures, enclosed courtyard layouts, cities centered on political functions, the use of jade ritual objects and bronze ritual vessels, square characters mainly based on meaning and form, social structures tied by blood relations and ancestor worship, etc., all indicate that Chinese civilization is an indigenous civilization that grew out of its own soil."

    See Xu Pingfang, Zhang Guangzhi, "The Formation of Chinese Civilization and Its Position in the History of World Civilizations," *Yanjing Journal*, new no. 6 (1999): 8–16.

2. The *Book of Han, Biography of Li Shiqi*: "For the sovereign, the people are supreme, while for the people, food is supreme."

3. Bu Gong, *The Chinese Model of Civilization Origin* (Beijing: Science Press, 2007).

4. Zhang Guangzhi, "Continuity and Disruption: A Draft of a New Theory on the Origin of Civilization," *Jiuzhou Academic Journal* 1, no. 1 (1986): 1–8.

5. Peter T. Furst, "Shamanistic Survivals in Mesoamerican Religion," in *Proceedings of the XII International Congress of Americanists, Mexico* 3 (1976): 149–157.

6. Xu Lianggao, "Ancestor Worship and Early States in China," in *Collected Papers from the Academic Symposium on the Civilization Process in the Central Plain Region* (Beijing: Science Press, 2006), 123–158.

7. Yan Wenming, "The Unity and Diversity of China's Prehistoric Culture," *Wenwu*, no. 3 (1987): 38–50.

8. Han Jianye, "On the Historical Position of Neolithic Culture in the Central Plain," *Jianghan Archaeology*, no. 1 (2004): 59–64.

9. Zhang Zhongpei pointed out that in northern China during the pre-Qin period, there were three relatively unified periods and three relatively fragmented periods. The three relatively unified periods were the "Miaodigou culture period," the upper Erligang culture, and the Western Zhou period; the three relatively fragmented periods were the middle Neolithic before Miaodigou culture period and the "Banpo culture" period, the late Yangshao to Longshan period, and the period after the upper Erligang culture.

    See Zhang Zhongpei, "Several Issues Regarding the Archaeology of the Eastern Inner Mongolia Region," in *Collection of Research Papers on the Archaeology and Culture of the Eastern Inner Mongolia Region* (Beijing: Marine Publishing House, 1991), 3–8.

10. Zhu Hong, "Ancient Ethnic Groups in Northeast China," *Cultural Relics Quarterly*, no. 1 (1998): 54–64; Zhu Hong, "Ancient Ethnic Groups in Southern China," *Social and Sciences Journal of Jilin University*, no. 3 (2002): 5–12; Zhu Hong, "Ancient Ethnic Groups in Northwest China," *Archaeology and Cultural Relics*, no. 5 (2006): 60–65.

11. The population in South China extending to Southeast Asia and the Pacific Islands may mainly belong to the Austronesian language family. See Jiao Tianlong and Fan Xuechun, *Fujian and the Austronesian Language Family* (Beijing: Zhonghua Book Company, 2010).

12. Han Kangxin, Tan Jingze, and Zhang Fan, *Research on the Ancient Inhabitants of Northwest China* (Shanghai: Fudan University Press, 2005); Wei Dong et al., "Measurement Characteristics of the Skulls Unearthed from the Hami Tianshan North Road Cemetery," *Acta Anthropologica Sinica* 31, no. 4 (2012): 395–406.

Index

A

agricultural and crafting tools
 adze, 30–31, 33–34, 40–41, 46, 50–51, 54–55, 58, 70, 76, 78, 80, 108, 110, 115, 117–18, 152–53, 159–60, 165–66, 168, 172, 175, 177, 184, 198, 202, 205, 207, 210, 213, 215, 217–19, 223–26, 244, 246, 252–53, 257, 259, 263, 265–69, 272
 axe, 33–34, 40–41, 46, 50–51, 54–55, 58, 67, 70, 76, 78, 80, 86, 106, 108–10, 115, 117, 145, 152–53, 159–60, 165–66, 168, 172, 175, 177, 179, 184, 198, 200, 202, 205, 207, 210, 213, 217, 219, 221, 223–24, 226, 241, 244, 246, 252–53, 255, 257–63, 266–69, 272
 axe with a short cylindrical tube attached, 242
 jue, 165, 198, 224
 si, 41, 46, 54, 78, 80–81, 109, 117
 weeder, 160, 163
 yue, 81, 84, 86, 97, 106, 113, 115, 120, 122, 125, 132, 142, 145, 156, 159–61, 163, 167, 172, 177, 180, 187, 190–91, 197, 200–201, 204–5, 207, 210, 215, 217–19, 223–24, 231, 233–36, 255, 257
 zhi, 45, 85

ancestor worship, 59, 90, 124, 189, 234, 278, 336, 339
ancient Chinese archaeological cultures, 66
 Baijia culture, 35, 39, 42–45, 51–53, 57, 59, 68, 149
 Baodun culture, 195, 216–17, 226–27, 235, 264
 Beigou culture, 223, 226
 Beixin culture, 66–67, 69, 78, 81–82, 90, 105, 110, 120, 287, 290–91
 Beiyinyangying culture, 112–14, 122, 124–25, 158, 169
 Cishan culture, 39, 49–51, 54, 56, 68–69
 Dawenkou culture, 84, 94, 109–10, 112, 120, 122, 125, 130, 132, 134, 141–42, 144, 153–54, 156, 158, 160, 169–70, 176–77, 179–80, 182–83, 187–92, 196, 198, 200, 205, 214–15, 217–18, 227, 233, 277, 287, 290–91, 296–97, 299, 301–2, 304–6, 329
 Daxi culture, 72, 74–75, 79, 81, 89–90, 94, 115–17, 120, 122–24, 140–41, 159, 166, 168, 170–71, 180, 182, 217, 301
 Dingsishan culture, 39, 41, 45, 75
 Erligang culture, 3, 239–40, 246–47, 249–54, 256, 261–62, 265, 267–69, 271–73,

277–80, 285, 314, 316, 331, 334
Erlitou culture, 240–46, 249–52, 256, 260–61, 264–65, 267–69, 271–73, 277, 279–80, 286, 288, 307, 310–14, 316, 318
Gantuoyan culture, 195, 225, 265
Gaomiao culture, 39, 52–53, 57, 59, 74–75
Gaotaishan culture, 240, 256, 258–59, 269, 278
Guangfulin culture, 195, 217–18, 228–29, 251, 306
Hamin Mangha culture, 175, 180
Hami Tianshan North Road culture, 240, 263, 266, 270
Haochuan culture, 195, 218, 223–24, 233, 251–52
Hemudu culture, 66, 76–79, 86, 88, 90, 120
Hougang culture, 195, 197–98, 203, 206–9, 226, 228, 234, 245, 255–56, 306, 309, 311
Houli culture, 39–42, 45, 51–52, 66–67, 78
Hutoupu culture, 195, 224, 265
Karuo culture, 131, 152–53, 183–84, 188, 226
Kayue culture, 240, 261–62, 268–70
Kuahuqiao culture, 39, 45–48, 52–55, 59, 76, 78
Laohushan culture, 195, 200, 202, 208–10, 212, 227, 231, 235–36, 253, 255, 306–7, 329
Liangzhu culture, 134, 142, 154, 160–61, 163–64, 169–71, 180, 182–83, 186–89, 191–92, 194–95, 203, 206, 217–18, 224, 233, 236, 251–52, 304, 330
Lijiagou culture, 28, 31
Longshan culture, 137, 142, 194–98, 200, 203, 206, 208, 211, 215, 218, 223, 226–28, 230–31, 233–35, 237, 249–51, 290, 305, 311, 317
Majiabang culture, 66, 75–76, 78–79, 81, 84, 112
Majiayao culture, 130–31, 138–39, 145, 148, 152–53, 183–84, 187–92, 194–95, 212, 217, 219–20, 226, 230, 233–34, 239, 263, 297, 307
Nanbaoligaotu culture, 176–78, 183, 189, 222
Nanmuyuan culture, 39, 52–53
Peiligang culture, 2, 4, 38–40, 42–45, 49–52, 54–59, 62, 65, 67–70, 89–90, 110, 327, 333, 336
Pengtoushan culture, 39, 41–42, 45–46, 48–49, 52–53, 55–56, 76
Pianbuzi culture, 176–78, 222–23, 258
pre-Xia culture, 288, 304, 306
Qijia culture, 195, 211–13, 221, 228–32, 234, 236, 240–41, 254–55, 260–62, 268–71, 307, 310, 331
Qujialing culture, 134, 137, 142, 164, 168–71, 182–83, 187–88, 190–92, 214–15, 235, 277
Sanxingdui culture, 240, 247, 264, 268, 271
Shangshan culture, 30, 34, 36, 39, 41, 45, 47–48, 53, 76–77
Shijiahe culture, 188, 203–4, 206, 211, 214–18, 227, 231, 233–37, 308–9, 330
Shuangdun culture, 39, 51–52, 59, 66, 69, 77
Shuangta culture, 28, 32–34, 50–51, 65
Shunshanji culture, 45, 52, 58, 76, 86
Siba culture, 240, 263–64, 269
Tangjiagang culture, 66, 72, 74–75, 81–82, 88
Tanshishan culture, 130, 164–66, 195, 218, 223–24, 228–29, 251, 306
Wangwan culture, 3, 195, 202–9, 214–16, 218, 226–28, 231, 234–35, 237, 244, 288, 305–6, 308–10, 312–13, 330, 334
Xiachuan culture, 24
Xiajiadian culture, 240, 245–46, 255–56, 258–59, 268–72, 277–79, 331
Xiantouling culture, 66, 72, 75–76, 225
Xiaojiawuji culture, 214–15, 227, 231, 309
Xiaozhushan culture, 66, 80, 84, 89, 94, 109, 122, 177–78, 180, 183, 195, 222–23, 226, 249, 258

Xiaqiyuan culture, 240–41, 245–46, 249, 268, 311
Xinglongwa culture, 39, 49–51, 55, 62, 64–65, 78, 81, 178
Xinguang culture, 195, 216, 225–26
Xinkailiu culture, 39, 54–55, 80, 85
Xinle culture, 39, 54–55, 79
Xueshan culture, 104, 138–39, 143–44, 154, 176, 178–80, 188–89, 207–9, 211–12, 220, 222, 226, 228, 245, 255–56, 297, 311
Yabuli culture, 66, 80, 86, 94, 118, 172
Yangshao culture, 2, 52, 66–72, 79–82, 84–86, 88–91, 93–97, 101, 103, 105–8, 110, 115–19, 123–24, 126, 129, 131–32, 134, 138, 140, 143–45, 151–52, 154, 167, 169–70, 175, 178–80, 182–83, 188–92, 200, 203, 205, 208–9, 211, 214, 219, 227, 286, 288, 290–91, 297, 299, 301, 304, 317, 334
Yueshi culture, 240, 243, 245–47, 249–52, 258–59, 268, 271–72, 278, 290, 314, 316
Zaolütai culture, 195, 204, 206–9, 217–18, 224, 226–27, 231, 249, 251, 305–6, 309–11
Zaoshi culture, 39, 52–54, 72
Zhaobaogou culture, 39, 54–55, 64, 79–81, 84, 88–89, 176
Zhenxing culture, 66, 80
Zhongba culture, 195, 216–17
Zhukaigou culture, 240, 242, 245, 253–56, 268–71, 273, 279, 316, 331
Zuojiashan culture, 54–55, 66, 80, 84, 86, 172, 177–79

B
Bagua, 62
Battle of Zhuolu, 290–93
Believing-the-Ancient – Doubting-the-Ancient – Interpreting-the-Ancient, 285
bone artifacts
  bone beads, 71
  bone flutes, 42, 62, 90

bone hairpin, 31, 46, 71, 176, 267
bone-handle stone-blade knife, 149
bone-horn-and-ivory instruments, 78, 81, 86
Book of Changes, 311, 314
Book of Documents, 7, 10, 289, 296, 302, 304, 306, 309–10, 312–15
Book of Zhou, 290
bronzeware, 257
burial pits, 97, 205, 208, 213, 234
burial positions
  extended on the side, 256
  extended prone, 150, 205, 221–22
  extended supine, 40, 43, 59, 67, 70–72, 132, 136–37, 148–49, 155, 159, 165, 167, 198, 201, 207, 210, 213, 217, 222, 252, 254, 256, 258, 261, 278
  extended supine burials, 45, 50, 79–80, 95, 101, 106, 108, 110, 114, 117, 140, 177, 244–45, 250, 262–63
  flexed burials, 26, 33, 41, 45, 50, 59, 75, 80, 177, 212, 217, 220, 222, 258, 267, 278
  flexed on the (left or right) side, 139, 220, 222, 254, 258, 261, 263, 266–67
  flexed supine, 144, 175
  prone burials, 79
  squatting flexed burials, 26, 41
  supine extended burial, 31, 267
burial types
  burial in the ground, 336
  house burial, 50
  infant urn burials, 40, 43, 59, 70–71, 86, 90, 205, 208, 213
  joint burial, 43, 62, 67, 72, 79, 101–3, 106, 110, 125, 132, 136, 139, 213, 215, 220, 222, 254, 261, 263, 302
  primary burials, 72, 258, 261
  secondary burial, 51, 67, 72, 80, 95, 106, 148, 167, 258, 261

C
cave, 20, 22, 24, 26–28, 30–32, 34, 40–41, 201

INDEX

cemetery, 4, 59, 71–72, 75, 90, 95, 115, 132, 142–44, 150, 156, 158–59, 161, 163, 167, 176, 192, 198, 200–201, 212, 219–22, 235, 255–57, 262–63, 267, 278–79
"centered three-tier structure," 65
Central Asian Bronze culture, 213
character-like symbols, 59, 160, 188
"China interaction sphere," 126–27
Classic of Mountains and Seas, 288, 290–91, 295–96, 299, 301, 309, 311
Commentary of Zuo, 291–92, 294, 296, 298–300, 303, 309–10, 312–13
construction techniques and materials
  beam-framed architectural houses, 187, 327
  clay strip coiling method, 26, 30–31, 42, 50–51, 184
  mortise and tenon, 34, 37, 58, 88, 118, 163, 171
  slab-building method, 26, 30, 40
  stilt house, 41, 58, 79
  timber-framed earthen wall construction, 41, 216
cooking and utility tools
  cauldron, 26, 28, 30, 32–34, 41, 45, 48, 52–53, 66–69, 71, 74–79, 84, 86, 96, 104, 113, 116–18, 136, 139, 164–65, 178, 204, 214, 218, 224–25, 242, 252, 264–65
  fire seed stove, 95, 103
  gui (cooking utensil), 122, 134, 153–54, 158, 160, 164, 177, 179–80, 182–83, 187, 194, 196–97, 202–3, 206, 208, 211, 214–15, 217–18, 223–24, 226, 230–31, 233, 239, 241, 244–45, 252, 256–57, 264, 268, 271, 281, 299
  range, 45, 57, 64–65, 69, 76, 96, 104, 110, 139, 146–47, 167, 175, 202, 289
  stove, 85, 136, 139, 200, 203, 211, 289
  zeng, 26, 57, 71, 113, 136, 139, 144–45, 166, 169, 183, 200, 202, 206–7, 209, 211, 214–15, 224, 241, 246–47, 258
cremations, 266, 278
cultural regions

northeast cultural region, 82
southeastern cultural region, 22–23
Yangtze River–South China cultural region, 81
Yellow River Basin cultural region, 66
cultural system
  bottle (pot)–earthen bowl (basin)–jar–*ding* cultural system, 66, 81–82, 84–85, 94, 120
  cauldron–concaved-bottom jar–high-foot plate cultural system, 240, 265
  cauldron–*ding*–round-foot plate–high-foot plate cultural system, 195
  cauldron–round-foot plate cultural system, 129
  cauldron–round-foot plate–high-foot plate cultural system, 39, 54, 56, 66, 81, 84–85, 94, 118, 120, 122, 130, 265
  cord-mark round-bottom cauldron cultural system, 28, 30, 34, 39, 41, 53
  cylindrical jar cultural system, 28, 32, 39, 50–51, 56, 66, 80, 82, 84, 94, 109, 118, 120, 122, 129–30, 195, 226, 259, 263, 266
  cylindrical jar–painted pottery jar–earthen bowl cultural system, 94, 120, 130, 171
  deep-belly jar cultural system, 28
  deep-belly jar–double-handle pot–earthen bowl cultural system, 39–40, 45, 52, 55
  ding–high-foot plate–pot–cup cultural system, 120
  ding–jia (li)–gui cultural system, 195–96
  ding–li–yan cultural system, 240, 260
  flat-bottom basin–round-foot plate–double-handle jar cultural system, 28, 30, 39
  jar–earthen bowl–basin–bottle cultural system, 131
  jar–pot cultural system, 240, 260
  jar–pot–earthen bowl–basin cultural system, 195, 219
  plain round-bottom cauldron cultural system, 28, 31–32, 39, 41, 52, 56

D

dry farming of millet grain and sorghum, 51, 96, 112

E

early China, 1–6, 9–18, 21, 25, 56–57, 65, 85, 91, 93–94, 126–27, 129, 131, 178, 180, 186–88, 192, 194, 226, 234, 237, 239, 266, 270–72, 277, 280–81, 285–86, 294–95, 310, 312, 316–21, 323, 328, 331–40
early Chinese cultural sphere, 1–2, 5, 9, 12, 14, 16, 56, 85, 93–94, 126, 130, 195, 240, 327, 333, 338–39

F

Five-Emperor Period, 1, 127, 286, 291, 317

G

geographical regions
  Central Plain, 1, 3–5, 7, 9–10, 12, 14, 28–29, 36, 38, 55–56, 84–85, 91, 93, 107–8, 116, 122, 127, 129, 131–32, 134, 141, 179, 187, 189–92, 196, 198, 211, 227, 229–37, 239, 241–42, 246, 258, 267, 270–73, 277–81, 286, 294, 305–7, 309–10, 312–13, 316–18, 323, 327–28, 331, 334, 337–38
  China's Second Ladder, 21–22
  Huai River Basin, 186, 229, 270, 280
  North China, 21, 24, 28–29, 31–34, 36, 49–50, 56, 65–66, 72, 81–82, 91, 120, 324, 339
  South China, 2, 21, 26, 28–30, 32–36, 39, 41, 45, 53–54, 56, 59, 66, 72, 84–86, 94, 117–18, 120, 123, 129–30, 164, 178, 195, 218, 229, 232, 240, 264–65, 268, 273, 281, 313, 326, 333, 339
  Xizang Plateau, 23, 130–31, 152, 184, 186, 194–95, 320, 324
  Yangtze River Basin, 2–4, 14–16, 36, 38, 55–56, 82, 85, 88, 106, 122–23, 152, 169, 187, 195–96, 226–27, 230–32, 240, 270, 273, 278, 316, 322, 326–27, 333, 337–39
  Yellow River Basin, 14–16, 38–39, 45, 52, 55–56, 66, 81–82, 84–85, 88, 118, 120, 123, 169, 180, 187, 195–96, 219, 226–27, 229, 231–32, 240, 263, 268, 270, 273, 278, 316, 322, 326, 330, 337–39
geological periods
  Holocene, 28–29, 35–36, 322–27
  Pleistocene, 18–21, 23, 26, 34, 36, 322, 325
  Quaternary period, 324
  Tertiary period, 324
grave goods, 40, 42, 45, 50–51, 103, 106, 114, 125, 132, 142–43, 156, 164–65, 167, 189, 235, 244, 258, 267, 279
gravel-lithic flake industry, 25, 333

H

Hag, 49, 51, 54–55
Homo erectus, 17–20, 325
  early Homo erectus, 18, 21, 325
  late Homo erectus, 19, 21
Homo sapiens
  early Homo sapiens, 17–20, 23
  late Homo sapiens, 17–20, 326
human development stages
  Bronze Age, 4, 12, 212, 220, 239–40, 242, 259, 266, 269–70, 272, 317, 332, 336
  Chalcolithic, 3, 12, 129–30, 179, 190, 192, 194–95, 220, 231, 234, 236, 317, 329, 334
  Mesolithic, 28, 35–36, 39, 55–56, 66, 85, 94, 118, 120, 130, 195, 266, 333
  Neolithic, 2, 4, 11–12, 17, 20, 26, 28–29, 31, 33–36, 38, 40–42, 45, 49–51, 55–56, 65, 68–69, 76, 81, 84–86, 93, 116, 152, 158, 166, 168, 178, 207, 216, 259, 271, 290, 317, 326–27, 331, 333–34, 337
  Paleolithic Age, 2, 4, 14, 17, 20–21, 25–27, 32, 36, 65, 266, 320, 325–26, 333, 336–37

J

jade forms
  bi, 78, 80, 109, 113, 138, 154, 159–61, 163, 172, 175, 180–81, 183, 189, 200–202, 204, 212–13, 218, 220, 223–24, 246, 256, 273
  bi with protruding teeth, 177, 183, 197, 200, 202, 227, 254
  chuan, 260
  cong, 134, 160–61, 163, 169, 182–83, 189, 201, 212, 336
  connected *bi*, 159, 172, 175, 180, 197, 254, 273
  dagger, 260
  gui, 242, 254–55, 273
  jade *huang*, 78, 84, 113, 159, 167, 177, 180, 200–201, 224, 246, 254, 273
  jade *jue*, 50, 55, 62, 64–65, 78, 86, 113, 159–60, 165, 167, 180, 225, 254–56, 265, 273
  jade pig-dragon, 62
  jade tubes, 45, 80
  jade wares in mouths, 158
  jade *ya zhang*, 242, 254, 265
  jade *zhang*, 197, 231
  tooth-shaped *bi*, 197, 200
  yuan, 202, 224

L

legendary Chinese rulers
  Emperor Ku, 286, 295–97, 300, 310–11, 317, 334
  Gonggong, 297–99, 304, 306, 309, 330
  Gun, 295, 306, 330
  Shun, 286, 295, 303–7, 317, 334
  Yan Emperor, 286, 288
  Yao, 286, 295, 303–5, 317, 334
  Yellow Emperor, 286, 288
  Zhuanxu, 286, 295–302, 305–6, 317, 334

M

modes of social development
  Central Plain Mode, 5, 126–27, 192, 236, 279
  Eastern Mode, 126, 192, 236
  Northern Mode, 126, 192, 236, 279
  "multi-petaled flower," 5, 56, 126–27, 337, 342

N

national evolutionary scheme
  archaic state–dynastic state–empire, 194, 316
  archaic state–regional state–empire, 194, 316
  state–dynastic state–empire, 194
Nine Provinces and Five *Fu*, 312–13, 317

P

patterns
  added relief decorations, 30, 32, 50–51, 78, 80, 96, 131, 133, 137, 142, 144, 151–54, 170, 177–79, 184, 190, 223, 226, 247, 250, 258
  animal-face patterns, 189, 233
  cloud-thunder pattern, 161, 176, 197, 218, 224, 241, 245, 249–51, 253–54, 265, 268, 272
  cord-mark pattern, 26, 41, 50, 68, 224
  corrugated pattern, 116
  dragon patterns, 200
  engraved pattern, 31, 50, 78, 169, 265
  fine-tooth comb patterns, 266
  fine-tooth comb patterns with clustered dot patterns, 31, 42, 50, 66, 74, 80, 88, 152, 179, 225, 259
  fine-tooth comb patterns with fine parallel stripes, 177
  god-human-animal-face patterns, 160–61, 163, 182, 189
  Hui pattern, 32, 82, 200, 221, 225, 241, 245, 249, 251, 268, 272
  imprinted pattern, 32, 41, 137, 241, 250–52, 265, 268
  marked-cord pattern, 160, 206, 217, 253, 262, 268

octagram pattern, 88, 179, 189–90, 297
overlapping-scale pattern, 88, 107, 131–32, 142–43, 154
round pit patterns, 31, 34, 40, 55, 80
stamped-dot patterns, 30, 118
stamped pattern, 67–68, 159, 170
Z-shaped pattern, 55, 80, 82, 109, 122, 172, 225, 249
pre-Shang culture, 245, 310–11, 314
pre-Xia culture, 306
Proto-East Asian, 2, 18–20, 25, 242, 329, 333, 338–39

R
Records of the Grand Historian, 287, 292–96, 299–300, 303, 305–6, 310–11, 313
rice farming system, 122
rice in the south and millet grain in the north, 36, 229
ring-pommel swords, 241, 254–55, 257–58

S
sand mound site, 118, 224, 265
shaman, 64, 90, 300, 302
shell mound site, 118, 166, 224, 265
state stage
    archaic state stage, 2–3, 186, 194, 236, 317–18, 334
    dynastic state stage, 3, 237, 281, 317–18, 334–35
stone tools
    lithic core-chopper, 21–22
    lithic flakes, 21–24, 30, 218
    microlith, 24, 55, 86, 178, 198, 203, 205, 207, 210, 223, 227, 246, 255, 329
    net pendant, 40–41, 50, 55, 66, 72, 81, 115, 117, 160, 165–66, 168, 179, 198, 223, 225, 245, 253, 257, 259
    stone grinding rods, 30, 40, 42, 50–51, 67, 70, 109, 178–79, 226, 267
Su Bingqi, 12, 25, 93, 108, 126–27, 175, 194, 286, 288, 316

T
Taiji, 4, 62, 124, 169, 336
Tan Qixiang, 8
types of crops
    barley, 222, 262
    carbonized cultivated rice, 41
    foxtail millet, 33, 103, 213
    great millet, 222
    hemp seeds, 150
    highland barley, 213, 230
    indica rice, 78, 163
    japonica rice, 30, 78, 115, 163, 165, 168, 171
    millet, 207, 229–30, 270, 323
    millet grain, 33, 36, 42, 50–51, 54, 56, 70, 72, 85, 96–97, 112, 122, 144–45, 148, 150, 153, 158, 168, 171, 186, 198, 213, 226, 229–30, 245, 250, 257, 262, 264, 267, 270–71, 288, 291, 322, 335
    rice, 15, 27, 36, 40–41, 56–57, 76, 78–79, 96–97, 111–12, 115, 117, 122, 148, 158, 163, 165–66, 168, 171, 186, 198, 202, 205, 207, 213, 215, 217, 226, 229–30, 245, 250, 252–53, 265, 270, 291, 322–23, 326, 335
    rye, 222
    shu, 213, 230, 270
    sorghum, 33, 36, 43, 51, 54, 70, 72, 96–97, 112, 122, 144, 148, 150, 153, 213, 221, 226, 230, 245, 257, 270, 291
    soybean, 213, 230, 245
    wheat, 38, 198, 202, 205, 207, 213, 221–22, 229–30, 237, 245, 262, 264–65, 267, 270–71, 322–23, 330
types of pottery
    painted pottery, 4, 44, 59, 70–71, 78, 82, 84, 88, 93, 96, 101, 104–10, 112–13, 115–16, 119, 124–25, 131, 138, 140–45, 149–50, 154, 168–69, 172, 175–76, 183, 187–89, 191–92, 194, 211–12, 230, 233,

239, 249, 256–57, 262–63, 265, 269, 278, 299, 328, 336
pottery shards, 31–32, 110, 148–49, 254

V

vessels and containers
basin, 28, 30, 32, 40–41, 51–52, 68, 76–77, 79, 81–82, 84–86, 95–96, 104, 110, 113, 116, 124, 131, 136, 138–40, 143–45, 150, 152, 166, 169, 176, 179, 184, 196–97, 202–4, 206–9, 211, 214, 219, 241, 245–46, 249, 252, 259, 263
bo, 90
bottle, 68, 70, 81–82, 84–85, 95–96, 101, 103–6, 112, 115, 119, 264, 288
bowl, 32, 42, 50–53, 68, 75, 78–79, 86, 106, 113, 115, 132, 136–37, 141, 143, 150, 166, 169, 177, 190, 200, 203, 206–9, 211, 214–18, 223, 225, 241, 251, 256, 258–59, 265–66
cauldron-shaped *ding*, 70, 105, 109, 122, 164, 247
chime stone, 201, 231
chopping block, 200
cockscomb-handle basin, 249–50, 264
cup, 30, 32, 51, 75, 77, 82, 105–6, 109–10, 113, 115–17, 120, 122, 134, 137, 141–42, 144, 151, 153–54, 156, 158–61, 164–66, 169–70, 172, 182–83, 196, 198, 200, 202–3, 206–8, 211, 214, 218, 220, 222–23, 225, 227, 233–34, 241, 247, 251, 253, 258–60, 263–67, 302, 308
ding, 4, 42, 52, 57, 66–68, 70–71, 76, 78, 81–82, 84–85, 94–96, 101–2, 104–5, 109–10, 112–13, 115–16, 119–20, 123, 125, 130–31, 133, 137, 139–43, 153–54, 158–60, 164–67, 169–70, 182–83, 187, 194–97, 200, 203–4, 206, 208, 214, 217–18, 223–25, 227, 229–31, 239–42, 245–46, 249–54, 258, 260, 268, 271–72, 280, 289, 299, 313–14, 336
dustpan-shaped vessels, 136, 148

earthen bowl, 26, 30–31, 40–43, 45, 48, 50–56, 66, 68–69, 72, 75–79, 81–82, 84–86, 89, 95–96, 101, 104, 107, 110, 113, 115, 119–20, 131, 136, 138–45, 150–52, 154, 167, 171, 176–77, 203–4, 207, 209, 216, 219, 224–26, 251, 258–59, 263–65, 267, 299
ge, 242, 246, 252–56, 265, 268, 272–73, 279
gu, 161, 200, 203, 241, 246, 250–52, 256, 264, 268, 272
gui, 116, 159, 165–67, 200–202, 204, 206, 218, 224, 245–46, 251, 253–54, 268, 272
he, 76, 78, 110, 113, 122, 137, 154, 160, 177, 179–80, 202, 204, 206, 209, 214–15, 218, 230, 241, 246, 252–53, 256–57, 260, 264, 271–72
high-foot plate, 30, 32, 34, 39, 45, 47, 52, 54, 56–57, 68, 76–79, 81, 84–86, 105–6, 109–10, 113, 115–16, 118, 120, 122, 132, 134, 137, 139, 141–42, 144, 153–54, 158, 160–61, 164–67, 169–70, 179–80, 182–83, 196, 200–203, 206–7, 209, 211, 214, 216–18, 221, 223–25, 241, 245–47, 249–54, 256, 258, 261, 263–68, 299
jar, 28, 30–34, 40–45, 47, 49–56, 65–66, 68–69, 71–72, 74–82, 84–86, 95–96, 101, 105, 107–9, 113, 116–18, 120, 122, 129, 131, 133–34, 136–45, 148, 150–54, 159–60, 164–67, 169–71, 175–80, 182, 184, 202–4, 206–9, 211, 214–19, 223–27, 235, 241–43, 245–47, 249–53, 256, 258–68, 299, 311
jars with spouts, 131, 141
jia, 134, 137, 139, 142, 187, 194–97, 200, 202–4, 207–9, 211, 214, 230, 241, 246–47, 249, 252–54, 268, 271–72, 281
jue, 241, 245–46, 249, 252, 254, 256–57, 268, 271–72, 280
lei, 197, 208, 246, 272
li, 194–97, 200, 202–4, 208–9, 211–12, 227, 230–31, 239–43, 245–47, 249,

INDEX

251–54, 256, 258–60, 262, 268–69, 271–72, 280, 300, 311, 314
lieyan, 197
mortar and pestle, 137, 241, 246, 251
pot, 30, 40, 42, 45, 49, 52, 54, 56–57, 66, 68–69, 71, 78–82, 84–85, 101, 109–10, 113, 116, 120, 132, 134, 136–37, 139, 141–42, 144–45, 150–51, 153–54, 158–60, 164–66, 169–70, 175–77, 179–80, 182–83, 196–97, 200–201, 203, 206–9, 211, 214, 216–25, 233, 241, 245–47, 250–51, 253–54, 256, 259–60, 263–65, 267, 299, 317
pottery, 2, 4, 26, 28–38, 40–44, 46–47, 50–53, 55, 57, 59, 65–66, 70–71, 74, 76–78, 81–82, 84–86, 88–90, 93, 95–96, 101, 103–10, 112–16, 118–20, 122–26, 131, 134, 136–45, 148–50, 153–54, 158, 160, 164–70, 172, 175–76, 178–80, 183–84, 187–92, 194, 196, 198, 204, 206–8, 210–12, 214, 216–22, 224–26, 229–30, 233–35, 237, 239, 241, 244, 246–49, 251–57, 259–63, 265–69, 271–72, 278–79, 297, 299, 305, 311, 326–28, 333, 335–36
pottery *xun*, 90, 231
qi, 200–201, 242, 273

tower-shaped knob lids, 166, 169, 211
urn, 71, 95–96, 131, 136, 139–40, 143, 150, 166–67, 170, 172, 204, 206–9, 211, 214, 216–17, 219, 221–23, 241–42, 245, 247, 251–54, 256, 258–59, 264, 269
vat, 55, 79, 106, 113, 115–16, 132, 134, 139, 151, 167, 169, 175, 182, 187, 206, 209, 214, 241, 247, 252, 264
yan, 113, 153–54, 160, 182, 196–97, 202–4, 206–9, 218, 224, 228, 230–31, 239–40, 242, 245–47, 250–54, 256, 258, 260, 268, 271–72, 280, 306, 311, 314
yi, 113, 160, 180, 196
you, 246, 272
yu, 50, 68, 223, 243, 252
zhi, 251
zun, 7, 134, 144, 151, 153, 156, 160, 169, 176, 179, 182, 187, 190, 196, 200, 206, 209, 214–18, 241, 245–46, 249, 252–53, 256, 258, 260, 264–65, 268–69, 272, 277, 314

Y

Yan Wenming, 12, 15–16, 56–57, 93, 103, 126–27, 182, 194, 286, 288, 290, 316, 319
yin and *yang*, 124

ABOUT THE AUTHOR

HAN JIANYE, born in 1967, is a native of Tongwei, Gansu Province. In 1982, he was admitted to the Longxi Normal School in Gansu Province and started teaching at the Gouchuan School in Tongwei County in 1985. In 1987, he was admitted to the Department of Archaeology at Peking University. After receiving his master's degree in 1994, he began to teach at the College of Applied Arts and Sciences at Beijing Union University. From 1996 to 2000, while working, he pursued and received a PhD in History at the School of Archaeology and Museology at Peking University. He is currently a professor in the Department of History and Museology at the College of Applied Arts and Sciences at Beijing Union University, the Director of the Comprehensive Experimental Teaching Center of Applied Arts, and the Director of the Archaeological Research Center. He has published over 80 academic papers and authored monographs, such as *Research on the Neolithic Culture in the Northern Region of China*, *Natural Environment and Cultural Development in the Pre-Qin Period in the Northwest Region of China*, *Bronze Age and Early Iron Age Culture in Xinjiang*, *Pre-Qin Archaeology in Beijing*, *Age of Five Emperors Period: Archaeological Observations on the Ancient History System Centered on Huaxia*, *Pre-Qin Archaeological Research: Cultural Lineage and Cultural Exchange*, *Pre-Qin Archaeological Research: Settlement Patterns, Man and Land Relations*, and *Early China*, and other works. He has also published archaeological excavation reports, such as *Daihai Archaeology (I): Laohushan Culture Site Excavation Report Collection*, *Daihai Archaeology (III): Yangshao Culture Site Excavation Report Collection*, and *Zhumadian Yangzhuang: Mid-Holocene Cultural Remains and Environmental Information in the Upper Reaches of the Huai River*, and more.